D1233438

Studies in Church History

47

SAINTS AND SANCTITY

SAINTS AND SANCTITY

EDITED BY

PETER CLARKE

and

TONY CLAYDON

PUBLISHED FOR
THE ECCLESIASTICAL HISTORY SOCIETY
BY
THE BOYDELL PRESS
2011

First published 2011

A publication of the Ecclesiastical History Society
in association with The Boydell Press
an imprint of Boydell & Brewer Ltd
PO Box 9, Woodbridge, Suffolk IP12 3DF, UK
and of Boydell & Brewer Inc.
668 Mt Hope Avenue, Rochester, NY 14620, USA
website: www.boydellandbrewer.com

ISBN 978-0-95468-098-5

ISSN 0424-2084

A CIP catalogue record for this book is available
from the British Library

The publisher has no responsibility for the continued existence or accuracy
of URLs for external or third-party internet websites referred to in this
book, and does not guarantee that any content on such websites is, or will
remain, accurate or appropriate.

Details of previous volumes are available from Boydell & Brewer Ltd

Produced by Toynbee Editorial Services Ltd

Papers used by Boydell & Brewer Ltd are natural, recyclable products
made from wood grown in sustainable forests

Printed in Great Britain by
CPI Antony Rowe, Chippenham and Eastbourne

CONTENTS

ILLUSTRATIONS

TABLES

PREFACE

The theme of 'Saints and Sanctity' was endorsed enthusiastically by the Ecclesiastical History Society committee when Prof. Andrew Louth, FBA, proposed it as the focus for his presidency of the society in 2009–10. It was both topical, given the growing number of saints canonized by the modern papacy (as discussed by Prof. Michael Walsh in this volume), and an extremely fertile theme, prompting a rich variety of papers dealing with issues ranging from the representation and promotion of saints to Protestant reactions against, and appropriations of, concepts of sainthood. The contributions edited here comprise six plenary papers given at the Summer Meeting in 2009 and the Winter Meeting in 2010, and a selection of the communications offered at the Summer Meeting.

The Editors are grateful to the members of the society who chaired communications sessions at the Summer Meeting and kindly devoted their time and expertise to reviewing those communications submitted for publication. We are also grateful to the authors for responding to editorial requests for revisions in a timely and co-operative manner, and wish to express our continuing indebtedness to Dr Tim Grass, whose tenacious efficiency in copy-editing this volume has once again ensured its publication. We thank the society for funding his vital post as Assistant Editor.

The society wishes to thank the staff of Durham University, and in particular St Aidan's College there, for hosting the Summer Meeting, and is grateful to Dr Barbara Bombi (the Conference Secretary), especially for arranging exhibitions at the Cathedral and University Libraries at Durham, and to Prof. Richard Gameson and the university library staff for curating these. The society is also indebted to Dr Stella Fletcher (the Secretary) for organizing the excursion at the Summer Meeting and to the Institute of Historical Research for accommodating the Winter Meeting. Sadly Prof. Tony Claydon and Dr Barbara Bombi decided to resign as society officers in 2010 owing to other commitments; the society is grateful for their valuable contributions and welcomes Dr Charlotte Methuen (incoming Co-Editor of SCH) and Prof. Michael Walsh (incoming Conference Secretary) as their successors.

The Summer Meeting concluded with a Round Table discussion, a recent innovation that has become an established feature. This brought together members of the society specializing in different periods of church history and explored what the function of saints and meaning of sanctity have been over the whole course of that history, in Catholic, Protestant and other religious traditions. It underlined the fundamental and continuing relevance of 'Saints and Sanctity' for our field.

Peter Clarke
University of Southampton
Tony Claydon
Bangor University

CONTRIBUTORS

Robert ANDREWS (*EHS postgraduate bursary*)
 Postgraduate student, Murdoch University

Clyde BINFIELD
 Professor Emeritus in History, University of Sheffield

Frans CIAPPARA
 Senior Lecturer in History, University of Malta

Sophia L. DEBOICK
 Postgraduate student, University of Liverpool

Bernard HAMILTON
 Professor Emeritus of Crusading History, University of
 Nottingham

Margaret HARVEY
 Senior Lecturer in History, Durham University (retired)

Joy HAWKINS (*EHS postgraduate bursary*)
 Postgraduate student, University of East Anglia

Colin HAYDON
 Reader in Early Modern History, University of Winchester

Josephine LAFFIN
 Lecturer in Church History, Flinders University

Pak-Wah LAI (*EHS postgraduate bursary*)
 Postgraduate student, Durham University

Oliver LOGAN
 Lecturer in European History, University of East Anglia
 (retired)

Andrew LOUTH (*President*)
 Professor of Patristic and Byzantine Studies, Durham
 University

Elena MARTIN
 Durham Doctoral Fellow, Department of Theology and
 Religion, Durham University

Aude DE MÉZERAC-ZANETTI
>Postgraduate student, Durham University / Université de Paris III

Maureen C. MILLER
>Professor of History, University of California, Berkeley

Gesine OPPITZ-TROTMAN
>Postgraduate student, University of East Anglia

Ariana PATEY
>Postgraduate student, Heythrop College, University of London

Patrick PRESTON
>Visiting Fellow, University of Chichester

Richard PRICE
>Reader in the History of Christianity, Heythrop College, University of London

Samantha RICHES
>Co-ordinator, Centre for North-West Regional Studies, Lancaster University

Salvador RYAN
>Professor of Ecclesiastical History, St Patrick's College, Maynooth

Sarah SCUTTS (*Michael J. Kennedy Postgraduate Prize; EHS postgraduate bursary*)
>Postgraduate student, University of Exeter

Rowan STRONG
>Associate Professor of Church History, Murdoch University

Katharine SYKES
>Lecturer in History, Harris Manchester College, Oxford

Alan THACKER
>Senior Research Fellow, Institute of Historical Research, University of London

Alexis TORRANCE (*EHS postgraduate bursary*)
>Postgraduate student, University of Oxford

Peter TURNER
>Independent scholar, Oxford

Christine WALSH
>   Independent scholar, London

Michael J. WALSH
>   Fellow, Heythrop College, University of London

Cordelia WARR
>   Senior Lecturer in Art History and Visual Studies,
>   University of Manchester

Martin WELLINGS
>   Methodist minister, Oxford

Chris WILSON (*EHS postgraduate bursary*)
>   Postgraduate student, University of Exeter

ABBREVIATIONS

ActaSS	*Acta sanctorum*, ed. J. Bolland and G. Henschen (Antwerp etc., 1643–)
Add. MS	Additional Manuscript
BAV	Biblioteca Apostolica Vaticana
BJRL	*Bulletin of the John Rylands University Library of Manchester* (Manchester, 1903–)
BL	British Library
BN	Bibliothèque Nationale de France
Bodl.	Bodleian Library
CChr	Corpus Christianorum (Turnhout, 1953–)
CChr.CM	Corpus Christianorum, continuatio medievalis (1966–)
CChr.SL	Corpus Christianorum, series Latina (1953–)
CathHR	*Catholic Historical Review* (Washington, DC, 1915–)
CHC	*Cambridge History of Christianity*, 9 vols (Cambridge, 2005–09)
ChH	*Church History* (New York / Chicago, 1932–)
CSCO	Corpus Scriptorum Christianorum Orientalium (Paris, 1903–)
CSEL	**Corpus Scriptorum Ecclesiasticorum Latinorum** (Vienna, 1866–)
CWS	Classics of Western Spirituality (Mahwah, NJ, and London, 1978–)
DBI	*Dizionario biografico degli Italiani* (Rome, 1960–)
DOP	*Dumbarton Oaks Papers* (Washington, DC, 1941–)
DSp	*Dictionnaire de spiritualité ascétique et mystique*, 17 vols in 21 (Paris, 1927–95)
EETS	Early English Text Society (London / Oxford, 1864–)
EHR	*English Historical Review* (London, 1886–)
EME	*Early Medieval Europe* (London, 1992–)
ET	English translation
JECS	*Journal of Early Christian Studies* (Baltimore, MD, 1993–)

JEH	*Journal of Ecclesiastical History* (Cambridge, 1950–)
JMedH	*Journal of Medieval History* (Amsterdam, 1975–)
JRS	*Journal of Roman Studies* (London, 1911–)
LCL	Loeb Classical Library (London and Cambridge, MA, 1912–)
MedH	*Medieval History* (Bangor, 1991–4; Oxford, 2002–)
MGH	Monumenta Germaniae Historica inde ab a. c. 500 usque ad a. 1500, ed. G. H. Pertz et al. (Hanover / Berlin etc., 1826–)
MGH AA	Monumenta Germaniae Historica, Auctores antiquissimi, 15 vols (1877–1919)
MGH Epp.	Monumenta Germaniae Historica, Epistolae (1887–)
MGH Epp. Sel.	Monumenta Germaniae Historica, Epistolae Selectae (1916–)
MGH L	Monumenta Germaniae Historica, Leges (1835–)
MGH S	Monumenta Germaniae Historica, Scriptores (in folio) (1826–)
MGH SRG	Monumenta Germaniae Historica, Scriptores rerum Germanicarum (1871–)
MGH SRM	Monumenta Germaniae Historica, Scriptores rerum Merovingicarum (1937–)
NPNF I	A Select Library of the Nicene and Post-Nicene Fathers of the Christian Church, ed. P. Schaff, 14 vols (New York and Edinburgh etc., 1887–92 and subsequent edns)
NPNF II	A Select Library of the Nicene and Post-Nicene Fathers of the Christian Church: Second Series, ed. P. Schaff and H. Wace, 14 vols (New York and Oxford etc., 1890–1900 and subsequent edns)
ns	new series
os	original series
PG	Patrologia Graeca, ed. J.-P. Migne, 161 vols (Paris, 1857–66)
PL	Patrologia Latina, ed. J.-P. Migne, 217 vols + 4 index vols (Paris, 1841–61)
PO	Patrologia Orientalis, ed. R. Graffin and F. Nau (Paris, 1907–)
PS	Parker Society (Cambridge, 1841–55)
RHC Oc.	Recueil des historiens des croisades: Historiens occidentaux, 5 vols (Paris, 1844–95)

RHC Or.	Recueil des historiens des croisades: Historiens orientaux, 5 vols (Paris 1872–1906)
RS	*Rerum Brittanicarum medii aevi Scriptores*, 99 vols (London, 1858–1911) = Rolls Series
s.a.	*sub anno* (under the year)
SC	Sources chrétiennes (Paris, 1941–)
SCH	Studies in Church History (London / Oxford / Woodbridge, 1964–)
SCH S	Studies in Church History: Subsidia (Oxford / Woodbridge, 1978–)
SCJ	*Sixteenth Century Journal* (Kirksville, MO, 1970–2006)
s.n.	*sub nomine* (under the name)
SS	Surtees Society (London / Durham etc, 1835–)
s.v.	*sub verbo* (under the word)
TNA	The National Archives
UL	University Library

INTRODUCTION

The subject of 'Saints and Sanctity' might seem a natural one for the Ecclesiastical History Society's meetings, given that the history of the Church is often popularly conceived of as a sequence of saints – and heretics – and the idea of the saint very easily captures the popular imagination: witness the, to some, surprising interest aroused by the recent (September 2010) beatification of John Henry Cardinal Newman, which advanced him a stage further towards formal canonization. Yet, although earlier meetings of the society have touched on aspects of sanctity – 'Martyrs and Martyrologies' (1992–3), 'The Holy Land, Holy Lands, and Christian History' (1998–9), and 'The Church and Mary' (2001–2) – the broad topic of 'Saints and Sanctity' has never been addressed before.

Anyone reading through the papers presented here will discover that it is a subject of very great diversity; no general message emerges from these pages. In one of the areas of my research – Late Antiquity and Byzantium – the topic has, over the last quarter of a century, been very much at the forefront of research (probably the reason for my lighting on the topic for the conferences during my period as president). Much of this interest was sparked off by Peter Brown's remarkable article, 'The Rise and Function of the Holy Man in Late Antiquity' (1971), which has spawned a shoal of articles and books which have pushed elements of Brown's approach beyond the boundaries of Late Antiquity at least as far as early medieval Europe and the world of Byzantium. The quarter-centenary of the publication of that article has been marked by several symposia devoted to its influence. Nevertheless, even though Brown's approach, drawing on sociological and social anthropological models, led to the phenomenon of the saint or holy man being understood in a particular way, later research (even that of Brown himself) has questioned or qualified such an approach as often as it has advanced it.

The aim of the Summer and Winter Meetings in 2009–10 was to take this interest further and to explore the whole notion of sanctity in Christian history. The response exceeded my expectations, and has resulted in the volume before you. Some feared it would be an excessively medieval topic, and while the chronological sequence takes longer to reach the early modern period than in the proceedings of some earlier conferences, there is no lack of exploration of the role of sanctity from the close of the Middle Ages to the present day.

The title of the conferences points to two questions – what is a saint? and what is sanctity? – that are naturally raised many times and in different ways. Is a saint a role model? someone with special powers? a patron and intercessor? Is sanctity something that is perceived in contemporary human beings? or are saints the noble dead? Who decides? Throughout Christian history we can detect an ambiguity between sanctity as the goal, perhaps rarely achieved, of the Christian life, that is, something to do with the inner life of the Christian, something hardly claimed by anyone for themselves (though there are exceptions to this), and sanctity as an aura of power, claimed for individuals by their friends, or more often by those who want to make use of the power thus acknowledged. Historians have perhaps been more attracted to the relationships of power in which claims to sanctity play a role, but several contributions to this volume try to look at sanctity as an inward quality. And there are Christian traditions, notably many forms of Protestantism, that call in question the very notion of attaining sanctity, in the name of a notion of justification by faith that marginalizes works.

One feature of the saint that seems to have been there from the beginning is the way in which the saint, though now a denizen of the heavenly courts, is still thought of as belonging to a particular locality. The cult of the saints is largely a cult of local saints. There is often a mismatch between the claims of a local see or particular monastery, and the local boys (rarely girls) on offer, which opens the door to the imagination of those seeking, by means of the saint, to promote local claims to power. A number of papers explore another element of this sense of the locality of the saint: what to do with the renown of saints that continued after the Reformation in a world of thought that had little place for the notion of sanctity? It is not surprising for a conference held in Durham that the question of the legacy of St Cuthbert is discussed in these pages.

The cult of the saints became a prominent feature of early

and medieval Christianity, and has continued to be important in those Christian traditions that repudiated or were unaffected by the Reformation. Within such cults, the saints had to be promoted. The *life* of the saint is the primary form of this, and this is explored in a variety of ways in this volume, including some examples of figures from the Protestant tradition in which the story of the life held up individuals for emulation and admiration, if not veneration. Saints' *vitae* need authors, and the intentions of such authors can be various and not always conscious. An author who knew the saint may be promoting himself as much as the saint by his association with him or her. More often the author of such lives is reduced to *topoi*, as he develops a story from very scanty material. One might argue that the very common case of an author of a saint's life – some humble monk, himself unknown, scribbling away in his monastery – is more interesting than the better informed author, as the lack of material about the saint brings to the fore the devotion to the saint that was expressed in the cult. Particularly interesting, too, though only glanced at in this volume, is the way in which female saints were generally promoted by male authors who promoted them by writing their lives, and often developing their cult, thereby making issues of gender doubly reflexive. Gender issues emerge in other ways: in some periods women saints seem very rare, in other periods they are much more prominent. How is one to account for this?

As well as the *vita*, the cult was supported by other ways of presenting or honouring the saint. The focus of the cult was generally the relics of the saint. Shrines and reliquaries could become ways of promoting the saint, as could visual depictions in statues and icons: there is rich material for exploration of the understanding of the role of the saint, and the nature of sanctity, to be found here. Again, we find that it is devotion to the saint that is prominent, how he or she is venerated, rather than traditions about his or her life. Gifts to a shrine – vestments (discussed in this volume in the case of St Cuthbert), statues, icons and adornments to these objects of devotion, often thank-offerings – are important indications of the extent and nature of his or her veneration. In modern times, photography, and the retouching of photographs, gives an interesting insight into the visual model it was thought important to project in the case of a saint, something particularly documented in the case of St Thérèse of Lisieux.

Local cults and traditions about saints are important in the genesis of the saint, but as time passed, and particularly in the second Christian millennium, some formal process of canonization was required for the recognition of a saint. These are mostly alluded to, rather than discussed, in these pages, but it is clear that such procedures were human, however much it was thought they were discerning something beyond the human. Politics often muscled in on claims to sanctity, hardly surprising as sanctity entailed a claim to power. The role of the Russian tsar in the canonization of the great Russian saint, Serafim of Sarov, is discussed, as is the record of the greatest maker (or acknowledger) ever of saints, the late Pope John Paul II. It becomes difficult to avoid the impression that the criteria that came into play involved considerations which were often very arbitrary.

All these and many other issues are raised and engaged with, though hardly finally answered, in the essays contained in this collection. However, to look for some overall conclusion is probably not appropriate. Variety seems to be of the essence in the matter of saints and sanctity – variety and locality. Perhaps the lesson which is most obvious from reading the contributions to this volume is the extent to which investigation of the phenomenon of sanctity invites a variety of approaches. Many of the papers here suggest that we look at something that has been missing in recent or traditional scholarship. As the phenomenon of saints and sanctity is multivalent, so too are appropriate ways of approaching the subject.

Andrew Louth
Durham University

HOLINESS AND SANCTITY IN THE EARLY CHURCH

by ANDREW LOUTH

In 1971 Peter Brown published his justly famous article, 'The Rise and Function of the Holy Man in Late Antiquity'.[1] It is no exaggeration to say that this article – and the host of articles and books that succeeded it[2] – have transformed the way we think about saints and their cult in late antiquity. This change is part of a wider transformation of the study of the world of early Christianity, a change that has much to do with the changing, not to say declining, place of Christianity in Western society. The very words Peter Brown used in the title of his article are emblematic of this changed perspective: holy, man, late antiquity. Others have noted the change of words from what one might have expected, or from what one would have expected a few decades, even years, earlier. Averil Cameron spoke of Peter Brown 'rightly avoiding the term "saint", for in this early period there were no formal processes of sanctification, and no official bestowal of sainthood'.[3] Put like that, it seems obvious why Brown talked about the 'holy man'. I want to suggest that the nature of the change involved is much less easy to track down, and furthermore that awareness of the specific suggestions implicit in Brown's choice of words will enable us to contemplate the world of late antiquity from the perspective Brown was largely inaugurating, while not

---

[1] Peter Brown, 'The Rise and Function of the Holy Man in Late Antiquity', *JRS* 61 (1971), 80–101; repr. in idem, *Society and the Holy in Late Antiquity* (London, 1982), 103–52. I have referred to the reprint.

[2] Several of Peter Brown's later articles are collected in part II of *Society and the Holy*, 81–332; books include *The Making of Late Antiquity* (Cambridge, MA, 1978) and *The Cult of the Saints* (London, 1981). The significance of Brown's original article is manifest from the fact that in March 1997 a conference was held in Berkeley, California, to celebrate the quarter-centenary of its publication, the proceedings of which were published in *JECS* 6.3 (Fall 1998), and from the publication of a symposium inspired by Brown's article: James Howard-Johnston and Paul Anthony Hayward, eds, *The Cult of Saints in Late Antiquity and the Early Middle Ages* (Oxford, 1999).

[3] Averil Cameron, 'On Defining the Holy Man', in Howard-Johnston and Hayward, eds, *Cult of Saints*, 27–43, at 27.

losing the other perspectives that were implicit in the language and concepts laid aside.

The very title of this paper is intended to point to a range of significance that can easily be narrowed down by the choice of specific words. English, because of its hybrid nature, often has two words where it might have been thought that one would have done: one of Latinate origin, another of Teutonic descent. And usually the two words have different ranges of meaning, as is the case here. The Teutonic word, holy, is much less clearly defined, and capable of a much wider range of reference. It is first of all an adjective and can be applied to a wide range of nouns: a person, a place, a text, a language, a country, a city, a feeling, an object – of jewellery, for instance, or an amulet – and so on. The Latinate word, though derived from an adjective *sanctus*, is in English a noun, and can scarcely be used save in reference to a person. There is an English adjective, 'saintly', but its reference is as limited as the noun from which it is derived, and its meaning rather diminished. There is, I have to admit, a usage of 'saint' amongst rather literal-minded Orthodox converts, who use it for the Russian, or Slavonic, *svatiy*, and end up with expressions such as the 'saint Trinity' or the 'saint Scriptures', but this is hardly English. There is also another word, 'sacred', presumably at some level related to 'saint', that has its own range of connotation, rather different from either holy or saint, though closer to the former. My point in mentioning these rather obvious facts of the English language is that the availability of such different but overlapping words makes it clear that there is a range of reference attached to the notion of the holy or the saintly or the sacred, and that the choice of words can determine a particular way of conceiving of the phenomenon or phenomena of holiness or sanctity.

We might illustrate these differences by considering what Peter Brown's article might have been like had it been differently worded, and called, let us say, 'The Rise and Function of the Saint in the early Church [or: in the Patristic Period]'. Peter Brown's speaking of the 'holy man' envisages possibilities excluded, that the use of the word 'saint' would not. Holy man: as opposed to holy place, or holy woman – both oppositions I think envisaged by Peter Brown, for whom Christianity came to be characterized by holy people rather than the pagan holy places, and by holy men rather than wise women. The first is a commonplace of scholarship on the

rise of Christianity, derived perhaps from some Christian perceptions of Christian distinctiveness. Once mentioned, however, one
wonders how accurate it is; it certainly did not take Christianity
long to develop its own sense of holy places, if, indeed, it had ever
abandoned the notion. The term holy men, as opposed to wise
women, opens up areas of gender or sex distinction that have been
very much to the fore in the scholarship of the last half-century;
talk of the 'saint' glosses over this or perhaps assumes that there is
nothing particularly distinctive about the case of the woman saint.

Nonetheless, what I want to do in the first part of this paper is
to suggest what might have been involved in an article on the rise
and function of the saint in early Christianity, by way of contrast,
and then by exploring the contrast suggest what the wider field
might look like that embraces both holiness and sanctity.

The beginnings of the notion of the saint in Christian use go
back to the New Testament, and more specifically to St Paul, who
in his epistles refers regularly to the members of the church in a
particular place as the saints, οἱ ἅγιοι.[4] This echoes a use of ἅγιος
found in the Septuagint, though nothing like as frequently.[5] The
biblical use of ἅγιος suggests that its primary use is in relation
to God, who is *the* Holy One,[6] and that this use is extended to
those who are close to God and to the place where God dwells;
so the angels are the holy ones, and the sanctuary of the temple is
referred to as τὰ ἅγια.[7] Holiness is then something bestowed, not
acquired, and bestowed by God. Its basic meaning, when applied to
those other than God, seems to be dedicated to God, 'set apart'. St
Paul's use of the term for baptized Christians seems to convey the
meaning of those who are 'in Christ', set apart from the world and
dedicated to God by baptism and their faith in Christ. There is also
likely a sense of the 'holy ones' derived from the apocalyptic literature, in which the holy ones are constituted by those who, in the
final struggle between good and evil, will fight on behalf of God.[8]

The next step in the evolution of the Christian notion of the
saint focuses on the figure of the martyr. The Greek word μάρτυς

---

4 e.g. Rom. 8: 25; 1 Cor. 1: 2; 6: 1; Col. 1: 2.
5 e.g. Pss 15: 3; 33: 10 (LXX).
6 Strikingly, Isa. 43: 15; very frequently, 'the Holy One of Israel', e.g. Isa. 1: 4; 5: 24.
7 e.g. Exod. 29: 30, and frequently in Heb.: 8: 2, 9; 13: 11.
8 e.g. Rev. 13: 7; 14: 12.

means 'witness', someone who bears testimony to something that he or she knows or has seen. The use of the word for someone who suffers, ultimately to the point of death, for what he or she believes is so common that we overlook the oddness of the word in what is now the normal sense. A century ago there was a good deal of debate as to why the word μάρτυς came to be used in this way. Karl Holl felt that the notion of eyewitness, someone who had seen something, must remain embedded in the word, and pointed to the fact that martyrs are sometimes recorded as having a vision of God at the point of death, the most obvious example being the first martyr Stephen, who dies after exclaiming, 'Behold, I see the heavens opened, and the Son of man standing at the right hand of God' (Acts 7: 56).[9] Like many of Holl's ideas, it is attractive, but more for its brilliance than its plausibility. The more generally accepted explanation was that early Christian martyrdom took place in a fundamentally juridical context in which the faithful Christian was bearing witness to his faith before a judge, often under torture, which was used to elicit valid testimony from the lower classes. The μάρτυς fulfils the purpose of the ἅγιος which is implicit in his baptismal confession. Running through the whole of the New Testament is the idea that those who confess Christ can be expected to have that confession tested in the context of persecution.[10] This is implicit in what the Apostle Paul says to the Romans: 'we rejoice in our tribulations, knowing that tribulation produces endurance, and endurance tests us, and such testing produces hope, and hope does not disappoint us, because God's love has been poured into our hearts through the Holy Spirit which has been given to us' (Romans 5: 3–5). Tribulation (θλῖψις) is very nearly a technical term in the New Testament for persecution: to endure persecution and its threat and to use it as a means to refine our hope and open our hearts to God's love is the aim of every Christian, every ἅγιος, and its fulfilment is seen in the martyr, the one who bears testimony to Christ in the face of death. So the true ἅγιος, the true saint, is seen in the figure of the martyr.

---

[9] Karl Holl, 'Die Vorstellung vom Märtyrer und die Märtyrerakte in ihrer geschichtlichen Entwicklung', *Neue Jahrbücher für dem klassischen Altertum* 33 (1914), 521–56, repr. in idem, *Gesammelte Aufsätze zur Kirchengeschichte*, 3 vols (Tübingen, 1928), 2: 68–102.

[10] e.g. Luke 21: 13–15; 1 Pet. 4: 12–14.

The notion of the saint and that of the martyr come to feed off one another, as it were, but in a way that from our historical perspective might seem strange. For example, the idea of the saint or martyr as a kind of role model seems to me to lie rather in the background, contrary to some modern presuppositions about the nature of sanctity. For the notion of the saint, as we have found it in the Apostle Paul, is essentially about a *community* set apart, dedicated to God. And this community, because it is the Church, the ἐκκλησία, shares the ambiguity implicit in the New Testament notion of the Church: it is both the local community and also the universal community, and in either sense it is a community incorporate in the risen Christ, and as such not limited to those who are still living this mortal life. The saints are those upheld by the intercession of the Holy Spirit (Romans 8: 27); they are also upheld by their own prayers one for another, and by more tangible means of support – for example, St Paul's 'collection for the saints' (1 Corinthians 16: 1). The martyr becomes pre-eminently one of the saints who has successfully and finally borne witness to Christ with his death; he achieved this through the prayers of the saints and, in return, his prayers can be sought for those saints who remain on earth. The martyr differs from the saints still on earth in that these saints may still be tested and fail, whereas he or she is victorious and beyond possibility of failing. For these reasons the notion of the saint, or the true saint, comes to be transferred to the martyr, but the martyr is still defined by the community of saints, the Church, and the layers of meaning that attach to that notion in the early Christian consciousness – both local and universal, both earthly and heavenly.

That early Christian consciousness was deeply affected by eschatological, apocalyptic ideas: the 'open heaven' that the protomartyr Stephen saw as he died was more real for the early Christians than the earthly life that they lived, it was there that their hopes were set, it was there that the martyrs now lived in the presence of God – in the vision of the Apocalypse, the Apostle John sees under the altar 'the souls of those slain for the word of God and for the witness they had borne' (Revelation 6: 9). But the local layer of the meaning of ἐκκλησία still preserves its power: the martyr, as saint, as he emerges in the second century, is a local figure; he belongs to the local community where, or for which, he had borne witness, and in imitation of the heavenly altar the relics of the martyr

ANDREW LOUTH

were soon to be found beneath the altar of the martyr shrine, the *martyrium*, and eventually required for any Christian altar.[11] As a local figure he can be expected to care for the local community from which he came; he is their heavenly patron.

It seems to me that it is difficult to underestimate the impact on the Church's self-understanding of that early experience of martyrdom, which lasted until the beginning of the fourth century and came to form the bedrock of the Church's memory. It is, of course, possible to exaggerate the threat of martyrdom: nothing the Roman authorities did was comparable with Stalin's attempt to exterminate Christianity in Russia in the last century. Nonetheless, persecution was an ever-present possibility. For that reason, as virtually everyone recognizes, the sudden change in the Church's fortune, from being persecuted by the Roman emperors to being favoured and eventually adopted as the imperial religion, involved for the Church a crisis of identity. But one of the constants in that crisis of identity was the determination of the Church to remain the Church of the martyrs, and that determination affected the evolution of the notion of sanctity. There were different ways of claiming this heritage, and a good deal of the interest in studying the fourth-century Church lies in tracing the different strategies that emerged. The most striking was the emergence of the monastic order. I use the somewhat anachronistic terminology deliberately, because other ways of putting it – especially anything suggesting the rise of asceticism – seem to me to raise even more fundamental questions. I would still endorse what I wrote some years ago in the *Cambridge History of Early Christian Literature*:

> The traditional story of the rise of monasticism as a fourth-century phenomenon, associated *par excellence* with the Egyptian desert, is a Catholic legend, which, unlike many others, was reinforced, rather than questioned, by Protestant scholarship, happy to regard monasticism as a late, and therefore spurious, development. The 'monastic movement' should perhaps be seen rather as a reform movement of an already existing, and flourishing, ascetic tradition: a reform inspired by the changes, both within the Church itself, and in the Church's relation

[11] See Canon 7 of the Second Ecumenical Council of Nicaea, in Norman P. Tanner, ed., *Decrees of the Ecumenical Councils* (London, 1990), 144–5.

6

to society, brought about by the gradual Christianization of the Roman empire that began in the fourth century with the conversion of Constantine.[12]

For Christian asceticism had already incorporated the tradition of martyrdom. The most obvious evidence is found in Clement of Alexandria and his fellow Alexandrian, Origen. Clement, for instance, says:

> If the confession of God is martyrdom, each soul that has conducted its affairs purely in knowledge of God and has obeyed the commandments is a martyr both in its life and in its speech, no matter how it may be released from the body, by pouring forth the faith like blood, as it were, during its entire life right up to its departure. For instance, the Lord says in the Gospel, 'whoever leaves father or mother or brothers' and the rest 'for the sake of the Gospel and of my name' is blessed, indicating by this not the simple, but the gnostic martyrdom, in which a person, by conducting his affairs according to the Gospel's rule through love towards the Lord, ... leaves his worldly family and wealth and possessions for the sake of living without the passions.[13]

The real – the gnostic – martyrdom is the lifelong radical following of Christ, as required in the gospel. In Origen's *Exhortation to Martyrdom*, we find the same ideal made more explicit:

> As to how the measure of bearing witness is filled up, or is not filled up but falls short, the following reflections may show. If during all the time of trial and test we give no place to the devil in our hearts, when he would defile us with evil thoughts of denial, as indecision or some inducement draws us away from martyrdom and perfection; if in addition we do

---

[12] Frances Young et al., eds, *Cambridge History of Early Christian Literature* (Cambridge, 2004), 373–81, at 373. There followed a reference to Richard Price's elegant discussion of the question, which has not had the impact it deserved, owing to its being hidden away in his introduction to his translation of Theodoret's *Religious History*: Theodoret of Cyrrhus, *A History of the Monks of Syria*, trans. with introduction and notes by R. M. Price, Cistercian Studies 88 (Kalamazoo, MI, 1985), esp. ix–xxxvii.

[13] Clement of Alexandria, *Stromateis* 4.4.15.3–5; David Brakke's translation, modified, is taken from from his *Demons and the Making of the Monk* (Cambridge, MA, 2004), 25.

not defile ourselves with any word that is incompatible with bearing witness; if we endure all the taunts of our adversaries, their insults, mockery, obloquy, and their pretended pity when they treat us as fools and madmen and say that we are mere dupes; and if besides we do not permit ourselves to be seduced either by love for our children or their mother or any one of those regarded as dearest to us in life, nor to be lured away to their possession and this kind of life; but if turning from all of these we give ourselves entirely to God and to life with him and near him with a view to sharing union with his only-begotten Son and those who have a share in him: then we can say that we have filled up the measure of bearing witness. But if we are wanting in as little as one of these points, we have not filled up, but rather defiled, the measure of bearing witness, and have mixed with it some foreign element; and we shall therefore be in need of the same as they who have built on a foundation of wood or hay or stubble.[14]

For Clement, the true martyrdom is to live ἀπροσπαθῶς (unperturbed by emotion); for Origen it is successfully to resist the attacks of the devil. This latter motif suggests a direct transition from the acts of the martyrs, for in the *acta* the persecuting authorities are often depicted as inspired by the demonic forces of evil. We should notice, too, that to see martyrdom and asceticism as struggle with demonic forces of evil is to see both in terms of the apocalyptic struggle with evil that characterized early Christianity. The lately popular notion of monasticism as 'interiorized apocalyptic', to use the expression of one who is also an Athonite monk,[15] belongs to this realm of ideas.

In this way the monk inherited the tradition of the martyr, and in inheriting that became a candidate for sanctity in the Church of the empire. The other principal strategy whereby the Church of the empire preserved its continuity with the Church of the martyrs was through fostering the cult of the martyrs. The

---

[14] Origen, *Exhortation to Martyrdom* 11; trans. J. J. O'Meara, Ancient Christian Writers 19 (New York, 1954), 151, quoted by Brakke, *Demons and the Making of the Monk*, 26.

[15] See Alexander Golitsin, ' "Earthly Angels and Heavenly Men": The Old Testament Pseudepigrapha, Niketas Stethatos, and the Tradition of "Interiorized Apocalyptic" in Eastern Christian Ascetical and Mystical Literature', *DOP* 55 (2001), 125–33.

evidence for this is manifold: sermons on the martyrs by the great preachers of the fourth century such as St Basil the Great and St John Chrysostom, and the promotion of the cult of the martyrs, particularly in Rome and especially by Pope Damasus. These two strategies are brought into juxtaposition by two of Prudentius's poems: the *Psychomachia*, which celebrates ascetic struggle, and his *Peristephanon*, which celebrates the sufferings of the martyrs. In a different way these two strategies are united in Athanasius's *Life of St Antony*, which depicts Antony as the ascetic martyr par excellence, while at the same time linking Antony with the martyrs in Alexandria whom he visits, and laying the foundations for the cult of the ascetic saints as continuing that of the martyrs.

Claims to define identity are claims to authority – and power. And so in this case: ascetics, on the way to becoming monks, claim to reinterpret the significance of martyrdom within the Christian Church, building on developments already present in the period of the martyrs; the cult of the martyrs continues the defining theme of the martyrs in a different way and becomes a valuable weapon in the hands of those who want a say in defining the nature of the Church. It is a weapon on which bishops in particular wanted to lay their hands, and were in a good position to do so. I have already mentioned Pope Damasus and Rome; the sermons on the martyrs, preached by bishops, fit into this pattern of claiming and interpreting the martyr heritage, and thereby defining sanctity. Bishops themselves not only seized the chance of defining sanctity through interpreting the martyr cult; they were themselves very soon candidates for sainthood themselves. This process was doubtless assisted by the phenomenon of ascetic bishops in the later fourth century: bishops who themselves belonged to the ascetic movement, such as Ambrose, Augustine and (in the East) Basil the Great and John Chrysostom. It is not clear how soon bishops themselves became the object of a cult. An early example might be St John Chrysostom, whose life, *Dialogue on the Life of St John Chrysostom*, was written by Palladius shortly after his death, and the return of whose relics to Constantinople in 438 could be said to mark the beginnings of his cult. Chrysostom, however, may not be a good example, as his uncompromising asceticism was perhaps as striking as his episcopal dignity. Another way in which the notion of martyr was adopted by bishops as a way of promoting their own sanctity, or at any rate applied to them, is manifest in the martyr language used to describe the experience of bishops who suffered at the hands of the emperors for their defence of what they regarded as orthodoxy, pre-eminently St Athanasius. The variety of ways in which the notion of the martyr was appropriated in the fourth century suggests that we are dealing with an issue of some complexity.

We are now well into the area redefined by Peter Brown in his article of 1971. In what way does it look different as a result of the route we have taken to arrive there? It might be said that all I have done is to spell out the background of the traditional Christian notion of sanctity that Peter Brown took for granted, but to have done that is to have shown that there *was* a traditional Christian notion of sanctity. Brown's essay leaves the notion of the holy undefined, and moves quickly to the way in which claims to holiness were claims to power, and then explores – with his customary skill and insight – the power relationships that appealed to the notion of the holy. But the notion of holiness in Christianity was not an undefined notion, capable of infinite interpretation; it was rooted in the classical texts of Christianity, notably the New Testament, and had a history that had evolved a notion of holiness that was far from undefined. The Christian notion of holiness or sanctity was already richly textured, and the emerging holy man had to work within the confines of a notion already current. This seems to me to be missing from Peter Brown's tracing of the lineaments of the holy man. His holy man is presented as emerging on a blank canvas. This is presented very clearly in his final paragraph:

> The predominance of the holy man, therefore, marked out Late Antiquity as a distinct phase of religious history. The classical period conjures up the image of the great temple; the Middle Ages, of a Gothic cathedral. In between, it is the portraits that strike the imagination, the icons of the holy men, the austere features of the philosophers, the ranks of staring faces in the frescoes and mosaics. For some centuries, the locus of the supernatural was thought of as resting on individual men.[16]

And Brown goes on to characterize this period in terms of

---

[16] Brown, 'Rise and Function of the Holy Man', 151.

the remote, inaccessible God of monotheism mediated to human beings by human institutions that sought to control the supernatural. By the Middle Ages, these are institutions – he mentions 'the medieval papacy, the Byzantine *lavra*, the Russian *starec*, the Muslim Caliphate … all, in their various ways, direct results of attempts of men to rule men under a distant high God'[17] – but the way was prepared for them by the holy man, who alone was God's man. It is hard not to be bewitched by the suggestiveness of Peter Brown's prose, but it seems to me that the suggestions that abound in these final pages are highly selective, and selective because of the way in which the notion of holiness has been narrowed down by being focused on the Syrian holy man, as presented by Brown. The general context in which Peter Brown is thinking is revealed in another sentence: 'Seen in this way, the victory of Christianity in late Roman society was not the victory of the One God over the many, it was the victory of men over the institutions of the past.'[18] The general background against which the phenomenon of the holy man is being placed is the triumph of the Church, the Christianization of Roman society. But too exclusive a concentration on that important issue can tend to obscure the fact that the Church which triumphed in the fourth and succeeding centuries already had a history, something which tends to be overlooked in Brown's overarching scenario: Roman – late antiquity – Christian Middle Ages. The figure of the saint certainly belongs to that scenario, but he also belongs to the more closely defined scenario suggested above: the crisis of identity faced by the Church of the martyrs in the fourth and fifth centuries. A crisis of identity entails an already existing identity, itself formed by history. And the Christian notion of holiness and sanctity is part of that identity and history; it is, as I have suggested, richly textured, not something fashioned, as it were *ex nihilo*, by the holy man of late antiquity.

Concentration on the holy man produces a kind of narrowing of our vision. The features of the holy man, discussion of which makes up the body of Brown's article, include: patronage; wielding of supernatural power; exorcism; and παρρησία (the right to approach and address) before the remote and stern God, conceived on the model of the Emperor. The last of these leads into a discus-

---

[17] Ibid. 152.
[18] Ibid.

sion of four more detailed features of the holy man: his resolving the contradiction between the remoteness and tenderness of God; his professionalism; his role as an allayer of anxiety; and his role as *décisionnaire universel* ('universal decision-maker') of his locality. Many of these ideas would have been familiar in another context to the attentive reader of Peter Brown. It was only four years before he published his article on the holy man that he had published *Augustine of Hippo*.[19] The features of the holy man overlap strikingly with the features of the late antique bishop, explored by Brown in that remarkable biography. Features not so prominent in that book – the power of the bishop, his παρρησία with God – might have found a place had Brown explored more thoroughly the liturgical role of the bishop, as Gerald Bonner had done in a number of important articles.[20] In his article, Peter Brown grants that '[t]he bishops might wield the *mysterium tremendum* of the Eucharistic sacrifice. In the hands of a courageous bishop this could be no mean weapon'[21] and refers to Ambrose's confrontation with the Emperor Theodosius over the massacre at Callinicum, but the bishop's daily presiding over the eucharist, made explicit as an act of παρρησία in a variety of ways in the different eucharistic prayers from late antiquity, was no less important. We hear about the extraordinary ways in which the Syrian holy man seized and wielded supernatural power not least because it fascinated Theodoret, but another part of the picture of late antiquity was the increasingly important role of the bishops in the local communities they served.

But our vision of, and understanding of, the holy is further narrowed down by the way Peter Brown presents the holy man as *the* locus of the holy in late antiquity. Let me give two examples. First, Brown suggests that Christianity shifts the focus from the pagan holy place – the temple, the sacred groves, the oracle – to the holy man. It is a perception embraced by Christian scholars, too, who want to emphasize how Christianity is a personal religion – a term more used than analysed. But Christians quickly came to

[19] Peter Brown, *Augustine of Hippo* (London, 1967).
[20] See esp. '*Vera lux illa est quae illuminat*: The Christian Humanism of Augustine', and 'The Church and the Eucharist in the Theology of St Augustine', items IV and VI in Gerald Bonner, *God's Decree and Man's Destiny* (London, 1987).
[21] Brown, 'Rise and Function of the Holy Man', 140.

lay store by their holy places, their churches, their basilicas. Already, within a few years of the so-called 'Edict of Milan', we find Eusebius of Caesarea preaching at the dedication of the new basilica in Tyre a sermon in which he gives a glowing account of the magnificence of the new basilica, itself redolent with symbolism, so that the earthly building symbolizes the Church as a community and the soul as an edifice of virtues in which God's presence is realized, as well as the cosmos itself, created by the Word of God, as his Temple:

> This cathedral is a marvel of beauty, utterly breathtaking, especially to those who have eyes only for the appearance of material things. But all marvels pale before the archetypes, the metaphysical prototypes and heavenly patterns of material things – I mean the re-establishment of the divine spiritual edifice in our souls. This edifice the Son of God himself created in his own image, and in every way and in every respect he endowed it with the divine likeness, an imperishable nature, a non-physical spiritual nature, remote from any earthly matter and actively intelligent ...
>
> Building truly in righteousness, he equitably divided the whole people in accordance with their powers. With some, he walled round the outer enclosure – that was enough for them – making unwavering faith the protective barrier ... To some he entrusted the entrances to the church proper, giving them the task of waiting at the doors to guide those entering ... Others he made under-props to the first outer pillars that form a quadrangle round the court, bringing them for the first time into touch with the letter of the four gospels ... There are also in this shrine thrones and an infinite number of benches and seats, all the souls, on which rest the Holy Spirit's gifts, just as in olden time, they appeared to the holy apostles, and others with them, to whom were revealed dividing tongues like flames of fire, fire which rested on each one of them ...
>
> Such is the great cathedral which throughout the whole world under the sun the great Creator of the universe, the Word, has built, Himself again fashioning this spiritual image of earth of the vaults beyond the skies, so that by the whole

creation and by rational beings on earth His Father might be honoured and worshipped …[22]

This sense of the church building as a microcosm, in which is reflected the human soul and the community of the Church, its creation and its redemption, was to dominate Christian history, and is still a powerful reality. In the Byzantine East, the great church of the Holy Wisdom in Constantinople, built by the Emperor Justinian, became the earthly model for generations of churches. The author who wrote under the title of Dionysius the Areopagite at the beginning of the sixth century had already provided an elaborate symbolic structure for the services that took place within the Christian church – and the title of one of his treatises, the *Celestial Hierarchy*, reminds us of the holy ones, the angels, whose presence defines the Christian holy place, and links it to the holy place of the divine presence in heaven. Maximus the Confessor (580–662) developed this in his *Mystagogia*, in which he uses the symbolic structure of the church building to lend the eucharistic liturgy a meaning, cosmic in scope and reaching into the hidden places of the human spirit.[23] He is followed by Germanos (Patriarch of Constantinople, 715–30), according to whom

> The church is the temple of God, a holy place (τέμενος ἅγιον), a house of prayer, the assembly of the people, the body of Christ. It is called the bride of Christ. It is cleansed by the water of his baptism, sprinkled by his blood, clothed in baptismal garments, and sealed with the ointment of the Holy Spirit … The church is an earthly heaven, in which God, who is beyond the heavens, dwells and walks about. It represents the crucifixion, burial and resurrection of Christ: it is glorified more than Moses' tabernacle of witness, in which are the mercy seat and the Holy of Holies. It is prefigured in the patriarchs, foretold by the prophets, founded in the apostles, adorned by the hierarchs, and fulfilled in the martyrs.[24]

---

[22] Eusebius of Caesarea, *History of the Church* 10.4.55–6, 63, 66, 69; trans. G. S. Williamson, 2nd edn (Harmondsworth, 1989), 318, 320–1.

[23] *I Mystagogia tou Agiou Maximou tou Omologitou*, ed. Ch. G. Sotiropoulos (Athens, 1993), esp. chs 1–7.

[24] St Germanos of Constantinople, *On the Divine Liturgy* 1; ed. and trans. Paul Meyendorff (Crestwood, NY, 1984), 57 [slightly modified].

Holiness does not just reside in saints, it is found in the holy building of the Church, and again the holiness found there is not some incomprehensible supernatural presence, but already the bearer of a richly textured meaning.

St Germanos was the Patriarch of Constantinople who resigned over Emperor Leo III's introduction of iconoclasm. Peter Brown has written illuminatingly on the subject of the icon, but in his 1971 article it is drawn into the magnetic field created by his conception of the holy man: 'the icons of the holy men, … the ranks of staring faces in frescoes and mosaics',[25] as we have already heard. There seem to me to be two aspects overlooked by such an approach to icons – aspects that seem closely related, and which bear directly on the concept of the holy employed and articulated by Peter Brown. For Brown, and I expect for most people, icons are icons of saints; we are struck by the frontal gaze of the figures depicted. It is, however, a striking feature of the iconoclast controversy that the arguments, at least, were rarely about icons of the saints; the arguments were about depicting Christ, the God-man, and were therefore about icons of Christ – and just as much about icons of the Virgin Mother of God, who is rarely depicted without the presence of Christ. The patristic quotations cited by the iconodules are often broader in reference and referred – or were taken to refer – to religious pictures in general, or to depictions of saints, but among the extant arguments I can only think of one place where icons of the saints are envisaged, where St John Damascene affirms that 'We represent Christ the King and Lord without divesting him of his army. For the saints are the army of the Lord'; he continues: 'I venerate the image of Christ as God incarnate; of the mistress of all, the Mother of God, as the mother of the Son of God; of the saints, as the friends of God, who, struggling against sin to the point of blood, have both imitated Christ by shedding their blood for him, who shed his blood for them, and lived a life following his footsteps'.[26]

One of the features of Peter Brown's argument in the Holy Man article, as we have seen, is his sense of the anxiety created by the transition from the world of the pagan gods, seen as close to

---

[25] Brown, 'Rise and Function of the Holy Man', 151.
[26] St John Damascene, *Against the Iconoclasts* 1.21; cf. 2.15; ET in *Three Treatises on the Divine Images,* trans. Andrew Louth (Crestwood, NY, 2003), 34–5.

human concerns, and the rise of the worship of the one, remote Creator God, characteristic of Christianity and Islam. Perhaps it was the consciousness of the way in which Islam partnered Christianity as ushering in the new world that succeeded the pagan Roman Empire – a consciousness spawned by his fascination with the Pirenne thesis, which made the rise of Islam, rather than the barbarian invasions, the decisive event in the fall of the Roman Empire in the West – that led Peter Brown to see the religious transition in terms of the change from the ever-present gods of paganism to the remote and transcendent God of monotheism. I am not sure, however, that assimilating Christianity to Islam is a good way of understanding it. For the Christian God is not remote. He is indeed the Creator, and, as uncreated, beyond any human conception, as fourth-century Christian theology came to emphasize (in common, it should be said, with contemporary pagan philosophy). But God is also present in creation through his providence, and even more has made himself one with the created order through the Incarnation. To speak of the Christian God as remote, as Peter Brown consistently does, is a half-truth that is virtually a falsehood (it is true, to be sure, that at one point Brown does speak of the Christian God as 'and yet, ideally, the ever-loving Father',[27] but 'ideally' seems to me to take away with one hand what he offers with the other). One of the fears St John Damascene had concerning imperial iconoclasm was that it would lose hold of the truth of the Incarnation and fall into a dualism in which God was utterly remote from the finite, created material world. At one point the Damascene exclaims:

> Of old, God the incorporeal and formless was never depicted, but now that God has been seen in the flesh and has associated with human kind, I depict what I have seen of God. I do not venerate matter, I venerate the fashioner of matter, who became matter for my sake and accepted to dwell in matter and through matter worked my salvation, and I will not cease from reverencing matter, though which my salvation was worked ... Therefore I reverence the rest of matter and hold in respect that through which my salvation came, because it is filled with divine energy and grace.

---

[27] Brown, 'Rise and Function of the Holy Man', 143.

And he goes on to list all those material things that are the object of Christian veneration: the wood of the cross; the holy places associated with Christ's crucifixion and resurrection; the 'ink and the holy book of the Gospels'; the Christian altar; the sacred vessels; and, 'before all these things', the holy body and blood of Christ received in the eucharist, which is matter.[28] For John, holiness is instinct in matter because it is created and has been used by God. God is not remote, but ever-present, and it is this truth that the iconoclasts endanger.

'Holiness and Sanctity in the Early Church': in the course of this paper I have tried to reflect on Peter Brown's article on the rise of the holy man in late antiquity, one of the most influential articles of the last half-century. That article itself could probably be set in the context of a concern throughout the last century with the notion of the holy, going back, at least, to Rudolf Otto's remark-able work, *Das Heilige*.[29] I have attempted to set Brown's reflections in a rather different context: that of the evolving notion of sanctity, or holiness, in the history of the early Church. Nothing I have said detracts from the brilliance and insight of Peter Brown's fascinating article, but rather suggests that the notion of holiness was already well developed and that the phenomenon of the Syrian holy man, at the heart of Brown's reflections, did not create the notion of holiness, but had to negotiate, as it were, with an already highly developed and richly textured notion that had evolved through the experience of the early Church. That experience itself was rooted in the experience of Israel, as found in what Christians came to regard as their Old Testament, and can be traced through the New Testament and the early Christian experience of martyrdom, which was determinative for the Christian notion of sanctity. Before we reach Brown's Syrian holy man, we find various attempts to rede-ploy the notion of the martyr as saint in the Christian Empire of Constantine and his successors. There were several contenders: not simply ascetics, but also bishops, who both sought to embody the notion of sanctity, and, just as important, to adjudicate on claims to sanctity through control of the cult of the saints. Sanctity and claims to holiness had to fit into an already highly developed

---

[28] St John Damascene, *Against the Iconoclasts* 1.16 (trans. Louth, *Three Treatises*, 29–30).

[29] Rudolf Otto, *Das Heilige* (Breslau, 1917).

matrix of interpretation. Holiness was one of the touchstones of authority in the Christian community, so the claims and counter-claims, and claims to adjudicate, become one of the continuing threads determining the authenticity of Christian experience. The struggle between institutional authority and Christian experience is one that characterizes many periods of Christian history; the notion of holiness, how it is defined and how it is articulated – and how it is recognized and acknowledged – is fundamental to our understanding of the dynamics of that conflict, as well as providing insight into the complex nature of Christian experience.

Durham University

THE MONK AS CHRISTIAN SAINT AND EXEMPLAR IN ST JOHN CHRYSOSTOM'S WRITINGS

by PAK-WAH LAI

By the time Augustine read the *Life of Antony* in 386, the biography had already become an international best seller in the Roman Empire.[1] Translated twice into Latin and read in places as far off as Milan and Syrian Antioch, the Egyptian *Life* also proved to be a significant influence upon hagiographical writing in the late fourth century, the most notable example being the *Lives* of St Jerome.[2] Consequently, scholars have often taken it to represent the dominant paradigm for sainthood in fourth-century Christianity and the centuries that followed.[3] But is this assumption tenable? The *Life of Antony* would in all likelihood be read only by the educated elite or by ascetic circles in the Church, and was hardly accessible to the ordinary Christian. More importantly, hagiographical discourse in the fourth century was not restricted to biographies, but pervaded all sorts of Christian literature. This is certainly the case with the writings of St John Chrysostom (c. 349–407), who often presents the Christian monk as a saintly figure in his monastic treatises and his voluminous homilies. Indeed, what emerges from his writings is a paradigmatic saint who is significantly different from that portrayed in the biographies, and yet equally influential among his lay and ascetic audiences. To be sure, Chrysostom's monastic portraits share some common features with that provided by Athanasius's *Life*. Never-

---

[1]   The biography's influence, as Leclercq observes, was to endure until the Middle Ages: Augustine, *Confessions* 8.6.15; Owen Chadwick, *John Cassian*, 2nd edn (Cambridge, 1968), 3; Jean Leclercq, *The Love of Learning and the Desire for God*, trans. C. Misranhi (New York, 1974), 125.

[2]   Carolinne White, *Early Christian Lives* (London, 1998), 73, 87; Gregory of Nazianus, *Oratio in laudem Basilii* 21.5; Palladius, *Historia Lausiaca* 8; John Chrysostom, *Homiliae in Matthaeum* [hereafter *Hom. Matt.*] 8; Jerome, *De viris illustribus* 88.

[3]   William A. Clebsch, Preface to *Athanasius: The Life of Antony and the Letter to Marcellinus*, trans. and intro. Robert C. Gregg, CWS (Mahwah, NJ, 1980), xiv.

theless, there are also stark differences between the two, and these are the focus of this paper.

The Lives and Chrysostom's Monastic Portraits: Similarities

Chrysostom was no stranger to the monastic vocation, having spent the first decade of his adulthood living as an urban ascetic and then as an anchorite in the Syrian mountains (368–78).[4] His enthusiasm for asceticism appears to have remained undimmed even after he became a priest in Antioch (c. 386) and later Bishop of Constantinople (397–404). Indeed, it was probably one of the factors which contributed to his eventual downfall and exile in 404.[5] This same ascetic vision would have informed his numerous monastic treatises, written most probably during the 370s, and the several hundred more homilies he preached in both Antioch and Constantinople.[6]

When one examines these writings, it is clear that Chrysostom's monastic portraits share several common narrative features with the *Life of Antony* and those *Lives* that come after it. Like Abba Antony, Chrysostom's monk is an icon of God's presence and a mediator of his power, being esteemed not only as an angel on earth, but also as a doer of miraculous works, whether it is the healing of the sick or the exorcism of demons.[7] As in the *Lives*, Chrysostom's monk is an exemplar of Christian living, a person who saturates his daily routine with prayer and the study of Scriptures, and who triumphs over demonic temptations or attacks by the aid of Christ.[8] Both writings also share an ascetic vision which parallels closely that of the Cynics and Stoics. Like their pagan counterparts, these narra-

---

[4]   J. N. D. Kelly, *Golden Mouth: The Story of John Chrysostom – Ascetic, Preacher, Bishop* (London, 1995), 14–30.

[5]   His reforms as a bishop, as Kelly points out, were shaped by his ascetic ideals and evidently unpopular among some clergy in the church of Constantinople: ibid. 211–17.

[6]   The genuine homilies of Chrysostom number more than eight hundred, making him the most prolific author of the Eastern Church: Wendy Mayer, *The Homilies of St John Chrysostom – Provenance: Reshaping the Foundations*, Orientalia Christiana Analecta 273 (Rome, 2005), 26.

[7]   This paradigmatic or symbolic feature, as Cunningham suggests, is one of the most important features of saints in general: Athanasius, *Vita Antonii* [hereafter *Vit. Ant.*] 3, 14–15; John Chrysostom, *Comparatio regis et monachi* [hereafter *Comp. reg. mon.*] 4; idem, *Adversus oppugnatores vitae monasticae* [hereafter *Oppugn.*] 2.6, 2.8, 3; Lawrence S. Cunningham, *The Meaning of Saints* (San Francisco, CA, 1980), 65, 73.

[8]   Chrysostom, *Comp. reg. mon.* 2; Athanasius, *Vit. Ant.* 3.

tives assume that the monk's life of ascetic practice, whether it is his frequent fasting or his lack of sleep, is meant to help him overcome his passions (*pathē*) and attain a state of freedom from being controlled by the passions (*apatheia*).[9] Furthermore, these writings are also characterized by the conviction that one's life should be lived in accordance with nature (*kata phusin*), a point that is clearly illustrated in Jerome's portrayal of Paul of Thebes, who is entirely dependent on a raven for his daily bread throughout the decades of his seclusion.[10]

CHRYSOSTOM'S MONASTIC PARADIGM: SOME DISTINCTIVE FEATURES

Where Chrysostom differs from the *Lives* is the way he recasts some of the narrative motifs commonly found in these spiritual biographies. The first is the notion of the monk as living a heavenly or indeed an angelic life. Like many of his contemporaries, Chrysostom believes that the *telos* of the Christian life is the recapitulation of Adam's bliss, or angelic life, in paradise.[11] Chrysostom is also convinced, however, that this angelic lifestyle involves not only a wholehearted dependence on God for one's needs, but also the enjoyment of the countless pleasures offered by this 'garden of delights', as it is translated in the Septuagint.

> Like some angel, in fact, man lived this way on earth, wearing a body, yet being fortunately rid of any bodily needs; like a king adorned with sceptre and crown and wearing his purple robe, he revelled in this life of freedom and great affluence in the garden.[12]

It is also within what we might call this hedonistic-theological framework that Chrysostom understands the role of human labour, namely as a means of preventing Adam from sliding into excessive indulgence and ultimately sloth or indifference (*rathumia*).[13]

---

9 Athanasius, *Vit. Ant.* 4, 7; Chrysostom, *Comp. reg. mon.* 1–2 (PG 47, 388, line 25); Luis E. Navia, *Diogenes of Sinope: The Man in the Tub*, Contributions in Philosophy (Westport, CT, 1998), 117–27.

10 Jerome, *Vita S. Pauli, primi eremitae* 10 (trans. in White, *Early Christian Lives*, 80).

11 Chrysostom, *Hom. Matt.* 55.6.

12 John Chrysostom, *Homiliae in Genesim* [hereafter *Hom. Gen.*] 15.14; ET in *Homilies on Genesis 1–17*, trans. Robert C. Hill, Fathers of the Church 74 (Washington, DC, 1985), 203.

13 Chrysostom, *Hom. Gen.* 14.8, 12.

Seen in this light, the monk's ascetic struggle and life *kata phusin* cannot simply be for Chrysostom a return to a life of simplicity. Neither is it merely about learning how to depend on God's providence, as is assumed in the *Lives* by Athanasius and Jerome. Rather, the monk, as an exemplar of Christian living, or indeed of Adam's bliss in paradise, is also a person who has learnt how to take great pleasure in God's daily provision. And with respect to work, or in his case the ascetic struggle, this is practised not only as a means of releasing himself from his lusts and desires, but also as a preventative measure against human indulgence and, ultimately, the sin of *rathumia*.[14]

It is certainly with this in mind that Chrysostom, in his *De virginitate,* would portray the prophets Elijah, Elisha and John the Baptist as ascetic figures who, despite having 'heaven for a ceiling, the ground for a bed, the desert for a table', would regard the barrenness of the desert' as 'a place of plenty'. Similarly, in his *Comparison between a King and a Monk*, Chrysostom would have no qualms about saying that the monk living an ascetic lifestyle in the wilderness is able to drink water 'with greater pleasure than others [such as the king] drink marvellous wine'.[15]

Apart from this hedonistic emphasis, Chrysostom also differs from the *Lives* in terms of how he understands the monk's public ministry. To be sure, Chrysostom would concur with Athanasius and Jerome that the primary function of the monk's feats, be it his teachings, exorcisms or miraculous healings, is to demonstrate his status as a worthy agent of Christ. 'The saint's identity', as Clebsch puts it, 'became that of the Saviour and the saint's deeds became deeds normally reserved for the work of divinity.'[16] Nevertheless, such a life of ministry often sits uneasily in the *Lives*, as may be seen in Jerome's Hilarion, who has to travel from Gaza to Alexandria, and later to Libya and Sicily, in order to escape the public attention generated by his miracles. Hence, within this spiritual

---

[14] Indeed, as Hill remarks, *rathumia*, in Chrysostom's theology, is the cause for Adam's Fall: Chrysostom, *Hom. Gen.* 14.12, 16.13 (trans. Hill, 186–7).

[15] Chrysostom, *Comp. reg. mon.* 3; ET in *A Comparison between a King and a Monk / Against the Opponents of the Monastic Life*, trans. David G. Hunter, Studies in the Bible and Early Christianity 13 (Lewiston, NY, 1988), 72–3.

[16] Clebsch, Preface to *Athanasius*, xv.

tradition, the contemplative life and the active life are often in great tension with one another.[17]

This, however, is not the case for Chrysostom. In his *Comparison between a King and a Monk*, he presents the monk as a philosophical figure who, when fully trained, is no different from the philosopher-king idealized in Plato's *Republic*, and who is, indeed, far more capable than an ordinary king in ruling over cities and men with kindness.[18] To be sure, such a portrayal of the monk is probably hyperbolic and undoubtedly skewed by the polemical concerns of his treatise. Nevertheless, its underlying emphasis on the monk's active life of ministry is clearly important for Chrysostom and is reiterated time and again in his writings elsewhere, as in the case of Book 3 of his *Against the Opponents of the Monastic Life*. Addressed to a hypothetical Christian parent, the treatise argues that the parent should not be dismayed by his son's monastic vocation, but rather be comforted by the fact that once his son has 'completed' his monastic training, he will become 'a light to all', being able to 'heal people suffering with incurable diseases', and be 'hailed [along with other monks] as benefactors, patrons and saviours to all'.[19] It is for the same reason, arguably, that Chrysostom would elsewhere criticize monks who refused ordination and ministry simply because they were afraid of sacrificing their life of contemplation.[20]

While several of his monastic portraits clearly affirm with their biographical counterparts that the Christian monk is the embodiment of spiritual perfection, Chrysostom also recognizes that the monk can be an equally powerful and inspiring symbol of Christian repentance. Written during his time as a member of an ascetic community in Antioch (368–72), the first letter of Chrysostom's *Exhortation to Theodore after his Fall* is a very touching attempt to persuade his dear friend Theodore (subsequently Bishop of Mopsuestia) to repent of his lapse and to re-embrace his monastic vows. Here, one of the main arguments that runs through the letter is Chrysostom's contention that God's loving kindness (*philanthrōpia*) is always available for the repentant sinner,

---

17 Jerome, *Vita S. Hilarionis eremitae* 3, 33–8.
18 Chrysostom, *Comp. reg. mon.* 2.
19 Chrysostom, *Oppugn.* 3.18 (trans. Hunter, *Comparison / Opponents*, 168).
20 Chrysostom, *Ad Demetrium de compunctione* 1.6.

no matter how far he has fallen away.[21] To reinforce his argument, Chrysostom appeals to a cycle of three narratives, each of which begins with a monk or Christian disciple who, having attained a mature level of ascetic practice, lapses into sin. Later, each monk repents of his sins and, in the case of the first two monks, attains an even more excellent life.[22] Clearly then, the monk's exemplary role here lies not in his spiritual strengths, but in his very human frailty. Indeed, it is by repenting of his sin that he becomes an encouragement to every sinner and an icon through whom one can appreciate the abundance of God's *philanthrōpia*.

Interestingly, the narrative motif of the monk as miracle worker is also brought into play in one of the stories here. In the second narrative, the monk falls into lust and visits a brothel. After regretting his sin, he promptly shuts himself in his hut, so that he may repent continually with many 'fastings, prayers and tears'. Some time later, by divine prompting, he is approached by others to pray and intervene for a drought. To his surprise, the monk finds his prayers answered and recognizes, therefore, that God must have forgiven him. In other words, the motif of the miracle worker is deployed here not so much as a feature of the monk's spiritual perfection but more as a sign of God's *philanthōpia* and forgiveness for the repentant.

As to the fourth difference between Chrysostom's monastic saint and those portrayed in the *Lives*, we have already hinted at it above: the monastic figure, for Chrysostom, is more an icon of virtue and divine grace than a spiritual hero for ascetics. This is evident in the fact that while the identity and biographical details of the monk are important narrative features for the *Lives*, it is much less the case in Chrysostom's writings. In contrast, Chrysostom's monk is almost always a nameless and unidentifiable figure. Even when his writings present the monk as a spiritual teacher, they, unlike the *Life of Antony*, display a clear lack of interest in the content of the monk's teachings. Indeed, his monastic portraits, as a whole, are rather anaemic sources for monastic wisdom and teaching.[23]

---

[21] Chrysostom, *Adhortationes ad Thedorum Lapsum* [hereafter *Thdr.*] 1.4; 1.6.22.

[22] Ibid. 1.18–19.

[23] There are ample references to the monk as a teacher in his monastic treatises. However, in none of them are these narratives used as a means of communicating monastic teachings and wisdom: cf. Chrysostom, *Oppugn.* 3.12. The *Life of Antony*, in

This, of course, does not mean that there is no monastic wisdom in Chrysostom's writings. There are spiritual gems everywhere in his writings, but his monastic portraits are not where you would find them.[24] Rather, these portraits are intended for a different purpose, namely, to embody and illustrate the virtues and ideals of Christianity in a way that would inspire Christians, whether lay or ascetic, towards greater spiritual progress and holiness.

This iconic nature of Chrysostom's monk may be better understood when we consider the fifth and final distinctive feature of his monastic paradigm. Unlike the *Lives*, whose literary styles are clearly influenced by their Greco-Roman biographical precedents,[25] the form and emphasis of Chrysostom's monastic portraits owe their origins more to the Greek rhetorical traditions in which he was trained under the renowned orator Libanius.[26] Indeed, many aspects of epideictic (ceremonial) oratory, such as its literary structure or rhetorical strategies, are evident in his monastic portraits. Take his *Homily 67 on the Gospel of Matthew*, for example. When Chrysostom employs the technique of *synkrisis*, or rhetorical comparison, to compare the life of a female ascetic with those of his audiences, he most certainly has in mind the paradigm of the *encomion*, in which a subject is praised on the basis of his or her origins, upbringing and deeds. At the same time, what emerges from this example is not a straightforward application of the *encomion* paradigm, but one that is both creative and subversive. The female ascetic who is the subject here was, as he reminds his audiences, a former Phoenician prostitute, notorious in Antioch and the regions of Cilicia and Cappadocia for ruining families and practising sorcery. Thus, whether it is in terms of her origins, upbringing or deeds, she was in the eyes of Greco-Roman society a member of the lowest class, to be despised by all. Yet, this same prostitute has now repented of her past and embraced an ascetic lifestyle.[27] For Chrysostom, the conversion of this former prostitute

contrast, devotes at least 29 chapters to the teachings of Antony: Athanasius, *Vit. Ant.* 16–44.

[24] For example, his perceptive discussion of the value of fasting is found not in such portraits but in one of his homilies on Genesis: Chrysostom, *Hom. Gen.* 10.2.

[25] Robert C. Gregg, Introduction to *Athanasius: Life of Antony and Letter to Marcellinus*, 5.

[26] Kelly, *Golden Mouth*, 7–8.

[27] Chrysostom, *Hom. Matt.* 67.3.

should be both an encouragement and a warning to his audiences. Those who still despair because of their moral bankruptcy should be greatly encouraged, since this prostitute, whose origins and upbringing are worse than theirs, has proved that it is possible for the worst sinner to attain great virtue. Yet, for those who are proud of their pedigree and moral achievements, the same spiritual feats of this prostitute should be a harsh warning to them, in view of the fact that she has achieved much more than them, despite her lowly background.[28]

Besides these, another rhetorical device which Chrysostom regularly uses to accentuate the iconic quality of the monk is the *ekphrasis*.[29] This is well illustrated in his *Homily 69 on the Gospel of Matthew*, where he describes the monks living in the nearby Syrian mountains. 'Let us go away', invites Chrysostom, 'to the tents of those men.' There, we see that nothing in 'their lodging-places [is] in a condition inferior to the heavens; for the angels lodge with them, and the Lord of the angels'. These, he explains, are men who have been 'delivered from the body, and in the flesh disregarding the flesh, ... pure from all covetousness, and full of self-denial'.[30]

> If any time they should be minded to feast more sumptuously, their sumptuousness consists of fruits, and greater is the pleasure there than at royal tables. There is no fear there, or trembling; no ruler accuses, no wife provokes, no child casts into sadness, no disorderly mirth dissipates, no multitude of flatterers puffs up; but the table is an angel's table free from all such turmoil.
>
> And for a couch they have grass only beneath them, like as Christ did when making a dinner in the wilderness. And many of them do this, not being even under shelter, but for a roof they have heaven, and the moon instead of the light of a candle, not wanting oil, nor one to attend to it; on them alone does it shine worthily from on high.[31]

He continues,

---

[28] Ibid. 67.4.
[29] An *ekphrasis* is a detailed description of a person, thing, occasion or place that is commonly used in Greek rhetoric to enhance the 'visual' impact and therefore the plausibility of the subject portrayed.
[30] Chrysostom, *Hom. Matt.* 69.4.
[31] Ibid. 49.4 (NPNF I 10, 424–5).

there are not master and slave; all are slaves, all free men. ...
They have no occasion to be in sadness when evening has
overtaken them ... They have no occasion after their supper to
be careful about robbers, ... neither to dread the other ills ...
And their conversation again is full of the same calm. ... [They
speak] always about the things to come, and seek wisdom; and
... as though they had migrated unto heaven itself, as living
there, even so all their conversation is about the things there.[32]

What we have here, then, is a very vivid or indeed idealized
picture of the monastic lifestyle, where, in the company of angels,
the monks enjoy much pleasure, despite the simplicity of their
lives, and where the malice, social rivalry and worries that usually
accompany life in the *polis* are entirely absent. Clearly, this *ekphrasis* is iconic in the sense that it particularizes, in the imagination
of his listeners, the idyllic heavenly life that every Christian is
meant to attain. Chrysostom, however, takes it further by recasting
it immediately as a *synkrisis* between the monks and his listeners.
Compared to these angel-like men, says Chrysostom, his audience
are 'worse than the brutes', since much of their time is spent in
covetousness and the pursuit of things superfluous to their lives.
In other words, Chrysostom also intends his *ekphrasis* to have a
cathartic effect for his listeners, awakening in them on the one
hand repentance for their spiritual lethargy and indulgence, and
on the other a deep desire to imitate the monks' angelic virtues
and lifestyle.[33]

Conclusion

This essay has shown clearly that even though Christians in the
late fourth century generally agreed that the Christian monk or
ascetic had succeeded the martyr as the new saint and exemplar of
the Church, they had yet to agree unanimously on what this new
saint might 'look' like. Contrary to common belief, Athanasius's
Life of Antony is most probably just one of many monastic para-
digms propounded in the late fourth century. Indeed, given the
rhetorical training of so many of the fourth-century bishops, such
as Gregory of Nazianus and Basil of Caesarea, it is not unlikely

---

[32] Ibid. 69.4 (NPNF I 10, 425).
[33] Ibid.

that their vision of the monastic saint might be closer to that of Chrysostom than to that of Athanasius. This calls for further study. Nevertheless, what we can say at present with greater confidence is that Chrysostom's vision of the Christian monk, as both a saint and an exemplar for Christians, has several unique attributes distinguishing it from its biographical counterparts. Besides being a sign of God's presence and power in the Church, the monastic figure for Chrysostom is also an inspiring and powerful symbol of what the Christian life ought to be: a life which thoroughly enjoys God's provisions, serves others in love and is confident of God's philanthropic love for the repenting sinner.

University of Durham

COMMEMORATION, REPRESENTATION AND INTERPRETATION: AUGUSTINE OF HIPPO'S DEPICTIONS OF THE MARTYRS

by ELENA MARTIN

Recent studies of martyrdom in early Christianity look beyond the traditional perception of martyr *acta* and *passiones* as historical documents that can help us to reconstruct the past.[1] While previously these texts had been deemed worthy of attention on account of their proven authenticity or historical veracity, now they are all valued as important sources that have much to tell us about the communities and environments in which they were produced.[2] This approach does not deny the historical value of the sources, but rather it appreciates that they are a special kind of historical document.[3] Texts and sermons about holy men and women never were created as objective accounts.[4] Every textual portrait of a martyr reveals a prior judgement that inscribes meaning and purpose into seemingly meaningless events to present condemned criminals as religious heroes, horrific tortures as divine

[1]   Key studies include Elizabeth Castelli, *Martyrdom and Memory: Early Christian Culture Making*, Gender, Theory and Religion (New York, 2004); Kate Cooper, 'The Voice of the Victim: Gender, Representation and Early Christian Martyrdom', *BJRL* 80.3 (Autumn 1998), 147–57; Lucy Grig, *Making Martyrs in Late Antiquity* (London, 2004), 146–51; Johan Leemans et al., *Let us Die that we may Live: Greek Homilies on Christian Martyrs from Asia Minor, Palestine and Syria (c. AD 350 – AD 450)* (London, 2003); Joyce E. Salisbury, *Blood of Martyrs: Unintended Consequences of Ancient Violence* (London, 2004). For a less recent but seminal study, see Peter Brown, *The Cult of the Saints* (Chicago, IL, 1981, repr. 1982).

[2]   For a succinct overview, see Grig, *Making Martyrs*, 146–51.

[3]   For example, Sebastian P. Brock and Susan Ashbrook Harvey, *Holy Women of the Syrian Orient*, Transformation of the Classical Heritage 13 (Berkeley, CA, 1987), 3: '[*acta* are] an important kind of historical evidence about how a given group understands its own history'. This shift in focus is linked with the influence of 'the linguistic turn' in early Christian studies; see further Elizabeth A. Clark, *History, Theory, Text: Historians and the Linguistic Turn* (Cambridge, MA, 2004), esp. 159: 'Christian writings from late antiquity should be read first and foremost as literary productions before they are read as sources of social data.'

[4]   Castelli, *Martyrdom and Memory*, 25: 'From the earliest of sources onward, it becomes clear that the early Christians positioned the historical experience of persecution almost immediately within a framework of meaning that drew upon broader metanarratives about temporality, suffering and sacrifice, and identity.'

gifts, and public deaths as cosmic dramas. Consequently, the various methods of representation that were used to construct depictions of the martyrs are significant elements in their own right, whether they are rhetorical devices, scriptural allusions, artistic embellishments or miraculous occurrences. These are the very details that make martyrs; they turn death into martyrdom, and the dead into martyrs.

By focusing on methods of representation, we become more aware that depictions of the martyrs are artificial in the sense that they are constructed by an author who works as a craftsman. Hence recent studies of martyrdom highlight the fact that martyrs are 'made' by a creative process of commemoration, representation and interpretation.[5] That is, a person does not naturally become a martyr at the moment of his or her death, but rather martyrs are made by individual or communal memory-work. As Elizabeth Castelli puts it: 'the designation "martyr" is not an ontological category but a post-event interpretive one'.[6]

This process of making martyrs was not natural or inevitable, but rather it was guided and controlled by authority figures who acted as artists and authors. Working with the freedom of artistic licence and authorial intent, these men were not constrained by fidelity to historical accuracy. Perceiving the past through the lens of the present, they appropriated the memory of the martyrs, inscribed their own experiences and concerns onto the historical figures, and transformed the martyrs into mouthpieces to communicate and validate their own opinions and beliefs. This weaving of the present into the past collapsed distances of time to result in a closer identification between the represented martyr and the audience to whom the representation was delivered. The audience was encouraged to identify with the martyr, take their words to heart and imitate their actions. In this way, the memory of the martyrs was adopted and adapted for pastoral, theological and ecclesiological purposes. The carefully constructed depictions of the martyrs became fertile and generative images that informed Christian identity, ethics, ideals and beliefs. Depictions of the martyrs were

---

[5]   See Castelli, *Martyrdom and Memory*; Grig, *Making Martyrs*; Salisbury, *Blood of Martyrs*.
[6]   Elizabeth Castelli, 'The Ambivalent Legacy of Violence and Victimhood: Using Early Christian Martyrs to Think With', *Spiritus* 6 (2006), 1–24, at 1.

not just *products* of a dynamic process, but they were also used as *tools* to produce, construct and edify the communities in which they themselves were formed.

This paper uses Augustine of Hippo's methods of depicting the martyrs as an example of this creative process of making martyrs.[7] A brief overview outlines his five main methods of representation: (1) removing narrative structure; (2) avoiding descriptions of the suffering body; (3) censoring female nudity; (4) deleting the martyrs' words; and (5) abstracting the martyrs' names. The example of Augustine illustrates that the process of making martyrs does not only involve elaboration, amplification and embellishment, but also abstraction, erasure, censoring and silencing; that martyrs are constructed not only by commemoration, but also by deliberate and wilful forgetting.

As we shall see, one of the most unusual characteristics of Augustine's depictions of the martyrs is the comparative lack of detail.[8] This stands in stark contrast to other sources of the period, particularly Greek martyr homilies, in which narrative details were embellished to create rich, vibrant and memorable portraits of the martyrs. Unlike his contemporaries, Augustine rarely tried to grasp the attention of his audience by reverting to lurid descriptions of torture, exciting his audience with narrative climax, or describing the naked bodies of female martyrs. Augustine's depictions of the martyrs are less explicit than Prudentius's poetic rendering of the dismemberment of Hippolytus, less evocative than Gregory of Nyssa's description of the frostbitten limbs of the Forty Martyrs

---

7   For background on Augustine's attitudes towards the martyrs, see Tarcisius J. van Bavel, 'The Cult of the Martyrs in St. Augustine: Theology Versus Popular Religion?', in *Martyrium in Multidisciplinary Perspective: Memorial Louis Reekmans*, ed. M. Lamberigts and P. van Deun, Bibliotheca Ephemeridum Theologicarum Lovaniensium 117 (Leuven, 1995), 351–61; Jan den Boeft, ' "*Martyres sunt sed homines fuerunt*": Augustine on Martyrdom', in *Fructus centesimus: Mélanges offerts à Gerard J. M. Bartelink à l'occasion de son soixante-cinquième anniversaire*, ed. A. A. R. Bastiaensen, A. Hilhorst and C. H. Kneepkens (Dordrecht, 1989), 115–24; A.-M. La Bonnardière, 'Les *Enarrationes in Psalmos* prêchées par Saint Augustin à l'occasion de fêtes de martyrs', *Recherches Augustiniennes* 7 (1971), 73–104; Peter Brown, 'Enjoying the Saints in Late Antiquity', *EME* 9 (2000), 1–24; W. H. C. Frend, 'The North African Cult of Martyrs', in *Jenseitsvorstellungen in Antike und Christentum: Gedenkschrift für Alfred Stuiber*, ed. E. Dassmann (Münster, 1982), 154–67; C. Lambot, 'Les sermons de Saint Augustin pour les fêtes des martyrs', *Revue Bénédictine* 79 (1969), 82–96.

8   See the brief comment in F. van der Meer, *Augustine the Bishop: The Life and Work of a Father of the Church*, trans. B. Battershaw and G. R. Lamb, 2nd edn (London, 1978), 492.

of Sebaste, less dramatic than Chrysostom's thrilling performances of devilish fury.[9] But Augustine's depictions of the martyrs are no less fascinating than those of his contemporaries. While he did not excite his audience with the thrill of blood, nudity or narrative climax, he aimed to captivate them with the more chaste enjoyment of articulate word-play, clever puns, and brief yet lucid similes. By focusing on a martyr's name or the hidden meaning of their martyrdom, he shifted the emphasis away from the single moment of the martyr's death to reveal the eternal truths that are expressed by martyrdom.

REMOVING NARRATIVE STRUCTURE

Most of Augustine's reflections on the martyrs are found in the sermons that he delivered at martyr festivals.[10] These festivals included liturgical readings that were often followed by the public reading of the martyr's *acta* or *passio*, that is, the written narrative describing the martyr's trial, torture and death.[11] This was followed by at least one sermon, which served as a direct commentary on the martyrdom narrative and often reflected or retold parts of the narrative. Bearing this in mind, we find that one of the most striking characteristics of Augustine's sermons on the martyrs is that most often he removed the narrative structure. He replaced the logical sequence of connected episodes found in the martyrdom narrative with a thematic structure organized around the analysis of a particular word or the explanation of a certain theological idea. He constructed his sermons from disconnected reflections inspired by the narrative but presented as individual units of information,

---

9   See further, Prudentius, *Peristephanon*, ed. and trans. H. J. Thomson, LCL 398 (London, 1953). For a range of examples in the martyr homilies of John Chrysostom and the Cappadocian Fathers, see Leemans et al., *Let us Die*; Wendy Mayer, *St. John Chrysostom: The Cult of the Saints* (New York, 2006).

10   Augustine's sermons are translated in John E. Rotelle, ed., *The Works of Saint Augustine: A Translation for the Twenty-First Century*, part 3, vols 1–11, trans. Edmund Hill (New York, 1990–7). Some of Augustine's sermons on the martyrs are included in the collection of his *Enarrationes in Psalmos*, in John E. Rotelle and Boniface Ramsey, eds, *The Works of Saint Augustine: A Translation for the Twenty-First Century*, part 3, vols 15–20, trans. Maria Boulding (New York, 2000–04). All references to the *Sermons* [hereafter *S.*] and the *Enarrationes in Psalmos* [hereafter *En. Ps.*] are taken from this series [hereafter *WSA*].

11   *S.* 274.1 (*WSA*, 3/8: 23), 280.1 (*WSA*, 3/8: 72), 299F.1 (*WSA*, 3/8: 271), 335A.1 (*WSA*, 3/9: 211). Martyrdom narratives were not available for all the martyrs: *S.* 315.1 (*WSA*, 3/9: 129).

such as thoughts on the trials of life, or comments on the fear of death. As a result, Augustine encouraged his listeners to remember only the small fragments of detail that he chose to bring to their attention. And yet Augustine did not avoid the narrative structure altogether, but rather his thematic approach extracted the martyrs from their historical narrative and superimposed them onto the grand narrative of salvation history. The martyrs are seen against the panoramic backdrop of the cosmic drama of creation, the Fall and redemption. This relocation from historical narrative to theological narrative is not concerned with the accuracy of historical truth as much as the atemporal significance of the theological framework into which the martyrs are placed and perceived.

Avoiding Descriptions of the Suffering Body

Unlike his contemporaries, Augustine avoided graphic descriptions of torture and death in his depictions of the martyrs. Descriptions of the suffering body were central to the memory of martyrdom in late antiquity.[12] This is particularly evident in Greek martyr homilies from the fourth century. Throughout the course of these homilies, many preachers referred to themselves as painters or writers, impressing images or inscribing words upon the minds of their listeners.[13] They presented their listeners with highly visual, chronological and episodic narratives, unfolding in cinematic progression from the occasion of the martyr's arrest through to the moment of his or her death.[14] The narrative is fleshed out as the graphic detail of torture is expanded and the suffering body is described with clinical precision. The preachers used the mnemonic device of violent and bloody images,[15] and

[12]   Brown, 'Enjoying the Saints', 6–7; Daniel Baraz, *Medieval Cruelty: Changing Perceptions, Late Antiquity to the Early Modern Period* (Ithaca, NY, 2003), esp. 39.

[13]   For example, John Chrysostom, *A Homily on the Holy Martyrs* 8 (trans. Mayer, *Cult*, 226); idem, *A Homily on Saint Barlaam* 10 (trans. Mayer, *Cult*, 186); idem, *On the Holy Maccabees and their Mother* 11 (trans. Mayer, *Cult*, 145); Basil, *Homily on the Martyr Gordius* 2 (trans. Pauline Allen, in Leemans et al., *Let us Die*, 59); idem, *Homily on the Forty Martyrs of Sebaste* 2 (trans. Allen, in Leemans et al., *Let us Die*, 68–9).

[14]   For example, Gregory of Nyssa, *Homily 1b on the Forty Martyrs of Sebaste* 145 (trans. Leemans, in Leemans et al., *Let us Die*, 98): 'let us then narrate everything about the martyrs step by step, in a way that brings their contest under your eyes on this very stage'.

[15]   For the mnemonic function of violent images, see Mary Carruthers, *The Craft of Thought: Meditation, Rhetoric, and the Making of Images, 400–1200*, Cambridge Studies in Medieval Literature 34 (Cambridge, 1998), 101.

made their words even more memorable by employing unusual similes to catch the attention of the listener.[16] For example, John Chrysostom described the martyrs lying on burning hot coals as if they were reclining on soft beds of roses; he compared the blood that poured out from their bodies with the saffron-coloured rays of the morning sun; he said that the lymphatic fluid that seeped from their wounds glowed brighter than the stars in the night sky.[17] Sensually evocative descriptions make the images even more memorable. We encounter the disturbing sight of disembowelled bodies, the smell of burning flesh, the chilling breath of ice-cold air, and the sound of bones being shattered and bodily fluids hissing amid the flames.[18] These preachers linger on the dark, grotesque and unsettling details of suffering, only to create a type of *chiaroscuro* in which the bright light of divine truth breaks through to illuminate and enhance the beauty and truth of martyrdom. The physical and tangible bodies of the martyrs become sites at which the *in*-visible and *in*-tangible presence of God is revealed.

Upon first glance it might seem that Augustine fits neatly into this scheme of preaching. Often he opened his sermons by equating the senses of hearing and seeing, as he described the reading of the martyrdom narrative as a visual, theatrical performance re-enacted in front of his listening audience: 'all those things, recounted in such glowing words, we perceived with our ears, and saw with our minds';[19] 'A tremendous spectacle has been set before the eyes of our faith. We heard with our ears, we saw with our hearts'.[20] This might lead us to expect that he would also construct vivid visual images of the martyrs. But Augustine did not excite his audience with the thrill of violence.

---

[16] Ibid. 131.

[17] Chrysostom, *On the Holy Martyrs* 4, 5 (trans. Mayer, *Cult*, 222); idem, *A Homily on the Martyr Julian* 2 (trans. Mayer, in Leemans et al., *Let us Die*, 132).

[18] For example, Basil, *Homily on the Forty Martyrs of Sebaste* 5 (trans. Allen, in Leemans et al., *Let us Die*, 71–2); Gregory of Nyssa, *Homily 1b on the Forty Martyrs of Sebaste* 153 (trans. Leemans, in Leemans et al., *Let us Die*, 105); Chrysostom, *A Homily on the Martyr Julian* 3 (trans. Mayer, in Leemans et al., *Let us Die*, 133); idem, *On the Holy Martyrs*, esp. 4, 8 (trans. Mayer, *Cult*, 221–2, 226); idem, *A Homily on Saint Romanus* 7 (trans. Mayer, *Cult*, 232).

[19] *S.* 280.1 (*WSA*, 3/8: 72).

[20] *S.* 301.1 (*WSA*, 3/8: 282).

Instead he spoke with an extraordinary subtlety to tame, sanitize and spiritualize the cruel deaths.

Augustine's reserved depictions of the martyrs seem to be out of place in what has been referred to as 'a world awash with blood'.[21] He described the suffering body only very rarely, and even then he did so with a great deal of reservation and moderation that reflects his general ambivalence towards the harmful power of mental images. His heavy-handed erasure of detail reduced the martyrs to hazy silhouettes and shadowy figures. He corrected the vision of his listeners by using variations of the slogan *non poena sed causa* ('it is not the suffering, but the cause [that makes a martyr]').[22] Repeating this pithy and memorable slogan, Augustine encouraged his listeners to look away from the suffering body, and towards the spiritual truths that are expressed through martyrdom: namely, the power of God; the presence of Christ; the working of the Holy Spirit; and the reality of eternal life.

CENSORING FEMALE NUDITY

Augustine constructed depictions of female martyrs in a similar way. Martyrdom narratives and sermons often emphasize the sexuality of female martyrs by describing them as young, beautiful and naked women, whose punishment sometimes includes a brief but unsuccessful stint in a brothel, and whose gruesome deaths are described with sexual innuendo. For example, in *The Martyrdom of Saints Perpetua and Felicitas* the narrator describes how the two women were stripped naked and brought into the amphitheatre in transparent nets. Felicitas had only just given birth in prison, and Perpetua, a recently nursing mother, still had milk dripping from her breasts.[23] In *The Martyrdom of Saints Carpus, Papylas, and Agathonicê*, we read that when Agathonicê was sentenced to death, she removed her clothing and 'when the crowd saw how beautiful she was, they grieved in mourning for her'.[24] In *The Martyrdom of Saint Crispina* the perse-

---

[21] Brown, 'Enjoying the Saints', 7.

[22] For example, *Letter*, 89.2 (*WSA*, 2/1: 359); S. 275.1 (*WSA*, 3/8: 26), 285.2 (*WSA*, 3/8: 95), 325.2 (*WSA*, 3/9: 168–9), 328.4, 7 (*WSA*, 3/9: 177–8, 179), 335.2 (*WSA*, 3/9: 209), 335C.5 (*WSA*, 3/9: 222–3), 335G.2 (*WSA*, 3/9: 244). See further den Boeft, 'Augustine on Martyrdom', 118.

[23] *The Martyrdom of Saints Perpetua and Felicitas* 20; trans. Herbert Musurillo, in idem, *The Acts of the Christian Martyrs*, Oxford Early Christian Texts (Oxford, 2000), 106–31, at 129.

[24] *The Martyrdom of Saints Carpus, Papylas, and Agathonicê* 6 (trans. Musurillo, *Acts*, 35).

cutor orders Crispina's head to be shaved so that her beauty would become her shame.[25] This is not just the case for martyr *acta* and *passiones*. In the fourth century, Prudentius described how the young Eulalia watched on happily as the executioners tore at her naked sides with metal claws.[26] Victricius of Rouen gives brief descriptions of several female martyrs, including one female martyr who, 'while her child went hungry, offered full breasts to the wild beasts', and a virgin martyr who 'submitted to the executioner a neck adorned with the necklace of virginity'.[27] Both Prudentius and Ambrose depict Agnes, a young girl martyr, in an openly sexualized manner.[28]

In contrast, Augustine's female martyrs are not stripped naked. Torture is not given sexual connotations; breasts are not exposed; beauty is not lamented; bare flesh is not attacked with metal claws. These conventions for representing female martyrs would have concerned Augustine for two main reasons: firstly, the memory of naked female bodies had the potential to haunt the dreams of chaste and holy men; secondly, the combination of erotic and violent elements seemed to invite perverse and voyeuristic desires to abuse and misuse the memory of the martyrs.[29] For these reasons Augustine effectively clothed his women martyrs by simply not referring to female nakedness, so that his silence would censor the account and allow the details to remain 'out of sight'. By choosing exactly what he wanted his audience to see (or rather, not see), he redirected his listeners' attention away from the corporeality of the female martyr's body and towards the spiritual sights that were seen with the eyes of the heart.

Erasing the Words of the Martyrs

The fourth method concerns a common feature of martyr sermons: the construction of long fabricated speeches that were delivered by the martyr during his or her trial or torture. John Chrysostom

---

[25] *The Martyrdom of Saint Crispina* 3 (trans. Musurillo, *Acts*, 307).

[26] Prudentius, *Peristephanon* 3 (LCL 398, 151–2).

[27] Victricius, *Praising the Saints* 12; trans. Gillian Clark, 'Victricius of Rouen: *Praising the Saints*', *JECS* 7 (1999), 365–99, at 399.

[28] See further Virginia Burrus, 'Word and Flesh: The Bodies and Sexuality of Ascetic Women in Christian Antiquity', *Journal of Feminist Studies in Religion* 10 (1994), 27–51; eadem, 'Reading Agnes: The Rhetoric of Gender in Ambrose and Prudentius', *JECS* 3 (1995), 25–46.

[29] For the power of mental images to arouse lust, see Augustine, *Confessions* 10.30, 41 (*WSA*, 1/1: 264); *S.* 151.8 (*WSA*, 3/5: 46).

and the Cappadocian Fathers invented fictitious speeches between the martyrs and their persecutors, which allowed their audiences to overhear conversations between the martyrs and their family members, and included monologues that enabled the martyrs to speak directly to the listening audience.[30] Similarly, in his poems Prudentius inserted long speeches into the mouths of his martyrs.[31] The inclusion of fictitious speech enlivened the martyr's story, imported a sense of humour, directly appealed to the emotions, and (most importantly) enabled preachers, poets and authors to convey their own beliefs and concerns through the mouths of the martyrs.[32]

Although Augustine did occasionally report the words of the martyrs from their martyrdom narrative, he did not tend to create imaginary speeches for them, but rather rendered them mute. An exception to this rule is found in the few instances where he created hypothetical situations in which an anonymous martyr was put to trial by a persecutor. In these cases, Augustine created imaginary speeches for imaginary characters, where the martyr's words are little more than a patchwork of scriptural quotations:

> Now set before your eyes the contest engaged in by the martyrs. Here comes the opponent, he's forcing them to deny Christ ... He promises riches and honours ...
>
> The faithful man, though, who was promised such things, despised them, and said, 'Shall I, just for the sake of riches, deny Christ? ... I mean to say, he is the one *who became poor for our sakes, though he was rich, so that we might be enriched by his poverty* (2 Cor. 8: 9). I mean to say, he's the one about whom again the apostle says, *in whom are all the treasures of wisdom and knowledge hidden away* (Col. 2: 30 [*sic*]) ... The things that the eye of the heart gazes on are better than what the eye of flesh can see. *For the things that can be seen are temporary, while the things that cannot be seen are eternal* (2 Cor. 4:18) ...'.
>
> 'You do not want', he says, 'to receive more ample gifts from me? If you do not deny Christ, I will take away what you have.'

30 Leemans et al., *Let us Die*, 33–4.
31 e.g. Prudentius, *Peristephanon* 3, on Eulalia (LCL 398, 142–56); ibid. 5, on Vincent (LCL 398, 168–203); ibid. 10, on Romanus (LCL 398, 290–3). See also Chrysostom, *A Homily on Saint Romanus* 8 (trans. Mayer, *Cult*, 233–4).
32 Leemans et al., *Let us Die*, 33–5.

'It is still against my superfluities that you are raging. *Like
a sharp razor, you have practiced deceit* (Ps. 52: 2). You shave off
the hairs, you do not cut the skin ... I used to do what Paul
advised: *Command*, he said, *the rich of this world, command them
not to think proudly of themselves, nor to place their hopes in the
uncertainty of riches* (1 Tm. 6: 17–19) ... *we brought nothing into
this world, but neither can we take anything away. Having food and
clothing, with that let us be content* (1 Tm. 6: 7–8).'[33]

Similarly, while Augustine silenced the voices of the martyrs,
he replaced their words with those of Scripture to make them
proclaim the Gospel and sing the Psalms.[34] So he says of the martyr
Vincent: 'When his flesh, which was a kind of tribute to the victorious Christ, was thrown into the sea from the boat, it silently said,
We are cast down, but not lost (2 Cor. 4: 9).'[35] In another sermon,
he explains that Vincent 'knew how to say, *In God I shall praise the
word, in the Lord I shall praise the utterance; in God I shall hope, I shall
not fear what man may do to me* (Ps. 56: 10–11) ... he knew to whom
he should say, *My God, rescue me from the hand of the sinner, from the
hand of the law-breaker and the wicked; since you are my patience* (Ps. 71:
4–5)'.[36] Here Augustine 'en-textualizes' the martyrs to make them
embody, fulfil and proclaim God's word. The authoritative words
of Scripture fix the meaning of martyrdom, colour the memory
of the martyrdom event, and present the martyrs as instruments of
God's self-revelation.

Abstracting the Martyrs' Personal Names

The final method concerns Augustine's abstraction and erasure of
the martyrs' personal names. We might expect that, after most of the
details have been stripped away from the memory of the martyrs,
Augustine would retain at least this final personal element. Yet, we
find that he took advantage of every opportunity to delve into
the hidden meanings and figurative significance of the martyrs'
names by creating puns that abstracted and depersonalized the

---

[33] S. 299D.4 (*WSA*, 3/8: 258–9); cf. S. 326.2 (*WSA*, 3/9: 171), 334.1 (*WSA*, 3/9:
204–5).

[34] For the martyrs proclaiming the Gospel, see *City of God* 18.50; trans. R. W.
Dyson, *The City of God Against the Pagans*, Cambridge Texts in the History of Political
Thought (Cambridge, 1998), 897–8; S. 318.1 (*WSA*, 3/9: 147).

[35] S. 274.1 (*WSA*, 3/8: 23).

[36] S. 277A.2 (*WSA*, 3/8: 48).

martyrs. So, for example, he explained that the names of Perpetua and Felicitas signified the perpetual felicity of eternal life,[37] and the name Vincent pointed towards the martyr's vanquishing of the Devil.[38] While these puns might appear to degrade the memory of the martyrs by denying their importance as human individuals, Augustine's intention was to amplify their importance by affirming the value of their memory for the whole Christian community. As members of the elect, the martyrs' names were predestined before time.[39] Their names extend beyond the limits of time and place, beyond individual persons and personality, to signify and support the journey of every Christian towards God.

But Augustine took this one step further. On many occasions, he did not mention the martyrs' names at all, but rather he was interested in the collective homogeneous group of 'the martyrs': one group united in motive and cause, conformed to Christ by their faith and actions, and bound together with the Christian community as one body extending through time and space. This erasure of personal names might give the impression that Augustine was embarking on a project of *damnatio memoriae* and was expressing a negative attitude towards the martyrs. But it is here that we find the driving force of the whole of Augustine's process of making martyrs. He replaced the personal names of the martyrs with repeated explanations of the Greek word *martys*, which translates into the Latin word *testis*, and evokes the judicial connotations of a witness bearing testimony to truth: 'People who were humiliated and subjected to various torments on account of their witness to Christ, and fought for the truth even to death, we call "martyrs" (*martyres*), using the Greek word even though we could just as well call them "witnesses" (*testes*) in our own tongue'.[40] For Augustine, a martyr is only ever a *witness* pointing to a truth that lies beyond: a thing that may be used but never enjoyed in and of

---

37 *S.* 281.3 (*WSA*, 3/8: 79), 282.1 (*WSA*, 3/8: 81).

38 *S.* 274.1 (*WSA*, 3/8: 23). Other examples include Cyprian: *S.* 313C.2 (*WSA*, 3/9: 102); Primus, Perpetua and Victoria: *S.* 335A.1 (*WSA*, 3/9: 212); Lawrence: *S.* 304.1 (*WSA*, 3/8: 316); 305A.4 (*WSA*, 3/8: 326–7); Quadratus: *S.* 306B.3 (*WSA*, 3/9: 30), 306C.1–2 (*WSA*, 3/9: 36–7).

39 *S.* 282.1 (*WSA*, 3/8: 81), 306B.3 (*WSA*, 3/9: 30).

40 *En. Ps.* 118(9).2 (*WSA*, 3/19: 379). See further Lucy Grig, 'Torture and Truth in Late Antique Martyrology', *EME* 11 (2002), 321–36, esp. 324–8.

itself; a means that must necessarily lead to an end; the object of our vision but never the focal point on which our eyes should rest.

CONCLUSION

At the end of this overview, we find a tension arising from Augustine's need and desire to remember the martyrs, and his reluctance to allow his listeners to form mental images of them. If the memory of the martyrs is too vivid or engaging, it becomes a useless and even dangerous memory that leads the mind away from God. Augustine's methods of abstraction and erasure reduce the martyrs to the bare essentials in order to emphasize only those details that direct our minds towards the spiritual message communicated through the martyrs. In this way, his methods of representation tame and control the dangerous process of remembrance by prescribing the exact details that his listeners should forget or recollect, and then providing an authoritative interpretation of those details to guide them away from the physical and temporal moment of martyrdom, and towards a perception of spiritual and eternal truth.

Augustine's depictions of the martyrs were part of his wider attempt to reform the way that people remembered the martyrs. But his influence was limited. While he stripped the martyrs of the details of their deaths, and dislocated them from their narratives, these were the very things that other people wanted to see and hear. Many later depictions of the martyrs linger on the gruesome and erotic elements that Augustine had tried so hard to conceal.[41] Yet his depictions of the martyrs do draw our attention to a more general observation that applies to all depictions of the saints: to understand their meaning and purpose fully, we need to pay attention not only to the details that are present in the image, but also to those details that have been erased. Often that which is omitted from the picture is just as important as that which is included.

University of Durham

---

[41] While it is beyond the scope of this study to explore this issue in further detail, see, e.g., Beth Crachiolo, 'Seeing the Gendering of Violence: Female and Male Martyrs in the *South English Legendary*', in Mark D. Meyerson, Daniel Thiery and Oren Falk, eds, *A Great Effusion of Blood? Interpreting Medieval Violence* (Toronto, ON, 2004), 147–63; Martha Easton, 'Pain, Torture, and Death in the Huntingdon Library *Legenda aurea*', in Samantha J. E. Riches and Sarah Salih, eds, *Gender and Holiness: Men, Women, and Saints in Late Medieval Europe* (London, 2002), 49–64.

HAGIOGRAPHY AND AUTOBIOGRAPHY IN THE LATE ANTIQUE WEST

by PETER TURNER

Peter Brown's classic essay of 1971, 'The Rise and Func-tion of the Holy Man in Late Antiquity',[1] is celebrated for applying the tools of sociology and anthropology to the study of late antique sanctity. It strove to remove holy men from the distorting literary texts through which we know them, and to place them instead in a rich context of everyday concerns. My starting point here, however, is not the essay itself but a no less interesting critique of it subsequently made by the author himself. In 1998, Brown offered a number of pieces of advice he would now give to a younger self embarking on the same topic. In 1971, he claimed, he had unwittingly colluded with the hagiographical texts by presenting holy men in dramatic, epic terms. Focusing on what holy men did for society, he had observed the phenomenon from a purely third-person perspective, and had neglected their own personal quest for sanctity.[2] Although he had located the holy man's activity in the everyday, he had effectively conceded that the ultimate locus of the holy man's holiness – his superior under-standing – was unknowable.

Indeed, to a very large extent, the sources render this aspect of sanctity very difficult to know. The vast majority of informa-tion about holy men (and indeed holy women) in late antiquity is written in the third person. This is partly a literary phenom-enon: hagiographies became, from the early fourth century, a distinctive and thriving genre of Christian writing in the West, so much so that even scholars interested in the period's non-religious history are often obliged to make use of them. In comparison, the period did not produce anything which we might term a genuine example of the autobiographical genre. With the notable excep-

---

[1]   Peter Brown, 'The Rise and Function of the Holy Man in Late Antiquity', *JRS* 61 (1971), 80–101.

[2]   Peter Brown, 'The Rise and Function of the Holy Man in Late Antiquity: 1971–1997', *JECS* 6 (1998), 353–76, at 368.

tion of Augustine's *Confessions*, and a few later works such as Paulinus's *Eucharisticon* and Patrick's *Confessio*, the period offers little in the way of first-person religious writing. The literary prominence of the *Confessions* and their seductive 'everyman' voice mean that broader extrapolations based on them must be made very cautiously. Furthermore, sacred biographies celebrate figures full of virtues often already visible in childhood, and therefore largely omit any aspect of change. Usually, any progress they record relates less to how holy men themselves evolved than to society's recognition of their greatness. By contrast, confession was virtually the only form late antique Christian autobiographical writing could take, and this stressed sinfulness and spiritual evolution. Almost by definition, then, the themes of first- and third-person Christian writing addressed different concerns. Indeed, they seem to concern not so much different aspects of religious experience as entirely different grades of human being.

Nonetheless, the aim of this paper is to explore their relationship. The formal differences between these two types of writing can, I believe, be very informative in allowing us to observe sanctity from differing viewpoints. Ultimately, this is because these viewpoints are less distinct than they initially appear. This is true partly in a literary sense: on the one hand, hagiography often allows its authors to make important autobiographical statements. On the other, autobiographical statements – both within and outside hagiography – may be shaped by literary traditions from third-person religious writing. But a comparison which examines these relationships is potentially of more than literary importance, for it allows us to consider how the idea of the holy man as a complete human being and the idea of the ordinary man as a progressing sinner were linked. Such an analysis may help fulfil the need identified by Brown for an understanding of sanctity which incorporates in the rather static image of the holy man the more dynamic phenomenon of personal religious experience. Although an approach of this kind could possibly be applied meaningfully to a large range of religiously-minded texts from late antiquity and the early Middle Ages, both Greek and Latin, pagan and Christian, the present discussion will focus on a small number of early Western Christian texts, suggesting wider parallels where relevant. My modest aim in doing so is to outline some possible new approaches capable of being developed further.

★ ★ ★

Hilarius's *Life of Honoratus* is one of the earliest Western hagiographies. It was delivered as an oration in 411 on the first anniversary of the death of its subject, briefly Bishop of Arles but better known as an ascetic hero and the founder of the monastery at Lérins, a previously desolate island off the Provençal coast, brought to life after the saint arrived there seeking solitude. Although the *Life* was written for a specific occasion, it was, as Pricoco has argued, strongly informed by the author's hagiographical reading which allowed Hilarius to depict his hero as a model of spiritual perfection.[3]

The section of immediate interest here occurs during Honoratus's period as abbot.[4] The author recounts how the saint left the island in order to recruit him personally to the monastery. Hilarius confesses his sinfulness and the difficulty he experienced in committing himself to the monastic life; he attributes to Honoratus's kindness and patience his eventual decision to make that commitment. Hilarius speaks of their subsequent intimacy, the familiar names the saint gave him – my tongue, my heart, my soul – and the fact that Honoratus could not bear his younger kinsman to be absent.

This passage has been chosen, of course, because in it the author characterizes himself, his own religious journey and his relationship to the saint: it is an autobiographical passage placed within a third-person biography. It is interesting, however, that even in this passage the biographical function is not actually replaced. The story serves chiefly as a means of depicting the saint's kindness and generosity, and one aspect of the author's role is as an eyewitness, lending a personal guarantee to the story. Such a concept requires a statement of humility on the author's part; it is precisely because of his unworthiness that Honoratus's love is so striking.

Late antique scholarship would benefit from a systematic comparative study of such personal interventions in hagiography. Although usually very brief, it is remarkable how common they are across the whole diverse gamut of late antique hagiography. Sulpicius Severus's personal acquaintance with his subject Martin

3 S. Pricoco, *Monaci, filosofi e santi. Saggi di storia della cultura tardoantica* (Messina, 1992), 59–61.
4 Hilarius, *Vita Honorati* 23–5, in *Vitae Sanctorum Honorati et Hilarii, Episcoporum Arelatensium*, ed. S. Cavallin (Lund, 1952), 65–8.

is one of the crucial claims of his famous hagiography.[5] Having been dedicated to the church from birth, Theodoret of Cyrus was virtually brought up amongst the Syrian holy men whose prayers helped his mother conceive and to whom he dedicated his work.[6] In pagan biographies too, a close bond between author and subject is often recorded. Porphyry recalls how his master Plotinus magnanimously travelled to Sicily to rescue him from a bout of melancholy;[7] Eunapius relates the heart-warming intervention of his teacher Prohaeresius after he had arrived as a student in Athens with a life-threatening fever.[8]

But the opportunity hagiography offers its authors for autobiographical statements is not the only point of contact between first- and third-person religious writing. Sometimes saints characterize themselves directly using expressions we would normally expect only from a hagiographer. An excellent example from the early sixth century is Severinus's self-portrait in the *Letter to Paschasius* which Eugippius uses to introduce his *Life of Severinus*. In this letter, Eugippius claims to have no relevant information about his subject's background since the saint himself refused to discuss it.[9] Severinus's decision is ideological: 'what use is it to the servant of God to name his country or race, when by keeping silent he can more easily avoid pride?'[10] For Eugippius, the suppression of detail about Severinus's earthly background emphasizes his far more important spiritual identity. This apparent rejection of biographical convention has parallels in earlier texts such as Porphyry's *Life of Plotinus*, which begins by reporting the philosopher's refusal to discuss his background, as one 'ashamed of being in a body'.[11]

This literary heritage may seem to add weight to those sceptical commentators who argue that Eugippius feigned ignorance of Severinus's background for effect.[12] But such doubts are prob-

---

5   Sulpicius Severus, *Vita Martini* 25 (CSEL 1, 134).

6   Theodoret, *Religious History* 9.5–8 (SC 234, 415–23); 13.16–17 (ibid. 503–7).

7   Porphyry, *De vita Plotini et ordine librorum eius* 11, in *Plotinus I: Porphyry on Plotinus, Ennead I*, ed. and trans. A. H. Armstrong, LCL 440 (London, 1966), 37.

8   Eunapius, *Vitae Philosophorum ac Sophistarum*, in *Philostratus and Eunapius: Lives of the Sophists* 485–6, ed. and trans. W. C. Wright (London, 1921, repr. 2005), 476–83.

9   Eugippius, *Epistula ad Paschasium* 7–11 (SC 374, 153–5).

10   Ibid. 9 (SC 374, 152–4).

11   Porphyry, *De vita Plotini* 1 (*Plotinus I*, ed. and trans. Armstrong, 3).

12   There has been extensive debate about the historicity of Eugippius's hagiography and, in particular, of the function of this device. For an introduction, see W.

ably misplaced. Severinus's mysteriousness seems to have been not only the first thing people remembered about him but a deliberate, consistent policy. His distinctive manner of speaking was not a single incident, but a habit, built up over time (*referre solitus erat*) and it is thus likely that what Eugippius reported was a genuine aspect of the saint's charismatic style. Nonetheless, he recognizes that the saint, when referring to his past life, speaks of himself 'in covert words as if of another' (*sermone clauso tamquam de alio aliquo*). His favoured way of describing himself, in other words, would have sounded more natural in the third person.

An example of just such a device in the third person comes from Hilarius's *Life of Honoratus*. As with Eugippius's later portrait, the saint's background is not revealed but here the policy of concealment is attributed to the writer, not the saint. Hilarius too rejects rhetorical convention: the function of recording an impressive lineage at the beginning of a eulogy, he claims, is to compensate for personal deficiencies in the subject – something clearly inapplicable to his hero:[13] 'None is more glorious in the heavenly places than are those who have ignored their pedigrees and chosen to be reckoned as fatherless except in Christ.'[14] But, through the complex interaction of first- and third-person voices, this statement is doubly interesting. Hilarius is Honoratus's episcopal successor and kinsman and, apparently, the only figure personally recruited to a monastery whose other members are presented anonymously. The ideological significance Hilarius attributes to his master's mysterious provenance inevitably also becomes a secret shared with the deceased saint and therefore part of his own identity in turn. Its importance for Hilarius as a church leader is confirmed in the *Life of Hilarius* written by his own follower, the younger Honoratus, in which the pattern of concealment (still presented as a rejection of convention, but fast becoming one in its own right) is repeated.[15]

Within late antique religious writing, then, we can observe

Pohl, 'Einleitung: Commemoratium – Vergegenwärtigungen des heiligen Severin', in W. Pohl and M. Diesenberger, eds, *Eugippius und Severin* (Vienna, 2001), 9–23.

[13] Hilarius, *Vita Honorati* 4.1.

[14] Ibid.; ET in F. R. Hoare, *The Western Fathers* (London, 1954), 250.

[15] Honoratus of Marseilles, *Vita Hilarii* 2 (*Vita Honorati et Hilarii*, ed. Cavallin, 81). Like his mentor, Hilarius was unknown in the city before the election. The parallel is observed, but goes undeveloped, by R. W. Mathisen, *Ecclesiastical Factionalism and Religious Controversy in Fifth-Century Gaul* (Washington, DC, 1989), 89. Other examples of late antique Western saints apparently concealing their own identity occur in the

a certain fluidity between the first- and third-person voices: undoubtedly this may take many different forms, of which we have mentioned only a few. Just as hagiographies could offer a space for personal expression, what we might consider character- istic of hagiography is sometimes expressed not in third- but in first-person terms. Though revealing, such an observation is not entirely surprising. Many hagiographies were written by close associates of their subjects. The two perspectives were inevitably combined when writers bore witness to what they themselves had seen. Similarly, that some saints' self-presentation should appear hagiographical seems understandable when we bear in mind that they were sometimes explicitly praised for their attentive readings of sacred *lives*.[16] Broadly speaking, such fluidity is in keeping with much contemporary literary theory, according to which genres are not distinct and exclusive categories but constantly influence one another in an ever-evolving system of expectations.[17]

But does this relationship between first- and third-person writing have a relevance beyond the purely literary level? Specifi- cally, how might it help answer Brown's suggestion that sanctity should be considered in not merely social, but also in individual terms? On a first reading, the relationship might seem to pose a serious challenge to the idea of humility which has always been such a central feature of Christian sanctity. Indeed, we might be tempted to think of saints as rather self-aggrandizing, even delu- sional figures. Honoratus's kindness to Hilarius may have been mentioned primarily as a demonstration of the saintly kindness of the former but, however undeserving its recipient proclaimed himself to be, the story inevitably advertised his exclusive relation- ship with his episcopal predecessor.[18] Similarly, whilst Severinus may have claimed to disguise his identity out of humility, the inevitable effect of doing so was to make it and him a magnet of

---

Lives of Germanus of Auxerre and Fulgentius: Constantius of Lyons, *Vita Germani* 31 (SC 112, 180); Ferrandus, *Vita Fulgentii* 12.24–5 (PL 65, 129).

[16] e.g. Ferrandus, *Vita Fulgentii* 12.23 (PL 65, 128); Gerontius, *Vita Melaniae Iunioris* 26 (SC 90, 178–80).

[17] For an excellent introduction, see J. Frow, *Genre* (London, 2006).

[18] As argued by J. M. Vessey, 'Ideas of Christian Writing in Late Roman Gaul' (unpublished D.Phil. thesis, University of Oxford, 1988), 116. The view is supported by C. Leyser, '"This Sainted Isle": Panegyric, Nostalgia, and the Invention of Lerinian Monasticism', in W. E. Klingshirn and M. Vessey, eds, *The Limits of Ancient Christianity* (Ann Arbor, MI, 1999), 188–208, at 199.

curiosity and fascination. This is particularly true if we imagine him consciously copying hagiographical models. Many hagiographers saw in a saint's reluctance to accept worldly renown proof of their worthiness; the pattern referred to in German scholarship as the *Fama Effekt* often culminates with saints being elected as bishop or abbot precisely because they have demonstrated the necessary reluctance and humility.[19] The sheer conventionality of this theme has long made historians highly sceptical. What is so richly attested in hagiography may have influenced real life, but only in the form of a polite and expected ritual performed in the pursuit of ambition.[20]

It would be rather unsatisfactory if explanations of this type remained the only way to connect third- and first-person spiritual accounts. Like other types of religious literature, hagiographies were presumably meant to be read in faithful humility. But with very little autobiography from our period, and very few descriptions of how hagiography was received, it is difficult to specify how the lives of saints were related by readers to their individual experience. One major exception to this is the famous conversion scene in Augustine's *Confessions*. Here is not the place to revisit this well-known passage in depth; let us limit ourselves instead to the role played in it by Athanasius's *Life of Antony*. As Michael Williams has convincingly argued, this was a critical element of the conversion.[21] It is well known that after hearing a child's voice over the garden wall chanting *tolle, lege*, Augustine recognized it as a divine instruction to read the first verse that struck his eyes after opening the Bible. Less often remembered is that this conviction took root only as Augustine recalled how he 'had heard that Anthony, on chancing to enter a church in the middle of the

---

[19] 'Der FAMA-EFFEKT beruht sich auf einem Paradoxon: Je mehr sich ein Anachoret von seiner Umwelt abschliesst, je mehr er den Kontakt zu den Mitmenschen zu meiden sucht, desto bekannter wird er': E.-M. Brunert, *Das Ideal der Wüstenaskese* (Münster, 1994), 411 ('The FAMA-EFFECT is based on a paradox: the more an anchorite cuts himself off from his environment, the more he seeks to avoid contact with his fellow men, the better known he becomes' [translation mine]).

[20] T. Hodgkin, *Italy and her Invaders*, 8 vols (London, 1880–9), 2: 248, speaks of 'the harmless comedy of the *nolo episcopari*, which was so commonly played in those days'. In a similar vein, Mathisen calls Hilarius's flight after Honoratus's death '*de rigueur*', suggesting that he was 'hoping, perhaps, to be able to fulfil the *topos* of being *raptus ad episcopatum*': *Ecclesiastical Factionalism*, 88.

[21] M. S. Williams, *Authorised Lives in Early Christian Biography: Between Eusebius and Augustine* (Cambridge, 2008), 150. My argument above is very close to that of Williams.

Gospel reading, had taken heed of what was being read as if it were addressed to himself'.[22] Significantly, this intense response to Antony's story was neither unique nor exceptional. Although Augustine does not state whether he himself had read the Latin translation of this Greek work at the time of his conversion, he had originally been told about the work by a former imperial officer, Ponticianus, whose own life was changed by reading it, as were those of his companions. The nature of this literary influence is as important as its impact. For Augustine, its message was that both the Bible and church history were of immediate relevance to every believer. As for Ponticianus, whose reading of the work had instantly made him 'ponder the shifting tides of his heart',[23] Augustine recognized the personal relevance of the great saint's story. Furthermore, Augustine's reaction only makes sense because he accepted the story as entirely historically true;[24] its emotional impact was in no sense merely cathartic or vicarious. Quite the contrary: what it encouraged in its readers was the immediate and direct literalization of the Christian message in their own lives, as had been the case in the lives of the saints. Seen in this way, the powerful impact of hagiographies upon individual spiritual lives is understandable.

Of course, one may or may not regard this realization as an indication of humility on Augustine's part: the fact that, when writing about themselves, religiously minded people in late antiquity saw their relationship with saints as relevant to their own religious identity can be judged in any number of ways. But what Augustine's experience effectively questions is a deeper assumption, namely the idea that the personal identities of religiously minded people were essentially stable and fully formed. In different ways, this assumption is shared both by hagiographers and by critical historians keen to reduce sanctity to more familiar phenomena. The former saw the characters of saints as already clear in childhood; the latter often attribute to religious authority an entirely

---

[22] Augustine, *Confessiones* 8.12.29; ed. J. J. O'Donnell, 3 vols (Oxford, 1992), 1: 101. The translations in the main text and at n. 24 below are from Augustine, *Confessions*, trans. P. Burton (London, 2001).

[23] Augustine, *Confessiones* 8.6.15.

[24] Ibid. 8.6.14: 'There was the strongest attestation for them [i.e. God's work through Antony]; they had occurred within living memory, and almost, indeed, within our own lifetimes.'

predictable and worldly logic. But the powerful influence exerted on religious people by the stories and experiences of others makes most sense when we recognize their personal identities as flexible and open to evolution. In a celebrated chapter of his masterpiece *Truth and Truthfulness*, the philosopher Bernard Williams argues against the deceptive idea that personal identities are most authentically created in isolation; rather, throughout our entire lives, they are a product of our interactions with other people who reinforce, encourage, challenge and correct them.[25]

Such a description may seem far too secular for an age as religiously minded as late antiquity. Ultimately, the very concept of holy men presupposes an identity derived not from society but ultimately from God. Nonetheless, what is striking about Augustine's case in particular is how prominent a role the responses of other people played in allowing his religious convictions to form. To put it another way, precisely because they could be seen as God's vehicles, the voices of others provided a crucial source of guidance in his spiritual quest. The theme of God speaking through other people is especially prominent in the *Confessions*.[26] For example, although he hears the child's voice when alone, the religious import of the episode is validated by his mother Monica and his friend Alypius as soon as he goes indoors. What he comes to realize, moreover, is not that God has finally spoken to him, but that he had been speaking to him all along. When he was an adolescent, Augustine's mother had consistently disapproved of his loose sexual behaviour; committing himself to celibacy, he now recognized that this disapproval had always come from God.[27] In other words, a view of personal identity which recognized God alone as the ultimate arbiter did not exclude a recognition of the role of other people. The influence exerted on him by a great man like Antony was entirely consistent with the attention he learned to pay to the voices of those immediately around him.

It would of course be unwise to assume that Augustine's religious experience was completely typical. However, I would suggest that the form it took and the influence of others upon him are capable

---

[25] B. Williams, *Truth and Truthfulness* (Princeton, NJ, 2002), ch. 8.

[26] See N. Wolterstorff, 'God's Speaking and Augustine's Conversion', in W. E. Mann, ed., *Augustine's Confessions: Critical Essays* (Oxford, 2006), 161–74.

[27] Augustine, *Confessiones* 2.3.7.

of providing a new interpretative tool for historians faced with rather conventional hagiographical devices like the *Fama Effekt*. The more we recognize that holy men, like others, had complex human identities, the less contrived such episodes appear. Late antique society needed confirmation of the true value of religious leaders before they could regard them as true holy men, and this could certainly involve a genuine demonstration of humility. But holy men too needed confirmation of their own vocation before they could commit themselves absolutely, just as Augustine, though intellectually persuaded by the ascetic life before he entered the garden, nonetheless required a external sign, as well the support of others in his new conviction. Whilst, ultimately, such confirmation could only be divine, it nonetheless emerged in the company of others.

Brown's suggestion that the study of sanctity should include a greater emphasis on the first-person perspective is valid. As I have argued here, the juxtaposition of third- and first-person religious writings is potentially a useful means of addressing this desideratum. In attempting to reconcile these apparently different perspectives, we come to recognize that they were never entirely separate in the first place, that holy men were not considered so remote from everyday life as to be personally irrelevant, that the experiences and views of others – whether encountered directly or through literature – were always an aspect of personal identity, and that holy men's identities were, like those of other people, neither rigid nor complete. In recent decades, our understanding of holy men and of the phenomenon of sanctity have improved enormously. Following Brown's lead, we have come to understand much more about the role of holy men in society. We still know much less about how they became holy men in the first place; in other words, about who they were not just in social, but also in personal terms. To begin to understand this issue, future research might reflect more deeply not just on the first- and third-person perspectives as alternative phenomena, but on their complex mutual relationship. This might begin with a question whose outline I have sketched in this paper: did holy men know they were holy men and, if so, how and why did this conviction form?

Oxford

POPES, PATRIARCHS AND ARCHBISHOPS AND THE ORIGINS OF THE CULT OF THE MARTYRS IN NORTHERN ITALY*

by ALAN THACKER

Although exceptional skill and learning have been devoted to the origins of martyr cult, undeniably this grand and highly distinguished tradition has been shaped by certain widely shared and long-standing assumptions. In particular, while great scholars such as Duchesne and Delehaye have exhibited a strong (and very proper) scepticism about particular legends, there has in general been a predisposition to accept at face value the underlying context as presented by the post-Constantinian Church. Most historians of the martyrs have followed hagiographical tradition and accepted that, as Pope Leo I claimed in the mid-fifth century, 'uncounted numbers' of the faithful had died in the imperial persecutions and were marked out as endowed with power 'to help those in danger, to drive away sickness, to expel unclean spirits and to cure infirmities without number'.[1] That carefully constructed picture, however, only emerges in the late fourth and fifth centuries, and it is the circumstances and processes which shaped its emergence that will be examined here.

This essay will focus on the Western patriarchate, and in particular northern Italy, where it remains extremely difficult to establish what exactly was handed down (in cultic terms) to the Church protected and empowered by Constantine. It will look especially at certain aspects of martyr cult as manifested in the crucial centuries immediately after the peace of the Church, to try to distinguish

* Versions of this essay were read to seminars at the Universities of York and Birmingham, and to the Winter Meeting of the Ecclesiastical Society, and I am grateful to members of all these gatherings for their helpful comments. The essay has also benefited greatly from discussion with Dr Mark Handley about the local epigraphic evidence and with Dr Tom Brown in the course of visits to Aquileia and Ravenna

[1] Leo I, *Tractatus septem et nonaginta* 5.4, 76.6 (CChr.SL 138, 24; 138A, 481); ET by Jane P. Freeland and Agnes J. Conway in *St Leo the Great: Sermons*, Fathers of the Church 93 (Washington, DC, 1996), 31–2, 338–9.

the driving forces which lay behind its early, and highly successful, development. Above all, it will examine veneration for the martyrs in certain churches and communities which could be said to be the seat of higher episcopacy – namely those sees whose ecclesiastical rulers had responsibilities wider than their own dioceses and bore such titles as pope, patriarch, archbishop or metropolitan. I have discussed the use of such titles elsewhere, but it is perhaps worth summarizing here what we know about their use and the organization which it implied.[2] Briefly, then, the main unit of organization throughout the late imperial Church as established by the time of Constantine in the early fourth century was the diocese presided over by a simple bishop. But above the bishop and weighing down upon him with varying degrees of authority lay senior managerial figures. The most immediate of these was the metropolitan, whose seat was the church of the metropolis of an imperial province and whose ecclesiastical authority corresponded to the secular governor of that province. Ideally, metropolitans convoked provincial synods and played a leading role in the consecration and disciplining of their suffragan bishops, but by the fifth century their authority seems to have been greater in the Eastern Empire than in the more disrupted West, where they were fewer in number and in places like Gaul more *primi inter pares* than genuine managerial superiors.

Certain metropolitans had greater powers still. At the apex of the hierarchy lay the holders of the five great sees, the *pentarchia* – Rome, Constantinople, Alexandria, Antioch and Jerusalem. Except for the New Rome, Constantinople, they were deemed to be of apostolic foundation and their holders bore variously the titles of pope, patriarch and archbishop.[3] In Isidore's phrase, they were the *patres principum*, 'the fathers of the chief prelates'.[4] And, of course, among them Rome enjoyed a primacy of honour as the see where Peter, chief of the apostles, was first bishop and was enshrined. Beneath the holders of these sees lay certain senior metropolitans

[2] For what follows, see A. T. Thacker, 'Gallic or Greek? Archbishops in England from Theodore to Ecgberht', in P. Fouracre and D. Ganz, eds, *Frankland: The Franks and the World of the Early Middle Ages* (Manchester, 2008), 44–69, esp. 45–55.

[3] V. Peri, *La Pentarchia: Istituzione ecclesiale (IV–VII sec.) e teoria canonico-teologica*, Settimane di studio nel Centro italiano di studi sull'alto medioevo 34 (Spoleto, 1988), 209–311.

[4] Isidore of Seville, *Etymologiae* 7.12.9 (*Isidori Hispalensis episcope etymologiarum sive originum libri xx*, ed. W. M. Lindsay, 2 vols, Scriptorum Classicorum Bibliotheca Oxoniensis (Oxford, 1911), I: 299).

with exceptional but not very clearly defined authority. Mostly seated at important cities which had at one time or another had the status of imperial capital, they too were styled archbishop, although the title was less widely used in the West than in the East, where by the sixth century the title was formally bestowed by the emperor.[5] Throughout this period the popes in their official correspondence were very sparing in their use of the title, confining it to the holders of those sees which the emperor had officially designated as archiepiscopal.

The title of patriarch has an equally complex history. By 539 when Justinian restricted its use to the five great sees already mentioned, in some areas it seems to have been adopted simply as means of expressing higher episcopal authority. Thus when Cassiodorus, in the name of Athalaric, king of the Ostrogoths, wrote to Pope John II in 533, he referred to the Italian metropolitans (including the pope) as patriarchs.[6] This usage seems to have continued in conservative Gaul until the early seventh century. The metropolitan bishop of Lyons, for example, styled himself *episcopus patriarcha* at a council in 585.[7] But such a usage in an official document such as the record of a council was very unusual.[8] It should be noted that again the popes did not use the term in this way in their correspondence.[9]

In late fourth-century northern Italy the complex arrangements just described were, as we shall see, in a very undeveloped state. While some sees were accorded a primacy of honour, the boundaries of metropolitan provinces had yet to be fully defined. There were, apparently, relatively few dioceses. New arrangements were forged under bishops such as Ambrose of Milan and Chromatius

---

[5]   In the East, it was also used as a title of honour, applied in particular to bishops who were not subject to a metropolitan but answerable only to their patriarch, a usage first recorded in the ninth century: J. Bingham, Origines Ecclesiasticae *or the Antiquities of the Christian Church*, 10 vols (London, 1710–22), 1: 191–4, 230–1. I am grateful to Andrew Louth for these references.

[6]   Cassiodorus, *Variae* 9.15.3 (MGH AA 12, 279).

[7]   Clearly this title was in the air in 585. In that year too Childebert, Guntramn's nephew, sent a letter to Bishop Laurence of Milan, whom he styled patriarch: 'Epistolae Austrasicae', in MGH Epp. 3, 155 (no. 45), cited by C. Sotinel, *Identité civique et christianisme: Aquilée du IIIᵉ au VIᵉ siècle*, Bibliothèque des Écoles françaises d'Athènes et de Rome 324 (Rome, 2005), 336. Cf. Peri, 'La Pentarchia', esp. 262–3.

[8]   In general the term was used unofficially – as in Gregory of Tours' reference to Nicetius of Lyons as *patriarcha*: *Libri historiarum X* 5.20 (MGH SRM 1.1, 227).

[9]   See pp. 75–6 below.

of Aquileia, and the hierarchy which emerged from their activities was intimately bound up with the promotion of the cult of the martyrs. Although only one among many areas where such cult was developing, northern Italy in this period fostered devotion to the martyrs in new and dramatic ways, which were to leave their impact not only on the region itself but upon the Latin West as a whole.

One last point: the evidence for western martyr cult. The textual record is highly problematic. A few martyrs are the subject of near-contemporary (and often horrific) accounts of their sufferings and execution, but these pre-Constantinian *Acta* or *Passiones* generally conclude with the death of their protagonist.[10] While, as was appropriate in Roman custom, they lay emphasis on the retrieval and decent burial of the corporeal remains, they say nothing about *post mortem* veneration and wonder-working, apart from a few appearances of the newly martyred in visions and dreams, encouraging those they had left behind.[11] In the West, as we shall see, it was not until well after the peace of the Church, in the late fourth century, that Bishop Ambrose of Milan flamboyantly boosted the power of the martyrs to intervene posthumously on earth, both through their corporeal remains and through relics derived from them.[12]

Many martyrological texts, in particular those devoted to the Roman martyrs, are little more than romances, often of highly uncertain date.[13] Archaeological evidence is perhaps more reliable, but has often been read in the light of later practice. It has disclosed a number of very early burials – either in sarcophagi or in *loculi*, the shelf-like spaces in the catacombs – where inscriptions characterize the inmate as 'martyr' (witness) or even 'most blessed martyr'.[14] It has also yielded a certain amount of evidence that from a very early date such burials might be distinguished by special attention and attract other burials around them; the nature of that attention and the traditions attached to it are, however, much more difficult to determine.[15]

[10] *Acts of the Christian Martyrs*, ed. H. Musurillo (Oxford, 1954).

[11] *Acts*, ed. Musurillo, 134, 182–4, 202, 222–4, 234.

[12] See pp. 57–61 below.

[13] For recent discussion, see C. Pilsworth, 'Dating the *Gesta martyrum*', *EME* 9 (2000), 309–24.

[14] V. F. Nicolai, F. Bisconti and D. Mazzoleni, *Les catacombes chrétiennes de Rome*, trans. and rev. J. Guyon (Regensburg, 1999), 174–5; and see pp. 64–74 below for Chrysogonus and Protus at Aquileia and Felix and Fortunatus at Vicenza.

[15] e.g. the burials around the tomb of St Peter at the Vatican: J. Toynbee and J.

Undoubtedly, however, the most influential evidence for the name and (overwhelming) number of the early Christian martyrs has been the so-called Hieronymian martyrology, the register of those who were believed to have suffered the extreme penalty during the imperial persecutions.[16] This work was little more than a list of names arranged calendrically (either according to the *dies natalis*, the day on which the martyr died, or the *depositio*, the day when the body was laid to rest), together with (usually) the location of the martyrdom and/or the place of burial. Wrongly ascribed to St Jerome, the earliest surviving form of the martyrology derives from a compilation made in France in the late sixth or even the early seventh century, although it is generally thought that that text was underlain by a much earlier redaction, probably made in the earlier fifth.[17] There is room for doubt about this.[18] But whatever the date of the original text, as transmitted in the earliest surviving manuscripts, the Hieronymian martyrology is a highly confused (and confusing) record. There are innumerable duplications and mutations; it was clearly the ambition of the compilers to magnify the number of saints, to impress posterity with the magnitude of the sacrifice under the imperial persecutors.[19] It is the nature of such a record to be worked over, enlarged and amended and in many – perhaps most – cases it is very difficult to ascribe a date to an entry.

The remainder of this essay will examine the north Italian evidence in more detail. It will start with a brief survey of the evidence from Rome, where martyr cult burgeoned in the late fourth century, and then look more closely at the emergence of

---

Ward-Perkins, *The Shrine of St Peter and the Vatican Excavations* (London, 1956), 145–62.

[16] *Martyrologium Hieronymianum,* in *ActaSS* Nov. 2/1, 2/2 [hereafter *MH* 2/1, 2/2], edited from the principal early surviving manuscripts: Paris, BN, lat. 10837 (E); Bern, Burgerbibliothek, Bongars 289 (B); Wolfenbüttel, Herzog August Bibliothek, Weissenburg 81 (W).

[17] J. Dubois, *Les martyrologes du Moyen Âge latin,* Typologie des sources du Moyen Âge occidental 26 (Turnhout, 1978), 29–37.

[18] See, e.g., F. Lifshitz, *The Name of the Saint. The Martyrology of Jerome and Access to the Sacred in Francia 627–827* (Notre Dame, IN, 2006), esp. 13–29.

[19] This tendency to repeat names in order to add to the list of the martyred is very evident in another witness to *MH*, the martyrology of Tallaght, at the core of which lies an abbreviated form of *MH* probably drafted in Northumbria in the later seventh century. Here names are repeated more or less randomly – apparently to 'punctuate' long lists of entries – and certainly without any regard to historical veracity: P. Ó Riain, 'The Northumbrian Phase in the Formation of the Hieronymian Martyrology: The Evidence of the Martyrology of Tallaght', *Analecta Bollandiana* 120 (2002), 311–63.

the two great metropolitan sees in the area, Milan and Aquileia. It will conclude with a survey of the role of apostolic and martyr cult in underpinning the pretensions of Aquileia and Ravenna to patriarchal status and independence from Rome.

THE MARTYR CULTS OF ROME

There is, of course, a vast literature.[20] What is crucial to this essay is the fact that, although by the late fourth century much emphasis is laid upon the countless number of Rome's martyrs by writers such as the Spanish poet Prudentius, it is really quite difficult to locate authentic martyrs executed in Rome in the record, especially in the relatively brief period of the Great Persecution.[21] And it is even more difficult to trace authentic evidence of continuing cult, as we might expect if the primary impetus to martyr cult came from below, from long-standing devotion originating in the period before the peace of the Church. Much effort has been expended on this and it is certainly possible to show that some tombs were treated as special and even that they attracted other burials, but that is not the same as the expectation of miracles in the presence of corporeal remains, or the distribution of portions of those remains as wonder-working relics; that almost certainly came later.[22] What, above all, is lacking is any memory of these figures as historic persons. We know nothing about almost any of the Roman martyrs apart from their names and (probably) the day on which they died or were laid to rest, preserved by the church as their feast day, *dies natalis* or *dies depositionis*. We have to remember that in fourth-century Rome the pope was only a middle-ranking imperial official; the prefect of the city was far grander, and the great extramural basilicas, such as St

[20]   Recently discussed in A. T. Thacker, 'Rome of the Martyrs: Saints, Cults and Relics, Fourth to Seventh Centuries', in É. Ó Carragáin and C. Neuman de Vegvar, eds, *Roma Felix – Formations and Reflections of Medieval Rome* (Aldershot, 2007), 13–49; idem, 'Martyr Cult within the Walls: Saints and Relics in the Roman *Tituli* of the Fourth to Seventh Centuries', in A. Minnis and J. Roberts, eds, *Text, Image and Interpretation* (Turnhout, 2007), 31–70.

[21]   T. D. Barnes has shown that, after the capture of the Emperor Valerian in 260, in the West at least it is unlikely that many Christians suffered martyrdom. The Great Persecution, which between 303 and 311 saw many hundreds of deaths in the East, only lasted from 303 to 306 in the West where it was only partially enforced; it saw no executions at all in Gaul and Britain: see esp. his 'Lactantius and Constantine', *JRS* 73 (1973), 29–46; *Constantine and Eusebius* (Cambridge, MA, 1981), 22–7, 28, 38–9, 358; *The New Empire of Diocletian and Constantine* (Cambridge, MA, 1982), 180.

[22]   Thacker, 'Rome of the Martyrs', 43–5.

Peter's, San Lorenzo fuori le mura and Sant' Agnese fuori le mura, were imperial foundations in the hands of imperial administrators.[23] They were also the site of imperial tombs, and it may be no coincidence that it was the saints associated with these foundations who became leading patrons of the Roman Christian community. As one French archaeologist has suggested of the basilica of SS Pietro e Marcellino, where the Empress Helena was buried, it was not the cults which attracted the imperial burial; rather it was the imperial burial which conferred prestige on the cults.[24]

Although a limited group of some fifty martyrs was already the subject of commemoration by the mid-fourth century when the first surviving Roman calendar was compiled, the real explosion of martyr cult takes place in the late fourth century during the troubled pontificate of Pope Damasus I (366–84). Damasus's famous inscriptions, distinctively branded with the calligrapher Filocalus's elegant lettering, stamped his presence on cult sites, including the great imperial burials, scattered around extramural Rome. They stressed the Roman-ness of the enshrined saints and thereby not only enhanced Damasus's prestige within Rome but also enhanced the prestige of the city as a Christian centre.[25] By 400, Prudentius could write of the countless number of the remains of saints adorning Rome identified by their incised *tituli* (inscriptions), many of them anonymous, their names known to Christ alone.[26] We are left with a strong sense that Damasus was not so much the publicist of an ancient tradition as the creator of a new phenomenon.

THE CULT OF RELICS IN MILAN

One crucial element of martyr cult in its finally achieved form was, however, absent from Damasus's activity: there is no convincing evidence that the pope ever distributed secondary relics as a concrete means of establishing contact with the martyrs and of obtaining

---

[23] See Thacker, 'Clergy and *Custodes* at Old St Peter's from the Fourth to the Eighth Century', forthcoming in R. McKitterick et al., eds, *Old Saint Peter's* (Cambridge, 2012)..

[24] J. Guyon, *Le Cimetière aux deux lauriers*, Bibiothèque des Écoles françaises d'Athènes et de Rome 264 (Rome 1987), 262.

[25] M. Sághy, '*Scinditur in partes populus*: Pope Damasus and the Martyrs of Rome', *EME* 9 (2000), 273–87; Thacker, 'Rome of the Martyrs', 30–8 and references therein.

[26] Prudentius, *Peristephanon* 11, lines 1–16; ed. and trans. H. J. Thomson, LCL 398 (Cambridge, MA, 1953), 304–6.

their intervention in earthly affairs.[27] In the West, that idea emerged in Milan, then capital of the Western Empire, only a few years after Damasus's activity in Rome. It seems clear that the pope's enterprise had impressed Bishop Ambrose. Hitherto, Milan had contained few if any martyrial sites.[28] The bishop set about remedying this partly by importing relics from elsewhere but most crucially by his famous *inventio* (literally a "finding") of the first martyrs native to Milan, the hitherto 'forgotten' martyrs Gervasius and Protasius, whose remains he exhumed and placed under the altar of his new church, the *basilica ambrosiana*. This event was marked by spectacular cures.[29] Much was made of the blood which emanated from the bodies on their discovery and Ambrose employed this to good effect by distributing throughout western Christendom phials of blood-soaked dust as corporal relics, which he identified as a potent means of accessing the intercessory and wonder-working powers of the two martyrs. He and his circle developed the doctrine that the saint was as present in the least particle of dust infused with his corporeality as he was in his body at the tomb. The initial *inventio* was soon followed by others and by further relic distribution.[30]

Alongside this development of local cult went the introduction of apostolic relics. Ambrose's establishment of the *basilica apostolorum* and the introduction of relics of the apostles John, Andrew and Thomas from the East (probably from Constantinople) is well known, and is the subject of two entries commemorating the *ingressus reliquiarum* into the city in the Hieronymian martyrology.[31] Again Milan became a centre for the diffusion of these relics to other western sees, not only in northern Italy but further afield in Campania and in France.

---

[27] Thacker, 'Rome of the Martyrs', 43–5.

[28] The martyrs Nabor and Felix were clearly established in Milan before the *inventio* of Gervasius and Protasius in 386. They had probably been brought there from Lodi before Ambrose's time, but it was Ambrose who popularized their cult: Paulinus of Milan, *Vita Ambrosii* 14, in *Vita di Sant'Ambrogio*, ed. M. Navoni, Storia della chiesa 6 (Milan, 1996), 75 and note; M. Humphries, *Communities of the Blessed* (Oxford, 1999), 223–4.

[29] Ambrose, *Epistula* 77 (22) (CSEL 82, 126–40); Paulinus, *Vita Ambrosii* 14 (ed. Navoni, 74–6).

[30] Discussed at greater length by A. T. Thacker, '*Loca sanctorum*: The Significance of Place in the Study of the Saints', in A. T. Thacker and R. Sharpe, eds, *Local Saints and Local Churches in the Early Medieval West* (Oxford, 2002), 1–43, at 5–14; G. Clarke, 'Victricius of Rouen: Praising the Saints', *JECS* 7 (1999), 365–99.

[31] Entry for 9 May: *MH* 2/1, 57 (occurs only in ms B); 2/2, 241–2. Entry for 27 Nov.: *MH* 2/1, 247; 2/2, 623. For *MH* mss E, B, W, see n. 16 above.

It is worth stressing two points about the Ambrosian programme: first, that (at least in the West) it was revolutionary and highly visible; and, second, that it was a potent means of articulating ecclesiastical patronage and defining superior sees. The pioneering aspect of Ambrose's activity is indicated by the fact that, shortly before the *inventio* of the saints Gervasius and Protasius, the Emperor Theodosius had sought to prohibit interference in martyrial tombs. Clearly, such events were just becoming an issue.[32] Ambrose's ostentatious translation of 386 advertised the martyrs' power to intervene on earth on behalf of their clients; it also promoted in a new way the distribution of corporeal or secondary relics. Indeed, it is difficult to show that such relics were at all a significant element in Christian cult before this date.[33] The theology developed by Ambrose's circle suggested that the saints themselves came visiting when relics sent, and they were received as if this was indeed the case. At Rouen, for example, to which Ambrose sent apostolic and martyrial relics in 396, Bishop Victricius came to meet and venerate them (he appears to have prostrated himself before them) and then accompanied them back to the city in a very public ceremony, intended to be comparable to an imperial *adventus*. They were then set up in a new basilica and clearly promoted as objects of public devotion.[34] Ambrose's gifts clearly enhanced his own standing as a bishop and the standing of his see. It established and bound together a circle of clients, who venerated the same saints and talked the same intense relic-language. Ambrose had ratcheted up the whole apparatus of martyr cult, through processes which went well beyond Damasus's activities in Rome.

Milan's activities need to be set in the context of the local ecclesiastical structure. Although by virtue of its status as the Western capital Milan was the senior Italian see after Rome itself, its metropolitan status took some time to be defined. Before Ambrose's episcopate, there seems to have been no formal hierarchy of rela-

32 *Codex Theodosianus* 9.17 ('De sepulchris violatis'), ed. Th. Mommsen and P. Meyer (Berlin, 1905), sections 6 (381), 7 (386).

33 For an authoritative expression of the received view of the development of relics, see P. Séjourné, 'Reliques', in A. Vacant, ed., *Dictionnaire de théologie catholique*, 15 vols (Paris, 1903–50), 13: 2312–76. Early African *Acta*, such as those of Perpetua and Felicitas, show that the faithful valued tokens of the martyrs, such as the ring which the living Saturus returned to Pudens as a *pignus et memoria sanguinis* after dipping it in his own blood: *Acts*, ed. Musurillo, 130 (ch. 21).

34 Clarke, 'Victricius'.

ALAN THACKER

tions between the relatively few existing sees of northern Italy.[35] At most, it can be said that some (such as Milan and perhaps Aquileia) were more influential than others, largely because they were located at major cities where the emperors from time to time resided rather than because (unlike Rome) they had some special status determined by their Christian past. All this began to change under Ambrose. He not only enhanced his own see by founding there a new and widely renowned cult, but he also established an ascendancy over other sees by making them the theatre of further martyrial *inventiones*. In particular, in 393 he orchestrated the *inventio* of the Bolognese martyrs Vitalis and Agricola, translating their remains to a church on the via Emilia to the east of the Roman city. Thereafter he consolidated his influence at Bologna by providing a successor to Bishop Eustathius (who had co-operated with him in the *inventio*) in the person of his deacon Felix.[36]

Ambrose followed this up by proceeding to Florence, where he was responsible for the consecration of a new basilica on which he bestowed what he termed *apophoreta* ('presents') brought with him from Bologna. These 'palms of the martyr' were secondary relics discovered at the *inventio*, evidently wood and nails allegedly used in the crucifixion of Agricola. They presumably played a role in the dedication of the Florentine church.[37] Again, Ambrose's action seems to have been followed by intervention in the affairs of the bishopric. Although Florence's first known bishop was recorded in 313, the figure who definitively established Christianity there was Zenobius, whose episcopate began c. 394, at the time of, or shortly after, Ambrose's visit.[38]

It is not entirely clear whether at Bologna and Florence Ambrose was dealing with well-established bishoprics or with new or recently revived ones. It is almost certain, however, that he was involved in founding new sees among established communities which had hitherto lacked a bishop.[39] Such activity was proper

[35] Sotinel, *Identité civique*, 188–9.
[36] Introduction to *Vita di Sant'Ambrogio*, ed. Navoni, 29; Ambrose, *Exhortatio Virginitatis* (PL 16, 347–79, at 351); F. Bonnard, 'Bologne', *Dictionnaire d'histoire et de géographie ecclésiastique* [hereafter *DHGE*] 9 (Paris, 1937), cols 645–60, at 650–1.
[37] Ambrose, *Exhortatio Virginitatis* (PL 16, 351, 354); N. Mclynn, *Ambrose of Milan: Church and Court in a Christian Capital* (Berkeley, CA, 1994), 347–50.
[38] C. C. Calzolai, 'Florence', *DHGE* 17 (Paris, 1971), cols 533–45, at 534–5.
[39] Humphries, *Communities of the Blessed*, 147–53, 173–5; Sotinel, *Identité civique*,

60

to metropolitans and set up dependent suffragans appropriate to metropolitan status. In the late fourth century there were ecclesiastical roles and hierarchies waiting to be carved out in northern Italy, and Milan clearly made the most of its opportunities.

To sum up: under Ambrose the see of Milan was establishing itself as the leading see in northern Italy. A crucial element in his strategy was a revolutionary new deployment of martyr cult. As with Damasus in Rome, the saints which emerged under Ambrose had very dubious origins. Indeed, in the case of Gervasius and Protasius they may have been complete inventions. And at the very least, others such as Vitalis and Agricola were figures, hitherto little more than names, to whom new identities were assigned. By moving western martyr cult along new and more demonstrative paths, Ambrose enhanced the prestige of his own see and secured spiritual *virtus* to underpin the extension of its authority over others and the establishment of new dependent suffragans.

THE RISE OF AQUILEIA

It is against this background that that we need to consider the development of martyr cult in another north Italian see, Aquileia. Aquileia was undoubtedly one of the principal cities of northern Italy. It functioned from time to time as an imperial residence in the fourth century and was capital of the province of Venetia-Istria, but generally remained second to Milan.[40] Aquileia's achievement of senior ecclesiastical status is a fascinating and complex story. Already by the late fourth century its standing is apparent from its choice as the venue for a church council to deal with the alleged Arianism of two Dacian bishops. The Bishop of Aquileia, Valerian, presided, sitting in an elevated position with Ambrose, the prime mover, beside him. Although Aquileia's position vis-à-vis other early sees in the area, such as Trent, Parenzo and Verona, is not entirely clear, it is evident that its bishop was setting up new sees in the late fourth century in Christian centres which had probably hitherto looked to it for leadership.[41] Our best evidence is from Concordia, a settlement between Aquileia and Venice, where the

---

199–212. Note that in all this Rome played no part; it was simply the senior (patriarchal) see by virtue of its apostolic status.

[40] Sotinel, *Identité civique*, 16–24.

[41] Ibid. 188–208; Humphries, *Communities of the Blessed*, 73–9, 140–5.

introduction of apostolic relics was accompanied by the consecration both of a church to receive them and of a bishop for the local community. The presiding bishop delivered a celebrated sermon at the dedication of the church which provides good evidence of the event and its context.[42] From this we learn that the relics were those of SS John the Baptist, John the Evangelist, Andrew, Thomas and Luke, all associated with Ambrose's *basilica apostolorum*. They may have come either directly from him or from the sources which supplied him. At all events they suggest that the sermon dates from the late fourth century; it has been plausibly ascribed to Chromatius, Bishop of Aquileia (387/8–407/8).[43] The sermon also tells us that the city of the presiding bishop had received relics of these saints. That perhaps accords with a *dedicatio basilicae* and *ingressus reliquiarum*, located at Aquileia and recorded in the Hieronymian martyrology on 3 September, in which the saints involved included Andrew, Luke, John and (perhaps) Euphemia, the saint of Chalcedon.[44] Like Milan and the new see at Concordia, Aquileia was to have its own *basilica apostolorum*.[45]

All this suggests that while the bishop of Aquileia was not so active in importing apostolic saints as Ambrose, when the opportunity arose he linked the arrival of apostolic relics with the establishment of suffragan bishoprics and the enhancement of his own see-city. It precedes, and is in many ways a pattern for, Victricius's activities at Rouen, which itself emerged as a metropolis in the fifth century.[46] Like Ambrose in Milan, Chromatius was feeling his way towards the expression of a hitherto largely unformulated

[42] Chromatius, *Sermones* 26 (CChr.SL 9A, 118–22). For the impact on Concordia of the importing of these relics, see G. Brusin and P. L. Zovatto, 'La trichora paleocristiana nel nuovo complesso monumentale di Concordia', *Felix Ravenna*, 3 ser. fasc. 35 (86; 1962), 74–94. The new basilica clearly had considerable prestige and was soon augmented by new tombs of those seeking burial near the saints – *ad limina apostolorum* – and eventually a second basilica was established beside it, perhaps developed from the tomb of the holy priest Mauricius.

[43] Chromatius, *Sermones* (SC 164, 103–8); J. Lemarié, 'Homélies inédites de Saint Chromace d'Aquiléé', *Revue Bénédictine* 73 (1963), 181–243, at 229–35.

[44] *MH* 2/1, 115; 2/2, 485–6. Euphemia is recorded in *MH* ms W as if she were an addition, but relics of the saint were certainly known in the West. They were imported into Milan by Ambrose and distributed to others of his circle: Paulinus of Nola, *Carmina* 27, lines 428–35 (CSEL 30, 281); *MH* 2/1, 57; 2/2, 242; G. Lucchesi, 'Eufemia di Calcedonia', *Bibliotheca Sanctorum* 5 (Rome, 1994), cols 154–9, at 158–9.

[45] G. Brusin, 'La *Basilica apostolorum* di Aquileia', in *Mullus: Festschrift Theodor Klauser* (Münster, 1964), 28–33.

[46] Judging by the rankings suggested by the order of episcopal attestations of

higher episcopacy. By the mid-fifth century, the standing of his see had clearly been recognized; in 442 Pope Leo I expressly referred to the metropolitan bishop of Venetia, undoubtedly Aquileia.[47] This status was retained, despite the city's destruction by the Hunnic king Attila in 452, from which it never fully recovered. Aquileia's special position alongside Milan in northern Italy continued to be demonstrated by the tradition, in place by the sixth century, that the bishop of the one city was always consecrated by his opposite number in the other.[48] We cannot be certain of the extent of the fifth-century province, but it has been suggested that in the earlier fifth century it was extended eastwards into Istria and Pannonia and northwards across the Alps to the Danube. Certainly by the sixth it included Istria with its important dioceses of Pola and Parenzo.[49]

Despite, then, the city's reversals in the secular sphere, its bishops retained and (as we shall see) even enhanced their standing in the later fifth and sixth centuries. Undoubtedly one reason for Aquileia's continuing ecclesiastical importance in the sixth century, despite its reversals in the secular sphere, was the collapse of episcopal authority in Milan. Already eroded by the removal of the imperial seat in 402 to Ravenna, that authority was further weakened when, at the onset of the Gothic wars in Italy, Bishop Datius fled the city. After the failure of imperial forces to defend Milan and its destruction by the Goths, Datius remained abroad in Constantinople until his death in 552. As a result, sees such as Trent and Verona, in the earlier fifth century on the frontier between the ecclesiastical provinces of Milan and Aquileia, had by the later sixth moved firmly into the hands of the bishops of Aquileia.[50] By the mid-sixth century, indeed, the latter had even assumed the

---

Frankish councils, 461–585: *Concilia Galliae* (CChr.SL 148, 148); MGH L Concilia 1, 9, 85, 96, 135, 145, 172.

[47]   Leo I, *Epistolae* 1, 2 (PL 54, 593–7, 597–8).

[48]   Referred to by Pelagius I as an established fact: *Epistulae quae supersunt* 24, ed. P. M. Gassó and C. M. Batlle, Scripta et Documenta 8 (Montserrat, 1956), 73–4.

[49]   G. Fedalto, *Aquileia: Una chiesa, due patriarcati*, Corpus Scriptorum Ecclesiae Aquileiensis 1 (Città Nuova, 1999), 66–70.

[50]   C. Sotinel, 'The Three Chapters and the Transformations of Italy', in C. Chazelle and C. Cubitt, eds, *The Crisis of the* Oikoumene, Studies in the Early Middle Ages 14 (Turnhout, 2007), 85–120, at 86–9; idem, *Identité civique*, 323–38.

title of patriarch. That aggrandizement, referred to disparagingly by
Pelagius I in 559, most certainly did not have papal recognition.[51]

How did the development of martyr cult play into this complex
political and ecclesiastical situation? In modern historiography,
Aquileia is renowned for the number and authenticity of its martyr
cults. One reason for this is undoubtedly the witness of the Hieronymian martyrology, which contains an exceptional number of
references to Aquileia (indeed, after Rome and Milan, more entries
than any other western see) and which features Bishop Chromatius together with Septimius, a fifth-century bishop of Altinum
(a suffragan see of Aquileia), as alleged patrons of the work in its
prefatory material.[52] Another is the striking and unusual archaeological evidence, including some early inscriptions to martyrs.[53]
Despite all this, as we shall see, Aquileia, like Milan, depended
primarily upon reinvention rather than secure tradition in its elaboration of martyr cult.

On the basis of the Hieronymian record, eleven saints have been
isolated as early martyrs at Aquileia and its environs. They are as
follows: Hilarius and Tatianus (16/17 March); the Cantii – Cantius,
Cantianus and Cantianilla (31 May); Protus (15 June); Herma-
chora and Fortunatus (12 July); Felix and Fortunatus (14 August);
and Chrysogonus (24 November).[54] The martyrological evidence,
however, is nothing like as simple as that list would suggest. The
following repetitions should be noted: Protus and Chrysogonus
also appear with the Cantii on 31 May;[55] Cantianella and Protus
appear together on 14 June;[56] Candidus, Cantianus and Chrisogonus
appear with Protus on 15 June;[57] Cantius, Cantianus and Cantiana
appear on 17 June;[58] Chrysogonus appears as martyred in Aquileia

[51] He referred dismissively to Bishop Paul of Aquileia as 'patriarch, as they suppose
(*ut ipsi putant*) of Venetia and Histria': *Epistulae*, ed. Gassó and Battle, 73–4; see pp. 75–6
below.

[52] *MH* 2/2, 1.

[53] See pp. 67–9 below.

[54] e.g. G. Cuscito, *Martiri cristiani ad Aquileia e in Istria*, Università degli studi
di Trieste, Facoltà di magistero, 3 ser. 25 (Udine, 1992), 9–10, 53; idem, 'I martiri
aquileiesi', in S. Tavano and G. Bergamini, eds, *Patriarchi. Quindici secoli di civiltà fra
l'Adriatico e l'Europa centrale* (Milan, 2000), 49; Sotinel, *Identité civique*, 373.

[55] *MH* 2/1, 69; 2/2, 283.

[56] *MH* 2/1, 78; 2/2, 318–19.

[57] *MH* 2/1, 78; 2/2, 319.

[58] *MH* 2/1, 79; 2/2, 322.

on 17 February[59] and as a martyr in Rome or in Aquileia in various entries for 23/24 November.[60] Even allowing for errors in copying over a long period of transmission, this is a disturbingly confused set of entries. We should also note the suspicious duplication. Fortunatus appears three times, twice in association with different saints,[61] while in the case of the Cantii, even the earliest textual witness felt it necessary to explain away at some length the curiously implausible similarity of their names.[62] It seems reasonable then to start from the premiss that the martyrology's record of these Aquileian saints has been corrupted.

This essay will focus mainly on Fortunatus and Felix, venerated in Aquileia itself, and on a group of five saints, Chrysogonus, Protus and the Cantii, whose cult was centred upon a settlement some six miles to the east of the city now known as San Canzian d'Isonzo. Let us look first at Felix and Fortunatus.[63] According to their *passio*, of uncertain date but not earlier than the later fifth or sixth century, they were brothers, from the environs of Aquileia,[64] arrested in the time of Diocletian for professing their Christian faith and executed on 14 May outside the walls beside the river which is next to the city (presumably the Isonzo). After their death, some of their compatriots (*provinciales eorum*) from Vicenza sought to take them to their own city, but the citizens of Aquileia would not permit this. Dissension broke out, but fearing the savagery of the Aquileian authorities the two parties came to an accord: one of the brothers should go to Vicenza while the other remained in Aquileia.[65]

---

59 *MH* 2/1, 22; 2/2, 102–3 (as Crisentianus).

60 *MH* 2/1, 146 (23, martyr of Rome (ms W); martyr of Aquileia (ms E); 24, *natalis* in Rome (ms E)); 2/2, 615, 618.

61 *MH* 2/1, 77, 90, 106 (*natalis* of Fortunatus only in mss B and W); 2/2, 314–15, 371, 442.

62 Maximus of Turin, *Sermo* 15 (CChr.SL 23, 57–8): 'Nec mirum si similes sunt nomine, qui sunt similes passione; si una est illis apud homines appellatio, quibus apud deum est una vocatio.' Although grand families, most notably of course that of the Emperor Constantine, did identify themselves by alliterative naming, the particular variant endings in this case, -ius, -ianus, -ianella, look distinctly formulaic and were perhaps confected from the nomen or cognomen Cantius: see p. 73 n. 95 below.

63 The origins of the cult are discussed by M. P. Billanovich, 'Appunti di agiografia aquileiese', *Rivista di storia della chiesa in Italia* 30 (1976), 5–24.

64 'de vicino loco, non longe ab hac civitate'.

65 *ActaSS* Jun. 2, 460–3; R. Bratož, *Il Cristianesimo aquileiense prima di Costantino* (Udine, 1999), 390–1; Billanovich, 'Appunti', 11.

This odd story clearly reflects the nature of the cult in the sixth century, when Venantius Fortunatus, who came from the Veneto, noted that the remains of Felix were venerated in Vicenza and those of Fortunatus in Aquileia.[66] Other, earlier, evidence is, however, less conclusive. Felix and Fortunatus feature in a mass preface attributed to Eusebius, Bishop of Milan (449–62), but this only discusses their sufferings and death in an unlocated city.[67] More significant, if genuine, is the sermon, now generally attributed to Bishop Chromatius, of which only the opening sentence survives: 'Today is the feast day (*natale*) of the holy martyrs Felix and Fortunatus who adorned our city with their glorious martyrdom.'[68] This would imply that the cult of Felix and Fortunatus had been introduced by then and provided with a context linking it to Aquileia. It should be noted, however, that there is room for doubt about the ascription of this lost sermon to Chromatius.[69] Apart from this, the only other early textual evidence for the veneration of Felix and Fortunatus is the garbled entries in the various early versions of the Hieronymian martyrology, which, if read in the light of Fortunatus's clear statements, again appear to record a cult divided between Aquileia and Vicenza.[70]

Also curious is the uncertainty about the feast day of these

[66] 'Felicem meritis Vicetia laeta refundit / et Fortunatum fert Aquileia suum' (Carmen 8, lines 165–6); he also refers to 'the urn of the blessed martyr Fortunatus in Aquileia' (*Vita S. Martini* 4, lines 658–60): MGH AA 4/1, 185, 369 respectively. It is clear that by the ninth century the community at Vicenza itself believed that it possessed only St Felix's body: L. Cracco Rugini, 'Storia totale di una piccolo città: Vicenza romana', in A. Broglio and L. Cracco Rugini, eds, *Storia di Vicenza* (Vicenza, 1987), 205–303, at 290–1.

[67] Bratoz, *Il Cristianesimo*, 390; *Sacramentarium Bergomense*, ed. A. Paredi (Bergamo, 1962); A. Paredi, *Le Prefazioni ambrosiani* (Milan, 1937), 160–2, 277–90.

[68] 'qui civitatem nostram glorioso martyrio decorarunt': Chromatius, *Sermones* 7 (CChr.SL 9A, 30–1).

[69] For this, see Lemarié, 'Homélies de Saint Chromace', 201–31. Against Lemarié's arguments must be set the fact that the sermon is anonymous, one of a group recorded in Ripoll in northern Spain in the twelfth century. Lemarié bases his attribution to Chromatius partly on stylistic resemblances, which can hardly be conclusive since only two sermons are securely attributable to the bishop. His crucial argument is that the sermon's opening sentence must refer to Aquileia. This, however, may well derive from the later *passio*, whose feast date (14 May) the preacher evidently followed (see p. 67 below). This matter will be addressed more fully in a forthcoming paper by Richard Sharpe and myself.

[70] *MH* 2/1, 106. As construed by Delehaye: 'In Aquileia Furtunati, Vicetiae Felicis': 2/2, 442–3, and perhaps best rendered: 'In Aquileia (the feast day of) Fortunatus, at Vicenza'.

saints. The martyrology indicates that the Aquileian feast fell on 14 August, whereas the *passio* gives 14 May as the date of their death, a date followed by the Ambrosian calendar in Milan.[71] The manuscript with the lost sermon ascribed to Chromatius (which also dates from the twelfth century) places that sermon under the same incipit as a sermon devoted to the Ascension, perhaps because the homily on the martyrs was preached at much the same time. If so, that would require a date in May or early June and hence would suggest that the place at which the sermon was preached also commemorated Fortunatus and Felix on 14 May.[72] A further entry in the martyrology, for 11 June, records a translation in Aquileia of Fortunatus, bishop and martyr.[73] Although no Aquileian bishop of this name is known, this may well refer to the arrival of Fortunatus in the city and the ascription to him of a local identity after he had arrived there. All this clearly indicates that the cult of Felix and Fortunatus was scarcely authoritatively recorded either in the martyrology or in Aquileian early sources.

One other pertinent piece of evidence is the existence of an extramural cemeterial church to the south of the city known in the Middle Ages as San Felice and only later as SS Felice e Fortunato. Excavation of this building, which was in ruins by the end of the eighteenth century, suggests that it dated from the fifth century, at the earliest from c. 400.[74] Inscriptions from the same cemetery refer to it as a place or neighbourhood of saints – unnamed but clearly in the plural.[75] More explicit than these is that which commemorates a sixteen-year-old girl called Aurelia Maria and concludes with a request to the (again unnamed) holy martyrs to keep her in mind. This last, which has been dated to the later fourth or early fifth century,[76] was carved on a stone which may

---

[71] V. Saxer, 'L'hagiographie ancienne d'Aquilée à propos d'un livre récent', *Mélanges de l'École française de Rome, Moyen Âge, temps modernes* 92 (1980), 373–92, at 376; *Sacramentarium Bergomense*, ed. Paredi, 243.

[72] Ibid. 375–6.

[73] *MH* 2/1, 77; *MH* 2/2, 314–15; Saxer, 'L'hagiographie', 380–2.

[74] Sotinel, *Identité civique*, 267–8.

[75] 'Sanctorum locus', 'sancta beatorum vicinia': Corpus Inscriptionum Latinarum [henceforth CIL] 5, *Inscriptiones Galliae Cisalpinae Latinae*, ed. Th. Mommsen, 2 vols (Berlin, 1872, 1877), nos 1678, 1698; J. B. Brusin, *Inscriptiones Aquileiae*, 3 vols (Udine, 1991–93), 3: 1089–90, 1105 (nos 3114, 3162); Sotinel, *Identité civique*, 214 n. 202; Billanovich, 'Appunti', 14–15.

[76] Although the name Aurelia would perhaps have seemed rather old-fashioned by then: J. G. Keenan, 'The Names Flavius and Aurelius as Status Designations in Later

be part of a sarcophagus, but is perhaps more likely to have been a slab closing a burial pit or *loculus*.[77] Recorded as discovered in an unidentified *vicus* near Aquileia, it too has been attributed to the cemetery of San Felice, although the lettering of the inscription and the pitted surface of the slab bear a notable resemblance to the martyrial sarcophagi located in San Canzian d'Isonzo.[78]

It is difficult to know what to make of all this. If the cult originated at Aquileia and the city retained one of the bodies, why is the church there dedicated to St Felix, the one whose body was lost? The relatively late date of that church is also noteworthy. That contrasts with the archaeological evidence from Vicenza, which is clearly earlier. At Vicenza we do indeed have evidence of a basilican *aula* dating from the late fourth or early fifth century, securely dedicated to both saints.[79] Moreover, this contains a slab – evidently the lid of a sarcophagus – on which was inscribed 'the blessed martyrs Felix and Fortunatus' and which was pierced by an opening (*fenestella*) through which the faithful could touch the relics or place objects upon them to be sanctified by contact. The inscription on the lid, which is a revised classical stele, could be of any date between the fourth and sixth century, but it has been suggested that it more probably belongs to the later fourth or early fifth.[80] Coins found in the urn containing the relics when it was opened in 1813 date from the reigns of Constantine, Constans and Constantius Gallus and could well have been placed there shortly after 351/354.[81]

As Claire Sotinel has pointed out, it looks as if the dual cult was

Roman Egypt', *Zeitschrift für Papyologie und Epigraphik* 11 (1973), 33–63; 13 (1974), 283–304; idem, 'An Afterthought on the Names Flavius and Aurelius', *Zeitschrift für Papyologie und Epigraphik* 53 (1983), 245–50. I am grateful to Mark Handley for these references.

77   CIL 5, no. 1636; Brusin, *Inscriptiones Aquileiae*, 3: 1030 (no. 2925); G. Vergone, *Le Epigrafi lapidarie del Museo Paleocristiano di Monastero (Aquileia)*, Antichità Altoadriatiche: Monografia 3 (Trieste, 2007), no. 8 (with illustration).

78   I am grateful to Mark Handley for this suggestion.

79   Cracco Rugini, 'Storia totale', 295–8; M. Mirabella Roberti, 'La tomba dei martyri', 'Gli eóifici', 'I musaici', *La Basilica dei Santi Felice e Fortunato in Vicenza*, 2 vols (Vicenza, 1979), 1: iii, 13–35, 37–55.

80   Billanovich, 'Appunti', 17–18, though she quotes G. B. de Rossi as thinking it could be much earlier: *La Roma sotterranea*, 3 vols (Rome, 1864–77), 3: 436. For a later dating, see Bratoz, *Il Cristianesimo*, 399 n. 153.

81   Roberti, 'La Tomba', in *La Basilica dei SS Felice e Fortunato*, 1: 9–11. The urn apparently contained the remains of only one individual, killed by decapitation, although that of course does not prove that originally both saints had been buried

more important to Vicenza than to Aquileia.[82] That is borne out too by the fact that the Vicenzan saint, Felix, is invariably named first in the record. It is, then, at least possible that Vicenza was the cult's place of origin and that, as with Concordia (perhaps indeed in the context of an attempt to establish a bishopric[83]), Aquileia obtained a share in relics from a dependent community as part of its assertion of superiority. The inconsistencies of the *passio* which claims that the saints came 'not far away' from Aquileia and yet had compatriots in Vicenza, and the story of the apportionment of the corporeal remains would make sense if that were the case. The lost sermon, if early, may well represent an attempt to justify the relocation to the metropolitan city. Equally, it may have been delivered in Vicenza, where as at Milan the feast day may originally have been 14 May. If (as is perhaps more likely) it is later, it would simply reflect the story as circulated in the *passio*.

Let us look now at the group of saints venerated at San Canzian d'Isonzo. The *pieve*, the ancient mother church there, is dedicated to the Cantii, and nearby, preserved in a sixteenth-century chapel dedicated to St Protus on the outskirts of the settlement, are two early sarcophagi, one inscribed to 'the most blessed martyr Protus', the other to 'the most blessed martyr Chrysogonus'. A marble stele or slab again inscribed to 'the blessed martyr Protus' is also preserved there and is perhaps rather earlier: it has been dated to the first decades of the fourth century.[84] It has been plausibly suggested that the marble slab adorned the original *loculus* or burial place of Protus and was placed in position perhaps shortly after the peace of the church, while the two sarcophagi represent later, more honoured, burials.[85] Excavations at the chapel itself revealed a much earlier building, which originated as a small *aula*, perhaps in the fourth century, and was later enlarged and floored with a mosaic pavement, perhaps at the end of the fifth. The internal arrangements suggest that this was possibly an early *memoria*,

---

beneath the slab: C. Corrain, 'Ricognizione antropologia, di tre resti scheletrici', in ibid. 1: 117–31, at 121–3.

[82] Sotinel, *Identité civique,* 215 n. 208.

[83] A bishop is first recorded in 590: W. Pohl, 'Heresy in Secundus and Paul the Deacon', in Chazelle and Cubitt, eds, *Crisis of the* Oikoumene, 243–64, at 253–6. Cf. Cracco Rugini, 'Storia totale', 286.

[84] Tavano and Bergamini, eds, *Patriarchi,* 65–7 (nos 4.24, 25, 27).

[85] Ibid. 65.

initially intended for Protus alone but later also containing the tomb of Chrysogonus.[86] The resemblances between the two coffins and the slab of Aurelia Maria invoking the saints suggest that all may have been the fruit of a single campaign of the later fourth century. Bishop Chromatius, with his evident interest in saints, martyrs and relics, is an obvious sponsor, or perhaps his predecessor Valerianus.

At the *pieve* itself equally interesting evidence was discovered during excavation there in the 1960s. To the north-west of the church and partly overlain by it, a rectangular basilica was detected. It had been floored with an elaborate mosaic carpet, probably dating from the late fifth or sixth century, of a type familiar from the early cathedral at Aquileia and from that built in the late sixth century at Grado by the Patriarch Elias.[87] There are indications that the walls of the rectangle themselves were earlier and that there had been an earlier mosaic floor. Several burials were discovered beneath the church floor, of which one was of particular interest. It lay some 7.5 metres from the east wall and a little to the south of the main north-south axis of the basilica, some 9 centimetres below the sixth-century mosaic floor. The tomb had a base formed from slabs of white Istrian marble and seems to have been covered with similar large slabs, of which one survived, worn by footfall; presumably, then, it was exposed and visible in the original earlier pavement of the basilica, but in the later one formed a special panel in the floor itself. To the east of it, and also covered by the sixth-century floor, lay an exedra, on the north-south axis of the basilica and open to the east. The tomb contained remains from three different skeletons, identified by the excavators as those of a man, woman and boy, possibly related.[88] These have been interpreted as the three Cantii, originally buried in some sort of *memoria* of which the exedra formed a part.[89]

[86] M. Mirabella Roberti, 'La memoria di San Proto a San Canzian d'Isonzo', *Aquileia Nostra* 31 (1961), cols 85–94.

[87] Tavano and Bergamini, eds, *Patriarchi*, 43–6 (nos 3.3–5); D. Gioseffi, 'I pavimenti del vescovo Elia', in *Grado nella storia e nell'arte*, 2 vols, = *Antichità Altoadriatiche* 17 (1980), 2: 325–49.

[88] C. Corrain, 'Resti scheletrici umani dagli scavi di San Canzian d'Isonzo', *Studi Goriziani* 39 (1966), 63–72. Dr C. Callow suggested in a personal communication that this is perhaps a maximalist interpretation; it is quite difficult to sex skeletons, especially of children.

[89] M. Mirabella Roberti, 'La basilica paleocristiana di San Canzian d'Isonzo', *Aqui-

Let us now look at the hagiographical evidence. Belief in the Cantii as a trio who suffered martyrdom during an imperial persecution at Aquileia certainly goes back to the early fifth century, when Maximus, Bishop of Turin (probably the bishop who died between 408 and 423), compiled a homily in their honour.[90] That work, however, is very short (the extant text is perhaps incomplete) and contains almost no biographical information beyond the fact that they were siblings. It makes much of the repetitious nature of their names, which the author evidently considered highly remarkable. The text also alludes to a *historia* of the Cantii and describes the circumstances of their deaths. After investigation by imperial officials, they sought to flee, taking a vehicle drawn by mules, but when one of the mules suddenly collapsed they willingly allowed themselves to be taken to their execution. Maximus makes much of this comparing the vehicle which took them to heavenly glory to the chariot which took Elijah into heaven.

The surviving *Acta* are much more elaborate.[91] They tell of two brothers, Cantius and Cantianus, and their sister Cantianella, descendents of the celebrated Roman family of the Anicii, who lived in the time of the Emperors Diocletian and Maximianus (286–305) and were educated in the Christian faith by Protus. When the emperors initiated a persecution of the Christians, for love of the Christian martyr Chrysogonus they came to Aquileia, where they had great estates. There they encountered a persecution more fierce than in Rome. They visited imprisoned Christians, inquiring after Chrysogonus, and learned that Chrysogonus had been martyred not far from the city *Ad Aquas Gradatas* and had been buried by the priest Zoilus. They started preaching, but hearing that they had come from Rome, the imperial official Dulcidius and his *comes* Sisinnius ordered them to sacrifice to the gods. They were threatened with execution if they did not comply.

When this sentence was brought to the Cantii, they ascended their vehicle, together with Protus and left the city, hastening to the body of the holy martyr Chrysogonus. They were pursued and captured by Sisinnius in the place known as *Ad Aquas Gradatas*

---

leia Nostra 38 (1967), cols 61–86; idem, 'Una basilica paleocristiana a San Canzian d'Isonzo', *Studi Goriziani* 39 (1966), 43–62.

90 Maximus, *Sermo* 15 (CChr.SL 23, 57–8); Saxer, 'L'hagiographie ancienne', 376–7.
91 *ActaSS Mai* 7, 428–30.

where Chrysogonus had been killed, their vehicle having broken down when one of the mules collapsed (the words here are the same as those used by Maximus in his sermon). The *Acta* then incorporate Maximus's comparison with Elijah. They conclude with the refusal of the Cantii and Protus to sacrifice to the gods, their execution by Sisinnius, and the burial of their bodies in a marble chest (*locellus*), next to Chrysogonus. This was said to have taken place on 31 May, *Ad Aquas Gradatas*, twelve miles from Aquileia across the river Isonzo; if, however, as seems likely, *Ad Aquas Gradatas* is indeed San Canzian,[92] the author got its distance from the metropolis seriously wrong and was presumably therefore not local.

The key to the Aquileian *Acta* is the figure of Chrysogonus. By the earlier sixth century, this Aquileian martyr, who may indeed have been one of the city's early bishops, had become a focus of cult in Rome. This seems to have arisen because he was identified with Chrysogonus, the presumed founder of one of the more important Roman *tituli*, the church in Trastevere which supplied priests to the cemeterial church of San Pancrazio. By the sixth century the Roman Chrysogonus had become so important that he was among the saints added to the *Communicantes* prayer in the Roman mass – that is to say, he joined a select group of apostles and martyrs continually invoked in the core text, the canon.[93] At some point in the later fifth or early sixth century, an elaborate romance had been concocted in Rome, associating Chrysogonus with Anastasia, who gave her name to the *titulus* of Sant' Anastasia, across the Tiber not far from San Crisogono.[94] Like Chrysogonus, Anastasia, also presumed to be a founder of an eponymous Roman church, had been transformed into a saint buried outside Rome (in her case Sirmium), another instance of Rome appropriating a non-Roman cult. In the so-called *Passio Anastasiae*, Chrysogonus is presented as a Christian Aquileian who corresponded with Anastasia and instructed her in the faith. Invited by Diocletian to abjure, he refused and was decapitated *Ad Aquas Gradatas*, his body being

---

[92] S. Tavano, 'Un monastero altomedievale a San Canziano', *Memorie storiche Foro-giuliesi* 45 (1962–64), 161–9.

[93] Thacker, 'Martyr Cult', 40–1, 46–7.

[94] P. F. Moretti, *La* Passio Anastasiae, Studi e testi Tardo Antichi 3 (Rome, 2006); H. Delehaye, *Étude sur le Légendier Romain: Les saints de novembre et décembre*, Subsidia hagiographica 23 (Brussels, 1936), 48, 151–71.

buried by the priest Zoilus in his house *in subterraneo cubiculo*. This Roman legendary cycle clearly furnished the creator of the surviving *Acta* with material in the story which he put together to link all the saints of Isonzo, just as the Roman author of the *Passio Anastasiae* sought to link the fictive patrons of two neighbouring Roman churches.

What are we to make of all this? It is clear that there were at least two early martyrs at San Canzian d'Isonzo – Protus and Chrysogonus, perhaps buried outside the city on an estate belonging to a local Christian family, the Cantii.[95] The burial arrangements ascribed to the Cantii themselves, if we do indeed accept the excavators' interpretation, are more ambiguous. They are quite different from those of the two indubitable martyrs. The formulaic repetitiveness of the names suggests that they may have been variants on the nomen or cognomen of the family which had established the Christian burial ground and the early memoria, and which had perhaps acquired sanctity by association.[96] It looks, then, as if the promotion of the Cantii was another example of late fourth-century saint-making, with which were associated two indubitably authentic martyrs who, as a consequence, acquired new identities.

By the later fourth or the earlier fifth century the Christian community at Aquileia seems to have been actively promoting the saints of Isonzo both within the diocese and without. In Aquileia itself by the sixth century the Cantii could be celebrated by Venantius together with Fortunatus as patrons of the city.[97] The fact that neither Maximus's homily nor the *Acta* were local works suggests that from a relatively early date they were also celebrated further afield. Although the dedication of the *chiesa parocchiale* at San Canzan d'Isonzo to all three saints remained unique, dedications to Cantianus were fairly widespread though the diocese and in the wider province.[98] In early sixth-century Trieste, then a suffragan see of Aquileia, the mosaic pavement of a martyrial basilica was funded by donors (commemorated in the work itself) whose names

---

[95] As suggested by an earlier (second/third-century) inscription recording a Lucius Cantius: Sotinel, *Identité civique*, 70.

[96] For a less sceptical view, see Sotinel, *Identité civique*, 67–72. But note that neither Maximus's homily nor the *passio* knew the distance of *Ad Aquas Gradatas* from Aquileia – i.e. their authors were not local.

[97] MGH AA 4/1, 368–9.

[98] Bratoz, *Il Cristianesimo*, 374–5.

included Crysogonus and Cantius.[99] By then the saints of the metropolitan see were clearly well known. The central role which they had acquired is also indicated by a silver reliquary, dating from the fifth century and probably of Aquileian workmanship, which was discovered in Grado under the high altar of the cathedral of Sant'Eufemia, the cathedral which replaced Aquileia when the bishops withdrew permanently to the lagoon after the Lombard invasion, c. 568.[100]

The evidence from Aquileia suggests, then, that we have to be very wary of assuming any degree of continuity in martyrial cult. Almost nothing is known of any of the figures venerated in what is often regarded as one of the major centres of such cult in Italy outside Rome. It is clear that, like Milan, in the late fourth and early fifth centuries the bishops of Aquileia were enhancing, probably reinventing, the city's deposit of sanctity as part of a growing sense of their importance in the ecclesiastical hierarchy. As we have seen, the acquisition of apostolic relics from Concordia and, perhaps, those of Felix and Fortunatus from Vicenza were part of this process. One pointer confirming this impression is the establishment of the cult of Chromatius's predecessor Valerian (d. 388), seemingly one of the earliest recorded elevations of a bishop to saintly status.[101] Another is perhaps the promotion of SS Hilarius and Tatianus, named only once in the Hieronymian martyrology as jointly venerated at Aquileia on 16/17 March.[102] An intramural centrally planned church recorded in modern times as dedicated to those saints has been thought to be a late antique *martyrium*, but was more probably built in the later sixth century under Byzantine influence.[103] At all events, Aquileia's promotion of the cult is evident as with the Cantii in the naming of the donors of a fifth-century mosaic floor at Grado.[104] The evidence, then, although far from conclusive, suggests that, as it developed its metropolitan

---

[99] G. Cuscito, 'La Basilica martiriale di Trieste', in idem, ed., *San Giusto e la tradizione martiriale Tergestina* = *Antichità Altoadriatiche* 60 (2005), 215–35, at 221–33; P. L. Zovatto, 'Il *Defensor ecclesiae* e le iscrizioni musive di Trieste', *Rivista di storia della chiesa in Italia* 20 (1966), 1–8, at 3–4.

[100] For a full bibliography, see Tavano and Bergamini, eds, *Patriarchi*, 52–4 (no. 4.5).

[101] Sotinel, *Identité civique,* 215–16. He appears as Bishop Valentinus in Aquileia, Nov. 26: *MH* 1/1, 147; 2/2, 621–2.

[102] *MH* 2/1, 33; 2/2, 147–9; Cuscito, *Martiri cristiani*, 61–3.

[103] Sotinel, *Identité civique*, 216, 300–2.

[104] Billanovich, 'Appunti', 20, 22; G. Marchesan-Chinese, 'La basilica di Piazza della Vittoria a Grado', in *Grado nella storia e nell' arte*, 2: 309–23.

authority, extending it over newly founded dioceses, the see of Aquileia, like Rome and Milan, began to systematize, flesh out and augment its roll-call of holy saints.

RIVALS TO ROME: AQUILEIA AND RAVENNA

Last of all, let us consider, albeit briefly, the emergence of the metropolitan of Aquileia's grandest title – that of patriarch. Bishop Paul (559–69) had evidently adopted the style at his consecration in 559, when the see was in conflict with the papacy over the condemnation of the Three Chapters, texts relating to the nature of Christ which had been adopted at the Council of Chalcedon, but which had provoked controversy and had been condemned by Justinian in 543/4.[105] Popes Vigilius and Pelagius I reluctantly endorsed the imperial condemnation, but they failed to carry much of the western patriarchate with them and in Italy were opposed by the metropolitans of Aquileia and Milan and their suffragans. By 559 the metropolitans and their supporters were deemed schismatic by the papacy. This remained the situation until 573 when Laurence, the metropolitan of Milan, was reconciled to Pope John III and submitted to Roman jurisdiction. His position had been seriously weakened by the Lombard invasion of northern Italy in 568, which had caused him to flee to Genoa, over eighty miles away, where he was cut off from the heartlands of his province. The Lombards had also caused the metropolitan of Aquileia to move his seat (but only by some five miles) from the mainland to the island of Grado. Unlike the bishop of Milan he remained in full contact with his suffragans and was thus left as the sole leader of the schismatics.[106]

As has already been indicated, there is good evidence that in the earlier sixth century the title of patriarch or *episcopus patriarcha* was used informally among the Franks and the Ostrogoths to designate metropolitan bishops. It has been suggested that the Aquileian title was similar to the Gallican usage (i.e. that it was a grand word for metropolitan) which simply persisted because of the schism.[107] That, however, seems doubtful. It emerged at a crucial period, when the bishop of Aquileia had become *de facto* leader of the schism

[105] For recent approaches, see Chazelle and Cubitt, eds, *Crisis of the* Oikoumene.
[106] Sotinel, 'Three Chapters', 85–120; idem, *Identité civique*, 306–38.
[107] See especially V. Peri, 'Aquileia nella trasformazione storica del titolo patriarcale', *Antichità Altoadriatiche* 38 (1992), 41–63.

and (as was not the case in Gaul) it was employed persistently in official documents, including (it seems) letters to the pope, and in local conciliar texts, such as that recording the Council of Grado in 579.[108] Pelagius's reaction to it in 559 would suggest that it bore implications beyond simple metropolitan jurisdiction, which in Aquileia's case had been recognized by the papacy for well over a century. At the very least the pope seems to have read it as a clear statement of full independence from the jurisdiction of Rome.[109]

With the assumption of patriarchal dignity went a further remodelling of Aquileian martyr cult. It seems likely, for example, that the aggrandizement of the cult of the Cantii at Isonzo dates from this period.[110] Also, the new prominence accorded to the cult of Euphemia, patron of Chalcedon and hence of Chalcedonian orthodoxy, manifest in the dedication to her of the new cathedral at Grado in 579, is surely from this time.[111] Even more significant, however, is a fresh initiative to establish the apostolic origins of the see.

That in the western patriarchate by the mid-sixth century possession of apostolic, even more than martyrial, cult was essential to patriarchal and archiepiscopal status is evident from the activities of Maximian of Ravenna. Ravenna, the imperial capital in 402 and later the capital of the Ostrogothic kings and Byzantine exarchs, had long sought metropolitan status, largely at the expense of weakened Milan.[112] By the mid-sixth century, indeed, it had achieved a degree of success. Although it seems to have remained in some sense under the jurisdiction of Rome, and although it apparently had no suffragans, its bishops had the power to consecrate bishops in provinces other than their own.[113] In the late 540s, when

---

[108] Pelagius I, *Epistulae* 24 (ed. Gassó and Battle, 73–4); MGH L Concilia 2/1, 586; Pohl, 'Heresy', 255.

[109] Pelagius I, *Epistulae* 24 (ed. Gassó and Battle, 73–4).

[110] Roberti, 'Basilica paleocristiana', esp. 63–5, 73–7.

[111] Fedalto, *Aquileia*, 111–12.

[112] Sotinel, *Identité civique*, 87.

[113] This power is first recorded as exercised by Bishop Peter I Chrysologus (c. 430–50). Although Deliyannis claims suffragan bishops for Ravenna, as she herself points out the ascription of suffragans to Peter I is a sixth- or early seventh-century forgery: D. Deliyannis, *Ravenna in Late Antiquity* (Cambridge, 2010), 84, 210, 335 nn. 261, 264; eadem, Introduction to Andreas Agnellus, *Liber pontificalis ecclesiae Ravennatis*, CChr.CM 199, 102–3. Despite being one of the bishoprics of Flaminia and hence a suffragan see of Rome, Ravenna had metropolitan rights over the province of Emilia and in the late sixth century also had jurisdiction in Istria and Liguria: T. S. Brown,

the papacy was seriously compromised over the issue of the Three Chapters, Justinian elevated Maximian, the new holder of the see, to the status of archbishop.[114] This led to a quest for apostolic and other martyrial relics to validate the new-found 'quasi-patriarchal' dignity.[115] According to the historian of Ravenna, Agnellus, writing in the ninth century, Maximian founded a church dedicated to the protomartyr Stephen, within which he placed relics (largely presumably secondary contact relics) of some twenty apostles and martyrs.[116] He also aggrandized the church of St Andrew in Ravenna, refurbishing it with columns of Proconnesian marble instead of the existing humble nut-tree wood, and allegedly sought to place within it the corporal remains of the apostle Andrew, stolen from Constantinople. The emperor, it seems, denied Maximian the apostolic body but allowed him to return with relics of many other saints, including St Andrew's beard, surreptitiously sliced from the apostolic chin during an all-night vigil. All this spells out the importance of relics – and in particular apostolic relics – for higher episcopacy in this period. For Agnellus, Maximian's failure to procure the apostolic body condemned his see to subordination to Rome. The historian concludes sadly: 'And it is a true thing, brothers, if he had buried the body of Andrew, brother of Peter the prince, here, the Roman popes would not have thus subjugated us.'[117]

It seems likely that similar attitudes to those of Maximian prevailed at Aquileia. The famous, and of course wholly bogus, contention that it had been founded by the evangelist Mark, senior disciple of St Peter, before he went on to found Alexandria, makes its first appearance in the record in the later eighth century.[118] It has recently been argued, however, that another text, the *Vita S. Siri*, takes it back at least to the early eighth century and prob-

---

'The Church of Ravenna and the Imperial Administration in the Seventh Century', *EHR* 94 (1979), 1–28, at 7–9.

[114] Deliyannis, *Ravenna*, 209–13.

[115] R. Markus, *Gregory the Great and His World* (Cambridge, 1997), 146.

[116] Agnellus, *Liber pontificalis* 72 (CChr.CM 199, 241–2).

[117] Ibid., no. 76 (CChr.CM 199, 244); Deliyannis, *Ravenna*, 256.

[118] Paul the Deacon, *Gesta episcoporum Mettensium* (MGH S 2, 261); Paulinus of Aquileia, *Carmen* 8 (MGH Poetae Latini Aevi Carolini 1, 140). This paragraph draws heavily on the work of Richard Pollard and I am most grateful to him for allowing me to read and cite his as yet unpublished doctoral thesis: 'Literary Culture in Ninth-Century Italy' (University of Cambridge, 2009), esp. ch. 4.

ably to the mid-seventh.[119] Although the origins of this myth are entirely obscure, when the archives of the two rival patriarchal sees of Aquileia-Grado and Aquileia-Cividale were examined in 827, it appeared that both laid claim to Marcan antecedents;[120] that suggests that the story was already being put about before 606, the year in which the patriarchate had split in two.[121] Associated with this invention is the equally fabricated story of Hermagoras, supposed disciple of Mark and alleged first bishop of Aquileia. His *Acta* are late but may have been built around an actual Aquileian martyr of that name. The confused nature of the entries relating to him in the Hieronymian martyrology has led to doubt that he featured in its earliest recensions.[122]

Conclusions

Martyr cult, then, was a dynamic developing tradition in northern Italy. In the late fourth century the activities of Damasus and Ambrose had rendered possession of martyrial remains a more or less essential concomitant to the establishment of an episcopal see; Ambrose in particular had made the ceremonial translation and importation of relics a crucial activity for sees with pretensions to higher episcopacy, and had made martyr cult instrumental in the subjugation of existing bishoprics and the establishment of new ones. Popes, patriarchs, archbishops and metropolitans rediscovered martyrs or gave existing martyrs new identities as the need arose. At Rome, secure in its Petrine tradition, Damasus simply multiplied the city's local deposit of sanctity. At Milan, lacking in local saints, Ambrose was faced with a more difficult problem, which

---

[119] N. Everett, 'The Earliest Recension of the Life of St Sirus of Pavia (Vat. Lat. 5771)', *Studi Medievali* 43 (2002), 857–957; Pollard, 'Literary Culture', 270–83.

[120] MGH L Concilia 2/1, 583–9. The patriarch of Aquileia-Grado returned to communion with Rome in 606, but the move provoked a most serious division in the province of Venetia-Istria. The bishops in the Lombard territories separated from Aquileia-Grado and adopted a new metropolitan, based eventually at Cividale but still retaining the title of patriarch of Aquileia. This remained so even after their eventual reconciliation with the papacy in 700.

[121] Thus Sotinel, *Identité civique*, 371–2; idem, 'Three Chapters', 118–19; Cuscito, *Martiri*, 43–4; but cf. Pollard who favours a later seventh-century date: 'Literary Culture', 281–2, 287. J.-Ch. Picard opted for the late seventh or eighth century: *Le Souvenir des évêques*, Bibliothèque des Écoles françaises d'Athènes et de Rome 268 (Rome, 1988), 696–7.

[122] *MH* I/1, 90; 'Passio S. Hermagorae', *ActaSS* Julii 3, 249–57; Saxer, 'L'Hagiographie', 380.

he triumphantly resolved. He imported apostolic relics, invented a local martyrial tradition, and put apostolic and martyrial remains to potent new uses. At Aquileia, usually seen as better endowed with local martyrs, if not with apostles, the bishops adopted a third approach. The martyrial tradition, hitherto probably confined to little more than names and perhaps death days, was reworked and rehoused to provide a suitable deposit of sanctity and suitable shrine centres in the late fourth and early fifth centuries, while apostolic relics were imported as at Milan. In the sixth century, when Aquileia by default acquired a pre-eminent role among the bishops of northern Italy, yet another new programme of martyrial cult was developed and associated with the establishment of new apostolic credentials. From the fourth century through to the seventh, martyr cult was a crucial instrument in the development of episcopal hierarchy, and as such was in a perpetual state of reinvention.

Institute of Historical Research

REPENTANCE AS THE CONTEXT OF SAINTHOOD IN THE ASCETICAL THEOLOGY OF MARK THE MONK

by ALEXIS TORRANCE

It seems fitting to begin with a tribute to the late Henry Chadwick, whose thorough, even-handed, and ever readable work contributed much to our understanding of the theme of sanctity in the early Church. In particular, his address at a conference on 'The Byzantine Saint' held in Birmingham in 1980 exemplified his capacity to identify and constructively pursue the broad issues at stake. In speaking of the early saints and the content of their lives, Chadwick explains, 'we are tempted either to tell the stories of their mortifications and then, as was said of Lytton Strachey, ostentatiously refrain from laughing, or we go in search of trendy non-religious explanations of the social needs that created them'.[1] He goes on to acknowledge, as most would, the importance of sociological interpretations and their potential for the study of sanctity, but warns that 'a stripping away of their religious motivation will leave the historian with a distorted picture'.[2] It is along this route of keeping the religious or theological motivations and presuppositions of sanctity in mind, that the present essay will proceed. It focuses on the neglected concept of μετάνοια or 'repentance' (lit. a 'change of mind') which dominates much of the ascetic theology of the early Christian East, particularly as expounded by the influential fifth-century theologian Mark the Monk (or 'the Hermit' / 'the Ascetic').

What makes the concept of repentance worthy of closer scrutiny in the context of views about sanctity in the early Church is the way in which it is used, particularly in Mark, as a term and an idea which sums up the path not simply of the ordinary Christian, but also of the near-perfect or perfected Christian. Repentance is, to be sure, the gateway to the holy in early Christian thought, but

---

[1]   H. Chadwick, 'Pachomios and the Idea of Sanctity', in S. Hackel, ed., *The Byzantine Saint* (London, 1981), 11–24, at 12.
[2]   Ibid.

it is also, as elaborated by Mark and others, conceivable in terms of the content of the holy, expressed through a loving – one might say Christ-like – repentance for one's fallen neighbour and for the fallen world at large.

MARK THE MONK

Comparatively little scholarly consideration has been given to the ascetical theology of Mark the Monk. His identity and date have perplexed several scholars, though placing him in the early fifth century, and linking him to Egypt and/or Syria, seems the most plausible approximation.[3] Despite the limited knowledge we have about the person of Mark, we know of his popularity in the Eastern Christian ascetic tradition. A simple attestation to this is the maxim that had apparently become commonplace amongst Eastern Orthodox monastics, and is mentioned in several Markan manuscripts: 'sell all and buy Mark'.[4] Mark's circle of influence spans such dignitaries of Eastern Christian monasticism and spirituality as Dorotheus of Gaza, John Climacus, Isaac the Syrian, Theodore the Studite, Symeon the New Theologian, Peter of Damascus, Gregory of Sinai, Gregory Palamas and Nicodemus of the Holy Mountain.[5] He figures widely and substantially in patristic florilegia, about six per cent of the *Synagoge* of Paul of Evergetis being made up of Markan quotations.[6] As such, he can safely be regarded as a mouthpiece for much Eastern Christian ascetic thought, and so deserving of the church historian's attention.

---

3 Studies of Mark include: K. T. Ware, 'The Ascetic Writings of Mark the Hermit' (unpublished D.Phil. thesis, University of Oxford, 1965); H. Chadwick, 'The Identity and Date of Mark the Monk', *Eastern Churches Review* 4 (1982), 125–30; O. Hesse, 'Was Mark the Monk a Sixth-Century Higumen near Tarsus?', *Eastern Churches Review* 8 (1976), 174–8; A. Grillmeier, 'Marco eremita e l'origenismo. Saggio di reinterpretazione di Op. XI', *Cristianesimo nella storia* 1 (1980), 9–58; M. Plested, *The Macarian Legacy: The Place of Macarius-Symeon in the Eastern Christian Tradition* (Oxford, 2004), 75–132; C. Carlton, '*Kyriakos Anthropos* in Mark the Monk', *JECS* 15 (2007), 381–405; and the introduction to the SC edition of Mark's works by G.-M. de Durand (*Traités I*, SC 445, 13–35).
4 On which see K. T. Ware, Introduction to *Marc le Moine: Traités spirituels et théologiques*, trans. C.-A. Zirnheld (Begrolles-en-Mauge, 1985), ix–li, at ix.
5 For more on the 'afterlife' of Mark, see Ware, 'Ascetic Writings', 457–69.
6 See J. Wortley, 'The Genre and Sources of the *Synagoge*', in M. Mullett and A. Kirby, eds, *The Theotokos Evergetis and Eleventh-Century Monasticism* (Belfast, 1994), 306–24, at 320.

Repentance in Mark the Monk

The basis for Mark's preoccupation with μετάνοια and its relationship to sanctity is, as with countless Christian ascetics and teachers, the gospel word. The need to bear in mind that Christ's public ministry begins, in the Gospels of Matthew and Mark, with the present imperative μετανοεῖτε ('repent ye' / 'keep repenting'), as well as that the term is key in many New Testament texts, cannot be overestimated when examining how the early ascetics approached the concept, particularly Mark. He opens his treatise Περὶ μετανοίας ('On Repentance') with an incisive exegesis of Christ's initial command as found in Matthew 4: 17 ('repent, for the kingdom of heaven is at hand'), one which serves as a fitting keynote to his whole vision of repentance. He writes:

> Our Lord Jesus Christ, the power and wisdom of God, foreseeing for the salvation of all what he knew was worthy of God, decreed the law of liberty by means of various teachings, and to all set a single goal, saying: 'Repent', so that we might understand by this that all the diversity of the commandments is summed up by one word: repentance.[7]

That repentance ought to be the foundation of Christian life, and that it should accompany the ascetic throughout the struggle for Christian sanctity, are not particularly striking ideas for anyone familiar with early ascetic literature. The need for an open and more nuanced idea of the early Christian understanding of repentance, one which includes not simply self-mortifications and desperate weeping, but also thanksgiving, forgiveness, faith, joy, hope and humble love (in short, all the Christian virtues), has been raised a number of times in different ways.[8] However, that repentance should not only be the means to, but in some sense the actual *goal*

---

7   *De Paenitentia* [hereafter *Paen.*] 1.1–7 (SC 445, 214).

8   See K. T. Ware, 'The Orthodox Experience of Repentance', *Sobornost* 2.1 (1980), 18–28; J. Chryssavgis, *Repentance and Confession* (Boston, MA, 1990); C. Rapp, 'For Next to God You are my Salvation: Reflections on the Rise of the Holy Man in Late Antiquity', in J. Howard-Johnston and P. A. Hayward, eds, *The Cult of Saints in Late Antiquity and the Middle Ages: Essays on the Contribution of Peter Brown* (Oxford, 1999), 63–81; C. B. Horn, 'Penitence in Early Christianity in its Historical and Theological Setting: Trajectories from Eastern and Western Sources', in M. Boda and G. T. Smith, eds, *Repentance in Christian Theology* (Collegeville, MN, 2006), 153–87; C. Trevett, ' "I have heard from some Teachers": The Second-Century Struggle for Forgiveness and Reconciliation', in K. Cooper and J. Gregory, eds, *Retribution, Repentance and Reconcilia-*

and content of sanctity (εἰς σκόπος)[9] has yet to be underlined and discussed. In order to understand how this works itself out in Mark and (by extension) in much Eastern Christian ascetical theology, his reasoning underlying the need for a continuing repentance should be unpacked.

Mark the Monk's theology has been noted chiefly for two of its emphases. The first is his dissection of the process of temptation and sin, which was to be taken up virtually *in toto* by John Climacus in his *Ladder of Divine Ascent*. The other is his detailed theology of baptism, something he developed in response to the threat of Messalianism, which emphasized the efficacy of ascetic effort over against that of the sacraments. More than perhaps any other ascetic writer, Mark depicts baptism as the one and only all-encompassing renewal for the human being.[10] Baptism does not simply launch Christian life for Mark, but contains within itself (μυστικῶς, 'secretly') the fullness of sanctity, which must be lived out ἐνεργῶς, 'actively', by the Christian through the keeping of Christ's commandments. It is within this framework of baptism, as containing in itself all the gifts of grace, that Mark's vision of repentance emerges. Mark claims that 'in all our activity, there is but one foundation of repentance – and that is the one baptism in Christ'.[11] This statement arises through Mark's interpretation of Hebrews 6: 1–6 and 10: 26, on the impossibility of restoring or renewing the apostate to repentance.[12] The purpose of these passages is by no means (μὴ γένοιτο), Mark insists, to question the validity or possible frequency of post-baptismal repentance. The 'renewal', 'enlightenment' and 'sacrifice' mentioned in these verses is not repentance but baptism: not, then, 'there is no second repentance', but 'there is no second baptism'. He uses this platform

---

tion, SCH 40 (Woodbridge, 2004), 5–28; R. Price, 'Informal Penance in Early Medieval Christendom', in ibid. 29–38.

⁹ *Paen.* 1.4 (SC 445, 214).

¹⁰ Baptism in Mark is discussed by K. T. Ware, 'The Sacrament of Baptism and the Ascetic Life in the Teaching of Mark the Monk', *Studia Patristica* 10 (1970), 441–52.

¹¹ *Paen.* 7.25–6 (SC 445, 238).

¹² *Paen.* 7–8 (SC 445, 234–44). The crucial verses are Heb. 6: 6, 'If they shall fall away, to renew them again unto repentance [unlike most modern translators, Mark took εἰς μετάνοιαν to mean 'unto / into repentance', not 'through repentance'], seeing as they crucify to themselves the Son of God afresh, and put him to an open shame'; Heb. 10: 26, 'For if we sin willfully after we have received the knowledge of the truth, there remains no more sacrifice for sins' (citations from the Authorized Version, slightly modified).

to argue that what is in fact being said is that baptism is the basis of repentance, its enabling. It is thanks to baptism that repentance is possible.[13]

Far from being a facet of Christian life that can and ought to be avoided, repentance is for Mark inescapable for the Christian, inasmuch as he understands the practice of repentance to be coterminous with the keeping of the gospel commandments: 'repentance, in my opinion, is neither limited to times or actions, but it is practised in proportion with the commandments of Christ'.[14] Just as we eat, drink, listen, and speak, so for the believer repentance is a necessity of nature, and to fix a term on it 'is to turn backwards and renew the falls of times past'.[15] Personal sanctity is necessarily the preserve, for Mark, of the repentant, and to deny repentance is tantamount, he says, to denying Christ, who is the guarantor of repentance.[16] Without repentance, the hallowed treasure hidden within through baptism remains buried, and the Christian's potential is stunted, not to say thwarted. Even the hypothetical absence of sin cannot be used as an excuse not to repent, Mark explains, given the status of repentance for him as the most basic and over-arching commandment of Christ: 'He who lives in faith lives for the sake of repentance, even if it was not because of our own sin, but because of the sin of the transgression, that we were purified by baptism and once purified, received the commandments'.[17]

---

[13] This interpretation is shared with Ambrose of Milan and John Chrysostom: Ambrose, *De Paenitentia* 2.2 (PL 16, 497C); John Chrysostom, *In epistulam ad Hebraeos* 9.5 (PG 63, 78). All three, incidentally, are explicitly reacting to the Novatianist interpretation of these verses (this is the only point at which Mark explicitly names a heretical group).

[14] *Paen.* 6.25–7 (SC 445, 232). This sentence, along with others in the same vein, is cited by the late seventh-century Syrian ascetic Dadisho Qatraya: *Commentary on Abba Isaiah* (CSCO 326–27), Discourse 14.6; cf. 15.43; 3.9.

[15] *Paen.* 12.3–5, 15–17 (SC 445, 252).

[16] 'Christ became the guarantor of repentance for us: the one who abandons it rejects the guarantor': *Paen.* 12.19–20 (SC 445, 252).

[17] *Paen.* 12.6–9 (SC 445, 252). It is suggested (Ware, 'Ascetic Writings', 199–200, 348) that this and two other passages (*Paen.* 10.15–38 (SC 445, 246–8); *On the Spiritual Law* [hereafter *Leg.*] 155 (SC 445, 114)) may imply a person repenting for original as well as actual sin. The point, however, in the passages from *Paen.* is not that there is a need to repent for original sin, but that original sin necessitates that all, even a perfect person, find salvation in Christ, who commands us to repent (and so repentance is unavoidable). The most natural reading of *Leg.* 155 is that a person should consider himself responsible for the vain chatter of others because of 'an old debt' in his own life, not 'the ancient debt' of Adam.

Even the saints then, need repentance. Indeed, if the righteous neglect repentance, they prove themselves to be like Samson, Saul, Eli and his sons, who may have gained a certain measure of sanctity, Mark says, but because of their rejection of repentance they suffered fearful deaths.[18]

This way of thinking leads Mark to consider the form of repentance carried out by the saints, since repentance without sin appears counter-intuitive. To begin with, Mark's sense of the devastation wrought by sin allows him to see a need for repentance even for those who have reached the measure of the saints. While there may be, he admits, people who live in perfection, they have not always done so. The sins of their past, however apparently slight (and here he cites the Sermon on the Mount and other texts related to this theme: anger towards another is like murder; an impure glance equals adultery; we are accountable for every vain word; and so on), sins such as these make even the apparently perfect 'in need of repentance until death'.[19] On a deeper level, however, the repentance of the saints is not so much preoccupied with their own past faults and flaws, but with something which we may call 'Christ-like repentance'. To this we now turn.

MARK THE MONK ON CHRIST-LIKE REPENTANCE

There is no doubt that Mark, together with the Christian East generally, would have considered the view that Christ needed to atone for his own failings heretical: Christ had no failings.[20] Yet when faced with the question of whether the sufferings Christ endured were for a personal debt (since he had argued that all sufferings have this as their source), Mark gives a nuanced answer:

'Tell me, those who fall into debt because of their own

---

[18] *Paen.* 11.10–13 (SC 445, 248–50).

[19] *Paen.* 10.1–14 (SC 445, 246): μετάνοιαν κεχρεώστηκεν ἕως θανάτου. Elsewhere he makes a comparable and striking point regarding the inability of present virtue to make up for past laxity: 'the greatest degree of virtue which we have accomplished today is a reproach for our past negligence, not a compensation for it': *On that there is no Justification by Works* [hereafter *Justif.*] 43 (SC 445, 142). Neither of these points mean that Mark considers forgiveness unattainable, only that, according to him, no matter how much we do (and we should always do as much as we can), we are not worthy of forgiveness.

[20] Mark twice alludes to Heb. 4: 15, speaking of Christ's humanity as full, only 'without sin': *On the Incarnation* [hereafter *Incarn.*] 49.22–3 (SC 455, 310); *To Nicholas* [hereafter *Nic.*] 9.6–7 (SC 455, 136).

borrowing, are they alone debtors or are their guarantors (ἐγγυώμενοι) also?'

The subordinate answered saying: 'their guarantors also of course.'

The old man went on: 'Know it well that in accepting us Christ constituted (κατέστησε) himself a debtor according to the holy scriptures: "the lamb of God who takes away the sin of the world", "the one who became a curse for us", "the one who took upon himself the death of all and died on behalf of all" '.[21]

This idea of Christ as 'guarantor' of humanity sums up what 'the repentance of Christ' (my phrase) in Mark entails. The Incarnation is the occasioning of Christ's underwriting or 'guaranteeing' human life with his own, becoming the focal point of all human failure and sin, and at the same time the focal point of their forgiveness, and of hope. If we are to speak of the repentance of the saints as 'Christ-like' in Mark, it must be shown, then, that it is in some way akin to this process of underwriting the life of humanity.

Mark does this at *De Paenitentia* 11: 'the saints are obliged to offer repentance for their neighbour, since without an active love it is impossible to be perfected'.[22] The end of repentance is not found for Mark in the forgiveness of one's own failings, but in an imitation of Christ's perfect and redemptive self-giving sacrifice. This reinforces for him the point that repentance is always incomplete in this life and can never be left aside.

The fullest exposition of the Christian imitating Christ in this way is found in *Conversation with a Lawyer* 18–20. Here Mark elaborates on the idea of suffering for others, involving what he calls 'the two types of communion': one of love, the other of evil. 'Because of this communion, without even knowing it, we stand surety for one another'.[23] Mark then briefly explains the communion of evil which begets involuntary sufferings in the one who enters it. The result of such entry is an overall increase of evil rather than its lessening.[24] This leads to his explanation

---

[21]   *Conversation with a Lawyer* [hereafter *Causid.*] 15.12–23 (SC 455, 70), citing John 1: 29; Gal. 3: 3; 2 Cor. 5: 14.

[22]   *Paen.* 11.15–17 (SC 445, 250).

[23]   *Causid.* 18.36–8 (SC 455, 80).

[24]   *Causid.* 19 (SC 455, 80–4).

of the communion of love and how the saints become sponsors (ἀνάδοχοι) for their fellows.[25] He begins by declaring that 'the sponsoring (ἡ ἀναδοχή) that comes from love is that which the Lord Jesus transmitted to us'.[26] Having taken on all our sufferings, and death itself, 'to his own apostles he passed on this law, as to the prophets, fathers, and patriarchs: the latter being taught before by the Holy Spirit, the former being shown the example through his immaculate body'.[27]

The essence of this teaching and law is encapsulated, says Mark, in the words 'no one has greater love than the one who lays down his life for his friends' (John 15: 13).[28] This law was perpetuated by the Apostles, who taught that 'if the Lord laid down his life for us, we also should lay down our lives for the brethren' (1 John 3: 16) and that we should 'bear one another's burdens, and so fulfil the law of Christ' (Galatians 6: 2).[29] Entering the communion of love entails suffering in imitation of Christ for our fellow human beings. Elsewhere he writes: 'Do not say that a dispassionate person (ὁ ἀπαθής) cannot suffer affliction; for even if he does not suffer on his own account, he is under a liability to do so for his neighbour'.[30] This, in short, is the meaning of Christ-like repentance in Mark. In the life of the believer it involves a radical enlargement of individual repentance in order to embrace and relieve the pain of his or her neighbour.

Such merciful repentance is, moreover, not simply a desirable attribute according to Mark, but the basis upon which the world continues to stand: 'Since ... the merciful will be shown mercy, through repentance, in my opinion, the whole world holds together (ὅλος ὁ κόσμος συνέστηκεν), one finding mercy through another according to the divine will'.[31] The act of mercifully reaching out to other people is the repentance that holds the world together. Without it, the cosmos itself would lose all coherence, and forfeit all meaning. Thus Christ-like repentance is for Mark an idea of

---

[25] This is interesting from an ecclesiological perspective, since this became the common term used for godparents at baptism in the Christian East.

[26] *Causid.* 20.5–6 (SC 455, 84).

[27] *Causid.* 20.21–4 (SC 455, 84).

[28] *Causid.* 20.27–9, 60–3 (SC 455, 84–8).

[29] *Causid.* 20.63–7 (SC 455, 88).

[30] *Justif.* 123 (SC 445, 166).

[31] *Paen.* 11.30–2 (SC 445, 250).

profound consequence, and becomes the goal towards which all repentance ought to strive. This is a goal traced and fulfilled for Mark in the life of Christ, a life which needed no repentance, but which nevertheless willingly repented on behalf of all and for all.

Conclusion

What has been briefly presented is an attempt, following the call of Henry Chadwick, to bring out a key aspect of the early Christian ascetic mindset regarding the nature and purpose of holiness. Mark proves a perfect focus for attention given both his unambiguous popularity among posterity, and his ability to take common tropes of the ascetic life and develop them within a theological frame-work more elaborate than those held (if at all) by the common monks of the late antique Christian world. But while others may not have completely shared his tendency to weave such a detailed ascetic theology of repentance, particularly regarding what I have termed 'Christ-like' repentance, the ideas and concepts he espoused regarding the concept were indeed a shared heritage and preoccupation among many Christian ascetics, both anterior and posterior to Mark. Examples are plentiful, and a representative sample might include: Abba Lot's carrying of half the burden of a disciple who had sinned grievously;[32] Poemen's compassion which 'leaves his own dead to weep over the dead of another';[33] Pachomius's giving himself up to mourning before the Lord for forty days on behalf of ten brothers who were murmuring;[34] the grief, described by Antony, which a monk feels for the whole Church;[35] Bassian the Solitary's feverish mourning for 'the delusion and captivity and destruction of the race of men';[36] Barsanuphius and John's bearing of the whole of their disciples' transgression;[37] the taking on of the sins of the community by the monks at a monastery near Alex-andria described by John Climacus;[38] Isaac the Syrian's merciful

---

[32] *Apophthegmata Patrum*, Lot 2 (PG 65, 256).

[33] *Apophthegmata Patrum*, Poemen 6 (PG 65, 320).

[34] *First Greek Life* 100, in *Pachomian Koinonia: The Lives, Rules, and other Writings of Saint Pachomius,* I, *The Life of Saint Pechomius and his Disciples,* trans. A. Veilleux, Cistercian Studies 45 (Kalamazoo, MI, 1980), 367.

[35] Epistle 5, *The Letters of Saint Antony the Great,* trans. D. Chitty (Oxford, 1975), 14–16.

[36] John of Ephesus, *Lives of the Eastern Saints* 41 (PO 18, 652–3).

[37] Barsanuphius and John, *Letter* 73 (SC 427, 348–50).

[38] John Climacus, *The Ladder of Divine Ascent,* Step 4.23 (PG 88, 685D).

heart which bleeds not only for other people, but for the whole of creation;[39] and so on. Mark's preoccupation with the theme of repenting for others is thus not an isolated one in the history of the ascetical theology of the Christian East, as these examples from the fourth to seventh centuries demonstrate. Rather Mark was giving theological justification to an idea that permeated the experience of the Christian ascetics before as well as after his time.

To the mind of many of these ascetics, embarking on the way of repentance was a journey with the goal not of individual perfection or personal salvation, but of cultivating and enlarging one's heart to repent for, and bear the falls and pain of, those around, trying, in however faltering or inadequate a way, to mimic and share in the example of Christ. Moreover, because of this grounding of sanctity in the concept of repentance, one also sees how the hope of living a saintly life was not altogether out of reach for the average monk and the average layperson, since every Christian life, to be Christian at all, was bound to the continuum of repentance. While the seasoned ascetics may not have expected that treading the path of repentance would always yield the heights of a Christ-like repentance in the lives of the average monk or layperson, they recognized an organic, even indissoluble link between all forms of repentance, exalted or lowly. Sanctity was attainable by all, in other words, because the path of sanctity intersected completely, from beginning to end, with the path of repentance.

Christ Church, University of Oxford

---

[39] Homily 71, *Ascetical Homilies of St Isaac the Syrian*, trans. D. Miller (Boston, MA, 1984), 344–5.

THE SIGNIFICANCE OF ST CUTHBERT'S VESTMENTS*

by MAUREEN C. MILLER

S anctity is a quality first perceived, then acclaimed, contested or affirmed. Most commonly the visual perception of sanctity took the form of witnessing miracles: individuals saw with their own eyes divine power working through another human being. The development of the cult of the saints in western Europe, however, gave rise to a rich visual and material culture. The tombs of saints and the churches dedicated to them were adorned with precious works of art intended to glorify the holy patron. This essay considers quite intimate gifts: articles of clothing laid on the body of a saint. It moves from a particular set of vestments left at a saint's shrine to wider considerations of what the clergy wore during the central Middle Ages. Liturgical attire might not only honour the sanctity of a long-venerated individual but might also be used to claim sanctity for others.

The clothing in question – several slender bands exquisitely embroidered with images of prophets, apostles and saints (figure 1) – came to light with the opening of St Cuthbert's tomb in Durham Cathedral on 17 May 1827.[1] They were subsequently identified as three pieces of ecclesiastical vesture: a stole, a maniple and a cincture or 'girdle'. Scholars of historic textiles and liturgical furnishings have long been aware of the significance of these vestments in the development of western embroidery arts and of

* The research for this paper forms part of my forthcoming book, *Clerical Clothing in Medieval Europe*. It was generously supported by the American Council of Learned Societies and by the Committee on Research and the Department of History of the University of California, Berkeley. A special grant from the Abigail Reynolds Hodgen Publication Fund at University of California, Berkeley, made possible both my travel to Durham and the publication of the illustrations included here. I am deeply grateful for this support, and to the participants in the Ecclesiastical History Society Summer Meeting who offered such stimulating suggestions to enrich this paper.

[1] On the background and politics of the opening of the tomb, see Richard N. Bailey, 'St Cuthbert's Relics: Some Neglected Evidence', in Gerald Bonner, David Rollason and Clare Stancliffe, eds, *St Cuthbert, His Cult and His Community to AD 1200* (Woodbridge, 1989), 231–46.

clerical apparel.[2] In these contexts they attest the skill, wealth and generosity of Anglo-Saxon royal women as well as to the early forms and materials of liturgical vestments. A broader significance will be suggested here by considering these embroideries in the contexts of the culture of the secular clergy in medieval Europe[3] and of the development of ideas about sanctity. Cuthbert's vestments are significant as the earliest extant examples of an ornate style of liturgical apparel that came to be widely diffused from the end of the tenth century and artfully deployed to support reform agendas in the late eleventh and twelfth centuries. Specifically, the wearing and representation of ornate golden vestments was used by reformers in the eleventh and twelfth centuries to make important claims to sacred status for the entire clerical order. The aura of sanctity was transmitted via clothing associated physically or visually with saints.

CUTHBERT'S VESTMENTS

Cuthbert's reputation for sanctity was well established by the late seventh century when it prompted a monk of Lindisfarne to write the earliest *vita*. It was much more broadly disseminated, however, through the verse and prose lives written by the Venerable Bede in 716 and 721 respectively. Born in 634, Cuthbert had been trained by Irish monks at Melrose and went on to become prior of the monastery of Lindisfarne. He was also drawn to the eremitic life and was living as a hermit on Farne Island when he was called to be Bishop of Lindisfarne in 685. His episcopate was brief: he died two years later in 687.[4] When the Lindisfarne community fled the Vikings in 875, Cuthbert's body accompanied the monks in their peregrinations through Northumbria and settled down with them

---

[2]   Joseph Braun, *Die liturgische Gewandung im Occident und Orient: Nach Ursprung und Entwicklung, Verwendung und Symbolik* (Freiburg im Breisgau, 1907), 110, 532, 596; Elizabeth Plenderleith, Christopher Hohler and R. Freyhan, 'The Stole and Maniples', in C. F. Battiscombe, ed., *The Relics of Saint Cuthbert* (Oxford, 1956), 375–432; C. R. Dodwell, *Anglo-Saxon Art: A New Perspective* (Ithaca, NY, 1982), 186; Jill Ivy, *Embroideries at Durham Cathedral* (Durham, 1992), 7–17; Anna Muthesius, *Byzantine Silk Weaving AD 400 to AD 1200* (Vienna, 1997), 59, 177–8; Elizabeth Coatsworth, 'The Embroideries from the Tomb of St Cuthbert', in N. J. Higham and D. H. Hill, eds, *Edward the Elder 899–924* (London, 2001), 292–306.

[3]   An approach also taken by Mary Frances Smith, Robin Fleming and Patricia Halpin, 'Court and Piety in Late Anglo-Saxon England', *CathHR* 87 (2001), 569–602.

[4]   B. Colgrave, 'St. Cuthbert and His Times', in Battiscombe, ed., *Relics*, 115–43, esp. 122–39.

at Chester-le-Street. In 995 the see and Cuthbert were moved to Durham. Multiple recognitions of his relics occurred, the first described by Bede as having taken place eleven years after the saintly bishop's death and revealing that his body was incorrupt. It was during the second recognition in 934 that King Æthelstan presented to the saint the stole, maniple and cincture discussed here.[5] Inscriptions on the reverse of the end panels of both the stole and maniple indicate that they were made at the command of Queen Ælfflaed (c. 900 – c. 918)[6] for Frithestan, Bishop of Winchester (909–31): 'ÆLFFLAED FIERI PRECEPIT / PIO EPISCOPO FRIDESTANO' (figures 2.1, 2.2).[7]

The ornate embroidered figures on these vestments and the precious materials used to make them were remarkable – topics to which I will return shortly – but gifts of clothing given by elite pious women to clerics were not. In a letter of 735, St Boniface acknowledged with gratitude the gift of *vestimenta* given to him by Abbess Eadburga, and Alcuin similarly thanked the 'sister in Christ' Gisla for a cloak (*cappa*) she had sent him.[8] Bede's prose life of St Cuthbert reveals that this holy man had also received such gifts. In chapter 37, at the beginning of the section narrating the bishop's last days as told to Bede by Herefrith, then Abbot of Lindisfarne, Cuthbert instructs that his body be placed in a stone coffin, 'wrapping it in the cloth which you will find there. I was unwilling to wear the cloth while alive, but, out of affection for the abbess Verca, a woman beloved of God, who sent it to me, I have taken care to keep it to wrap my body in'.[9] More commonly, bishops left the

---

[5]   On the various recognitions, see C. F. Battiscombe, 'Introduction', in idem, ed., *Relics*, 1–114. In addition to depositing the vestments, Æthelstan had a *testamentum* placed within the coffin beside the saint's head. The document gives a complete list of the gifts offered by the king. There is also some evidence for a movement of Cuthbert to Norham in the early ninth century: Historia de Sancto Cuthberto: *A History of Saint Cuthbert and a Record of His Patrimony*, ed. Ted Johnson South (Cambridge, 2002), 48–9, 58–9, 64–7, 84–5, 96–101, 108–9.

[6]   I use here the dates given by Sheila Sharp for Ælfflaed's marriage to Edward (after the death of his father Alfred in 899) and for when the king probably put her aside (917 or 918) in order to marry Eadgifu: 'The West Saxon Tradition of Dynastic Marriage', in Higham and Hill, eds, *Edward the Elder*, 79–88, at 82.

[7]   Plenderleith, Hohler and Freyhan, 'Stole and Maniples', 375; Ivy, *Embroideries*, 7, 9 (figs 4–5).

[8]   *Die Briefe des heiligen Bonifatius und Lullus*, no. 35 (MGH Epp. Sel. 1, 60); *Epistolae Karolini Aevi tomus II*, no. 84 (MGH Epp. 4, 127).

[9]   'In hoc corpus meum reponite, involuentes in sindone quam inuenietis istic. Nolui quidem ea vivens indui, sed pro amore dilectae Deo feminae, quae hanc michi

vestments given to them as gifts to their sees. When he died in 542, Bishop Caesarius of Arles left to whoever succeeded him in the see 'all the paschal vestments that were given to me ... together with the better quality shaggy cloak, the better quality tunic, and the thick cloak, which I have left behind'. The rest of his clothes, with the exception of his hooded cloak, were to be divided among his clerical and lay servants.[10] Theodred, Bishop of London in the late tenth century, left a chasuble 'and all that belongs to it' (perhaps a matching stole and maniple) to each of four individuals, specifying the colours – one white, one red and two yellow, one ornamented and one not – and mentioning that he had bought two of them at Pavia. In the same period Bishop Alfwold of Crediton left his cope 'to Edwin the mass-priest' and a set of mass vestments to his see.[11]

As liturgical apparel, the stole and maniple were associated with the major orders of the priesthood, diaconate and subdiaconate – that is, the clergy whose service at the altar particularly associated them with the eucharist.[12] The stole was usually eight to ten

misit, Vercae videlicet abbatissae ad obvoluendum corpus meum reservare curavi': *Two Lives of Saint Cuthbert: A Life by an Anonymous Monk of Lindisfarne and Bede's Prose Life*, ed. and trans. Bertram Colgrave (Cambridge, 1940), 272–3. Aristocratic Anglo-Saxon women were notably generous in this regard: see Smith, Fleming and Halpin, 'Court and Piety', 591–2; Dodwell, *Anglo-Saxon Art*, 179–80, 182, 185. And Anglo-Saxon elite culture notably valued precious textiles: J. Campbell, 'Elements in the Background to the Life of St Cuthbert and his Early Cult', in Bonner, Rollason and Stancliffe, eds, *St Cuthbert*, 3–19, esp. 9.

[10] 'Sancto et domino meo pontifici, qui mihi indigno digne successerit, licet omnia in sua potestate sint, tamen si iubet et dignum ducit, vestimenta paschalia, quae mihi data sunt, omnia illi serviant, simul cum casula villosa meliore et tunica vel guanape quod melius dimisero. Reliqua vero vestimenta mea excepto birro auricularii mei tam clerici quam laici cum gratia et ordinatione domini episcopi sibi ipso iubente immo donante dividant': *Sancti Caesarii Arelatensis Opera Omnia*, ed. G. Morin, 2 vols (Maredsous, 1937, 1942), 2: 284–5; PL 67, 1140A; ET *Caesarius of Arles: Life, Testament, Letters*, trans. William E. Klingshirn, Translated Texts for Historians 19 (Liverpool, 1994), 72.

[11] *Councils and Synods with other Documents relating to the English Church*, 1, A.D. 871–1204, ed. D. Whitelock, M. Brett and C. N. L. Brooke (Oxford, 1981), part I (871–1066), 81, 385–6.

[12] Fernand Cabrol and Henri Leclercq, eds, *Dictionnaire d'archéologie chrétienne et de liturgie*, 15 vols (Paris, 1907–53), s.vv. 'étole', 'manipule'; Joseph Braun, *Die liturgischen Paramente in Gegenwart und Vergangenheit: Ein Handbuch der Paramentik* (Freiburg im Breisgau, 1924), 81–4, 127–35; Louis Duchesne, *Christian Worship: Its Origin and Evolution*, trans. M. L. McClure, 5th edn (London, 1956), 390–4; Braun, *Die liturgische Gewandung*, 101–17, 515–620; Janet Mayo, *A History of Ecclesiastical Dress* (New York, 1984), 16, 177; Roger Reynolds, 'Clerical Liturgical Vestments and Liturgical Colors', item VI in idem, *Clerics in the Early Middle Ages: Hierarchy and Image* (Aldershot, 1999), 2–4.

feet long and two to three inches wide. Priests wore it around
the neck with the ends draping down the front of the body, and
deacons draped it over one shoulder. The maniple was a shorter
and narrower band worn over the left forearm. It probably originated as a handkerchief or towel, but quickly lost this function
and became a purely ornamental ritual object. Although worn
by priests, deacons and subdeacons, by the tenth century it was
considered the special apparel of the subdeacon and bestowed
in the ordination rite for this order.[13] The cincture or girdle was
belted around the waist over the long white tunic, or alb, that was
the most basic liturgical garment. It was particularly associated
with the clerical virtue of chastity in liturgical commentaries and
in the vesting prayers recited by clerics as they donned liturgical
attire.[14]

It is interesting that the stole, maniple and cincture that Queen
Ælfflaed is said to have had made for Frithestan appear not to have
been preserved at his see of Winchester. They were obviously in
the possession of her stepson, King Æthelstan, who brought them
to Cuthbert's tomb.[15] This may well have been because of the
extraordinary wealth invested in these precious vestments. Worked
on a foundation net of white silk, the embroidery employs silk
but mostly gold thread. The gold is very pure: it was beaten into
thin sheets (1/7000 inch thick) that were cut into strips (1/90
to 1/150 inch wide) and then wound around a core of thin red
silk. The gold thread was densely attached to the foundation with
fine interlocking couching stitches done in red silk thread: on the

---

[13] Braun, *Die liturgischen Paramente*, 127–34; Mayo, *Ecclesiastical Dress*, 16, 177; Reynolds, 'Clerical Vestments', 3–4.

[14] See, e.g., Hrabanus Maurus, *De institutione clericorum libri tres* 1.17; ed. Detlev
Zimpel, Freiburger Beiträge zur mittelalterlichen Geschichte, Studien und Texte 7
(Frankfurt, 1996), 310. Vesting prayers will be discussed fully in my book on clerical
clothing, but a common form for the cincture is: 'Ad zonam. Praecinge, Domine,
cingulo fidei et virtute castitatis lumbos mei cordis et corporis, et exsiccando extingue
in eis humorem libidinis, ut jugiter in eis sit honor totius castitatis': Edmund Martène,
De antiquis ecclesiae ritibus libri tres, 4 vols (Antwerp, 1763–4), 1: 190 (Troyes); cf. 192
(Tours), 194 (Figeac-Moissac).

[15] Battiscombe, 'Introduction', 33; Ivy, *Embroideries*, 7; Coatsworth, 'Embroideries
from the Tomb', 296. I thank Sarah Foot for her observation that the vestments may
have been completed after King Edward repudiated Ælfflaed to marry his third wife,
Eadgifu, and thus came into the royal treasury instead of being given to Frithelstan
or the see of Winchester; see her forthcoming book in Yale's English Monarchs series,
Æthelstan (New Haven, CT, 2011).

maniple, as many as 128 gold threads per inch were employed. In sum, a fortune in gold was invested in these objects.[16]

Uncommon skill and artistry were as well. The stole and maniple have full-length figures – the height of each roughly five inches – separated by foliage and identified through inscriptions (figure 3). The stole was in five pieces, and already damaged when removed from the tomb in 1827, and several panels are clearly missing.[17] The design, however, is evident: a quatrefoil enclosing an image of the Lamb of God is at the centre, which would have rested at the nape of the bishop's neck, and from this cascade depictions of the Major and Minor Prophets. On either side of the Lamb are Jeremiah and Isaiah. Daniel follows Jeremiah; the figure below Isaiah is missing but was surely Ezekiel. The sequence continues on the right with Amos, Obadiah (Abdias), and Nahum, and on the left with Hosea (Osee), Joel, Habakkuk, Jonah and Zechariah (Sophonias). Missing appear to be the Minor Prophets Micah, Zephaniah, Haggai and Malachi. Two small square end panels have portrait busts of the Apostles James and Thomas, perhaps because, as Christopher Hohler suggested, one was revered as a missionary to the far west (Spain) and the other to the far east (India).[18] Although the Prophets are depicted, as is customary, with long hair and beards, clothed in classicized tunics and cloaks, there are unconventional features: instead of scrolls, most hold books and palms.

The maniple also has some unorthodox characteristics. The right hand of God descends in a quatrefoil at the centre. It is flanked by full-length images of Pope Gregory the Great and Pope Sixtus II, each of them followed by depictions of the deacons with whom they were associated: Peter the Deacon next to Gregory and St Lawrence following Sixtus. These four clerical figures wear liturgical vestments. Square end panels feature portrait busts of St John the Baptist (holding a palm and book) and St John the Evangelist (holding a palm and chalice). Because the figures face alternately left and right, a symmetrical imperative leaves Gregory and Lawrence wearing their maniples draped over their right, rather than their left, arms and results in Gregory offering a blessing

---

[16] Ivy, *Embroideries*, 10; Plenderleith, Hohler and Freyhan, 'Stole and Maniples'. 376–91.

[17] Ibid. 375; Ivy, *Embroideries*, 8.

[18] Plenderleith, Hohler and Freyhan, 'Stole and Maniples', 400.

with his left hand.[19] The cincture or girdle is decorated with a rich foliate design done in red silk on the same gold couched background used in the stole and maniple.[20]

Gold ornamented garments were highly prized in Anglo-Saxon culture by both laymen and ecclesiastical institutions. Although monastic observers criticized lay preoccupation with such finery, once such ornamented textiles passed to religious uses they became associated with sanctity. They were considered appropriate gifts for saints and for ecclesiastical communities dedicated to saints.[21] As gifts, some did reach the Continent, but there are limits and a distinct chronology to the diffusion of this opulent style of liturgical garb. Scholars examining the development of western liturgy have recently questioned long-held assumptions of ever-increasing liturgical uniformity according to Roman 'norms' and underscored both the tenacity of local traditions and the creative exchanges across time and space that yielded extremely complex, and interesting, patterns of liturgical development.[22] These advances in the study chiefly of liturgical texts are extremely useful in reconsid-

---

[19] Ibid. 398–408; Ivy, *Embroideries*, 13.

[20] Ibid. 17; Plenderleith, Hohler and Freyhan, 'Stole and Maniples,' 388–91. Elizabeth Coatsworth noted that while the stole and maniple were clearly made for ecclesiastical use, this cincture or girdle could have been a piece of secular dress adapted to liturgical uses: 'Embroideries from the Tomb', 302–5.

[21] Dodwell, *Anglo-Saxon Art*, 170–87.

[22] The complexity of liturgical development became evident in the first half of the twentieth century as Michel Andrieu and others worked on the *Ordines Romani*. Key essays in describing the complex patterns of exchange that came out of this manuscript work are: Cyrille Vogel, 'Les échanges liturgiques entre Rome et les pays francs jusqu'à l'époque de Charlemagne', in *Le chiese nei regni dell'Europa occidentale e i loro rapporti con Roma sino all'800*, 2 vols, Settimane di studio del Centro italiano di studi sull'alto medioevo 7 (Spoleto, 1960), 1: 185–295; and Niels Krogh Rasmussen, 'Célébration épiscopale et célébration presbytérale: Un Essai de typologie', in *Segni e riti nella chiesa altomedievale occidentale, 11–17 aprile 1985*, Settimane di studio del Centro italiano di studi sull'alto medioevo 33 (Spoleto, 1987), 581–607. Examples of recent work emphasizing local traditions include: Giacomo Baroffio, 'I manoscritti liturgici italiani tra identità universale e particolarismi locali', in Sergio Gensini, ed., *Vita religiosa e identità politiche. Universalità e particolarismi nell'Europa del tardo medioevo* (San Miniato, 1998), 449–64; M. A. Claussen, *The Reform of the Frankish Church: Chrodegang of Metz and the Regula canonicorum in the Eighth Century* (Cambridge, 2004); Yitzhak Hen, 'The Recycling of Liturgy under Pippin III and Charlemagne', in Geert H. M. Claassens and Werner Verbeke, eds, *Medieval Manuscripts in Transition: Tradition and Creative Recycling* (Leuven, 2006), 149–60.

ering the material culture of the liturgy. Cuthbert's vestments are a case in point.

When assessing possible stylistic influences on the stole and maniple, for example, it has been asserted that silk hangings and vestments brought back from Italy by Anglo-Saxon pilgrims may have been models.[23] Rome, however, was definitely not the source of this new style.

Roman evidence indicates that in the early Middle Ages precious textiles and ornament were reserved for the decoration of churches and altars, not clerical bodies. The *Liber pontificalis* gives abundant evidence that the highest quality luxury fabrics were available in ninth- and tenth-century Rome in significant quantities: included in most papal biographies are long lists of precious textiles, and other valuable objects made of gold and silver, donated to churches. These include various grades of purple silks, including the most coveted murex-dyed, and those with intricate woven patterns.[24] The *Liber* indicates, however, that these textiles were used as *vela* (veils) hung from architraves and between columns to create spatial divisions within churches, and as altar coverings.[25] Only in the twelfth century are vestments found among the gifts

---

[23] Ivy, *Embroideries*, 12; on Anglo-Saxon contacts with the Eternal City, see W. J. Moore, *The Saxon Pilgrims to Rome and the Schola Saxonum* (Fribourg, 1937); and D. J. Birch, *Pilgrimage to Rome in the Middle Ages: Continuity and Change* (Woodbridge, 1998). My thanks again to Sarah Foot for suggesting these sources. Freyhan argued for Byzantine sources in his contribution to 'Stole and Maniples', 409–23. This is a possible connection worth pursuing; see Warren T. Woodfin, 'Presents Given and Presence Subverted: The Cunegunda *Chormantel* in Bamberg and the Ideology of Byzantine Textiles', *Gesta* 47 (2008), 33–50; Karl Leyser, 'The Tenth Century in Byzantine-Western Relationships', in Derek Baker, ed., *Relations Between East and West in the Middle Ages* (Edinburgh, 1973), 29–63, esp. 42–4.

[24] The lists are so lengthy and detailed that Paolo Delogu did an economic study of them, complete with bar-graphs of import rates over the ninth century: 'L'importazione di tessuti preziosi e il sistema economico romano nel IX secolo', in idem, ed., *Roma medievale – aggiornamenti* (Florence, 1998), 123–41. The *Liber pontificalis* also gives evidence of silk patterns much more elaborate than those used later in vestments, such as the *chrysoclaba* that had biblical scenes and images of Christ, the Apostles and angels woven into them. Two precious examples of these, depicting the Annunciation and the Nativity, survive from the Sancta Sanctorum (now in the Vatican Museums): Muthesius, *Byzantine Silk Weaving*, 175, entry M35 and plates 20A–B.

[25] The *vestes* listed in the *Liber* are *Vestes altaris*: *Le Liber pontificalis*, ed. Louis Duchesne, 2nd edn, with additions and corrections by Cyrille Vogel, 3 vols (Paris, 1955–57), 1: 418–19, 421, 432, 435, 500; 2: 2–3, 8–11; John Osborne, 'Textiles and their Painted Imitations in Early Medieval Rome', *Papers of the British School at Rome* 60 (1992), 312–21.

made by popes to Roman churches: the *Descriptio Lateranensis ecclesiae* recorded that Pope Innocent II (1130–43) gave a fine cloth woven of gold to the basilica, from which altar cloths and a chasuble were made, while Anastasius IV (1153–54) donated a white chasuble hemmed all around with precious gold embroidery.[26]

The visual evidence of Roman mosaics and frescoes accords with the textual evidence of the *Liber pontificalis*. Roman artists were perfectly capable of depicting ornamentation on clothing, but they deployed these skills only when rendering images of elite lay people and, more importantly, holy personages. The use of gold on garments was restricted to images of Christ, the Virgin Mary and saints. Clerics were represented with an elegant, but sober, demeanour: their vestments were depicted in a limited range of colours and without ornamentation (figure 4). This changed in the eleventh and twelfth centuries. Along with changes in the representation of the forms and colours of vestments, a new opulence in ornamentation – particularly the use of gold – is strikingly evident. Just a few examples of depictions of embroidered ornament on clerical vestments are the golden collar, sleeve and hem bands on Saint Stephen's dalmatic in the 'Universal Judgment' panel painting (1061–71) now in the Vatican Pinoteca; similar decorative bands on the tunicle of the thurifer attending St Clement in the late eleventh-century mass fresco in the lower basilica at San Clemente (figure 5); and the hems, sleeves and pallia of the ecclesiastics in the apse mosaic of the 1140s from Santa Maria in Trastevere (figure 6).[27]

Although these depictions of embroidered features on liturgical vestments reveal simple non-figural patterns, they do represent the use of gold to ornament clerical attire. This was clearly not a long-standing Roman tradition. Where did it originate?

THE GENESIS OF A NEW STYLE

Since Cuthbert's vestments are the earliest extant example of liturgical vestments decorated with gold embroidery, and such vestments are widely attested in English texts, Anglo-Saxon England

---

[26] Roberto Valentini and Giuseppe Zucchetti, eds, *Codice topografico della città di Roma*, 4 vols, Fonti per la storia d'Italia 81, 88, 90, 91 (Rome, 1940–53), 3: 349, 352.

[27] Serena Romano, *La pittura medievale a Roma 312–1431, 4. Riforma e tradizione 1050–1198* (Milan, 2006), 50, 139, 308–9.

has the strongest claim to be the birthplace of this style. Inventories of ecclesiastical treasuries reveal the presence of such vestments, and something of their diffusion, on the Continent. Their earliest reference to gold ornamented liturgical attire there comes in 851 from the Benedictine monastery of Saint Bavo in Ghent, which owned 'stolam I auream et alias II cum auro. Manipulas I cum auro et aliam II'.[28] Other references occur after 900, becoming relatively common from the late tenth century, with a notable cluster of references from Bavaria, lower Saxony and the eastern edge of Alemannia.[29] Most interesting is a document from 903 that begins by announcing the intention of fostering the custom among noble and religious men of giving of their own possessions to augment the goods of God's churches. Before a 'public synod' attended by many counts and other noble men, the chor-bishop Madalwinus gave over to Bishop Burchard of Passau and his advocate 'his entire liturgical apparatus, that is, what that one was accustomed to wear at mass: a purple cope decorated with gold, a purple chasuble made of costly silk, two stoles with a maniple ornamented with gold and gems'.[30]

Although there is a mid-ninth century reference to King Æthelwulf donating an alb with gold embroidery to St Peter's, it seems most likely that the fashion took root in Rome through Ottonian influence in the late tenth century. We know, for example, that other liturgical innovations, such as the pontifical, were transferred across the Alps and embraced in Rome during this period.[31] What

---

[28]   Otto Lehmann-Brockhaus, *Lateinische Schriftquellen zur Kunst in England, Wales und Schottland vom Jahre 901 bis zum Jahre 1307*, 5 vols (Munich, 1955–60), 3: 354–410, gives no early entries from inventories; the textual evidence for textiles is predominantly from chronicles, saints' lives and charters, with very few references before the eleventh century. For the Continent, and this specific inventory from Ghent, see Bernhard Bischoff, ed., *Mittelalterliche Schatzverzeichnisse, Erster Teil: Von der Zeit Karls des Großen bis zur Mitte des 13. Jahrhunderts* (Munich, 1967), 38.

[29]   Ibid. 83 (Regensburg, St Emmeram, 993), 120 (Passau, 903, Pfävers, 974), 124–5 (Freising, 957–94).

[30]   'totum apparatum suum, id est sicut ipse paratus ad missam solitus fuerat stare, pluviale purpuream auro paratam, casulam purpuream siricam de sirico precioso, stolas II cum anfanone auro et gemmis paratum': Bischoff, ed., *Mittelalterliche Schatzverzeichnisse*, 120.

[31]   Cyrille Vogel and Reinhard Elze, eds, *Le Pontifical romano-germanique du dixième siècle*, 2 vols (Vatican City, 1963); succinctly summarized in Cyrille Vogel, *Introduction aux sources de l'histoire du culte chrétien au Moyen-Âge* (Spoleto, 1973), 182–203 (ET *Medieval Liturgy: An Introduction to the Sources*, trans. William G. Storey and Niels Krogh Rasmussen (Washington, DC, 1986), 225–39).

I would like to emphasize here, however, is how the new style was used.

In their Anglo-Saxon context, gold ornamented garments communicated elevated status in both lay and ecclesiastical worlds. Frithestan, for whom the Durham vestments were made, was later venerated as a saint: he may have had a reputation for holiness during his lifetime that prompted the queen's gift. Cuthbert, of course, was a widely venerated saint when the vestments were brought to his tomb. Golden gifts were appropriate for saints: the reliquaries and shrines built for them reinforced this association. Sacred books also were covered in gold and gems, and over the course of the early Middle Ages ecclesiastical legislation more and more firmly specified that the chalice should be of gold or other precious materials. But when did the men serving at the altar merit attire of gold? In the example mentioned above, neither the chor-bishop Madalwinus (who publicly handed over his gold-ornamented cope, stoles and maniple) nor Bishop Burchard of Passau (who received them) was a saint.

The migration of this marker of sanctity from saints to the clergy more generally has not been fully traced. One vector was probably the celebration of saints' feast days: it may have seemed appropriate for golden vestments offered to saints to be worn by those attending their tombs and solemnizing their veneration. The tomb of a saint figures prominently in the transfer of sanctity to clerics via liturgical garments. A late ninth-century Roman *ordo* reveals the custom of incubating the stoles to be bestowed in diaconal and priestly ordinations on the 'confession' or tomb of St Peter. Just as the pope was placing his hands on the head of the ordinand, the archdeacon is instructed 'to remove from the confession the stoles, which had been placed there the day before, and put them on them [the ordinands]'.[32] Although generic blessings for *linteamina*,

---

[32] 'Accedens autem archidiaconus tollit orarios [*sic*] de confessione, qui de esterna die repositi sunt ibi, inponet super eos': Michel Andrieu, *Les Ordines Romani du haut Moyen Âge*, 5 vols, Spicilegium sacrum Lovaniense, Études et documents 11, 23–4, 28–9 (Louvain, 1931–56; repr. 1960–5), 4: 198 (*Ordo* 36.19); two manuscripts have the correct accusative plural, 'oraria'. A *confessio* in Roman usage could be any niche, usually below the altar, that allowed contact with the relics or tomb venerated in the church; see Sible de Blaauw, *Cultus et decor: Liturgia e architettura nella Roma tardoantica e medievale*, 2 vols, Studi e testi 355–6 (Vatican City, 1994), 1: 84. St Peter's, of course, came to be the most visited *confessio* of the city, and *Ordo* 36.13 specifies (Andrieu, *Ordines*, 4: 197) that the ordination rituals described took place 'ad sanctum Petrum'.

things used on or at the altar, are included in church dedication rites from the eighth century and in early sacramentaries, blessings specifically for vestments appear first in the Romano-Germanic pontifical of the mid-tenth century.[33]

In the rich artistic evidence of medieval Rome, however, the transfer of the visual markers of sanctity from holy personages to ordinary clerics can be traced with some precision: golden ornament appears on the vestments of ecclesiastical figures who are not saints in the late eleventh century and is well established in the twelfth. In some representations, even though the clergy attending a saint wear comparably rich attire, a halo does clearly denote the individual to be venerated. But in other images, such as the apse of Santa Maria in Trastevere, all the ecclesiastics wear ornamented vestments and none have haloes. Five of the six, indeed, were saints; Pope Innocent II, however, was not. We have here two examples of the ways in which the opulent new style of vestments were used. At Santa Maria in Trastevere, sanctity is visually asserted for the church's patron, Innocent II, through both association – a long-standing technique – and liturgical attire. The more significant claim is the more generalized visual assertion of sacred status for the clergy, even the minor clergy in the San Clemente frescoes.

Extreme claims for the superior status of the clergy on the basis of their spiritual powers were, of course, being made by ecclesiastical reformers at this time. Pope Gregory VII, writing to Bishop Hermann of Metz in 1081, for example, asserted not only that there is 'nothing in this world more pre-eminent than priests' but also that 'a greater power is granted to an exorcist when he is constituted a spiritual emperor to drive out demons, than may be bestowed upon anyone of the laity on account of secular

---

[33] Andrieu, *Ordines,* 4: 397–402 (*Ordo 42*), 339–47 (*Ordo 41*), esp. 346 for the 'linteamina vel omnia ornamenta ecclesiae, seu vasa sacra quaecumque ad cultum Dei ad ecclesiam pertinere'. The eighth-century Gelasian sacramentaries have separate prayers for the chalice, paten, *lentiaminum* and a general benediction 'ad omnia in usu basilice': *Liber Sacramentorum Romanae Aeclesiae Ordinis Anni Circulu (Cod. Vat. Reg. lat. 316 / Paris Bibl. Nat. 7193, 41/56) (Sacramentarium Gelasianum),* ed. Leo Cunibert Mohlberg, Rerum Ecclesiasticarum Documenta, Series maior, Fontes 4 (Rome, 1968), 109–10; *Liber sacramentorvm Engolismensis: Manuscrit B.N. Lat. 816. Le Sacramentaire Gélasien d'Angoulême,* ed. Patrick Saint-Roch (CChr.SL 159C), 363–5. For the Romano-Germanic pontifical, see Vogel and Elze, eds, *Le pontifical romano-germanique,* 1: 152–4 (40.79–81).

domination'.[34] But the long chronology of the emergence and diffusion of golden vestments makes it clear that reformers were drawing upon earlier associations within the culture of the secular clergy. How precious textiles appropriate to saints were appropriated for lesser clerical bodies merits further research. Let me suggest in conclusion that royal courts and ecclesiastical institutions enjoying royal patronage were clearly important sites of transfer and that elite status surely facilitated this migration of connotations of the holy. Golden vestments worn by bishops from elite lineages serving important sees would have prompted less concern than similar attire donned by men of lesser status by virtue of holy orders. It was certainly the uses of the holy to subvert social hierarchies that provoked fierce resistance to the more radical voices of late eleventh-century reform. The significance of the ornate style of liturgical attire first visible to us in Cuthbert's vestments lies not only in its exquisite workmanship, but also in the symbolic work it was able to perform.

University of California, Berkeley

---

[34] *The Register of Pope Gregory VII 1073–1085*, trans. H. E. J. Cowdrey (Oxford, 2002), 391 (8.21).

Figs 2.1, 2.2. Inscriptions, St Cuthbert's Stole, Cathedral Treasury, Durham (courtesy of Durham Cathedral).

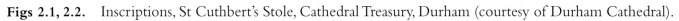

Fig. 3. Detail of Peter the Deacon, St Cuthbert's Maniple, Cathedral Treasury, Durham (courtesy of Durham Cathedral).

Fig. 4. Apse mosaic, S. Prassede, Rome (Scala / Art Resource, New York).

Fig. 5. Detail, The Mass of Saint Clement, Church of San Clemente, Rome (Istituto Superiore per la Conservazione ed il Restauro – Archivio per la documentazione dei restauri, Rome).

Fig. 6. Apse mosaic, S. Maria in Trastevere (Scala / Art Resource, New York).

WHY DID THE CRUSADER STATES PRODUCE SO FEW SAINTS?

by BERNARD HAMILTON

The crusading movement was an important part of the attempt by the papal reformers of the eleventh century to integrate the turbulent and powerful warrior class of western Europe into Christian society. Pope Urban II's aim was to persuade these fighting men to use their skills in defence of Christendom, and to form an armed force directed by the Church. Crusading would enable the warriors to combine their military abilities with the practice of the Christian life. This ideal later came to be accepted as normative by the armies of all Western states.

The First Crusade was successful. In 1099 it captured Jerusalem, and subsequently western settlers established control over a swathe of territory stretching from northern Mesopotamia to the Sinai peninsula. The crusaders who settled in the East and those westerners who joined them there were guardians of the Holy Places. The Catholic West regarded their work as supremely important, and huge new crusading expeditions were sent to the Levant during the next two centuries, to defend Jerusalem when it was threatened, or, after it had been lost in 1187, to recover it.[1]

Latin rule in the Holy Land led to a great increase in western pilgrimage there, and the spiritual life of some individuals was shaped by this experience, for example, that of St Raineri, the patron saint of Pisa, who spent some ten years in the Holy Land praying at the shrine churches before returning to the West, and that of St Godric of Finchale, whose two journeys to Jerusalem led him to become a hermit.[2] The beneficial consequences for western spirituality of Latin rule in the Crusader States were recognized by many western churchmen, of whom the most vocal was St Bernard of Clairvaux. He gave his enthusiastic support to the Knights

---

[1] See the very important work of W. J. Purkis, *Crusading Spirituality in the Holy Land and Iberia c. 1095 – c. 1187* (Woodbridge, 2008), 1–119.

[2] Colin Morris, 'San Ranieri of Pisa; The Power and Limitations of Sanctity in Twelfth-Century Italy', *JEH* 45 (1994), 588–99; *Libellus de vita et miraculis s. Godrici auctore Reginaldo Dunelmensis*, ed. J. Stevenson, SS 20 (1845).

Templar, founded to protect the pilgrimage routes in the Kingdom of Jerusalem,[3] and his benevolent interest in the Latin East was believed to have continued after his death in 1153. When King Amalric was campaigning in Egypt in 1167, St Bernard appeared to him in a vision; Amalric attributed his subsequent victory to the saint's intercession, and sent the True Cross reliquary which he wore round his neck to Clairvaux as an act of thanksgiving.[4]

It would be reasonable to expect that some of the western settlers in the Crusader States, who devoted their lives to the maintenance and protection of the Holy Places, would have become saints, and, indeed, some of them did, but virtually all of those were members of religious communities. Some Benedictine monks of the Mount Tabor monastery, who were killed by Muslim raiders in 1113, were later commemorated as martyrs in some French Benedictine communities.[5] The Franciscan Order honoured as martyrs the friars and the Poor Clares killed by the Mamluks when they sacked Acre in 1291.[6] Helinus, the first prior of the Premonstratensian community of St Habbakuk near Jerusalem, was revered as blessed by his order.[7] But the greatest number of saints was to be found among the Carmelites. The Latin Hermits of Mount Carmel, from whom the order evolved, received their first rule from St Albert, Latin Patriarch of Jerusalem (1205–14). As Andrew Jotischky has shown, later historians of the order claimed that the hermits of Mount Carmel could trace their descent from the prophet Elijah and his disciples, and the list of saints which the order claimed as members grew out of this myth of origins. From the crusading period came 'Berthold, the first prior-general, and his successor Brocard, who received the Rule from Albert; Cyril the visionary, who corresponded with Joachim of Fiore; Angelo the martyr, another ascetic

---

[3] 'Liber ad Milites Templi: de laude novae militiae', in *S. Bernardi Opera,* ed. J. Leclercq and H. M. Rochais, 8 vols (Rome, 1957–77), 3: 312–39; ET *In Praise of the New Knighthood,* intro. M. Barber, trans. M. C. Greenia, Cistercian Fathers 19B (Kalamazoo, MI, 2000).

[4] *Vita s. Bernardi Clarevallensis abbatis auctore Gaufrido monacho* 3, in *Acta SS* Aug. 4, 327. Amalric's gift is recorded in a list of reliquaries belonging to Clairvaux: A. Manrique, ed., *Cisterciensium seu verius ecclesiasticorum annalium a condito Cistercio,* 4 vols (Lyons, 1642–59), 2: 548 (*s.a.* 1173, ch. 6, section 9).

[5] Feast day 4 May: *Acta SS* Maii 1, 437. The attack is described by Albert of Aachen, *Historia Ierosolimitana* 12.9–11; ET S. B. Edgington, Oxford Medieval Texts (Oxford, 2007), 836–40.

[6] *Acta SS* Maii 4, 135.

[7] *Acta SS* Aug. 4, 398.

and visionary of the thirteenth century'. The historical evidence for the existence of some of these saints is slight.[8] The Carmelites also promoted the cult of the Patriarch Albert who had given them their rule. He had been murdered in 1214 during an ecclesiastical procession. This was not a martyrdom, but a revenge killing: a former master of the Hospital of the Holy Spirit at Acre, whom he had deposed as unsuited to hold office, stabbed him. Albert was an able and efficient patriarch who may have merited canonization, but he does not appear in the universal calendar of the Catholic Church, only in that of the Carmelite Order.[9]

In the Western Church the most common form of canonization in the twelfth and thirteenth centuries was by popular acclaim. Devotion centred on the relics of the 'saint', or, where appropriate, on his or her tomb, and votaries sought the saint's help for a variety of needs. Such cults had to receive approval from a diocesan bishop or from a provincial synod, and the local clergy often kept records of miracles which were reported to have been worked at such shrines.[10]

Although it was a widely held view among participants in the First Crusade that those who died on campaign, whether from natural causes or in battle, were martyrs for the faith, this view was never endorsed by the Church.[11] Nevertheless, popular cults grew up around some participants who died on crusades to Jerusalem, but this occurred in their homelands, not in the Latin Kingdom. For example, Thiemo, Archbishop of Salzburg, who accompanied Welf IV of Bavaria on the Crusade of 1101 and went missing at the Battle of Heraclea, was considered a martyr at Salzburg. His *Passio* claimed that he had not been killed in battle but had been taken prisoner, and that his captors, who knew that he was a skilled metal worker, wanted him to repair a Muslim idol [*sic*]. When he

---

[8]   A. Jotischky, *The Perfection of Solitude: Hermits and Monks in the Crusader States* (University Park, PA, 1995), 139–51; idem, *The Carmelites and Antiquity: Mendicants and their Pasts in the Middle Ages* (Oxford, 2002), 190–210, at 191.

[9]   A. Jotischky, 'Albert of Vercelli (1149/1152–1214)', in *The Crusades: An Encyclopedia*, ed. A.V. Murray, 4 vols (Santa Barbara, CA, 2006), 1: 28.

[10]   See the case study: T. Head, *Hagiography and the Cult of Saints: The Diocese of Orléans 800–1200* (Cambridge, 1990).

[11]   B. Hamilton, ' "God wills it": Signs of Divine Approval in the Crusade Movement', in K. Cooper and J. Gregory, eds, *Signs, Wonders, Miracles: Representations of Divine Power in the Life of the Church*, SCH 41 (Woodbridge, 2005), 88–98, at 90–1.

refused to do this, they killed him.[12] The only example which I have found of a popular devotion of this kind relating to Frankish settlers in the Crusader States is eccentric. This is the cult of SS William and Peregrine of Foggia who, according to the inscription on their reliquary recorded in 1630, had been born in Antioch and had come to Foggia in Apulia during the reign of Frederick Barbarossa (1152–90). The chronology is plausible, since they may have been refugees from the Crusader States who fled to Sicily in the aftermath of Saladin's invasion in 1187. The *Acta* which give a biography of the saints and an account of the miracles which had been performed through their intercession are of little historical value, since they were written in 1630 in order to secure confirmation of the traditional cult, which was duly licensed.[13]

I have found no evidence of any cults of this kind in the Crusader States, but because no bishops' registers survive it is difficult to be certain about this. Arguably the most important sources of evidence for such cults are saints' lives, and these have received very full attention. The standard scholarly collection of such works is the *Acta Sanctorum* edited by the Bollandist Fathers, which is arranged calendrically in accordance with the date of the saints' feast day. The first two volumes of January saints were published in 1643, but the project, which is still ongoing, has not yet reached the end of November. The work now consists of sixty-seven folio volumes.[14] In 1897, when the Bollandists had reached the end of October, Charles Kohler produced an index of the materials in this great work relating to the Latin East. This revealed that the only cults of western settlers in the Crusader States were those sponsored by religious communities, to which I have already referred. I should add that there is no archaeological evidence of cults of this kind, nor is any mention made of them in the numerous pilgrim narratives from this period.[15]

Part of the reason for this is that the Frankish population did

---

[12] *Passio Thiemonis archiepiscopi* (MGH S 11, 28–33, 51–62); P. Riant, 'Le martyre de Thiemo de Salzburg', *Revue des questions historiques* 39 (1906), 218–37.

[13] Feast day 26 April: *Acta SS* Apr. 3, 464–6.

[14] See David Knowles, 'The Bollandists', in idem, *Great Historical Enterprises: Problems in Monastic History* (London, 1963), 1–32.

[15] D. Pringle, *The Churches of the Crusader Kingdom of Jerusalem: A Corpus*, 4 vols (Cambridge, 1993–2009); S. de Sandoli, *Itinera Hierosolymitana Crucesignatorum (saec. XII–XIII)*, 4 vols (Jerusalem, 1978–84).

not predominate in the majority of settlements, and the eastern Christian communities alongside whom they lived already had well-established cults of local saints. The Frankish settlers were happy to invoke those saints. In 1156, for example, the nobleman Henry of Antioch and his wife Isabella built a church in honour of St Barsauma, an important saint in the Syrian Orthodox Church, to whose prayers they attributed the healing of their son.[16] There is no evidence that the indigenous population paid religious honour to Frankish holy men and women who lived and died among them. This appears to be further evidence of the reserve which existed at a deep level between the indigenous Christians and the Franks, to which Claude Cahen drew attention.[17]

The other method of canonization available in the Latin Church in the twelfth century was to institute formal proceedings. A provincial synod might recommend that a man or woman be canonized, but papal ratification was needed, and after 1234, when the Decretals of Gregory IX were published, the process of canonization was reserved to the pope alone.[18] Such procedures involved considerable expense and also persistence. Witnesses had to attend the papal Curia and present evidence about the good life of the saint and of the miracles with which he or she had been credited since his or her death, and proceedings could take a long time. The English crown petitioned for the canonization of Edward the Confessor in 1138, but the process was not completed until 1161.[19] Philip III of France initiated the canonization process of his father, Louis IX, in 1282. Louis had led the Crusade against Egypt in 1249–50, and, after that had failed, had stayed in the Holy Land for another four years to protect Frankish interests. In 1270 he led a second crusade and died at Carthage while planning an attack on Tunis. John of Joinville was one of the witnesses called to give evidence at the process and the notes which he made then almost certainly formed the basis of his *Life of St Louis*. Louis IX was canonized by Boniface VIII

---

[16] Michael the Syrian, *Chronicle* 17.13; Syriac text ed. with French trans. by J. B. Chabot, *Chronique de Michel le Syrien*, 4 vols (Paris, 1899–1924), 3: 303–4.

[17] C. Cahen, 'Indigènes et croisés', *Syria* 15 (1934), 351–60.

[18] E. W. Kemp, *Canonization and Authority in the Western Church* (London, 1948), 56–141; M. Goodich, 'Vision, Dream and Canonization Policy under Pope Innocent III', in J. C. Moore, ed., *Pope Innocent III and his World* (Aldershot, 1999), 151–63; idem, *Miracles and Wonders: The Development of the Concept of Miracle, 1150–1350* (Aldershot, 2007), 69–99. See also A. Vauchez, *Sainthood in the Later Middle Ages* (Cambridge, 1997).

[19] F. Barlow, *Edward the Confessor* (London, 1970), 256–85.

in 1297, but although crusading zeal formed an important part of the evidence adduced in his favour, his just government of France was considered equally significant.[20] To be successful, canonization proceedings normally needed the support of a powerful corporate body, such as a religious order or a royal dynasty.

It might have been expected that the Latin kings of Jerusalem would have wanted at least one of their number to be canonized, because of the prestige that this would confer on their realm. Godfrey of Bouillon would seem to have had all the right qualifications for sainthood. His mother, Blessed Ida of Boulogne, was beatified.[21] He had been one of the chief vassals of the Western Emperor but had abandoned this position to take the cross. He had led the crusaders to victory at Jerusalem in 1099 and had been elected as ruler of the new state. Moreover, his moral character was said to have been irreproachable. In the later Middle Ages he was numbered among the Nine Worthies as one of the three greatest Christian rulers, yet no attempt was made to have him canonized.[22]

I would suggest that there were two reasons for this. Firstly, although his brother and successor, Baldwin I (1100–18), would have had an incentive to initiate canonization proceedings which would, if successful, have brought honour to his dynasty, he would have needed the cooperation of the patriarch of Jerusalem to present the case at the papal court. Yet throughout most of his reign the patriarchate was weakened by disputes about whether the holders of this office had been validly appointed.[23] Secondly, Baldwin II (1118–31), though a distant kinsman of Baldwin I, was not his direct heir, but was in effect the founder of a new dynasty: a considerable change of personnel took place at his court and among the chief officers of state when he came to the throne.[24] He had no incentive to promote Godfrey's cult.

---

[20] Jean de Joinville, *Histoire de Saint Louis*, ed. N. de Wailly (Paris, 1872); J. Richard, *Saint Louis, Roi d'une France féodale, soutien de Terre sainte* (Paris, 1983).

[21] 'B. Idae Vita, auctore monacho Wastensi coevo', *Acta SS* Apr. 2: 141–5.

[22] William of Tyre, *Chronicon* 9.5 (CChr.CM 63, 426–7). The Nine Worthies were Joshua, King David and Judas Maccabeus; Hector, Alexander the Great and Julius Caesar; King Arthur, Charlemagne and Godfrey of Bouillon.

[23] The Latin Patriarchs were Arnulf of Chocques (elected but not consecrated, July–December 1099); Daimbert of Pisa (December 1099 – 1101); Evremar of Chocques (1102–08); Gibelin of Arles (1108–12); Arnulf of Chocques (1112–18): B. Hamilton, *The Latin Church in the Crusader States: The Secular Church* (London, 1980), 12–16, 52–64.

[24] A. V. Murray, *The Crusader Kingdom of Jerusalem: A Dynastic History 1099–1125*,

The only attempt to promote the canonization of a member of the military aristocracy of the Crusader States was initiated by Peter of Blois. He was present at the papal court in the autumn of 1187, representing Archbishop Baldwin of Canterbury in a legal dispute, when news reached the pope of the defeat of Hattin and the loss of Jerusalem. Peter stayed in Rome until after 26 January 1188, when Clement III finally pronounced judgment in the Canterbury dispute. During that time Peter wrote three works in support of a new crusade: a lament for the loss of Jerusalem; an exhortation to Archbishop Baldwin to take the cross; and the *Passio Raginaldis*, an account of the life and death of Reynald of Châtillon, former Prince of Antioch and Lord of Montréal and Hebron.[25]

Peter was informed about the battle of Hattin by the members of the military orders who brought news of the defeat to Rome. Reynald was the only member of the lay nobility taken prisoner at Hattin to be killed by Saladin, the rest being held to ransom.[26] When the crusader army was encircled by Saladin, Reynald did not attempt to escape, but stood by King Guy of Lusignan until they were forced to surrender. When they were brought before Saladin, Reynald was offered the choice of conversion to Islam or death, and when he refused to apostatize Saladin beheaded him himself. Peter of Blois provides the earliest western account of Reynald's death, but the facts he gives are confirmed by Muslim historians.[27] Peter clearly hoped that Reynald would be canonized and would become a symbol of the steadfast crusader, and that this would aid recruitment for the new crusade. Peter later accompanied Archbishop Baldwin on the Third Crusade and revised his text of the

Prosopographica et Genealogica 4 (Oxford, 2000).

[25] Peter of Blois, 'Passio Raginaldis principis Antiochie', in *Petri blesensis tractatus deo* (CChr.CM 194, 31–73); R. W. Southern, 'Peter of Blois and the Third Crusade', in *Studies in Medieval History presented to R. H. C. Davis,* ed. H. Mayr-Harting and R. I. Moore (London, 1985), 207–18.

[26] Saladin did not allow the Templars and Hospitallers captured at Hattin to be ransomed, but ordered them to be executed: Abu Shama, *The Book of the Two Gardens* (RHC Or. 4, 277–8).

[27] Ibid. 275–6, 284–5, 298–9, 305; Kamal ad-Din, *History of Aleppo*, French trans. E. Blochet, *Revue de l'Orient latin* 4 (1896), 180–1; Baha al-Din Ibn Shaddad, *The Rare and Excellent History of Saladin,* trans. D. S. Richards (Aldershot, 2001), 74–5; *The Chronicle of Ibn al-Athir for the Crusading Period,* trans. D. S. Richards, 3 vols (Aldershot, 2006–8), 2: 323–4.

Passio while in the Holy Land as a result of information supplied by King Guy's brother, who had also been present at Hattin.[28]

No attempt was made to promote Reynald's cause using Peter of Blois's evidence. The reasons for this are, of necessity, speculative, but I would advance the following suggestion. The natural supporters of Reynald would have been the Lusignan family, but as Guy had lost his kingdom, his French kin would not have had sufficient influence to promote Reynald's cause at the papal Curia. They would have relied on the support of their overlord, Richard I of England, and they might have received it had not Richard been held to ransom at the critical point, between late 1192 and early 1194, by Leopold, Duke of Austria.[29] By the time he was released the Emperor Henry VI had gained control of the Kingdom of Sicily and become the dominant power in Italy and at the papal court, and he was hostile to Richard.[30] Although Hohenstaufen influence in Rome ended with Henry's death in 1197, Richard himself died eighteen months later. His successor, his brother John, married Isabella of Angoulême in 1200, despite the fact that she was betrothed to Hugh VIII of Lusignan, thereby alienating the Lusignan family.[31]

The *Passio* did not have a wide circulation,[32] whereas an alternative account of Reynald's role in the affairs of the Latin East reached a very large audience. This was contained in the Old French Chronicle attributed to Ernoul, which is closely related to the various recensions of the Old French translation and continuations of William of Tyre's Chronicle, known as the *Estoire d'Eracles*. The account which these sources give of events leading up to Hattin is based on information supplied by the survivors, of whom the most important was Balian of Ibelin, one of a group of knights who had fought their way through Saladin's encircling forces at Hattin, aban-

---

[28] Peter does not specify which brother this was: Geoffrey of Lusignan and Aimery of Lusignan, Constable of the Kingdom and later King of Cyprus and of Jerusalem, were both present at the Battle of Hattin.

[29] J. Gillingham, *Richard I* (New Haven, CT, 1999), 222–53.

[30] I. S. Robinson, *The Papacy 1073–1198: Continuity and Innovation* (Cambridge, 1990), 510–22; Brenda M. Bolton, 'A Matter of Great Confusion: King Richard I and Syria's *Vetus de Monte*', in A. D. Beihammer, M. G. Parani and C. D. Schabel, eds, *Diplomatics in the Eastern Mediterranean 1000–1500: Aspects of Cross-Cultural Communication* (Leiden, 2008), 171–203.

[31] W. L. Warren, *King John* (London, 1964), 64–76.

[32] R. B. C. Huygens, Introduction to *Petri Blesensis tractatus duo* (CChr.CM 194, 8–13).

doning the king and the relic of the True Cross.[33] These men were concerned to justify their own part in the crisis and to lay the blame for the loss of the kingdom on Guy of Lusignan and his supporters, most of whom were dead and of whom Reynald of Châtillon had been the most important.[34] Once the *Eracles* began to circulate in western Europe, it would have been difficult to refute the account of Reynald's activities which it gives.

In the thirteenth century the social and religious position of the Franks in the reduced territories which they continued to govern did not differ substantially from that of the twelfth century, and this continued to inhibit the growth of popular cults of potential Frankish saints. Between 1192 and 1229 the crown of Jerusalem was held by women, and the husbands of those queens, all of whom came from outside the kingdom, brought their own retinues with them and placed their followers in positions of power.[35] This was an impediment to the institution of canonization proceedings in regard to earlier rulers and their aristocratic supporters, which, to be successful, would almost certainly have needed persever-ance over a long period of time, as well as considerable expendi-ture. From 1229 to 1286, when there was no resident king in the Crusader States, the problems of initiating a canonization process were insuperable.[36] That, I would suggest, is why the Crusader States produced no saints apart from some clergy whose cults were promoted by the religious orders.

University of Nottingham

[33] *La Chronique d'Ernoul et de Bernard le Trésorier,* ed. L. de Mas Latrie (Paris, 1871); *L'Estoire d'Eracles empereur et la conqueste de la terre d'Outremer* (RHC Oc. 1–2); P. W. Edbury, 'The French translation of William of Tyre's *Historia*: The Manuscript Tradi-tion', *Crusades* 6 (2007), 69–105. For the complex relations between the text of Ernoul and the *Eracles* in the years leading up to Hattin, see B. Hamilton, *The Leper King and his Heirs* (Cambridge, 2000), 6–11.

[34] M. R. Morgan, *The Chronicle of Ernoul and the Continuations of William of Tyre* (London, 1973), 136.

[35] The Queens regnant of Jerusalem were Sybil (1186–90), wife of Guy of Lusignan; Isabella I (1190–1205), wife of (1) Conrad of Montferrat (d. 1192), (2) Henry of Troyes (d. 1197), (3) Aimery of Lusignan, King of Cyprus (d. 1205); Maria (1205–12), wife of John of Brienne; Isabella II (1212–28), wife of the Emperor Frederick II: B. Hamilton, 'King Consorts of Jerusalem and their Entourages from the West from 1186–1250', in H.-E. Mayer, ed., *Die Kreuzfahrerstaaten als multikulturelle Gesellschaft*, Schriften des historischen Kollegs, Kolloquien 37 (Munich, 1997), 13–24.

[36] J. Riley-Smith, *The Feudal Monarchy and the Kingdom of Jerusalem, 1174–1277* (London, 1973).

SANCTITY AS A FORM OF CAPITAL

by KATHARINE SYKES

his paper uses Bourdieu's model of the three forms of
capital – economic capital, social capital and cultural
capital – to explore the complex relationship between the
spiritual and temporal spheres described in medieval hagiographical texts. It focuses on the *vita* of Hugh of Avalon, Bishop of
Lincoln, composed in the early thirteenth century during a period
of important procedural developments in the process of papal
canonization.[1] This paper argues that the two necessary prerequisites for canonization by the beginning of the thirteenth century,
namely miracles and sanctity of life, can be analysed as forms of
symbolic capital, which could be transformed into material goods
through the mechanism of divine providence. Thus sanctity – in
particular, a reputation for ascetic behaviour – was not merely a
form of capital: it was also the mechanism through which one
form of capital could be transformed into another.

HAGIOGRAPHY AND HISTORIOGRAPHY

England in the twelfth and thirteenth centuries witnessed not only
a considerable outpouring of hagiographic texts: it also experienced rapid social, economic and religious change.[2] Yet whilst the

---

[1]   The place of Hugh's canonization within broader trends is discussed in Robert
Bartlett, 'The Hagiography of Angevin England', in P. R. Coss and S. D. Lloyd, eds,
Thirteenth Century England V: Proceedings of the Newcastle upon Tyne Conference 1993
(Woodbridge, 1995), 37–52, at 52; Benedicta Ward, *Miracles and the Medieval Mind:
Theory, Record and Event 1000–1215* (London, 1982), 174–5, 190–1.

[2]   For economic and social developments, see Richard H. Britnell and Bruce
M. S. Campbell, eds, *A Commercialising Economy: England 1086 to c. 1300* (Manchester,
1995); for legal and administrative developments, see M. T. Clanchy, *From Memory to
Written Record: England 1066–1307*, 2nd edn (Oxford, 1993); for religious developments,
see Andrew Brown, *Church and Society in England, 1000–1500* (Basingstoke, 2003).
For the reactions of canonists and theologians to these developments, see John W.
Baldwin, *The Medieval Theories of the Just Price; Romanists, Canonists, and Theologians in
the Twelfth and Thirteenth Centuries* (Philadelphia, PA, 1959); John Gilchrist, *The Church
and Economic Activity in the Middle Ages* (London, 1969), 23–82; Jacques Le Goff, *Your
Money or Your Life: Economy and Religion in the Middle Ages* (New York, 1988); Lester
K. Little, *Religious Poverty and the Profit Economy in Medieval Europe* (London, 1978),
173–83.

impact of legal and bureaucratic developments on the writing of hagiography has been widely studied, the impact of commercialization, urbanization and monetarization upon the genre has received less attention.[3]

A partial exception is to be found in Simon Yarrow's *Saints and their Communities*, which explores a series of twelfth-century miracle collections, including the relic tour of the canons of Laon, which generated money for the rebuilding of the cathedral after a disastrous fire.[4] As the tour demonstrates, authors of hagiographical texts did display considerable interest in the economic and material benefits of sanctity; their works can be supplemented by records kept at cathedral shrines that reveal the considerable profit which could be generated by the presence of a saint.[5] Yet for Yarrow, gifts of money or objects to saints and their shrines are symbolic rather than economic: the gifts to the canons of Laon, for example, express a series of 'social exchanges', in which 'money lost its practical, economic function and became a symbolic expression of largesse, hospitality and charity'.[6] I do not propose to question the idea that money can gain symbolic meanings, but rather the idea that in so doing, it loses its economic functions.[7]

This dichotomy between *economism* (everything is reducible to economic forces) and *semiologism* (everything is symbolic communication) was addressed by the sociologist Pierre Bourdieu in an article first published in 1983. In it he set out two forms of 'hidden' or symbolic capital, namely social capital and cultural capital, which provide the link between the symbolic and economic realms.[8] In

---

[3]   A notable exception is Henry Mayr-Harting, 'Functions of a Twelfth-Century Recluse', *History* 60 (1975), 337–52.

[4]   Simon Yarrow, *Saints and their Communities: Miracle Stories in Twelfth-Century England* (Oxford, 2006), 63–99.

[5]   For the economic benefits brought by the presence of a shrine, including Hugh's own shrine at Lincoln, see Ben Nilson, *Cathedral Shrines of Medieval England* (Woodbridge, 1998), 144–90, 211–41.

[6]   Yarrow, *Saints and their Communities*, 87–88, drawing on Marcel Mauss, *The Gift: The Form and Reason for Exchange in Archaic Societies*, trans. W. D. Hall (London, 1990), 3.

[7]   For an analysis of the shift from the 'gift economy' to the 'profit economy', see Little, *Religious Poverty*, 3–41.

[8]   Originally published as Pierre Bourdieu, 'Ökonomisches Kapital, kulturelles Kapital, soziales Kapital', in Reinhard Kreckel, ed., *Soziale Ungleichheiten*, Soziale Welt, Sonderheft 2 (Göttingen, 1983), 183–98; ET by Richard Nice as 'The Forms of Capital', in J. Richardson, ed., *Handbook of Theory and Research for the Sociology of Education* (New York, 1986), 241–58. All quotations in this paper are taken from the

his formulation, 'cultural capital' is 'a disposition of mind and body', roughly translatable as personal development or self-improvement; the cultivated air resulting from long years of study and immersion in cultural activities. In its embodied or personal form, the acquisition of cultural capital requires sacrifice and self-discipline, and although primarily an individual attribute, cultural capital can be passed on via intimate relationships (Bourdieu concentrated on the home, but an alternative medieval example might be the relationship between a master and his disciples). It can also be 'objectified' or transmitted to a particular object (in the form of a famous painting or work of literature, or in our context, a relic or shrine) and 'institutionalized' (in the form of academic qualifications, or, in our context, papal canonization). Cultural capital operates as a 'hidden form' of economic capital for two reasons. Its initial generation requires economic capital, either in the form of a direct financial outlay (such as fees, or the purchase of books and materials) or, indirectly, in the form of lost earnings; secondly, it can be transformed back into economic capital in the form of higher wages and other material benefits.[9]

Social capital, on the other hand, is the profit derived from group membership; that is, the resources on which individuals can draw as the result of membership of a particular group, such as a political party, or the nobility (two obvious medieval alternatives are membership of a religious community or the ecclesiastical hierarchy, although as this paper will demonstrate, noble status was also clearly important). Social capital, too, represents a hidden form of economic capital as it requires some form of financial outlay (such as membership fees, or the expenditure required to meet formal and informal standards imposed by the group) or, again, loss of earnings. It pays out in the form of the resources of the group, which depend on its size, its connections and the capital (economic or cultural) of individual members.[10] In further articles, Bourdieu spoke of a fourth type of capital, religious capital, defined as 'accumulated symbolic labour' or 'the goods of salvation', rituals and symbols which are often mastered and monopolized by religious

latter. A more extended discussion can be found in Pierre Bourdieu, *Distinction: A Social Critique of the Judgement of Taste*, trans. Richard Nice (London, 1984).

9   Bourdieu, 'Forms of Capital', 243–8.
10   Ibid. 248–54.

specialists; this has received considerable attention from sociologists and economists.[11]

However, this paper will stick to the original tripartite formulation: in the text examined here, religious capital was viewed as an integral part of social and cultural capital, not as an optional but related extra. Put simply, for Hugh's biographer, sanctity – expressed primarily in Hugh's behaviour, and perceptions of his behaviour, but also in his miracles – generated a range of material as well as spiritual benefits for his cathedral, his diocese and his order.

THE TEXT

Adam of Eynsham's *Life of St Hugh* is composed of five books, the first of which is the shortest and which concerns Hugh's early career in Burgundy. Hugh of Avalon was born c. 1140 and entered a nearby house of canons, Villarbenoît, as a child. At twenty-five, captivated by the Carthusian way of life, he transferred to the Grande Chartreuse. The second book describes his leadership of the Carthusian community of Witham in England, to which he was transferred as prior c. 1179, and the third book his promotion to the bishopric of Lincoln in 1186. Adam served as Hugh's chaplain from 1197 until his death in 1200, and much of the material in the third, fourth and fifth books of the *Life* was drawn from his personal recollections and from interviews with those who had known Hugh.[12] Adam's *Life*, composed c. 1212, also incorporates material from other *vitae*, including one of the two versions composed by Gerald of Wales.[13]

In composing the text, Adam demonstrates his awareness of the new prerequisites for papal canonization, namely miracles and sanctity of life, which had been set out by Innocent III in a series

[11] Pierre Bourdieu, 'Genesis and Structure of the Religious Field', *Comparative Social Research* 13 (1991), 1–44, at 9. For subsequent discussion, see Bradford Verter, 'Spiritual Capital: Theorizing Religion with Bourdieu against Bourdieu', *Sociological Theory* 21 (2003), 150–74.

[12] Adam of Eynsham, *Magna Vita Sancti Hugonis* [hereafter *Magna Vita*], ed. D. L. Douie and D. H. Farmer, 2 vols, Nelson Medieval Texts (Edinburgh, 1961–2), 1: 45.

[13] Adam of Eynsham, *Magna Vita*, ed. Douie and Farmer, 1: xii, xiv. Gerald wrote two lives of Hugh, both of which are printed in *Giraldi Cambrensis Opera Omnia*, ed. J. S. Brewer et al., 8 vols, RS 21 (London, 1861–91), 7: 73–80 (as part of the *Life of Remigius*), 83–147 (*Life of St Hugh*).

of judgements from 1199, the year before Hugh's death.[14] The main theme of the work is, unsurprisingly, the presentation of evidence of Hugh's sanctity; drawing in large part upon his ascetic life-style, but also supported by several well-attested *pre* and *post mortem* miracles. However, Adam also reveals considerable interest in the temporal economy and in the theme of 'capital', which works on at least three levels within the text.

On one level, the *Life* is avowedly anti-materialist. In keeping with the spirit of papal and episcopal reform, Hugh and his biographer are quite clear that there are two separate economies: the spiritual economy of the *sacerdotium* and the temporal economy of the *regnum*.[15] Hugh's primary concern was with the former. On hearing of his election as bishop, Hugh focused less on 'the prospect of luxury and wealth' or 'the advantages of a position of rank and authority' and more on 'the bitter loss of the contemplative life and of quiet and tranquillity for meditation and prayer'.[16] His preparations for office were spiritual rather than material: he prayed and meditated, preparing his soul rather than his wardrobe or equipage, and prepared a lasting feast of nourishment for the souls of his flock, rather than 'perishable food to fill the belly'.[17] Thus, on one level, Hugh's reputation for sanctity – his spiritual wealth – derived from his explicit rejection of material wealth.

This antithesis between temporary temporal rewards and eternal spiritual rewards is a particular feature of Hugh's dealings with three successive Angevin kings. In one such episode, Satan, operating through the medium of royal courtiers, persuaded Richard I that the bishop of Lincoln owed an annual tribute of a mantle, non-payment of which had generated considerable arrears. Hugh negotiated a release from the tribute in return for the enormous sum of three thousand marks, which he intended to pay by returning to Witham to live as a hermit, setting aside money from his episcopal revenues rather than extorting payments from his flock. However, Hugh's clergy were so anxious not to lose his

---

[14] Innocent III's development of the canonization procedure is discussed in E. W. Kemp, *Canonization and Authority in the Western Church* (Oxford, 1948), 104–7; see also A. Vauchez, *Sainthood in the Later Middle Ages* (Cambridge, 1997), 27–30, 36–40.

[15] See Le Goff, *Your Money or Your Life*, 10–11.

[16] Adam of Eynsham, *Magna Vita*, ed. Douie and Farmer, 1: 100.

[17] Ibid. 1: 99. See also ibid. 1: 76.

leadership that they provided the money to pay the release from their own revenues.[18]

This brings us to the second, related use of the language and concept of capital in the text. Hugh and his biographer insisted that the two separate economies had two separate currencies: merit and marks. Spiritual wealth, particularly sanctity of life, was measured in one coin; material wealth in another. It was this which prompted him to negotiate the release from the tribute demanded by Richard I, however high the cost: 'Nothing seemed to him more shameful or intolerable than that the bride of the King of Heaven, or he himself, her temporary steward, should pay taxes or tribute to any human being.'[19] For the most part, discussion of the spiritual and temporal economies respected this separation and uses different terms. The temporal economy was described in concrete numismatic or commercial terms, in quantities of specific coin or fixed prices.[20] Discussion of the spiritual economy, on the other hand, made use of familiar agricultural, pastoral or viticultural metaphors.[21] Yet the two strands, one spiritual and one commercial, did meet in the metaphor of the talent.[22] In describing the financial centre of Hugh's spiritual economy, Witham, Adam described the monks as 'expert money-changers who could weigh, examine, and judge with him the shape, weight and metal of the talents of the Lord, lest any light, alloyed or false ones should be discovered among them'.[23] In a passage in the fourth book, Adam of Dryburgh, the former Premonstratensian prior who became a Carthusian convert at Witham, mixed metaphors in his advice to Hugh:

> But what must I think of the talents given you to trade with? What profits and interest do you pride yourself on having

---

[18] Ibid. 2: 33–8.

[19] Ibid. 2: 35.

[20] Compare Wulfric's miraculous discovery of two newly minted coins in his purse: Mayr-Harting, 'Functions', 342.

[21] Adam of Eynsham, *Magna Vita*, ed. Douie and Farmer, 2: 71, 153.

[22] For the relevant biblical texts and the underlying tension between condemnation and praise of wealth, see Gilchrist, *Church and Economic Activity*, 50–1.

[23] Adam of Eynsham, *Magna Vita*, ed. Douie and Farmer, 2: 45 (drawing on John Cassian, *Conferences* 1: 20–2): '(Erant uero ibi plurimi) probabiles trapazete qui librarent, examinarent atque diiudicarent secum figuram et pondus et metallum eorum que tractabat dominicorum talentorum, ne quid forte in leue, ne quid minus uel purum uel legitimum inueniri potuisset.'

acquired in comparison with those holy merchant venturers who had knowledge of all the perils of land and sea, and not only planted but enriched and defended the church with their blood?[24]

In their references to money-changers and merchants, profits and interest, the two Adams, although drawing on biblical and patristic imagery, revealed an understanding of commerce and trade which went beyond the allegorical. The mid- to late twelfth century was a period of rapid economic, commercial and bureaucratic growth in England, which neither Hugh nor his biographer could afford, quite literally, to ignore. In such circumstances, money and capital appeared frequently in a third sense, in their literal as well as their metaphorical guises; as desirable objectives, as well as rhetorical antitheses. Hugh's sanctity, in the form of both his ascetic reputation (part of the 'sanctity of life' required for papal canonization by the beginning of the thirteenth century) and his miracles, provided the mechanism for transmuting merit into marks, as well as marks into merit.

Discussions of capital as a desirable object appeared most frequently in reference to Hugh's role as an earthly as well as a spiritual steward: first at St Maximus, a cell of Villarbenoît; then at the Grande Chartreuse; then Witham; and finally at Lincoln. As steward, Hugh was required not simply to defend the estates and chattels of his communities, but to secure, if possible, their increase. This required careful negotiation of a very narrow path, a synthesis of competing spiritual and temporal needs, and occasional intervention by the divine regulator. As before, on one level Adam insisted that the two economies were separate, and that Hugh's duties as steward were purely spiritual. At Lincoln, Hugh was alleged to have refused to oversee the auditing of his accounts: 'He interpreted the counsel of the Apostle that a bishop should be a good steward of his household as meaning that he should lay this task on men renowned for their honesty and prudence, and acted up to this.'[25]

[24] Adam of Eynsham, *Magna Vita*, ed. Douie and Farmer, 2: 54: 'Quid vero de commissorum tibi negotiatione talentorum sentiemus? Que lucra, quas usuras reportaturum te confidis inter illos egregios institutores qui, omnia terre marisque pericula experti, non modo plantauerunt set etiam ornauerunt et munierunt ecclesiam sanguine suo?'

[25] Ibid. 2: 152.

In the early years of his career, Hugh was able to preserve this distinction with little trouble. Upon his appointment as prior of the cell of St Maximus, its estates 'barely sufficed for the adequate maintenance of one canon and a small household'.[26] However, after handing over the temporal assets (sheep and vineyards) to devout peasants, and devoting himself to the spiritual assets (through prayer and study), 'the Lord, on account of his faith in his mercy, took charge of him and his companions and provided bountifully for them ... Thus, in a short time the church was endowed with goods and the people with virtue, and both acquired fame and a high reputation in the neighbourhood.'[27]

Yet in his dealings with the Angevin kings, Hugh was required to take an increasingly active approach to securing and defending the temporal assets of the Church. At Witham, Hugh was forced to use considerable skill to secure prompt payment for the extensive building programme. As Henry II's interest in the project began to wane, envoys were sent from Witham to ask him to settle the bills, returning with 'empty promises, but no gifts' (*verbum, non datum*).[28] Eventually, Hugh travelled to petition the king in person, accompanied by another member of the community, Gerard. Provoked by Henry's evasive tactics, Gerard exploded, asserting that he preferred to return to his 'barren Alpine crags, rather than to struggle with a man who regards anything spent on his salvation as mere waste'.[29] The king could keep his treasure: 'neither Christ nor any good Christian will deign to share it'.[30] Hugh, meanwhile, had maintained a studious silence. Henry turned to him, and asked if he too planned to return to the Grande Chartreuse. Hugh replied that he had not lost faith in Henry, and was sure that with God's help he would complete the task. Henry settled the outstanding bills at once.

This conflict between strict asceticism, represented by Gerard's barren Alpine crags, and the need to collect what was owed to the Church was brought into even sharper focus by Hugh's promotion to the episcopate. As Bishop of Lincoln and steward of the 'estate' of the Blessed Virgin Mary, Adam depicted Hugh's constant battle

---

[26] Ibid. 1: 18.
[27] Ibid. 1: 18–19. See also ibid. 1: 42.
[28] Ibid. 1: 64.
[29] Ibid. 1: 66.
[30] Ibid.

against Angevin encroachments on the spiritual and temporal resources entrusted to his care. In this battle, Hugh drew on spiritual weapons, namely anathema and excommunication, to prevent confiscation of temporal assets following his refusal to supply a contingent of knights to serve overseas,[31] and again to protect the temporal goods of the diocese from the depredations of the Exchequer after his death.[32]

Although Adam repeatedly insisted that the spiritual and temporal economies were separate, he was also adamant that temporal goods could and should be used for spiritual purposes.[33] This underlay Hugh's refusal to grant benefices to royal officials, 'since their holders should not serve at court, at the treasury or the exchequer, but as the Scripture enjoins, at the altar'.[34] Such a position also received divine sanction: one of Hugh's clerks had a vision in which he was instructed to tell the bishop to deliver a stern rebuke to the archbishop of Canterbury regarding the practice of farming out churches to the highest bidder, regardless of their unsuitability:

> Thus churches are let to make money for an annual rent to the highest bidder in the same way as taverns or shops. They never think of the cure of souls or of using the revenues of the church to assist the needy, but all the time greedily strive to stuff their money-bags, either to be dissipated by luxury or to be kept locked by avarice till rust eats them away.[35]

Thus, for Adam, the interconnection of the two spheres legitimated the use of spiritual sanctions such as anathema to preserve temporal goods and to prevent their misappropriation, particularly when recourse to legal arguments or instruments, such as wills, might not provide sufficient protection. It also meant that temporal capital could be transformed into spiritual capital, either by the meritorious acts just mentioned, namely the cure of souls and

---

[31] Ibid. 2: 98–116; discussed by K. J. Leyser, 'The Angevin Kings and the Holy Man', in H. Mayr-Harting, ed., *St Hugh of Lincoln: Lectures delivered at Oxford and Lincoln to Celebrate the Eighth Centenary of St Hugh's Consecration as Bishop of Lincoln* (Oxford, 1987), 49–73, at 61–8.

[32] Adam of Eynsham, *Magna Vita*, ed. Douie and Farmer, 2: 186–7.

[33] For discussions of stewardship, see Gilchrist, *Church and Economic Activity*, 29–37.

[34] Adam of Eynsham, *Magna Vita*, ed. Douie and Farmer, 1: 115.

[35] Ibid. 2: 87–8.

poor relief, or through the commissioning of objects and buildings designed to magnify the Lord and his saints. Hugh's interest in building projects, initiated at Witham, continued at Lincoln, 'which Hugh's immense zeal for the beauty of the house of God had caused him to begin to rebuild from the foundations'.[36] On another occasion, he used the consecration of a particularly beautiful and expensive chalice as an opportunity to praise those who lavished time and money on the liturgy and its vessels, and to rebuke those 'who, although enriched by the Church's revenues, did not endow their churches with books, vessels and other necessities, but rather tried to despoil than to adorn the poor churches of Christ with all these things'.[37] Hugh was also an avid collector of saintly relics, whether by purchase or by theft, and amassed a considerable array of them.[38]

Relic thefts aside, the acquisition of temporal capital for spiritual projects presents something of a problem in the text. It could not be acquired by force: Hugh handed back a magnificent Bible to its original owners at Winchester upon learning that it had been requisitioned from them by Henry II;[39] nor was he prepared to extort money from his flock to settle his debts in the affair of the mantle.[40] Gifts and donations from the laity, and from the royal family in particular, were acceptable sources of income, but they too had to be acquired under the correct circumstances. They could not be sought, unless already pledged as in the case of the rebuilding programme at Witham, but they could be received. In the third book, following a lengthy passage in which Adam sets out Hugh's utter disregard for the trappings of high office as demonstrated by preparations for his consecration as Bishop of Lincoln, he remarks that Henry was so pleased that the ceremony had finally been carried out after much delay that he gave Hugh many gold and silver vessels, and 'defrayed the immense cost of the ceremony'.[41] Last, but by no means least, Hugh was rewarded for his zeal for burying the dead and his parsimonious lifestyle on

---

[36]   Ibid. 2: 189.
[37]   Ibid. 2: 85–6, at 86.
[38]   Some of Hugh's 'acquisitions' are detailed in ibid. 2: 153–4, 167–71.
[39]   Ibid. 1: 85–8. Hugh's precise term is 'defrauded' (*fraudavit*).
[40]   See n.18 above.
[41]   Adam of Eynsham, *Magna Vita*, ed. Douie and Farmer, 1: 92–103, at 103.

earth with a magnificent burial, 'in addition to the reward reserved for him in heaven'.[42]

This is where miracles, the second prerequisite for papal canonization by the beginning of the thirteenth century, come in. In the text, Hugh's ostentatious asceticism provided a mechanism for generating further temporal capital, just as anathema provided the mechanism for securing existing goods that were already in the Church's possession. Hugh's ascetic behaviour generated merit in heaven, which, through the mediation of divine providence, was transmuted into material benefits in the temporal sphere. This intertwining of the temporal and spiritual economies helped to reconcile an apparent tension in the text between asceticism and aestheticism. As his building works at Witham and Lincoln demonstrate, Hugh had a highly developed aesthetic sense that he also displayed in his appreciation of reliquaries, manuscripts and liturgical vessels. Personal display and misappropriation of funds was one thing; temporal outlay on behalf of the spiritual estate of which Hugh was the steward was quite different.

Sanctity as Cultural and Social Capital

We have seen, then, that in Hugh's *vita* capital features heavily not simply in its metaphorical or symbolic guise (the talent) but in its material guise (the mark). But how does this relate to the original proposition, that sanctity is a form of capital?

On the one hand, for Adam, Hugh's sanctity and saintly reputation were the result of individual actions, representing an embodied form of cultural capital. Hugh was well educated and intelligent, and his reputation drew scholars to Witham from far and wide.[43] As bishop his opinion was often sought in legal cases in which his considerable skills, derived not from legal training but from divine favour, were seen by contemporaries as literally miraculous.[44] However, the chief cause of Hugh's saintly reputation was his ascetic behaviour, which was also the key mechanism in the text for the generation of capital. During his lifetime, his ascetic behaviour had brought dividends to his order and his diocese in

---

[42]   Ibid. 2: 1. Hugh's burial is described in more detail in the fifth book: ibid. 2: 217–32.

[43]   Ibid. 1: 77–8.

[44]   Ibid. 2: 150.

the form of relics, new buildings, liturgical vessels and ornaments. As bishop, Hugh had access to considerable temporal resources, but his *vita* emphasized the reserves generated by his ascetic lifestyle. These reserves, primarily spiritual but occasionally temporal (as demonstrated by his desire to retire to Witham to save money from his episcopal revenues), could be spent in turn in both the spiritual and temporal spheres. After his death Hugh's embodied cultural capital, generated primarily by his asceticism, was 'objectified' in the form of his shrine and his relics, and 'institutionalized' by his canonization.

On the other hand, Hugh's successful canonization also drew on his considerable reserves of social capital. By the beginning of the thirteenth century saintly reputation and posthumous miracles were not enough, on their own, to secure canonization: what were also needed were powerful supporters and a significant outlay of capital, both economic and symbolic. Hugh was a member of two important groups, the nobility and an ascetic religious order, which had helped to secure his promotion to a third, the episcopate.[45] In a period in which candidates for canonization were increasingly drawn from the episcopate (who were recruited in turn, in large part, from the nobility and from the religious orders), Hugh's membership of these three groups significantly increased his chances of inclusion in a fourth and final group: the communion of saints, which brought considerable rewards for Hugh and for his diocese.[46] A successful canonization bid, as the institutionalization of cultural capital, required not only a reputation for sanctity generated by asceticism and wisdom, but also social capital generated by membership of influential groups.

CONCLUSION

This examination of Adam of Eynsham's *Life of St Hugh* suggests that Bourdieu's concept of three forms of capital provides a useful tool with which to unlock the double- and quadruple-entry bookkeeping in thirteenth-century hagiographical texts. Adam's life reveals a complex financial system, fed by asceticism and regu-

---

[45] For the electors, Hugh was the only candidate 'who combined all the virtues with good breeding': ibid. 1: 94. See also Vauchez, *Sainthood*, 279–83.

[46] For statistics on social status and canonization, see Vauchez, 249–84. For the economic rewards, see Nilsen, *Cathedral Shrines*, 158–60, 222–6.

lated by anathema, excommunication and, ultimately, divine providence, in which credits could be made in one currency (merit) and withdrawn in another (money and material gifts). Bourdieu's theory not only provides a model for exploring different types of cultural capital which translated into a reputation for sanctity; it also provides a model for examining the relationships between successful and unsuccessful canonization attempts, and between social and cultural capital.

Yet the medieval evidence also suggests that we should look again at Bourdieu's assertion that 'economic capital is at the root of all the other types of capital'.[47] Adam of Eynsham, along with many of his contemporaries, perceived two separate but overlapping economies, one spiritual and one secular. Secular wealth was no guarantor of spiritual wealth or merit, and in many respects served as its antithesis. However, conscious rejection of secular rewards in the form of ascetic behaviour, an important component of a reputation for sanctity, could generate both symbolic capital (in the form of merit and miracles), and material capital, which was paid out, increasingly, in marks.

Harris Manchester College, University of Oxford

---

[47] Bourdieu, 'Forms of Capital', 252.

SAINT AND MONSTER, SAINT AS MONSTER: EXEMPLARY ENCOUNTERS WITH THE OTHER

by SAMANTHA RICHES

The concept of the monstrous is tremendously powerful as a cultural signifier of Otherness, not least when it is embodied into a physical form such as a dragon or other fantastical and threatening creature which can be clearly contrasted with a human hero. A wide range of saints' narratives – written and visual – which emanate from the Middle Ages include an encounter with a monster; the motif offers an excellent opportunity to present the saintly figure with a foil, not only in simple terms of good human versus evil beast, but also by demonstrating the contrast between the civilized nature of a form of perfected humanity and the untamed wilderness which is the natural habitat of monsters.[1]

In the best-known cases – the legends and iconography of St George, St Michael and St Martha, for example – the encounter takes on a violent aspect,[2] culminating in the death of the monster at the hands of the saint or their followers, but in other narratives a far more subtle paradigm is used where violence, or a threat of violence, forms an element in the trajectory of the story but does not appear in the concluding episode. The Cornish saint Carantoc, for example, uses a ferocious dragon as a teaching aid,[3] but far from killing the creature, as he was asked to do, he lets it fly away to safety when the people have learned their lesson. St Petroc and St Simon Stylites are both credited with healing injured dragons who came to them for help, and other saints' lives include tropes such as the employment of dragons as bodyguards,[4] or the contain-

---

[1]   For fuller discussion of the place of the monstrous in medieval understandings, and an extensive bibliography on the topic, see B. Bildhauer and R. Mills, eds, *The Monstrous Middle Ages* (Cardiff, 2003).

[2]   Versions of the lives of St George, St Michael and St Martha may be found in Jacobus de Voragine, *The Golden Legend: Readings on the Saints*, trans. William Granger Ryan, 2 vols (Princeton, NJ, 1993), 1: 238–41; 2: 201–10; 2: 23–6 respectively.

[3]   For the life of St Carantoc, see G. H. Doble, *The Saints of Cornwall*, 4 vols (Llanerch, 1960–5, repr. 1997–8), 4: 31–52.

[4]   For the life of the Blessed Ammon, see H. Waddell, *Beasts and Saints* (London,

ment of ferocious monsters by the division of an island into the realm of the beasts and the realm of the humans.[5] Some narratives subvert the model of the saint-as-dragon-slayer still further – we find self-description of an early medieval Irish saint as 'a mangling dragon'.[6] These saints who encountered and utilized monsters, or, more precisely, those who are constructed with monstrosity as an element of their sanctity, were all venerated to a greater or lesser extent during the Middle Ages; whilst their individual cults may not have been particularly widespread, the prevalence of such motifs can illuminate an important yet largely overlooked means by which saints were constructed as powerful advocates for humanity.

This paper focuses on a range of encounters between saints and monsters in which the monster is shown to be contained and controlled rather than killed outright. This trope is particularly interesting because it indicates some of the ways in which the saint's negotiation with the Other – encoded in the body of a monster – can be used to present particular messages to the saint's adherents. This pedagogic interpretation relates to the etymological roots of the term 'monster': the Latin *monstro* translates as 'to show',[7] and is found today in the English term 'demonstrate'. Thus, whilst the stories presented here may appear to be drawn purely from the realm of fantasy, the trope of the encounter between the saint and the monster arguably provides potential for devotees to consider a paradigm of containing the Other which could be employed in everyday struggles of faith. Although these saints' lives may have been understood as literal truth by at least some of their audience, a more important understanding of their function is perhaps that of a parable – these stories would surely have been discussed by the people who heard them told. It is important to note that within these saints' legends monsters can be presented by the narrator as hallucinatory, for example in the stories of St Margaret and St Perpetua,[8] or as apparently real beasts, as in the story of St Martha,

1934), 8–12.
  5 For the life of St Hilary, see de Voragine, *Golden Legend*, trans. Ryan, 1: 87–9.
  6 For a transcription of the life of Mac Creiche, see C. Plummer, ed., *Miscellanea Hagiographica Hibernica*, Subsidia Hagiographica 15 (Brussels, 1925), 53–91.
  7 See, e.g., the definitions of *monstro* and *monstrum* in W. Smith and J. Lockwood, *Chambers Murray Latin-English Dictionary* (Edinburgh, 1976, first publ. 1934), 444.
  8 For St Margaret's legend, see de Voragine, *Golden Legend*, trans Ryan, 1: 368–70.

and they can be understood as forms of the devil, or evil more generally, in either guise; they also exhibit divergent abilities to withstand the power of prayer and force of arms. This kind of variation, which does not seem to relate clearly to either chronology or geography, indicates the range of understandings associated with monsters in medieval understanding and emphasizes the range of cultural work which monsters could undertake within narrative, the visual arts and other kinds of expression.

The model of peaceful coexistence which is found in some of these stories could be interpreted as a form of longsuffering and transcendence, motifs which are commonly invoked in medieval discussion of the Christian life, particularly when saints – especially martyrs – are presented as exemplars.[9] It has much to recommend it as a strategy for dealing with fortune's trials, not least because it is more widely applicable to real life than the rather more dramatic trope of violent subjugation. Examples of this model of containment of the Other are found quite widely, and I have elsewhere discussed in detail the legends and iconography of some saints who encounter monsters in a non-violent way;[10] in some cases these saints' narratives are relevant to this paper too, but only brief references are given here. This paper offers some more complex examples of this particular aspect of alterity in saints' cults, especially where narratives seem to move between different discourses; it forms part of an ongoing project which considers the full panoply of meanings encoded within the topos of the saintly encounter with the monstrous.

Initially, we should be clear that the group of legends we are considering here represent a deviation from the normative encounter between the saint and the monster. St George rescuing the princess from the dragon is an instantly recognizable archetype of what a saint can reasonably be expected to do when confronted with a monster: he – or, less frequently, she – should ensure the

---

St Perpetua had a vision of a hideous dragon guarding a ladder, strewn with knives and swords, which reached to heaven; see de Voragine, *Golden Legend*, trans. Ryan, 2: 342.

9 Cf. my 'St George as a Male Virgin Martyr', in S. J. E. Riches and S. Salih, eds, *Gender and Holiness: Men, Women and Saints in Late Medieval Europe* (London, 2003), 65–85.

10 See my 'Virtue and Violence: Saints, Monsters and Sexuality', in A. Harper and C. Proctor, eds, *Medieval Sexuality: A Casebook* (London, 2007), 59–78.

safety of one or more persons threatened with predation by tackling the creature through either physical or spiritual force, or indeed a combination of the two. Thus St Petroc took on a dragon in order to safeguard a town which was threatened by its predatory behaviour,[11] whilst St Martha subdued the predatory Tarasque with the sign of the cross, stepping aside to let local Provençal people beat the creature to death with sticks and stones.[12] Meanwhile, the case of St Margaret offers us an interesting commentary on the perceived role of saintly violence: the saint is frequently depicted plunging a cross-topped lance into her attacker, even though there is no violent attack on the dragon within the written narrative.[13] However, there is a clear subset of saints who do not employ violence in their encounters with monsters – or do not have violence attributed to them by the taletellers and artists – although we should note that some of these pacific saints will also, when occasion demands, invoke violent means. Thus, for example, the Blessed Ammon, whose history was recorded in the eighth century,[14] gives us three different attitudes to monsters in one story, with two examples of the topos of non-violent interface and a third episode which accords with the classic violent encounter found in the legend of St George and the dragon. Ammon's third dragon, like St George's foe, and invades human space in an unacceptable way, in sharp contrast to the other two monsters, which live peaceably alongside the holy man either in a separate part of the desert, or actively helping him by guarding his monastery. It could be that these motifs of benign indifference and co-operation are meant to be read as the ideal relationship between humans and the natural world, even when the natural world has a clear potential for threat; when the potential becomes actual threat, the saint is shown to take action to eliminate it.

The encounter between saint and monster offers an opportunity to demonstrate the power of the saint, spiritual as well as physical. The *Golden Legend* narrative of St Matthew recounts an episode in which the power of the saint's faith is so strong that dragons are drawn to him, and are subdued by his presence to the

[11] K. Jankulak, *The Medieval Cult of St. Petroc* (Woodbridge, 2000).
[12] De Voragine, *Golden Legend*, trans. Ryan, 2: 23–6.
[13] See my 'Virtue and Violence'.
[14] Waddell, *Beasts and Saints*, 8.

extent that they lose consciousness.[15] A similar level of power is exhibited by another apostle, St Philip: he banished a dragon 'to a desert place where he could do no harm to anyone'.[16] Again, the dragon is not overcome by violence: saintly power alone forces the monster into exile. Another interesting example of a non-violent interface is offered by the Irish saint Senán: here we find the monster keeping an island free from human sinfulness, and it simply leaves when requested to do so by the saint.[17] The monster is described as 'hideous, uncouth, ruthless, awful ... keen, savage, froward, angry, edged, crimson, bloody, cruel';[18] the language used of the monster is very redolent of violence – and hence the danger into which the saint is putting himself by confronting the beast – but it also perhaps has connotations of the sins of anger and violence that could have been visited on this agent of God if an ordinary mortal had approached it.

St Serf, or Servanus, a Scottish saint with multiple connections to dragons, has a narrative that presents us with examples of encounters with monsters which end violently as well as instances in which a monstrous threat is contained by a simple act of blessing that could be intended to indicate the power of Christian belief, and also perhaps the power of the institutional Church. It is unclear quite how far his cult extended beyond eastern and central Scotland, but his narrative does give us some sense of the potential which this kind of trope could offer for encouraging devotees to put their trust in a local rather than universal saint.

Serf is dated to the period 490–550, and his story is preserved in a thirteenth-century manuscript, held in Marsh's Library in Dublin.[19] The chronological gap between the events described and the time of recording indicates that we cannot be certain of the

---

[15] De Voragine, *Golden Legend*, trans. Ryan, 2: 184.

[16] Ibid. 1: 267.

[17] Notably, this monster is not presented as a direct embodiment of sin but rather as a prophylactic against sin: this is a clear example of the wide range of meanings which can be attributed to dragons and similar beasts. For further discussion, see my 'Encountering the Monstrous: Saints and Dragons in Medieval Thought', in Bildhauer and Mills, eds, *Monstrous Middle Ages*, 196–219.

[18] This description is found in 'The Life of Senán Son of Gerrgenn', in *Lives of Saints from the Book of Lismore*, ed. Whitley Stokes (Oxford, 1890), 213.

[19] MS Z 4.5.5, fols 3ʳ–3ᵛ. See A. Macquarrie, '*Vita Sancti Servani*: The Life of St Serf', *Innes Review* 44 (1993), 122–52; I am grateful to Simon Taylor for drawing this text to my attention.

extent to which this manuscript offers a true picture of the way that St Serf was understood in the early medieval period. However, it is notable that several of our monster-encountering saints share this motif, in that a late medieval manuscript contains a narrative set in a much earlier period. This may simply be testament to a shift from oral to written culture, or indeed a coincidence of survivals, but it may also be suggestive of a late medieval interest in the alterity of remote time periods as well as the alterity of monsters.

The manuscript presents a fascinating account of the trip that St Serf is supposed to have made from Rome to Scotland, accompanied by a veritable host of followers. During his journey across the Alps, Serf spent the night in the Black Valley, or Valley of Beasts, where he knew that his faith would be tried. A biblical verse is invoked: 'You will tread upon the asp and the serpent, and trample down the lion and the dragon' (Psalm 91: 13); this is glossed by saying that by holding fast to the faith of the Holy Trinity, believers will tread upon the asp and serpent (namely, on the devil and his pride) and nothing will harm them. As soon as the verse was recited,

> there came a pestilential cloud of vapour over the valley where they were. Then came great earthquakes, thunder and lightnings, hailstones, and fires of sulphur, and all kinds of two-legged and four-legged beasts, and these filled the valley around them. Then came gnats having horny beaks, dragons, winged serpents, and all the torments of hell which Satan can show to men. Seeing all these things, a great part of the crowd fell dead. But St Serf, seeing that his companions could not endure these things, arose and blessed the valley. So all these things vanished and returned to nothing, and never troubled anyone further.[20]

A pointing hand was inscribed in the margin of the Dublin text, probably during the fifteenth century, to highlight this passage about the monsters: this seems to indicate that a level of meaning beyond simple fantasy is intended to be drawn. Indeed, there are several striking aspects of this element of the narrative, not least

---

[20]   Macquarrie, '*Vita Sancti Servani*', 147–8.

the apparent distinction between 'dragons' and 'winged serpents',[21] but here we should focus on the means by which St Serf defeated these monsters. His use of a blessing instead of a more concrete weapon is paralleled in the *vitae* of some of the other saints we have mentioned, such as St Margaret and St Senán, both of whom were threatened by physical violence but prevailed by spiritual force; like St Margaret's dragon, these monsters seem to have been insubstantial, though none the less dangerous for that, as the deaths of many of Serf's followers indicate.[22]

This episode seems to underline Serf's spiritual power, as he stood unharmed whilst mere mortals fell dead around him, but in his second bout of monster-slaying, which took place near his chapel at Dunning – his first and favourite foundation – in Perthshire, he employed a more physical approach than the simple blessing he used in the Black Valley. The Aberdeen Breviary of 1510 relates that:

> In a place called Dunnyne, the inhabitants were harassed by a dreadful dragon which devoured both men and cattle, and kept the district in continuous terror. St Serf, armed with the breastplate of faith, attacked the monster in its lair and slew it with a blow of his pastoral staff.[23]

A tradition noted in the Dublin life relates that his staff was hewn from the same tree that produced Christ's cross, but the legend of St Martha, as well as those of many secular dragon-slayers, demonstrates that even ordinary materials would do the job. The significance of the use of a weapon, especially in conjunc-

---

[21] This distinction is intriguing, for one widely accepted definition of a dragon is that it is a large serpent that is frequently endowed with wings. It may be that the author here means something different – more Other? – with this usage, and this points up the useful ambiguity of the concept of dragons.

[22] It is also worth noting that the trope of making the sign of the cross is presented as an alternative to a more physical means of defeating a monster in some versions of the life of St George, including the earliest written account of the dragon legend, from the twelfth century, though this quickly gave way to a physical combat. See my *St George: Hero Martyr and Myth* (Stroud, 2000), 25. Meanwhile, in the *vita* of St Martha the blessing acts as a prelude to a properly physical death: as noted above, the saint subdued the Tarasque by making the sign of the cross and asperging it with holy water, and then stood aside so that the people could kill it with sticks and stones.

[23] *Breviarium Aberdonense*, ed. W. Blew, Bannatyne Club (London, 1854), 430; a digital version of this text is available at <http://www.archive.org/details/breviariumaber9603cathuoft>.

tion with the clearly metaphorical 'breast-plate of faith' of the *miles Christianus*,[24] is unclear: the author seems to be combining different discourses here, perhaps in an effort to indicate both the physical and spiritual heroism of St Serf in one easy move. Serf thus stands as an example of the extent to which one saint's dealings with dragons were capable of being constructed in multiple ways.

The complex legend of the Irish holy man Mac Creiche also moves effortlessly between different discourses. His life survives in one manuscript dated to the seventeenth century, although the saint himself is located in the fifth or sixth century;[25] the story is set in County Tipperary. The narrative is long and complex, with many references to the saint's power, some of which appear to encode evil and threat in the form of monsters.

> Wondrous illustrious miracles were done by Mac Creiche when great pestilences attacked all Ireland ... viz. the long-clawed griffin ... and the 'broicsech' [badger monster][26] ... a monster [*pést*] most vehement, strong, malignant, unwearied, with its bestial rage upon it ... And this is what it would do; it would open its ravenous raging maw like a mad dog, with its jaws all on fire, and emit a broad terrifying stream of harsh magical (literally 'pagan') breath ... and every man whom that

[24] Imagery of the soldier of Christ occurs in a variety of places in the New Testament, including a reference to the 'breastplate of faith and charity' in 1 Thess. 5: 8.

[25] Brussels, Koninklijke Bibliotheek, MS 2324–40, fols 87–98; this was transcribed in 1634 from a copy made in 1528; see Plummer, *Miscellanea*. I am grateful to Gilbert Markus for the reference.

[26] The invocation of a monstrous badger conjures up quite a curious image. It can perhaps be interpreted as a means of localizing this embodiment of the Other by reference to something with which local people would be familiar; it is known that any new concept must have some recognizable aspect in order to be meaningful. A useful analogy can be drawn with the German term *unheimlich*, which is usually glossed as 'uncanny'. The word contains the term *heimlich*, which carries implications of security and familiarity. The element 'un-' gives us an opposite meaning, of course, but the term makes clear reference to something which is known and familiar. Similarly, the concept of the monstrous badger draws upon the known world, but indicates that what is being described is far beyond any real-life badger. Whilst they do not threaten people, badgers are known for their destructive power, particularly towards hedgehogs and other small mammals, and it could be that this aspect is being invoked here. In the same way, the 'gnats having horny beaks' mentioned in the narrative of St Serf in the Black Valley may be intended to invoke the midges of the Scottish Highlands: small but menacing, and almost certainly familiar to the audience of the tale. I am indebted to Simon Taylor for drawing this reading of the episode to my attention.

poisonous breath touched and every animal, died a premature
and sudden death ... so that it stripped almost the whole land
of its good men, and a great number of them left it altogether;
and this was the extent of their losses, to wit, men and women
to the number of sixty every day.[27]

Here we see a similar approach to that found in the narrative of
St Senán, where the threat of the monster is carefully established
through the violent language used to describe it; furthermore,
familiar tropes associated with dragons are invoked, such as the
aspect of pestilential breath.[28]

Initially the people tried to scare the monster off themselves,
but this only served to make it more fierce. Then everyone fasted,
and the archangel Victor appeared in a vision to say that he would
sing the monster a lullaby so that it would sleep for three days,
giving them time to summon Mac Creiche. When the saint arrived
it duly awoke and pursued the people. They cried piteously, knelt
before Mac Creiche and offered themselves to him in servile rent
of service, and to his monks after him, if only he would come to
their aid.

The storyteller then excels even the description of the *broicsech*
with an inspired rendering of the encounter between saint and
monster, which took place at a weir. The monster discharged balls
of fire from its maw, and Mac Creiche struck back with the aid
of his bell:

> he struck the bell fiercely, so that the monster started, and
> reared itself on its hind legs so that it was higher than a bushy
> tall-topped eminent tree, or a bell-tower set on a hill; and the
> numerous claws and talons growing out of it were horrible,
> and great fear seized the clerk ... And then it hurled itself on
> to the weir with dreadful, horrible, unnatural fury; and with
> such fury did it discharge its balls of fire through its ravening
> raging maw, and through its nostrils, and raise its bestial wrath
> upon it, that its bristles could be seen standing on end, with a
> dew-drop of blood on every single hair of its body from ear to

---

27 Plummer, *Miscellanea*, 76.

28 St George's dragon is the obvious example of a monster which spreads conta-
gion: it was initially fed sheep, and then humans, as a means of persuading it to stay
away from the city of Silene and hence protecting the inhabitants from its breath; see,
e.g., de Voragine, *Golden Legend*, trans. Ryan, 1: 238.

tail … After this Mac Creiche smote the bell twice while the monster was traversing the weir with enormous strides, and his maw all aflame, and at the third stroke a ball of fire shot from the bell into the monster's maw, and its maw caught fire. And when the monster perceived that its gullet was on fire, it turned back on the weir with a horrible scream and screech, and both hosts arose, and set up great universal clamorous cries of triumph.[29]

Mac Creiche drove the monster into the waters of the loch, which turned red. In a dramatic twist worthy of a modern horror film the monster suddenly rose up again in the loch, causing panic amongst the crowd. Mac Creiche is described as ashamed of his failure to finish it off; he took hold of his cowl (or possibly hat or skullcap) and threw it over the monster. The garment magically grew and pressed down on the monster; it seemed to be 'like a cowl of smelted iron'[30] which sank the monster down to the bottom of the loch. It did not drown, but it would not rise again until the brink of the Day of Judgement. Everyone rejoiced and again offered themselves in servile labour. Mac Creiche accepted this thank-offering, but threatened that if proper tribute were not paid in the future – even to his relics after this death – a curse would come down on the people and cause pestilence and disease, and a malignant demon would cause strife in the tribe.

This image of a saint who curses as well as saves may strike some modern readers as rather off-key, but it is a trope found in a number of accounts of saints, and particularly perhaps Irish ones. We should note too that Mac Creiche speaks of himself in the following terms:

> (But) I will be a mangling dragon [*uil-pheist ledartach*],
> If I hear the contest;
> I will be opposed to them,
> If they destroy my increase.[31]

Here we see Mac Creiche harnessing the power of the defeated monster in the most extreme way, by identifying himself as a dragon. The threat of pestilence within his curse is drawn from

---

[29] Plummer, *Miscellanea*, 81.
[30] Ibid. 82.
[31] Ibid. 73.

this same discourse, for it invokes the pestilential breath of the *broicsech* itself, and indeed other dragons, and hence underlines Mac Creiche's self-identification as a monster.[32]

We noted earlier the concept of monsters as demonstrators; the narratives of St Serf and Mac Creiche both allow space for lessons to be drawn, even in the absence of a pointing hand in the margin highlighting the relevant passage. We know from the example of the medieval bestiary that moral lessons could be drawn from even apparently unpromising material, and the lives of saints must have seemed very fertile by comparison. The paradigm of the violent encounter between hero and monster was clearly well established as a mainstay of medieval culture, and it is possible that the trope of containing the threat of the monster was a particularly useful motif, as it represented ongoing defeat; this is arguably a more powerful concept than a single outright victory. These stories each confirm the status of the saint as a powerful figure who can advocate the cause of their adherents, whilst the absorption model seems to represent the logical extension of the underlying motif of a power relationship and the harnessing of the potential for violence that discussion of saints overcoming monsters inevitably invokes. In this context, it is a particularly clear example of the confirmation of the status of the saint as a figure of power.

Lancaster University

---

[32] This self-identification as a monster is a trope which can also be found in wider society, outside the discourse of saints' narratives. For example, the heraldic popularity of dragons derives to some extent from the same concept, for dragon-slayers were thought to absorb the powers of their defeated foe and this force could be passed on to future generations of the same family. In this way the saint's narrative seems to be in step with a more general understanding of the roles played by monsters in medieval culture. On the topic of dragon-slaying in relation to heraldry, especially where the story of a dragon-slayer in an earlier age arises in order to explain pre-existing family imagery, see J. Simpson, *British Dragons* (Ware, 2001).

PENANCE, MERCY AND SAINTLY AUTHORITY IN THE MIRACLES OF ST THOMAS BECKET*

by GESINE OPPITZ-TROTMAN

The miracle stories of St Thomas Becket, recorded first by Benedict of Peterborough (d. 1193) and then by his successor in the task, William of Canterbury (of whom little is known), comprise the largest collection of miracles of the high Middle Ages, and describe the nature of medieval sanctity in manifold ways. The two writers went about their task in markedly contrasting ways, with William generally the more ambitious of the two. He frequently returned to records entered by Benedict to adapt, correct or expand upon them.

The following essay addresses the penitential dimensions of Becket's miracle stories in order to suggest an important connection between St Thomas's power as an administrator of penitential obligation and the establishment of his sanctity. It suggests that the form of Thomas's saintly visitations, as described particularly by William of Canterbury, negotiated the complex and delicate problems of the period between martyrdom in December 1170 and the royal penance at Canterbury in the summer of 1174, and the years afterwards. Both miracle collections allow for a cautious inclusion of royal authority, despite the naturally anti-royalist emphasis of Becket's cult and the largely unspoken contemporary anxiety that Henry II may have been more directly responsible for the archbishop's death than could be admitted by the king's subjects.

Becket left behind him a career strewn with acrimony and, while his death lifted him above a multitude of conflicts both minor and major, the controversy could not be erased entirely by martyrdom. This left the hagiographers of St Thomas facing a legacy which was difficult to reconcile with sainthood. One way in which this was achieved was by showing a relatively merciful saint

* I would like to thank Nicholas Vincent for reading an extended version of this paper and offering much helpful advice.

in absolute symbolic command of the penitential duties of others. Miracles have a kind of affinity with scenes of penance. As Mary C. Mansfield suggested, 'public penance acts out a utopian dream: it declares the hope that God's justice can be made visible on earth'; this is also true of miracles.[1] A further aim of this paper, therefore, will be to indicate the importance of revelation and publicity within St Thomas's cult, and to suggest in conclusion how such miracles, as publicized expressions of inner truth, interacted with the increasing emphasis placed by twelfth-century theologians on inward contrition.

Becket's murder incriminated as many people as he had condemned during his tumultuous career. After the shaky peace established with Henry II in late July 1170 at Fréteval, Thomas had returned to England. Yet he came bearing fresh excommunications, partly in reaction to the infringement upon the primacy of his see that the archbishop of York had committed in crowning the young Henry. Moments before he was martyred, the knights demanded angrily that Thomas revoke these punishments. This was significant, because it was the journey made across the Channel by Gilbert Foliot of London, Roger de Pont l'Evêque of York and Jocelin of Salisbury, to protest against their excommunications, that provoked Henry II to the rash words that set the knights on their course back to England and the murder they eventually committed there. According to the eyewitness Edward Grim and other chroniclers, Thomas, invoking the bishop's privilege of binding and loosing, refused the knights' demand that the excommunications be retracted: 'no penance has been made,' he said, 'so I will not absolve them'.[2]

---

[1] Mary C. Mansfield, *The Humiliation of Sinners: Public Penance in Thirteenth Century France* (London, 1995), 17. Pilgrimages, the journeys often involved in the reporting of miraculous stories, also have an almost essentially penitential dimension, as Raymonde Foreville pointed out: 'Les "Miracula S. Thomae Cantuariensis"', *Actes du 97ᵉ congrès national des sociétés savantes* (Nantes, 1972), 443–68, at 452; repr. in eadem, *Thomas Becket dans la tradition historique et hagiographique* (London, 1981), 443–68, at 452.

[2] Edward Grim, 'Vita S. Thomae', in James Craigie Robertson, ed., *Materials for the History of Thomas Becket, Archbishop of Canterbury (Canonized by Pope Alexander III. A. D. 1173)*, 6 vols (London, 1876), 2: 353–450, at 436. John of Salisbury, among others, omits this. But Grim was present, and it is too prosaic a detail, given the situation, to be put down to embellishment. William fitzStephen includes it: 'Vita Sancti Thomae, Cantuariensis archiepiscopi et martyris', in Robertson, ed., *Materials*, 3: 1–154, at 132–3.

Marcus Bull has noted William of Canterbury's preoccupation with Henry's trip to Ireland (October 1171 – April 1172), as well as the fact that the monk mentions these political events to the exclusion of more immediate concerns, such as the fire that devastated Canterbury Cathedral in 1174 or the tumultuous events of the rebellions of 1173–74. Indeed, the story of St Thomas's appearances to a timid fisherman, chosen as a messenger and sent to ask the king to come to the shrine at Canterbury, specifically mentions the Irish situation, as Bull notes.[3] This account, set during late August or September 1171, is possibly the clearest within William's collection concerning the problems of Henry II's guilt and contrition.[4] The fisherman Alfred of Gloucester subsidized a man buying fish for the monastery, formerly a porter of Becket's. In so doing, Alfred honoured St Thomas by showing respect not only to the monastic institution but also to one who had known the saint when he was alive. The following night Alfred received a spectacular visitation from St Thomas, among a dazzling array of lights, 'sitting on a white steed, above the waters flowing past [Alfred's] cottage'. Among other tasks given to Alfred, to which we shall return below, he was instructed to pass a message to the king himself:

> Your king drove my person into exile. Nothing which he undertakes will come to a favourable end unless he come to my shrine, and there win the mercy of divine indulgence. It will be made known to him that it is unnecessary he travel abroad, neither to Rome nor to Jerusalem, in search of mercy.

The invitation is clearly to visit Canterbury: as Colin Morris notes, pilgrimage to Rome and Jerusalem was viewed with some degree of ambivalence, perhaps particularly amongst monks, as its popularity increased.[5] During the course of the twelfth century several significant shrines had appeared, and competition was growing for pilgrims' attention among the major centres of pilgrimage: not only Rome or Jerusalem, but also Compostela, Bari, Cologne, Vézelay and Canterbury itself.[6] In the case of Alfred's

---

[3]   Marcus Bull, 'Criticism of Henry II's expedition to Ireland in William of Canterbury's Miracles of St Thomas Becket', *JMedH* 33 (2007), 107–29, at 119–20.

[4]   William of Canterbury, 'Miraculorum gloriosi martyris Thomae, Cantuariensis archiepiscopi', in Robertson, ed., *Materials*, 1: 137–546, at 275–6.

[5]   Colin Morris, *The Sepulchre of Christ and the Medieval West* (Oxford, 2005), 200–5.

[6]   On shrine competition, see Debra J. Birch, 'Selling the Saints: Competition

mission to the king, we see the obligation to visit a particular place coinciding with a specific penitential duty.

While Bull skilfully draws attention to the range of attitudes to the Irish developments voiced by William's text, he perhaps understates what contemporary commentators saw as the major problem: the fact that the king's presence in Ireland delayed his return to Normandy and to the initial penance he eventually observed there, where papal legates had awaited him some months before.[7] After all, as the cult and the renown of the saint grew, all eyes must have been on the king, but his return from Dublin, where he had probably wintered, was delayed by bad weather.[8] A crucial symbolic moment thus arrived when the saint reappeared a second time to remind the fisherman of his mission, predicting where Henry would dismount from his horse as he rested on his journey across to Ireland, and assuring Alfred that this place would be close to his home. 'Listen,' Thomas rebuked the sleeping fisherman, 'you did not perform my command.' Like the king, Alfred seemed to procrastinate. But he travelled to the place revealed by the saint, and sought a chance to confront Henry:

> As the king was dismounting in the place near that predicted by the saint's speech, with warlike hand and great splendour, the man, mindful of his duty, intended to seize the king's reins; but seeing him diverted by various thoughts ... repressed the words on his trembling lips out of servile fear.

Thus the message went unspoken, but there was no punishment for Alfred. The miracle serves not to make an example of this put-upon fisherman, but to signal Henry II's apparent ignorance of public expectation.[9]

---

among Pilgrim Centres in the Twelfth Century', *MedH* 2 (1992), 20–34; eadem, *Pilgrimage to Rome in the Middle Ages: Continuity and Change* (Woodbridge, 1998), esp. 150–5.

[7]   See esp. Gervase, who saw the expedition as an evasion of this responsibility: *Opera Historica*, ed. W. Stubbs, 2 vols, *RS* 73 (1879–80), 1: 234–5.

[8]   Anne Duggan thinks Henry was there from around 11 November 1171 until late February 1172: '*Ne in dubium*: The Official Record of Henry II's Reconciliation at Avranches, 21 May 1172', *EHR* 115 (2000), 643–58, at 643–4.

[9]   Nevertheless, nobody could suppose that the king was unaware of the damage the murder had done to his reputation. A description of Henry's instant realization that the infamy of the murder would mark his reputation and guarantee the opprobrium of posterity can be found in the third fragment of Lansdowne MS 398 (London, BL), abridged in Robertson, ed., *Materials*, 4: 158–85, at 159.

Indeed, Alfred's other task was to pass news of his mission to others. St Thomas bade him go forth to Canterbury on pilgrimage in search of the hair-shirt relic, the sign of Becket's secret penitential discipline, discovered beneath his robes by the monks in the aftermath of the martyrdom. The account leaves it unclear whether he should take this with him on his mission to the king. Crucially, however, this is strongly implied. St Thomas continued: 'Returning, you shall communicate with your neighbours; and you shall speak to the abbot your lord, and brother Richard, in order that they be started on the same cause as yourself.' Thus the miracle story was much more concerned to reflect a public expectation of royal penance than it was with the actual enforcement of the saint's wishes.

Underlying William's description of Alfred's 'servile fear' was the entire problem of how to confront the king with the implication of attributable guilt. The fact that a fisherman was chosen clearly opened the door for association with the call of Peter and Andrew (Matthew 4: 17–19). This fairly obvious allusion may have provided a framework of interpretation for a largely monastic audience with intimate knowledge of Scripture, and lends subversive dimensions to William of Canterbury's language at other points in his narrative. William's reference elsewhere in this story to Henry II's 'subjugation' to his authority of the 'kinglets of the tetrarchy' (*rex regulos tetrarchas ditioni suae bello metuque subjugasset*) certainly alluded to the 'traditional ways of dividing Ireland', as Bull notes.[10] However, considering the miracle story's main object, these words made another bold allusion, either to the tetrarchy of Judea ruled over by Herod the Great (d. 4 BC), whom Matthew (2: 16) accuses of ordering the Massacre of the Innocents, the original Christian martyrs,[11] or to the tetrarchy founded by Diocletian (284–305). Certainly the latter interpretation would have reflected the tumult of the Angevin domains before Henry II recovered his position at the time of his Canterbury penance, but any hint of comparison between Henry and Constantine, the liberator of Christianity,

---

[10] Bull, 'Criticism of Henry II's Expedition', 119–20. Gerald of Wales recorded, with typical gusto, Henry II's expedition to the 'occidental kinglets, [subsequently] stupefied by his thunderbolts': *Giraldi Cambrensis Topographia Hibernica et Expugnatio Hibernica*, ed. James F. Dimock (Wiesbaden, 1964; first publ. 1867), 149.

[11] The apocryphal second-century *Protoevangelium of James* is the only source to repeat Matthew's claim.

is undercut by the alternative reference suggested by the use of Matthew, and may thus be read as ironic. William's text is alive to such allusions and ambiguities; shot through with reference to the Gospel of Matthew, this miracle story is subtle and complex in its reproach of the king.

Another story tells of paralysis inflicted on the child of a woman who had mocked Thomas's sanctity. Vitally, this mockery occurred in the context of an invitation to visit Hugh de Morville, one of Becket's murderers. De Morville had held back the onlookers in the cathedral. The tale is related by both Benedict of Peterborough and his successor, William, who greatly modified and expanded the tale.[12] William describes how a wealthy man, Robert, was dining at the house of a certain Stephen, when he received an invitation from his old friend Hugh de Morville to visit. This Robert refused out of pious deference to St Thomas, prompting an outburst against the saint on the part of Stephen's wife, and her persuasion of the reluctant Robert to accept the invitation from de Morville, a man described by William as the 'infamy of our age'.[13] Stephen, subsequently hearing news of St Thomas's miraculous works, suggested a pilgrimage, to which his wife agreed. However, the younger of their sons, apparently influenced by his mother's lack of caution, protested, unwisely wondering aloud why the martyr should be someone to care about. Paralysis struck one of his arms shortly after. William places an emphasis on the mother's sense of her own guilt, and her remorse: 'And God saw her penitence and contrition.' In consequence of this, St Thomas appeared to her sick son, healing him with the command 'Esto sanus' and bidding him become a monk.

Crucially, William's version attributes this miracle partly to the presence nearby of what he calls 'certain of the king's agents' (*quidam de ministris regis*). These accompanied the young man to the

---

[12] This tale is related by William of Canterbury, 'Miracula', in Robertson, ed., *Materials*, 1: 195–98; and Benedict of Peterborough, 'Miracula Sancti Thomae Cantuariensis', in ibid. 2: 21–298, at 219–20. The divergence in some fundamental details between the two versions makes their exact relationship ambiguous.

[13] This is a further reference to the ostracizing of the murderers. Roger of Howden describes Hugh de Morville's isolated existence at Knaresborough: *Gesta Regis Henrici Secundi Benedicti Abbatis*, ed. William Stubbs, 2 vols, RS 49 (1867), 1: 13. Knaresborough is only ten miles or so from Fountains Abbey, a Cistercian house where the said Stephen's younger son was apparently sent to become a monk, according to Benedict.

Canterbury tomb to give thanks 'more thoroughly'.[14] Clearly, the miracle story in William's version was intended as a further rebuke to the king. By noting various details, in particular the reference to Hugh de Morville and the presence of the king's servants, William imbues his retelling with a powerful sense of the political climate in a way his predecessor Benedict had not. Like the careless mother, Henry II similarly had to do penance for careless words uttered in anger: the context of Hugh de Morville's guilt, and Henry's presence as a proxy via his servants, allow the narrative to connect Hugh de Morville's act with the king's complacency, as if Hugh were an unruly son.[15] William reiterates the resistance of the parents to their son enlisting in Cistercian orders.[16] The boy's hesitation brought about further visions of St Thomas. As William relates it, the saint warned: 'I have spoken to you twice in secret. The third time I will appear unto thee, and the entire region (*tota regio*) will know it.' It is unclear whether this is a further threat, but the difference between quiet recommendation and public, spectacular reproof would have been felt keenly by all sides in England amidst what Frank Barlow memorably termed 'the deafening silence' concerning the king's guilt.[17]

We might compare this with a simpler, more visceral story: that in which pilgrims to Jerusalem, endangered at sea, were saved by St Thomas on the condition that they prayed for the soul of Reginald FitzUrse.[18] This was the knight who, it is thought, first struck the archbishop.[19] The miracle story itself, in Book IV of

[14] William of Canterbury, 'Miracula', in Robertson, ed., *Materials*, 1: 197.

[15] In his *Vita*, William had uniquely included an anecdote describing the deceit and sinfulness of de Morville's mother, which he supposed de Morville to have inherited: 'Vita et passio S. Thomae', in Robertson, ed., *Materials*, 1: 1–136, at 128. On the wider significance of this anecdote, see Roger Dahood, 'Hugh de Morville, William of Canterbury, and Anecdotal Evidence for English Language', *Speculum* 69 (1994), 40–56.

[16] The manuscripts of both miracle collections probably circulated widely through Cistercian networks, possibly to advertise the translation of Becket's remains, initially planned for May 1186. Henry II had made threats against the order and its property in the 1160s, at the height of the dispute with Becket, whom the order supported. Anonymous I (formerly thought to be Roger of Pontigny) describes the presentation of Henry's warning to the General Chapter, in 'Vita Sancti Thomae, Cantuariensis archiepiscopi et martyris', in Robertson, ed., *Materials*, 4: 1–79, at 65. On the Cistercians' role in the Becket conflict, see Martin Preiss, *Die politische Tätigkeit und Stellung der Cisterzienser im Schisma von 1154–1177* (Halle, 1934).

[17] Frank Barlow, *Thomas Becket* (London, 1986), 252.

[18] William of Canterbury, 'Miracula', in Robertson, ed., *Materials*, 1: 363.

[19] Abbott's account of the martyrdom remains one of the most detailed and

William's manuscript, is brief but extraordinarily dramatic, with a vivid description of a violent storm, the appearance of St Thomas 'through a vision', and the pilgrims' reward the following day as they sighted Palestine. The story doubtless referred to the penitential trip to the Holy Land on which the murderers were sent by Alexander III, undertaken in 1173 (by which time the situation in England had become fairly dangerous for them). The dating of this particular miracle is important, especially if we are to compare it to the miracle involving de Morville discussed above, which clearly dates from the time de Morville and his co-conspirators (including FitzUrse) were ensconced in Knaresborough. It seems likely that Book IV of William's collection derives from the period between the murderers' departure from England in 1173 (in the footsteps of de Tracy, who had travelled to Rome in apparent panic in 1171–72), and the penance of Henry II himself in July 1174.[20]

The miracle story involving FitzUrse strongly implies that the pilgrims, on their way to Jerusalem, were asked to pray for him because they found themselves in a symbolically similar situation; indeed, William may have been able to imagine that FitzUrse was making such a journey at more or less the same time as he recorded this miracle. William's Book IV seems preoccupied with pilgrimage abroad, particularly to Rome and Jerusalem. Even compared to other descriptions of danger at sea elsewhere in his collection, in this example William does everything to emphasize the pilgrims' complete powerlessness: with three masts broken, two tillers destroyed, and gaping cracks in the ship itself, the seafarers were helpless (*inopia*), at the mercy of the wind and the waves (*aestum maris et raptum ventorum*), and in grave danger of falling victim to wreckers. We can quickly perceive that the travellers' disrupted pilgrimage stands for the crisis of their own souls; St Thomas helped them complete the penitential journey, but on the condition that they showed mercy to FitzUrse, one almost

---

comprehensive, despite its idiosyncrasies: Edwin A. Abbott, *St Thomas of Canterbury: His Death and Miracles*, 2 vols (London, 1898), 1: 27–174; on Morville's role in particular, see 124–5.

[20] Although questions concerning the highly complex provenance of various sections of St Thomas's *Miracula* must remain beyond the scope of the present discussion, a letter in Book IV from the prior of Wenlock in Shropshire, validating a cure of leprosy, suggests a *terminus ad quem* of 1175, for its 'frater Humbaldus' was Prior Humbald (1155–75): William of Canterbury, 'Miracula', in Robertson, ed., *Materials*, 1: 338–9.

universally despised. William's oblique inclusion of the murderers in such miracles hints not only at the king's potential dereliction of penitential obligation, but even more at the failure of Henry II to punish the murderers properly in the immediate aftermath of the murder. Indeed, it is only recently that the king has been given some credit for punishing them at all.[21]

The cult of St Thomas was therefore one with a very particular kind of penitential flavour, and it may now be possible to attribute the immense amount of wealth acquired by Christ Church from visiting pilgrims and their donations to more than simple popularity.[22] Charitable gifts consolidated the monastic ownership of property in Canterbury, comprising between a third and a half of the city by the end of the century.[23] Among these was a fee paid to the lepers' hospital at Harbledown by the king, begun on the day of Henry's penance (12 July 1174), and taken over by Canterbury citizens in 1234. This was being paid regularly well into the twentieth century. Amanda Martinson has detailed Henry II's engagement with Christ Church throughout his reign, noting that his largest donations as patron occurred, unsurprisingly, after Becket's murder.[24] As Knowles has noted, a very large number of bishops and abbots came from Christ Church, Canterbury, in the late twelfth and early thirteenth centuries.[25] Robert of Hastings, one such man, was appointed Abbot of Chester with the support of Henry II as well as Archbishop Baldwin, and himself paid for the construction of four shops in Burgate Street, Canterbury, bestowing these on the monks along with other properties.[26] Such

[21] See Nicholas Vincent, 'The Murderers of Thomas Becket', in Natalie Fryde and Dirk Reitz, eds, *Bischofsmord im Mittelalter / Murder of Bishops* (Göttingen, 2003), 211–72.

[22] For some details of Becket's spectacular shrine and the types and quantity of donations, see Ben Nilson, *Cathedral Shrines of Medieval England* (Woodbridge, 1998), 144–90, 211–15, 234.

[23] William Urry, *Canterbury under the Angevin Kings* (London, 1967), 23. Urry also observes that many ecclesiastics from Christ Church were promoted in the years that followed: ibid. 29.

[24] Amanda M. Martinson, 'The Monastic Patronage of King Henry II in England, 1154–1189' (unpublished Ph.D. thesis, University of St Andrews, 2007), esp. 261.

[25] David Knowles, *The Monastic Order in England* (Cambridge, 1940), 177 n. 1. Indeed, Benedict himself became prior of Christ Church in 1175, and Henry II helped him to obtain the abbacy of Peterborough just two years later. Benedict's replacement of Odo in Canterbury was foretold by St Thomas, as described by William of Canterbury, 'Miracula', in Robertson, ed., *Materials*, 1: 542–3.

[26] Urry, *Canterbury*, 29.

gifts *pro anima* ('for the soul') signified the even stronger bonds of obligation which such a cult could create around a place and those involved with it.[27] The very act of donation could indicate, paradoxically, the giver's absolution, for the saint would sometimes refuse gifts from sinners.[28]

On 12 July 1174, Henry II made a pilgrimage to the crypt of St Thomas, entering the city in sackcloth, barefoot, mute and 'in the sight of all' (*in omnium conspectus*).[29] A version of William of Canterbury's *Miracula* from 1174 provided the first account of the king's visit.[30] Its details were confirmed by Grim's early *Vita*: having publicly confessed to indirect responsibility for the murder, the king was flagellated by the monks and spent the night prostrate before the tomb, naked.[31] The thoroughness of his purgation was subsequently 'shown' by an astonishing and almost immediate reversal of his political and military fortunes, which would in itself have certified his genuine contrition in the eyes of his contemporaries.[32]

Alexander Murray has observed the increasing emphasis throughout the eleventh and twelfth centuries on the crucial role played by contrition in theories of penance.[33] Henry II's pilgrimage

---

[27] See Stephen D. White, *Custom, Kinship, and Gifts to Saints: The* Laudatio Parentum *in Western France, 1050–1150* (London, 1988), esp. 19–39. White too sees giving as an important interface between ecclesiastical and lay communities. 'By giving a gift to a saint, a lay benefactor established with his monastic beneficiaries an ongoing social relationship that was supposed to last forever and to link him indirectly to one of the saints and to God': ibid. 27.

[28] For example, we are told that St Thomas rejected oblations from a couple living in sin: William of Canterbury, 'Miracula', in Robertson, ed., *Materials*, 1: 288–9.

[29] For a detailed comparison of the royal penance at Avranches with this visit to Canterbury, see Anne Duggan, 'Diplomacy, Status, and Conscience: Henry II's Penance for Becket's Murder', in *Forschungen zur Reichs-, Papst- und Landesgeschichte: Peter Herde zum 65. Geburtstag von Freunden, Schülern und Kollegen dargebracht*, ed. Karl Borchardt and Enno Bünz, 2 vols (Stuttgart, 1998), 1: 265–90, repr. in eadem, *Thomas Becket: Friends, Networks, Texts and Cult* (London, 2007), VII. Duggan argues that the Canterbury penance was far more voluntary and conscientious than the sequence of political demonstrations at Avranches. 'Avranches had reconciled the public man; Canterbury absolved the private person at a much more fundamental level': ibid. 285. However, the division of public humiliation and private penance was perhaps less clear-cut.

[30] William of Canterbury, 'De adventu regis ad tumbam martyris Thomae' [part of his 'Miracula'], in Robertson, ed., *Materials* 1: 487–9.

[31] Edward Grim, 'Vita', in Robertson, ed., *Materials*, 2: 445–7.

[32] e.g. ibid. 2: 447.

[33] Alexander Murray, 'Confession before 1215', *Transactions of the Royal Historical Society* ser. 6, 3 (1993), 51–81, at 62–3.

was a carefully orchestrated series of symbolic gestures designed to express complete humility and remorse. The dividing line between the famously 'interiorizing emphasis' suggested by Peter Abelard's prioritization of the 'disposition and intention of the sinner' and the structuring role played by publicity, not only in Henry's pilgrimage but also in St Thomas's cult itself, was certainly indistinct.[34] Anne Duggan surmises that the king may have intended to do his initial penance at Avranches on 7th April, Maundy Thursday, the traditional day for public penitents.[35] It was only the very poor weather that made keeping this schedule a logistical impossibility. His later relationship to the cult was one characterized by sustained, even strategic, penitential activity, visiting the shrine at least ten times;[36] according to Herbert of Bosham, the most fiercely loyal of Becket's *eruditi*, Henry made the journey each time he returned to England thereafter.[37]

Whilst Henry II's exact motivations for enacting penance at the tomb were probably complex and without doubt largely political, the saintly authority of St Thomas was closely tied by his hagiographers to his intercession in relation to problems of penitential obligation, particularly in relation to this highest of secular authorities.[38] One miracle recounts a dream of Henry II in which he is forced to turn to St Thomas for help, and in the wake of which he granted Christ Church long-promised liber-

[34] D. E. Luscombe, 'The *Ethics* of Peter Abelard: Some Further Considerations', *Peter Abelard: Proceedings of the International Conference, Louvain, May 10–12, 1971* (Leuven, 1974), 65–84, at 82; for Abelard's views on inner contrition, see his *Ethics*, ed. and trans. D. E. Luscombe, Oxford Medieval Texts (Oxford, 1971), esp. 88–9, where he describes the 'sigh and contrition of heart' (*gemitu et contritione cordis*) by which 'we are instantly reconciled with God'. For a deconstruction of the notion of 'private penance', see Mansfield, *Humiliation*.

[35] Duggan, 'Ne in dubium', 644.

[36] See Thomas Keefe, 'Shrine Time: King Henry II's Visits to Thomas Becket's Tomb', *Haskins Society Journal* 11 (2003), 115–22.

[37] Herbert of Bosham, 'Liber melorum', abridged in Robertson, ed., *Materials*, 3: 535–54, at 546.

[38] On Angevin kingship and pilgrimage, see Nicholas Vincent, 'The Pilgrimages of the Angevin Kings of England, 1154–1272', in Colin Morris and Peter Roberts, eds, *Pilgrimage: The English Experience from Becket to Bunyan* (Cambridge, 2002), 12–45. On Henry II's pilgrimage to Rocamadour in 1170, which presaged his reconciliation with the exiled Becket, see Anne Mason, '"Rocamadour in Quercy above all other Churches": The Healing of Henry II', in W. J. Sheils, ed., *The Church and Healing*, SCH 19 (Oxford, 1982), 39–54.

ties.[39] In turn, apparently isolated examples of the penitential discipline St Thomas demanded from people throughout the miracle
collections are related to the broader hagiographical problem of
royal and saintly authority, particularly in William of Canterbury's
collection. During his lifetime, Thomas Becket was unpopular with
the monks of Christ Church and perceived by many as a man of
secular interests entirely unsuited and unqualified for the highest
ecclesiastical seat in England. The monks' discovery of a concealed,
lice-ridden hair-shirt beneath his robes as they sought to wash his
corpse was probably the crucial moment in the establishment of
his cult.[40] This revelation made the exposure of penitential discipline central to the truth of St Thomas's sanctity. The emphasis
on penance in the miracle collections, and the suspense created
by the delay of appropriate action, underlined his particular kind
of holiness. As an arbiter of penitential obligation and generous
forgiveness in his miracles, he commanded a certainty of moral
authority absent from his earthly career. Becket's longstanding feud
with the Bishop of London, Gilbert Foliot, his chief ecclesiastical
antagonist, was registered by one miracle story in which he saved
the bishop from illness after Gilbert appealed to him on the advice
of the bishop of Salisbury, another of Becket's former enemies.[41]
It was this kind of authority to create and dissolve obligations and
penitential bonds that formed the basis of Thomas's sanctity.

University of East Anglia

---

[39] William of Canterbury, 'Miracula', in Robertson, ed., *Materials*, 1: 275–6, 493–4.

[40] See R. W. Southern, *The Monks of Canterbury and the Murder of Archbishop Becket*
(Canterbury, 1985), 13–14.

[41] William of Canterbury, 'Miracula', in Robertson, ed., *Materials*, 1: 470–1. Foliot
had also made penitential promises at the tomb when he accompanied Henry II in
1174, for which (within another account of Henry's penance) see Ralph de Diceto,
Radulfi de Diceto Decani Lundoniensis Opera Historica, ed. William Stubbs, 2 vols, *RS* 68
(London, 1876), 1: 383–5.

SEEING THE LIGHT? BLINDNESS AND SANCTITY IN LATER MEDIEVAL ENGLAND

by JOY HAWKINS

The fifteenth-century collection of miracles attributed to Henry VI and collated as evidence for his canonization proceedings includes the tale of John Robbins of Worcestershire, who, it is reported, 'rashly insulted the blessed King Henry, heaping many rebukes upon him'. The late king punished the irreverent Robbins, striking him blind. When Robbins repented, and 'vowed with many tears to visit [Henry's] holy tomb, he recovered his faculty of sight'. Robbins appears to have been understandably embarrassed about the event: when he later made his pilgrimage to Windsor, he failed to reveal the whole story to the shrine official.[1] In late medieval England, a common moral justification for disease was that God and his saints inflicted infirmity on sinners as a punishment for their transgressions, providing the opportunity for repentance and atonement.[2] However, blindness could also be regarded as a divine gift, offering protection from worldly distractions and allowing holy individuals to communicate more easily with God. Indeed, a lack of earthly sight allowed potential saints to demonstrate that they possessed the intrinsic values of humility and patience deemed necessary to achieve sanctity. This paper examines these two different theological explanations for blindness.

Although wide-ranging and comprehensive studies have been made of leprosy, insanity and the religious responses to disability, the common affliction of blindness has not received nearly as much scholarly attention.[3] The purpose of the present survey is to begin redressing this issue, exploring the relationship between sanctity

---

[1]   *The Miracles of Henry VI: Being an Account and Translation of Twenty-Three Miracles*, ed. R. Knox and S. Leslie (Cambridge, 1923), 112–13.

[2]   P. B. R. Doob, *Nebuchadnezzar's Children: Conventions of Madness in Middle English Literature* (London, 1974), 3.

[3]   Carole Rawcliffe, *Leprosy in Medieval England* (Stroud, 2006); Basil Clarke, *Mental Disorder in Earlier Britain: Exploratory Studies* (Cardiff, 1975); Irina Metzler, *Disability in Medieval Europe* (London, 2006); C. M. Woolgar, *The Senses in Late Medieval England* (New Haven, CT, 2006). Moshe Barasch, *Blindness: The History of a Mental Image in*

and blindness during the later Middle Ages, whilst demonstrating that being deprived of one's sight could be an important element in attaining sanctity. It was believed that blind saints possessed qualities which others did not. Furthermore, saints who suffered from visual impairments during life often, in turn, gained a reputation for curing eye complaints after their death. It is not surprising, therefore, that shrine-keepers advertised the efficacy of their saint's healing powers in order to attract pilgrims. The ability to restore the sight of the blind offered 'proof' of God's omnipotence and the power he invested in his agents.[4]

The first understanding of blindness was as a physical manifestation of divine punishment. The ability to inflict blindness upon the impious underlined the saints' special status as God's agents, with the power to punish earthly mortals who irreverently committed sacrilege or succumbed to the sins of gluttony or pride. Sinners could be encouraged to improve their conduct by being blinded temporarily, as we have seen in the case of John Robbins above.[5] Throughout the Middle Ages hagiographers appear to have relished recounting stories of the saints meting out blindness upon the impious. For instance, in the immensely popular thirteenth-century *Golden Legend*, one tale describes how a vain English woman visited the shrine of Thomas Becket at Canterbury to request that he change her eye colour to make her more attractive. Her reward for such a trivial request was to be smitten with blindness until she repented of her coquettish behaviour.[6]

Blindness was believed to be an appropriate chastisement because it denied the individual the ability to see the 'light of heuen'.[7] Indeed, losing the sense of sight enclosed the individual in a private world of darkness, providing an enforced opportu-

Western Thought (New York, 2001), concentrates on the representations of the blind rather than the medieval understanding of, and reactions to, visual impairment.

4   S. J. Roth, *The Blind, the Lame and the Poor: Character Types in Luke-Acts* (Sheffield, 1997), 16, 106.

5   Robert Bartlett, *Gerald of Wales: A Voice of the Middle Ages* (Stroud, 2006), 93.

6   Jacobus de Voragine, *The Golden Legend: Readings on the Saints*, trans. William Granger Ryan, 2 vols (Princeton, NJ, 1993), 1: 62. For a continental comparison, see *The Book of Sainte Foy,* trans. Pamela Sheingorn (Philadephia, PA, 1995), 50–1, 151–2, 162–4.

7   Tob. 5: 10; biblical citations are taken from *The Holy Bible containing the Old and New Testaments in the Earliest English Versions made from the Latin Vulgate by John Wycliffe and his Followers*, ed. J. Forshall and F. Madden, 4 vols (Oxford, 1850).

nity for reflection. It also, of course, acted as a visual deterrent to others. A fifteenth-century chantry priest, John Audelay, who lost both his sight and hearing, looked upon his physical afflictions as a punishment sent by God for his previous follies and lax way of living.[8] He wrote a collection of poems as a warning, urging his readers to make a full confession of their sins while they still had the ability.[9] If a person's impairment was deemed to have been caused by gluttony or pride, or was punishment for a felony, he or she would often be shunned by the community.[10] The blind were further disadvantaged because they were unable to participate fully in Christian rituals, including the mass, which during the later Middle Ages was predominantly a visual experience.[11] Taking its evidence from the Book of Leviticus, the Church taught that anyone who had a blemish in the eye, or was blind, should be forbidden from consuming, or even approaching, the bread of God.[12] This had severe repercussions for priests with eye complaints as there was understandable fear that a blind priest might spill the wine or drop the host, a potentially excommunicable offence.[13] Consequently, men with only slight problems with their sight had to receive special dispensation from the pope before they were allowed to join the priesthood.[14]

There was, however, a contrasting understanding of blindness which explains why, on occasion, a blind priest was allowed to retain his benefice. A lack of physical sight could shield against earthly temptations, and thus was often viewed as a divine gift bestowed upon the fortunate few. It was widely accepted that the eyes were the main passageways for sin to enter the body; sight, therefore, ranked as the most dangerous of the senses, constantly

---

[8] *The Poems of John Audelay*, ed. E. K. Whiting, EETS os 184 (1931), 49, 93–4, 111, 123.

[9] Ibid. 101.

[10] *Calendar of the Patent Rolls Preserved in the Public Record Office: Edward I, A.D. 1281–1292* (London, 1893), 192.

[11] Eamon Duffy argues that 'seeing the Host became the high point of the lay experience of the Mass': *The Stripping of the Altars: Traditional Religion in England, c. 1400 – c. 1580*, 2nd edn (New Haven, CT, 2005), 96.

[12] Lev. 21: 16–21.

[13] Nicholas Vincent, *The Holy Blood: King Henry III and the Westminster Blood Relic* (Cambridge, 2001), 31, 49.

[14] *Calendar of Papal Registers: Letters and Petitions, 1198–1492*, 15 vols (London, 1894–1961), 4: 540; 5: 540. Similarly, men who had blinded another, even accidentally, also had to receive dispensation before they could enter the priesthood: ibid. 4: 355.

and unexpectedly threatening a person's morals.[15] Preachers and theologians warned that an 'unchaste eye' was a sign of 'an impure mind'.[16] Bernard of Clairvaux (c. 1090–1153) described the dire consequences for those who failed to guard their eyes against licentious or otherwise corrupting sights and permitted spiritual pollution to enter the body. An uncontrolled roving eye could transmit an overabundance of foul images to the brain, contaminating the whole body 'with intolerable filth'.[17] The belief that the eye had the potential for iniquity remained popular: one fourteenth-century preachers' handbook warned that the 'eyes are very quick to harm [the] soul', 'goading' the rest of the body into committing crimes, and explained that 'for this reason some call their eyes their worse enemies'.[18] The blind were protected from the threats associated with a wanton gaze. The handbook provided a striking *exemplum* for preachers to illustrate and reinforce the moral message of their sermons. The tale begins with two hermits cultivating a vineyard. One pierces his eye on a small, sharp branch, but rather than lament his loss, he rejoices, crying: 'I have lost a grievous enemy … God be praised, I have lost one. If I had lost both, I could be quite sure of my soul's salvation.'[19]

Members of the congregation listening to such examples would be made to understand that suffering the torments of blindness was not necessarily a dreadful fate. Indeed, the Gospel of St Matthew warned that any man who 'seeth a womman' and 'coueite hire' has already committed adultery with her 'in his herte'. Thus readers are instructed that 'yif thi right eiye sclaundre thee, pulle it oute, and cast it fro thee; for [better that] oon of thi membris perishe, than al thi body go in to helle'.[20] It was far preferable to have the offending eye plucked out than to endure the everlasting torments of hell. As John Trevisa's translation of Bartholomaeus Anglicus's encyclopaedia succinctly observed, it was 'bettir [for] thee to goo

---

[15] Woolgar, *Senses*, 176–7.

[16] Gerald of Wales, *The Jewel of the Church: A Translation of* Gemma ecclesiastica, trans. J. Hagen (Leiden, 1979), 182–3; Robert Mannyng of Brunne, *Handlyng Synne*, ed. Frederick J. Furnivall, EETS os 119, 123 (1901, 1903), I: 242, 258, 280.

[17] Bernard of Clairvaux, 'On Conversion', in *Bernard of Clairvaux: Selected Works*, ed. G. R. Evans, CWS (New York, 2005), 11.

[18] *Fasciculus morum: A Fourteenth-Century Preacher's Handbook*, ed. Siegfried Wenzel (London, 1989), 651–3.

[19] Ibid. 653.

[20] Matt. 5: 29–30.

vniyed [one-eyed] into lif than to haue tweye [two eyes] and be sent into fure [fire] with outen ende'.[21] A lack of sight, therefore, freed blind men and women from vulnerability to many of the cardinal sins, including gluttony, avarice and lust.[22]

A similar assumption prompted Teresa de Cartagena (b. 1415) to come to terms with her deafness. In her *Grove of the Infirm*, the Spanish nun reflected on the spiritual benefits of her disability. She believed it to be liberating because it defended her against the noisy, earthly world so that she was able to hear God's voice with greater clarity:

> Since God has placed such cloisters on my hearing [he shows] me clearly by increasing my suffering that it is His will that I avoid any worldly chatter and maintain complete silence in order to better understand what with the din of worldly distractions I would not be able to hear. ... Certainly these words thanking God for having removed all my obstacles and hindrances should be a very helpful example for others.[23]

Teresa's wisdom could apply equally to those who had lost their sight rather than their hearing. Sensory impairment was often seen as a divine blessing to be utilized by future saints to strengthen their belief and bring them closer to God, while also creating the potential for spiritual wisdom. As reworked in Jacobus de Voragine's *Golden Legend*, the tale describing Saul's conversion on the road to Damascus provided a graphic illustration of the last of these gifts. The narrative explained that Saul 'was blinded to be enlightened in his darkened intelligence. Hence it is said that in the three days during which he remained blind, he was taught the Gospel.'[24] Only while his body was suffering from hunger and thirst, and otherwise immune to distractions, could Saul hear God's voice. It can be argued that the biblical precedent of his temporary infirmity served as a model for later accounts in which the sinner was persuaded to repent after a period of enforced reflection. For

[21] *On the Properties of Things: John Trevisa's Translation of Bartholomaeus Anglicus' De proprietabus rerum*, ed. M. C. Seymour, 3 vols (Oxford, 1975–88), 1: 365–6.

[22] S. Shahar, *Growing Old in the Middle Ages: 'Winter Clothes us in Shadow and Pain'*, trans. Y. Lotan (London, 1997), 55.

[23] *The Writings of Teresa de Cartagena*, trans. Dayle Seidenspinner-Núñez (Woodbridge, 1998), 28–9.

[24] De Voragine, *Golden Legend*, trans. Ryan, 1: 120.

instance, one twelfth-century miracle, attributed to the hand of St James preserved at Reading Abbey, describes how Gilbert, a keeper of hounds 'who was over-fond of the vanity of the chase', had his sight taken away as a penance for hunting on the saint's feast day.[25] Only through the consequent adversities Gilbert faced was he able to recognize and testify to God's power. The themes of punishment and repentance recurred in later medieval saints' lives, as has been shown with the fifteenth-century example of John Robbins.

Individual *vitae* and collections of stories about the saints suggest that blindness was bestowed by God not only as a necessary precursor to the attainment of sanctity, but as a sign of holiness revealing the prospective saint's true nature to those around him or her. Indeed, a visual impairment could magnify an individual's exemplary virtues, which, although not necessarily associated with his or her disability, might otherwise have remained hidden. For example, St Gilbert, who founded the Gilbertine Order at Sempringham about 1131, suffered from deteriorating eyesight as he grew older. Significantly for Gilbert's original thirteenth-century biographer, despite his being almost completely blind Gilbert's intellectual abilities and spiritual awareness did not diminish. In fact, it appeared that 'in return for having lost light from his body, he received the illumination he merited from the greater and more important blessing of the spirit. Although he was infirm, sick and blind he lost none of his mental energy.'[26] Moreover, because of his disability, Gilbert was no longer troubled by 'secular preoccupations' and thus was able to dwell 'entirely among the things of heaven', escaping from the worldly distractions which had been thrust upon him as abbot. Gilbert's blindness allowed him to transcend the mundane so that he could concentrate on 'good deeds of pious activity' and meditation, which had led him originally to found his own religious order.[27]

In the fifteenth-century Middle English version of Gilbert's *Life*, translated and expanded by John Capgrave (1393–1464), the author explains that Gilbert's blindness was not inflicted by God as an enemy, but bestowed by a friend, 'prouokyng a man to batayle and

---

[25] 'The Miracles of the Hand of St James', trans. Brian Kemp, *Berkshire Archaeological Journal* 65 (1970), 1–19, at 13.
[26] *The Book of St Gilbert*, ed. R. Foreville and G. Keir (Oxford, 1987), 87.
[27] Ibid. 89.

behestyng victorie to him'. Capgrave believed that Gilbert's blindness served to promote a greater degree of holiness than would have been possible had the abbot remained fully sighted. Gilbert's disability provided him with 'grete perfeccion of vnderstanding in his soule', filling him with the 'grace of the Holy Goost',[28] thereby emphasizing that his impairment was an essential element to his sanctity. Not surprisingly, this conviction originated with the first *Life*, which insisted that, despite Gilbert's pious and copious weeping, his blindness was not self-inflicted but was, in fact, a sign of the Lord's clemency:

> we know that he [Gilbert] weakened [his] eyes with frequent floods of tears while he was preaching, and that he suffered much harm from winds, dust, vigils ... we do not blush for it, since the same thing happened to Isaac, Jacob, and many other holy men; on the contrary we give thanks all the more fervently because we know that this was proof not of God's anger and indignation, but of his mercy.[29]

Gilbert was not alone in shedding 'frequent floods of tears'; in their moments of ecstasy, saints often wept copiously. Tears were not perceived as signs of weakness: indeed, it has been suggested by Richard Kieckhefer that weeping reflected the saints' heightened awareness of the 'gulf which unfortunately separated themselves from God. In their raptures and in their identification with the crucified Saviour they sought to close this gap.'[30] Francis of Assisi's blindness was also attributed to his 'tears of contrition'.[31] His early biographers held up the saint's courage as an *exemplum* of how to cope with pain.[32] One early *Life* describes how the medical practitioners consulted by Francis decided to try cauterization:

---

[28] John Capgrave, *Lives of St Augustine and St Gilbert of Sempringham*, ed. J. J. Munro, EETS os 140 (1910), 95–6.

[29] *Book of St Gilbert*, ed. Foreville and Keir, 87.

[30] Richard Kieckhefer, *Unquiet Souls: Fourteenth-Century Saints and Their Religious Milieu* (Chicago, IL, 1984), 180–2.

[31] St Bonaventure, 'Major Life of St Francis', trans. Benen Fahy, in Marion A. Habig, ed., *St Francis of Assisi: Writings and Early Biographies* (Chicago, IL, 1983), 627–787, at 668. For the Latin text, see St Bonaventure, 'Legenda maior S. Francisci', ed. Michael Bihl, *Analecta Franciscana* 10 (1926–41), 557–626, at 580. Rachel Fulton discusses 'tears of contrition' in greater detail: *From Judgment to Passion: Devotion to Christ and the Virgin Mary, 800–1200* (New York, 2002), 165, 171, 175.

[32] Bonaventure, 'Major Life of St Francis', 664–70 (ed. Bihl, 578–81); de Voragine, *Golden Legend*, trans. Ryan, 2: 226.

[The surgeon] put a searing-iron in the fire in preparation for the operation. Francis trembled with fear, but then he began to encourage his body, addressing the fire like a friend ... . he made the sign of the cross over the red-hot instrument and waited unafraid. The sizzling iron was plunged into the soft flesh and drawn from his ear to his eye-brow ... when the doctor saw the extraordinary strength of his spirit which was revealed in his frail body, he hailed it as a miracle.[33]

The blindness from which Francis suffered enabled him to exercise the saintly qualities of courage, patience and humility, particularly when faced with the prospect of painful treatment. Such exemplary behaviour showed that saints could act as role models for the faithful to follow. Ordinary men and women were taught that, in order to emulate holy figures and to secure their place in heaven, or at least to reduce their time in purgatory, they needed to face their pain meekly. The possibility that God had protected St Francis from the agony of cauterization because he had such a strong faith would have given patients a modicum of comfort when such stories were repeated.

Upon other future saints God conferred blindness as a form of spiritual armour, shielding them from their enemies. In the famous case of St Lucy, who willingly embraced Christianity in the face of persecution, God gave the virgin martyr the strength to mutilate herself. According to legend, Lucy, determined to live a chaste and devout life, plucked out her own eyes and presented them to her pagan suitor on a plate. Lucy's act revealed to her persecutors the depth of her courage and provided a clear sign of her trust in God. Although she preserved her virginity, she was killed by her would-be husband for her stubborn insubordination. An early and widespread cult developed and she was quickly canonized.[34] Later, Lucy became the patron saint of the blind and she was often depicted bearing her eyes on a dish as a reminder of the torments she suffered.[35] Lucy's martyrdom thus associated the removal of

---

[33] Bonaventure, 'Major Life of St Francis', 668–9 (ed. Bihl, 580–1).

[34] David Sox, *Relics and Shrines* (London, 1985), 118.

[35] Emil F. Frey, 'Saints in Medical History', *Clio Medica* 14 (1979), 35–70, at 42–3; K. A. Winstead, *Virgin Martyrs: Legends of Sainthood in Late Medieval England* (London, 1997), 1–3; Greg Buzwell, *Saints in Medieval Manuscripts* (London, 2005), 61.

earthly sight with faith and righteousness, a connection which could be made in cases where blindness was deemed to be self-inflicted. Moreover, Lucy's strength of belief and fidelity to God was rewarded with the miraculous restoration of her eyes.[36] This would have reassured the blind and purblind that loyalty to God in the face of adversity could reap physical and spiritual benefits.

Throughout the later Middle Ages, a connection was increasingly made between physical blindness and the possession of spiritual wisdom, which together granted the visually impaired the ability to 'see' God. Artists frequently portrayed bishops and saints wearing spectacles, promoting the belief that poor sight was a gift from God allowing the opportunity for personal redemption and even sanctity.[37] For example, Matthew the Evangelist was sometimes depicted needing a reading aid to consult his gospel.[38] There is a fine example on the rood screen at St Agnes Church, in Cawston, Norfolk, where he appears with a pair of glasses on his nose and holding the Bible. Such images would have reassured the hypermetropic (long-sighted) members of the congregation that declining vision did not preclude them from having inner sight. It could be argued that only the blind and purblind were truly able to see God as they were not distracted by material goods. Furthermore, blind men and women could turn to the saints in the hope of a cure because celestial helpers had the ability both to remove and to restore a person's sight.

The blind were prominent figures in the gospels, singled out by Christ as worthy recipients of healing. In the annual re-creation of the story of the 'Healing of the Blind Man', performed by the Glovers' Guild as part of the fifteenth-century Chester Mystery Cycle, the actor playing Jesus informed the crowd that he had performed this miracle to 'set forth God's great glory' and to demonstrate the magnitude of divine power.[39] The imitation of Christ through healing the blind was considered an important part of the saints' miraculous repertoire and clear proof of their sanctity. In an attempt to secure the canonization of Henry VI, his miracles were investigated and collated; particularly prominent are those of

[36] David Farmer, *The Oxford Dictionary of Saints*, 4th edn (Oxford, 1997), 312.
[37] Richard Corson, *Fashions in Eyeglasses* (London, 1967), 22, 24–7; for later examples, see ibid. 34–5.
[38] Farmer, *Oxford Dictionary of Saints*, 340.
[39] *The Chester Mystery Cycle*, ed. David Mills (East Lansing, MI, 1992), 223.

men and women receiving their sight through the intervention of
the late king.[40] For instance, a Lancashire man, Richard Herdman,
unable to distinguish day from night, devoutly appealed to Henry
for help. Within a short time he 'recovered clearness of vision in
both eyes'.[41]

The cure of Herdman can be located within a long tradition
of similar cures throughout medieval England. Although blindness was often regarded as the bestowal of divine favour, for many
the promise of a reward in the afterlife was insufficient and they
wanted instant relief from their ocular complaint.[42] Consequently,
those suffering from painful and debilitating eye diseases or inju-
ries sought the intercession of the saints, who were considered
to be 'a source of power to be tapped'.[43] It is not surprising that
medieval men and women suffering from eye complaints should
turn to those saints who had themselves suffered from blindness
during their earthly lives. It was believed that physical remains,
relics or any material possessions left behind by a saint emitted a
form of 'holy radioactivity', secreting healing powers through the
shrine; thus intimate contact with the relic, shrine or *feretrum* could
lead directly to thaumaturgical healing.[44] For example, placing
one's head on the spot where St Ethelreda had reputedly first
been buried was believed to cure all maladies of the eyes.[45] Water
in which a holy body or relics had been washed was regarded as
beneficial for the alleviation of many ills, and in particular blindness and eye disease.[46] After St Gilbert of Sempringham's body had
been washed, the water was used to cure pilgrims of their ocular
complaints, including Ysouda of Pickworth, who had suffered from
painful and inflamed eyes for the space of a month before she

---

[40]   *Miracles of Henry VI*, ed. Knox and Leslie, 54, 73, 74, 111, 119, 136, 148, 189, 204,
214.

[41]   Ibid. 204–5.

[42]   Examples can be found in several *vitae*, e.g. *The Canonization of Saint Osmund*, ed.
A. R. Malden (Salisbury, 1901), 45, 75; Thomas of Monmouth, *The Life and Miracles of
St William of Norwich*, ed. A. Jessop and M. R. James (Cambridge, 1896), 167–8, 181–2,
228–31. For other examples, see Metzler, *Disability*, 129–38.

[43]   Duffy, *Stripping of the Altars*, 175.

[44]   Ben Nilson, *Cathedral Shrines of Medieval England* (Woodbridge, 1998), 1.

[45]   Richard of Cirencester, *Speculum Historiale de Gestis Regnum Angliae*, ed. J. E. B.
Mayor, *RS* 30, 2 vols (1863–9), 1: 209.

[46]   C. Grant Loomis, 'Hagiological Healing', *Bulletin of the History of Medicine* 8
(1940), 636–42, at 637.

bathed her eyes in St Gilbert's water.[47] As we saw above, Gilbert's sight dimmed as he grew older; it seemed natural to his biographer that the holy man should relieve others of their blindness when they invoked him.[48]

Further investigation is needed to discover whether medieval pilgrims searching for cures deliberately selected and appealed to saints who had had comparable disabilities during life.[49] Nonetheless, it is clear that those suffering from visual impairments identified particularly with those saints who had themselves endured a similar trial. A sense of empathy and intimacy could develop between the saint and supplicant when there was a shared experience; the blind could confidently invoke the help of Lucy or Gilbert to bear their pain humbly in order to reap the spiritual rewards from their physical ordeal.[50] Blindness gave saints a special quality: this is evident from the time of St Paul. Paul's blindness gave him an inner vision that enabled him to distinguish the true path from the deceptions of this world. Building on the Old Testament book of Isaiah, medieval men and women were taught that 'God he shal come and sauen vs. Thanne shul ben opened the eyen of blynde men'.[51] Although this exhortation might be read as a metaphor for spiritual enlightenment, it also promised that, if the blind accepted their pain and afflictions with patience and humility, they would be rewarded with paradise.

University of East Anglia

---

[47] *Book of St Gilbert*, ed. Foreville and Keir, 301.

[48] Ibid. 315–17.

[49] For the post-1588 period, see Jacalyn Duffin, *Medical Miracles: Doctors, Saints, and Healing in the Modern World* (Oxford, 2009), 40.

[50] Duffy, *Stripping of the Altars*, 180.

[51] Isa. 35: 4–5; Roth, *The Blind, the Lame and the Poor*, 105.

THE VISION OF ST FURSA IN THIRTEENTH-CENTURY DIDACTIC LITERATURE[*]

by CHRIS WILSON

The vision of the otherworld seen by St Fursa (c. 590 – c. 649) and recorded in a *Vita* and in Bede's *Ecclesiastical History* achieved a high level of popularity in England and France during the thirteenth century, especially through its inclusion in preaching aids for the friars and the *pastoralia* (the various guides and manuals for priests on the care and confession of their congregation) produced before and after the Fourth Lateran Council of 1215.[1] This essay will discuss how compilers of this material altered, rearranged and summarized Fursa's vision, and what these changes reveal about shifting attitudes towards sanctity in the thirteenth century. In some of these redactions, Fursa's sainthood was sidelined or ignored completely. In others, the point at which Fursa is described as a saint varies and the emphasis of the vision shifts from a reward for a saintly life to the purgation of a sinful priest. It will be suggested that these modifications to Fursa's role in the vision were linked to the genre and audience of the redactions and to other thirteenth-century theological preoccupations, including debates over the sinfulness of usury and the emergence of the doctrine of purgatory.[2]

[*] This paper is a sample of my wider current research into the dissemination of visions of the otherworld in the long thirteenth century. I would like to thank Sarah Hamilton, Catherine Rider and Kati Ihnat for their comments on this paper.

[1] Fursa is also known as Fursey, Fursy, Forseus, Fursis and Furseus. Nine manuscripts of Fursa's *Vita* survive. It is edited, omitting Fursa's first two visions (Fursa's second vision is the focus of this communication), in *Vita virtutesque Fursei abbatis Latinacensis passiones* (MGH SRM 4, 423–40). The first two visions which originally formed part of the *Vita* are included in 'Le visioni di S. Fursa', ed. M. P. Ciccarese, *Romanobarbarica* 8 (1984–5), 231–303. The earliest surviving manuscript of this work is London, BL, MS Harley 5041, fols 79–98, which was probably copied in northern France in the eighth century. This manuscript has formed the basis of a recent transcription and translation: Oliver Rackman, *Transistus Beati Fursei* (Norwich, 2007). This is a helpful addition to the scholarly literature on the saint, although Rackman somewhat misleadingly introduces his own subtitles into the account. The vision appears in Bede, *Historia ecclesiastica* 3.19; ed. and trans. Bertram Colgrave and R. A. B. Mynors, *Bede's Ecclesiastical History of the English People* (Oxford, 1969), 268–77 [hereafter: *HE*].

[2] For a discussion of the relationship between purgatory and visions, see Carl

Fursa's vision of the otherworld lends itself well to a study of attitudes towards sanctity as, unlike the newer visions in circulation at the end of the twelfth century where saints were usually otherworldly guides or residents, the visionary was actually a saint himself.[3] Nonetheless, Fursa's vision contains many of the same features as the rash of visions of the otherworld that appeared at the end of the twelfth century, and these should be seen as the immediate context for the account's thirteenth-century popularity. Usually these visions took place when a monk, or sometimes a layperson or knight, was seriously ill, almost always on his deathbed. The soul of the visionary was then taken out of his body and given a tour of the otherworld, a combination of heaven, hell, the earthly paradise and purgatory. The flourishing of these new visions at the end of the twelfth century has attracted considerable interest.[4] Earlier visions, including Fursa's account as recorded by Bede, have also attracted attention, particularly in respect to the dating of the emergence of the doctrine of purgatory.[5] In contrast, the plentiful later redactions of Fursa's vision have generally been ignored. In order to look at these redactions in more detail, this paper will sketch out the life of Fursa and his vision as it appeared in Bede's *Ecclesiastical History*, before discussing a selection of didactic texts in which the vision appeared in the long thirteenth century.

Fursa was the first recorded Irish missionary to Anglo-Saxon England. He lived in East Anglia before travelling to Frankia and Péronne, where he was buried.[6] His story survives in a *Vita* (known as the *Vita Prima* or *The Passage*), in which four separate visions are

Watkins, 'Doctrine, Politics and Purgation: The Vision of Tnuthgal and the Vision of Owein at St Patrick's Purgatory', *JMedH* 22 (1996), 225–36.

3   For a list of saints involved in these visions as inhabitants, see Alison Morgan, *Dante and the Medieval Other World* (Cambridge, 2002), 75–6.

4   For an overview of the genre of otherworldly visions, see Peter Dinzelbacher, *Vision und Visionsliteratur im Mittelalter* (Stuttgart, 1981); Claude Carozzi, *Le Voyage de l'âme dans l'au-delà d'après la littérature latine* (Rome, 1994).

5   This debate was prompted by Jacques Le Goff, *La Naissance du purgatoire* (Paris, 1981); trans. Arthur Goldhammer as *The Birth of Purgatory* (Chicago, IL, 1983). See, most recently, Marilyn Dunn, 'Gregory the Great, the Vision of Fursey and the Origins of Purgatory', *Peritia* 14 (2000), 238–54, at 238; eadem, *The Vision of Saint Fursey and the Development of Purgatory,* Fursey Occasional Papers 2 (Norwich, 2007); Sarah Foot, 'Anglo-Saxon "Purgatory"', in Peter Clarke and Tony Claydon, eds, *The Church, the Afterlife and the Fate of the Soul,* SCH 45 (Woodbridge, 2009), 87–96.

6   The Fursey Pilgrims, a nondenominational society devoted to maintaining the memory of Fursa's mission to East Anglia and fostering new scholarship about the saint, was founded in 1997 to mark the 1400th anniversary of his birth.

recorded. A continuation to the *Vita* was added during the seventh century and a ninth-century compilation of his miracles, known as the *Virtues of Fursa,* was also produced.[7] A second life of Fursa was written in the eleventh or twelfth century in Continental Europe, with a preface by Arnulf, Abbot of Lagny, who died in 1106.[8] The original *Vita* formed the basis of Bede's brief description of Fursa's life and he mentioned it several times.[9] Most of the thirteenth-century redactors worked from Bede's version of Fursa's life, and it is the saint's longest vision on which they all focus.

In the *Ecclesiastical History,* after describing the monastic and saintly context of Fursa's life, Bede redacted three of his visions. He described two short visions of angels, and then summarized a longer experience in which the visionary saw 'not only the very great joys of the blessed but also the fierce onslaughts of the evil spirits ... who sought to prevent his journey to Heaven'.[10] He chooses one section of the vision to redact in more detail, because he thought it might be helpful (*commodum*) to his readers.[11] He describes how, once the visionary was taken to a great height, he was told to look down on the world. There he saw four fires, which gradually merged together and moved towards him. Because of Fursa's saintly life, the angels were able to fight off the fire (and the demons that inhabited it), clearing his path to a fuller (*copiosior*) vision of the heavenly hosts, including some Irish saints.[12] After his visit to heaven, on the journey back to his body, the most widely reproduced part of the vision occurred. Fursa was attacked by a group of demons who threw a soul that they plucked from the flames at him, striking his shoulder and jaw. The wounds that were inflicted were visible for the rest of Fursa's life. The reason for the attack was explained by the angels: the soul had belonged

---

7   This compilation is appended to the earlier *Vita* in MGH SRM 4, 440–9.

8   *ActaSS* Ian. 2, 44–54.

9   Bede, *HE* 3.19 (ed. and trans. Colgrave and Mynors, 270–1, 276–7).

10   Ibid. Bede altered the order of the visions from the *Vita* to emphasize Fursa's monastic vocation and the parts of his story that took place in England. The four visions from the *Vita* can be found as follows (note that the MGH edition of the *Vita* does not include the first two visions and the Ciccarese edition does not include the third and fourth visions): first vision, 'Le visioni', ed. Ciccarese, 280; second vision, ibid. 283; third vision, MGH SRM 4, 436; fourth vision, ibid. 437. Bede started with the *Vita's* fourth vision before redacting the first and second accounts, and he omitted the third vision.

11   Bede, *HE* 3.19 (ed. and trans. Colgrave and Mynors, 272–3).

12   Ibid.

to a man who had given some of his clothing to Fursa as the saint attended his deathbed.

THE VISION IN THIRTEENTH-CENTURY *EXEMPLA* COLLECTIONS

In the thirteenth century the Dominican and Franciscan friars designed and used a growing number of *exempla* collections in order to facilitate their itinerant preaching. These collections had evolved from the unstructured and localized collections of miracles produced in Cistercian monasteries and from sermon collections in which the *exempla* were integrated into the orations. These collections, often arranged thematically, owed much both to the English tradition of the imaginative narrative and to the Scholastic culture of Paris.[13] At first glance, these *exempla* collections seem to take very different approaches to the vision of Fursa and its moral significance for preaching. The account of Fursa's vision became so diverse that one early fourteenth-century manuscript has three different versions of the vision, seemingly from two different traditions.[14] Given the wide availability and popularity of Bede's *Ecclesiastical History,* this might not be surprising. Many compilers would have been able to redact their own versions of the account, rather than relying on standard shorter versions already in circulation. In fact, several of the collections refer specifically to Bede's redaction in the margin.[15] But despite these references the *exempla* compilers made some revealing changes to the narrative which they inherited. By discussing a selection of *exempla* this essay will now survey these changes briefly and assess their significance.

All the *exempla* focus on the burning of St Fursa by the soul. In most cases the visionary is named as a saint but, given the short length of the accounts, there is little space for information about Fursa's life or about his other visions. He is never, for example, described as a monk. Most of the *exempla* simply leave Fursa's

---

[13] David L. D'Avray, *The Preaching of the Friars: Sermons Diffused from Paris before 1300* (Oxford, 1983), esp. 64–70; see also Claude Bremond, Jacques Le Goff and Jean-Claude Schmitt, *L'Exemplum*, Typologie des sources du Moyen Âge occidental 40 (Turnhout, 1982). For the older Cistercian *exempla* collections, see Brian Patrick McGuire, 'The Cistercians and the Rise of the Exemplum in early Thirteenth Century France: a Reevaluation of Paris, BN Ms. Lat. 15,912', *Classica et Medievalia* 34 (1983), 211–67; *Collectaneum exemplorum et visionum Clarevallense e codice Trecensi 946*, ed. Olivier Legendre (CChr.CM 208).

[14] London, BL, MS Harley 268, fols 30ʳ, 34ʳ, 114ʳ.

[15] See, e.g., BL, Add. MS 11284, fol. 3ʳ.

sanctity undiscussed, and the changes occur to other parts of the narrative. The most notable of these changes concerns the reason that Fursa is punished, and it is tied to his relationship with the burning soul. In Bede's account, the soul that was thrown at Fursa was described simply as a sinner whose sin was left unspecified (*peccatoris*).[16] Fursa remembered that when the man had died he received some of his clothing. Bede's narrative reveals a specific concern, inherited from the *Vita,* with the pastoral care of dying sinners.[17] In fact, as Fursa returned to earth, one of the angels gave Fursa 'helpful advice as to what should be done for the salvation of those in the hour of death'.[18] The narrative in the *exempla* tradition took on another dimension. In these versions, the sinner had been a usurer and the cape that Fursa accepted is seen as a profit from that sin. The moral of the narrative is about avoiding the taint of usury, an issue not discussed in either the *Vita* or the *Ecclesiastical History.* Although it does not directly affect Fursa's description as a saint, the introduction of the issue of usury, combined with the lack of information regarding his deathbed responsibilities, lessens the spiritual distance between the visionary and the audience of the *exempla.*

Jacques de Vitry (c. 1160s – 1240) is one *exempla* compiler who is especially explicit in this regard. He was a renowned Dominican preacher and his *exempla* originally formed part of one of his sermon collections, the *Sermones vulgares* (or *ad status*).[19] The vision of Fursa is attached to a sermon addressed to people caring for the sick.[20] In Jacques's version of the vision the soul is thrown at

16 Bede, *HE* 3.19 (ed. and trans. Colgrave and Mynors, 274–5); *Vita* 16 ('Le visioni', ed. Ciccarese, 301).

17 The theme of correct clerical behaviour is even more clearly drawn out in the *Vita,* in which the Irish saints Beoan and Meldan lectured Fursa on the issue: *Vita* 13 ('Le visioni', ed. Ciccarese, 294).

18 Bede *HE,* 3.19 (ed. and trans. Colgrave and Mynors, 272–3).

19 J.-B. Pitra, ed., *Analecta novissima spicilegii Solesmensis: Altera continuatio,* 2 vols (Paris, 1888), 2: 189–93 (Prologue), 344–6 (list of sermons), 443–61 (list of *exempla*).

20 'Sermo XL. Sermo ad hospitalarios et custodes infirmorum', in Pitra, ed., *Analecta novissima,* 2: 345, 450. The sermon is based on Prov. 16: 6: 'By mercy and truth iniquity is purged.' By the mid-thirteenth century *exempla* were circulating in individual collections, separate from sermons. One such early fourteenth-century English collection of Jacques de Vitry's *exempla* is BL, MS Harley 463; the vision of Fursa is at fol. 6ᵛ. References below are taken from Jacques de Vitry, *Exempla ex sermonibus,* ed. Thomas Crane (New York, 1890). Crane extracts the *exempla* from Paris, BN, MS Lat. 17509. All translations are my own.

the saint because he had 'accepted a cape from a certain usurer'.[21] No reference is made to the circumstances in which Fursa had come to own the cape. In a further addition to the Bede's narrative, Fursa is forced to return to his body to do penance. The *exemplum* culminates with a moral summary attached to the end of the narrative, which seems to indicate a new audience for the account. The focus is on the method for purchasing goods, and the reader or listener is told 'that the holy man [Fursa] did not know that the cape he had obtained came from the usurer, but he ought to have enquired thoroughly'.[22] The audience is urged to try and trace the source of their goods 'in the same way that they thoroughly stretch out meat, bought at the market, to see whether it is sound or diseased or bad smelling'.[23]

The theme of usury was deployed in a similar way in all of the *exempla* accounts of the thirteenth century, often appearing in thematic sections devoted to the sin.[24] The punishment given to Fursa for owning the cape of a usurer strikes a conservative theological note in a period when canonists were beginning to come to terms with the economic reality of the practice.[25] In the period when these *exempla* were in circulation, legislation against usury, as Helmholz has shown, was only effectively applied when the rates

---

[21] De Vitry, *Exempla*, 46 (no. 99).

[22] Ibid.

[23] Ibid.

[24] In Odo of Cheriton's 'Parabolae' it appears after the story of St Laumer and the usurer: BL, MS Arundel 231, fol. 105[r]. Fursa's vision does not appear in all of the versions of the 'Parabolae' and is missing from the only published edition of the text: *Fabulistes Latins: Depuis le siècle d'Auguste jusqu'à la fin du Moyen Âge.* 4: *Études de Cheriton et ses dérivés*, ed. L. Hervieux (Paris, 1896), 177–255. In the anonymous 'Speculum laicorum', it appears as the first *exemplum* in ch. 2, entitled 'De acquisitis injuste et eorum periculo'. It is followed by six usury stories, including one about incorrect trading practices in Greece and the account of St Laumer and the usurer: BL, Add. MS 11284, fol. 3[v]. In the anonymous *Fasciculus morum* it appears at the end of a sermon devoted to avarice: *Fasciculus morum: A Fourteenth-Century Preacher's Handbook,* ed. and trans. S. Wenzel (University Park, PA, 1989), 22–3. It is given a slightly different stress in Arnold of Liège's 'Alphabetum narrationum', in which it is placed in a chapter entitled 'elemosina': BL, MS Harley 268, fol. 114[r]. In both the French *Manuel des Peches* and the Middle English *Handlyng Synne* it is paired with a story about how usurers should be detested. They are edited side by side in William de Wadington and Robert Mannyng of Brunne, *Handlyng Synne, with those Parts of the Anglo-French Treatise on which it was Founded*, Manuel des pechiez, ed. F. J. Furnival, EETS os 119, 123 (1901, 1903; repr. as one vol. 1973; repr. 2006), 88.

[25] John Gilchrist, *The Church and Economic Activity in the Middle Ages* (London, 1969), 67.

of interest reached exorbitant levels.[26] In addition, in nearly all of these *exempla,* the punishment for usury is located in hell, another markedly conservative feature given Jacques Le Goff's argument that purgatory was increasingly seen as the location for usurers in the afterlife.[27] The decision to locate the punishment of usury in hell also clears up some of the ambiguity about the 'space' of the otherworld as it is described in Bede's version.

The introduction of usury and hell had little direct effect on Fursa's sanctity. However, in one strand of the vision's transmission there was a more direct attempt to suppress the holiness of the visionary. This seems to be part of an attempt to change the perspective of the vision, making it more useful for preaching to the laity. This redaction of the vision was more popular in mainland Europe, but it does feature in at least one English manuscript.[28] It contrasts in several places with Bede's narrative of the vision. Fursa is no longer named at all and the anonymous visionary who replaces him is no longer described as a saint. In addition, the visionary is no longer the beneficiary of a dying sinner's cape – he is actually wearing the coat of a usurer and is dying himself.[29] At the end of the vision he is granted the right to return to his body and die for a second time, not wearing the cape. The perspective of the account shifts very clearly from the saintly, priest's-eye view of the deathbed to the position of a dying sinner. Fursa's sanctity and sainthood are completely eroded and he is no longer any different from one of the lay people listening to this redacted version of the account.

The Vision in Robert of Greatham's *Miroir*

Robert of Greatham (*fl.* early to mid-thirteenth century) negoti-

---

[26] R. H. Helmholz, 'Usury and the Medieval English Church Courts', *Speculum* 61 (1986), 364–80.

[27] Jacques Le Goff, 'The Usurer and Purgatory', in Fredi Chiappelli, ed., *The Dawn of Modern Banking* (New Haven, CT, 1979), 25–52; idem, *La Bourse et la vie: Economie et religion au Moyen Âge* (Paris, 1986),   trans. Patricia Ranum as *Your Money or Your Life: Economy and Religion in the Middle Ages* (New York, 1988), esp. 65–84. Despite the general propensity to place the vision in hell, I have found one example in which the vision takes place in purgatory: BL, MS Royal 12.E.i, fol. 160ᵛ. In the fourteenth century Dante infamously placed usurers in the lowest sub-circle of the seventh circle of hell.

[28] BL, MS Harley 268, fol. 30ʳ.

[29] Ibid.

ated Fursa's sainthood and sanctity in a more subtle way. He placed the vision of Fursa at the end of a sermon for the second Sunday after Easter in his Anglo-Norman *Miroir* (c. 1250s).[30] This vernacular sermon collection seems to fit into a tradition of *pastoralia* more explicitly connected with the Fourth Lateran Council and the growing role of the parochial clergy than with the preaching of itinerant friars.[31] Robert's use of the vision of Fursa and his alteration of the visionary's role in the account fits this context. The vision was used to illustrate a sermon that seems to reflect the clarification of the relationship between the clergy and the laity outlined in the canons of the Fourth Lateran Council in 1215 and the Oxford Council of 1222.[32] The changes in the narrative of the vision also hint at developments in eschatological doctrine that had gathered pace from the end of the twelfth century.

As we shall see, the content of Robert's version of the vision suggests that he may have had access to the earlier *Vita* as well as to Bede's account. Robert was probably an Augustinian canon, perhaps a priest from a priory or abbey. His introduction indicates that he composed the work for a lady of high status, but the way in which his sermons are addressed and the number of surviving manuscripts suggest that he may have had a wider audience in mind.[33] At the beginning of the fourteenth century the *Miroir* was faithfully translated into Middle English.[34] It also had considerable influence in shaping Robert Mannyng of Brunne's *Handlyng Synne* (1303).[35]

---

[30] Robert of Greatham, *Miroir des Evangiles*, ed. Saverio Panunzio (Bari, 1974), 232. All translations are my own.

[31] Leonard E. Boyle discusses the impetus for the increase in the production of these manuals in 'The Inter-Conciliar Period 1179–1215 and the Beginning of Pastoral Manuals', in Roberto Tofanini, ed., *Miscellanea Rolando Bandinelli, Papa Alessandro III. Studi raccolti da Filippo Liotta* (Siena, 1986), 43–56.

[32] For the English context of this literature, see M. Dominica Legge, *Anglo-Norman Literature and its Background* (Oxford, 1963), 212–13; Marion Gibbs and Jane Lang, *Bishops and Reform 1215–1272* (Oxford, 1934; repr. 1962), esp.106–31.

[33] The following thirteenth-century manuscripts are extant: Nottingham, UL, MSS WLC/LM/3; WLC/LM/4; Cambridge, UL, MS Gg.I.i; Cambridge, Trinity College Library, MS B.14.39 (323); York, Chapter Library, MS 16.K.14.

[34] *The Middle English 'Mirror': An Edition based on Bodleian Library, MS Holkham misc. 40*, ed. Kathleen Marie *Blumreich,* Medieval and Renaissance Texts and Studies 182 (Tempe, AZ, 2002). See also Thomas Duncan, 'The Middle English Mirror and its Manuscripts', in *Middle English Studies Presented to Norman Davis*, ed. D. Gray and E. G. Stanley (Oxford, 1983), 115–26.

[35] As such it can be seen as one of the forerunners of the 'second wave' of vernac-

Robert's approach to St Fursa's vision was different from that of the *exempla* compilers described above. In some respects he was more faithful to his earlier sources, focusing on the pastoral responsibility of priests. Yet he radically altered the order of the narrative, moving details of Fursa's sainthood to the end of the account and changing the position of the visionary's burning. Some of these changes have been discussed in a literary context by Fritz Kemmler with regard to the development of narrative and Robert's intended audience.[36] But the changes have a theological dimension as well, linked into the development of the doctrine of purgatory, the provisions of the Fourth Lateran Council, and the newer visions of the otherworld that were in circulation during the thirteenth century.

Unlike the *exempla* discussed above, Robert devoted his redaction of the vision to the correct pastoral practice of priests and he was seemingly uninterested in the potential to discuss usury. The vision was attached to a sermon on John 10: 11–16, *ego sum pastor bonus,* traditionally used in reference to the behaviour of the clergy.[37] He mentioned *prestres* or *prestre* eight times and *pastur* once in the *exemplum* alone.[38] Robert proceeded to link Fursa's burning to his pastoral role at the deathbed (as it had been in the *Vita* and the *Ecclesiastical History*).[39] If anything, Robert made the link more explicit, noting that the visionary was responsible for dealing with the dead man's will.[40] His concluding moralization was equally revealing. He addressed parsons and priests, urging them to look to their end when they took other men's alms and to consider St Fursa who had forgotten what he had taken rightfully, and what he had not.[41] Whether this actually means he intended the *Miroir* to be used by priests (or even chapter canons) is unclear, but the

ular penitential *pastoralia* identified in Leonard E. Boyle, 'The Fourth Lateran Council and Manuals of Popular Theology', in Thomas J. Heffernan, ed., *The Popular Literature of Medieval England* (Knoxville, TN, 1985), 30–43, at 35.

36   Fritz Kemmler, *'Exempla' in Context: A Historical and Critical Study of Robert Mannyng of Brunne's 'Handlyng Synne'*, Studies and Texts in English 6 (Tübingen, 1984), 127–29.

37   Robert of Greatham, *Miroir,* 232.

38   Ibid. 243 (line 326), 244 (line 351), 245 (lines 378, 383), 246 (lines 407, 414), 247 (lines 426, 438).

39   *Vita* 16 ('Le visioni', ed. Ciccarese, 301); Bede *HE,* 3.19 (ed. and trans. Colgrave and Mynors, 274–5).

40   Robert of Greatham, *Miroir,* 246.

41   Ibid. 247.

monastic context of the vision, so prevalent in the Bede and *Vita* versions, as in the *exempla* collections, disappears once again.

This focus on clerical duty may be one reason why Robert denied his readers knowledge of Fursa's sainthood until the end of the *exemplum*. He noted that on Fursa's return to his body he lived well and wisely and had 'amended his life so that he is now called Saint Fursi [Fursa]'.[42] Yet there were other influences at work here as well. Robert seemed to make a link between the trial that Fursa underwent during the vision and his eventual canonization. This suggests that the vision was operating as the cleansing of an everyday priest, rather than as the spiritual reward for a saint.

A reader of the *Ecclesiastical History* or the *Vita* is given the impression that St Fursa was granted this vision *because* of his worthy life that he had led since his early childhood, if not birth. In Bede's version, before the visionary is taken by the angels we are told that 'from his boyhood days he had devoted all his energy to the study of sacred books and to the monastic discipline; furthermore as a saint should, he earnestly sought to do whatever he learned to be his duty'.[43] Similarly the *exempla* compilers introduced Fursa as a saint and, perhaps due to the length of the accounts, did not discuss any development in his character. By contrast, Robert was writing a longer narrative and in his redaction there was space for the vision to have a reforming influence on the visionary. In this way, Fursa's cleansing has parallels with the other longer visions that were in circulation during the thirteenth century. After their visions, the Cistercian novice Gunthelm was no longer tempted to leave his monastery; the lay person Dryhthelm (his vision was also recorded in Bede's *Ecclesiastical History* and widely disseminated) took the monastic habit; and Tundal embarked on a more austere form of life.[44] In various versions of Owein's visit to Saint Patrick's Purgatory, including Marie de France's Anglo-Norman redaction, the visionary was inspired by his experience to go on crusade.[45]

---

[42] Ibid.

[43] Bede, *HE* 3.19 (ed. and trans. Colgrave and Mynors, 270–1); MGH SRM 4, 434; *Vita* 1 ('Le visioni', ed. Ciccarese, 279).

[44] Helinand of Froidmont, whose work is the focus of some of my research, includes all of these visions in his thirteenth-century *Chronicon*: PL 212, 791C–793C (*Vision of Dryhthelm*), 1038D–1055D (*Vision of Tundale*), 1060C–1063D (*Vision of Gunthelm*).

[45] Marie de France, *L'Espurgatoire Seint Patrice,* ed. Yolande de Pontfarcy (Louvain, 1995).

The cleansing and transformational aspects of Robert's account were not only achieved by the careful deployment of the information he inherited regarding Fursa's sanctity; there is a clearer presentation of the process of purgation, which relies on a restructuring of the otherworld.[46] The most substantial change that Robert made in this respect was relocating Fursa's burning. As we have seen in the Bede and *Vita* versions the burning of Fursa occurred *after* his extended vision of heaven, on his return to his body. In the *Miroir*, this incident occurs on the way to heaven as an extension and alteration of the 'four fires' part of the narrative inherited from Bede and the *Vita*. In Robert's version Fursa's guide 'led him into many places and showed him many things: the depth of Hell and the pains that were there and then (*e puis*) he led him towards (*vers*]) Heaven'.[47] On this journey, in an area clearly distinguished from hell, he comes across a single large fire (Fursa is no longer asked to look down on the earth and is instead always moving upwards and heavenwards). It is this single fire in the air that contained the demons which eventually assaulted him with the soul of the sinner, and the issue of usury is not mentioned at all.[48]

There are a variety of other stylistic changes which seem to suggest that Robert was trying to fit the narrative into the more structured genre of visionary accounts that emerged at the beginning of the thirteenth century. First, Fursa is only guided by a single angel, rather than an entourage of four.[49] Second, he plays a more active role in his journey, moving himself towards the fire rather than watching the fire approach him.[50] Finally, on returning to his body he spends a considerable time (three days) on his deathbed.[51] Even the part of the vision which appears to

---

[46] Although it is by no means certain that Robert was one, the Augustinian Canons were regarded as some of the greatest promoters of the doctrine of purgatory. In the twelfth century they were responsible for the promotion of Lough Derg and St Nicholas of Tolentine (d. 1305), the first member of the order to be canonized and the patron saint of souls suffering in purgatory.

[47] Robert of Greatham, *Miroir*, 244.

[48] Ibid.

[49] Ibid. 243.

[50] Ibid. This particular alteration could also be influenced by the spread of romance literature. A possible parallel may be seen in Robert Easting, 'The South English Legendary "St Patrick" as Translation', *Leeds Studies in English* 21 (1990), 119–40.

[51] Robert of Greatham, *Miroir*, 246.

be most anachronistic, the location of purgatory in the air, had contemporary parallels. Gervase of Tilbury, operating in the same Anglo-Norman milieu as Robert, recorded a story in which a girl communicated with her dead father who categorically stated: 'Purgatory is in the air'.[52]

CONCLUSION

Robert uses Fursa's sainthood and sanctity as part of a package of changes that seem concerned with the 'space' of the otherworld and the newer visions in circulation. His decision to focus on Fursa's role as priest and only to reveal his sanctity at the end of the account demonstrates the pastoral environment after Lateran IV, a fact highlighted by the sermon that the *exemplum* illustrates. By and large the *exempla* compilers seem less concerned with Fursa's own role in the vision and more interested in altering the account to introduce the topic of usury, a concern generally (although not exclusively) associated with the preaching of the friars. When changes to Fursa's status were introduced by the *exempla* authors, they tended to reduce the spiritual distance between the saint and the lay audience at which they were targeted, perhaps in line with the wider devotional trends that saw an increasing focus on Christ's humanity. In the case of the vision of Fursa it seems to be the ambiguity of the earlier narrative in Bede's *Ecclesiastical History* that offered later compilers and authors a blank canvas on which to paint their own ideas of the account and its moral significance. But it also demonstrates a wider editorial flexibility which later compilers employed when they redacted visions of the otherworld. This flexibility was utilized even when redacting highly revered texts, such as the work of the Venerable Bede, and could be applied to such basic concepts as the sanctity of the visionary.

University of Exeter

---

[52] Gervase of Tilbury, *Otia Imperialia* 3.103, in *Gervase of Tilbury, Otia Imperialia: Recreation for an Emperor*, ed. and trans. S. E. Banks and S. W. Binns, Oxford Medieval Texts (Oxford, 2002), 764, 768.

'ERAT ABIGAIL MULIER PRUDENTISSIMA': GILBERT OF TOURNAI AND ATTITUDES TO FEMALE SANCTITY IN THE THIRTEENTH CENTURY

by CHRISTINE WALSH

For many people in the Middle Ages it was the belief in the intercessory powers of saints at the court of heaven which drove individual acts of veneration.[1] However, saints were not just sources of assistance in times of need; they could also be perceived as role models both for those who wanted to live a religious life and for the broader laity. Not surprisingly, the lessons drawn from a particular saint's life tended to reflect individual attitudes and beliefs, and the same saint could be used to justify contradictory forms of behaviour. This paper examines two contrasting responses to the cult of St Katherine of Alexandria and what they tell us about attitudes to women and female sanctity in the thirteenth century.[2]

These contradictory interpretations of Katherine's life derive from the complex nature of her *Passio*. In many ways it is no different from other martyr stories with its tale of a Christian virgin executed by a Roman emperor, and it was her chastity and her martyrdom which constituted Katherine's claim to sanctity.[3] However, the *Passio* also presents Katherine as an educated and powerful woman. In one of the most well-known passages she makes a public defence of her faith against fifty pagan philosophers, converting them all to Christianity. Katherine's cult was growing in popularity in the thirteenth century, and explaining

---

[1]   A good general introduction to saints as intercessors is B. Ward, *Miracles and the Medieval Mind: Theory, Record and Event 1000–1215*, rev. edn (Aldershot, 1987).

[2]   Katherine is supposed to have died c. 305 but there is no evidence that she ever existed. Her *Passio* probably dates from the eighth century. For a discussion of the origins of her cult, see C. Walsh, *The Cult of St Katherine of Alexandria in Early Medieval Europe* (Aldershot, 2007).

[3]   Her intercessory powers are emphasized in the earliest versions of the *Passio* when, as she is led out to her execution, Katherine prays that whosoever shall pray for assistance in her name shall have their prayers answered and a heavenly voice is heard granting her request. See, e.g., the tenth-century Greek *Passio* by Simeon Metaphrastes published by J.-P. Migne with a Latin translation by Surius (PG 116, 275–302).

why it was acceptable for her to preach was a problem for the medieval Church, which wanted to reserve preaching to licensed male preachers.[4] Hence we can see that as Katherine joins the holy dead, sanctified by her virginal martyrdom, she also presents an example of a woman acting beyond the role usually assigned to women. It is this dichotomy which goes to the heart of differing attitudes to the saint. At one and the same time she is the model of a chaste holy woman and of an unconventional spirituality. The medieval Church sought to resolve this dichotomy by representing Katherine in traditional terms, emphasizing her virginity and obedience to Christ as the attributes to be followed by other women. In contrast, her preaching was represented as an exception to the norm, a unique gift from the Holy Spirit to her alone.[5]

One way in which the Church constructed its representation of Katherine was through sermons. However, although there is a large and growing body of work on sermons and preaching, little work has been done on sermons about St Katherine.[6] The starting point for any analysis of sermons remains the comprehensive collection contained in Schneyer's *Repertorium*.[7] Using a sample of 183 sermons by named authors all dated before 1350 and identified by Schneyer as being on the theme of St Katherine, it is possible to draw some preliminary conclusions. The most common incipit text used is Psalm 44: 14 [45: 13], 'All the glory of the king's daughter is within in golden borders', which occurs in ten sermons.[8] A further six sermons use other texts from Psalm 44 [45] as their starting point. This psalm is full of royal imagery, which,

4   See A. Blamires, 'Women and Preaching in Medieval Orthodoxy, Heresy and Saints' Lives', *Viator* 26 (1995), 135–52.
5   Mary Magdalene was the other saint associated with female preaching and similar attempts were made to show her as an exception. See K. L. Jansen, *The Making of the Magdalen: Preaching and Popular Devotion in the Later Middle Ages* (Princeton, NJ, 2000), esp. ch. 2; Blamires, 'Women and Preaching', 141–5; R. Rusconi, 'Women's Sermons at the End of the Middle Ages: Texts from the Blessed and Images of the Saints', in B. M. Kienzle and P. J. Walker, eds, *Women Preachers and Prophets through Two Millennia of Christianity* (Berkeley, CA, 1998), 173–95, esp. 179–82.
6   For an introduction to recent historiography on sermons, see C. Muessig, 'Sermon, Preacher and Society in the Middle Ages', *JMedH* 28 (2002), 73–91.
7   J. B. Schneyer, *Repertorium der lateinischen Sermones des Mittelalters für die Zeit von 1150–1350*, 11 vols (Munich, 1969–90), 2: 282–318.
8   All biblical quotations are from the Latin Vulgate. Those in English are from the Challoner revision of the Douai-Reims translation of the Latin Vulgate. Where the Authorized Version reference differs, it is given in parentheses.

given that Katherine is always portrayed as a princess in art and literature, might be thought appropriate. However, the imagery stresses female beauty, not intelligence, and its use can be seen as another way of constructing Katherine in conventional terms. More interestingly, there is a thirteenth-century sermon on the theme of St Katherine by the Franciscan theologian and preacher Gilbert of Tournai (c. 1200–84).[9] When set in the context of other known works by Gilbert, this sermon can be shown to reflect contemporary concerns about religious women and in particular beguines.[10]

Gilbert's starting text is an unusual one. He uses a quotation from 1 Kings [1 Samuel] 25: *Erat Abigail mulier prudentissima.*[11] This is the only time, of which I am aware, that Gilbert uses this text, and so far I have only found two other instances of its use. One is in a sermon, also on St Katherine, by Dionysius Cartusianus (1402–71).[12] The fact that this text is used twice in this way implies that both sermon-writers thought that there was a useful comparison to be made between the biblical heroine Abigail and St Katherine. The other instance is in a sermon attributed to the leading Franciscan, Bonaventure (1221–74).[13] This sermon is a general one for virgin saints. I have not been able to examine it, but given Gilbert's known propensity for drawing on the sermons of others

---

[9]   Vatican City, BAV, MS Vat Lat 11444, fols 10[rb]–12[ra], dating from the thirteenth century.

[10]   Gilbert studied at Paris University, where he taught for some years before joining the Franciscans shortly before 1240. He was a prolific writer and his works include many sermons; Schneyer lists 457 by him, although only two are on the theme of St Katherine. Gilbert was well connected and was commissioned by Pope Alexander IV (1254–61) to produce two collections of his sermons, and by Louis IX (1226–70) to write a manual on good government. For a summary of Gilbert's life and works, see *DSp, s.n.* 'Guibert de Tournai'. See also D. L. D'Avray, *The Preaching of the Friars: Sermons Diffused from Paris before 1300* (Oxford, 1985), 120–4, 144–6. For a list of Gilbert's sermons, see Schneyer, *Repertorium*, 2: 282–318.

[11]   1 Kgs 25: 3 [1 Sam. 25: 3]: 'and the name of his wife was Abigail. And she was a prudent and very comely woman.'

[12]   *Repertorium der lateinischen Sermones des Mittelalters für die Zeit von 1350–1500* [CD–ROM] from the unpublished papers of J. B. Schneyer, ed. L. Hödl and W. Knoch (Münster, 2001) [This is a continuation of Schneyer's *Repertorium*, referred to above, which was compiled after his death from notes that he left. Unless otherwise specified, all references are to Schneyer's original *Repertorium*, not to the CD–ROM].

[13]   Charleville, Bibliothèque Municipale, MS 92. See Schneyer, *Repertorium*, 7: 224 (no. 159); *Catalogue général des manuscrits des bibliothèques publiques des départements*, 7 vols (Paris, 1849–85), 5: 589–90. Gilbert knew Bonaventure well and accompanied him to the Council of Lyons in 1274.

it may well be related to his sermon on Katherine.[14] Although the specific audience for Gilbert's sermon is unknown, many of his *de sanctis* sermons were composed for the Paris clergy so this may have been its intended audience. It is structured conventionally with a series of *distinctiones* supported by a large number of biblical quotations on the twin themes of *sapientia* and *prudentia*.[15] The date of composition is not known but is unlikely to have been earlier than the mid-thirteenth century.

Abigail was the wife of Nabal, a wealthy farmer, and is described as a 'prudent and very comely woman'. Her husband, however, is described as 'churlish and very bad and ill natured'. When David, who is hiding in the desert from Saul, asks Nabal for provisions for his men in return for having protected Nabal in the past, he refuses and so David swears to destroy him. When Abigail hears of her husband's refusal she brings provisions to David and begs him not to destroy Nabal. David is captivated by Abigail and agrees, and when her husband dies shortly afterwards David takes her as one of his wives.

The comparison of Katherine with Abigail supports the contention, made earlier, that the Church sought to contain Katherine's exceptional gifts within the boundaries of acceptable female behaviour and to use her as an exemplar of traditional female sanctity. Abigail is presented as a beautiful, intelligent woman well able to argue her cause successfully in public. However, throughout her story Abigail acts with deference and humility. She bows low before David and constantly refers to herself as a 'handmaiden' to the point that her response to his offer of marriage is: 'Behold, let thy servant be a handmaid, to wash the feet of the servants of my lord.'[16] Abigail also presents a model of wifely virtue as, although her first husband was a bad man, she behaves honourably and seeks to protect him.

Gilbert begins by saying that it is appropriate to adopt the description of Abigail as 'very prudent and comely' in order to praise Katherine.[17] The first reason for this is the similarity in

---

[14] See C. T. Maier, *Crusade, Propaganda and Ideology: Model Sermons for the Preaching of the Cross* (Cambridge, 2000), 250–63.

[15] See R. H. and M. A. Rouse, 'Biblical Distinctions in the Thirteenth Century', *Archives d'histoire doctrinale et littéraire du Moyen Âge* 29 (1974), 27–37.

[16] 1 Kgs [1 Sam.] 25: 41.

[17] BAV, MS Vat Lat 11444, fol. 10rb, lines 24–26: 'convenientes possunt assumi verba

their marital situation. Abigail had two worldly marriages, one bad, one good, whilst Katherine had two spiritual ones, one bad, one good. Firstly, he says that Katherine was 'the bride of the devil on account of the stain of Original Sin'. She then converts and becomes betrothed to Christ.[18] The imagery of Katherine as Christ's bride occurs in several places in the sermon.[19] Although the virgin as the bride of Christ is a traditional image and Gilbert does not stray outside convention in the emphasis that he lays on it, we can see the beginnings of the story of Katherine's mystical marriage to Christ, which was to become an important part of her Legend in subsequent centuries. Indeed, it is around the time that Gilbert was writing that the first evidence for this addition to her story appears.[20]

Gilbert deals with the issue of Katherine's intellectual prowess through a series of biblical quotations concerning the concepts of *prudentia* and *sapientia*. Although the two words have slightly different shades of meaning, they are closely related.[21] By using both of them Gilbert manages to use the more practical nuances of meaning associated with *prudentia* to tone down the more intellectual concept of wisdom associated with *sapientia*. He also reinforces the exceptional nature of Katherine's abilities by including texts which emphasize how both *prudentia* and *sapientia* come from God.[22] However, this leaves open the possibility that other women might claim to have similar gifts from God and does not address the controversial issue of women preaching. Gilbert deals with these matters indirectly by citing several biblical texts praising wise

proposita ad commendationem beate virginis Katarine'.

[18] Ibid., lines 32–34: 'Sic beata Katerine primus fuit sponsa diaboli propter macule originalis infectionem et postea sponsa Christi'.

[19] e.g. ibid., fol. 10[vb], lines 11–12: 'electa mea sponsa, mea spetiosa'.

[20] The earliest surviving reference to Katherine's mystical marriage is in an Old French poem dated to 1251 (Paris, BN, MS Arsenal 3645). It is not mentioned in the influential *The Golden Legend*, written c. 1260. See S. Nevanlinna and I. Taavitsainen, *St Katherine of Alexandria: The Late Middle English Prose Legend in Southwell Minster MS 7* (Cambridge, 1993), 22–3; K. J. Lewis, *The Cult of St Katherine of Alexandria in Late Medieval England* (Woodbridge, 2000), 107–10; Jacobus de Voragine, *The Golden Legend: Readings on the Saints*, ed. and trans. William Granger Ryan, 2 vols (Princeton, NJ, 1993), 2: 334–41.

[21] See C. T. Lewis and C. Short, eds, *A Latin Dictionary* (Oxford, 1996), s.v. *sapiens*, where there is a cross-reference to *prudens*.

[22] e.g. BAV, Ms Vat Lat 11444, fol. 11[ra], lines 16–17: 'Proverbs 2 Dominus dat sapientiam et ex ore eius scientia et prudentia' ('the Lord giveth wisdom and out of his mouth cometh prudence and knowledge').

men who keep their own counsel.[23] The implication is that even if one has intellectual abilities they are better kept private.

The issue of Katherine's intellectual abilities continued to be a theme in sermons. There is a paper by D'Avray that picks up on this theme of female scholarship and examines a sample of sermons about Katherine to elucidate how it is handled. He concludes that sermons popularized the concept of the woman intellectual as an aspect of female sanctity in Germany during the later Middle Ages.[24] Even so, it is worth noting that in two of the four sermons D'Avray cites emphasis is placed on the divine source of Katherine's preaching.[25]

So far I have concentrated on the positive aspects of Gilbert's views on holy women. However, there was another category of religious women for whom he had little time. These were the beguines. The term 'beguine' covered a wide variety of women, some of whom formed communities under clerical control while others were more independent or even followed a solitary religious life.[26] They were a problem for the church authorities, who found it difficult to control some of the more radical women, and even when they submitted to church supervision their way of life caused hostility in some quarters. In particular, even when they formed settled communities, they tended to interact with the lay world to a far greater extent than enclosed nuns, which laid them open to accusations of immorality. Sometimes this interaction was

---

[23] e.g. ibid., fol 11[va], lines 19–21: '(Ecclesiasticus 19: 28 [20: 1]) est tacens et ipse est prudens. Amos 5 prudens in tempore illo tacebit etc' ('there is one that holdeth his peace and he is wise. Amos 5 the prudent shall keep silent in that time etc').

[24] D. L. D'Avray, 'Katherine of Alexandria and Mass Communication in Germany: Woman as Intellectual', in N. Bériou and D. L. D'Avray, eds, *Modern Questions about Medieval Sermons: Essays on Marriage, Death, History and Sanctity* (Spoleto, 1994), 401–8.

[25] Ibid. 405.

[26] The following works provide a good starting point for modern research on the beguine movement: H. Grundmann, *Religiöse Bewegungen im Mittelalter: Untersuchungen über die geschichtlichen Zusammenhänge zwischen der Ketzerei, den Bettelorden und der religiösen Frauenbewegung im 12. und 13. Jahrhundert und über die geschichtlichen Grundlagen der deutschen Mystik*, 2nd edn (Darmstadt, 1961), ET *Religious Movements in the Middle Ages*, trans. S. Rowan (Notre Dame, IN, 1995); E. McDonnell, *The Beguines and Beghards in Medieval Culture: With Special Emphasis on the Belgian Scene* (New Brunswick, NJ, 1954); R. Lerner, *The Heresy of the* Free Spirit *in the Later Middle Ages* (Berkeley, CA, 1972); W. Simons, *Cities of Ladies: Beguine Communities in the Medieval Low Countries 1200–1565* (Philadelphia, PA, 2001); T. S. Miller, 'What's in a Name? Clerical Representations of Paris Beguines (1200–1328)', *JMedH* 33 (2007), 60–86.

due to the economic necessity of earning a living, and sometimes they took on more pastoral or even preaching roles.

Gilbert's views on beguines were forcibly expressed in his work *Collectio de scandalis*, written for the Second Council of Lyons in 1274.[27] This council had been called by Pope Gregory X with the objective of reinvigorating the Crusade movement. Underlying Gregory's desire to promote the Crusade to the Holy Land was his view that, for the Crusade to be successful, reform of Church and society was needed. Gilbert is known to have been a strong supporter of the Crusades and was supportive of Gregory's views on the need for reform.[28] The *Collectio de scandalis* was written very much in this vein and covered a wide range of issues which Gilbert thought the Council should address and reform. It is in its closing passages that he deals with beguines.[29] He accuses them, amongst other things, of translating the Bible into the vernacular and of seeking to interpret the mysteries of the Scriptures which were barely accessible to those well versed in such matters.[30] Gilbert claims to have handled personally a Bible translated into French by beguines, which he says was generally available in Paris. He makes it clear that he strongly disapproves of such things and believes that their books should be destroyed before they lead others astray. It has been suggested by a number of scholars that Gilbert's hostility to the beguines was, in part, due to a desire to divert attention from the Franciscans, who were themselves under attack at the Council of Lyons.[31] While Gilbert may have a mixture of reasons for his attack on the beguines there can be no doubt of his contempt for them. This is clear from the scathing terms in which he addresses them: he calls them 'little women' (*mulierculas*) living irreverently in 'little convents' (*conventiculas*). These women are the opposite of the ideal woman presented in his sermon on Katherine.

However, this is not how the women saw themselves. From

[27] J. J. I. von Döllinger, *Beiträge zur politischen, kirchlichen und cultur-Geschichte der sechs letzen Jahrhunderte*, 3 vols (Vienna, 1882), 3: 180–200.

[28] See, e.g., three sermons by Gilbert in support of crusades in Maier, *Crusade, Propaganda and Ideology*, 176–209.

[29] Von Döllinger, *Beiträge*, 199–200.

[30] Ibid. 199: 'Habent interpretata scripturarum mysteria et in communi idiomate gallicata, quae tamen in sacra scriptura exercitatis vix sunt pervia'.

[31] J. Le Goff, 'Le Dossier des mendiants', in *1274: Année charnière, mutations et continuités: Lyon–Paris, 30 septembre – 5 octobre 1974* (Paris, 1977), 211–22.

their perspective they were deeply religious women who only wanted to live a truly Christian life. Although some of their behaviour might be controversial, they also conformed to some of the fundamental religious practices of the day. Of relevance here is their participation in the cult of saints. Certain saints were of more significance to beguines than others, and the lessons they drew from these saints were different from those drawn by clerics such as Gilbert. Finding evidence for what beguine women themselves thought is difficult as they have left few written records from this period; however, it is possible to approach them indirectly and infer something of their views.

The general devotion to Katherine can be seen from the number of beguinages dedicated to the saint. In his study of beguinages in the Low Countries, Simons has found seventy-eight whose patron saint can be identified.[32] Unsurprisingly, the Virgin Mary was the most popular with twenty-one dedications, but she is closely followed by Katherine of Alexandria with fifteen, whilst Elizabeth of Hungary has thirteen. Many beguines had been married before turning to the religious life, and Elizabeth, a married woman with three children who had followed a harsh penitential life in her widowhood, might well appeal to such women. Katherine's appeal, however, was of a different order and was related to her distinctive attributes of scholarship and preaching.

There is considerable evidence to show that beguines were interested in scholarship and education. We have already heard from Gilbert of Tournai that the Paris beguines had translated the Bible into the vernacular and discussed and debated religious matters. While it is not clear exactly who had done the translation, it is clear that at least some beguines must have been able to read it and that there was a significant interest in theological matters. It is also the case that many beguines earned a living as teachers, and some beguinages had schools attached to them as early as the thirteenth century.[33] Direct evidence of preaching by beguines is harder to come by, but, for example, there is evidence that Agnes of Oinches, the Mistress of the Paris beguinage, preached to her fellow beguines.[34]

32 Simons, *Cities of Ladies*, 87–8.
33 Ibid. 80–5.
34 Miller, 'What's in a Name?', 79–80.

There is also artistic evidence of beguine devotion to Katherine. In a study of thirteenth-century psalters and books of hours from the diocese of Liège, Oliver has identified several psalters as being produced for use by beguine women.[35] Multiple images of Katherine are to be found in these psalters. Oliver contrasts this with the fact that images of Katherine are rarely found in other Flemish psalters produced for lay patrons, which highlights the importance of the saint for beguines.[36] Oliver has made a detailed study of one of the psalters which she has dated to 1265–75.[37] This psalter was broken up and various leaves scattered but Oliver has managed to reconstruct much of it. Amongst the material which remains are five scenes from the life of St Katherine.[38] One of the scenes depicts Katherine studying as a child. This is rare for the thirteenth century, when stories of Katherine's childhood were only just starting to appear, and its inclusion hints at the importance placed on education by the owner of the psalter.[39]

This paper has tried to show how differing responses to the cult of St Katherine can be related to conflicting views of female sanctity and acceptable female behaviour. To the beguines she was a woman who personified their aspirations to live a religious life while remaining active participants in the world. Her emblematic qualities as a teacher and preacher made her a role model for their own activities in these fields. In contrast the established Church sought to present Katherine in more conventional terms. Sermons were an important channel for promulgating this view of the saint. This highlights the importance of the study of sermons

---

[35] J. H. Oliver, *Gothic Manuscript Illumination in the Diocese of Liège (c. 1250 – c. 1330)*, 2 vols (Leuven, 1988) 1: 112–14. The Psalters cited by Oliver are: Baltimore, Walters Art Gallery, MS 37 (ibid. 2: 239–41); Brussels, Koninklijke Bibliotheek, MSS IV–36 (ibid. 244–6), IV–1066 (ibid. 248–50); Cambridge, Fitzwilliam Museum, MS 288 (ibid. 250–2); Liège, Bibliothèque de l'Université, MS 431 (ibid. 259–62); New York, Pierpont Morgan Library, MS 440 (ibid. 280–3); Oxford, Bodl., Douce MSS d. 19, fols 10–39; 381, fols 63–5; Philadelphia, Free Library, Lewis European MSS 3:1–28 and 8: 1–4 (ibid. 285–6); Paris, BN, lat. MS 1077 (ibid. 287–9).

[36] Ibid. 1: 114.

[37] J. H. Oliver, 'Medieval Alphabet Soup: Reconstruction of a Mosan Psalter-Hours in Philadelphia and Oxford and the Cult of St Catherine', *Gesta* 24 (1985), 129–40.

[38] Ibid. 137.

[39] Beguine devotion to Katherine can be shown to have continued into later centuries. See, e.g., certain fifteenth-century wills in A. de la Grange, 'Choix de testaments tournaisiens anterieurs au XVIᵉ siècle', *Annales de la Société historique et archéologique de Tournai*, ns 2 (1897), 1–365, at 141 (no. 464), 220 (no. 775), 227 (no. 798), 265 (no. 934), where various bequests are made to the saint.

in understanding the way in which the lives of the saints were interpreted (and reinterpreted) within a specific historical context. The example of the sermon on St Katherine by Gilbert of Tournai exemplifies this process. In it we see how the judicious use of biblical quotations emphasizes Katherine's humility and obedience to her celestial spouse, Christ, whilst her intellectual abilities and public speaking are portrayed as heavenly gifts to her alone rather than as something to be copied by other women.

The tension between these two views of female sanctity mirrors the social tensions between the Church and beguine women. More work on the reception of Katherine's cult and in particular sermons on the saint would almost certainly illuminate further the range of ideas on female sanctity and spirituality that existed in the thirteenth century, and how these changed over subsequent centuries.

London

LITURGICAL CHANGES TO THE CULT OF SAINTS UNDER HENRY VIII[*]

by AUDE DE MÉZERAC-ZANETTI

The origin of the word 'canonization' is a timely reminder of the liturgical nature of the cult of saints. Up to the ninth century, including a new saint in the canon of the mass was one of the two steps, along with the translation of his or her relics, leading to the creation of a new cult.[1] The cult of saints is essentially a liturgical matter.[2]

Under Henry VIII, pilgrimages and the veneration of relics were banned, lights placed before images extinguished, images taken down and shrines dismantled. More generally, the cult of saints came under scrutiny as numerous summer holy days were abrogated and the intercession of a long list of saints was no longer sought in the new litany of 1544, while the doctrinal basis for such practices was being re-examined. The demise of these practices has been richly documented.[3] This paper will examine the liturgical dimension and the consequences of the reassessment of the cult of saints in the 1530s and 1540s, when divine service was purged of anything that might be used to question the royal supremacy or, more generally, Henry VIII's policies for reforming the Church.

Changes to the cult of saints are usually approached through the prism of high politics and law enforcement. But the reactions of the clergy and laity on the receiving end of the enforcement effort are more difficult to assess; if disobedience left records, conformity and obedience usually did not. The liturgical celebration of the saints was a privileged point of contact between high theology and practical devotion; elaborate ceremonies were performed before a

---

[*] I would like to thank my supervisors, Alec Ryrie and Frank Lessay, as well as the editorial team of Studies in Church History, for their comments on earlier versions of this paper.

[1]   E. W. Kemp, *Canonization and Authority in the Western Church* (Oxford, 1948), 1–2.

[2]   Three of the seven modalities of the cult of saints are purely liturgical: ibid. 1–2.

[3]   Eamon Duffy, *The Stripping of the Altars: Traditional Religion in England c. 1400 – c. 1580*, 2nd edn (London, 2005), 394–5, 398, 407, 408, 443; Diarmaid MacCulloch, *Thomas Cranmer* (New Haven, CT, 1996), 327–8; G. W. Bernard, *The King's Reformation: Henry VIII and the Remaking of the English Church* (New Haven, CT, 2005), 288–9, 292.

laity usually well aware of the powers of saintly intercession and eager to collect the spiritual benefits to be reaped from church attendance. Reconstructing liturgical performances of the past is an impossible task, since once the *Ave* bell had sounded, there was nothing left to behold; rituals are thus one of the most evanescent subjects of study. The solution to this methodological difficulty may reside in the study of the liturgical texts from which ceremonies were conducted.[4] The approach offered here is based on a survey of a significant corpus of service books which offers a unique perspective on the local implementation of liturgical changes to the cult of saints. The conservative bias of the corpus is unquestionable, for all service books should have been destroyed in 1549 when the first Book of Common Prayer came into use. Moreover, these books may owe their survival to chance and local circumstances; consequently the corpus is not necessarily representative geographically or ideologically. Yet they show not only how dramatically the pope and St Thomas Becket were expunged from the liturgy, and how liturgical performance could be affected by these changes, but also how Becket's was not the only cult affected by the Henrician Reformation.

★ ★ ★

In the aftermath of the break with Rome, the Bishop of Bath and Wells, John Clerk, issued a detailed list of changes to be made in the liturgy.[5] Of course, the saints who once bore the papal title were affected, since the clergy were to cross out every utterance of the word *papa*.[6] John Clerk also ordered subtle alterations to be made to reflect the new understanding of the relationship between English saints and the papacy that the regime sought to promote. St Augustine of Canterbury was sent by the 'bishop of Rome' to convert the English, and his consecration was no longer referred

[4]   On the hermeneutical possibilities and dangers of studying service books, see Richard W. Pfaff, *Liturgical Calendars, Saints, and Services in Medieval England* (Aldershot, 1999).
[5]   Kew, TNA, State Papers 6/3, fols 42–44ᵛ; very briefly summarized in J. S. Brewer, J. Gairdner and R. H. Brodie, eds, *Letters and Papers, Foreign and Domestic: Henry VIII*, 22 vols (London, 1862–1910), 8: 293. For an edition of this text, see Aude de Mézerac-Zanetti, 'Reforming the Liturgy under Henry VIII: The Instructions of John Clerk, Bishop of Bath and Wells', forthcoming in *JEH*.
[6]   TNA, SP 6/3, fol. 44ʳ.

to as being effected by papal prerogative, *jussu pape*.[7] Although few breviaries contain this particular alteration, in the newly printed *Portiforium* of 1544, the printers Grafton and Whitchurch, who had been granted the monopoly for printing service books, replaced the words *jussu pape* by *jussu regis*. This provided a historical precedent of sorts to shore up the king's claim to exclusive power over the appointment of bishops.[8] Although meaningful, these were still modest revisions to the liturgy of the saints, meant mainly to de-papalize the worship of the Church.

In a further effort to undercut papal claims to the headship of the Church, John Clerk lavished most attention on the feasts of St Peter. Indeed, he ordered the suppression of several passages asserting the temporal power of Peter and his power to remit the sins of all men. St Peter was no longer described as the temporal overlord established by Christ to rule over the world, and his title of Prince of the Apostles (*apostolorum princeps*) was deleted from the liturgy.[9] The response to the fifth lesson in the feast of SS Peter and Paul was carefully edited. *Tu es pastor ovium princeps apostolorum: tibi tradidit Deus omnia regna mundi. Et ideo traditae sunt tibi claves regni caelorum* is abridged to: *Tu es pastor ovium: tibi tradidit Deus claves regni caelorum*.[10] Another passage exalting Rome as the head of the world (*caput mundi*) was also removed.[11] Furthermore, in the hymn *Aurea jam luce*, sung at the beginning of matins on all the feasts of St Peter,[12] the clergy were to substitute *tuis* for *cunctis* in the phrase:

---

7   For instance, Worcester, Cathedral Library, SEL.A.51.5, a breviary that belonged to one John Foxe, possibly related to Richard Foxe, Bishop of Winchester, whose obit is in the calendar. See also Oxford, Bodl., Gough Missals 56, MS Laud misc. 299; York, Minster Library, XI.G.19/1. However, in many manuscript missals the expression *jussu pape* does not occur.

8   *Portiforium secundum usum Sarum, noviter impressum et plurimis purgatum mendis* (London, 1544), sig. AAii[v].

9   TNA, SP 6/3, fol. 44. For the precise passages, see F. Procter and C. Wordsworth, eds, *Breviarium ad usum insignis ecclesiae Sarum*, 3 vols (Cambridge, 1879–86), 3, col. 371; F. H. Dickinson, ed., *Missale ad usum insignis et praeclarae ecclesiae Sarum* (Burntisland, 1861–83), cols 132–3, 299–300.

10   The original translates as: 'You are the shepherd of the sheep, Prince of the Apostles. God granted you all the kingdoms of the world. And for that reason, the keys of the kingdom of heaven were given to you.' As amended, it reads: 'You are the shepherd of the sheep. God granted you the keys of the kingdom of heaven': TNA, SP 6/3, fol. 44[v]; cf. Procter and Whitworth, eds., *Breviarium*, 3, col. 371.

11   TNA, SP 6/3, fol. 44[v]; cf. Procter and Whitworth, eds., *Breviarium*, 3, col. 368.

12   The verse starting *jam bone pastor* was sung at all three feasts of St Peter (the Feast of the Chair of St Peter, SS Peter and Paul, and St Peter in Chains): Procter and

peccati vincula / Resolve tibi potestate tradita / Qua cunctis caelum verbo claudis, aperies.[13] Thus the power of remission of sins granted to Peter and his successors no longer applied to all men wherever they might live, but only to the people under the jurisdiction of the bishop of Rome. The liturgy of St Peter was thus subtly refashioned to accommodate the royal supremacy, reflecting the denial by Henrician reformers of the pope's primacy and temporal overlordship of the Church.[14]

In the context of the break with Rome, it was necessary to defuse attempts to use the *lex orandi* to attack the changes effected to the *lex credendi*, in other words to challenge the supremacy on liturgical grounds. The effect of these adjustments was cumulative. Taken as a whole, they deeply affected the liturgy; and the impression produced by encountering a breviary that is so thoroughly reformed is rather striking, since many passages are illegible and the modern reader is bound to be surprised by the lack of reverence with which these books were treated. For instance, the priest of the parish of Arlingham, Gloucestershire, an ardent defacer, blotted out with a red crayon more than a dozen passages from the feasts of St Peter, St Thomas, the Visitation and Corpus Christi, as well as those of St Osmund and St Aldhelm.[15] In practice, the result must have been radically altered liturgical celebrations of these saints, for many prayers and readings for their feasts were completely illegible.

Accustomed as they were to the hitherto unchanged pattern of worship, compliant clergy and their congregations must have felt this transformation acutely. There were also practical implications: since the responses suppressed from the feast of SS Peter and Paul were sung passages, the new text would require changes in the plainsong melody. The gradual erosion of the sense of continuity

---

Whitworth, eds., *Breviarium*, 3, cols 172, 365, 565–6; and the hymn *Aurea luce* itself was also sung at vespers and at matins during the Octave of SS Peter and Paul: ibid., cols 438–9.

[13] The word 'yours' is substituted for the word 'all': 'Unbind the fetters of sin by the power transmitted to you, by which you open and close heaven to all with your word.'

[14] G. R. Elton, *The Tudor Constitution,* 2nd edn (Cambridge, 1982), 361–2, 366. See contemporary debates on Matt. 16: 19 and John 20: 23 in Malcolm B. Yarnell, 'Royal Priesthood in the English Reformation' (unpublished D.Phil. thesis, University of Oxford, 2000), 208–15. For the evolution of the figure of St Peter under Elizabeth and James, see Karen Bruhn, 'Reforming Saint Peter: Protestant Constructions of Saint Peter the Apostle in Early Modern England', *SCJ* 33 (2002), 33–49.

[15] Salisbury, Cathedral Library, MS 152.

that the liturgy had provided was certainly compounded by two other Henrician policies: the abrogation of numerous holy days and the displacement of the feast of the dedication of a parish church from day which had been observed locally to the first Sunday of October. In 1536, in the context of a possible diplomatic rapprochement with Lutheran princes, Parliament put forth the *Ten Articles,* a new formulary of faith endorsed by the king, in which the traditional notion of patronage was questioned and faith in the saints' specialized powers denied.[16] All this affected the immediacy of the relationship between the faithful and the saints, while the rewriting of the liturgical texts subtly highlighted the revised models of sanctity in Henry's Church. The direct involvement of the king and the impact of the political context on the definition of sainthood are best exemplified by the complete reassessment of the life and death of the most popular of English saints, St Thomas of Canterbury.

★ ★ ★

According to the traditional hagiography, Thomas Becket, Archbishop of Canterbury, had died a martyr for the liberties of the Church, and the liturgy in his honour was unambiguous in the celebration of his feast.[17] The reading of Becket's life as that of a martyr and a good pastor was never completely unchallenged.[18] Indeed, the events that led to his murder in the cathedral can be given a variety of interpretations ranging from saintly abnegation to haughty provocation. The story was revised in the latter direction by Henry VIII: Thomas had fled to France and to the pope after quarrelling unnecessarily with Henry II, and had attempted to have just laws repealed by a foreign potentate. Later, in a dispute over primacy with the archbishop of York, he had refused to acknowledge the validity of the coronation of the young king in 1170. Finally, he had died a traitor to his king, the immediate cause of death being his resisting lawful arrest.[19] His Canterbury shrine was dismantled and the celebrations of his feast day (29 December)

---

[16] Gerald Bray, *Documents of the English Reformation* (Cambridge, 1994), 172; Duffy, *Stripping of the Altars,* 393.

[17] *The Sarum Missal done into English,* trans. A. Harford Pearson (London, 1884), 30.

[18] Anne Duggan, *Thomas Becket* (London, 2004), 200, 213, 236.

[19] Paul Hugues and James Larkin, eds, *Tudor Royal Proclamations,* 3 vols (New Haven, CT, 1964), 1: 276. See also G. R. Elton, *Policy and Police* (Cambridge, 1972),

and his translation (7 July) were discontinued, in an effort to wipe his spirit from the collective memory. Study of the missals and manuals suggests that the clergy complied: on average the feasts of St Thomas Becket appear more aggressively and more consistently defaced than the prayers for the pope. Yet the liturgy was rendered completely illegible in only a minority of books. In other cases, the word *vacat* was added in the margin, suggesting that even if the service was still legible, the order to cease its celebration was well understood. A common practice was to scratch out the name 'Thomas' from the liturgy, making the attack all the more personal. Finally there is no evidence from letters written to the king's vice-gerent in spiritual affairs, Thomas Cromwell, that these feasts were celebrated after 1538. Furthermore, the eradication of the cult of Becket also required the rededication of churches, institutions and even individuals named after him.[20] So then, by un-canonizing Thomas Becket, the regime was asserting its authority to define who deserved to be inscribed in the catalogue of saints and thus honoured.

★ ★ ★

The demise of Becket's cult is well known, but an extensive survey of the liturgical books reveals that the cults of other saints were changing too. In ten out of twenty-nine missals, manuals and breviaries according to the use of York, St William of York was subjected to the Becket treatment.[21] Furthermore, in seven of these books, part or all of the services honouring SS Wilfrid, Cuthbert and John of Beverley were also crossed out. Usually the service for St William was defaced less aggressively than that for St Thomas but more than those for the three others, suggesting that these alterations were either not all made at the same point in time or else not with the same aim in mind. Nothing in these liturgies is likely to have displeased the regime, so, in the absence of a surviving order

257 n. 1; Robert E. Scully, 'The Unmaking of a Saint: Thomas Becket and the English Reformation', *CathHR* 86 (2000), 579–602.

20 One wonders how this might have affected Thomas Cromwell, Thomas Cranmer and the countless Thomases of Tudor England. For examples of rededications, see Scully, 'Unmaking of a Saint', 597; for a misdirected effort, see Brewer, Gairdner and Brodie, eds, *Letters and Papers*, 17: 881.

21 Cambridge, UL, F.150.a.41; Durham, UL, Cosin V.I.2; Leeds, UL, MS Ripon 7; London, BL, C.35.b.4; Oxford, Bodl., Douce B.243, Gough Missals 21, MS Gough liturg. 1; York, Minster Library, Stainton 12, MS XVI.A.9, MS Add. 69.

from the temporal power or the ecclesiastical hierarchy, the explanation for these defacings must be reconstructed from elements taken from the political and religious context in Yorkshire.

It is best to look at these defacings as two separate phenomena. We may focus first on the pair of archbishops and then on the Anglo-Saxon saints. This strategy is further validated by the evidence, since in three books St Thomas's and St William's are the only feasts that were crossed out.

The life of St William does not present much evidence to justify the eradication of his cult.[22] His election to the archbishopric of York was hotly contested for years, mainly by the Cistercians and Augustinians in Yorkshire, but also by St Bernard of Clairvaux, who wrote several letters to successive popes to discredit William's candidacy. Shortly after William arrived at York, he was taken ill and died. Although he may have been murdered, his death could not be interpreted as martyrdom, regardless of the wishes of the local clergy. However, his afterlife may have appeared more repellent to the Henrician regime. During the Interdict on England (1208–14), his relics attracted much attention; miracles occurred and were exploited by the clergy in the dispute between the king and the Church centred on York.[23] His canonization in 1226 was effected by Rome, as the papacy started to claim the exclusive right to canonize.[24] This could have contributed to the depiction of St William as a 'Roman saint' rather than an English saint.

Looking at St William from a comparative perspective may offer a better explanation. The promotion of the cult of St William closely parallels that of Becket: a spattering of miracles took place in York between 1173 and 1177, just after the death and immediate canonization of St Thomas. In 1226, the York saint was canonized, only a few years after the munificent translation of the relics of Thomas. At last the northern province and the city of York had the local saint and shrine that they desperately needed as they strove to equal Canterbury.[25] Conversely, the suppression of the cult of St William could be seen as parallel to that of St Thomas, creating a symmetry between the two provinces. After Canterbury

---

[22] This brief account of William of York's life is based on Christopher Norton, *William of York* (Woodbridge, 2006).

[23] Ibid. 198.

[24] Ibid. 192–4.

[25] Ibid. 195–6.

had dismantled their shrine and suppressed a much-loved saint, eager reformers in York might have felt pressure to do the same to their local canonized archbishop.

★ ★ ★

The three late seventh-century saints, SS Wilfrid, Cuthbert and John of Beverley, had all been active at a time of assertion of Roman traditions in the English Church (epitomized by the Synod of Whitby in 664) and of conflict between the provinces of York and Canterbury. Wilfrid himself offers a striking contrast to the type of godly behaviour Henry VIII required of his subjects. He engaged in disputes with King Ecgrith of Northumbria, encouraging the queen to make a vow of chastity, the type of clerical meddling that Henry VIII would have found particularly distasteful. Wilfrid appealed to Rome twice, sought consecration in France because he doubted the validity of an English consecration, defended the Roman party at Whitby, promoted curial traditions in connection with the cult of relics and encouraged the continental form of monastic life. In his afterlife, he became an example of *pius pater* according to the Roman model.[26] The lives of Cuthbert and John are less distinctly offensive, although the former is known to have been a promoter of the Benedictine rule in England and his shrine in Durham was one of the most visited by pilgrims.[27]

Beyond these biographical details, the political context of the Pilgrimage of Grace of 1536[28] offers the clearest insights into why the liturgies of these northern saints were suppressed. This evidence is particularly convincing since none of these saints were suppressed from Sarum service books. The shrines of William, John, Cuthbert and Wilfrid were located in York, Beverley, Durham and Ripon respectively. These four places were strategic locations during the Pilgrimage of Grace, and musters or risings of armed men took place in all of them. The banner of St Cuthbert was one of the two

---

[26] William Trent Foley, *St. Wilfrid of York as* pius pater: *A Study of Late Roman Piety in Anglo-Saxon England* (Ann Arbor, MI, 2000).

[27] On the impact of the Reformation on the cult of St Cuthbert, see, in this volume, Margaret Harvey, 'The Northern Saints after the Reformation in the Writings of Christopher Watson (d. 1580)', 258–69.

[28] The rebellion started in Lincolnshire and swept through Yorkshire and parts of other northern shires. The pilgrims' demands were principally focused on the restoration of traditional religion.

main rallying signs of the pilgrims, along with the banner of the Five Wounds. In all likelihood the banner of the patron saint of the Percy family, St John of Beverley, which had been used in battle on numerous occasions, would also have been displayed by the rebels.[29] The rebels demanded that the liberties of the cathedrals and churches of Durham, St Peter of York, Beverley and Ripon be restored.[30] The enlisting of these saints by the pilgrims could well have sparked revenge from zealous reformers, anxious to suppress local cults, which had featured prominently in the rebellion. Moreover the shrines of William, Wilfrid and John of Beverley were only dismantled belatedly, at the prompting of the king, after a visit to the city of York in 1541. It is possible that this tardy response singled out these northern saints for special treatment at the hands of a local clergy eager to embrace the Henrician Reformation.

In several cases, the deleted passages hint at the entirely liturgical nature of the change at hand. In 1536, the king had abrogated many of the holy days that occurred in summer. In practice, this meant that many saints' days were no longer to be days of rest and prayer; the clergy could still celebrate these feasts by a mass and divine office, but attendance was no longer mandatory, and laymen were to busy themselves with harvesting or other forms of work. It is possible that some of the light crossings out reflect the downgrading of a feast to a ferial (i.e. ordinary) day. Indeed, in the two missals, only the sequences of St John and St Wilfrid were crossed out, since the presence of such liturgical poems always signalled the high rank of the feast. At Hutton Rudby, the priest lightly crossed out the lessons of the office of matins for John, Wilfrid and Cuthbert. In the breviary from the parish of Swine, in the East Riding of Yorkshire, which was heavily defaced, the feasts of Thomas and William were either cut out or completely scratched out, whereas the offices of Cuthbert, John and Wilfrid were merely crossed out; in consequence, perhaps, the proper of these saints was suppressed and replaced by the common of bishops (set liturgical texts for the feast of any saint of episcopal rank, to be used when no specific

---

[29] Wilson, *John of Beverley*, 114, 121–2. On the Percy host, see Michael Bush, *The Pilgrimage of Grace: A Study of the Rebel Armies of October 1536* (Manchester, 1996), 187–215.

[30] See the Pontefract Articles, as edited in R. W. Hoyle, *The Pilgrimage of Grace and the Politics of the 1530s* (Oxford, 2001), 460–3, at 462.

liturgy was provided in the service book).[31] Even though there are irregularities, as can be seen from the table, these practices would be consistent with the downgrading of a special feast to a ferial day. And this interpretation is reinforced by the surviving calendar of the Cottingham breviary, in which most of the abrogated holy days were suppressed from the list of feasts of obligation.

Unsurprisingly, the restoration of these feast days was one of the demands of the pilgrims. The suppression of St Wilfrid's feast in particular had caused uproar in the parish of Watton, north of Beverley, that soon turned to rebellion as the Pilgrimage of Grace spread from around Hull to Beverley and the rest of the East Riding.[32] On 12 October 1536, St Wilfrid's Day, musters were held at Skipwith Moor, Hunsleigh Beacon, Arram and Sutton Ings, as the rebels marched towards Beverley.[33] St Wilfrid's patronage would undoubtedly have been mobilized by the rebels. The strict enforcement of the suppression of saints' days, especially that of St Wilfrid, in the aftermath of the defeat of the rebels, is a very plausible act of revenge by Henrician supporters.

In this case study, the systematic analysis of liturgical books has highlighted unknown victims of the assault on the cult of saints. By taking into consideration a series of factors, historical, political and liturgical, a compelling set of reasons for the suppression of local cults emerges.

★ ★ ★

Liturgical continuity is usually taken for granted before the advent of the Book of Common Prayer, and yet the service books in use during the period tell another story. The break with Rome required multiple adaptations of the devotional material honouring the saints, in particular where St Peter was concerned, and also led to a reassessment of the virtues that made a saint. The royal Head of the Church took on the right to decide whether a saint deserved to be honoured, by whom (clergy alone or all the faithful), and with what degree of solemnity. The abrogation of the feasts of all

---

[31] For more on the propers and commons of saints in missals and breviaries, see Andrew Hughes, *Medieval Manuscripts for Mass and Office: A Guide to their Organization and Terminology* (Toronto, ON, 1982), 153–6; 237–8.

[32] Brewer, Gairdner and Brodie, eds, *Letters and Papers*, 12/1: 201; Duffy, *Stripping of the Altars*, 395; Bush, *Pilgrimage of Grace*, 34–5.

[33] Bush, *Pilgrimage of Grace*, 427–8.

but a few scriptural saints, followed by the restoration of several of these in July 1541, along with the de-canonization of Thomas Becket, emphasize the mutability of the liturgical cult of saints in the 1530s and 1540s.[34] The liturgical approach also allows for innumerable localized analyses that convey the immense diversity of practices found in Henry's Church. Local and national politics deeply affected worship practices and altered lay and clerical devotion to saints, as, indeed, in the aftermath of the Pilgrimage of Grace, when clergy from the diocese of York suppressed the liturgical texts honouring SS William of York, Cuthbert, Wilfrid and John of Beverley, whose patronage had been invoked by the rebels in support for their cause.

University of Durham / Université de Paris III

---

[34] Duffy, *Stripping of the Altars*, 430.

Table 1. Liturgical Texts defaced in several York Service Books

Book	Missal	Missal	Breviary	Breviary	Breviary	Breviary	Calendar
Repository	Oxford, Bodl.	Cambridge, UL	BL	York, Minster Library	Durham, UL	Oxford, Bodl.	Leeds, UL
Shelfmark	Douce B. 243	F 150.a.41	C.35.b.4	MS Add 69	Cosin V.I.2	MS Gough liturg.1	MS Ripon 7
Provenance	unknown	unknown	unknown	Swine	Hutton Rudby	unknown	Cottingham
Thomas	mass	mass	office	office	office	missing	defaced
William	sequence	mass	office	office	office	office	defaced
Wilfrid	sequence	sequence	intact	office	lesson ii & iii	office	defaced
John	sequence	sequence	intact	lesson ii	office	office	defaced
Cuthbert	sequence	intact	office	office	office	office	defaced
Other	11,000 virgins		Sylvester	Sylvester, Corpus Christi, Margaret, Egidius, Feast of Relics	Margaret	11,000 virgins, passages from Egidius and Edward	abrogated days and others

'I, TOO, AM A CHRISTIAN': EARLY MARTYRS AND THEIR LIVES IN THE LATE MEDIEVAL AND EARLY MODERN IRISH MANUSCRIPT TRADITION

by SALVADOR RYAN

Veneration of the martyrs as powerful intercessors and exemplars of Christ-like fortitude is one of the earliest and most powerful manifestations of Christian religious practice. Not only were martyrs thought to be assured of salvation, but the blood which they shed was conceived by Tertullian as 'seed' for the upbuilding of the Christian Church. As legends of their lives and, more importantly, the manner of their deaths developed over time, martyrs would also function as valuable instructors in the essentials of the Christian life, their speeches before death often assuming a sermon-like quality. By the fifth century recourse to the relics of martyrs was also already well established.[1] The cult of the martyrs would have a long future.

This paper examines part of that future: late medieval and early modern Gaelic Irish devotion to the early Christian martyrs as evidenced in the vernacular manuscript tradition. It is argued here that, from the fifteenth century onwards especially, one can discern an increasing appetite, among literate lay people of means in particular, for vernacular lives of some of the most popular Christian martyrs. This set in train a process whereby Latin originals were acquired and translated for the consumption of a more assertive and confident native Irish aristocracy – sometimes relatively faithfully and at other times less so. In the case of the latter, the introduction of peculiarly Irish elements to the narratives was not uncommon and facilitated their becoming embedded in the vernacular. Tales of early Christian martyrs might claim additional importance in an Irish context, filling a lacuna in the Irish Christian tradition, which did not lay claim to any native martyr figures

---

[1]   John Anthony McGuckin, 'Martyr Devotion in the Alexandrian School: Origen to Athanasius', in Diana Wood, ed., *Martyrs and Martyrologies*, SCH 30 (Oxford, 1993), 35–45, at 45.

from the period of the Christianization of the Irish in the fifth and sixth centuries.

Systematic research on the cult of the martyrs in late medieval Ireland has yet to be undertaken. While some Irish lives of individual martyrs have been edited and translated, often with some commentary, a broader analysis of their appearance in the medieval and early modern manuscript tradition has not yet been attempted. What follows is a preliminary examination of the martyrs who appear in a select number of vernacular manuscripts. This demonstrates that some of the most popular of Christian martyrs (found widely also in England, Wales and Scotland, and across the Continent) are also to be found in native Irish collections from the outset. However, in the cases of two of the most popular female martyrs, Catherine of Alexandria and Margaret of Antioch, at least from the evidence of the manuscript tradition, very different futures would lie ahead.

Perhaps the most illuminating of extant Irish devotional collections is that of a Donegal noblewoman named Máire Ní Mháille who commissioned a 'Book of Piety' for her own use in 1513. This collection included a range of popular legends such as the Finding of the True Cross by St Helena, and devotional lists such as the *merita missae* or benefits accrued for hearing mass. One of Ní Mháille's requests was the inclusion of a life of the virgin martyr St Catherine of Alexandria. On completing the account, the Tory Island scribe Ciothruadh Mág Fhindghoill penned the following note:

> So that so far is the life and death of Catherine the Virgin and it was Enóg Ó Giolláin and I myself who drew it from the Latin and a curse on all my implements, and everyone who shall read or listen to, or memorise it will gain Heaven for himself and three others he most likes *et reliqua*.[2]

With this note, the Donegal scribe indicated how such a life was meant to be used: it would ideally be read by the literate and presumably heard read aloud by others with the expectation that they would memorize the tale and, one imagines, draw lessons from

[2] *Leabhar Chlainne Suibhne: An Account of the Mac Sweeney families in Ireland with Pedigrees*, ed. P. Walsh (Dublin, 1920), xlvi. For an edition of this life, see 'Betha ocus bás Chaitreach Fína', ed. Gearóid Mac Niocaill, *Éigse* 8 (1956–7), 231–6.

it. The promises attached to fulfilling these terms were, indeed, great: salvation for oneself and a very select group of favourites. This should not necessarily be interpreted as a straightforward quid pro quo arrangement, however; the memory of Catherine's passion, or at least the broad outline of the story, would presumably incline those nearing death to turn to the saint as intercessor in their time of greatest need. After all, in her last moments the saint is recorded in the *Legenda Aurea*, a famous thirteenth-century dossier of saints' lives compiled by Jacobus de Voragine, as petitioning God that 'anyone who honours the memory of my passion, or who invokes me at the moment of death or in any need, may receive the benefit of your kindness', to which a voice from heaven replied 'to those who will celebrate your passion with devout minds, I promise the help from heaven for which you prayed'.[3] In other versions of the legend, the benefits accorded those who recalled Catherine's passion extended to worldly preservation also, as in a mid-fifteenth-century English manuscript (Harvard University, Houghton Library, MS Richardson 44): 'Let plague and hunger, disease and storm and all disturbances of weather be far from them, and may their lands have healthy air and an abundance of grain and fruit'.[4] The Donegal scribe Mág Fhindghoill would also ensure that he himself would not be excluded from the boons to be gained from the virgin martyr Catherine, even if it seems that the virginal life may not have been foremost in his thoughts. In a personal note, he writes 'I beseech the mercy of God through the intercession of Catherine the Virgin, and it is not easy to steal me away today from Síle.'[5]

Collections such as the one compiled for Máire Ní Mháille were routinely commissioned by the Gaelic Irish or Anglo-Norman aristocracy in the later Middle Ages and into the early modern period, and were brought to fruition largely by lay scribes who were usually members of hereditary learned families. In the main, however, such late medieval Irish manuscripts were not strictly devotional in composition, instead comprising a wide variety of

---

3   Jacobus de Voragine, *The Golden Legend: Readings on the Saints*, trans. William Granger Ryan, 2 vols (Princeton, NJ, 1993), 2: 339.

4   Claire M. Waters, *Virgins and Scholars: A Fifteenth-Century Compilation of the Lives of John the Baptist, John the Evangelist, Jerome and Katherine of Alexandria* (Turnhout, 2008), 409.

5   *Leabhar Chlainne Suibhne*, ed. Walsh, xliv–lxiii.

texts including hagiographical, homiletic, topographical and gene-
alogical material, in addition to secular sagas of both native and
continental origin. What makes Ní Mháille's collection useful is
that we know the date of its compilation, the scribes involved
and also something about the patron herself. When one can piece
together many relevant strands of evidence such as these, some
fundamental assumptions can be made regarding the selection
of elements which make up the work as a whole. This I have
attempted to do in a previous study.[6] Máire Ní Mháille's collection
features the lives of both Catherine of Alexandria and Margaret
of Antioch, both hugely popular female saints in the Middle
Ages. However, only one of these competing females would make
significant inroads into early modern and modern Irish devotional collections. This can be observed in the table below and
may point to a rationalization of sorts of female martyr figures
in the eighteenth-century manuscript tradition. Before exploring
this question further, some discussion of the appearance of other
martyrs in native Irish collections is warranted. There were many
other (sometimes less well known) early martyrs whose lives were
clearly sought by the Gaelic Irish, and these are also the subject
of this survey.

One of the best known Irish devotional collections of the early
fifteenth century is the *Leabhar Breac* or 'Speckled Book', most
probably the work of a single scribe called Murchadh Riabhach
Ó Cuindlis of Baile Locha Deacair in east Galway between 1408
and 1411.[7] This miscellany, which is comprised largely of Middle
Irish and Hiberno-Latin religious material, was in the hands of
the professional legal family of Mac Aodhagáin of Duniry in the
sixteenth century.[8] The passions of the Apostles feature prominently in this collection, including those of Peter and Paul, James,
Bartholomew, Andrew and Philip; in addition, however, are found
passions of St Longinus (the centurion who pierced Christ's side),

    [6] Salvador Ryan, 'Windows on Late Medieval Devotional Practice: Máire Ní
Mháille's "Book of Piety" (1513) and the World behind the Texts', in Rachel Moss,
Colmán Ó Clabaigh and Salvador Ryan, eds, *Art and Devotion in Late Medieval Ireland*
(Dublin, 2006), 1–15.
    [7] Tomás Ó Concheanainn, 'The Scribe of the Leabhar Breac', *Ériu* 24 (1973),
64–79.
    [8] Brendan Jennings, *Mícheál Ó Cléirigh, Chief of the Four Masters and his Associates*
(Dublin, 1936), 89.

St John the Baptist, St George, St Christopher and St Marcellinus, erstwhile apostate pope of the fourth century. The passions found in the *Leabhar Breac* are generally longer and contain more dialogue than those found in the thirteenth-century *Legenda Aurea*. The popularity of early martyrs among the native Irish aristocracy is further evidenced by surviving wall paintings at Ardamullivan Castle, an O'Shaughnessy tower house in County Galway, and Ballyportry Castle, an O'Brien tower house in County Clare, which include images of St Christopher and St Sebastian respectively.[9]

The story of Marcellinus relates how his cure of a certain abbot Paphnutius (also the subject of legends in his own right in the Irish manuscript tradition) provoked the ire of the emperor Diocletian (who had ordered Paphnutius's right eye to be struck out) and thus set in train the great persecution against the Church. Marcellinus, out of fear, worships the pagan idol and thus abjures his faith. This results in a great council of bishops flocking to Rome to prompt him to repent, which he duly does with great sorrow, and asks for sentence to be passed over him in confession. However, none of the bishops are prepared to judge the heir of Peter; instead, they recall to him Peter's denial of Christ and his weeping of tears of blood. The reference to bloody tears, which does not occur in the *Legenda Aurea*, points to a common feature of medieval Irish literature which underlines depth of sorrow.[10] Here it might be noted that vernacular Irish lives of universal martyrs were not averse to introducing elements which would have particular resonance with native audiences. Jane Cartwright has identified similar additions in the case of Welsh lives of female saints.[11] Marcellinus ends up passing judgement on himself, abdicates and presents himself as a confessor before the authorities, declaring 'I am a Christian', in full knowledge of his fate. This is not before he instructs his bishops that his body is to be left without burial on pain of excommunication. Diocletian duly has Marcellinus beheaded and his body is cast out without burial for thirty days. It is only on the appointment

---

[9]   Karena Morton, 'Aspects of Image and Meaning in Irish Medieval Wall Paintings', in Moss, Ó Clabaigh and Ryan, eds, *Art and Devotion*, 51–71, at 64.
[10]   See Vernam Hull, 'Celtic Tears of Blood', *Zeitschrift für celtische Philologie* 25 (1952), 226–36.
[11]   Jane Cartwright, *Feminine Sanctity and Spirituality in Medieval Wales* (Cardiff, 2008).

of his successor, Marcellus, who receives a vision from St Peter instructing him to bury Marcellinus next to him, that the apostate pope finds rest.[12]

Other passions in the *Leabhar Breac* occasionally exhibit some particularly Irish features, as in the legend of Longinus, who 'brought a long spear in his hand with which he wounded Christ in his side and split his heart in twain, so that blood and wine came out'.[13] References to Christ's *fionfhuil* or 'wine-blood' are very common in Irish religious literature of this period, especially in bardic religious poetry.[14] In the *Leabhar Breac* account, based largely on the *Acta Longini*, Longinus goes on to profess belief in Christ in the manner of the centurion in Mark's Gospel; better known variations of this story allude to his blindness – he is called *An Dall* or 'the Blind Man' in medieval Irish literature – and to his being cured by the blood of Christ which runs down the shaft of his spear after the piercing. In the *Leabhar Breac*, his subsequent career as a monk puts him on a collision course with the authorities, who proceed to knock the teeth out of his head and cut the tongue from his mouth in an effort to persuade him to honour the gods. However, Longinus persists in requesting that he be allowed to have a go at smashing the images of the gods to see whether they would take revenge on him. When he succeeds in driving the demons from the idols, the prefect is fearful and orders that his tongue be cut out a second time (given that Longinus had miraculously continued to speak, perhaps the governor suspected that the first removal had been botched). However, this time, as many 'medieval' saints were wont to do, Longinus replies in kind, beseeching the Lord for vengeance on the ruler who is himself struck blind and whose bowels and entrails became terribly twisted. The prefect pleads for mercy and Longinus explains that this can only be achieved for him through Longinus's own beheading. When this is accomplished, the prefect prostrates himself beside the body of Longinus in repentance and his sight is restored.

---

[12] *The Passions and Homilies from the Leabhar Breac: Text, Translation and Glossary*, ed. Robert Atkinson (Dublin, 1887), 295–9.

[13] Ibid. 300.

[14] For a discussion of this term, see Salvador Ryan, 'Reign of Blood: Aspects of Devotion to the Wounds of Christ in Late Medieval Ireland', in Joost Augusteijn and Mary Ann Lyons, eds, *Irish History: A Research Yearbook* 1 (Dublin, 2002), 137–49, at 147–8.

The passion of St John the Baptist, which occurs in the *Leabhar Breac*, likewise exhibits variation from that of the *Legenda Aurea*, and attributes the request for John's head to Herodias's two daughters, Salvisa and Neptis.[15] Moreover, an inclusion later in the manuscript regarding the so-called *Scuab a Fanait* or 'Broom out of Fanad' is also worthy of note. This was a plague that was expected to visit Ireland in revenge for the beheading of John the Baptist, for which the Irish were thought to be directly responsible, in the person of an Irish druid called Mog Ruith, seemingly a disciple of Simon Magus.[16] This tradition, which is quite early, is found in a note on 29 August (the feast day of the decollation of St John the Baptist) in the ninth-century *Félire Oengusso* or Martyrology of Oengus.[17]

Some of the martyrs discussed above occur in other fifteenth-century manuscripts, most notably British Library MS Egerton 91, which contains both the decollation of St John the Baptist (although in this instance, after the version in the *Legenda Aurea*) and the legend of Mog Ruith and also the passion of Pope Marcellinus. The scribe in this case was Uilleam Mac an Leagha, one of the most prolific of his day. The same scribe was responsible for the lives of the martyrs St George and St Longinus (Paris, Bibliothèque Nationale MS Ancien. Fond. 8175), in addition to the life of St Juliana of Nicomedia. This lesser-known female martyr was quite popular in the Irish manuscript tradition, appearing in collections as late as the eighteenth century. Irish translations of her Latin life were made during the fifteenth century (see especially Royal Irish Academy MS 23 0 48 and British Library MSS Egerton 136 and 1781) and, of course, she appears in the *Legenda Aurea*, which was already well known in medieval Ireland.[18] The tale recounts how the young African virgin spurns the Roman prefect of Nicomedia to whom she is betrothed, because he will not accept the Christian faith. Her father has her stripped and beaten as a result; the bulk of the tale, however, is devoted to a

---

15 Martin McNamara, *The Apocrypha in the Irish Church* (Dublin, 1984), 65.

16 Ibid. 65–7.

17 *Félire Oengusso Céli Dé / The martyrology of Oengus the Culdee*, ed. and trans. Whitley Stokes, Henry Bradshaw Society 29 (London, 1905).

18 Máirtín Mac Conmara, 'An léann eaglasta ag baile, 1200–1500', in Máirtín Mac Conmara, ed., *An léann eaglasta in Éirinn, 1200–1900* (Dublin, 1988), 102–38, at 115; for an Irish version of her life, see J. Vendryes, 'Betha Iuiliana', *Revue celtique* 33 (1912), 312–23.

battle of wits between Juliana and her would-be husband, who desires that she sacrifice to the gods. Having been imprisoned and hung up by the hair of her head, Juliana succeeds not only in holding out against the prefect but also in exposing a demon who visits her in disguise to try to change her mind. As in the case of Longinus, Juliana is not averse to using force on the demon, tying his hands behind his back, flinging him to the ground and violently thrashing him with her chains until the demon invokes Christ crucified to be allowed to go free.[19] When Juliana is finally released, she emerges from the prison dragging the demon after her along the ground and finally depositing it in a sewer. Juliana is subjected to a number of horrific tortures including being broken on the wheel and immersed in a bath of molten lead, but on each occasion she overcomes these instruments of torture until finally she is beheaded. The prefect and his companions are subsequently shipwrecked after which their bodies are devoured by wild birds on the shoreline.[20]

It has long been recognized that the fifteenth century experienced a flowering of devotional texts in the Irish language, many of them translations of Latin originals. This period coincided not only with a renaissance of sorts in Gaelic areas, but also the observant reform movement among the mendicant orders, particularly the Franciscans. The epicentre of the observant reform could be found in Gaelic areas, where most of the ninety new friaries established between 1400 and 1508 were located.[21] In addition, ever closer ties between mendicant orders and local ruling families and, indeed, between scribes and their patrons would lead to the formation of new intellectual networks which enjoyed important ties with England and the Continent. The production of manuscripts in the north-western counties of Cavan, Leitrim and Donegal is particularly noteworthy from the end of the fifteenth through the middle of the sixteenth centuries, as observed recently by Raymond Gillespie, many of these containing translations of Latin lives of

---

[19] In the version found in the *Legenda Aurea* it is Juliana and not Christ crucified that the demon invokes.

[20] Vendryes, 'Betha Iuiliana', 312–23.

[21] Peter O'Dwyer, *Towards a History of Irish Spirituality* (Dublin, 1995), 135; also Colmán N. Ó Clabaigh, *The Franciscans in Ireland, 1400–1534: From Reform to Reformation* (Dublin, 2002).

saints.[22] A careful study of manuscripts and their subjects from this area reveals some degree of commonality of interest.[23] However, evidence for a degree of overlap in subject matter is not confined to one geographical area, as is evident in the British Library MSS Additional 30512, owned by the Fitzgeralds of Desmond (Munster) in the sixteenth century, and Egerton 1781, written by members of the Mac Parrtháláin family (well-known scribes and dependants of the Mac Samhradháin, lords of Tullyhaw in Cavan), at the house of one Niall Ó Siaghail in County Offaly: both of these late fifteenth-century manuscripts include the lesser-known legends of James Intercisus and also Ciricus and Julitta.

In both manuscripts, the tale of James Intercisus is that found in the *Legenda Aurea*. James Intercisus (or James 'cut into pieces'), a nobleman from the city of Elape in Persia, was induced by some friends to worship idols, after which his family sent him a letter disassociating themselves from him and banning him from their house on account of his having 'traded truth for a lie'.[24] Thus rejected, he wept bitterly and resolved to do penance. News travelled to the ruler of the land that James was a Christian and he was brought before the authorities who threatened him with all manner of torture because he had confessed to being a 'Nazarene', a sorcerer in their eyes. James professed himself untroubled by death, which he termed a mere sleep, and asserted his belief in resurrection. He was thus sentenced to be put to death by being dismembered piece by piece. The account relates the severance of each finger, after which on each occasion James is offered the opportunity to surrender but instead responds with biblically inspired maxims. For instance, with the eighth finger taken, James recalls Christ's circumcision on the eighth day; with the ninth, the hour Christ yielded up his spirit on the cross, and with the tenth, the Ten Commandments.[25] Sometimes these aphorisms have an almost comical quality to them; for instance, having had the toes removed from his right foot and in anticipation of the same proce-

---

[22] Raymond Gillespie, 'Saints and Manuscripts in Sixteenth-Century Breifne', *Breifne* 11.44 (2008), 533–56.

[23] See Salvador Ryan, '"Wily women of God" in Cavan's Late Medieval and Early Modern Devotional Collections', in Brendan Scott, ed., *Culture and Society in Early Modern Breifne / Cavan* (Dublin, 2009), 31–47.

[24] Jacobus de Voragine, *Golden Legend*, trans. Ryan, 2: 344.

[25] Ibid. 345.

dure on his left, beginning with the smallest toe, James commented 'Little toe, be comforted, because the big and the little will all rise again, and not a hair of the head will perish.'[26] The structure of the legend of James Intercisus, with its gradual denouement of martyrdom, accompanied by James's various utterances, presented valuable pedagogical opportunities for those wishing to impress upon the minds of hearers elements of the Christian message.

The second legend that these two manuscripts have in common is that of Ciricus (Quiricus) and Julitta, child and mother respectively, whose cult had already been widespread since late antiquity. Called before the governor of Tarsus while holding her three-year-old child in her arms, Julitta is charged with being a Christian and is asked to sacrifice. She refuses and is separated from her child and brought away to be scourged while Ciricus sobs loudly. The governor attempts to calm the child with kisses, but instead the three-year-old attacks him viciously, clawing at his face with his fingernails and crying out 'I too am a Christian!', at which point the governor throws him down a series of steps to his death. Julitta rejoices that her child has gone to heaven before her, and soon after is beheaded.[27] The feast day of Ciricus was recorded in the Irish *Félire Oengusso* as early as the ninth century and in the *Martyrology of Turin*, which may have been composed for a convent of Augustinian nuns at Lismullin, County Meath, in the first half of the twelfth century;[28] the entry for Quiricus (recorded as Círic here) is in majuscule, underlining its significance. The earliest reference to Ciricus in Irish literature, however, is to be found in the work of the early eighth-century Irish poet Blathmac.[29] The relative popularity of Ciricus and Julitta in medieval Ireland may also have something to do with their reputation as patrons of women in childbirth. The cults of Quiricus and Julitta enjoyed some popularity in Cornwall too, with church dedications at Luxulyan, Veep

---

[26] Ibid. 346.

[27] Ibid. 324.

[28] Pádraig Ó Riain, ed., *Four Irish Martyrologies: Drummond, Turin, Cashel, York* (London, 2002), 129. I am grateful to Prof. Pádraig Ó Riain and Dr Dagmar Ó Riain-Raedel for drawing my attention to this reference. See also Ryan, '"Wily Women of God"'.

[29] *The Poems of Blathmac, son of Cú Brettan*, ed. James Carney (Dublin, 1964), 87.

and Calstock, in addition to Tickenham near Bristol and Swaffham Prior in Cambridgeshire.[30]

By far the most popular female saints in late medieval Ireland were Catherine of Alexandria and Margaret of Antioch, the former famous for having exploded four specially prepared wheels studded with iron saws and sharp nails, designed for her torture, killing four thousand pagans in the process, and the latter for having exploded out of the belly of the devil, who had taken the form of a dragon, by making the sign of the cross, thus earning the position of patroness of women in childbirth.[31] Catherine's fame spread quickly in Ireland and one indication of this is the rededication of one of the seven penitential beds of St Patrick's Purgatory, Lough Derg, to the saint in the later Middle Ages. Catherine would now claim a place among an exclusively native list of early Irish saints, including Patrick, Bridget, Columcille, Brendan, Molaisse and Dabheog, displacing Columcille's biographer Adomnán in the process.[32] As noted above, the lives of both Catherine and Margaret are contained in the 1513 'Book of Piety' of Máire Ní Mháille. What sets these saints apart in the manuscript tradition, however, is the varying longevity of their cults. While the cult of Catherine of Alexandria largely peters in the manuscript tradition after 1600,[33] with the occasional notable exception such as that of British Library MS Egerton 184, a Galway manuscript of 1726, the reverse is the case for Margaret of Antioch. Indeed, the latter saint's *Life*, while already found in manuscripts of the fifteenth and sixteenth centuries, nevertheless achieves near ubiquity in the eighteenth-century manuscript tradition. There is no other *Life* that even comes close to matching Margaret's performance in this regard; it has been estimated that in all the *Life* of St

---

[30] 'Christ Church Nailsea with St Quiricus and St Julietta Tickenham' <http://www.tickenhamchurch.org.uk>, accessed 13 January 2009. There are also seven recorded dedications to Ciricus in the Database of Dedications to Saints in Medieval Scotland, <http://webdb.ucs.ed.ac.uk/saints/index.cfm?fuseaction=home.searchadhoc>, accessed 20 July 2009.

[31] For a useful comparison with the popularity of female martyrs in medieval England, see Eamon Duffy, 'Holy Maydens, Holy Wyfes: The Cult of Women Saints in Fifteenth- and Sixteenth-Century England', in W. J. Shiels and Diana Wood, eds, *Women in the Church*, SCH 27 (Oxford, 1990), 175–96.

[32] Peter Harbison, *Pilgrimage in Ireland: The Monuments and the People* (London, 1991), 65.

[33] For a collection of a variety of evidence concerning St Catherine's cult, see Arthur Spears, *The Cult of St Catherine of Alexandria in Ireland* (Rathmullan, 2006).

Margaret appears in at least ninety manuscripts.[34] While the prevalence of one particular saint over another in the scribal tradition is not always a very reliable barometer of the popular cult, and other manifestations of devotion to the saint must necessarily be taken into account, nevertheless, the contrast is striking and invites further study. It could be argued that the legend of Juliana, which survives somewhat better than Catherine into the early modern period (and which is essentially an amalgam of both the Catherine and Margaret legends) rendered the older cult redundant. This apparent rationalization of female martyr cults in the later manuscript tradition might also be better appreciated when one takes into account the degree of overlap between certain female martyr figures. For instance, although it does not appear as her principal emblem, the 'Catherine wheel' was also the choice method of torture for Juliana in many accounts of her martyrdom, as observed by Karen Winstead; similarly, although Agatha was allowed to lay almost exclusive claim to the topos of having one's breasts struck off, she was not the only figure to have undergone such torture.[35]

Lives of early Christian martyrs, both well known and obscure, were clearly in great demand among the native Irish aristocracy through the late medieval and early modern periods. A preliminary examination of the manuscript evidence demonstrates that from the fifteenth century vernacular appropriations of Latin lives became increasingly common, as wealthy Gaelic families ensured that the most popular lives were included in their devotional collections. These lives were most often designed to be read aloud and their details memorized, the accomplishment of which promised many benefits. These benefits were an incentive to hear and remember the message within, exemplified in the general example of Christian witness and fortitude or the more practical enumeration of the Ten Commandments as seen in the James Intercisus legend. Visual reminders of the martyrs and their sufferings are also in evidence on the walls of medieval dwellings, in what were perhaps private chapels. However, as seen in the case of female martyrs such as Catherine of Alexandria, Juliana of Nicomedia and Margaret of

---

[34] Diarmuid Ó Laoghaire, 'Beathaí naomh iasachta sa Ghaeilge' (unpublished Ph.D. thesis, University College, Dublin, 1967), xxx.

[35] Karen A. Winstead, *Virgin Martyrs: Legends of Sainthood in Late Medieval England* (Ithaca, NY, 1997), 3.

Antioch, the unevenness of their later appearance in the manuscript tradition suggests that a downsizing of female martyr cults
was in operation during the course of the eighteenth century. A
comprehensive examination of the lives of female martyrs in Irish
manuscript sources over this period, in conjunction with manifestations of these cults in other media, now needs to be undertaken
in order to establish the reason for this phenomenon. This might
also encourage further research into the fate of the larger body of
early Christian martyrs in the Irish devotional landscape of the
early modern and modern periods.

St Patrick's College, Maynooth

Table 1. Preliminary Findings of Lives of Martyrs in Irish Manuscripts

Name of martyr	Number of occurrences	15th century	16th century	17th century	18th century
Catherine	4	BL, Egerton 1781	RIA, 24 P 25 BL, Add. 33993		BL, Egerton 184
Christopher	2	RIA, 23 P 16 RIA, 23 O 48			
Ciricus and Julitta	3	BL, Egerton 1781 BL, Add. 30512 King's Inns, MS 10			
Eustathius	3	RIA, 23 O 48	RIA, 23 O 4		BL, Egerton 180
George	5	RIA, 23 P 16 RIA, 23 E 29 RIA, 23 O 48 NLI, G9			RIA, 23 O 41
James Intercisus	2	BL, Egerton 1781 BL, Add. 30512			
John the Baptist	3	RIA, 23 P 16 BL, Egerton 91 RIA, 23 O 48			
Juliana	6	RIA, 23 E 29 RIA, 23 O 48 BL, Egerton 1781		BL, Egerton 136	RIA, 23 M 50 RIA, 24 L 11

Name	No.				
Laurence	2	BL, Add. 30512			BL, Egerton 190
Longinus	2	RIA, 23 P 16		BL, Egerton 136	
Marcellinus	2	RIA, 23 P 16 BL, Egerton 91			
Margaret	16	Bodl., MS Laud Misc. 610 BL, Egerton 1781	RIA, 24 P 25		BL, Egerton 190 BL, Egerton 188 RIA, 23 O 35 RIA, 23 L 12 RIA, 23 L 29 RIA, 23 L 38 RIA, 23 H 15 NLI, G 123 NLI, G 140 RIA, 23 I 35 RIA, 23 L 31 RIA, 23 C 7 King's Inns, MS 28
Sebastian	1				King's Inns, MS 19
Thomas of Canterbury	2				RIA, 23 M 50 King's Inns, MS 19

Note: The manuscripts are housed at the following repositories: Oxford, Bodl.; London, BL; Dublin, King's Inns; Dublin, National Library of Ireland (NLI); Dublin, Royal Irish Academy (RIA)

ST PIUS V (1504–72) AND STA CATERINA DE' RICCI (1523–90): TWO WAYS OF BEING A SAINT IN COUNTER-REFORMATION ITALY

by PATRICK PRESTON

Recent students of the Counter-Reformation in Italy have not neglected the subject of sanctity. For example, one such student, Peter Burke, has dealt with it in a general and theoretical way,[1] while others, such as Gabriella Zarri, have concentrated on certain classes of saints, in her case female saints and *beatae*.[2] Scholars, however, whose interests are in the particular rather than the general, have tended to prefer to study the lives and times of individual saints, and the perceptions of them by their contemporaries.[3] A different approach altogether has been to study a particular aspect of sanctity, such as hagiography or canonization.[4] Similarly, some scholars have concentrated on the salient aspects of the contribution that particular individuals made to the work of the Church militant, for example church reform in the case of Charles Borromeo or the repression of heresy in that of Michele Ghislieri.[5]

The approach adopted in this paper is somewhat similar to the last of those listed above, but the intention is to produce a compar-

---

[1]   Peter Burke, 'How to be a Counter-Reformation Saint', in idem, *The Historical Anthropology of Early Modern Italy: Essays on Perception and Communication* (Cambridge, 1987), 48–62.

[2]   Gabriella Zarri, *Le santé vive. Cultura e religiosità femminile nella prima età moderna* (Turin, 1990).

[3]   For Neri, see, e.g., G. Papàsogli, *Filippo Neri. Un secolo, un uomo* (San Paolo, 2002); Maria Teresa Bonadonna Russo and Niccolò del Re, eds, *San Filippo Neri nella realtà romana del XVI secolo. Atti del convegno di studio in occasione del IV centenario della morte di San Filippo Neri (1595–1995), Roma, 11–13 maggio 1995* (Rome, 2000). For Borromeo, see, e.g., Fernando-Vittorino Joannes, *Vita e tempi di Carlo Borromeo* (Brescia, 1985).

[4]   See e.g., Lorenzo Polizzotto, 'The Making of a Saint: The Canonization of St Antonino, 1516–1523', *Journal of Medieval and Renaissance Studies* 22 (1992), 353–81. For another example of this approach, see Angelo Turchini, *La fabbrica di un santo. Il processo di canonizzazione di Carlo Borromeo e la Controriforma* (Casale Monferrato, 1984).

[5]   For Church reform, see, e.g., John M. Headley and John B. Tomaro, eds, *San Carlo Borromeo: Catholic Reform and Ecclesiastical Politics in the Second Half of the Sixteenth Century* (Washington, DC, 1988). For the prosecution of heresy, see, e.g., M. Firpo and D. Marcatto, eds, *Il processo inquisitoriale del Cardinal Giovanni Morone* (Rome, 1981–95).

ative study of two saints as the basis for a further exploration of the topic. The exploration has been significantly extended by bringing out the differing attitudes of the two saints concerned towards Girolamo Savonarola (1453–98), another remarkable Observant Dominican who remained a dominant influence within the order in Italy long after his death at the stake. Savonarola, a native of Ferrara, entered the Dominican Order at San Domenico, Bologna, in 1475. He was twice posted to San Marco in Florence, in 1482–4 and then in 1490–8, a period that terminated sensationally with his condemnation on a charge of heresy and subsequent execution. It was during this second period at San Marco, a time of great instability in inter-state politics in Italy and Europe which culminated in the first period of the Italian Wars, that Savonarola made his reputation, first as a preacher of repentance threatening his hearers with scourges, tribulations and the wrath to come, and then as an apocalyptic prophet promising a glorious future for the city of Florence, which he described as an 'elect nation'. He preached to vast audiences, particularly after he had correctly predicted the French invasion of 1494, and, following the collapse of the Medici government, had succeeded in diverting an impending sack of the city by the army of Charles VIII. Subsequently, he was instrumental in the creation of a new, popular government on republican lines, a 'governo largo' in which ultimate power was vested, not in a Signoria of about three hundred members, as with the Medici, but in a Consiglio Grande of about three thousand members. The foreign policy of this new government was to be based on a French alliance.

Savonarola responded to the *fin de siècle* European longing for a renewal of Church and society. His plan was to achieve this first in San Marco, then in Florence, the 'elect city', and ultimately in the whole of the Church, via a thoroughly uncompromising programme of religious purification. If at first he had trusted in renewal from above, by means of an 'angelic pope', who would bring about the long-awaited renewal, by the beginning of 1494 he had moved to the idea of renewal from below. Ultimately he came to believe that renewal could come only by force. It would be a spiritual and moral renewal not only of the Church but of the whole of society. From the pulpit he railed at the moral laxity prevalent in Florence: gambling; sodomy; superfluous ornamentation in dress; and worldly festivals. His ideals were austerity and sobriety. While Florence was still in danger from war, the citizens supported him, but ultimately, when the threat of war receded, it was this austerity and his obstinacy in trying to carry out his programme without the assent of the papacy and against the will of many of the citizens, that led to his downfall. He continued to preach his message when the Church forbade him to do so. He compounded his disobedience by threatening to call a council against Pope Alexander VI. Eventually the apocalyptic prophet lost support in the government of the city. He was then at the mercy of his enemies. He was tried and condemned on a charge of heresy and schism, and executed without delay. His followers never accepted that the trial was just.[6]

Savonarolism survived the death of Savonarola: for the next forty years, Savonarola's San Marco followers continued to propagate his message, and tried to implement the Savonarolan programme of reform. They finally lost heart in the face of the development of the Counter-Reformation Church on the one hand, and the creation in Florence of the absolutist government of Duke Cosimo de' Medici on the other. However, Savonarola's memory was still cherished by many in the Dominican Order, though they tended to emphasize his spirituality rather than his revolutionary political and social message.

The divergences between the two saints studied in this paper are refracted in their differing attitudes to Savonarola, as will be shown later. A necessary preliminary to this exploration of sanctity in Counter-Reformation Italy is the clarification of the terms used. Counter-Reformation Italy here means sixteenth-century Italy, and a Counter-Reformation saint means not one who was canonized in the sixteenth century, but one who was either born or died during that time. On this definition, there were less than a dozen Italian Counter-Reformation saints. In addition to Caterina de' Ricci and Michele Ghislieri, the subjects of this essay, there were Angela Merici (1474–1540), founder of the Ursulines; Gaetano da Thiene (1480–1547), co-founder of the Theatines;

---

[6] There is a huge literature on Savonarola. Notable works published in English during the last forty years are D. Weinstein, *Savonarola and Florence: Prophecy and Patriotism in the Renaissance* (Princeton, NJ, 1970); L. Polizzotto, *The Elect Nation: The Savonarolan Movement in Florence, 1494–1545* (Oxford, 1994). In Italian, there are F. Cordero, *Savonarola*, 4 vols (Rome, 1986–8); S. Dall'Aglio, *Savonarola e il savonarolismo* (Bari, 2005).

Filippo Neri (1515–95), founder of the Oratorians; Alessandro Sauli (1535–92), the Barnabite 'Apostle of Corsica'; Carlo Borromeo (1538–84), Cardinal Archbishop of Milan, papal administrator and reformer; Francesco Caracciolo (1563–1608), co-founder of the Minor Clerks Regular; Maria Maddalena de' Pazzi (1566–1607), Carmelite mystic; and Aloysius Gonzaga (1568–91), Jesuit visionary and ascetic.[7]

I have chosen to discuss the lives of two Observant Dominicans, firstly because the comparison between them illustrates the variety of the distinctive contributions that could be made to the development of the Counter-Reformation Church; secondly because this comparison throws light on the relationship between sainthood and sanctity; and thirdly because it provides a convenient basis for investigating the Counter-Reformation prerequisites for beatification.

We shall consider first Caterina de' Ricci, the more complex personality of the two.[8] Born in 1523 into an important Florentine family – the de' Ricci were *ottimati,* influential patricians who were a force to be reckoned with in the political life of the city, even during the period of Medici domination in the second half of the fifteenth century – Caterina de' Ricci seems from an early age to have been marked out for a career in the service of the Church. If this was the will of her family, it was plainly a will with which she wholly identified. The only question was perhaps what precise form her career in the Church would take, in other words, which order of nuns she would enter. When in 1535 at the age of thirteen she entered the cloister in the Observant Dominican convent of San Vincenzo at Prato, the choice was her own:[9] in

---

7   On Gonzaga, see, in this volume, Oliver Logan, 'San Luigi Gonzaga: Princeling-Jesuit and Model for Catholic Youth', 208–27.

8   For Caterina de' Ricci, see G. M. Bertini, *Santa Caterina de' Ricci* (Florence, 1935). Otherwise, the literature on her is very sparse, except for what is to be found in *the Collana Ricciana. Fonti,* a large collection of sources that have been published under the editorship of Guglielmo Di Agresti: *Fonti I. Santa Caterina de' Ricci. Testimonianze sull'età giovanile* (Florence, 1963); *Fonti II. Libellus de Gestis di Fr. Niccolo Alessi,* 2 vols (Florence, 1964).

9   F. Capes, 'St. Catherine de' Ricci' (1908), <http://www.newadvent.org/cathen/03444a.htm>, accessed 8 July 2009. Though the choice was her own, she had no doubt been influenced by the fact that her family on both sides were *piagnoni.* The term *piagnone* – 'weeper' – was applied to the followers of Savonarola by his enemies. It was one of a battery of such terms of abuse that the characteristic attitudes and behaviour of the Savonarolans attracted. Eventually the *piagnoni* came to be proud of

other words, she deliberately settled for an austere and severe way of life devoted to the pursuit of holiness in a convent where the cult of Savonarola was well established and where, consequently, his works were read and his relics collected.[10]

It is now possible to follow the vicissitudes of Ricci's existence as a cloistered Third Order Dominican nun in the documents, all written by contemporaries,[11] collected by Padre Guglielmo di Agresti, and published in the series *Collana Ricciana* in 1963 and 1964. Ricci's career as a Dominican divides uncontroversially into two fairly clearly demarcated parts. In the first of these she overcame the initial prejudice against her; revealed the true nature of her gifts; convinced all critics that her sanctity was not simulated; established an international reputation; and suggested, in her practice of the Dominican way of life, a pattern of self-reform that could easily be adopted by others. In the second part, which begins about 1552, she also emerged as the unchallenged leader of her community of over a hundred nuns, a skilful administrator, and the correspondent and adviser of princes, cardinals and bishops. She was first elected Prioress of San Vincenzo in 1552, and was thereafter always prioress or sub-prioress; she was prioress seven times.[12] Since one object of this paper is to illustrate the variety of the contributions that could be made to the development of the Counter-Reformation Church, it is the first period of Caterina Ricci's life as a Dominican that is important here, as it is during this period that the nature of her distinctive contribution became clear.

this pejorative description. In the early summer of 1497, Alexander VI had excommunicated Savonarola. That June, the *Piagnoni* drew up a petition in an attempt to convince the pope to lift the excommunication. The list of signatories to this petition is an important source for determining the strength of Savonarola's support. The name of Francesco de' Ricci appears among them. Caterina's mother was a Ricasoli, her stepmother a Diacceto, and members of the Ricasoli and Diacceto families also signed it. See Polizzotto, *Elect Nation*, 18, 451, 457.

[10]   San Vincenzo had been founded in 1503 by nine ladies who had been followers of Savonarola. The foundation was under the jurisdiction of the Vicar General of the Congregation of San Marco, at that time Fra Francesco Salviati. The monastery became a library of Savonarola's works, and a memorial chapel to his memory where his relics were kept. Though Ricci was not a channel for the spirituality of books and relics, she nourished herself with the former and collected the latter: Agresti, *Fonti II*, 2: lxxxviii–ix.

[11]   Since the documents concerned were all produced during Ricci's lifetime, they are probably devoid of hagiographical elaboration.

[12]   In 1552, 1558, 1566, 1572, 1576, 1582 and 1586.

Although by entering San Vincenzo she had got what she had asked for, she did not at first flourish in the cloister. In fact, she created a very poor impression, being considered hysterical, stupid and good for nothing.[13] The main reason why she was regarded in this way may well have been the onset of an incapacitating affliction. Like all accounts of Ricci's early career, the documentation in *Fonti I* and *II* refers to the *ratti* ('seizures') to which she was subject. It is not entirely clear what is meant by the word *ratto*. It is unlikely to have been either rapture or ecstasy in the common acceptance of these terms, since they both suggest delight and joy, whereas it is known that Ricci's *ratti* were frequently accompanied by fearful pain. Something like catatonia, which is characterized by muscular rigidity and mental stupor, sometimes alternating with great excitement and confusion, may well have been involved. There is nothing to suggest that Ricci ever experienced this affliction during childhood. The first attack apparently occurred when she entered the Dominican Order but at that time it occasioned little comment.[14] Though these incapacitating seizures undoubtedly recurred between 1535 and 1540, she remained silent about them, and was consequently misunderstood.

Professed in 1536, she was deeply unhappy and increasingly unwell. Virtually confined to bed from 1539 to 1540, she suffered from a variety of illnesses including hydropsy, fever, kidney stones and asthma. Since she occasionally spat blood, she may also have been suffering from tuberculosis. Nevertheless, on 22 May 1540 she was instantly cured of renal calculus when she emitted thirty to thirty-two kidney stones without pain or suffering,[15] a feat that doctors considered impossible without a miracle.[16] At this juncture, the attitude of the San Vincenzo community towards her softened somewhat. Some were still against her; others thought that they had misjudged her; some did not know what to think. Among these last were her superiors, the most important of whom

---

[13] Domenico di Agresti, 'L'interpretazione savonaroliana di S. Caterina de' Ricci', *Memorie Domenicane* n.s. 29 (1998), 281–340, at 289, 299.

[14] Agresti, *Fonti I*, 27.

[15] How painful the affliction normally is may be judged from the account given of it by John Calvin, a fellow sufferer; see B. Gordon, *Calvin* (New Haven, CT, 2009), 329.

[16] Agresti, *Fonti II*, 2: 348.

was her confessor, her uncle Fra Timoteo Ricci.[17] Was his niece really favoured by God? When eventually it dawned on him that he might well be responsible for a potential charismatic, Timoteo Ricci was fully aware of the importance and the difficulty of his task: he must respect the will of God, but not encourage a merely simulated sanctity. He therefore needed to draw up a full account of all her spiritual experiences. He was assisted in delving into her conscious mind by Suor Maddalena Strozzi, a senior nun, whom he appointed as his niece's guardian.

The fact that her privacy could no longer be respected caused Caterina de' Ricci great distress: she liked neither to talk about herself nor get herself talked about,[18] but it was inevitable. For one thing, there was no possibility of leaving the rest of the community in the dark. By 1542, her gifts had declared themselves visibly through such manifestations as the stigmata. At this stage, Fra Timoteo and the nuns of San Vincenzo were convinced that she was not a sham. Finally the secret leaked out of San Vincenzo when the monastery was subject to official visitation by the superiors of the Dominican Order. Ricci's European fame was virtually inevitable. Requests for her prayers came from members of the French royal family, among others. Much more significant, perhaps, was the interest shown in the case by Filippo Neri, an admirer, like Caterina Ricci and many others at Prato, of Savonarola. It is to be noted, however, that the public response to the future saint was not necessarily favourable. One opponent was the formidable Observant Dominican polemicist and hammer of heretics Fra Ambrogio Catarino, who was a papal theologian at Trent at the very time that Ricci's star was in the ascendant. He also opposed the San Vincenzo cult of Savonarola to which Ricci subscribed.[19]

Ricci's health continued to improve, allegedly with the benefit of divine assistance, but a series of visions was the dominant feature of her spiritual experience in 1541. The series actually began in church on 25 December 1540, when Jesus, Mary and Savonarola exhorted Ricci to lead a virtuous life. The fact that Savonarola was included along with the two members of the Holy Family

---

[17] Agresti, *Fonti I*, 13.
[18] Ibid.
[19] Ambrosio Catharino Polito [sic], *Discorso contra la dottrina e le profetie di Fra Girolamo Savonarola* (Venice, 1548), 22.

suggests that in the minds of the San Vincenzo *piagnoni*, Savon-arola was already a saint. There were twelve more visions in the following year. They varied in content, location, duration, timing and emotional impact. One, a three-hour vision of the Virgin on 25 March 1542, strongly suggests her commitment to the Marian devotion.

In the meantime, however, her career as a visionary was over-shadowed when, at the beginning of February 1542, the *ratti* recurred in a very dramatic and sensational fashion.[20] There was a seizure that lasted from 6 p.m. on Thursday to 10 p.m. on Friday,[21] during which Ricci experienced in her own person the events of Christ's passion.[22] Though there was apparently no way of knowing this at the time, this 'passion ecstasy' was to recur every week for the next ten years. This extraordinary turn of events virtually coincided with the canonical visitation of the monastery by Fra Francesco Romeo da Castiglione, Prior of San Marco, Florence, and Provincial of the Dominican Order. Shortly afterwards, on 31 March, doubtless as part of a 'passion ecstasy', Ricci's body received the marks of the flagellation of Christ.[23] The early spring of 1542 was rich in sensational developments. Two of them occurred on the night of 9–10 April, when, Ricci alleged, she first visited limbo, and then, before dawn, was mystically married to Christ, who appeared to her in glory accompanied by the Queen of Heaven, St Mary Magdalen, St Thomas Aquinas and other saints.[24] Two days later, she was in ecstasy for six hours,[25] and two days after that she received the stigmata permanently.[26]

Were these mystical experiences genuine? The only way in which the authorities could answer this question was by interview and cross-examination, the procedure adopted by Fra Timoteo. They duly arrived at San Vincenzo in order of importance. On 30 March 1543, the Dominican General Alberto Las Casas himself

---

[20] Agresti, *Fonti II*, 2: 348.

[21] Agresti, *Fonti I*, 28–29.

[22] Ricci's passion ecstasies were not unprecedented, as the case of the *beata* Stefana Quinzani shows: see Cordelia Warr, 'Performing the Passion: Strategies for Salvation in the Life of Stefana Quinzani (d. 1530)', in Peter Clarke and Tony Claydon, eds, *The Church, the Afterlife and the Fate of the Soul*, SCH 45 (Woodbridge, 2009), 218–27.

[23] Agresti, *Fonti II*, 2: 348.

[24] Agresti, *Fonti I*, 32.

[25] Agresti, *Fonti II*, 2: 349.

[26] Ibid.

visited the monastery.[27] Cosimo de' Medici, who in 1545 was to expel the San Marco *piagnoni* from his territories,[28] likewise needed reassurance. In 1543, Duke Cosimo sent his wife, Eleanora di Toledo, to inquire on his behalf.[29] Finally, at some point before 1549, Cardinal Roberto Pucci made investigations on behalf of Pope Paul III.[30] None of these visitors could find any evidence for supposing that Ricci was a fraud.

After 1544, her visions became infrequent. She gradually assumed a more important role in the running of the monastery: on 29 September 1547, she was named vicar;[31] on 21 December of the same year she was named sub-prioress.[32] Ricci was elected prioress for the first time in 1552.[33] In the meantime she had probably been slowly recovering from her illness, for if an attack came on while she was performing one of the liturgical functions required of an official in the monastery, she was nevertheless able to carry on, though no doubt with some difficulty.[34]

It is clear that by 1552 Caterina de' Ricci was no longer a controversial or suspicious figure in the Church. Had she been so, she would never have been appointed Prioress of San Vincenzo. It had therefore taken at least fourteen years for the nature of her remarkable gifts to make itself plain and for her to win full acceptance. We have then an account – the account of Ricci's contemporaries – of her career in the Dominican Order up to 1552. How is this account to be understood? I propose the following interpretation.

It is necessary to concentrate on the *ratti*, which, I contend, were in the first place the manifestation of a neurological disorder that led to periodic fits, perhaps catatonic in nature. They occurred only after she had entered the Dominican Order, where they threatened her participation in the life that she ardently desired: since they were recurrent, she was potentially a chronic invalid, totally unsuitable for the rigours of life in an Observant Dominican convent. In

---

[27] Ibid.
[28] Polizzotto, *Elect Nation*, 432–3.
[29] Agresti, *Fonti II*, 2: 349.
[30] Agresti, *Fonti I*, 49.
[31] Agresti, *Fonti II*, 2: 349.
[32] Ibid.
[33] Ibid. 350.
[34] Agresti, 'L'interpretazione', 289.

that case the prospect of rejection and return to her own family in Florence stared her in the face. Dejection and lack of involvement in the life of the San Vincenzo community would be a perfectly comprehensible reaction to this situation.

The turning point in her life came when instead of bewailing her condition, she accepted it as the will of God: 'Nella sua voluntate è nostra pace'. In accepting her affliction as the will of God, she was imitating Christ. Her suffering in the 'passion *ratti*' ran parallel to his on the cross. The reproduction on her own body of the stigmata and the marks of the Flagellation was the psycho-somatic consequence of her identification with Christ. She was the martyred but living image of Christ crucified. The culmination of the suffering came in the Thursday to Friday *ratti*, but was certainly involved in the *ratti* on other days.[35] Her suffering had a shocking and terrifying effect on those who saw it. It demanded a change in the life of all spectators. Her appearance seemed tinged with the supernatural. She was 'one of Christ's snares to drag us to a continual meditation on his passion and life, in order to make us perfect'.[36]

Ricci's preoccupation with Savonarola was predictable, given her family background and the strong *piagnone* influence on the foundation of the monastery and on the ethos of the San Vincenzo community. There are in the documentation at least three signs of this commitment: one is the vision of 25 December 1540 mentioned above when Jesus, Mary and Savonarola exhorted Ricci to lead a virtuous life; another is the fact that she attributed several of the 'cures' through which her health improved to the influence of Savonarola;[37] and the third is that on 18 December 1541 she had a vision of Savonarola, who warned her about her conduct and announced that the city of Florence was threatened with the wrath of God and imminent scourges (as, according to Savonarola, it had been in 1494 and earlier).[38] The strongest evidence of the Savonarolan commitment is her wholehearted participation in the San Vincenzo cult of Savonarola, which included, for instance, the procession of 23 May 1549 in his honour,[39] but more particularly

---

[35] Agresti, *Fonti I*, 9–10.
[36] Agresti, *Fonti I*, 10.
[37] Agresti, 'L'interpretazione', 284.
[38] Ibid. 287.
[39] Ibid. 294.

the view that Savonarola was a saint, prophet and martyr, a view epitomized by the community's collection of ashes, together with images of the 'saint' either in wood or stone, with the words 'saint and martyr' written on them, as Catarino relates.[40] But in fact much in the Savonarolan message must have been indifferent or even uncongenial to her, notably his active involvement in the political life of the city and his promise of a glorious future for the city of Florence if the citizens remained faithful to their inspirational leader, though she would, no doubt, have sympathized with the attempts of the *piagnoni* to make arrangements for the care of the poor and the sick. Savonarolan spirituality, mysticism and theology of the cross were, of course, close to her own.

Ricci's modified commitment to Savonarolism was in accordance with the spirit of the Counter-Reformation: the closer the Church came to 1545 and the Council of Trent, the less relevant the Savonarolan reform programme became,[41] but the more Savonarola himself, stripped of his revolutionary, prophetic and apocalyptic mantle, could be presented as a potential Counter-Reformation saint, 'the very model of conformity and of the reforming zeal demanded by the Counter-Reformation Church'.[42] If, as is claimed, the central theme of Ricci's correspondence was the spiritual reform of the Church, it was not, apparently, a problem that she confronted before 1552. If, as is also alleged, her spirituality was above all conceived as a combat,[43] then firstly the combat would have been fought in every aspect of everyday life, especially perhaps in prayer, and it would have been against all the forces of the world, the flesh and the devil by which she was deflected from the identification with Christ and the total subjection to his will that she sought. However this may be, the spiritual combat was

---

[40] Polito, *Contra la dottrina et le profetie di Savonarola*, 18ʳ.

[41] The Savonarolan reform programme originated at a time when the Church, at a very low ebb during the pontificate of Alexander VI, seemed to ignore the obvious need for reform. When the Lutheran revolt made church reform essential, the problem was still evaded by the Medici popes Leo X and Clement VII, but Paul III eventually took the necessary step of calling a Council. Thereafter, the papacy became increasingly intolerant of all independent inititatives, such as that of Savonarola. The Counter-Reformation Church spoke for itself.

[42] Polizzotto, *Elect Nation*, 440.

[43] 'The Friars Preachers in Italy', translation [1963?] of Part B of the article in *DSp*, <http://www.domcentral.org/study/ashley/ds02ital2.htm>, accessed 14 August 2009.

surely moderated by that other great influence in Ricci's life, the Marian devotion.[44]

Ricci's outstanding contribution to the Counter-Reformation Church was the unwitting outcome of her response to illness. It was based on a radical version of the imitation of Christ. Though it was individual it had a wider reference. The sight of her suffering demanded a change in the life of all spectators. Unlike Savonarola's ambitious programme for church reform, Ricci's version of the imitation of Christ offered no challenges or threats to the hierarchical Church.

★ ★ ★

It is difficult to think of anyone whose way of living the Dominican life was more opposed to that of Caterina de' Ricci than Pope Pius V.[45] The use of his title, rather than his name, is indicative of the fact that the contrast was most acute during the six years from 1566 to 1572 when Michele Ghislieri occupied the throne of St Peter, but the contrast had a long history. Whereas Ricci was born into a prosperous Florentine family, Ghislieri was born at Bosco in 1504 into a poor Piedmontese family of shepherds, and was himself a shepherd when young. At fourteen, he entered the Dominican Order at Voghera, and presumably educated in the normal Dominican-Thomist way in philosophy and theology. He was ordained in 1528. His employment with the Inquisition began shortly afterwards, but there is no information available about the way he was trained for the job. In fact we know very little about him before, by his diligence and perseverance in his post, he attracted the attention of the head of the Inquisition, Cardinal Gian Pietro Carafa.[46] He was thereafter rapidly promoted, and promotion made him an object of public interest. Thus, for instance, at the beginning of the conclave of 1565–6 Cosimo de' Medici, Duke of Florence, described Ghislieri as devout, but obstinate and unbending.[47] He was, in fact, a zealot,

---

44 On the Marian devotion of Caterina de' Ricci, see G. di Agresti, 'Mediazione mariana nell' Epistolario di Santa Caterina', *Rivista di ascetica e mistica* 3 (1958), 243–55.

45 For Pius V, see L. von Pastor, *The History of the Popes from the Close of the Middle Ages*, ed. and trans. F. I. Antrobus and R. F. Kerr, 24 vols (London, 1929), vols 17, 18; Anon., *San Pio V e la problematica del suo tempo* (Alessandria, 1972); Nicole Lemaître, *Saint Pie V* (Paris, 1994); M. Guasco and A. Torre, eds, *Pio V nella società e nella politica del suo tempo* (Bologna, 2005).

46 See M. Firpo, 'Introduzione', in Guasco and Torre, eds, *Pio V*, 9–25, at 10.

47 Pastor, *History*, 18: 11.

very determined and with a strong sense of duty. In other words, he would shirk none of his many responsibilities, even though for most of them he was totally unprepared by experience. Here is an outline of the many problems with which Ghislieri had to deal during his short pontificate.

His first problem was to put his own house into order. He was, after all, Bishop of Rome, and it was therefore his duty to act like any good bishop in administering and organizing his diocese. He refused to have this done by proxy. The pope himself therefore visited all the churches in Rome.[48] He was outraged by the prevalent moral laxity, and since he always preferred justice to mercy,[49] all such offences, especially blasphemy, sodomy and concubinage, were ruthlessly punished.[50] All prostitutes were to be driven out of the Borgo;[51] and all defamatory pamphlets against princes, prelates and their officials were prohibited.

The machinery of papal government was also his personal responsibility. The Curia had long been a byword for corruption and inefficiency. The reform of the Datary,[52] the Penitentiary,[53] the Apostolic Camera[54] and the Segnatura[55] duly followed. Likewise, as bishop, it was his duty to introduce the reform decrees of the Council of Trent into the diocese of Rome.[56] One of the most important of these reform decrees required the bishops to reside in their own dioceses. It was particularly important for the pope to make this his responsibility since the reason why many bishops did not reside in their own dioceses was that they resided in Rome instead.[57] The pope could of course grant a dispensation to regularize non-residence, but all bishops who could not provide a legitimate reason for non-residence were forthwith returned to their duties elsewhere. Moreover, the Tridentine legislation required not

[48] Ibid. 17: 179–81.
[49] Ibid. 101, 136.
[50] Ibid. 86.
[51] Ibid. 90.
[52] Ibid. 172–3.
[53] Ibid. 175. See also E. Göller, *Die päpstliche Pönitentiarie von ihrem Ursprung bis zu ihrer Umgestaltung unter Pius V*, 2 vols in 4 parts, Bibliothek des königlich Preussichen historischen Instituts in Rom 3, 4, 7, 8 (Rome, 1907–11), 2/1: 128–31.
[54] Pastor, *History*, 17: 178.
[55] Ibid. 179.
[56] Ibid. 98.
[57] Ibid. 148, 187–90, 216–18.

only the establishment of seminaries for the training of priests,[58] but also the production of a Roman Catechism,[59] the reform of the Breviary[60] and the publication of an error-free version of the Vulgate.[61] Only the last of these was delayed. In the meantime Pius made arrangements for the reform of the religious orders.[62]

These labours, substantial though they were, were probably less onerous than those Ghislieri had to undertake in directing papal policy in areas outside Italy. Some of his responsibilities outside Italy were continuous with those inside. This was particularly the case with the implementation of the decrees of the Council of Trent. Others were the consequence of the Protestant Reformation. What areas lost to Protestantism could be recovered by the Church? The importance of this issue is underlined by the work of St Peter Canisius (1521–97) in Germany, Austria, Bohemia and Switzerland. In areas like France and the Low Countries, where Protestantism had not replaced Catholicism but was nevertheless strongly represented, what could be done to aid the Catholic party? Even where Protestantism had, formally at any rate, triumphed, as in England and Scotland, those who persisted in Catholicism could still be supported. Sometimes the problem was complicated by the attitude of the secular authorities. Spain was a particular problem. There was trouble enough with the Iberian peninsula. Philip II had a very exalted idea of his rights over the Church in Spain, but he was also the ruler of a vast empire in Europe and America. How far, for instance, was he prepared to tolerate papal attempts to legislate for the Indies? The case was much the same with Portugal and the Portuguese seaborne empire in Brazil, India, the East Indies and Japan. The cooperation of the monarch could not be taken for granted. However, Pius V's greatest diplomatic success was, perhaps, the formation of the Holy League – the coalition of Spain, the Republic of Venice, the Republic of Genoa, the Duchy of Savoy and the Knights Hospitallers that fought the successful battle against the Turkish fleet at Lepanto in 1571.[63]

Despite the enormous claims on Pius V's time and energy implied

---

[58] Ibid. 211.
[59] Ibid. 193.
[60] Ibid. 196.
[61] Ibid. 199.
[62] Ibid. 240–87.
[63] Ibid. 18: 353–99.

by the activities outlined above, his main preoccupation during the short period when he was pope was the elimination from Italy by means of the Inquisition of every trace of the Protestant heresy. The fact is that the Inquisition, in one form or another, had been the main object of his concern and interest since shortly after 1528, when he was ordained. *Pace* the hagiographers, he never had an academic career.[64] It is therefore surprising that he was ever able to become an inquisitor, since as Michael Tavuzzi has recently shown the usual practice in the Lombard Congregation was to appoint as inquisitors only middle-aged men who were well qualified both by education and experience.[65] But certainly he was well fitted for the job by his stubborn determination to carry out his duties even at the risk of death,[66] and so was promoted in due course. At first he had merely been an inquisitorial vicar, but he became inquisitor of Como in 1546 and inquisitor in Bergamo by 1548 at the latest. Sometime in the late 1540s or early 1550s, Gian Pietro Carafa, Grand Inquisitor and subsequently Pope Paul IV (1555–9), a kindred spirit, recognized his talents. His promotion was assured: First Commissary of the Holy Office, 1551–7; Bishop of Sutri and Nepi, 1556; Bishop of Mondovì, 1560; Grand Inquisitor, 1557–66.[67]

The high-profile cases which he instigated or in which he was involved as an inquisitor make very interesting reading. Listed in the order in which the *processi* culminated in a hearing before the Inquisition tribunal, the names of the accused and the dates when the *processi* were heard are as follows:

> 1555–60: Lorenzo Davidico;[68]
> 1557–9: Giovanni Morone;
> 1558: Girolamo Savonarola;
> 1566–7: Pietro Carnesecchi;[69]

---

[64] It is true that he eventually held the degree of master of theology, but that was conferred on him by Julius III *ex apostolica auctoritate* in 1553; see M. Tavuzzi, *Renaissance Inquisitors* (Leiden, 2007), 210.

[65] Ibid. 38–44.

[66] Ibid. 210.

[67] For these details of his early career, see ibid.

[68] For details of the Davidico trial, see D. Marcatto, ed., *Il processo inquisitoriale di Lorenzo Davidico (1555–1560)* (Florence, 1992); M. Firpo, *Nel labirinto del mondo. Lorenzo Davidico tra santi, eretici, inquisitori* (Florence, 1992).

[69] For details of the Carnesecchi trial and its importance, see M. Firpo and D. Marcatto, eds, *I processi inquisitoriali di Pietro Carnesecchi (1557–1567)*, 2: *Il processo sotto Pio V* (Vatican City, 2000); also M. Firpo and P. Simoncelli, 'I processi inquisitoriali

1569–70: Niccolo Franco;
1567–9: Aonio Paleario;
1566–76: Bartolomé Carranza.

These are the facts, but how they are to be understood is the subject of debate. The first four names in the list figure in a very influential interpretation of the history of the Church in sixteenth-century Italy that we owe to Massimo Firpo,[70] who claims that the conventional interpretation of Italian religious history in this period developed by Hubert Jedin, for example, is profoundly mistaken. Whereas the conventional view is that of a smooth continuity in which the Church was reformed by the implementation of the canons and decrees of the Council of Trent, Firpo sees almost the reverse of this. For him, the initiative was seized by the Congregation of the Inquisition, which ruthlessly imposed its own priorities on the rest of the Church. This policy originated with Gian Pietro Carafa, who was the first Grand Inquisitor after the reconstitution of the Roman Inquisition by the bull *Licet ab initio* of 1542. For him the great nightmare was that the Catholic Church would be perverted and corrupted by hidden heretics in high places. His suspicions centred in particular on two cardinals, Pole and Morone, both of whom in due course would be *papabile*. At all costs, they had to be prevented from occupying the throne of St Peter. From 1542 onwards, Carafa began to collect evidence against them, and to move against the small fry who could be coerced into providing the appropriate information. As part of this campaign, the Inquisition systematically scuppered the chances of all those of whom it disapproved in all the conclaves of the sixteenth century after 1542. Wherever possible, it promoted its own candidates. Only two of these ever attended the Council of Trent, which Carafa himself thought unnecessary.[71] The ruthlessness of the campaign against suspected sympathizers with Luther and others generated an atmosphere of fear and uncertainty. The Inquisition propagated

---

contro Savonarola (1558) e Carnesecchi (1558–1567). Una proposta di interpretazione', *Rivista di storia e letteratura religiosa* 18 (1982), 200–52.

70   For an introduction to Firpo's views, see M. Firpo, *Inquisizione Romana e Controriforma. Studi sul Cardinal Giovanni Morone e il suo processo d'eresia* (Bologna, 1992), 7–28.

71   Marcello Cervini attended the first phase of the Council (1545–7), when he was one of the legates along with del Monte and Pole; Felice Peretti di Montalto attended the last phase (1562–3).

a view of itself as the privileged instrument in a providential design for the safeguarding of the truth and of the Church, the invincible custodian of the truth. Ultimately, faith became synonymous with obedience to the dictates of the Church, and heresy with disobedience. The cultural consequences of all this, especially the lazy authoritarian conformism, were disastrous.

Firpo's is of course a highly controversial view, and this paper is no place for reviewing the controversy. But if he is even partly correct, he has transformed our view of Pius V. Pius V is, of course, important for his contribution to the Church in implementing the decrees of the Council of Trent,[72] safeguarding Catholic interests against the encroachments of powerful monarchs, and weakening Ottoman sea power, if only temporarily, via the Holy League. But he is immensely more important as the Inquisitor Pope of Firpo's account, who re-established the Carafa policy after the dangerous hiatus of the papacy of its opponent, Pius IV, and passed it on unimpaired to Felice Peretti di Montalto (Sixtus V, 1585–90) and Giulio Antonio Santoro, two dedicated inquisitors whom Ghislieri himself had elevated to the cardinalate. On Firpo's hypothesis Pius V was therefore one of the creators of Tridentine Catholicism and therefore one of the creators of the modern Western world. He was certainly a saint, because the Church made him one, and the Church cannot be wrong in canonization. Aquinas argued this, and, in the sixteenth century, Catarino argued it too.[73] But whether we can describe Ghislieri, devout though he was, in terms of sanctity and saintliness, is not so certain. Do determination, zeal, integrity, severity, inflexibility, austerity and intransigence, either singly or in combination, constitute saintliness or sanctity? There may, it seems, be more to sanctity than being a saint, spirituality for instance. 'Devoid of spirituality' is a charge that could never be made against Caterina de' Ricci, the *piagnone* mystic, the hub of whose life was the Marian devotion, the theology of the cross and the imitation of Christ.

Nevertheless, however different these two Dominican saints were, Ricci resembled Ghislieri in one important respect: she never

---

[72] This judgement remains true, although Gigliola Fragnito has recently shown that Pius V was working to modify the Trent decrees that he implemented; see G. Fragnito, 'Pio V e la Censura', in Guasco and Torre, eds, *Pio V*, 129–58.

[73] Ambrosius Catharinus Politi, 'De certa gloria, invocatione ac veneratione sanctorum disputationes', in idem, *Opuscula* (Lyons, 1542), 2–88, esp. 10–18, cf. Thomas Aquinas, *Quaestiones de quodlibet*, IX.a.16.

challenged the authority of the Apostolic See. How important conformity in the Counter-Reformation and the post-Tridentine Church was can be suggested in a variety of ways, but only two examples will be given here.

In the first place, consider Paul IV's reaction when in consistory in 1558 the Jesuit Laynez read out some parts of an anti-Savonarolan tract that the Dominican polemicist Catarino had written at some time around 1548.[74] Catarino had derided Savonarola's prophecies and tried to show that the prophet's doctrine was Lutheran *avant la lettre*. In this work, he also, without naming her, virtually dismissed Caterina de' Ricci as a weak, fragile, ignorant and gullible woman, and rejected the cult of Savonarola to which she subscribed. What Paul IV saw in Catarino's tract was not an exposé of doctrinal error – Lutheranism *avant la lettre* – but something that he found much more objectionable: a defiance, like that of Luther, of papal authority, 'He turned to the consistory and began almost to shout, "This is Martin Luther, this doctrine of his is pestiferous, what are you doing. Very Reverend Monsignori, what are you waiting for? This doctrine must be prohibited, take it away, do you not see how this man is fighting against the Apostolic Church" '.[75]

A *processo* against Savonarola was the consequence. It was presided over by Ghislieri as Grand Inquisitor from 1557 to 1566. Nevertheless, the Dominican Order rallied to Savonarola's defence, their advocates cleverly arguing before the Inquisition tribunal not on doctrinal grounds but on the grounds of canon law. The upshot was that Savonarola was declared innocent: he was no schismatic, but one who had always defended the supreme power and authority of the pope. Changes nevertheless had to be made to some of Savonarola's published works and some were placed on the Roman Index. The Savonarola who survived the *processo* of 1558 was not the apocalyptic millenarian prophet, but a pious friar, an ascetic, a writer of devotional works, a model of Counter-Reformation conformity and reforming zeal, who on perfectly respectable grounds had disregarded his excommunication by Pope Alexander VI. It seemed, therefore, that there was no objection in principle to beatifying him and then, when the time was ripe, to canonizing him. Yet Savonarola has never been beatified.

---

74 Polito, *Contra la dottrina et le profetie di Savonarola*.
75 Firpo and Simoncelli, 'Processi inquisitoriali', 216.

The second example that I have chosen to suggest the importance of conformity in the Counter-Reformation and the post-Tridentine Church starts from that fact. Why was he not beatified? It was certainly not for want of trying. His cult continued during the pontificate of Clement VIII (1592–1605), for example. Clement VIII, who came from a *piagnone* family and had close relationships with Filippo Neri and Caterina de' Ricci, gave many *piagnoni* the impression that the canonization of Savonarola was within reach.[76] But nothing happened. The cult was revived in the middle of the nineteenth century when the Dominican Convent of San Marco in Florence became the meeting place for a group of devotees known as the *New Piagnoni*.[77] This group included Fra Vincenzo Marchese, Luigi Passerini, Isidoro del Lungo, Cesare Guasti and Alessandro Gherardi. Savonarola's biographer, Pasquale Villari, shared their ideals and objectives.[78] Again nothing happened. Only in the twentieth century, when the movement for the canonization of Savonarola began anew on the grounds that his excommunication and execution were not legal, do we get a clear idea of what is wrong: there was strong opposition from the Jesuits, among others, who believed that Savonarola's attacks on the papacy constituted a serious crime.[79] Both the movement for canonization and the opposition to it continued right up to the end of the century.[80]

It seems reasonable, therefore, to infer, firstly, that the Counter-

---

[76] Dall'Aglio, *Savonarola e il savonarolismo*, 186.

[77] Weinstein, *Savonarola*, 3.

[78] Ibid. 4.

[79] Anon., 'Girolamo Savonarola', 24 July 2009, <http://simple.wikipedia.org/wiki/Girolamo_Savonarola>, accessed 10 August 2009.

[80] <http://findarticles.com/p/articles/mi_m1141/is_12_35/ai_53705898/>, accessed 20 July 2009. The *National Catholic Reporter* of 22 January 1999 carried an article by John L. Allen Jr with the title 'Jesuits and Dominicans square off anew over Savonarola – Dispute over whether to Canonize Dominican Friar Girolamo Savonarola'. This article referred to the historical commission convened in 1998 by Cardinal Silvano Piovanelli in conjunction with the five-hundredth anniversary of Savonarola's death. The commission, it seemed, was likely to issue a positive report, which could clear the way for an investigation by the Congregation for the Causes of Saints. In the summer of 1998, *L'Osservatore Romano*, the semi-official newspaper of the Holy See, paid tribute to Savonarola, referring to him as 'a tireless preacher for the moral reform of civil society'. Yet, in spite of these favourable omens, nothing has happened so far. One possible reason for this may be the attitude of the Jesuits. At the beginning of 1999, the Jesuit journal *La Civiltà Cattolica* referred to Savonarola in disparaging terms, and on 7 January 1999 the Jesuit journalist Fra Ferdinando Castelli told the *Daily Telegraph* that 'Savonarola rebelled against ecclesiastical authority. We do not believe that he was a religious man worthy of sanctification.'

Reformation view that faith is synonymous with obedience to the dictates of the Church and heresy with disobedience is remarkably tenacious; secondly, that, as things stand at the moment, conformity and obedience to the demands of the Church are necessary, but not sufficient, conditions for beatification; thirdly, that the exoneration of Savonarola in the *processo* of 1558 may have served the interests of the Inquisition at that time (Firpo and Simoncelli argue that it was the price that Ghislieri was prepared to pay for the support of the Dominican Order in the prosecution of Morone)[81] but it had no other significance; Savonarola's defiance of Alexander VI was neither forgotten nor forgiven. However, despite Catarino's attempt to inculpate all *piagnoni* who practised the cult of Savonarola, especially those at San Vincenzo, and Ricci chief among them, Ricci, though an ardent supporter of Savonarola, was safe because she had never criticized the Church.[82]

The Counter-Reformation, as understood in this paper, did not merely counter the Reformation: as H. O. Evennett argued,[83] it was a multi-dimensional phenomenon. For instance, while Ghislieri, as inquisitor and pope, did indeed devote most of his life to stamping out the Protestant heresy, Ricci, the Third Order Dominican nun, contributed to the development of Counter-Reformation spirituality and mysticism. The contrast between these two saints suggests that sanctity is not the invariable concomitant of sainthood. Nor is it sufficient for beatification, as we learn from the case of Savonarola, whose disciple Ricci was: even when purged of his prophetic aspirations and political ambitions, the inspirational prior of San Marco remains unforgiven.

University of Chichester

---

[82]   There is no evidence whatsoever that the Inquisition ever contemplated a *processo* against Ricci, even though Catarino might have been pointing in that direction. See Polito, *Contra la dottrina et le profetie di Savonarola*, 24^r–24^v: 'It would be good and necessary, a part of the bishop's job, in cities where there are people who have images or relics of Fra Girolamo, to give strict instructions that such images or relics be declared and that under the penalty of grave censures, no one should have the effrontery to venerate them. All conventicles where sacrifices are made and common prayers directed to Fra Girolamo against the express command of the sacred Canons … should be prohibited.'

[83]   H. O. Evennett, *The Spirit of the Counter-Reformation* (Cambridge, 1968).

VISUALIZING STIGMATA: STIGMATIC SAINTS AND CRISES OF REPRESENTATION IN LATE MEDIEVAL AND EARLY MODERN ITALY

by CORDELIA WARR

At the time of the Lord Pope Benedict XII [1334–42] it happened that in a city near Avignon in which the [Franciscan] brothers had a convent, on a certain day while all the friars were in the choir celebrating the holy office, two friars belonging to a different order arrived and walked around. Then one of them saw the image of St Francis with the holy stigmata depicted on the wall, [and] he said to his companion: 'Those friars minor want their saint to be like Christ'. And he took up his knife and said: 'I want to efface those stigmata from that image so that he [St Francis] does not appear like Christ'. And having said this, he carried out the deed. And when he had expunged the five stigmata, they began to shed blood abundantly. Seeing this, greatly amazed, he said to his companion, 'Aah! What shall I do?' His companion replied: 'You've really committed a mortal sin! I advise you to run quickly to a confessor and confess'. He did this. … The confessor counselled him that he should run to the pope and tell him everything about this and receive advice from him about what should be done. … When the pope heard this, he asked him if it was truly thus. The friar declared with an oath that it was thus. Then the pope said: 'I particularly want to see this miracle'. And when he came to that place, he saw blood flowing abundantly from those holy stigmata in the image. Then, greatly amazed, the pope knelt down in front of the image: [and] raising his hands to heaven he said: 'St Francis, forgive the sin of this miserable sinner, because I promise to you that I want to institute that the feast of your stigmata should be celebrated, and above all I want to enjoin your friars that throughout the whole order they must solemnly celebrate the feast of your stigmata'. And as soon as the lord pope had made this vow, the blood ceased to flow.[1]

This mid-fourteenth-century text brings to the fore some of the issues surrounding St Francis of Assisi's miraculous stigmata and their representation in the visual arts. Other miracle stories from the thirteenth and fourteenth centuries, such as those included in the *vitae* of St Francis written by Thomas of Celano and Bonaventure, could be cited.[2] They show that many experienced difficulty in giving credence to such an unusual miracle and that they objected to the perceived intention on the part of the Franciscans to promote their founder as a saint who conformed more closely to Christ than any other saint. They also reflect the very real resistance to depictions of Francis with the stigmata, which resulted in violent reactions in the decades after his death, including effacing and erasure.[3]

St Francis (d. 1226) is probably the best known stigmatic, yet he

[1]   Ferdinandus Doelle, 'De institutione festi SS. Stigmatum e Cod. Wratislaviensi narratio', *Archivum Franciscanum Historicum* 3 (1910), 169–70, quoting from a codex in Wroclaw University Library (XV.I.F.280(5) fol. 291ʳ): 'Tempore domini pape Benedicti XII accidit prope Auinionem in una civitate, in qua fratres habent claustrem, quadem die, dum fratres omnes essent in choro in officio divino, venerunt duo fratres alterius religionis et per ambitum transierunt. Tunc unus illorum vidit ymaginem sancti Francisci cum sacris stigmatibus in pariete depictam, dixit socio suo: "Illi minores volunt sanctum suum Christo assimilari". Et accepit cultellum suum et dixit: "Ego volo stigmata illa effodere ymagini isti, ut non appareat Christo similis". Et sic dictum opere perfecit. Et cum illa quinque stigmata effodisset, tunc inceperunt largiter sanguinem emanare. Quod ille videns, valde stupefactus, dixit socio suo: "Eya, quid faciam?" Qui respondit: "Valde mortale egisti. Sed consulo, cito curre ad confessorem et confitere". Quod et fecit. ... Qui consuluit sibi, ut curreret ad papam, et sibi omnia hec intimaret et consilium ab eo reciperet, quid facturus esset. ... Quod papa audiens, quesivit ab eo: si res in veritate sic esset. Tunc ille iuramento firmavit sic esse. Tunc papa ait: "Ego utique videre istud mirum volo". Et cum illuc venisset, vidit de illis sacris stigmatibus ymaginis sanguinem largiter emanare. Tunc dominus papa valde stupefactus, flexit genua ante ymaginem; extensis manibus in celum dixit: "Sancte Francisce, dimitte hanc noxam illi miserrimo peccatori, quia promitto tibi, quod volo instituere festum tuorum stigmatum celebrandum, et precipue volo precipere fratribus tuis, ut per totum ordinem debent celebrare festum tuorum stigmatum sollempniter". Et statim voto facto a domino papa, sanguis cessavit manare.'

[2]   See St Bonaventure, 'Major Life of Saint Francis', trans. Benen Fahy, in Marion Habig, ed., *Saint Francis of Assisi* (Chicago, IL, 1979), 749–50 (2.1.4), 752–3 (2.1.6); Thomas of Celano, *The Life of Saint Francis of Assisi and the Treatise of Miracles*, trans. Catherine Bolton (Assisi, 1997), 332–3 (2: 6–7), 333–4 (2: 8–9).

[3]   André Vauchez, 'Les Stigmates de Saint François et leurs détracteurs dans les derniers siècles du Moyen Âge', *Mélanges d'archéologie et d'histoire de l'École française de Rome: Moyen Âge et temps modernes* 80 (1968), 595–625, at 603.

was only one out of an increasing number in the thirteenth, four-teenth and fifteenth centuries, many of whom were Dominicans and the majority of whom were women. One, St Catherine of Siena (d. 1380), was, like St Francis, the subject of controversy both in respect of her receipt of the stigmata and her representation with the stigmata. Her biographer, Raymond of Capua (d. 1399), had been quite clear in his *vita* that at the moment Catherine received the stigmata the saint had successfully requested that they remain invisible, although they caused her incredible pain until her death.[4] Therefore, even those who accepted the fact of Catherine's stigmatization often had serious reservations about their depiction in paintings, prints or sculpture. In Catherine's bull of canonization in 1461 Pius II had avoided the question of the stigmata.[5] Indeed, some commentators actively denied that Catherine had stigmata. The Franciscan preacher Roberto Caracciolo da Lecce (d. 1495)[6] asserted that no mention had been made of the stigmata on the day of Catherine's canonization and used this to pour doubts on claims that she was a stigmatic:

> I, a sinner, who wrote this sermon, … was in Rome in the year of Our Lord 1461, in the third year of the pontificate of Pius [II], when the aforementioned pope, the Holy Spirit wishing it, canonized St Catherine with solemn celebrations. No mention was made then about the stigmata either in the life or the miracles of Catherine; no picture with the stigmata was reported; moreover no mention was made about the stig-mata in the bull [of canonization] … Furthermore, on the day of the canonization, in the afternoon, I gave a sermon to the people in the church of the Minerva [Santa Maria sopra Minerva] belonging to the order of preachers [Dominicans] …[7]

4   Raymond of Capua, *The Life of Catherine of Siena*, intro. and trans. Conleth Kearns (Washington, DC, 1994), 186 (2.6.195).
5   An Italian translation of the bull of canonization is published in Alfonso Capel-celatro, *Storia di Santa Caterina e del papato del suo tempo* (Florence, 1858), 477–86 (Schiarimento XI).
6   See Hughes Oliphant Old, *The Reading and Preaching of the Scriptures in the Worship of the Christian Church*, 3: *The Medieval Church* (Grand Rapids, MI, 1999), 566–7, for a short biography of Roberto.
7   Quoted in Saturnino Mencherini, *Codice diplomatico della Verna e delle SS. Stimate di S. Francesco d'Assisi nel VII° centenario del gran prodigio* (Florence, 1924), 94–5: 'Ego peccator, qui hunc sermonem confeci, … eramque Rome anno Domini 1461, anno

Speaking on the day of the canonization, Fra Roberto wasted no time in sowing doubts in the very church where Catherine was buried. His concern to argue against St Catherine's stigmata was just one element in a campaign on the part of the Franciscan Order to deny either the existence of Catherine's stigmata or their importance in comparison with those of St Francis, and also to ensure that they were not represented in visual art. The list of papal pronouncements on the subject of the represention of Catherine's stigmata is long. Pope Sixtus IV, for example, strongly supported his brother Franciscans. On 6 September 1472, he prohibited stigmata being painted in images of Catherine, with excommunication as the penalty for those who disobeyed, and this was reiterated in 1475 and 1480. The controversy rumbled on until, on 27 November 1599, Clement VIII instituted a commission of cardinals to make a decision about Catherine of Siena's stigmata and their representation, but it was not until 1630 that Urban VIII officially decided in favour of Catherine's stigmata.[8]

This paper will focus on the crisis of representation elicited by depictions of Catherine's stigmata, using the writings of two of her Dominican apologists: Tommaso Caffarini (d. 1434) and Gregorio Lombardelli (d. 1613). Their discussions demonstrate some of the wider issues surrounding the representations of saints and how these were articulated at the beginning of the fifteenth and the beginning of the seventeenth centuries, before and after the Council of Trent. The council had stressed the pedagogical importance of religious images and the central role of the bishop in ensuring that no images were allowed 'which give occasion of dangerous error to the unlettered'.[9] Some of its deliberations were pertinent

tertio Pii pontificis maximi, quando Pontifex praefatus, volente Spiritu Sancto, sanctam Catherinam solemni celebritate canonizavit. Nulla tunc a referentibus et vitam et miracula Caterinae de Stigmatibus facta est mentio; nulla pictura cum Stigmatibus fuit delata; nulla insuper in Bulla … de Stigmatibus mentio habita est. Ego insuper in die Canonizationis sermonem ad populum habui post prandium in ecclesia Minervae ordinis Praedicatorum'. Roberto Caracciolo's sermon is discussed by Diega Giunta, 'La questione delle stimmate alle origini della iconografia cateriniana e la fortuna del tema nel corso dei secoli', in Luigi Trenti and Bente Klange Addabbo, eds, *Con l'occhio e col lume* (Siena, 1999), 319–48, at 319–22.

8   Ibid. 322–4. The relevant texts are published in Mencherini, *Codice diplomatico*, 109–11, 117–23, 134–5, 178.

9   N. P. Tanner, ed., *Decrees of the Ecumenical Councils*, 2 vols (London, 1990), 2: 775 (session 25, 3–4 December 1563). The classic study of art after the Council of Trent

to depictions of those things, like Catherine's stigmata, which were invisible: uneducated people were to be taught that 'the Godhead is not pictured because it cannot be seen with human eye or expressed in figures or colours'.[10] Such concerns demonstrate the importance of visual images as a part of religious experience. Both before and after the council they were used as aids to meditation and teaching, preachers would refer to them in their sermons, and people would keep small private devotional paintings in their houses as well as having access to larger, more prestigious works in local churches. The correct depiction of saints was, therefore, of considerable concern to those charged with ensuring religious orthodoxy. The debate over the representation of Catherine of Siena's stigmata can help to elucidate how discussion of images of saints changed and evolved as the ability to articulate complex questions surrounding religious images developed.

Tommaso Caffarini was born in Siena and entered the Dominican Order around 1364. He had met Catherine of Siena and was the author of a number of hagiographical works, including the life of Maria Stornioni of Venice. From 1394 until his death he resided in Venice and was prior of SS Giovanni e Paolo from 1409 to 1411.[11] Like Caffarini, Gregorio Lombardelli came from Siena and joined the Dominican Order. He trained as a doctor of theology and was a consultor to the Sienese Inquisition. He was also a prolific author of hagiographical literature and wrote lives of a number of Sienese holy people, including the ninth-century shoemaker Blessed Sorore, reputedly the founder of the Ospedale di Santa Maria della Scala in Siena; Saint Galgano (d. 1180/1); and Aldobrandesca Ponzi (d. 1309). Lombardelli paid particular attention to recording the lives of those holy people who had joined or been influenced by the Dominican Order, such as the Blessed

remains Émile Mâle, *L'Art religieux après le Concile de Trente: Étude sur l'iconographie de la fin du XVIe siècle, du XVIIe, du XVIIIe siècle* (Paris, 1932). See also Rudolf Wittkower, *Art and Architecture in Italy 1600–1750*, 6th edn, rev. by Joseph Connors and Jennifer Montagu, 3 vols (New Haven, CT, 1999).

[10] Tanner, ed., *Decrees of the Ecumenical Councils*, 2:775.

[11] For brief biographical details, see the introduction to 'Caffarini' [Thomas Antonii de Senis], *Libellus de supplemento: Legende prolixe virginis beate Catherine de Senis*, ed. Iuliana Cavalli and Imelda Foralosso (Rome, 1974), vi–xii; Gaudenz Freuler, 'Andrea di Bartolo, Fra Tommaso d'Antonio Caffarini, and Sienese Dominicans in Venice', *Art Bulletin* 69 (1987), 570–86, at 571–3.

Franco da Grotti (d. 1291) and the Blessed Bonaventura Tolomei (d. 1348).[12]

Caffarini's *Libellus de supplemento* was written in the first decades of the fifteenth century,[13] and Lombardelli's *Sommario della disputa a difesa delle sacre stimate di Santa Caterina da Siena* was published in 1601.[14] The *Libellus* is divided into three parts, with the subject of *Tractatus VII* of the second part being 'de stigmatibus virginis et de omnibus speciebus stigmatum et proprietatibus seu conditionibus eorundem'.[15] This section is by far the longest of part two. It was probably originally composed as a separate work, possibly before 1412,[16] and may have been based on a series of sermons which Caffarini had given in Venice between 1394 and 1396.[17] The length of the *tractatus* on the stigmata indicates that even at this stage, just over thirty years after Catherine's death and more than half a century before Sixtus IV's intervention on behalf of the Franciscans, there was already considerable discussion on the subject. Lombardelli's *Sommario* is an abbreviated version of a manuscript written in Latin for Clement VIII which went through the arguments against Catherine as a stigmatic and the representation of her as such and put forward detailed counter-arguments.[18] Its publication in a shortened vernacular version allowed Lombardelli to widen his audience.

A number of Dominican authors who published their work in the sixteenth or early seventeenth century discussed or listed those who were reputed to be stigmatics. Francesco Silvestri, master general of the Dominican Order in the years leading up to his death in 1526,[19] published in 1505 a Latin life of Osanna

[12] For information on Lombardelli, see Jacques Échard and Jacques Quétif, *Scriptores ordinis praedicatorum recensiti, notisque historicis et criticis illustrati*, 2 vols (Paris, 1719–21), 2: 384–5. For a list of Lombardelli's works on Sienese saints, see Domenico Moreni, *Bibliografia storico-ragionata della Toscana*, 2 vols (Florence, 1805), 1: 522–4.

[13] For information on the possible dates for the composition of the *Legenda minor*, with further bibliography, see 'Caffarini', *Libellus*, xxiii–xl.

[14] Gregorio Lombardelli, *Sommario della disputa a difesa delle sacre stimate di Santa Caterina da Siena* (Siena, 1601).

[15] 'Caffarini', *Libellus*, 121–266.

[16] Ibid. xxx–xxxi.

[17] Freuler, 'Andrea di Bartolo', 575.

[18] Lombardelli, *Sommario*, 5.

[19] On Silvestri, see Tamar Herzig, *Savonarola's Women: Visions and Reform in Renaissance Italy* (Chicago, IL, 2008), 148–9, 152–3, 159–60, 175; Échard and Quetif, *Scriptores*, 2: 59–69.

Andreasi (d. 1505), who had experienced the pain of the stigmata, and an Italian translation appeared in 1507.[20] He also planned to write a brief tract on Osanna. In a letter to Isabella d'Este dated 1 February 1510 he indicated that this would include a discussion of female stigmatics.[21] The Italian translation of Michele Loth de Ribera's Latin *vita* of Maria Raggi (d. 1600), published in 1609 by Paolo Minerva da Bari, stated that the greatest of all God's gifts to Maria was that of having the stigmata for fifteen years. Other stigmatics are then named, including Lidwina of Schiedam (d. 1433), Gertrude the Great (d. 1301/2), Elizabeth of Spalbeek (d. 1304), Stefana Quinzani (d. 1530), Helen of Hungary (d. c. 1270), Francis of Assisi and Catherine of Siena.[22] The writings of these Dominicans responded to the debate about who could be regarded as a true stigmatic, in other words about the nature and definition of stigmata as argued in works such as the Franciscan Samuele Cassini's *De stigmatibus sacris Divi Francisci et quomodo impossibile est aliquam mulierem, licet sanctissimam, recipere stigmata* (Pavia, 1508). Cassini explicitly set out to refute any possibility that women could receive stigmata, thus at one stroke denying the existence of most Dominican stigmatics.

Caffarini used his *tractatus* to counter claims that St Francis was the only true stigmatic and to support Catherine of Siena and a number of other holy people as stigmatics. He argued for an expanded definition of stigmata in direct opposition to the restricted Franciscan understanding of the term, stressing that it could relate to all those wounds received by Christ during his passion, not just the wounds received on the cross, and that true stigmatization was not purely a miraculous phenomenon.[23] Caffarini's discussion of the different types of stigmata goes back to an understanding of the term valid before St Francis, in which 'it was used in a general sense, rather than with specific reference to Christ's wounds'.[24] According to Caffarini, St Dominic (d. 1221),

---

[20] Francesco Silvestri, *Beatae Osannae Mantuanae de tertio habitu Ordinis Fratrum praedicatorum vita* (Milan, 1505); *La vita e stupendi miraculi della gloriosa vergine Osanna mantovano del Terzo ordine de' Frati Predicatori* (Milan, 1507).

[21] Herzig, *Savonarola's Women*, 148.

[22] Paolo Minerva da Bari, *Vita della venerabile suor Maria Raggi da Scio* (Naples, 1609), 65–7.

[23] 'Caffarini', *Libellus*, 147, 174–7.

[24] Giles Constable, *Three Studies in Medieval Religious and Social Thought* (Cambridge, 1995), 199.

for example, qualified on account of his self-flagellation. Caffarini also recognized St Bridget of Sweden (d. 1373) as a stigmatic
because she burnt herself with lighted candles placed directly on
her bare skin, and St James the Apostle because of the scar on
his knee from repeated genuflections.[25] Miraculous mutations of
the heart also qualified as stigmata, and Caffarini named Margaret
of Città di Castello (d. 1320), Clare of Montefalco (d. 1308) and
St Ignatius of Antioch (d. c. 98/117).[26] Those beaten by demons
or humans, resulting in wounds and then in scars, included St
Euphrasia (d. circa 412).[27] Catherine of Siena suffered in this way,
and Caffarini went on to list some saints who were beaten, or who
had themselves beaten, such as St Elizabeth of Hungary (d. 1231),
the Dominican Margaret of Hungary (d. 1271) and St Thomas
Becket (d. 1170).[28]

Having made the argument for an expanded definition of
stigmata, Caffarini discussed the representation of stigmatics. The
text indicates both the importance which he attached to visual
images and his involvement with the visual imagery of stigmatics, particularly Catherine of Siena. In the *Libellus*, Caffarini
mentioned his activities as a commissioner and claimed to have
ensured, where possible, that only those who genuinely were stigmatics were represented as such.[29] Stating that 'truth conquers over
everything',[30] he reasoned that stigmatics should be represented
as such even when this might cause scandal. However, when the
image is not accurate, for whatever reason, it should be removed.
To demonstrate his point, Caffarini made extensive use of the
case of Margaret of Hungary, whose cult in Italy included a belief
in her stigmatization.[31] There are a number of surviving Italian
images from the fourteenth century showing Margaret as a stigmatic: in the panel of *Christ and the Virgin Mary with Dominican
Saints* in Santa Maria Novella, Florence, ascribed to the Master of
the Dominican effigies and dated to c. 1340; in a fresco from the

---

[25] 'Caffarini', *Libellus*, 123–5.
[26] Ibid. 128–9, 138–9.
[27] Ibid. 139.
[28] Ibid. 140.
[29] Ibid. 403–4, 409; see Freuler, 'Andrea di Bartolo', 573.
[30] 'Caffarini', *Libellus*, 156.
[31] For the cult of Margaret of Hungary in Italy, see Gábor Klaniczay, 'Le stigmate di
santa Margherita d'Ungheria. Immagini e testi', *Iconographica* 1 (2002), 16–31, at 16–18.

second half of the fourteenth century in San Niccolò, Treviso; in a fourteenth-century fresco in San Domenico, Perugia; and in a fresco from the first half of the fifteenth century in the church of San Domenico in Città di Castello.[32] Caffarini's interest in stigmatics had led him to investigate the case of Margaret of Hungary and he had received information from the Prior Provincial of the Hungarian Dominicans that, in fact, Margaret was not a stigmatic, rather it was her older contemporary Helen of Hungary.[33] Because of this, Caffarini opposed the representation of Margaret as a stigmatic and, he claimed, took steps to ensure that any such images were removed from the churches in Venice, including SS Giovanni e Paolo.[34] The opinions expressed make it clear that there was no excuse for showing stigmata on the basis of misguided belief. However, Caffarini supported the representation of stigmata where the evidence indicated their existence. He discussed the case of the Dominican Blessed Walter of Strasbourg, who is mentioned in Gerard of Frachet's mid-thirteenth-century *Vitae Fratrum*.[35] Quoting almost directly from the *Vitae Fratrum*, Caffarini said:

> While he [Walter] was in Colmar, in the house of the Friars Minor of Colmar, praying and considering the bitterness of the Lord's passion, he then felt such a great pain in five places upon his body that he was not able to contain himself without crying out with a great groan.[36]

On the basis of this evidence, Caffarini approved an image which he had seen of 'the same blessed Walter depicted at the moment of receiving the five stigmata, on the facade of the church

---

[32]   Ibid. 18–20.

[33]   Ibid. 16; 'Caffarini', *Libellus*, 172.

[34]   'Caffarini', *Libellus*, 156–7.

[35]   Ibid. 176–7. Caffarini stated that he found his information on Walter of Strasbourg 'in scriptis de Vita fratrum primitivorum eiusdem ordinis parte quarta capitulo ultimo'.

[36]   Ibid. 177: 'Cum quodam semel esset in Columbaria, in domo Fratrum Minorum, orans et volvens amaritudinem dominice passionis, ex tunc sensit in suo corpore in quinque locis tantum dolorem quod se contenere non potuit quin cum mano rugitu clamaret.' Gerard of Frachet, *Vitæ Fratrum Ordinis Prædicatorum,* ed. Benedictus Maria Reichert, Monumenta Ordinis Praedicatorum Historica I (Louvain, 1896), 223 (4.25): 'Idem frater, cum esset in Columbaria in domo fratrum minorum orans volvebat in corde amaritudinem dominice passionis; et ex tunc sensit in suo corpore in V locis vulnerum domini tantum dolorem, quod se continere non potuit, quin cum magno rugitu clamaret.'

of Saint Eustorgius in Milan, which image, I believe, remains there to this day'.[37]

Caffarini then proceeded to comment on the correct way to depict acknowledged stigmatic saints. He remarked that there were 'defects' in the images of stigmatics which he had seen, and noted that this was due to their not following relevant sources accurately.[38] Earlier he had given specific examples:

> [W]henever the Blessed Catherine of Siena is depicted with five visible stigmata on her hands and on her feet and with the seraphic apparition it was not done well, since neither from her own legend nor from any other place can it be found that it was thus, and so similarly whenever the Blessed Francis is depicted with blood-stained stigmata on his hands and on his feet and with the appearance of blood-stained rays touching the five places of his body, also it does not seem to have been done well, since mention is made regarding the said things neither in his legend nor elsewhere.[39]

Caffarini went on to say that he had arranged for Helen of Hungary, Walter of Strasbourg, Catherine of Siena and Francis of Assisi to be depicted 'here' so that the reader could see demonstrated the correct way of depicting them.[40] 'Here' refers to Caffarini's *Libellus*. There are two illustrated manuscripts of the *Libellus*: one in the Biblioteca communale degli Intronati in Siena (MS Segn. T.I.2), and a copy made shortly afterwards which is now in the Biblioteca universitaria in Bologna (cod. Lat. 1574). Both were completed in Caffarini's scriptorium in SS Giovanni e Paolo 'and their drawings are identical in number, correspondence to the text, and subject matter'.[41] The full page illustration

---

[37] 'Caffarini', *Libellus*, 177: 'Vidi etiam ego eundem beatum Gualterium depictum ad modum recipientis quinque stigmata, in facie ecclesie de Mediolano sancti Eustorgii, que image, ut puto, usque hodie perseverat ibidem.'

[38] Ibid. 181.

[39] Ibid. 156: 'quod quemadmodum ubi beata Catherina de Senis depingeretur cum quinque stigmatibus visibilis in manibus et in pedibus et cum apparitione seraphica non esset bene factum, cum nec ex legenda sua aut ex alio quod ita fuerit reperiatur, ita consimiliter ubi beatus Franciscus depingatur cum stigmatibus sanguinolentis in manibus et in pedibus et apparitione radiorum sanguinolentorum ad quinque sui corporis loca pertingentium, etiam non videtur bene factum, pro quanto de dictis nec in legenda nec alibi fit aliqua mentio'.

[40] Ibid. 181.

[41] Emily A. Moerer, 'The Visual Hagiography of a Stigmatic Saint: Drawings of

relevant to this section of the text in both the Bologna and Siena manuscripts is divided into four, showing Helen, Walter, Catherine and Francis at the moment of their stigmatization. However, as noted by Fabio Bisogni, the relationship between text and image is not clear: in both manuscripts rays emanate from the seraph and Catherine shows visible stigmata.[42] Narrative images, they show the point at which the stigmata were received in response to the reference in the text, but not in complete accordance with the sources to which Caffarini referred. Other stigmatics represented in the manuscripts are shown without any narrative context as single figures with their 'attributes' clearly delineated. Thus, for example, the Blessed Clare of Montefalco holds up her heart with the small relief sculpture of the instruments of the passion visible inside, and the Blessed Margaret of Città di Castello also holds out her heart with the three tiny sculpted stones which rolled out of it when her body was opened appearing on stalks attached to the top of the heart.[43] These images raise other questions, not explicitly addressed by Caffarini, about the legitimacy of making stigmata visible outside the narrative context of their reception, in short about issues relating to visibility and invisibility, time and space.

By the time that Gregorio Lombardelli published his *Sommario*, nearly two centuries after Caffarini wrote the *Libellus*, these aspects of the depiction of Catherine of Siena were deemed worthy of lengthy discussion, which bore directly on the issue of how images could, and should, be understood. For Lombardelli the argument centred on the legitimacy of showing Catherine of Siena with stigmata. He wrote after multiple objections had been voiced as to the representation of Catherine's invisible stigmata and used a variety of arguments to counter these. Lombardelli was clearly familiar with Caffarini's text. His definitions of the different types of stigmata followed Caffarini closely, for example.[44] He also took

Catherine of Siena in the *Libellus de Supplemento*', *Gesta* 44 (2005), 89–102, at 89. For a discussion of Caffarini's scriptorium, see Silvia Noventini, 'Lo "scriptorium" di Tommaso Caffarini a Venezia', *Hagiographica* 12 (2005), 79–144.

[42] Fabio Bisogni, 'Il "Libellus" di Tommaso d'Antonio Caffarini e gli inizi dell'iconografia di Caterina', in Trenti and Addabo, eds, *Con l'occhio*, 253–68, at 262.

[43] For a discussion of Clare of Montefalco and Margaret of Città di Castello, see Cordelia Warr, 'Re-reading the Relationship between Devotional Images, Visions, and the Body: Clare of Montefalco and Margaret of Città di Castello', *Viator* 38 (2007), 217–49.

[44] Lombardelli, *Sommario*, 63–4.

care to note that, according to Caffarini, both Catherine of Siena and Francis of Assisi received the same type of stigmata, thus claiming for Catherine the most prestigious type of miraculous stigmata.[45] Yet despite Lombardelli's reliance on Caffarini in the matter of definitions of stigmata, the two texts are significantly different, and this is evident in the development of arguments relating to the depiction of stigmatics.

Like Caffarini, Lombardelli specifically mentioned a number of images:

> [I]mmediately after her death, Saint Catherine was painted with the stigmata; and in our church of San Domenico di Camporeggi in Siena, one can find her painted like this, in the [following] years: 1392, 1426, 1475, 1492, 1508, and 1526, and in more recent times; and above the choir of the aforementioned church there is a very old wooden statue [which shows her] stigmatized, about which there is no knowledge about when it was done; but one believes [that it was executed] immediately after her death, since she is in the habit which she wore when she was alive …[46]

It is very difficult to be clear about the types of images to which Lombardelli referred since although he gave specific dates and locations, these may not be accurate and there is no mention of the artists and little in the way of description. However, it is possible to attempt an identification for 1526, when Sodoma (Antonio Bazzi, d. 1549) painted two frescoes for the Chapel of Saint Catherine in San Domenico: the *Swooning of Saint Catherine of Siena after the Stigmatization* and the *Vision of Saint Catherine of Siena after the Stigmatization*.[47] Both images show Catherine with blood-red wounds on her hands and it is this aspect of them which was of most importance for Lombardelli as he sought to legitimize representations of Catherine which included the stigmata.

---

45   Ibid. 50–1; 'Caffarini', *Libellus*, 177.
46   Lombardelli, *Sommario*, 80: 'a pena era morta S. Caterina, che si dipigneva con le Stimate; e nella Chiesa nostra di S. Domenico di Camporeggi di Siena, si trova così dipinta, l'Anno 1392. 1426. 1475. 1492. 1508. e 1526. e ne' più vicini tempi; e sopra il Coro di detta Chiesa v'è in statua di legno stimatizata antichissima, che non si trova memoria, quando fusse fatta; ma si crede, doppo la morte subbito, per essere nell'Abito, che vivendo portava'.
47   Andrée Hayum, *Giovanni Antonio Bazzi – 'Il Sodoma'* (New York, 1976), 196–201.

In chapter 1 of the second part of the *Sommario*, Lombardelli began by defending Catherine's stigmata as real in that they caused her physical pain. It is this which justifies their representation. The Dominicans:

> wanted her [Catherine] to be depicted with them [the stigmata] in order to express the pain which she felt, and in order to show that, if indeed the wounds were not seen by everyone, it does not follow on account of this that she did not have the wounds; because Balaam did not see the angel, and yet the angel was there, and the ass saw the angel.[48]

Lombardelli then went on to cite the argument that pictures are the books of the illiterate. However, he made one important change. He said that: '[P]ainting is a book for the learned because through painting they may recall what they have read, and for the uneducated because they may learn through it that which they do not know how to read in books'.[49]

The parallel between books for the educated and pictures for the uneducated was a commonplace justification for religious art.[50] Some writers such as Bede (d. 735)[51] and Bonaventure (d. 1274),[52] both cited by Lombardelli, had addressed the issue of painting as memory aid but had not linked this explicitly to the ways in which the educated used painting. Nonetheless, Lombardelli went on to ascribe this view, with greater or lesser accuracy, to a long list of individuals and councils, as would have been expected, in order to

---

[48] The story of Balaam can be found in Num. 22: 1–35. Lombardelli, *Sommario*, 31: 'voglion, che si dipinga con esse, ad exprimere il dolor, ch'Ella sentiva, & a manifestar, che, se bene non eran da tutti vedute le Piaghe, non per questo vale la conseguenza, adunque non haveva la Piaghe; perche Balaam non vedeva l'Angelo, e pur v'era l'Angelo, e lo vedeva il Somaro'. Caffarini also dealt with the issue of painful invisible stigmata, but did not go on to link this into any argument about their representation: *Libellus*, 147.

[49] Lombardelli, *Sommario*, 32: 'essendo la pittura un libro di i Dotti, acciò in esso imparino quel, che hanno letto: e de gli Ignoranti, acciò in essa imparino quel, che no[n] sanno legger ne i libri'.

[50] See Lawrence Duggan, 'Was Art really the "Book of the Illiterate"?', *Word and Image* 5 (1989), 227–51.

[51] *Vita sanctorum abbatum monasterii in uyramutha et gyruum* 6, in Bede, *Opera Historica*, ed. and trans. John Edward King, 2 vols, LCL 246, 248 (London, 1930), 2: 405–7. For a discussion of Bede, see Thomas F. X. Noble, *Images, Iconoclasm, and the Carolingians* (Philadelphia, PA, 2009), 111–16.

[52] St Bonaventure, *Opera Omnia*, ed. Patres Collegii a S. Bonaventura, 10 vols (Quaracchi, 1882–1902), 3: 203–4.

substantiate his argument. These included John of Damascus (d. c. 750) and Thomas Aquinas (d. 1274). He did not specify the writings he had used. John of Damascus's treatises *On the Divine Images* were the subject of renewed interest when Lombardelli was writing, with nine editions published during the sixteenth century.[53] However, it is likely that he was referring to John's *Exposition of the Orthodox Faith*, which dealt with the arguments for allowing images in chapter 15 of Book 4 ('Concerning Images'), since this source was specifically mentioned by some of the sixteenth-century writers to whom Lombardelli referred.[54] Thomas Aquinas's commentaries on the *Sentences* of Peter Lombard[55] are likely to have formed part of Lombardelli's formal Dominican education.[56]

Amongst the more recent sources cited by Lombardelli, there are a number of Dominicans, including Silvestro da Prierio (d. 1527),[57] Bartolomeo Fumo (d. 1545)[58] and Giovanni Cagnazzo da Taggia (d. 1521).[59] Indeed, Lombardelli's sixteenth-century sources are notably Dominican, and Spanish or Italian, including his fellow Sienese Constantino Ghini. There are exceptions, such as the inclusion of the Spanish Franciscan theologian Alfonso de Castro (d. 1558)[60] and the exclusion of Lancelotto Politi (d. 1553), a fellow

---

[53] Andrew Louth, *St John Damascene: Traditions and Originality in Byzantine Theology* (Oxford, 2002), 198–9.

[54] See, e.g., Constantino Ghini, *Dell'immagini sacre* (Siena, 1595), 78–9; cf. John of Damascus, *Exposition of the Orthodox Faith* 4.16 (NPNF II 9, 88).

[55] Thomas Aquinas, *Scriptum super sententiis magistri Petri Lombardi*, ed. M. F. Moos, 4 vols (Paris, 1947–56). For the defence of the use of painting in churches, see 3*: 213 (distinctio IX, articulus II, quaestiuncula II).

[56] Lombardelli describes himself as a master of theology on the title page of the *Sommario*. William A. Hinnebusch, *The History of the Dominican Order*, 2: *Intellectual and Cultural Life to 1500* (New York, 1973), 58–71, discusses the evolution of the curriculum for degrees in theology.

[57] On Silvestro Mazzolino da Prierio, see Michael Tavuzzi, *Prierias: The Life and Works of Silvestro Mazzolini Da Prierio, 1456–1527* (Durham, NC, 1997). Lombardelli is probably referring to Mazzolino's *Summa Summarium: que Silvestrina dicitur* (Bologna, 1514–15); for the section on images, see ibid. 327–8.

[58] Bartolommeo Fumo wrote the *Summa casuum conscientiae, aurea armilla dicta* (Venice, 1550): Quétif and Échard, *Scriptores*, 2: 123.

[59] Lombardelli refers to Giovanni Cagnazzi da Tabia as 'Giovanni da Tabia'. For biographical information, see Quétif and Échard, *Scriptores*, 2: 47. Cagnazzi's major work was the *Summa summarum quae tabiena dicitur* (Bologna, 1517); for the section on images, see ibid. 260.

[60] Alfonso de Castro, *Adversus omnes haereses* (Paris, 1534). The section on images is in lib. 8, 138–9. See Teodoro Olarte, *Alfonso de Castro (1495–1558): Su vida, su tiempo y sus ideas filosóficas-juridicas* (San José, Costa Rica, 1946).

Dominican and native of Siena who had contributed *De certa gloria, invocatione ac veneratione sanctorum disputationes* to the first round of Counter-Reformation publications supporting religious art.[61] As a rule, Lombardelli did not cite those authors who produced the first works of the Counter-Reformation defending religious images, such as Nicholas Harpsfield or Nicholas Sanders,[62] nor did he cite those who used these publications in their own subsequent publications on images, such as Gabriele Paleotti (d. 1597) or Johannes Molanus (d. 1585).[63] There is one exception: his use of Conrad Braun (d. 1563). Towards the end of his *Sommario*, Lombardelli put forward one final justification for images of St Catherine with visible stigmata, stating that 'if the picture is founded upon truth, upon history, if there is a tradition, and if there is the habit of painting in this way' and if removing the image would dishonour the saint in question, then the pope must order the reinstatement of the image.[64] Lombardelli cited here Braun's *De imaginibus* published in 1548, specifically chapter 21,[65] and Jacobus Simancas's *De catholicis institutionibus*.[66] The roll-call of theologians occasioned by the argument that pictures are the books of the uneducated (as well as the educated) ended with a further extrapolation that: 'just as in books, one reads things, that teach the invisible through the visible; just so the visible wounds of St Catherine, in images, teach [about] the invisible [wounds] which she carried whilst alive; and therefore it is no error to paint her with the stigmata'.[67]

The issue of legitimately showing the invisible is something discussed by a number of the early sources citied by Lombardelli,

[61] Ambrosius Catharinus Politi [Lancelotto de' Politi, 1484–1553], *De certa gloria, invocatione ac veneratione sanctorum disputationes* (Lyons, 1542).

[62] Anthony Blunt, *Artistic Theory in Italy, 1450–1600* (Oxford, 1940), 107.

[63] Gabriele Paleotti, *De sacris et profanis imaginibus libri V* (Bologna, 1582); Johannes Molanus, *De picturis et imaginibus sacris* (Louvain, 1570).

[64] Lombardelli, *Sommario*, 97: 'Ma, se la pittura sia fondata sopra la verità, sopra l'Istoria, s'habbia dalla tradizione, e sia consuetudine di cosi dipingnersi'.

[65] Conradus Brunus, *Iure consulti opera tria* (Mainz, 1548), 138–43 (ch. 21). The argument used was that images which are used correctly, in this case not idolatrously, should not be removed: ibid. 142.

[66] Jacobus Simancas, *De catholicis institvtionibvs Iacobi Simancae Pacensis episcopi, liber ad praecauendas et extirpandas hereses admodum necessarius* (Rome, 1575), 253–4 (tit. 33 'dell'Imagini', no. 12). Simancas used the same argument as Braun, citing Braun, *De imaginibus*, ch. 21.

[67] Lombardelli, *Sommario*, 32: 'come ne i libri, si leggono le cose, che insegnano l'invisibili per le visibili; così le visibili Piaghe di S. Caterina, nelle pitture, insegnano l'invisibili, che portò vivendo: e però, non è error nessuno a dipinderla con le Stimate'.

and can be traced back to eighth-century arguments against icon-oclasm.[68] It allowed Lombardelli, in chapter 2 of the second part of the *Sommario*, to engage with the question of what it was reasonable for the viewer to expect to see, and understand, in an image. Using a number of different comparisons, he argued essentially that viewers did not expect to see a 're-presentation' of what those who had seen St Catherine during her life had observed, and he touched tangentially on the issue of the relationship of images to explicit points of time, questioning: 'Why is it an error to paint Saint Catherine with visible wounds, which may represent invisible [wounds], or indeed may represent visible [wounds], which now in the aforementioned foot and hand can still be seen?'[69]

Lombardelli was referring here to the relics of St Catherine. The stigmata became partially visible after Catherine's death, and Lombardelli therefore used sight as evidential proof.[70] He recounted that, having gone to Rome in 1600, on 10 June he touched the hand of St Catherine, and he saw, clearly sculpted, the stigma.[71] To assume that viewers could not make a distinction between what could be seen with the eye at a single point in time and what was known to exist and must therefore be represented was, according to Lombardelli, incorrect and, moreover, insultingly simplistic. This is apparent in the opening sentences of chapter 2, which explicitly countered the opinions of Roberto Caracciolo:

> No one, with any common sense, and in their right mind, will make the mistake of maintaining, as Roberto tacitly implies, when they see an image of St Catherine with visible stigmata that it affirms that she received them in visible form, just as no one is deceived when they see the divine persons, the Father in the form of an old man; the Son crucified on the cross, or flagellated at the column, or crowned with thorns; or the Holy

---

[68]   Erik Thunø, *Image and Relic: Mediating the Sacred in Early Medieval Rome* (Rome, 2002), 140.

[69]   Lombardelli, *Sommario*, 33–4: 'perche è errore il dipigner S. Caterina con le visibili Piaghe, le quali rappresteno l'invisibili, ò vero che rappresentino le visibili, che ora in detto piede, e mano si vedon tuttavia?'

[70]   Ibid. 51. About the stigmata, Lombardelli states: 'nella morte furono vedute, e toccate; si come infin' oggi con mano si tocca, e si vede co[n] gli occhi questa verità'.

[71]   Ibid. 52: 'viddi, toccai, guardai, e riguardai la predetta santissima Mano, serbata in quel Monasterio; e viddi scolpita, chiara, e bella la prefata Stimata, e Piaga; la quale è di figura quadra. & non solamente la viddi, e rividdi, ma la feci vedere, e riveder da tutti'.

Spirit in the form of a dove, or a cloud, or fire, or of tongues; because no-one would dare to say that the Holy Trinity appear thus in glory.[72]

Lombardelli also drew comparisons between the representation of saints with their symbols – Peter with his keys; John with the chalice and serpent; Bartholomew with the knife. He pointed out how ridiculous it would be for anyone to infer from this that, for example, Peter was the custodian of a house.[73]

Lombardelli then advanced on two fronts. He pointed out that the Dominicans were not scandalized 'when we see an image of St Francis with red wounds on his feet and hands from which blood flows, even though blood did not flow from them, neither was he seen to have wounds: but he had nails made out of his own flesh'.[74] In an ingenious inversion of Caffarini's insistence on close adherence to the written sources, Lombardelli argued that if the Franciscans had no objection to representations of their founder which did not show the stigmata as they were described, why should they object to St Catherine's stigmata being visualized in images? Both saints were acknowledged to have had stigmata. Neither saint was represented with the stigmata as they had appeared (or not appeared!) during their lifetime. Lombardelli went on to claim that he had never seen Francis's stigmata represented in images as they were described in the main sources. He criticized the Franciscans for, on the one hand, advocating the view that images are no more than a re-presentation of what is seen by the eye and, on the other hand, for not taking note of their own advice on what should be represented in paintings commissioned by them. Again, he made a comparison with instances where invisible things, or those without form, were legitimately described or painted:

---

72   Ibid. 32–3: 'Nessuno, che sia di giudizio, e di mente sana, piglierà mai errore, come tacitamente inserisce Roberto, mentre vede l'immagine di S. Caterina con le Stimate visibili, si ch'affermi, che visibilme[n]te le ricevesse, come non lo prende chi vede dipinte le Persone Divine, il Padre in forma di Vecchio; il figlio in Croce co[n] fitto, ò alla Colonna Flagellato, ò Incoronato di Spine; ò lo Spirito Santo in forma di Colomba, du Nube, di Fuoco, ò di Lingue; poiche nessuno ardisce dir, che così in Gloria sia la Trinità Santissima.'

73   Ibid. 33.

74   Ibid.: 'non ci scandeliziamo noi, mentre che vediamo l'immagine di S. Francesco con le Piaghe de'piedi, e mani rubiconde, e versanti sangue, benche esse non versassero sangue, né si vedesser le Piaghe: ma della propria carne vi havesse i chiodi'.

and if it is permitted for doctors and painters to describe a soul, or to paint it separated from the body, or in the form of some animal, or of a star … why may one not paint her [Catherine] with them [the stigmata], when form is given to things which do not have any material form and for no other reason if not to express the properties and conditions which they had whilst they were alive?[75]

For Lombardelli, therefore, the purpose of images was to show what was known to be, bringing together knowledge across spatial and temporal barriers, rather than what could be seen by the naked eye at one fixed moment in time. Images were re-presentations of amassed knowledge, the result of different types of sight. In short, images ordered knowledge. This ordering of knowledge implied that the viewer must be equipped to understand the difference between what was seen and what was represented, and also to understand the different components of representation. Lombardelli stressed that images could not be understood correctly without mediation and instruction. When discussing the bull *Spectat ad Romani* of Pope Sixtus IV, issued in 1472,[76] he discussed the length of time during which the order not to depict Catherine with stigmata should have been enforced, and argued that in such cases once the cause of the prohibition had been removed – in this instance, the possibility that a viewer could think that Catherine had visible stigmata during her life – then the prohibition itself was no longer in force.[77] This argument is explicit within much Counter-Reformation literature and is in line with the provisions of the Council of Trent on the need for bishops to instruct their flock on 'the legitimate use of images' of saints and the use of images in 'recalling the articles of our faith'.[78] It is also present in many of the earlier writers cited by Lombardelli, such as Bede, Bonaventure and Aquinas. The so-called 'Gregorian dictum' that 'what writing offers to those who read it, a picture offers to

---

75 Ibid. 33–4: 'e se è lecito a' Dottori, & a' Pittori descriver' in'anima, ò dipignerla separata dal corpo, in forma di qualche Animale, ò di Stella … perche non si può Essa dipigner con esse, mentre che alle cose, che no[n] hanno nessuna material forma, è data forma, e non per altra cagione, se non per esprimer le proprietà, e co[n]dizioni, che havevan coloro, mentre vivevano?'

76 Mencherini, *Codice diplomatico*, 109–11, 117–23, 693.

77 Lombardelli, *Sommario*, 72–4.

78 Tanner, ed., *Decrees*, 2: 774–5 (session 25, 3–4 December 1563).

the ignorant who look at it' was true only in so far as the meaning of both writing and images might be clearly understood following instruction, memorization and explanation.[79]

The arguments employed by Lombardelli were partly different and partly evolved from those used by Caffarini. The *Libellus* and *Sommario* demonstrate some of the changing ways in which Dominican supporters of Catherine justified representations in which her stigmata were shown. They also give evidence of long-running crises of representation with regard to the relationship of what is known and what is seen to what is represented. Whilst Caffarini's text demonstrates a developed definition of different types of stigmata, closely adhered to by Lombardelli, his arguments concerning the representation of stigmatics can seem either simplistic – adherence to the written sources – or to be avoiding the issues – the invisibility of Catherine of Siena's stigmata. By contrast, Lombardelli's discussion shows a nuanced understanding of the purpose of visual images within the context of religious belief and the promotion of sanctity, one which draws on a sound theological training. Lombardelli took care to rely on carefully considered and well-referenced arguments in the greater part of his *Sommario*. However, in order to present a fully rounded case, he also supported the depiction of Catherine of Siena with the stigmata by reference to miracles. As a balance to the story quoted at the beginning of this paper, it seems appropriate to end with an example from the end of the third part of the *Sommario* which concerns two young men who were in Paris and who:

> one day, pushed by the Devil, took knives and went to the church of St Eustace in Paris, where St Catherine was painted with the stigmata, and without any respect or fear, they erased them [the stigmata], giving themselves to believe that they were making a sacrifice to God, when they were sacrificing to the Devil, and they went back to their houses happy, and celebrating, but the unfortunates, encouraged by the heat, went to the river Seine in order to wash themselves. There wasn't that much water there which could, according to the

[79]   Celia M. Chazelle, 'Pictures, Books and the Illiterate: Pope Gregory I's Letters to Serenus of Marseilles', *Word and Image* 6 (1990), 138–53, at 139; Noble, *Images, Iconoclasm*, 42–3; Duggan, 'Was Art really the "Book of the Illiterate"?', 229–30, 232.

natural course [of things], have drowned someone; and [yet] they were submerged. Everyone judged that it was a miracle.[80]

University of Manchester

---

[80] Lombardelli, *Sommario*, 67: 'Questi, vessati dal Diavolo, un giorno, presi i coltelli, andarano nella Chiesa di S. Eustochio di Parigi, ove era dipinta S. Caterina co[n] le stimate, e senza alcun rispetto, ò timore, le rasero, dandosi a creder di far sacrifizio a Idio, mentre sacrificarono al Diavolo, anda[n]dosene alle lor case lieti, e festeggianti. Ma gli infelici, invitati dal caldo, andarono al fiume Sequana, per lavarsi, là dove non era tan'acqua, che potesse, per corso naturale, annegare alcuno; e si sommersero; giudicando ognuno, che fusse stato miracolo'.

SAN LUIGI GONZAGA: PRINCELING-JESUIT AND MODEL FOR CATHOLIC YOUTH

by OLIVER LOGAN

Luigi (Alvise) Gonzaga (1568–91), heir to the principality of Castiglione delle Stiviere, renounced his succession in 1585 to enter the Jesuit novitiate, in the course of which he died of plague, evidently contracted while ministering to the sick. He was beatified with extraordinary rapidity in 1605, four years before Ignatius Loyola and Francis Xavier.[1] Admittedly the figure of the 'angelic youth' Luigi, as presented in the life written by the promoter of the cause for his canonization, Virgilio Cepari, and finally published in 1606, was more conventional and more calculated to seize the popular imagination than the uncharismatic Loyola, who enjoyed a very limited cult initially and was slow to deliver miracles.[2] But, more significantly, the beatification was a matter of dynastic politics: it was promoted not only by the Jesuits but also, and more insistently, by the Gonzaga dynasty, supported by the Holy Roman Emperor and by allied dynasties. A phase of bureaucratization of canonization processes, already under way, was intensified shortly after Luigi's beatification. Moreover, the criteria for sainthood would seem to have shifted somewhat in the first half of the seventeenth century. Luigi was not canonized until

---

[1] The first published life was Virgilio Cepari, *Vita del Beato Luigi Gonzaga della Compagnia di Gesù* (Rome, 1606). Subsequent editions appeared in Italian, Latin and other languages with varying titles, the Milan 1728 and Venice 1839 editions bearing the addition: *Con la terza parte nuovamente composta da un altro religioso della medesima compagnia* (the revised Part III contains expanded accounts of *post mortem* miracles). Citations here are from *Vita di San Luigi Gonzaga DCDG*, ed. Friedrich Schroeder (Einsiedeln, 1891), published on the tercentenary of Luigi's death (there were also German, English, French and Spanish editions). Part III of this edition follows the original format; the Appendix includes some material from Part III of the 1728 edition and also contains documents extending to 1891. Scholarly notices on Luigi's life include *DSp, s.n.* 'S. Louis de Gonzague', primarily on his writings; *DBI, s.n.* 'Luigi (Aluigi) Gonzaga, santo'. On iconography, see two exhibition catalogues: Luigi Bosio, ed., *Mostra iconografica aloisiana* (Castiglione delle Stiviere, 1968); Gianluigi Arcari, *L'immagine a stampa di San Luigi Gonzaga*, 2 vols (Mantua, 1999–2000); the latter contains valuable historical notes.

[2] Miguel Gotor, *I beati del papa. Santità, inquisizione e obbedienza in età moderna* (Rome, 2002), 57–9.

1726, under Benedict XIII. In 1729 the same pope pronounced him the patron of students in Jesuit educational institutions and apparently also of students more generally. This provided the basis for the cult of Luigi in the nineteenth century as the patron of 'Catholic youth', that is both adolescents and young adults. This development was linked to a novel understanding of adolescence as a specific age group and also to the Church's battle against secularism. Thus the cult acquired a new relevance long after the princely world that had pressured for Luigi's canonization had passed away. The legal history of canonization processes substantially explains the delay in Luigi's canonization, but this delay is also partly explicable by the very complexity and ambiguity of Luigi's image as both child and man, which served in the long term to give ever new life to his cult.

The international role of the Gonzaga dynasty helps to show why the pressures for his beatification were so powerful. The history of tensions within the dynasty, moreover, suggests that, in the eyes of its leaders, the apotheosis of Luigi, who had been an agent of internal pacification in life, could help to maintain unity. The various branches of the family held sundry territorial principalities (duchies and marquisates), notionally fiefs of the Holy Roman Empire, in the Po valley area. These branches looked to the emperor to upgrade their titles and also to resolve territorial disputes between the different family branches. The Gonzagas of Mantua were the senior branch. All branches were engaged in military entrepreneurship, providing troops for the campaigns of the Spanish monarchy. The numerous Gonzaga cardinals were the chief negotiators of Spanish interests at the court of Rome. Among the Gonzaga, vicious territorial disputes could be followed by spectacular reconciliations and hence did not altogether prevent the pursuit of overall dynastic interests, particularly in the ecclesiastical sphere. Luigi came of a cadet branch, as indicated, that of Castiglione delle Stiviere.[3] His father Ferrante was both a military figure and an important diplomatic link between the Spanish and the Austrian Habsburgs.[4] Luigi's younger brother Francesco, a major instigator of his beatification cause, who eventu-

---

[3]   Giuseppe Coniglio, *I Gonzaga* (Milan, 1967), esp. 482–5 on the Castiglione delle Stiviere branch. The entries on individuals in *DBI*, vol. 57, are a valuable source on the dynasty.

[4]   *DBI*, *s.n.* 'Gonzaga, Ferrante'.

ally succeeded to the marquisate of Castiglione, mainly served the Austrian branch as a diplomat.[5]

The foundation in 1588 of the Congregation of Rites, a committee of cardinals for whom *auditori di Rota* did the spadework, marked a major stage in the formalization of beatification and canonization procedures. In 1605, however, procedures were still relatively casual and furthermore there was still limited control over early manifestations of cult of those had died in 'odour of sanctity', that is with a strong reputation for holiness and in an exceptionally edifying manner.[6] On the morrow of his death, Luigi was revered as a saint both by fellow students and by Jesuit fathers of the Collegio Romano where he had died; the collection of relics began immediately.[7] In 1604 Fra Francesco Gonzaga, of the Gazzuolo branch, the Franciscan Bishop of Mantua, who had allegedly supported Luigi's Jesuit vocation and felt a special tie to him, called a diocesan synod to petition Pope Clement VIII for Luigi's canonization.[8] From May 1605 petitions were made to Pope Paul V by the dead youth's brother Francesco, then imperial ambassador in Rome, hand-in-glove with the powerful Austro-Moravian Cardinal Franz von Dietrichstein (a former fellow student of Luigi), and by a host of dynastic figures who were either related to Luigi or had enjoyed personal connections with him in the courts of Europe. Paul V declared Luigi a *beatus* on 26 September 1605.[9]

Bishop Francesco proclaimed him co-patron of Mantua, albeit Luigi's birthplace was then actually in the diocese of Brescia and he had had limited connections with Mantua; he had, however, come there to resolve an intra-dynastic dispute in 1589. Notwithstanding the acute tensions between the Mantuan and Castigli-

---

5   *DBI*, *s.n.* 'Gonzaga, Francesco'.

6   Gotor, *I beati*, 127–202; idem, *Chiesa e santità nell'Italia moderna* (Rome, 2004), 34–53; Simon Ditchfield, 'Tridentine Worship and the Cult of Saints', in R. Po-Chia Hsia, ed., *CHC 6: Reform and Expansion 1500–1660* (Cambridge, 2007), 201–24, at 207–10. The *Congregatio Beatorum*, founded in 1602, had the primary function of establishing central control over the early stages of cults before formal petitions for beatification were made to the papacy,

7   Cepari, *Vita*, 223–38.

8   Roberto Brunelli, *Diocesi di Mantova* (Brescia, 1986), 123–30, 138–9; *DBI*, *s.n.* 'Gonzaga, Francesco'; Cepari, *Vita*, 58–9.

9   Schroeder, Appendix to Cepari, *Vita*, 283–5, 291–3. There does not appear to be a published version of the bull confirming the beatification, the most relevant document being the grant to Francesco Gonzaga and his successors of a privilege regarding the printing of Cepari's *Life*: ibid. 403–5.

onese branches of the Gonzaga, the senior branch embraced Luigi. Together with other Padine princely houses, it was accustomed to having client prophetesses in nunneries who foretold golden futures for the dynasty[10] and it was not going to let go the opportunity of having a family saint. Perhaps, too, the cult of Luigi could be a pacifying factor within the dynasty. Bishop Franceso and Grand Duke Ferrante pressed for a special mass office in honor of Luigi. This was granted by Pope Urban VIII in 1618 for all the Gonzaga dominions. The Grand Duke organized splendid celebrations in Mantua and declared Luigi the special patron of the city.[11] Luigi's beatification was not peculiar in being the outcome of pressures by grand aristocracy linked to the 'candidate' by kinship or other personal connections,[12] but the pressures mobilized here were exceptionally weighty.

Virgilio Cepari, as indicated, had been the official promoter of Luigi's cause and his life of the latter, prior to its publication, seems to have been a key document in the beatification process. Cepari was the spiritual director of the ecstatic visionary nun Maria Maddalena de' Pazzi in the convent of the Angeli in Florence.[13] In 1600, he gave a first draft of the life to Maria Maddalena. The latter subsequently went into rapture, proclaiming Luigi to be a great saint.[14] The *Life* was probably addressed, in its various stages of composition, to several audiences: Jesuit novices; nuns; Jesuit superiors; and the bureaucrats of the Congregation of Rites.

In the description of Luigi's early life it was highly conventional. He was portrayed as an extraordinarily pious child, initiated into piety by his mother, but rapidly taking his own direction. He never felt sexual urgings. Starting from the basis of an innate innocence, he had, as youth and man, constantly made progress in the spiritual life. He pursued his intention to enter the Society of Jesus (according to the rule of which he would be excluded from high Church office) with great determination in the face of opposition

---

[10] Gabriella Zarri, *Le sante vive. Profezie di corte e devozione femminile tra '400 e '500* (Turin, 1990, with differing titles on cover and title page), 51–81.

[11] Schroeder, Appendix to Cepari, *Vita*, 286–8. Note the strong Jesuit position in Mantua under Gonzaga patronage; see Brunelli, *Diocesi di Mantova*, 136–7.

[12] On the making of saints in the Kingdom of Naples in the seventeenth and eighteenth centuries, see Jean-Michel Sallmann, *Naples et ses saints à l'âge baroque* (Paris, 1994), 154–76.

[13] *DSp*, *s.n.* 'Cepari (Virgilio)'.

[14] Schroeder, Appendix to Cepari, *Vita*, 267–72.

and diversionary wiles on the part of his family. The description
of his life as a trainee Jesuit was more innovatory in terms of
hagiography, related as it was to issues of Jesuit community life
and of the Jesuit mission to both nobles and paupers. Luigi studi-
ously avoided any privileges attaching to his noble status, strictly
adhering to the Jesuit rule. He sought out the shabbiest dress and
coarsest food available. He performed the most menial tasks. He
practised an apostolate through giving catechism classes, and he
died as a result of ministering to the sick. All this was combined
with great kindliness and charm. Cepari portrays him as a charismatic figure whose charisma derived from an intense inner life.
One has the impression of an aristocrat both of the world and of
the spirit. Cepari asserts that he was a powerful example both to
his fellow students and to his Jesuit teachers and his own concern
in writing Luigi's life was to ensure that this example was not lost.
Cepari downplayed the importance of miracles *post mortem* but
recounted Luigi's nonetheless. Even here, the latter's extraordinary
effect on other people seems to be indicated: those sufferers who
were first inspired or advised to pray to Luigi did so with great
warmth and confidence.[15]

Clearly Cepari saw him as a model for Jesuit trainees. Arguably, too, he saw him as exemplifying the Jesuit soteriology, which
emphasized human cooperation with divine grace. In depicting
Luigi as a holy child, Cepari followed a topos with a long history,[16]
but one which came to be regarded with suspicion; this was probably the reason why this work was placed on the Index in 1684.[17]
But further, he described the mature Luigi as a person of 'heroic
virtue'. The concept of 'heroic virtue' was at that time making
its first entry into the documentation of canonization procedures and the related canonical literature, the first known reference being in a petition of 1602 for the beatification of Teresa of
Avila. In general terms the concept came to mean an extraordinary
virtue, beyond mere justice. There was also often the idea that
it entailed the overcoming of difficulties.[18] This idea would seem

[15] Cepari, *Vita*, xix–xx, 3–266.
[16] Donald Weinstein and Rudolph M. Bell, *Saints and Society: The Two Worlds of Western Christendom, 1000–1700* (Chicago, IL, 1982), 19–72.
[17] Gotor, *Chiesa e santità*, 119–20.
[18] Romeo De Maio, 'L'ideale eroico nei processi di canonizzazione della contror-iforma', in idem, *Riforme e miti della Chiesa del cinquecento* (Naples, 1973), 257–78;

to be present with Cepari, but he specifically links the accolade to Luigi's strict observance of Jesuit discipline and to his pursuit of his goal notwithstanding the sense of desolation which God visits as a test upon those who seek to seek to serve him.[19] Cepari portrayed Luigi as an intensely spiritual and ascetic figure, even to the point of being rather *distrait* in relation to minor things. But what leading Jesuits emphasized in canonization proceedings was his great prudence; several said that they had expected him to hold high office in their order. Indeed one realizes that Luigi was a young man of great worldly experience gained in sundry courts and in accompanying his father in his military activities; moreover, he had helped to resolve a dispute between his brother Rodolfo and Duke Vincenzo of Mantua over the duchy of Solferino. The position of these Jesuit witnesses doubtless reflected a recent shift in the ethos of their order away from mystical spirituality towards a practical piety.[20] Cepari's own position perhaps synthesized the new ethos with the older one.

The years following Luigi's beatification saw an increased bureaucratization of beatification and canonization processes and greater caution therein; this reached its climax under Urban VIII (1623–44), but received further touches to the end of the seventeenth century. This process entailed an ever-increasing supervision by the Congregation of the Holy Office (Inquisition) of the proceedings of the Congregation of Rites, together with ever-increasing central control of the early stages of the cult of persons who had died 'in odour of sanctity'.[21] However, the way in which Luigi's beatification had been conducted perhaps had something to do with it. This showed glaringly how the pope needed protection from the pressures of interested parties. In the course of the seventeenth century there was a slowing down of canonization procedures. For the Jesuits, the canonizations of Loyola and Xavier

---

Pierluigi Giovanucci, 'Genesi e significato di un concetto agiologico: La virtù eroica nell'età moderna', *Rivista di storia della chiesa in Italia* 58 (2004), 433–78.

[19] Cepari, *Vita*, 98–100.

[20] José Martinéz Millán, 'Transformacion y crisis de la Compañia de Jésus (1578–1594)', in Flavio Rurale, ed., *I religiosi a corte. Teologia, politica e diplomazia in antico regime* (Rome, 1998), 101–29, at 106–7.

[21] Gotor, *I beati*, 243–418; idem, *Chiesa e santità*, 79–96, 110–20; Ditchfield, 'Tridentine Worship', 211–18.

were a priority and Luigi's canonization cause, initiated in 1607, was 'put on the back burner'.[22]

Luigi was eventually canonized in 1726, a vintage year for new saints, under Benedict XIII, on the same day as Stanislaus Kostka, another Jesuit novice-saint. Previously, as Archbishop of Benevento, the pope had promoted Luigi's cult in his archdiocese.[23] The bull of canonization obviously owed much to Cepari's *Life*. It emphasized Luigi's total chastity and the fact that he had preserved it among the enticements of the Spanish court. Significantly, it referred to the vision of Maria Maddalena de' Pazzi (canonized in 1669).[24] As already indicated, Benedict XIII in 1729 proclaimed Luigi, *qua* model of youth, to be the patron of all categories of Jesuit educational establishments, adding somewhat ambiguously: 'and indeed of others'.[25] This proclamation had particular relevance to the Marian Congregations which the Jesuits promoted within their colleges among both their own trainees and extern students and which formed old-boy networks among their alumni. Right into the late nineteenth century at least, the Jesuits propagated the Marian Congregations in the wider world; they were affiliated to the mother congregation in the Collegio Romano and San Luigi, who had been a strong devotee of the Virgin Mary, was their patron. The original model was followed by many other congregations which were not founded or controlled by the Jesuits.[26]

The cult of San Luigi became widespread in nineteenth-century Italy, primarily in the north. This development was linked to the fact that 'youth', understood as the group of adolescents, was seen as requiring specialized pastoral care, whether as a pastoral problem or as the milieu from which future generations of Catholic militants were to be recruited. The context of official secularization

---

[22] For attempts to reactivate the process and for liturgical concessions: Schroeder, Appendix to Cepari, *Vita*, 295–302.

[23] Ibid. 302. The prefect of the Congregation of Rites between 1712 and 1728 was Prospero Lambertini, the future Pope Benedict XIV, a very precise scholar aligned with the Bollandists and author of the standard text on canonizations, *De servorum Dei beatificatione et beatorum canonizatione* (Bologna, 1734–8): see Gotor, *Chiesa e santità*, 121–7.

[24] Bull of 31 December 1726, in *Bullarum Diplomatum et Privilegium Sanctorum Romanorum Pontificum*, 24 vols (Turin 1857–72), 13: 483–7; for contemporaneous canonizations, see ibid. 464–9.

[25] Text of 22 November 1729, in Schroeder, Appendix to Cepari, *Vita*, 406 n.; not in *Bullarum*.

[26] *DSp, s.v.* 'Congrégations de la Sainte Vierge'.

and of militant secularism in unified Italy is significant here. Public
secondary education was secularized and universities were seen as
hotbeds of secularist political radicalism. In the paranoid mental
world of Italian clericalism, which aspired to the restoration of
a mythic golden age of ecclesiastical hegemony in society and
which saw the Church and the community of the faithful as now
besieged by 'paganism', the threat to the 'purity' of male youth
was perceived as part of a general decadence of society. Previous
reservations about the model of the youthful saint were now
abandoned. San Luigi was the patron of young males, Sta Agnes
of girls.[27] Already in the era of French occupation *Compagnie di
San Luigi* were spreading in Piedmont and Lombardy.[28] 1868 saw
papal approval of *Gioventù Cattolica* (Catholic Youth), the oldest
component of the so-called 'Catholic lay movement', what came
to be known in the twentieth century as 'Catholic Action'. (It
became affiliated to the umbrella Catholic lay organization the
Opera dei Congressi founded in 1874.) Under the leadership of prestigious mature adult cadres, it was a militant clericalist organization

[27] Pietro Stella, 'Santi per giovani e santi giovani nell'Ottocento', in Emma
Fattorini, ed., *Santi, culti, simboli nell'età della secolarizzazione (1815–1915)* (Turin, 1997),
563–86 (for Luigi, ibid. 563–8, 575); Dario Cervato, *Diocesi di Verona* (Padua, 1999), 674,
669; Roberto Rusconi, 'Una Chiesa a confronto con la società', in Anna Benevenuti
et al., *Storia della santità nel cristianesimo occidentale* (Rome, 2005), 331–86, at 340–1. On
the nineteenth-century discovery of 'adolescence': Monica Turi, 'Il "brutto peccato".
Adolescenza e controllo sessuale nel modello agiografico di Maria Goretti', in Anna
Benevenuti Papi and Elena Giannarelli, eds, *Bambini santi. Rappresentazioni dell'infanzia
e modelli agiografici* (Turin, 1991), 119–46. In the diocese of Brescia, 24 churches and
chapels were dedicated to San Luigi, as against 150 to San Rocco, 58 to San Carlo
Borromeo and 42 to St Francis of Assisi; see A. Fapanni, 'Religiosità e pieta', in A.
Caprioli, A. Rimoldi and L. Vaccaro, eds, *Diocesi di Brescia* (Brescia, 1992), 357–424, at
388. Details of altars dedicated to San Luigi in the Veneto extant in the nineteenth
and early twentieth centuries are to be found in the calendars of pastoral visitations
in *Thesaurus ecclesiarum Italiae (secoli XVIII–XX)*, sub-series Veneto, 19 vols (Rome,
1969–85). Particularly significant references in bishops' pastorals of the ecclesiastical
province of Milan are: P. M. Corna Pellegrini Sandre, Bishop of Brescia (1891), in
Xenio Toscani and Maurizio Sangalli, eds, *Lettere pastorali dei vescovi della Lombardia*
(Rome, 1998), 57; A. C. Ferrari, Bishop of Como (1893), ibid. 103; G. Benaglio, Bishop
of Lodi (1858), ibid. 268; G. B. Rota, Bishop of Lodi (1891), ibid. 277; G. Sarto, Bishop
of Mantua (later Pope Pius X; 1891), ibid. 319–20; A. G. Riboldi, Bishop of Pavia
(1891), ibid. 399; P. G. De Gaudenzi, Bishop of Vigevano (1891), ibid. 492. Among
pastorals from the province of Venice, see E. Dalla Costa, Bishop of Padua (1926), in
Marcello Malpensa, ed., *Lettere pastorali dei vescovi del Veneto* (Rome, 2002), 268. Albums
of signatures presented at the tercentenary celebrations in Rome in 1891 reveal an
enthusiasm for Luigi among Catholics in all areas of Europe; see n. 30 below.
[28] Stella, 'Santi', 565.

campaigning for the rights of the 'prisoner in the Vatican'. It was the first body in Italy to organize mass pilgrimages to Rome and other Italian shrines.[29] Understandably it had an attachment to San Luigi and it organized the grandiose celebration of the tercentenary of his death in the church of S. Ignazio in Rome (20–28 June 1891). Naturally ordinands and Catholic Youth groups figured prominently among those present.[30]

Jesuit commentators put a strongly clericalist gloss on the commemoration. Luigi was celebrated as a model of Catholic values as counter-posed to the 'paganism' of secular society and as a Catholic hero set against the anti-clerical secularists' icon Giordano Bruno, whose statue had been erected in Rome in 1899.[31] On Luigi's feast-day (21 June) Leo XIII formally recognized the heroic virtues of the young worker Nunzio Sulpizio, who had allegedly taken San Luigi as his model.[32]

In the Fascist era, Luigi's example served to present a Catholic alternative to the militaristic cult of the body.[33] In the long term, however, the image of the aristocratic eunuch was bound to lose appeal. As an exemplar of youthful chastity, Luigi was to be somewhat outclassed by the proletarian 'heroine of chastity' Maria Goretti, the twelve-year-old from the grim Pontine marshes, murdered while resisting rape and canonized in 1950.[34] In the late 1960s came a certain reinterpretation, in the light of historical studies on Luigi's milieu, of the raw material provided by Cepari. A strong emphasis was placed on that milieu's superficiality, corruption and viciousness, something that Cepari had

---

[29] Gabriele de Rosa, *Il movimento cattolico in Italia. Dalla Restaurazione all'età giolittiana,* 5th edn (Rome, 1979), 49–55; Luciano Osbat and Francesco Piva, eds, *Il movimento cattolico dopo l'Unità 1868-1968* (Rome, 1972).

[30] 'Cronaca 16–30 giugno 1890', *Civiltà Cattolica* [hereafter *CC*] ser. 14, 7 (1890), 232–3; 'Cronaca 16–30 settembre 1890', *CC* ser. 14, 8 (1890), 231–2; Leo XIII, letter to the council of Gioventù Cattolica Italiana, 29 October 1890, in idem, *Acta* (Rome, 1885–1901; photographic reproduction, 23 vols in 8, Graz, 1971), 10: 272–3; 'Cronaca 1–15 dicembre 1890', *CC* ser. 14, 9 (1891), 111–12; 'Cronaca 16–30 giugno 1891', *CC* ser. 14, 11 (1891), 223–37. *CC* (1850–) has been published fortnightly in four vols per year.

[31] 'Cronaca 16–31 giugno 1891', 222–3, 225; 'Dopo le feste centenarie di S. Luigi Gonzaga', *CC* ser. 14, 11 (1891), 129–42.

[32] 'Cronaca 16–31 giugno 1891', 232–3.

[33] Stated with particular force by Elia Dalla Costa in his pastoral of 1926.

[34] Canonized 26 June 1950: *Osservatore Romano*, 149–50 (26–7, 28 June); Turi, 'Il "brutto peccato"', 119–46.

indicated only obliquely. This gave a nuance to the nineteenth-century clericalist vision. Luigi was 'God's rebel', in revolt against his own background; he had rejected the false values of court society with stoical resolve and mastered in himself the congenital Gonzaga temper.[35] Hence, while a man of his milieu, he had an exemplary value in a modern corrupt world. The emphasis had shifted from Luigi as a paradigm of chastity to Luigi as a rejecter of false mundane values.

Cepari's *Life* was a complex document which elicited varying responses in diverse contexts. For a long time it was the rather effete image of the 'angelic youth' which dominated in the Catholic imagination and was conveyed by iconography, but, political pressures apart, it had probably been the more 'establishment' image of the mature Luigi as obedient novice and practitioner of an active piety that were crucial for his beatification, although not perhaps for his canonization. Increasingly Luigi became an exemplar for young laity and not just for religious, and all the more so in the battle against secularism of the nineteenth and twentieth centuries; the Jesuit novice became an exemplar for novice Catholic Action militants. In the seventeenth and eighteenth centuries, canonizations had generally been the outcome of collaboration between social elites and religious orders. In the nineteenth century, however, aristocratic pride was barely a factor. Petitions for persons to be raised to the honours of the altar now came primarily from orders and congregations (mini-orders) of priests and sisters whose often impressive financial resources, which enabled them to fund canonization processes, came from mass donations or from the proceeds of teaching or nursing, not from aristocratic patronage. Canonizations and hagiography became more than ever instruments for asserting Catholic values, now in the face of secularism and materialism rather than Protestantism, as the Church sought to secure its mass base. In this context, even if saints of humble origin now had to be found, the cult of Luigi waxed rather than waned as his image was redefined.

University of East Anglia

---

[35] Giorgio Papàsogli, *Ribelle di Dio. Il mondo e la giovinezza di Luigi Gonzaga* (Milan 1968), esp. Preface by Domenico Mondrone, who was a leading writer on *CC*. See also Domenico Mondrone, 'Luigi Gonzaga ribelle che sceglie la libertà', *CC* anno 119, 1 (1968), 437–62. For a more conventional approach, see Mario Scaduto, 'L'azione di un mistico (In margine al centenario aloisiano)', *CC* anno 119, 4 (1968), 540–66.

THE NORTHERN SAINTS AFTER THE REFORMATION IN THE WRITINGS OF CHRISTOPHER WATSON (d. 1580)

by MARGARET HARVEY

Regional identity in medieval Durham depended crucially on St Cuthbert.[1] The property and privileges of the diocese were presented as possessions of an originally Celtic community which had carried the miraculously incorrupt body of the saint from Lindisfarne to a final home in Durham. Tradition added other holy abbots, bishops and kings, remembered as obedient to the Roman tradition after the Synod of Whitby in 664. The Durham story included the expulsion at the Conquest of married guardians of Cuthbert in favour of proper monks, a change corroborated by miracle stories and holy lives, such as that of Godric in the dependent cell of Finchale.[2] Increasing possessions were given to the saint; miracle stories showed him punishing violators of his shrine.[3] Relics, including the head of King Oswald and remains of Bede, linked the priory with these traditions. These ideas had penetrated the local identity; the notion of the *Haliwerfolc*, the community of the liberty of St Cuthbert, the lands belonging to the saint, remained strong in the late Middle Ages for people 'between Tyne and Tees'.[4] Nonetheless, in the 1570s Christopher Watson attempted a history which denigrated Cuthbert's life and miracles and those of other Durham saints.[5]

Watson was a native of Durham city, baptized in St Oswald's Church in 1545 and dying in 1580.[6] He was a King's Scholar of

---

[1]   G. Bonner, D. Rollason and C. Stancliffe, eds, *St Cuthbert, his Cult and his Community to A.D. 1200*, (Woodbridge, 1989); Symeon of Durham, *Libellus de exordio atque procursu istius, hoc est Dunelmensis ecclesie*, ed. and trans. D. Rollason [hereafter LDE] (Oxford, 2000), for edition and sources of main history; D. Rollason, ed., *Symeon of Durham: Historian of Durham and the North* (Stamford, 1998).

[2]   *LDE*, 172–5; 224–9; note 29 below.

[3]   *LDE*, index under 'Cuthbert, assistance rendered, retribution inflicted'.

[4]   C. D. Liddy, *The Bishopric of Durham in the Late Middle Ages: Lordship, Community and the Cult of St Cuthbert* (Woodbridge, 2008), ch. 5, esp. 205.

[5]   *ODNB, s.n.* 'Watson, Christopher (1545/6–1580/1)'; this contains no information about Watson's Durham family or kin.

[6]   A. W. Headlam, ed., *The Parish Register of St Oswald's Church, Durham, Containing*

Durham School;[7] from 1562 he studied at Cambridge, first at St John's College (BA 1566) and then at Corpus Christi (MA 1569).[8] He may then have become a schoolmaster.[9] He married and was ordained at least as a deacon, as he is described in 1578;[10] his will describes him as 'a minister of God's word', which may indicate a priest.[11]

Of his history, in British Library MS Cotton Vitellius C IX, only Book I is complete, dated 1574;[12] the rest is a jumbled collection of notes. Three books were projected, the first covering the period from the origins of Christianity in England to the coming of Augustine; the second from Augustine to the Synod of Whitby and the departure of the leading Celt, Colman, in 664; and the third continuing to the mid-fourteenth century, when his medieval manuscript sources failed. Watson's Durham declined from the purity of early Lindisfarne following the Synod of Whitby, with further decay after the Conquest.

Celtic saints often won Watson's approval, the Roman tradition never. Though he approved of Bede ('a budde of blessed memory') he did not use him in Book I, because his work was corrupted 'so is it pestred with the pernitius poppye develishe dernell and troble from tares of dreames, visions and monasticall miracles'.[13] About Cuthbert he was entirely negative: he talked of 'this God of the Northe as they call him, an Irisse man and bastard borne',

---

the Baptisms, Marriages and Burials from 1538–1751 (Durham, 1891), 5.

7   Durham, Cathedral Muniments [hereafter DCM], L/BB/1, fol. 10ʳ; L/BB/2, fol. 9ʳ, from 1557/8 to 1562.

8   J. and A. Venn, *Alumni Cantabrigenses*, 10 vols (Cambridge, 1922–54), 1/4: 348.

9   For his schoolmastering, see Catechism, n. 10 below; he wrote his history in Grimstone Hall, home of William Cavendish: London, BL, MS, Cotton Vitellius C IX [hereafter Vitellius], fol. 93ᵛ (Cavendish is abbreviated in this manuscript as 'Candys'). Richard Cavendish, William's brother, produced verses for Watson: C. J. Wright, *Sir Robert Cotton as Collector: Essays on an Early Stuart Courtier and his Legacy* (London, 1997), 369; R. Surtees, *The History and Antiquities of the County Palatine of Durham*, 4 vols (London, 1816), 4: facing 170. On Richard Cavendish, see *ODNB, s.n.* 'Cavendish, Richard (c.1530–1601)'.

10   Watson, as author of *Briefe Principles of Religion Collected for the Exercise of Youth and Simpler Sort of People* (London, 1578), is called 'de' (i.e. deacon).

11   Kew, TNA, PROB 11/62, fols 393ᵛ–394ʳ. I must thank Dr Paul Botley for showing me this. Watson's children, listed in the will, are also given in London, BL, MS Cotton Titus A II [hereafter Titus], last folio.

12   Book I: *Th'istorye of Duresme now furst published Anno 1574 by C. W. Deira-grantus* [a play on his Durham and Cambridge connections]; Vitellius, fols 105ʳ–126ʳ.

13   Vitellius, fol. 107ᵛ; the allusion was to the Parable of the Sower in Matt. 13: 24–30.

who was brought from Scotland 'to hatche sum of his devilish doctryne in England'.[14] Cuthbert represented Roman influence and superstition; his body was 'their great god'. 'This is that great man in whos banner was put more confydence than in the crosse and victorye of Christ, yet a sinfull man God knoweth, yea born in sin'.[15] Explaining how the monks took the body from place to place, he called it 'an idoll of great profett'.[16] He thought that Cuthbert's habit of inflicting retribution was not the way true saints should behave.[17]

He utterly disapproved of Wilfred, the prominent defender of the Roman side at Whitby in 664, and of Benet Biscop, who founded the monastery at Jarrow.[18] They learned superstition in Rome, so that 'not content with the reules of Christ's gospel nor satisfied with the glad tidyngs of there redemption preached by Aydan, Finan and Colman [Celts] … but drawinge out an uther order of lyffe from the confused chaos of man's brane',[19] they introduced a religion contrary to the Gospel. Biscop was criticized for introducing Roman liturgy.[20] To enter a monastery for salvation revealed that kings of Northumbria such as Ceolwulf 'wer farr deceaved, not knowing the salvation comynge from God to be geven by free grace to all thatt fathfully beleave in Christ Jesu'.[21]

Equally he disliked Godric, the twelfth-century hermit of Finchale.[22] Not only was Godric's life punctuated by miracles, but among the qualities celebrated were celibacy and sexual abstinence. Godric was quarrelsome and unquiet; his attempts to quell his sexuality simply illustrated that: 'Dispysynge His [God's] ordinary helpe, for all the dayes of his lyfe he lyved in stinkynge vilynye, and, so (yff it be true that of the papistical legend is reported), he leapt into the bramble bushes there to convert his lewd lust to

---

[14] Vitellius, fol. 64[r]. Watson derived the 'Irish' legend of Cuthbert from *Nova Legenda* (London, 1516), called 'Capgrave' in the sixteenth century; ed. C. Horstman, 2 vols (Oxford, 1901), 1: 216–44.

[15] Vitellius, fol. 68r.

[16] Vitellius, fol. 74[v].

[17] Vitellius, fol. 84.

[18] Vitellius, fol. 98[v].

[19] Vitellius, fol. 98[r].

[20] Ibid.

[21] Vitellius, fol. 69[r].

[22] For this legend and miracles, see Reginald of Durham, *Libellus de vita et miraculis sancti Godrici, heremitae de Finchale*, ed. J. Stephenson, SS 20 (1847).

sorrow'.[23] The expulsion of the Durham clerks in favour of monks and the imposition of clerical celibacy showed further decline from true Christianity.[24]

To explain why such a history was written, one must understand how fundamentally the medieval account of Durham's history was incompatible with Elizabethan Protestantism. The story of Christianity in Britain was rewritten by Bale, Foxe and finally Archbishop Parker to give it an apostolic origin, grounded not on Rome but on an earlier, purer tradition which the Celts at the Synod of Whitby in 664 had wished to preserve against Romanizers.[25] Parker described a Church gradually corrupted by Rome from the time of Augustine of Canterbury, with continuing decline thereafter, the pattern which Watson followed. Attitudes to saints and sanctity were also changing with the development of Protestant theology.[26] An emphasis on justification by faith alone meant that holiness was redefined. Monasticism was condemned as unscriptural and often corrupt; most Protestants rejected clerical celibacy and monastic vows.[27] Strong insistence on Christ as the only mediator of salvation meant that invocation of the saints was repudiated. Cults of the saints were attacked from the 1530s, and by 1562 Article Twenty-Two of the Articles of Religion condemned the 'Romish' doctrine of worship and adoration of images and relics and the invocation of saints as 'a fond thing vainly invented'.[28] If the saints did work miracles, they were the work of Satan. This doctrinal shift was combined with practical efforts to eradicate saints' cults by destroying shrines and images and reinterpreting their lives.

In Durham, the shrine of St Cuthbert was dismantled in 1538 and the body disinterred.[29] Later reburial of Cuthbert's remains

---

[23] Vitellius, fol. 89[r].

[24] Vitellius, fol. 76[v].

[25] J.-L. Quantin, *The Church of England and Christian Antiquity* (Oxford, 2009), esp. 22–87.

[26] H. L. Parish, *Monks, Miracles and Magic: Reformation Representations of the Medieval Church* (Abingdon, 2005); Idem, '"Impudent and abhominable fictions": Rewriting Saints' Lives in the English Reformation', *SCJ* 32 (2001), 45–65.

[27] P. Marshall, *The Catholic Priesthood and the English Reformation* (Oxford, 1994), ch. 5, esp. 163–5, 173; H. L. Parish, *Clerical Marriage and the English Reformation: Precedent, Policy and Practice* (Aldershot, 2000), 62–3, 138–60.

[28] E. Duffy, *The Stripping of the Altars: Traditional Religion in England c. 1400 – c. 1580* (New Haven, CT, 1992), 407–10, 450, 458, 568.

[29] N. Harpsfield, *Historia Anglicana ecclesiastica* (Douai, 1622), 105.

left the shrine desecrated; pilgrimage and processions ceased. The monastery which had housed and cared for the shrine was dissolved in 1539, but was refounded in 1541 by the King as a cathedral with canons and much the same franchises and endowments (so that the bishop still had some quasi-royal powers over the area) but rededicated, omitting Cuthbert's name.[30] The anonymous *Rites of Durham*, written from memory in the 1590s to describe the pre-Reformation church of Durham, shows the cathedral now shorn of images and shrines.[31] The stages by which this stripping took place are largely lost, but it was probably complete by the time of the Northern Rebellion in 1569. Emphasis on the royal supremacy over the national Church meant that when Durham tried to defend its ecclesiastical privileges under Elizabeth it succeeded not by proving 'long use' (which often meant a grant 'to the saint') but by showing the royal grant of 1541.[32]

Clearly well read, both in the medieval histories of Durham and in Protestant criticism, Watson was probably in touch with the Parker circle collecting material for ecclesiastical history.[33] In his will, one of the guardians for his daughter Bezabell was a 'Mr Jossline', probably to be identified with John Joscelyn (1529–1603), the archbishop's chaplain and Latin secretary.[34] Watson also included evidence from 'The Antiquity of Our British Church', to draw attention to the book because its rarity meant he could only 'obtain a superficiall sight thereof',[35] and no doubt thought that others might not see it at all. This was Parker's *De Antiquitate Britannicae ecclesiae* of 1572, published in a very limited edition of about fifty copies.[36]

---

[30] J. Field, *Durham Cathedral: Light of the North* (London, 2006), 97–9.

[31] *Rites of Durham*, ed. J. T. Fowler, SS 107 (1903), esp. 68–9, 77.

[32] B. Till, *York against Durham: The Guardianship of the Spritualities in the Diocese of Durham Sede Vacante*, Borthwick Paper 84 (York, 1993), esp. 4–5, 6; for the arguments produced, see, e.g., Durham, UL, Archives and Special Collections [hereafter DUL, ASC], DDR/EJ/CCG/2/1, fols 143[r–v].

[33] For the whole Parker enterprise, with full bibliography, see T. Graham and A. G. Watson, *The Recovery of the Past in Early Elizabethan England: Documents by John Bale and John Joscelyn from the Circle of Matthew Parker*, Cambridge Bibliographical Society Monograph 13 (Cambridge, 1998).

[34] *ODNB, s.n.* 'Joscelin [Joscelyn], John (1529–1603)'; Graham and Watson, *Recovery*, 5–12.

[35] Vitellius, fols 119[r–v].

[36] M. McKisack, *Medieval History in the Tudor Age* (Oxford, 1971), 44–5; Matthew Parker, *De antiquitate Britannicae ecclesiae et privilegiis ecclesiae Cantuariensis* (London, 1572).

Watson relied for his outline narrative on manuscript sources, some of which he owned.[37] This is not the place to discuss the complicated history of the sources for Durham history in the Middle Ages. It will suffice to say that Watson refers to one of his sources for the history after Whitby as *Status Ecclesie Dunelmensis*,[38] which is the twelfth-century history of Durham, known as *Libellus de exordio*, by Symeon, with a continuation.[39] He also mentioned works by 'Gyffreye the sacriste of Coldingham', 'Robert' (Graystanes) and 'William Chambers', with whose work, 'for want of a pilot', he was forced to end his Durham story in the fourteenth century. His references show that he had before him Durham material by Geoffrey of Coldingham, Robert Graystanes and William 'Chambre', continuing the chronicles of Symeon, in other words the narratives now printed as *Scriptores Tres*.[40] But he owned or used at least three copies of Symeon, which he compared.[41] Watson explained that at first he became stuck where Geoffrey ended, but then in 1573 his cousin Anthony gave him 'certeyn pamphletts in volume and ould text hands' and he was able to finish.[42]

The manuscripts gave Watson the medieval narrative; contemporary works provided the critique. Foxe's *Ecclesiastical History*, in the edition of 1570, was the most important.[43] John Bale's *The Actes ... of the Englysche Votaryes*, first published in 1546, showed the vices

---

[37] Including, in addition to the Durham histories, Cambridge, Emmanuel College, MS 85 (a Wycliffite tract on Roman ceremonies); Oxford, Bodl., MS Laud Misc. 207 (a Wycliffite version of Matthew and Mark's Gospels), MS Digby 81 (a miscellaneous volume, showing an interest in the date of Easter); London, BL, MS Royal 18 B III (a Brut Chronicle), all with Watson's notes or his name.

[38] Vitellius, fols 107^v–108^r.

[39] His main manuscript covered the period from 635 to 1152, to 'Sancta Barbara the bishoppe of Durham'. Titus (a Symeon manuscript of *LDE* with Coldingham and Graystanes among other items), has the rubric 'Liber de statu Lindisfarnensis id est Dunelmensis ecclesie'; it includes a continuation 'Tribus dehinc annis': *LDE*, xxxi.

[40] *Historiae Dunelmensis Scriptores Tres*, ed. J. Raine, SS 9 (1839), 2–156, is the printed version of Geoffrey, Robert and 'Chambre', which are continuations of Symeon and which occur in this order in some MSS of Symeon. All Symeon MSS are described in Rollason's edition of *LDE*. Titus has notes and personal material.

[41] His notes are in part III of BL, MS Cotton Vespasian A VI; see *LDE*, xxxiii–iv.

[42] Vitellius, fol. 93^r. *Scriptores Tres*, 31, shows where Geoffrey ended.

[43] Watson referred to Foxe's work as 'History Ecclesiastical': Vitellius, fol. 66, citing 'first tome, padge 165'; for other references, see fols 68, 69^{r-v}, 70^{r-v}; 89^{r-v}, 92^{r-v}. For editions of Foxe's work, see J. Roberts, 'Bibliographical Aspects of John Foxe', in D. Loades, ed., *John Foxe and the English Reformation* (Aldershot, 1997), 36–51, esp. 46–8; D. Loades, ed., *John Foxe: An Historical Perspective* (Aldershot, 1999), Introduction. References to Foxe also in Titus, fols 10^v, 39, 86, 87, 90, 114.

and frauds of monks, and *Legenda Nova* (1516) provided medieval saints' lives.[44] John Jewel's *Defence of the Apology* (1567)[45] convinced Watson that Bede's *Ecclesiastical History* edited in Catholic Louvain had been falsified by its editors, so he did not use it for the early history. His attack on Augustine relied almost wholly on Jewel's *Defence* and *Reply* to Harding (1566), part of Jewel's sustained anti-Catholic polemic.[46] For a repudiation of spurious visions, he quoted the Swiss Reformed theologian Ludwig Lavater, whose *De Spectris* was translated into English in 1572.[47] To attack Catholic attitudes to images, ceremonies, false miracles and shrines with relics, he noted, several times with exact references, James Calfhill's *Answer* (1565) to the Catholic John Martiall's *Treatise of the Cross* (1564), all part of the fierce polemic against recusants during this period.[48]

The need for a new narrative must have been emphasized when in 1569 the Northern Rising shook the whole Durham area. Public executions occurred in the city itself.[49] Many participants, rightly accused of favouring Catholicism, did public penance and a John Watson of Durham, perhaps Christopher's father, sought a pardon.[50] Though there is no evidence that Christopher's father was a rebel, he may have felt frightened.[51] Punishment after the Rising was arbitrary and the Watson family may in any case have favoured the Nevilles, who were among the rebel leaders. Christopher's attitude to the Neville family can be seen in his first work (a translation of Polybius's *History*, Book I), of 1568, to which he joined a *Life* of Henry V.[52] A prefatory letter to the *Life* explained that he had been

44 J. Bale, *The Actes … of the Englyshe Votaryes*, various editions between 1546 and 1560; cf. Vitellius, fols 86ʳ, 94ʳ.

45 *The Works of John Jewel, Bishop of Salisbury*, ed. J. Ayre, 4 vols, PS (London, 1844–50), 3: 150–206, esp. 163–6; G. W. Jenkins, *John Jewel and the English National Church* (Aldershot, 2006), esp. chs 2, 3.

46 *Works of Jewel*, ed. Ayre, 1: 81–552.

47 Ludwig Lavater, *Of Ghosts and Spirites Walking by Nyght*, trans. Robert Harrison (London, 1572), cf. Vitellius, fol. 81ʳ.

48 Titus, fols 35ʳ, 37ʳ, 131ʳ; James Calfhill, *An Aunsere to the Treatise of the Crosse* (London, 1564); ed. R. Gibbings, PS (London, 1846).

49 K. J. Kesselring, *The Northern Rebellion of 1569: Faith, Politics and Protest in Elizabethan England* (Basingstoke, 2007), esp. 124–5.

50 *Calendar of the Patent Rolls Preserved in the Public Record Office, Elizabeth I, 5: 1569–72* (London, 1976), no. 728.

51 Kesselring, *Northern Rebellion*, 126–30.

52 *The Hystories of the Most Famous and Worthy Chronographer, Polybius … , Englished by C.W.* (London, 1568); cf. H. B. Lathrop, *Translations from the Classics into English from Caxton to Chapman* (New York, 1932, repr. 1968), 187–8.

particularly struck by a speech attributed by Hall's *Chronicle* to the Earl of Westmorland.[53] Watson commended himself to the Westmorland family, the Nevilles, 'trusting so much to their bountiful benevolence and accustomed gentleness, which is naturally planted in the stock, so that they would gratefully accept my good will towards them'.[54] In 1568 this commendation applied particularly to Charles, the Sixth Earl, soon to be a leader of the Rebellion, for which he was attainted and died in 1571 in exile.[55]

Watson was certainly aware that cults of the saints lingered among the residual Catholicism of his native Durham. His comment about St Cuthbert's banner shows that it was still remembered.[56] Carried into battle before the Reformation, it appeared for the last time during the Pilgrimage of Grace (1536) and was finally destroyed by the Protestant wife of James Whittingham, dean until 1579.[57] Cuthbert's desecrated shrine was still visited in the 1570s.[58] To attack Catholic 'superstition' of this kind, Watson quoted extensively from James Pilkington's ('our worthy Durham bishop') work on Haggai, against 'the superstitious observance of teimes and days' for the benefit of Pilkington's diocese 'by resonne of ther ethnike idolls'.[59] Watson's own section on Cuthbert included:

> Thus much concerning B Cuthbert … to the entent that his acts fully displayed to the world and wayed in indifferent balance many (my countrymen especially) long deceaved by ignorance might attayne to a perfytt certenty and sum of his actions, therebye to iudge the better how to receave … what they hear of him.[60]

As a further assault on the cult of the saints Watson denigrated local oral history. He describes how, near Whitby, 'salynge alongst that cost I was shewed the place' where there were serpents turned to stone by St Hilda, the legend which explained the existence of

---

53 See McKisack, *Medieval History*, 105–11, for Hall.

54 Vitellius, fols 102[r–v].

55 Kesselring, *Northern Rebellion*, index under 'Westmorland (sixth earl of)'.

56 See above, n. 22.

57 *Rites*, ed. Fowler, 26–7.

58 *Dobsons Drie Bobbes: A Story of Sixteenth Century Durham*, ed. E. A. Horsman (London, 1955), 83.

59 Vitellius, fols 106[v]–107[r]; part verbatim, part summary from *The Works of James Pilkington. B.D.*, ed. J. Scholefield, PS (Cambridge, 1842), 16–17.

60 Vitellius, fol. 84[v].

ammonites.[61] Sceptical as ever, he explains that exactly the same tale is told in *Nova Legenda* about St Keyna.[62]

The refusal to identify with the *Haliwerfolc* implied in Watson's work may also indicate that he needed to identify with Protestants among his own divided kin. His family had been in Durham since a great-grandfather paved its marketplace.[63] Before the Reformation his grandmother had lived in the priory almshouses,[64] with one son, Roger, a monk of Durham and another, John (Christopher's father), in Elvet. The latter, a yeoman, described himself as 'an officer and a servant' of the priory from 'six yeres before the Dissolucion' (1533).[65] When he died aged eighty in June 1580, St Oswald's Church recorded him as 'for wisdom, gravyte, honest sobryete and other godly vertues worthe to be praised'.[66] Of John senior's five sons and three daughters, John junior, a rich Newcastle merchant, was sheriff there in 1567 and mayor in 1574.[67] Another son, William, preceded Christopher to Cambridge and perhaps into schoolmastering.[68]

Some of this family were Protestants. Roger, the monk, became a canon at the Dissolution and accepted the religious settlement immediately in 1559.[69] He was a deputy commissioner for the

---

[61] Vitellius, fol. 63[r]; *Nova Legenda*, ed. Horstman, 2: 29–33.

[62] *Nova Legenda*, ed. Horstman, 2: 102–4.

[63] For his great-grandfather (Richardson), see Vitellius, fol. 89[v]; *Records of the Borough of Crossgate, Durham, 1312–1531*, ed. R. Britnell, SS 212 (2008), index, esp. no. 493★.

[64] For Christopher's grandmother, see n. 69 below.

[65] Durham, Cathedral Library, Hunter MS 32A, fols 60[v]–62[r], a deposition from 1577. See also DCM, Dean and Chapter Register 2, fols 197[r–v]; Dean and Chapter Register 3, fol. 81[v].

[66] *Register*, ed. Headlam, 25; for his will, see *Wills and Inventories from the Registry at Durham*, ed. J. C. Hodgson et al., SS 112 (1906), 84–5. See also DCM, Dean and Chapter Register 1, fols 168[v]–169[r].

[67] For John Watson, junior, see *History of Newcastle and Gateshead*, ed. R. Welford, 3 vols (London, 1887), 3: 37; *Extracts from the Records of the Merchant Adventurers of Newcastle upon Tyne,* ed. J. R. Boyle and F. W. Dendy, SS 93 (1895), 93 n.; DCM, Dean and Chapter Register 2, fol. 227.

[68] William is mentioned as being at Cambridge in Roger's will (n. 69 below); for his being a pensioner at Christ's 1560, see Venn and Venn, *Alumni*, 4/1: 350. The Clergy of the Church of England Database (CCED) 1540–1835, <http://www.theclergydatabase>, ID 74706, accessed 27 April 2009, mentions William Watson as a schoolmaster with Walter Harlakenden at Tunstall in Kent in 1579. A Mr Harlakindon was another guardian in Christopher's will.

[69] Roger Watson, alias Bell, *The Durham Liber Vitae*, ed. D. and L. Rollason, 3 vols (London, 2007), 3: 423, C. 1329. This replaces all biographical material for Durham monks. See also A. I. Doyle, 'Further Monastic Books', *The Durham Philobiblion*, 1.7

visitation afterwards.[70] His will in 1561 gave Christopher £40 and books, on condition that he 'apply the school' [*sic*].[71] Christopher's papers throw new light on this uncle (his account of how this ex-monk became a Protestant being unique for Durham).[72] At first he 'continued a massynge sacrificer' and only later, influenced by Luther, Bucer and Calvin, 'of whose works he was a great student as witness thos books notid with his owen hand which I have to show' became 'a zelus and sure professor of the gospel'. Christopher quoted two of his sermons, one proving the truth of justification by faith. 'My cosyne and freand Anthony Watson, a fellow … in Crists colledge',[73] from Thorpe Thewles, who lent Christopher manuscripts, became a Fellow of Christ's in 1573 and later Almoner to the Queen and finally Bishop of Chichester.[74]

But other Watson cousins were at least religiously conservative. William Maurice alias Watson, a former chaplain to the last prior of Durham, was from 1557 Vicar of Bedlington;[75] in 1569 he was indicted and confessed to having participated when the rebels held a mass and other services in the cathedral.[76]

Another cousin, Miles White,[77] at Durham School with Christopher in 1558, became – and continued – a lay singing man of the cathedral.[78] In 1561 Roger bequeathed him the living of Norham if he would accept ordination but he did not; at his death in 1611 St Oswald's recorded him as 'a man of verie good accounte'.[79] He was, however, indicted and did public penance for participating in

(May 1952), 45–8. I thank Dr Doyle for all his help. For the will, see DUL, ASC, DPR 1/2/2, fols 17ᵛ–18ʳ. See also *The Royal Visitation of 1559*, ed. C. J. Kitching, SS 187 (1975), 22–7, 28.

[70] D. Marcombe, 'The Dean and Chapter of Durham, 1558–1603' (unpublished Ph.D. thesis, University of Durham, 1973), 165.

[71] For the will, see n. 69 above.

[72] Vitellius, fols 103ʳ⁻ᵛ.

[73] Vitellius, fol. 93ʳ (1573).

[74] *ODNB, s.n.* 'Watson, Anthony (d. 1605)'; for Anthony's will, see Surtees, *Durham*, 3: 83 n.

[75] *Liber Vitae*, ed. D. and L. Rollason, 3: 432, C 1369, under Maurice. For his will, see DUL, ASC, DPR 1/2/4, fol. 49ᵛ.

[76] *Depositions and Other Ecclesiastical Proceedings from the Courts of Durham Extending from 1311 to the Reign of Elizabeth*, ed. J. Raine, SS 21 (1845), 147.

[77] For John senior's will, see n. 66 above; for Anthony's, n. 74.

[78] B. Crosby, 'The Choral Foundation of Durham Cathedral 1350 – c. 1650' (unpublished Ph.D. thesis, University of Durham, 1992), Appendix VI, 129.

[79] *Register*, ed. Headlam, 50.

the Roman liturgy in 1569 and being reconciled to Rome.[80] He stayed continuously with prebendary William Todd, who for refusal to subscribe in 1559 was in 1566 under house arrest in the nearby village of Croxdale.[81] Miles also helped George Errington who was finally captured with John Boste (a famous Catholic martyr) and executed for conveying seminary priests in 1596.[82] With Errington was caught John Spede, probably a relative of Todd's, executed in Durham in 1594.[83] Spede wrote from prison to Miles for help. It is not surprising that Tobie Matthew, hunting recusants in 1596, described White to Burghley as 'a close dangerous fellow … none the better for his undeserved favour'.[84]

Christopher must therefore have felt impelled to demonstrate devotion to right religion. Book I of his history was offered 'to yow reverend fathers' (the Dean and Chapter), asking them to take it as

> this sclender dischardge of that indebted duetye which I owe to my contrye and your societye … drawne therto by a settled desyre to continew the honour and fame of my native soile and your worthi benefactors … driven by an earnest desire worthely to commende thes constitutions and rayse ther ancient renowne.[85]

He noted that Colman, the leader of the Celtic party at Whitby in 664, 'professed the same doctryne published by the reverend father in God which now enionethe [enjoieth?] … that sea and seat'.[86] Anyone who now complains must 'understand that (blessed be God) [the bishop] now sitting at Durham with his fellow bishops (under the protection of our good and most worthy sover-

---

[80] *Depositions*, ed. Raine, 133, 152–3.

[81] Durham, County Record Office, D/Sa/L 20.2, fols 1–15.

[82] Marcombe, 'Dean and Chapter', 181; *Unpublished Documents Relating to the English Martyrs, 1: 1584–1603*, ed. J. H. Pollen, Catholic Record Society, Record Series 5 (1908), 125–8, 220–1.

[83] J. Morris, *The Troubles of Our Catholic Forefathers Related by Themselves*, 3rd series (London, 1875), 183, 192; *Unpublished Documents*, ed. Pollen, 239.

[84] Marcombe, 'Dean and Chapter', 181; *Calendar of State Papers, Domestic Series, Elizabeth, 1595–97*, ed. M. E. A. Green (London, 1869), 183.

[85] Vitellius, fol. 108ᵛ.

[86] Vitellius, fol. 104ᵛ.

eign Queen Elizabeth) hath sought outt the ould wayes and them have found good'.[87]

Watson's enterprise shows how the attack on saints and their cults worked out locally. Local saints had various functions. Thomas Becket, for instance, could easily have made Canterbury a centre of resistance to the royal supremacy and so his story had to be rewritten.[88] Durham's identity had been fashioned round Cuthbert with a story equally incompatible with Protestantism. Watson was attempting to produce a new identity. For him, the Crown and not the saint was the benefactor (after God) of Durham.[89] True religious tradition was pre-Whitby and Celtic, not Roman. He hoped to convert his ignorant fellow Northerners out of their love of Cuthbert to the royal supremacy and true religion. He may also have hoped for a job!

Durham University

---

[87] Ibid.
[88] Parish, *Monks, Miracles*, 92–105.
[89] Vitellius, fols 69^r, 72^r, 72^{r-v}.

'TRUTH NEVER NEEDED THE PROTECTION OF FORGERY': SAINTHOOD AND MIRACLES IN ROBERT HEGGE'S 'HISTORY OF ST. CUTHBERT'S CHURCHES AT LINDISFARNE, CUNCACESTRE, AND DUNHOLME' (1625)*

by SARAH SCUTTS

Robert Hegge's 'History of St. Cuthbert's Churches at Lindisfarne, Cuncacestre, and Dunholme' was one of many texts produced in the early modern period which portrayed and assessed the Anglo-Saxon Church and its saints.[1] This Protestant antiquarian work fits into a wider tradition in which the medieval past was studied, evaluated and employed in religious polemic. The pre-Reformation Church often played a dual role; as Helen Parish has shown, the institution simultaneously provided Protestant writers with historical proof of Catholicism's league with the Antichrist, while also offering an outlet through which to trace proto-Protestant resistance, and thereby provide the reformed faith with a past.[2] The Anglo-Saxon era was especially significant in religious polemic; during this time scholars could find documented evidence of England's successful conversion to Christianity when Pope Gregory the Great sent his missionary, Augustine, to Canterbury. The See of Rome's irrefutable involvement in the propagation of the faith provided Catholic scholars with compelling evidence which not only proved their Church's prolonged existence in the land, but also offered historic prec-

* I would like to thank Alexandra Walsham, Julia Crick, Jane Dawson, Bill Sheils, Margaret Harvey and Tamsin Rowe for their comments and advice on this paper.

[1]   Other versions of this manuscript exist; however, this paper only deals with London, BL, Add. MS 27423, Robert Hegge, 'History of St. Cuthbert's Churches at Lindisfarne, Cuncacestre, and Durham' (1625). Subsequent references to Hegge's work are to this manuscript. For other versions, see esp. BL, Sloane MS 1322, Robert Hegge, 'The Legend of St. Cuthbert, with the Antiquities of the Church of Durham' (1628); Durham, Cathedral Library, Add. MS 62, R. H., 'Saint Cuthbert or the Histories of his Churches at Lindisfarne, Cuncacestre & Dunholme' (after 1627); Oxford, Bodl., Madan MS 36593, R. H., 'Saint Cuthbert or the Histories of his Churches at Lindisfarne, Cuncacestre & Dunholme' (1626).

[2]   Helen L. Parish, *Monks, Miracles and Magic: Reformation Representations of the Medieval Church* (London, 2005).

edent for England's subordination to Rome. In contrast, reformed writers engaged in an uneasy relationship with the period. Preferring to locate the nation's Christian origins in apostolic times, they typically interpreted Gregory's conversion mission as marking the moment at which Catholic vice began to creep into the land and lay waste to a pure primitive proto-Protestant faith.[3] In order to legitimize the establishment of the Church of England, Catholicism's English foundations needed to be challenged. Reformers increasingly placed emphasis upon the existence of a proto-Protestant 'strand' that predated, but continued to exist within, the Anglo-Saxon Church. Until the Norman Conquest, this Church gradually fell prey to Rome's encroaching corruption, and enjoyed only a marginal existence prior to the Henrician Reformation in the 1530s. Thus Protestants had a fraught and often ambiguous relationship with the Anglo-Saxon past; they simultaneously sought to trace their own ancestry within it while exposing its many vices. This paper seeks to address one such vice, which was the subject of a principal criticism levied by reformers against their Catholic adversaries: the unfounded creation and veneration of saints. Protestants considered the degree of significance the medieval cult of saints had attached to venerating such individuals as a form of idolatry, and, consequently, the topic found its way into countless Reformation works. However, as this essay argues, reformed attitudes towards sainthood could often be ambivalent. Texts such as Hegge's prove to be extremely revealing of such ambiguous attitudes: his own relationship with the saints Cuthbert, Oswald

---

[3] For early modern attitudes to the Anglo-Saxon Church, see esp. S. J. Barnett, 'Where was your Church before Luther? Claims for the Antiquity of Protestantism Examined', *ChH* 68 (1999), 14–41; Allen J. Frantzen, 'Bede and Bawdy Bale', in idem and John D. Niles, eds, *Anglo-Saxonism and the Construction of Social Identity* (Gainesville, FL, 1997), 17–39; Felicity Heal, 'Appropriating History: Catholic and Protestant Polemic in the National Past', *Huntington Library Quarterly* 68.1/2 (2005), 109–32; Colin Kidd, *British Identities before Nationalism* (Cambridge, 1999); Hugh A. MacDougall, *Racial Myth in English History: Trojans, Teutons and Anglo-Saxons* (Montreal, ON, 1982); Anthony Milton, *Catholic and Reformed: The Roman and Protestant Churches in English Protestant Thought 1600–1640* (Cambridge, 1995); Benedict Scott Robinson, 'John Foxe and the Anglo-Saxons', in Christopher Highley and John. N. King, eds, *John Foxe and his World* (Aldershot, 2002), 54–72; Glanmor Williams, 'Some Protestant Views of early British Church History', in idem, ed., *Welsh Reformation Essays* (Cardiff, 1967), 207–19. On antiquarianism more broadly, see esp. Graham Parry, *The Trophies of Time: English Antiquarians of the Seventeenth Century* (Oxford, 1995); Daniel Woolf, *The Social Circulation of the Past: English Historical Culture 1500–1730* (Oxford, 2003).

and Bede appears indistinct and, in numerous instances, his under-standing of sanctity was somewhat contradictory.

★ ★ ★

Hegge, an antiquary and writer, was born in Durham and educated at Corpus Christi College, Oxford. Although he has received scant attention from recent historians, we are able to piece together that during his time at university he engaged in activities ranging from lecturing on theology to compiling an illustrated treatise on the theory and construction of sundials.[4] His academic interests also extended to the history of his native county, which led him to compile his work on St Cuthbert and the history of Durham. By drawing on the works of medieval scholars such as William of Malmesbury, Simeon of Durham and Bede, Hegge produced an extensive account of the hermit's life.[5] While undoubtedly a work of local patriotism seeking to promote and celebrate the diocese's past, it is important to recognize that Hegge's Protestant faith played no small part in his representation of the saint and of Cuthbert's contemporaries.

At Corpus Christi Hegge was exposed to numerous currents of Arminian thought; figures such as Thomas Jackson, a member of the Durham House group (a collection of High Church Anglicans), and Gabriel Bridges, a fellow of the institution, frequently preached anti-Calvinist sermons at the college. While the Oxford colleges may have subscribed to varied religious schools of thought, Hegge's attitude was in keeping with those of his contemporaries at Corpus Christi who, disenchanted with Calvinism, advocated Arminianism from the turn of the seven-teenth century. The author's Arminian beliefs have been further recognized by Nicholas Tyacke, who highlighted the antiquarian's enthusiastic appreciation of ecclesiastical renovations in his native county.[6] Hegge remarked that under Bishop Neile 'the church

---

[4]   *ODNB*, *s.n.* 'Hegge, Robert', <http://www.oxforddnb.com>, last accessed 30 April 2009; Philip Pattendon, 'Robert Hegge of Durham and his St. Cuthbert', *Transactions of the Architectural and Archaeological Society of Durham and Northumberland* 5 (1980), 107–23.

[5]   An extensive, though as yet unpublished, overview of Robert Hegge's sources has been conducted by Margaret Harvey.

[6]   Nicholas Tyacke, *Anti-Calvinists. The Rise of English Arminianism c. 1590–1640* (Oxford, 1987), 119–20.

of Durham seems to renew her age, and … take on a new lease of eternitie, who for the internal beauty of her high altar, cathedral music, and sacred laver and other ornaments, may challenge her sister churches for prioritie'.[7] Indeed, during this time the diocese underwent a series of changes; in 1617 Durham Cathedral's communion table was moved to an altar-wise position, and in the early 1620s it was entirely replaced with a marble altar, decorated, according to a contemporary, with 'many cherubims'.[8] For puritans these changes represented a throwback to the pre-reformed era, and produced a sense of anxiety at a possible return to Catholicism. In contrast, Arminians demonstrated a less hostile attitude towards the medieval Church than their puritan counterparts; they recognized that the establishment had some redeeming features which still deserved a place within reformed worship.[9] This is not to say that such individuals did not engage in anti-Catholic polemic. As I will show, Hegge's portrayal of St Cuthbert and his fellow Northumbrian monks is highly critical; he holds them responsible for spreading Catholic vice and contributing to the deterioration of English religion. However, his understanding of sanctity contains numerous contradictions and ambiguities and opens up interesting questions regarding early modern perceptions of sainthood and the utility of saints in religious polemic.

★ ★ ★

Hegge's denigration of Cuthbert takes on a guise which is fairly typical in the writings of sixteenth- and seventeenth-century Protestant scholars. As in the polemical works of figures such as John Bale and John Foxe, we find 'The History of St Cuthbert's Churches' providing an extensive compendium of medieval Catholic vices, littered with snide asides designed to undermine the Church of Rome.[10] The text presents a detailed narrative of the

7   Robert Hegge, *The Legend of St Cuthbert*, ed. J. B. Taylor (Sunderland, 1816), 61, quoted in Tyacke, *Anti-Calvinists*, 120.

8   Bodl., Rowlinson, MS D. 821, fol. 4, in Tyacke, *Anti-Calvinists*, 118.

9   Michael Questier provides an insightful discussion of religious beliefs in the early seventeenth century in his 'Arminianism, Catholicism and Puritanism in England during the 1630s', *Historical Journal* 49 (2006), 53–78; Anthony Milton's *Catholic and Reformed* (Cambridge, 1995) discusses the reassessment of the medieval Church under Archbishop Laud and his circle.

10   For similar texts, see John Bale, *The Actes of Englysh Votaryes* (Antwerp, 1546); John Clapham, *The Historie of Great Britannie* (London, 1606); John Foxe, *Actes and*

saint's life. Having witnessed the soul of the esteemed bishop Aidan ascend into heaven, Cuthbert dedicates himself to the Lord. He begins an arduous journey to Lindisfarne, is subjected to numerous tests by the devil, and eventually arrives at the priory where he resides as a hermit for nine years. We read of a number of miraculous happenings which occurred during Cuthbert's time on the isle, from corn growing 'without Tillage' to the occasion when two 'sea-monsters' came 'kneeling to him'.[11] After his death we are further told of how his body remained uncorrupted; a testament to the piety and devotion in which he lived his life.[12] While Hegge recorded these wonders, his tone was not without a degree of scepticism and mockery. He suggested, for example, that the reader might like to 'borrow an optick-glasse from superstition' to better understand the saint's miracles.[13] There is a sense that these wondrous feats were being exposed as ridiculous delusions, and used as evidence with which to prove medieval Catholicism's corruption and the need for reform.

Hegge clearly believed that saints, and the miracles they performed, were instruments by which a deceitful Catholic clergy could exploit the populace to gain wealth and influence. The island of Lindisfarne, for example, was described as being 'as voide of men, as full of Devils, [and] becam the scene and stage whereon Saint Cuthbert acted all his miracles'.[14] The implication that Cuthbert's island home constituted a 'stage' implies that the events which transpired during his hermitage were rehearsed and part of a performance. Hegge was not alone in associating aspects of Catholicism with the theatre. Samuel Harsnett's *A Declaration of Egregious Popish Impostures*, first published in 1603, compared the Roman priesthood to a company of actors, who transformed public spheres into their theatrical stages.[15] Hegge's suggestion

---

Monuments (London, 1570); Raphael Holinshed, *The First and Second Volumes of Chronicles* (London, 1587); John Speed, *The History of Great Britaine* (London, 1611).

[11]   Hegge, 'History', 14–17.

[12]   For further information on St Cuthbert's life, see Bertram Colgrave, ed. and trans., *Two Lives of Saint Cuthbert* (Cambridge, 1985); *ODNB, s.n.* 'Cuthbert [St Cuthbert]' <http://www.oxforddnb.com>, last accessed 20 November 2009; John Michael Wallace-Hadrill, *Bede's Ecclesiastical History of the English People: A Historical Commentary* (Oxford, 1988).

[13]   Hegge, 'History', 17.

[14]   Ibid. 15.

[15]   Samuel Harsnett, *A Declaration of Egregious Popish Impostures* (London, 1603), ed.

that the saint's actions and miracles were not genuine was further asserted later in the text, when he exclaimed:

> … what advantage [the] Monks took of the blinde devotion of that age: whose whole practice was, to devise and relate miracles of their Saints: which (as superstition is allway credulous) were as easily believ'd. thus to gaine a reverend opinion from the Pagans of Christianitie; they thought it but a pious fraud, to cosen the people with Legends of wonders who, whiles they defended truth by falsehood, and their impostures discovered to wiser ages, have made religion rather suspected, then any way advanc'd it. For truth never needed [the] protection of forgerie: but will carrie away the victorie without hypocrisie.[16]

Thus Anglo-Saxon monks manipulated what Hegge called the 'superstition' of the age. While he apparently acknowledged the utility of the miraculous in converting heathens to the Christian faith, the author took issue with the clerics' liberal 'creation' of such spurious wonders. False marvels, such as those promoted by Cuthbert and his contemporaries, only served to associate Christianity with deceit and fraud. Instead, the author maintained, the monks of Lindisfarne should have let the religion speak for itself, believing that true faith did not need embellishment to convert or inspire.

Indeed, Hegge argued, the Anglo-Saxon Church was all too easily able to adorn itself with false saints and miracles. According to the text, Cuthbert, driven by vainglorious pride, sanctified himself. Through his adoption of an ascetic life, and by spreading a plethora of wondrous stories, he was able to secure his own canonization, and essentially turn himself into a god. '[I]f I were to make his funeral oration', wrote Hegge, 'I would not insert among his praises [that] he was an Anchorite. For thus to un[n] man himself, to contemplait himself into a Deitie, argued more pride, then Religion'.[17] He later concluded, '[t]hus St Cuthbert sainted himself in his lifetime, and gave them notice, what precious Relique he should be when he was dead'.[18] Instead of an absti-

---

and repr. by F. W. Brownlow as *Shakespeare, Harsnett, and the Devils of Denham* (London, 1993), 191–335.

[16] Hegge, 'History', 17.

[17] Ibid. 21–2.

[18] Ibid. 24.

nent and pious individual, Cuthbert was, in contrast, presented as a devious manipulator, concealing his narcissistic aspirations behind a mask of eremitical holiness. Furthermore, Anglo-Saxon religion was exposed as idolatrous. The monks at Lindisfarne could undermine the Lord's omnipotence with apparent ease, and elevate a mortal being, such as Cuthbert, to the status of a god. Moreover, such a challenge to God's supremacy went unopposed by contemporary individuals, indicating that by the seventh century Roman Catholic corruption was already taking hold of the nation.

These transgressions were symbolic of Catholicism's relegation of Holy Scripture; the Bible's importance appeared somewhat diminished. Not content with celebrating biblical figures, the Church of Rome sought to create its own sacred souls; scriptural characters thus became redundant in a world in which the clergy could produce its own saints and marvels. For Hegge, this was one of the papacy's principal vices, and constituted significant justification for reform. Instead of venerating the fraudulent Cuthbert, the author challenged medieval concepts of sanctity and stressed that those who wished to see a true representation of a hermit should:

> ... look upon Nebuchadenezzar, in his curse: he was driven from men, and did not eat grasse as [the] oxen: when his bodie was not w[i]th the dewe of heaven, til his heares became as eagles feathers, and his nailes as [the] claws of birds. Thus therefore for an hermite to excommunicate himself from being a citizen of [the] world, what is it else; then to sinne against the commonweal, and definition of a man: to whose societie is as naturall, as to be a Creature. So that whiles others think it devotion in him: I shall deem it a melancholie-distemper.[19]

The Book of Daniel details how Nebuchadnezzar was humbled by the Lord and, losing his sanity, lived in the wild like a beast. After seven years, however, both his regal position and his reason were restored to him, which in turn prompted him to 'praise and extol and honour the King in heaven'.[20] In contrast to Cuthbert who chose his eremitical existence, this Babylonian king had this ordeal divinely inflicted upon him; this distinction was important to Hegge. It was the combination of divine interest, and his spir-

[19] Ibid. 22–3.
[20] Dan. 4: 37.

itual journey as a result of his banishment in the wilderness, which led to Nebuchadnezzar's venerated status. In contrast, Cuthbert's asceticism was self-imposed; furthermore, according to Hegge, it was symbolic of a melancholic affliction. Such motivations were not deserving of canonization; Protestants believed the importance lavished upon abstinence by the medieval Church was misplaced. Although all Christians were called to self-denial, the degree of bodily humiliation that Cuthbert put himself through was not advocated by the Bible; reformers considered it a pious distraction which served to tempt the faithful away from God's true teachings. Cuthbert's hermitage, and the extent to which it was commended, was further evidence of the medieval Church's promotion of artificial sanctity and the degradation of pure Christianity.

Not only were the inhabitants of Lindisfarne charged with rejecting sacred Scripture in order to promote a monk of their own; they were further accused of mimicking biblical passages and applying their wonders to false idols such as Cuthbert. Hegge claimed they:

> ... defloured all the miracles of saints in holy-writ, and bestowed them upon their St. Cuthbert: so barren-braind Monks they were, that could not invent new ones, but such as were writ before ... For Adam could not be the commander of the creatures, in the state of innocencie: but St Cuthbert also must have the savage beasts to do him homage. Abraham could not entertain 3 Angells under an Oak, but Saint Cuthbert must have Angells for his guests, at the monasterie of Rippon ...[21]

Medieval Catholic monks, it seems, were not particularly inventive; Hegge alleged that they were devoid of all originality. As he had stressed earlier in his text, when acknowledging the utility of saints and wonders in converting pagans to the faith, Hegge believed that the Bible alone provided all that was necessary to extol the virtues of Christianity. Biblical figures such as Nebuchadnezzar were never formally canonized; however, Hegge's text identified such individuals as men of virtue, those who provided an example to be mimicked. Thus, in this sense, sainthood was not a prerequisite for respect or emulation, but rather it distracted from those figures that were deserving of recognition and could truly

---

[21] Hegge, 'History', 32–3.

promote God's message. The Lord no longer needed to endow individuals with miraculous abilities to demonstrate the glory of the faith. As such, any non-biblical figures were not divinely blessed, but rather fraudulent deceptions, symbolic of the 'superstition' and ignorance of the society which created them. Cuthbert's status as a saint, and the devotion which had been lavished upon him by his cult, therefore, represented the escalating contamination which existed within the Anglo-Saxon Church.

Thus Hegge's perception of St Cuthbert was highly critical. It has been suggested that the role of Cuthbert's banner in Catholic movements such as the Pilgrimage of Grace might have caused Protestants to be particularly hostile towards this saint.[22] This symbol of Catholic and Northumbrian pride accompanied those who journeyed from Durham to York in 1536, and as a result contemporary Protestants would have associated this Anglo-Saxon hermit with both the Roman Church and idolatry.[23] As such, it would not be unexpected for reformed writers to employ Cuthbert in such a way; furthermore, this may account for the fact that an Arminian was engaging with medieval sainthood with a similar degree of vehemence to that of zealous reformers such as John Bale and John Foxe in the previous century. Already considered popish by the hotter sort of Protestants, Arminians such as Hegge would have wanted to distance themselves from any association with Catholicism. However the saint's banner cannot account by itself for his denigration of Cuthbert; for Hegge, Cuthbert's hagiography encapsulated the corruption of Catholicism and provided precedent for reform. Throughout, the reader is presented with an

---

[22] Many thanks to Bill Sheils who commented on this point when this paper was presented at the Ecclesiastical History Society's Summer Meeting in 2009. See also, in this volume, Aude de Mézerac-Zanetti, 'Liturgical Changes to the Cult of Saints under Henry VIII', 181–92.

[23] C. S. L. Davies, 'Popular Religion and the Pilgrimage of Grace', in Anthony Fletcher and John Stevenson, eds, *Order and Disorder in Early Modern England* (Cambridge, 1985), 58–91, at 87. The banner, however, was not used during the Northern Rising of 1569 as Katherine Whittingham, John Calvin's sister and wife to the dean, had previously supervised its burning. For the destruction of St Cuthbert's banner, see A. Fowler, ed., *The Rites of Durham* (Durham, 1903), 27, 217; K. J. Kesselring, '"A Cold Pye for the Papists": Constructing and Containing the Northern Rising of 1569', *Journal of British Studies* 43 (2004), 417–43, at 426 n.; David Marcombe, 'A Rude and Heady People: The Local Community and the Rebellion of the Northern Earles', in idem, ed., *The Last Principality: Politics, Religion and Society in the Bishopric of Durham, 1494–1660* (Nottingham, 1987), 117–51, at 134.

exploitative medieval Church, an institution which both created and venerated false idols. With regard to Cuthbert, the text presents his sanctity as a fraudulent mask designed to appear pious while in actuality detracting from the Bible and enticing the laity to 'monkery' and superstition. While we might anticipate that Protestant authors would be disparaging towards Catholic saints, Hegge's text also presents a number of ambiguities and contradictions. As we shall now see, the manuscript is not disparaging of all Anglo-Saxon sainted figures, which implies that Hegge's attitude towards sanctity is more complex than one might expect.

★ ★ ★

There is no doubt that Hegge's text was both polemically and patriotically driven. Exposing the corrupting influence of the Roman Church upon English religion constituted only one half of the author's agenda. The text also sought to demonstrate the importance and success of the diocese, and represented a celebration of local worthies. This motivation, however, was apparently often in tension with the polemical dimension so apparent in Cuthbert's legend. Daniel Woolf has recently shown how there was a danger of antiquarians appearing popish, as their 'fondness for antiquities' was often in tension with their religious beliefs.[24] This becomes apparent when contrasting Hegge's critical discussion of the hermit Cuthbert with his exaltation of the Northumbrian king Oswald. Oswald, martyred in the seventh century by the pagan king Penda, was well known as a promoter of the faith. Having sent for a Scottish bishop, Aidan, this king translated sermons for his people and successfully converted them to Christianity. He was later 'culted' as a saint and his arm preserved as a relic, having remained miraculously uncorrupted due to his acts of charity. The reader is introduced to Oswald at the beginning of the text with Hegge calling him '[t]he first of the Saxon Kings (who made conquest as well of religion, as men) that in this province was dipt in the sacred Laver of Baptisme … [he] is observed by Malmesbury to be the first of the English race, that was illustrious by miracles'.[25] While Oswald's association with the miraculous is attributed to William of Malmesbury, Hegge does

24 Woolf, *Social Circulation*, 186.
25 Hegge, 'History', 4–5.

nothing to dispute this claim. The reader is instead provided with a comprehensive account of the martyr king's life and death. Hegge's use of his medieval sources is apparently selective; while Malmesbury's account of Oswald was unchallenged, Cuthbert's miracles were labelled as false wonders. Thus, we can see how these two saints served different functions for the author; Oswald's sanctity illustrated the divine status of both the king and the diocese of Durham, while in contrast Cuthbert's was symbolic of Catholic vice.

The text continued to underline the magnificence of this king:

> This great monarch [the] pious Founder of [Lindisfarne] … in battle with a Pagan Prince, lost his life, and the day: but with this advantage, that whiles Penda laft him not an head to meake a Crowne: he received a more glorious Diadem of Martyrdome. And as furie prosecuting revenge aftre death, toare his bodie in pieces: So the Devotion of the time dispersed his reliques to several places …[26]

Hegge underlined how the devotion of the time was responsible for the scattering of Oswald's relics. This is somewhat ambiguous. As has been demonstrated with Cuthbert, the author was happy to critique the Anglo-Saxon Church explicitly, and to accuse its monks of being 'barren-brain'd'. This passage, however, reads much more factually; Hegge apparently does not wish to pass judgement on this point. Instead, the text draws its audience's attention to the king's martyrdom and his role as a converter, a role which symbolized the monarch's authority in the religious affairs of his kingdom. We are told how Oswald was the pious founder of the faith in Northumberland, and that he laid down his life defending Christianity. The description is littered with praise; this selfless king is glorified and exalted as one of the region's heroes. This portrayal, however, raises a number of questions. Why, for example, would Hegge wish to celebrate a monarch who essentially promoted and died for Catholicism, the very religion his text sought to discredit? And why was Oswald's sanctity more acceptable than Cuthbert's?

These issues are further complicated by the author's inclusion of Oswald's miracles. The text's account of the king's uncorrupted limb is reasonably detailed, and treated with a degree of accept-

---

[26] Ibid. 5–6.

ance. Unlike the miracles attached to Cuthbert's hagiography, there is no sense of mockery. 'Lastly his arme was preserved in a sylver casket', wrote Hegge:

> This sacred Relique retain'd the blessing of Aidanus. And was honour'd as monument of incorruption: an historie which, to this effect, is related by Beda; that upon an easter day, as the King sate at dinner, his servant tolde him of some poore people, that expected almes at his gate: who forthwith bid him both carry them the meate, & divide the platter (which was of sylver) and distribute it among them. With which fact of charitie, Aidanus the Bishop, who sate by hime, much delighted, tooke him by the right arme. With this hearty wish: Never let this arme perish.[27]

While Aidan recognized the king's virtue and blessed his arm, it was the king who embodied divine abilities. Hegge was evidently proud of this monarch and employed him as evidence of his diocese's glory. The contradictory representations of Cuthbert and Oswald suggest that Hegge understood their sanctity in different ways. Certainly Oswald's royal position would have played no small part in the author's perceptions. As a monarch, the Northumbrian king had already been divinely appointed, arguably legitimizing his miraculous abilities. Furthermore, and perhaps more significantly, his martyrdom was representative of a personal sacrifice for both his people and his faith, whereas, as we have already seen, Cuthbert's trials were self-inflicted. Thomas Freeman and Brad Gregory have both recently shown the centrality of martyrdom to Reformation polemic and the extent to which martyred individuals were commended as objects of admiration and imitation.[28] While the majority of their work focuses upon perceptions of contemporary or recent martyrs, it might also be argued that a similar degree of importance was attached to this historical monarch. As such, Oswald's sanctity served to demonstrate not only a pious and charitable individual, but also a monarch who laid down his life for the Christian faith. Such a king would have assisted in patrioti-

---

[27] Ibid. 7–8.
[28] Thomas S. Freeman and Thomas F. Mayer, eds, *Martyrs and Martyrdom in England 1400–1700* (Woodbridge, 2007); Brad S. Gregory, *Salvation at Stake: Christian Martyrdom in Early Modern Europe* (Cambridge, 1999).

cally elevating the significance of not only Durham but also the English nation. While it is tempting to attribute Hegge's conflicting portrayals of sanctity to the fact that Oswald was a king and martyr, this does not explain the text's treatment of the monk Bede. Bede, a native of Jarrow, compiled his *Ecclesiastical History of the English People* in 731. This was an exceedingly influential text which enjoyed a pre-eminent scholarly reputation throughout the medieval and early modern periods. Bede's cult as a saint was established less than fifty years after his death.[29] Hegge presented this Northumbrian saint as a victim of Catholic 'monkery', unwittingly spreading their deceptions in his eighth-century history. When Cuthbert's bodily preservation was discussed the seventeenth-century author remarked: '[t]his miracle of incorruption St Beda reports, who was eleeven yeare olde at St Cuthberts death; in relating wherof he made no lye, but told one. The historie of whose life, and death, he writ and took upon trust, from the information of the Monks of Lindisfarne'.[30] Hegge partially exonerated Bede of responsibility in promoting Roman Catholic deception, attributing the legend's inclusion in the *Ecclesiastical History* to Bede's trusting nature and his fellow monks' exploitation of this.

So why did Hegge celebrate Bede and Oswald but not Cuthbert? It appears that their patriotic significance was too influential; Hegge did not want to discredit two of Durham's most prized historical figures. Thus we can see that Hegge was selective in his representation of sanctity and the religious past. He rejected aspects of medieval Catholicism which did not fit into a Protestant framework, such as asceticism and idolatry; however, he promoted other saintly characteristics, such as martyrdom and charity, as they served his patriotic agenda.

★ ★ ★

It can be argued that these three saints served two different functions for the author. While Cuthbert provided an excellent prism through which to expose the corruption of Catholicism and

---

[29] Bede's importance to Durham is discussed in Donald Matthew, 'Durham and the Anglo-Norman World', in David Rollason, Margaret Harvey and Michael Prestwich, eds, *Anglo-Norman Durham* (Woodbridge, 1998), 1–22, at 14–15.

[30] Hegge, 'History', 32.

the need for reform, Oswald and Bede gave Hegge two examples of Durham's glory and antiquity. Thus an ambivalent attitude towards sanctity is revealed. We can clearly see that there is a struggle between upholding traditional and patriotic representations of the past, and employing history as a polemical tool. Robert Hegge's manuscript nicely represents the ambiguities which emerged during the religious debates of the sixteenth and seventeenth centuries. While instinctively seeking to dismiss medieval sainthood as a manipulative tool with which a deceitful Catholic clergy tempted the faithful away from God, Hegge also recognized its utility in elevating the status of his native diocese. 'The History of Saint Cuthbert's Churches' further reveals that Arminians had a complex and ambivalent relationship with the medieval Church and ideas of sanctity. While it may have been less acute, this relationship, however, was not materially different from that of other types of Protestantism. Indeed, there is a sense of irony that Hegge's manuscript went on to be printed in 1663 by Richard Baddeley, the former secretary to the recently deceased Calvinist Bishop of Durham, Thomas Morton.[31] It is clear that the text cut across the spectrum of ecclesiastical orders, and that its anti-Catholic sentiment appealed to both Arminians and Calvinists. This further illustrates the complexities of seventeenth-century Protestant perceptions of the medieval Church, and how far attitudes within Protestantism itself differed or overlapped.

University of Exeter

---

[31] Robert Hegge, *The Legend of St. Cuthbert with the Antiquities of the Church of Durham* (London, 1663).

SIMULATED SANCTITY IN SEVENTEENTH- AND EIGHTEENTH-CENTURY MALTA

by FRANS CIAPPARA

Revelations, apparitions, voices, stigmata and ecstasies were extraordinary phenomena and profoundly emotional, in which God was perceived as communicating with human beings through bodily phenomena. It was up to churchmen to regulate and control divine intervention in daily life and separate truth from deceit. But attempting to fulfil this pastoral duty was a complicated matter. Were these experiences authentic, really proceeding from God or were they illusions of the devil, the deceiver par excellence and able to capture human trust? Furthermore, besides the devil's deceit, might there not also be an element of human simulation or 'false sanctity', that is, a mixture of lies and hypocrisy?[1] This was the art of the actor, who makes the audience believe what is untrue. Hypocrites have one sole aim: to obtain praise and fame through the exercise of sham virtues.

Pope Sixtus V in 1588 set up the Congregation of Rites, which established a more rigid approach to the canonization of saints.[2] All the same, the form that 'true' sanctity was to assume was a complex matter. The difficulty arose because there were diverse models of sanctity. There was, for instance, the search for the experience of martyrdom for the faith, which pushed young men to enter missionary orders and to set sail for non-European lands. However, besides this heroic type of sanctity, exclusively male, there was an alternative type of devotion, restricted to a tiny circle and especially evident among women, which culminated in ecstasies and raptures.

---

[1] Gabriella Zarri, 'Living Saints: A Typology of Female Sanctity in the Early Sixteenth Century', in Daniel Bornstein and Roberto Rusconi, eds, *Women and Religion in Medieval and Renaissance Italy* (Chicago, IL, 1996), 219–303.

[2] Miguel Gotor, *Chiesa e santità nell'Italia moderna* (Rome, 2004), 34–41; Simon Ditchfield, *Liturgy, Sanctity and History in Tridentine Italy: Pietro Maria Campi and the Preservation of the Particular* (Cambridge, 1995), 215–17; idem, 'Tridentine Worship and the Cult of Saints', in R. Po-Chia Hsia, ed., *CHC 6, Reform and Expansion 1500–1660* (Cambridge, 2007), 201–24; Peter Burke, 'How to be a Counter-Reformation Saint', in Kaspar von Greyerz, ed., *Religion and Society in Early Modern Europe 1500–1800* (London, 1984), 45–55.

This paper analyses the context of this kind of religiosity in seventeenth- and eighteenth-century Malta. It examines fourteen women who came to the attention of the Holy Office between 1677 and 1772 because of their supposed special privileges from heaven. Who were these women and what made them feign holiness? What strategies did they adopt to make their audiences think of them as saints? Why were they perceived as a substantial threat to the Church? And how was it that the Roman Inquisition got involved with such matters? Finally, was it always for reasons of 'religion' that the inquisitors proceeded against them?

★ ★ ★

These female aspirants to sanctity came from the lower social classes. One was the wife of a corsair, another was married to a blacksmith, and a third one to a fisherman. Angelica Casha, a seventy-year-old *bizocca* or tertiary from St Helen's, wove cotton and linen, while Anna Zammit's father was a mason. Catarina Piscopo lived on the alms she received and what little she earned by knitting socks. Yet, for all their simplicity, these 'holy women' succeeded in achieving visibility. What made this possible?

They were influential in part because there were a number of them. Friar Saverio in 1765 identified one at the parish of Cospicua, another at Lija and a third one at Birchircara; others were to be found at Vittoriosa, Senglea, Qormi, Valletta, Zebbug and Balzan. They impressed the circle of devotees surrounding them with the exemplary life they led, being hailed as 'living saints'.[3] They predicted their own demise, distributed alms to the poor, read people's innermost thoughts and healed bewitched persons. They bolstered their reputation for sanctity by intervening beneficently in the spiritual destinies of the living, who asked to be remembered in their prayers. They undertook fasts and penitential discipline on behalf of sinners and used their gifts of prophecy to tell people whether they were in a state of grace or would fall into mortal sin. They were particularly helpful at death, when they urged the dying to repent for their sins, instructing them in the prayers which Our Lady imparted to them in visions. Maria Aquilina was allegedly present at the judgement of a soul: the devil

---

3   Mdina, Archives of the Inquisition, Malta, Proceedings 115A, fol. 141^r [hereafter: AIM and Proc.]

claimed it his own but Our Lady prayed Our Lord 'by the milk she had given him' not to condemn it to hell.[4]

These wayward women did not just make people die a good death. They supposedly communicated with the next world and revealed the destination of deceased souls. Angelica Casha answered people's earnest prayers about the fate of their loved ones. She saw the souls in purgatory at night as she was in her room meditating on God's attributes of mercy and divine justice: they were dressed in black and white and recited the rosary in a most sweet voice.[5]

The reputation of these women was founded especially on their mystical experiences. They were assumed to live for days on communion alone[6] and were often communicated miraculously, either by Jesus Christ[7] or the host coming directly from the altar into their mouth.[8] Reportedly they had visions of saints, especially of the Virgin. She defended them in the battles they waged with the devil, who assailed their chastity or, in the form of a fat pig, scratched their faces and would not let them go to church.[9]

Christ was their chief comforter. He snatched away Antonia's heart from her breast and gave her his own.[10] He helped Francesca Protoplasta wash the clothes by drawing water from the well for her.[11] Angelica Casha took him in her arms, perhaps a vision born of her frustrated desire for the sensual and emotional satisfaction of pregnancy and motherhood.[12] Anna Zammit pretended that he helped her distribute bread to the poor. He was also supposed to have taken her for a walk when three months of age, holding her hand in his. Plausibly taking her cue from the life of St Catherine of Siena, she recounted how they were mystically married at the age of nine. Early one morning as she was hearing mass and

4   Proc. 109B, fol. 535ᵛ.
5   Proc. 114A, fols 123ᵛ–126ᵛ.
6   For one such woman, see Fulvio Tomizza, *Heavenly Supper: The Story of Maria Janis*, trans. Anne Jacobson Schutte (Chicago, IL, 1991). On this topic, consult Caroline Walker Bynum, *Holy Feast and Holy Fast: The Religious Significance of Food for Medieval Women* (Berkeley, CA, 1987).
7   Proc. 80, fol. 112ᵛ.
8   Proc. 110B, fols 571ʳ⁻ᵛ.
9   Proc. 86B, fol. 561ʳ.
10   Ibid., fol. 547ᵛ.
11   Proc. 80, fol. 129ʳ.
12   Proc. 114A, fol. 107ʳ.

contemplating the marriage of St Joseph with Our Lady, she was accosted by a young man who put a ring on her finger.[13]

Experiencing Christ's passion demonstrated that God's favour had been bestowed upon these women.[14] They may have felt in their heart Christ's cross and the instruments of his passion.[15] Maria Formosa's accounts of her spiritual experiences included hearing the Virgin telling her, while holding a crucifix covered with blood, 'This is what sinners do with their sins'. She experienced another vision, this time of Christ's wounds exuding blood. She asked him to take her on his lap and started to cry so that her tears washed his blood away.[16]

A great part of the popular charm of these women was due to their purported somatic experiences. Salvatore Dorell testified in 1732 that Catarina Piscopo would go into what seemed to be ecstasy as she recited the rosary.[17] The sexton at Zurrieq could not bring Maria Formosa out of these trances, in which sometimes she stayed from morning till night.[18]

But for all the accounts of the saintliness of these women, other witnesses were sceptical of their alleged revelations. They suspected them of being possessed by the devil or made fun of their playing the saint, sarcastically dubbing them mad.[19] They failed especially to win the approval of the ecclesiastical authorities and fell gradually prey to attacks at the hands of the Roman Inquisition. This problem of 'affected piety' had been unthinkable at the time of the battle against Luther. Then it was the roar of battle and the contest between theologians which menaced the walls of the Church; now it was the search for perfection. Nobody ever thought, Adriano Prosperi claims, that a structure set up to resist the attack of a series of sharp and aggressive theological 'truths', born of a tormented and Augustinian sense of guilt, would have found itself combating

---

[13] Proc. 96C, fol. 953ʳ.

[14] For Stefana Quinzani's sufferings of the passion, through which she helped souls in purgatory, see Cordelia Warr, 'Performing the Passion: Strategies for Salvation in the Life of Stefana Quinzani (d. 1530)', in Peter Clarke and Tony Claydon, eds, *The Church, the Afterlife and the Fate of the Soul*, SCH 45 (Woodbridge, 2009), 218–27.

[15] Proc. 80, fol. 128ʳ.

[16] Proc. 110B, fol. 565ʳ.

[17] Proc. 115A, fol. 116ʳ.

[18] Proc. 110B, fols 567ʳ⁻ᵛ.

[19] Proc. 135B, fol. 796ᵛ.

a crowd of candidates claiming sanctity.'It was a phenomenon of the first order in the story of post-Tridentine religion'.[20]

Three reasons may be offered to explain how feigned sanctity came to be regarded as a heresy. Firstly, it marked the successful attempt by the Roman Inquisition to extend its powers progressively, even after the Protestant emergency had abated. The second is that there was a firm connection between the Congregation of Rites, which examined candidates for canonization, and the Roman Inquisition, which was responsible for the prosecution of heretics. The assessor of the *Sant'Uffizio*, for example, was always a member of the *congregazione dei riti*. In other words, the inquisitors were directly involved in both saint- and heretic-making.[21] Thirdly, I would suggest that it reflected the influence of the Spanish Inquisition, which since 1529 had started cracking down on the so-called *beatas*.[22]

But why did the Church exhibit so much alarm at these 'servants of God' who represented themselves as perhaps excessive but enthusiastic practitioners of the ways of spiritual perfection? Public order was not an issue in Malta, as these women had no impact at all on national politics.[23] No Lucrecia de León prophesied the doom of the government; nor did any Maria Teresa or Bernardina Renzi predict that the expulsion of the Jesuits in 1768 would bring harmful consequences to Malta.[24] However, these women, who pretended they could peer into the souls of priests to discover their faults, did subvert church order. They did not criticize the contemporary state of the Maltese Church but they did challenge the clergy as the leaders of the community.[25] For instance, they dared

---

[20] Adriano Prosperi, *Tribunali della coscienza* (Turin, 1996), 434. For a discussion of these developments see also Andrea Del Col, *L'Inquisizione in Italia dal XII al XXI Secolo* (Milan, 2006), 659–80.

[21] M. Gotor, *I beati del papa. Santità, inquisizione e obbedienza in età moderna* (Florence, 2002).

[22] Andrew W. Keitt, *Inventing the Sacred: Imposture, Inquisition, and the Boundaries of the Supernatural in Golden Age Spain* (Leiden, 2005).

[23] On this topic, consult for Italy Gabriella Zarri,'Pietà e profezia alli Corti Padane. Le pie consigliere dei principi', in eadem, *Le santé vive. Profezie di corte e devozione femminile tra '400 e '500* (Turin, 2000), 51–86. For Spain, see Jodi Bilinkoff, *The Avila of Saint Teresa: Religious Reform in a Sixteenth-Century City* (Ithaca, NY, 1989).

[24] Richard L. Kegan, *Lucrecia's Dreams: Politics and Prophecy in Sixteenth Century Spain* (Berkeley, CA, 1990); Marina Caffiero, 'Le profetesse di Valentano', in Gabrielle Zarri, ed., *Finzione e santità tra medioevo ed età moderna* (Turin, 1991), 493–517.

[25] For the case of Francisca de los Apóstoles who in 1574 demanded the return of

to usurp the priestly office of confession by absolving people from venial sins. And, furthermore, did they not tend to do away with priestly mediation when they assured their followers that God willed them to eat meat on a Friday[26] or cheese during Lent?[27]

This inversion of gender-based hierarchy, which threatened traditional religious authority, was especially evident in the relations these women had with their confessors.[28] St Teresa of Avila emphasized the need of finding a competent spiritual director.[29] He could break the spirit of a penitent who may have actually been receiving divine communication but he could also lead her along the most secure path to spiritual perfection. It was an unpredictable road and some confessors were incapable of managing the women.[30] They became so enthusiastic about the marvellous events in the lives of their penitents that they became willing accomplices and the chief witnesses to their supposed piety. The Jesuit Sant'Albano was one of these credulous priests. He showed an absurd degree of respect for his penitent, Catarina Caunel of Valletta, but, according to a doctor who examined her, she had punctured her skin to simulate stigmata. Even her going for days without food was a sham; her sister discovered a box with food under her bed, containing bread, cheese and salami.[31]

In Malta, unlike Italy and Spain, no examples have yet been found of confessors ordering the portrait of a 'saintly woman'.[32] Nor are there instances of these females writing their autobiog-

---

Archbishop Bartolomé Carranza to his see of Toledo from Rome, see T. W. Ahlgren, ed. and trans., *The Inquisition of Francisca: A Sixteenth-Century Visionary on Trial* (Chicago, IL, 2005).

[26] Proc. 96C, fol. 982ʳ.

[27] Proc. 86B, fol. 547ᵛ.

[28] On this topic, see Giovanna Paolin, 'Confessione e confessori al femminile. Monache e direttori spirituali in ambito veneto tra '600 e '700', in Zarri, ed., *Finzione e santità*, 366–88.

[29] St Teresa of Avila, 'The Book of her Life', in *The Collected Works of St. Teresa of Avila*, trans. Kieran Kavanaugh and Otilio Rodriguez, 3 vols (Washington, DC, 1976), 1: 43.

[30] Anne Jacobson Schutte, 'Tra scilla e cariddi. Giorgio Polacco, donne e disciplina nella Venezia del seicento', in Gabriella Zarri, ed., *Donna, disciplina, creanza cristiana dal XV al XVII secolo* (Rome, 1996), 215–36.

[31] Proc. 92A, fols 56ʳ–63ᵛ.

[32] Anne Jacobson Schutte, '*Questo non è il ritratto che ho fatto io*: Painters, the Inquisition, and the Shape of Sanctity in Seventeenth-Century Venice', in *Florence and Italy: Studies in Honour of Nicolai Rubinstein*, ed. Peter Denley and Caroline Elam (London, 1988), 419–31.

raphies.[33] However, contrary to Urban VIII's constitution *Caelestis Hierusalem Cives* of 1634, which prohibited the recording of such experiences,[34] several priests undertook to honour them by writing their *vitae*.[35] For instance, Don Domenico Hellul, the parish priest of the Church of the Annunciation (Balzan), recorded the visions of Maria Borg.[36] To promote the spiritual prodigies of the tertiary Protoplasta, the minor conventual padre Ghimes, besides proposing a hagiographic composition, also distributed her shirt and veil as relics, while her girdle was reputed to cure tertian fever.[37]

The situation was regarded as truly dangerous when women developed inappropriate relations with their confessors, thereby seriously compromising the priests' souls. Antonia Schembri recounted to the inquisitor in 1685 that three years previously on a Tuesday, while she was hearing mass, St Thomas Aquinas appeared to her, his chest resplendent with light. He told her it was God's will to marry the Dominican Domenico Zammit. 'How can that be?', she asked. 'The omnipotence of God consists in doing whatever He wants', he answered. The woman described this vision to the friar and they had sex in a cave nearby.[38] As a further proof of this role reversal, Anna Zammit made Don Bartolomeo Bonnici suck her breasts as manifestation of his subordination to her, 'telling me that with this she treated me as her spiritual son'.[39] The father–daughter relationship of the sacrament of confession was thus transformed into a mother–son one, the penitent becoming a 'spiritual mother'.[40]

This brings us to one of the fundamental themes regarding these 'holy women'. They were prosecuted, not just because they flouted the 'abyssal difference' which Trent set between the clergy and the laity, but also because they were women. Jean Gerson (d. 1429), a

---

[33] For a rare case from Italy, see Cecilia Ferrazzi, *Autobiography of an Aspiring Saint*, trans. and ed. Anne Jacobson Schutte (Chicago, IL, 1996).

[34] Miguel Gotor, 'La riforma dei processi di canonizzazione dalle carte del Sant'Uffizio 1588–1642', in *L'Inquisizione e gli storici. Un cantiere aperto* (Rome, 2000), 279–88.

[35] For the validity of these *vitae*, and whether they reflected the thoughts of the women or were tempered with by the confessor, see Anne Jacobson Schutte, 'Un caso di santità affettata. L'autobiografia di Cecilia Ferrazzi', in Zarri, ed., *Finzione e santità*, 329–42, at 329–30.

[36] Proc. 141, fols 6^r–17^v.

[37] Proc. 80, fol. 112^v.

[38] Proc. 86B, fols 572^r–573^v.

[39] Proc. 96C, fol. 956^v.

[40] John Coakley, 'Gender and the Authority of Friars: The Significance of Holy Women for Thirteenth-Century Franciscans and Dominicans', *ChH* 60 (1991), 445–60.

French theologian and chancellor of the University of Paris, was a chief exponent of this misogyny. He questioned the canonization of Bridget of Sweden (d. 1373) before the fathers of the Council of Constance in 1415. But his initiative to regard female spirituality with suspicion far antedated his challenge to Bridget. His first treatise 'On Distinguishing True from False Revelations' written in 1401, already associated women with a dangerous lack of moderation in asceticism.[41] And in 'On the examination of doctrine' (1423) he claimed that these *mulierculae* (little women) – gullible, weak and voluble – were easily led astray by their fervour and by an unsavoury degree of curiosity. Above all, he associated many mystical phenomena with pathological disorders. Female bodies were colder and wetter than men's; this greater humidity and softness made them more impressionable and exposed to malign forces. Physically feeble and morally fragile women were naturally inclined to all mortal sins and rarely able to resist the assault of temptation.[42]

Gerson's writings were taken up by the Roman Inquisition when it started treating feigned sanctity as a prosecutable offence in the 1620s and 1630s.[43] They figure in Cesare Carena's *Tractatus de Officio Sanctissimae Inquisitionis* (1636) but more prominently in Cardinal Desiderio Scaglia's *Prattica per procedere nelle cause del S. Offizio* (c. 1635), which circulated widely in manuscript.[44] These manuals helped the inquisitors subject the women to great scrutiny

[41] Moshe Sluhovsky, *Believe not every Spirit: Possession, Mysticism, and Discernment in Early Modern Catholicism* (Chicago, IL, 2007), 175–9; Dyan Elliott, 'Seeing Double: John Gerson, the Discernment of Spirits, and Joan of Arc', *American Historical Review* 107 (2002), 26–54.

[42] Dyan Elliott, *Proving Woman: Female Spirituality and Inquisitional Culture in the Later Middle Ages* (Princeton, NJ, 2004), 266–9. For a virulent tirade against the female sex, see H. Kramer and J. Sprenger, *Malleus Maleficarum*, trans. Montague Summers (London, 1971), 111–25.

[43] For his inquisitorial procedure, see Brian Patrick McGuire, 'Education, Confession, and Pious Fraud: Jean Gerson and a Late Medieval Change', *American Benedictine Review* 47 (1996), 310–38, at 330–3. See also Elliott, *Proving Women*, 283–5.

[44] For one such copy, see AIM, Miscellanea [hereafter: Misc.] 2. On this treatise, see Albano Biondi, 'L'"inordinata devozione" nella *Prattica* del Cardinale Scaglia (ca. 1635)', in Zarri, ed., *Finzione e santità*, 306–25. Scaglia was also the author of the *Instructio* which condemned the abuses practised in the pursuit of witches; see John Tedeschi, 'The Roman Inquisition and Witchcraft: An Early Seventeenth-Century "Instruction" on Correct Trial Procedure', in idem, *The Prosecution of Heresy* (Binghamton, NY, 1991), 205–27.

and challenge.[45] What was the cause of their fantasies? And what was the degree of responsibility they bore for holding them?[46] One focus of interrogation was their personality. Could not the marvellous feats of mystic saints have fired their imagination? Teresa of Avila was canonized in 1622, Maria Maddalena de' Pazzi in 1669 and Rosa of Lima in 1671. The women's illiteracy barred them from access to books but five of them were members of third orders while the others could get such knowledge of the lives of the saints from their confessors or from what they heard in sermons.

Besides, was not taking pride in divulging visions and boasting of having reached 'true perfection' an inappropriate bid for sanctity?[47] Did not disobeying one's religious superiors go against humility? Was not quarrelling with one's parents and using harsh words to them damaging to one's reputation for holiness?[48] Did the women use their saintly reputation to improve their lot financially, through the contributions for masses for the suffrage of the souls in purgatory?[49] Did they exhibit an intense religious devotion or only what was expected of ordinary mortals? The Jesuit Don Giovanni Cassar, who in 1729 was sent to interview Maria Formosa, commented on her ignorance of mental prayer and her being unable to 'tame her passions'.[50]

There was another sign by which false saints were known – whether the content of their revelations conformed to the beliefs of the Church. Teaching erroneous doctrine was one of the clearest cases that could be made against the veracity of visions. Was it theologically sound, for instance, to call on the devil for help or to say that Judas or Pontius Pilate's wife had been liberated from hell 'through the piety of God and the prayers of Holy Mary'?[51] And did not Anna Zammit's actions smell of Quietism or Molinism, the doctrine which declares that man's highest perfection consists in psychical self-annihilation, when the mind no longer thinks or

---

[45] For the care and rigour of inquisitorial investigation of 'pretence' cases, see Christopher Black, *The Italian Inquisition* (New Haven, CT, 2009), 156–7.

[46] Stephen Haliczer, *Between Exaltation and Infamy: Female Mystics in the Golden Age of Spain* (Oxford, 2002), 125–45.

[47] Proc. 86B, fols 551[r–v].

[48] Proc. 92A, fol. 60[r].

[49] Proc. 115A, fol. 143[r].

[50] Proc. 110B, fols 570[r]–571[v].

[51] Proc. 80, fol. 112[v]; Proc. 86B, fols 552[v], 546[r].

wills on its own account?[52] She convinced her followers that she freed them from the temptation of the flesh and rendered them unable to sin by touching their 'shameful parts' with her own genitalia.[53] Antonia Schembri contradicted another basic tenet of the Catholic faith: her conviction that God had dispensed her from the need to confess implied that the sacraments, through which grace was mediated by the institutional Church, were unnecessary.[54]

The tribunal often wore these women down with its pitiless questioning to the point where they admitted their guilt: 'I realise that I have sinned and ask pardon from God and this tribunal, placing myself at your mercy'.[55] However, not all behaviour could be judged as hypocritical, based on wilful simulation. At first Antonia Schembri's good faith could not be shaken. She vigorously rebutted all the charges against her and defended her innocence to the last. She was also disposed, though, to recognize that she could be mistaken: 'I have said only the truth. Whether these revelations and apparitions are from God or truly from the devil I don't know. What I do know well is that I did not invent them myself'.[56] But her effort to mount a defence was unavailing. Her seemingly supernatural raptures and revelations could be imaginary or self-generated delusions. In fact, the two doctors who examined her on 10 January 1687 reported that she was mentally ill and in need of assistance:

> We ... state emphatically that she only suffers from hypochondriasis, that is she believes she is truly suffering from complaints which only exist in her imagination. This illness results from changes in the bowels, which bring about an alteration in the volume of blood, thereby giving rise to the symptoms she suffers from. Her malady is of course curable if the appropriate medicaments are administered.[57]

---

52 This heresy was condemned in 1687 by Pope Innocent XI, in the bull *Coelestis Pastor*. On 15 November of that same year, Inquisitor Vidoni issued a decree ordering all books and manuscripts relating to this heresy to be burnt: Proc. 86A, fol. 150ʳ. For a general overview, besides Massimo Petrocchi, *Il Quietismo italiano del seicento* (Rome, 1948), see the more recent Marilena Modica, *L'«infetta dottrina». Misticismo e Quietismo nella seconda metà del seicento* (Catania, 2001).
53 Proc. 96C, fols 949ʳ–1021ᵛ.
54 Proc. 86B, fol. 548ʳ.
55 Proc. 96C, fol. 974ʳ.
56 Proc. 86B, fol. 563ʳ.
57 This report was confirmed by two exorcists, who affirmed that, rather than

To the inquisitor, these females appeared particularly dangerous and were to be strictly controlled. Nuns endowed with ecstatic powers acted within the darkness of the monastery. Their mysticism was confined within the massive walls of the convents.[58] On the contrary, these lay women lived their visionary experiences in direct contact with the faithful.[59] They were therefore forced into seclusion either at home or in the dungeons of the Inquisition. They were also to refrain from having visitors to whom they might boast of their sanctity and false revelations.[60] Above all, no posthumous cult was to be promoted. Their memory was to be abolished and their writings collected and burned. In the case of *suor* Protoplasta, who had died in an odour of sanctity, her corpse was exhumed and buried in a common grave, lest devotion should develop around its tomb.[61]

★ ★ ★

To conclude, these women sought to gain the esteem of the public by publicizing their own sanctity. For a time they achieved power and overcame the limitations that society placed on them. But the Inquisition, equally afraid of a characteristically female style of spiritual expression and wishing at the same time to protect the hierarchy and its authority, eventually unmasked them as frauds and discredited them in the eyes of their followers. Just as at Seville, in Malta they were transformed from 'a symbol of holiness into one of illusion and deceit', and retreated into the obscurity from which they had briefly emerged.[62] The *vox populi* was no longer *vox Dei* and in certain cases it tended to be identified with the *vox diaboli*.[63]

University of Malta

---

being possessed, she was 'misled by her own imagination': ibid., fols 583^r–584^r.

[58] On how the inquisitor was to proceed with these nuns, see AIM, Misc. 2, 65–8. For one such nun, Benedetta Carlini, see Judith C. Brown, *Immodest Acts: The Life of a Lesbian Nun in Renaissance Italy* (Oxford, 1986).

[59] David Gentilcore, *Healers and Healing in Early Modern Italy* (Manchester, 1998), 166–7.

[60] AIM, Proc. 96C, fols 1020^v–1021^r.

[61] AIM, Corrispondenza13, fol. 204^r: Barberini to Visconti, 4 June 1678.

[62] Mary Elizabeth Perry, 'Beatas and the Inquisition in Early Modern Seville', in Stephen Haliczer, ed. and trans., *Inquisition and Society in Early Modern Europe* (London, 1987), 148.

[63] André Vauchez, *Santi, profeti e visionari. Il soprannaturale nel medioevo* (Bologna, 2000), 247.

ST WINIFRED, BISHOP FLEETWOOD AND JACOBITISM*

by COLIN HAYDON

During the Middle Ages, the cult of St Winifred was the most important of the many Welsh cults centred on wells. Winifred's story was recounted in two medieval Lives: the *Vita prima* by Pseudo-Elerius (c. 1100), written from a Welsh perspective, and the *Vita secunda* by Robert, prior of Shrewsbury, written after the translation of the saint's supposed relics to his abbey in 1138. According to these, Winifred (fl. c. 650) was educated by St Beuno in North Wales; and, although she had vowed herself to virginity, she inspired the lust of a local prince, Caradog, who, when repulsed, decapitated her. Where her head fell, a spring erupted; and Beuno restored Winifred to life and killed Caradog with a curse. Winifred subsequently became abbess at Gwytherin and, after her death, the spring's waters were held to cure the sick miraculously. The spring, at Holywell in Flintshire, attracted countless pilgrims in the later Middle Ages, and Henry VII's mother, Lady Margaret Beaufort, encased it in a fine building.[1] At the Reformation, however, the cult of saints was abolished, the Twenty-Second of the Thirty-Nine Articles specifically denouncing their invocation.

Holywell is the subject of numerous studies. Recently, Alexandra Walsham has meticulously investigated its post-Reformation history from different perspectives: *inter alia*, the shrine's survival despite Protestant hostility; Holywell's importance as a Counter-Reformation missionary centre; Protestants' theological explanations of the waters' healing properties; and the re-evaluation from the seventeenth century of cures accomplished by the spring and other holy wells, prompted by the development of spas.[2] This essay

* I am grateful to Alex Walsham and John Walsh for commenting on a draft of this essay.

[1]   *ODNB*, *s.n.* 'Gwenfrewi [St Gwenfrewi, Winefrith, Winifred] (*fl. c.* 650)'; 'Shrewsbury, Robert of (d. 1168)'.

[2]   Alexandra Walsham, 'Reforming the Waters: Holy Wells and Healing Springs in Protestant England', in Diana Wood, ed., *Life and Thought in the Northern Church c.*

examines two further topics: St Winifred as both a Catholic and
Jacobite totem in the late seventeenth and early eighteenth centuries; and resulting Protestant attacks on her cult and her shrine.
Political dissidents and oppositions – and not just established
regimes and churches – have sustained saints' cults in a variety of
contexts; and this study provides one example of this.

★ ★ ★

In the seventeenth century, Holywell's finest hour was when James
II visited. On 29 August 1687, the King, on a royal progress, went
there from Chester via Flint and prayed that, through St Winifred's
intercession, Mary of Modena would bear a son. James and Mary
plainly wished to revive Holywell as a royal shrine. Earlier, James
had made the Queen its proprietor; she had entrusted its care to
the Jesuits and planned to repair the building. Now, he gave the
chapel a lock of his hair, encased in a crystal.[3] In return, Thomas
Pennant later noted sourly, the 'prince who lost three kingdoms for
a mass ... received ... a present of the very shift in which his great-
grand-mother *Mary Stuart* lost her head'.[4] It seemed a peculiarly
appropriate gift: for Catholics, both St Winifred and Mary, Queen
of Scots, were decapitated for their steadfast faith. St Winifred's
healing miracles and the sacred Stuart monarchy were further
linked when, while at Holywell, the King 'was pleased to Heal for
the Evil'.[5] And, early on the pilgrimage, the Church of England's
clerics, presumably aware of James's later itinerary, were obliged to
scrape: at Flint, 'His Majesty was received by the Lord Bishop of
St. Asaph and his Clergy with all dutiful Respect.'[6] When, a little
over nine months later, Prince James Francis Edward was born and

1100 – c. 1700, SCH S 12 (Woodbridge, 1999), 227–55; eadem, 'Holywell: Contesting
Sacred Space in Post-Reformation Wales', in Will Coster and Andrew Spicer, eds,
Sacred Space in Early Modern Europe (Cambridge, 2005), 211–36; eadem, 'Sacred Spas?
Healing Springs and Religion in Post-Reformation Britain', in Bridget Heal and Ole
Peter Grell, eds, *The Impact of the European Reformation* (Aldershot, 2008), 209–30.
   3   Walsham, 'Holywell', 230.
   4   Thomas Pennant, *The History of the Parishes of Whiteford, and Holywell* (London,
1796), 230.
   5   *London Gazette*, 1 September 1687.
   6   Ibid. James probably derived malicious satisfaction from this: Bishop Lloyd was
fiercely anti-Catholic and, as the Vicar of St Martin's-in-the-Fields, had played a notable
part in the 'uncovering' of the Popish Plot. One recalls Macaulay's judgement on
James: 'to bend and break the spirits of men gave him pleasure': Lord Macaulay, *The
History of England from the Accession of James the Second*, ed. Charles Harding Firth, 6

the Catholic succession seemed assured, thanks were offered to St Winifred and Mary of Modena paid for mass at Holywell.[7]

Unsurprisingly, St Winifred's chapel was attacked at the Revolution.[8] Nevertheless, Catholic gentlemen and priests continued to promote the shrine and pilgrims continued to resort there. Celia Fiennes visited in 1698 and described the 'abundance of the devout papists on their knees all round the Well'.[9] In the early 1710s, Holywell was 'crowded with zealous *Pilgrims*, from all Parts of *Britain*'.[10] Philip Metcalf, the Jesuit chaplain of Powis Castle, published a new edition of St Winifred's life in 1712. Besides Catholics, humble local Protestants still went to the spring, to the dismay of their pastors.[11] Belief in its thaumaturgy seemed unbreakable. As Jean Bolland had gleefully recounted in the *Acta Sanctorum Januarii* (1643), 'Hereticks', knowing the waters' powers, continued to frequent the shrine while roundly declaring that 'they neither cared, nor minded, what their Ministers prated in the Pulpit'.[12] If this reputation endured, how easily might their descendants be seduced to Popery!

And not only to Popery but to Jacobitism too! Jacobites had influence in North Wales, with their secret society, the Cycle of the White Rose; and Holywell, given its association with the birth of 'James III', appeared a Jacobite redoubt in the Whig authorities' eyes. According to *Little Preston*, a Whig '*Heroi-Comick Poem*' published in 1717, it was for Jacobites ' "Distinguish'd as the Seat of Loyalty" '.[13] Further, the doggerel maintained:

> When Royal *James* the *British* Throne ascends,
> With high Rewards he'll grace … [his] zealous Friends.
> Methinks I now read in the Book of Fate,
> How from St. *Asaph* he'll the See translate
> To *Holy-Well* …[14]

---

vols (London, 1913–15), 2: 934. Lloyd was one of the Seven Bishops who opposed the King's ecclesiastical policy in 1688, and he subsequently supported the Revolution.

7   Walsham, 'Holywell', 230.

8   Ibid.

9   *The Journeys of Celia Fiennes*, ed. Christopher Morris (London, 1947), 181.

10   [Philip Metcalf], *The Life, and Miracles, of S. Wenefride* (n. pl., 1712), 175.

11   [William Fleetwood], *The Life and Miracles of St. Wenefrede* (London, 1713), 14.

12   Ibid. 9, 10.

13   Anon., *Little Preston: An Heroi-Comick Poem, upon the Late Action at Holywell* (London, 1717), 10.

14   Ibid. 9.

Holywell was easily accessible from Lancashire, the heartland of
Catholic Jacobitism. In 1715 Jacobites rose in both England and
Scotland, hoping to topple the Protestant Hanoverian dynasty and
to restore the exiled Stuarts; and Lancashire provided the backbone
of the English, predominantly Catholic, rebel army. After that army
was defeated at the battle of Preston, Nicholas Blundell, the recu-
sant squire of Little Crosby near Liverpool, probably sheltered a
fugitive rebel;[15] in the years before the rising he and his wife had
undertaken pilgrimages to Holywell, and after it they resumed
them.[16] Moreover, according to *Little Preston*, High Church Tories,
as well as Papists, frequented the shrine:

> 'Twas in the Place, where Popish Legends tell
> Fair *Winny*'s Blood produc'd a *Holy Well*:
> O wond'rous strange! the Maid, 'tis gravely said,
> Ev'n suffer'd Death to save her Maidenhead.
> But *Tory* Saints and Non-resisting Dames
> Now plunge and frisk in the polluted Streams:
> And chilly Girls, with warm Carresses ply'd,
> Oft yield up that for which poor *Winny* dy'd.[17]

★ ★ ★

William Fleetwood, Bishop of St Asaph from 1708 to 1714,
thought Holywell the eyesore of his diocese. Fiercely anti-Papist,
he had been chosen to preach the Fifth of November sermon
before the Commons in 1691, and in it had denounced Popery's
corrupt doctrines, superstitious practices, 'Doctrines of ill Nature'
and its 'Practices of Cruelty and Blood'.[18] He strongly disliked the
pilgrimages to St Winifred's shrine, and was stung by Bolland's
taunt concerning popular disregard for the Protestant ministers'
'prating'.[19] Furthermore, Fleetwood was an expert on miracles. In
1701 he had published his influential *Essay on Miracles*, based on
material which he had assembled for one of the important Boyle

[15] *The Great Diurnal of Nicholas Blundell of Little Crosby, Lancashire*, ed. J. J. Bagley,
3 vols, Record Society of Lancashire and Cheshire (Chester, 1968–72), 2: 152.
[16] Ibid. 1: 40, 60, 142–3; 2: 23, 105–6; 3: 49–50, 190.
[17] Anon., *Little Preston*, 6, cf. 11–12.
[18] William Fleetwood, *A Sermon Preached before the Honourable House of Commons,
at St. Margaret Westminster, on Thursday, the 5th of November, 1691* (London, 1691), 28.
[19] [Fleetwood], *St. Wenefrede*, 10, 14, 15, 19.

lectures, endowed for the refutation of the arguments of unbe-
lievers.[20] He believed that no 'considering Man either does or can
deny, that God may work Miracles, *whensoever, wheresoever*, and by
whomsoever he pleases';[21] but equally confidently he proclaimed 'I do
not ... believe, that any Miracles have been wrought at *Holy-well*,
either before or since the *Reformation*, because I see none proved'.[22]
Fleetwood was well equipped to engage in historical debate too.
He knew much history and had studied historical method; even
Thomas Hearne, who disliked him, grudgingly admitted that he
was 'a man ... of some learning in antiquity'.[23]

The grumbling Tory Hearne's dislike stemmed partly from
Fleetwood's resolute Whiggism. Fleetwood was appalled at the
High Church and High Tory revival produced by Dr Henry
Sacheverell's notorious sermon of 1709 denouncing Protestant
Dissenters, their Whig allies and Revolution principles. Impeached
before the Lords, though receiving a mild sentence, Sacheverell
was presented by an admirer to the St Asaph living of Selattyn,
Shropshire, and predictably Fleetwood, who had voted him Guilty,
delayed the institution (he was doubtless incensed by the fire-
brand's triumphant progress there in 1710). Between 1710 and
1714 the bishop was at loggerheads with the Tory government. He
opposed its peace plans in 1711–12 and the Schism Bill (designed
to smash the Dissenting academies) in 1714. The preface to his
Four Sermons, published in 1712, so offended the Tories that it was
burnt by the common hangman. Furthermore, Fleetwood detested
Jacobitism. He saw 1688 as 'that *great Deliverance*';[24] and he feared
that the Tories were crypto-Jacobites. In 1712, he opposed the bill
granting toleration to those likely Jacobite rebels, the Scotch Epis-
copalians.[25] Might not the Tories even contrive to ensure that the
'Popish Pretender' succeeded Queen Anne? 'I did not indeed think,
a few Years ago,' Fleetwood declared in 1713, 'that one should have
wanted an Apology for speaking or writing against Popery'. But
now, he continued, 'to betray any Fears of its returning ... [seems]

---

[20] Jane Shaw, *Miracles in Enlightenment England* (New Haven, CT, 2006), 29, 170–1;
ODNB, s.n. 'Fleetwood, William (1656–1723)'.

[21] [Fleetwood], *St. Wenefrede*, 39.

[22] Ibid. 11.

[23] *ODNB, s.n.* 'Fleetwood'.

[24] [Fleetwood], *St. Wenefrede*, 38.

[25] *ODNB, s.n.* 'Fleetwood'.

a Mark ... of ill Design and Disaffection to the Government'.[26] 'I should be glad to see Men somewhat more afraid of their Inveterate Enemy,' he stated, 'talk somewhat louder against *Popery* both from the Pulpit and the Press, and tell the People, That if that Superstition ever settles here again upon the Throne, there is an End of their Religion, Liberty, and Property, and every thing besides, that Life is worth the living for.'[27]

Since St Winifred was now an icon of both Popery and Jacobitism, Fleetwood conceived 'the Design of discrediting ... [her] Story'[28] – a small contribution to the anti-popish campaign that he envisaged.

★ ★ ★

Fleetwood prepared carefully for his task, reading the earliest lives of St Winifred (which he endeavoured to date) in the Bodleian and Cotton Libraries, and also later works.[29] He published *The Life and Miracles of St. Wenefrede ... with Some Historical Observations Made thereon* in 1713. It comprised two introductory sections, totalling forty-five pages, a reprint (with annotations) of Metcalf's *Life*, and two adjuncts. Despite its title, Fleetwood's work was, naturally, in part, theological. The Bishop reiterated Protestant attacks on the invocation of saints: there was no scriptural command to pray to saints and no proof that they could either hear mortals' prayers or work miracles.[30] But he was principally concerned to demonstrate that St Winifred had never even lived. His work began with an ostentatious display of even-handedness, praising the Maurist Jean Mabillon and promising to use Bolland's 'Rules concerning the Credibility of History' when assessing the evidence for the Saint's life.[31] Perceptive readers, however, doubtless noted the low, warning growl in the book's opening words, '*BOLLANDUS* the *Jesuit*'.[32]

Fleetwood contemptuously observed that 'there is no Author either in Manuscript, or in Print, who lived within 500 Years of

<hr/>

[26] [Fleetwood], *St. Wenefrede*, 19.

[27] Ibid. 20.

[28] Ibid. 15.

[29] Ibid. 15–18; and see 127.

[30] Ibid. 13–14, 118. Fleetwood strongly disliked the claim that pilgrims who were not cured at Holywell received rewards after death, seeing it as a 'Fetch of the crafty Monks' to encourage repeated, lucrative visits to the shrine: ibid. 103–4 note i.

[31] Ibid. 3, 8; Bolland ranked the credibility of various types of source.

[32] Ibid. 3.

… [St Winifred's] Time, that does so much as name her Name, or say a Word about her' life.[33] A *Calendarium* of Welsh saints, 'above 500 Years old', did not do so;[34] neither did English historians, from Bede to Matthew Paris, nor Welsh historians, such as Asser, Geoffrey of Monmouth and Giraldus Cambrensis.[35] Likewise, Fleetwood maintained that there was no 'Author, either written or printed, who mentions any *Parish*, *Church*, or *Well*, to have been in the Place where *Holy-well* now stands, beyond the Year 1130'.[36] Catholic claims about an *'uninterrupted Tradition'* were preposterous.[37] Displaying his learning, and discriminating sensitively between different types of source, Fleetwood carefully collated and analysed the various texts, noting discrepancies, and paraded inaccurate translations or embellishments by writers in later periods.[38] He tartly castigated the belief in any miracle, however improbable, of Papists who intoned that 'it was not impossible to God'.[39] Overall, Fleetwood was sure that the sources permitted no certainty of the sanctity or existence of 'St Winifred'.[40] 'I affirm not one single Point … [about St Winifred]', Fleetwood declared triumphantly, 'is, or can be proved, by any Rules of History'.[41]

The pretence of scholarly objectivity was belied by the Protestant rhetoric and hackneyed anti-popish charges which studded *The Life and Miracles of St. Wenefrede*. Fleetwood stressed that the Saint's virginity was not praiseworthy, though Papists had proclaimed 'strange, exalted, hyperbolical Things in Commendation of that State, which was never appointed or commanded of God'.[42] Monasticism was useless; relics often cheats;[43] prayers for the dead unnecessary. 'Voluntary Vows of Poverty, honouring Reliques, and praying for the Dead … are … great Snares, Occasions of many Errors, and the Foundation of a World of superstitious Practices … and by feeding the Fire of Purgatory, they provide a good

---

33 Ibid. 36.
34 Ibid. 41.
35 Ibid. 45–6.
36 Ibid. 23.
37 Ibid. 62–3 note k.
38 Ibid. 28, 30, 33, 34, 35, 51–2 note d, 62–3 note k, 83 note t.
39 Ibid. 62–3 note k.
40 Ibid. 117–18.
41 Ibid. 115.
42 Ibid. 40; cf. 54 note g.
43 Ibid. 43.

Income for the Priests.'[44] It was greed for 'a good Income' which principally explained the legend of St Winifred: a silly tradition was 'dress'd up by a *Monk*, who was employed to steal her Bones, and thereby bring the Advantage of *Oblations* to his Monastery'.[45] Robert of Shrewsbury was, indeed, so anxious for 'more Offerings' that he did not scruple to lie or conceal weaknesses in his *Vita*.[46] Bolland's jibe at Protestant ministers ended too 'just as it should when told by a *Jesuit*, i. e. *equivocally*'.[47] That pilgrims still visited the shrine, Fleetwood snorted, showed that there were 'still a great many crafty Priests ... [and] a great many weak deluded People'.[48] Catholics' morals were corrupted by indulgent confessors,[49] and Protestants gulled by superstition there. Furthermore, responding to the charge that infidelity had grown in England since the Revolution of 1688, Fleetwood contended that it was 'the grossest Corruptions of *Popery*' which begot, 'promote[d] and increase[d] Contempt of all *Revealed Religion*', thereby multiplying the numbers of deists and atheists.[50]

More scorching than Protestant rhetoric were sarcasm and simple abuse. 'Jesuit' and 'monk' were used derisively, as, naturally, were 'Jesuitical', 'monkish' and 'Popish'. The author of the *Vita prima* was 'some good *Welchman*', Robert of Shrewsbury's life 'a poor, miserable, suspicious Legend', and all the lives, in both manuscript and print, 'so much Trash'.[51] 'Apologizing' for his 'Levity', Fleetwood mocked Robert's laboured scrupulosity in omitting from his account unverifiable details of Winifred's life, such as her supposed visit to Rome: for why should 'a Man ... scruple to believe ... [the Saint] made a Journey to *Rome*, who firmly believed that she lived at least fifteen Years, after her Head was cut off, and set on again?'[52] As for Winifred's 'extraordinary Merit' and sanctity, was there 'any one honest Maid in all *Flyntshire* that would

44 Ibid. 45.
45 Ibid. 118.
46 Ibid. 31, 35.
47 Ibid. 12.
48 Ibid. 11–12; cf. 117.
49 Ibid. 49 note a.
50 Ibid. 38.
51 Ibid. 15, 16, 118.
52 Ibid. 31.

not do as much as *Wenefrede* did to avoid a furious Ravisher, and save her Virtue?'[53]

Ignoring these 'monstrous Stories', how were the cures at Holywell — the *irregular* cures, Fleetwood stressed — to be explained?[54] Very simply: through God's providence, it is 'a very cold Spring, and is good, as other cold Springs are, in many Cases'.[55] 'What Pity it is,' snapped the Bishop, 'that some great Saint or other has not taken Possession of the Waters of the [*sic*] Bath, *Tunbridge, Astrop, Sunning*, and other Places'.[56] How sad that, although cures were annually effected at spas, there was 'not a *Miracle* among them all, because, forsooth, they are under the Protection of no particular tutelar Saints'![57]

Bishop Fleetwood's hammer-blows were vigorously repeated. There was no 'Certainty and Assurance of … [the] Life, and Death, and Sanctity' of St Winifred;[58] there could be no certainty of her 'Existence, Life, and Death';[59] there were no 'undoubted Proofs' that 'she ever wrought any undoubted Miracles, either living or dead'.[60] '*Holy-well* is a Fountain of great Superstition', Fleetwood concluded: 'Never was so ridiculous a Legend [as St Winifred's] founded on so weak a Bottom.'[61]

★ ★ ★

In his *Life and Miracles of St. Wenefrede*, William Fleetwood described medieval Wales as 'a poor, ignorant, obscure, and superstitious Corner of the Land'.[62] Quite possibly, he thought the Principality remained so; and, like other bishops in Welsh sees, longed for translation to an English diocese. If so, Fleetwood was fortunate. The Jacobites' schemes, which he had so dreaded, soon lay in ruins; and, within four months of George I's accession, his resolute Whiggism was rewarded when he was translated to the diocese of Ely. When the 'Fifteen was crushed, Fleetwood rejoiced: 'had the Rebels

---

[53] Ibid. 41.
[54] Ibid. 37, 103–4 note i.
[55] Ibid. 12.
[56] Ibid. 98 note f.
[57] Ibid. (italics mine).
[58] Ibid. 22.
[59] Ibid. 36.
[60] Ibid. 40.
[61] Ibid. 41, 47.
[62] Ibid. 118.

prevailed,' he declared, 'the Evils then must have been numberless and endless'.[63] And, unsurprisingly, the rising had repercussions at the hated shrine of St Winifred.

In 1717, after the Act of Grace ended the rebels' trials, some 'Rebel Gentlemen' were released from Chester Castle; and on 5 August they went to Holywell 'to make use of the Waters of their Legendary Saint Winifred'.[64] Crying '*Long Live King* James *the Third, &c.*', and assaulting those who disapproved, they were 'at length ... joyned by a considerable Number of Papists and other Disaffected Persons', and then proceeded to the market cross 'where, with their Swords drawn, they proclaimed the Pretender in the most solemn manner'.[65] Upon this, the 'Loyal Part of the Town ... rose upon them with Clubs, Pitchforks, &c. and a Battle ensued'; one Jacobite was killed and many were wounded, and the troublemakers fled.[66] *Little Preston* (for it was this incident that that doggerel commemorated) scorned the Jacobite ringleaders, stressing their cowardice – youths who had fled from defeat at Preston and now attacked or frightened women and children.[67] The Whig *Original Weekly Journal* emphasized their perverse ingratitude in proclaiming the Pretender and 'forgetting ... [George I's] singular Mercy'.[68]

The demonstration of 1717 again spotlighted Holywell as a Catholic and Jacobite stronghold.[69] The following year, a correspondent reported in the London press that, during the summer, there were still '*vast Numbers of Papists* at Holywell, from several Parts, especially Lancashire, and that the Town ... [abounded] with them'.[70] In June, the Hanoverian regime accordingly decided to assail the shrine:

> The government having notice that the Roman Catholics

[63] William Fleetwood, *A Sermon Preach'd at Ely-House Chapel in Holbourn; on Thursday June 7, 1716* (London, 1716), 6.
[64] *Original Weekly Journal*, 17 August 1717.
[65] Ibid. 31 August 1717.
[66] Ibid.
[67] Anon., *Little Preston*, 7–8, 9–10, 12, 14, 19.
[68] *Original Weekly Journal*, 17 August 1717.
[69] According to *Little Preston* (8), there were also Jacobite celebrations at Holywell in 1715, when a false report of a Hanoverian defeat reached the town. This is probably correct: *Little Preston*, while not contradicting the metropolitan newspapers' accounts of the 'Battle', displays much additional local knowledge, including the leading Jacobites' names.
[70] *St. James's Post*, 11 July 1718.

were about to celebrate the feast of St. *Winifred* [22 June], at *Holiwell* in *Wales*, with great solemnity, sent down a party of dragoons thither, who seized their priest as he was officiating, with the image, plate, and other utensils; and found a parcel of writings, which discovered several estates settled to several superstitious uses.[71]

The uncovering of estates supporting 'superstitious uses' was ominous. In 1716, Parliament had passed an Act appointing commissioners to locate and sequestrate, *inter alia*, property in the realm that yielded income for the popish Church: once starved of such funds, the government reasoned, Catholicism's decay was ineluctable.[72] The Forfeited Estates Commission's papers also show that Holywell was worth plundering and reveal its patrons' generosity. The chapel at the Star Inn contained crucifixes, candlesticks, chalices and patens, each piece in both gold and silver, and a large silver tabernacle and lamp. There were reliquaries too. In the chapel at the Cross Keys Inn, there were silver candlesticks, chalices, lamps and a crucifix.[73] Nevertheless, impressive though such treasures were, their value, one commentator emphasized, was greatly surpassed by the information about the various estates.[74]

★ ★ ★

St Winifred's well outlasted the persecution following the 'Fifteen. According to Daniel Defoe, whose *Tour through the Whole Island of Great Britain* was published in the mid-1720s, 'numbers of pilgrims' still resorted to it, while 'good manners' ensured that a blind eye was turned to the 'very numerous', thinly disguised priests.[75] Protestants at Holywell in the 1730s tactfully called the pilgrims' religion 'the old faith'.[76] The shrine survived the 'Forty-five: Catholic rebels were far fewer than in 1715. Pennant noted that the number of devotees had greatly decreased by the 1790s, when he thought

---

[71] *The British Chronologist*, 3 vols (London, 1775), 2: 45–6; Kew, TNA, SP Dom. 35/12/74; cf. Cambridge, UL, Cholmondeley (Houghton) MS P78/1a.

[72] 1 Geo. I, Stat. 2, c. 50.

[73] TNA, FEC 1/1724.

[74] *The Political State of Great-Britain* 16 (1718), 70.

[75] Daniel Defoe, *A Tour through the Whole Island of Great Britain*, ed. G. D. H. Cole and D. C. Browning, 2 vols in 1 (London, 1974), Part 2: 66; cf. P. J. Corfield, *The Impact of English Towns 1700–1800* (Oxford, 1982), 57.

[76] London, Westminster Diocesan Archives, MS A 39, 101, (v).

that, 'with Protestants, and temperate Catholics, [the tale of St Winifred carried] ... with it self-confutation'.[77] Defoe ascribed the spring's healing properties to its mineral content, while Pennant observed that the waters were 'indisputably endowed with every good quality attendant on cold baths'.[78] Nevertheless, '[e]very element proves to us a medicine or a bane, as suits ... [God's] unerring dispensation', Pennant, rather sententiously, added: the spring's 'natural qualities ... [were] implanted ... by the divine Providence, in order to fulfil his will'.[79] This (now commonplace)[80] formula obviated the need to refute the story of St Winifred laboriously, though Pennant disbelieved it and its underpinning theological suppositions; and he referred the reader to Fleetwood's *Life* 'for proofs against the truth of the tale'.[81]

Nearly two centuries after the early Tudor reformers had rejected the cult of saints, it is astonishing that St Winifred remained an anti-popish totem, with her sanctity and very existence contested, and Holywell a bastion of opposition, a place of open Catholic and Jacobite pilgrimage.[82] The authorities' faltering attempts to suppress her cult resemble less Protestantism's often brutal iconoclasm than local officialdom's embarrassment at the apparitions at Lourdes or those at Marpingen during the *Kulturkampf*: a theme worthy of further exploration. No doubt the shrine's survival was aided by its location in 'a poor ... [and] obscure ... Corner of the Land'; and by the appointment, as Fleetwood's successor at St Asaph, of the more moderate John Wynne.[83] No doubt, too, the little town's leaders were as greedy for 'a good Income' from pilgrims as Fleetwood's stereotypical popish priests and monks.[84] Nevertheless, during the 1710s St Winifred's chapel was probably fortunate to escape destruction, given Bishop Fleetwood's pungent anti-Catholicism, the growing Jacobite threat and the 'Fifteen.

University of Winchester

[77] Pennant, *Whiteford, and Holywell*, 230, 231.
[78] Defoe, *Tour*, Part 2: 66; Pennant, *Whiteford, and Holywell*, 231.
[79] Pennant, *Whiteford, and Holywell*, 231.
[80] Walsham, 'Sacred Spas?', 218–20.
[81] Pennant, *Whiteford, and Holywell*, 231.
[82] Her shrine at Shrewsbury was desecrated during the Henrician Reformation: Walsham, 'Holywell', 217.
[83] *ODNB*, *s.n.* 'Wynne, John (1665/6–1743)'.
[84] See Defoe, *Tour*, Part 2: 66.

'MASTER IN THE ART OF HOLY LIVING': THE SANCTITY OF WILLIAM STEVENS

by ROBERT ANDREWS

The following paper explores the sanctity of the late eighteenth-century High Church Anglican layman, William Stevens (1732–1807), as seen through the eyes of his biographer, Sir James Allan Park (1763–1838). A largely unstudied figure,[1] Stevens, a prosperous London hosier who dedicated most of his adult life to philanthropic, theological and ecclesiastical concerns, arguably represents one of the most important figures within pre-Tractarian High Churchmanship.[2] Park was a close friend of Stevens. A judge of the Common Pleas and a founding member of Stevens's 'Club of Nobody's Friends', Park shared Stevens's interest in theology and church-related concerns, even publishing in 1804 a short discourse directed towards young people, on the need for a frequent reception of Holy Communion.[3] In focus here is a facet of Stevens's life that came to be closely associated with his many achievements as a lay divine and activist within the pre-Tractarian Church of England, namely, his personal sanctity; this was marked by a close connection between faith and works, a strict dedication and devotion to the Church of England's services and sacraments, and a rejection of 'enthusiasm' in its pejorative sense – all of which he held while maintaining a strong sense of cheerfulness and zeal. A portrait of sanctity that conforms to what is known about pre-Tractarian spirituality, the *Memoirs* may additionally be viewed as offering a representative understanding of what constituted holiness for this Anglican tradition.[4]

[1]   Since Park, the only account of Stevens's life has been Geoffrey Rowell, *The Club of 'Nobody's Friends' 1800–2000* (Durham, 2000), 1–31.
[2]   See, e.g., E. A. Varley, *The Last of the Prince Bishops: William Van Mildert and the High Church Movement of the Early Nineteenth Century* (Cambridge, 1992), 8–9, 63–4; James J. Sack, *From Jacobite to Conservative: Reaction and Orthodoxy in Britain c. 1760–1832* (Cambridge, 1993), 190–3; and Peter B. Nockles, *The Oxford Movement in Context: Anglican High Churchmanship 1760–1857* (Cambridge, 1994), 14 nn. 47, 50.
[3]   See James Allan Park, *An Earnest Exhortation to a Frequent Reception of the Holy Sacrament of the Lord's Supper* (London, 1804).
[4]   The term 'pre-Tractarian' distinguishes traditional Anglican High Churchmanship

In 1812, Park, a close friend of Stevens during his later years, produced the first edition of Stevens's memoirs.[5] The *Memoirs* had grown out of an obituary of Stevens which Park had written for the *Gentleman's Magazine* in 1807.[6] A devout layman of the pre-Tractarian High Church tradition, Park was very similar to Stevens in his commitment to Anglicanism, dedicating (albeit to a much lesser extent) a great portion of his life to similar church-related activities.[7] Along with Stevens and other notable laymen of that period, such as John Bowdler (1746–1823), William Cotton (1786–1866) and Joshua Watson (1771–1855), in addition to numerous bishops and clerics, Park played a role in fostering what is now widely agreed to have been an influential period of High Church renewal during the late eighteenth and early nineteenth centuries.[8]

According to Park, Stevens's life was a model of the highest sanctity within the Anglican tradition – a 'master in the art of holy living', as he put it,[9] thus linking Stevens with the High Church tradition of personal sanctity exemplified in the writings of Jeremy Taylor and William Law. Indeed, as is indicated by the phrase 'holy living', it seems almost certain that Park was borrowing from Taylor's well-known mid-seventeenth-century work that came to be designated by the same phrase.[10]

For Park, the sanctity evidenced by Stevens's life was both illustrative and instructive for those wishing to engage in a life of holy living, especially the young, whom he singled out as the

---

from its post-1830s Tractarian divergence. Pre-Tractarian High Churchmanship is a tradition within Anglicanism which emphasized its catholic, sacramental and monarchical roots, whilst not rejecting its reformed and Protestant heritage as Tractarianism often did. The pre-Tractarians are also referred to as the 'Orthodox'.

   5 See James Allan Park, *Memoirs of William Stevens, Esq.* (London, 1812). Citations here are from the fourth edition, *Memoirs of William Stevens, Esq.: Treasurer of Queen Anne's Bounty* (London, 1825). A fifth edition appeared in 1859, though this was edited by Christopher Wordsworth, junior (see [G.E. Colcayne] *Biographical List of the Members of 'The Club of Nobody's Friends'* (London, 1885), 4), who, aside from taking the liberty of substantially cleaning up and simplifying the grammar of what appears to be the fourth edition, also added a preface. Though it makes for easier reading, the 1859 edition is not, therefore, by Park alone and has thus not been used here.

   6 *Gentleman's Magazine* 77 (1807), 173–5.

   7 *ODNB, s.n.* 'Park, Sir James Alan (1763–1838)'.

   8 See Nockles, *Oxford Movement*, 1–43.

   9 Park, *Memoirs*, 131.

  10 Originally published as *The Rules and Exercises of Holy Living* in 1650, the work was also known by the shorter title, *Holy Living*. For a critical edition, see Jeremy Taylor, *Holy Living*, ed. P. G. Stanwood (Oxford, 1989).

section of his readership which he thought would benefit most from Stevens's example as an industrious layman who was able to make religion a part of his whole life, despite having to work in a trade that was highly demanding on his time.[11] In writing the life of Stevens, it thus became Park's hope to illustrate not only the life and sanctity of his subject, but also to display that life and sanctity in a manner that would enable his readership to emulate Stevens's example:

> One view, therefore, which the Author has in submitting this sketch of the life of Mr. Stevens to the world is to prove, and particularly to the young, how much every man has it in his power, even under very discouraging circumstances, by diligence, fidelity, and attention, to advance himself, not only in worldly prosperity, but in learning and wisdom, in purity of life, and in moral and religious knowledge.[12]

In Park's view, biography was best employed when it possessed the ability of conveying to its reader a model of piety and sanctity that was capable of emulation. Most biographies, he argued, could often be faulted because they failed to contain this important catechetical element. Furthermore, Park observed that most biographies were about lives and deeds which were ultimately unable to communicate with their readers on a level with which they themselves were familiar, because the subjects were too often drawn from the ranks of the famous and influential.[13] Stevens, on the other hand, was in his view a model more capable of emulation by a general readership, and thus it was 'of inestimable benefit to all mankind to know by actual facts, that a life of cheerful piety and purity, of temperance and humility, being that which all ought to imitate, is that to which all may attain.'[14]

The mention of a 'life of cheerful piety and purity' was another aspect which Park hoped to highlight in Stevens's life. It seemed a matter of concern to him that holy living be interpreted, especially by the young readership to whom he was attempting to speak, not

---

[11] Park, *Memoirs*, 6–8.
[12] Ibid. 3.
[13] Ibid. 1–3.
[14] Ibid. 2.

as a life of unhappiness, but as one of cheerfulness and joy. 'In no man', he claimed,

> was this truth more fully exemplified than in the subject of the following Memoir, whose uniform and habitual cheerfulness, whose lively but inoffensive wit, made the young and the gay delight in his society to the last week of his life; because his whole life and conversation proved that *in him* true and unde-filed religion, undebased by superstition on the one hand, or fanaticism on the other, had had her perfect work.[15]

There were many facets to Stevens's sanctity, though according to Park the most observable was his 'extensive' commitment to philanthropy.[16] As in his use of the biographical method as a means of demonstrating and inspiring sanctity, Park had reason for detailing to his readers Stevens's many charitable works and financial contributions.

> Many persons are disposed to be charitable, and to do good; but it is not everyone who understands the true and proper mode of doing it. This art was never better understood, nor more extensively practised, than by Mr. Stevens; and, there-fore, it is, that I am more diffusive in these narratives than I otherwise should be; entertaining the hope, that all, who have the desire to do good, will, from him, learn the happy mode of doing it; and that those, who *have* the power, not having hitherto exerted it, may be led by the lustre of his bright example, to shew themselves deserving of the blessings, which a gracious Providence has showered upon them: and that all may emulate this good, this excellent, this charitable man – and go and do as he did.[17]

Stevens was, for example, meticulous in how he distributed his wealth. It is claimed by Park, who evidently had access to Stevens's financial records, that Stevens used to divide his accounts under three headings: 'Clericus', 'Pauper' and 'Gifts', each heading signi-fying the three areas in which he distributed his money.[18] As their

---

[15] Ibid. 3.
[16] Ibid. 23.
[17] Ibid. 29.
[18] Ibid. 23–5.

names imply, 'Clericus' and 'Pauper' signified the clergy and the poor; 'Gifts', on the other hand, was a special category that Park claims Stevens used to catalogue particularly large sums of money as well as gifts that Stevens felt could not justifiably be referred to as true acts of charity.[19] From Park's information we can infer that throughout his lifetime Stevens would have donated tens of thousands of pounds to various charitable causes. Park, for example, notes that in one year (the exact date is not given) Stevens's total income was £1,200. Out of this, £600 went to charitable causes, while his personal expenses were about £300.[20] The recipients of Stevens's financial aid included many of the charities and societies of which he was a personal member, and which he served on a voluntary basis. These included: The Festival of the Sons of the Clergy; The Corporation for the Widows of the Clergy; The Clergy Orphan School; The Society for the Propagation of the Gospel in Foreign Parts; The Society for Promoting Christian Knowledge; and a number of London hospitals.[21] Additionally, though it was a commitment mostly of time rather than of money, Stevens distinguished himself as the Treasurer of Queen Anne's Bounty, a charitable fund for the relief of poorer clergy incorporated by Queen Anne in 1704; he held this office from 1782 to 1807.[22]

Though Park claimed that such acts of philanthropy were, on Stevens's part, 'founded … in the purest Christian motives',[23] it is fair to say, as Park further claims, that Stevens's charitable concerns flowed naturally from his deep and active piety which, in the classic High Church tradition, emphasized the strong link between faith and works.[24] Stevens, Park wrote, 'never conceived that faith and works, which God had united, could be lawfully disjoined'.[25] This meant Stevens's life of active philanthropy had in his view been evidence of a true and lively faith. For as Park observed, 'whenever the whole of a man's conduct is uniform, where you find charity to man, attended by piety to God, and always proceeding from his

---

[19] Ibid. 24.
[20] Ibid. 25.
[21] Ibid. 26–7.
[22] Ibid. 26.
[23] Ibid. 23.
[24] Ibid. 35. See also Nockles, *Oxford Movement*, 256–61.
[25] Park, *Memoirs*, 35.

command, *"to do good unto all men,"* then we may be assured, that this is true charity and pure religion'.[26]

As important as Stevens's life as a philanthropist was, however, it would have been nothing for Park had it not been for Stevens's strong commitment to Anglicanism in its High Church expression.[27] There is certainly no reason to doubt Park's claim that Stevens 'was a firm and conscientious believer in all the doctrines of religion, as professed in the Church of England', as well as being 'an attentive observer of all her ordinances'.[28] Indeed, for Park, evidence of this appeared to abound. Sundays, for example, saw Stevens usually attend two services, as well as frequently receive Holy Communion.[29] In addition, though Park notes that the practice was not widespread during Stevens's day, Stevens was also attentive in attending services on weekdays.[30] Aside from all this, however, his private devotional life was no less attentive: for example, Stevens read the daily lessons for Morning Prayer in their original languages of Hebrew and Greek before leaving his chamber for the day's work.[31]

'All this attention to public religious duties', Park claims, was performed

> without the least tincture of enthusiasm – his devotion was rational, calm, and placid. He was one of those who thought that a clouded countenance is not the natural result of true devotion: but on the contrary, was of the opinion that nothing tends more to enliven the heart, and cheer the face of man, than a constant and earnest endeavour to discharge with fidelity and regularity the duties of piety to God, beneficence and good-will to man.[32]

'Enthusiasm' here carries with it an especially pejorative meaning that was often employed by pre-Tractarian High Churchmen. At a basic level the term implied religious deviations such as excessive emotionalism, a belief in personal revelation, or supersti-

---

[26] Ibid.
[27] Ibid. 37.
[28] Ibid.
[29] Ibid. 37–8.
[30] Ibid. 38–9.
[31] Ibid. 41.
[32] Ibid. 40.

tion.[33] Methodists and Dissenters were the usual groups suspected of displaying these traits, though even Church of England Evangelicals sometimes endured such criticisms from High Churchmen.[34] This negative attitude is seen, for example, in the writings and sermons of Stevens's close friend, the cleric William Jones of Nayland (1726–1800),[35] though more important is the opinion of Stevens himself, who, in an appendix to the 1859 edition of the *Memoirs*, made reference to the writings of George Bull (1634–1710) as 'being confutations of the pernicious doctrines of the enthusiasts' and are thus 'equally useful in our time, as the *Methodists* are propagating the same pestilential notions now, as the *Puritans* did then'.[36]

However, despite this disapproval, it is important to note Park's clear implication that a piety 'without any tincture of enthusiasm' did not on that account lack warmth, cheerfulness, fervour and zeal. Stevens, Park stresses, possessed all these characteristics, evidence that at least in Stevens's case, the type of pre-Tractarian High Church spirituality that has often (albeit misleadingly) been labelled with the Tractarian-inspired pejorative, 'high and dry',[37] was in fact the very opposite.

Though painted as an ideal exponent of Anglican piety, there is evidence that Stevens – fully in the tradition of sainthood – was also somewhat of a maverick when it came to his religious life. In church, for example, it is observed by Park that Stevens always used to stand 'when the praises of God were sung, even though in a congregation, where he might be the solitary instance of this decorous and becoming usage'.[38] Moreover, in his later years Stevens appears to have dressed remarkably like a cleric, wearing black clothes and donning a large clerical wig.[39] Park records that this once appeared to have had the effect of fooling one clergyman

---

[33] John Mee, *Romanticism, Enthusiasm and Regulation: Poetics and the Policing of Culture in the Romantic Period* (Oxford, 2005), 25–37.

[34] Nockles, *Oxford Movement*, 191.

[35] See, e.g., William Jones, *The Theological, Philosophical and Miscellaneous Works of the Rev. William Jones, M.A., F.R.S.*, 12 vols (London, 1801), 1: 245–300, esp. 278–82.

[36] Park, *Memoirs* (1859 edn), App. II, 157.

[37] See Nockles, *Oxford Movement*, 40–1.

[38] Park, *Memoirs*, 38.

[39] Ibid. 39–40. For confirmation of this, see *London Literary Gazette, and Journal of Belles Lettres, Arts, Sciences, etc.*, no. 90 (10 October 1818), 655.

whose parish Stevens had attended for a service into thinking that he was indeed a cleric.[40]

His eccentricities aside, there is no major reason to doubt the general contention that Stevens's life reveals a very pious and dedicated figure whose high degree of personal sanctity was clearly evident. At the same time, however, it is also true that Park has created a hagiographic image of a pre-Tractarian High Church 'saint' who lived an unrealistically spotless life that admitted of few, if any, defects. To an extent this is an obvious point to make: many saints' lives, when re-examined in a more critical light, reveal figures that are more human, capable of failings and weaknesses. Not surprisingly, the same phenomenon is evident in Stevens's personal correspondence with his close friend, the exiled Loyalist clergyman who had served in North America, Jonathan Boucher (1738–1804). There, for example, we find Stevens revealing that he had been experiencing feelings of melancholy,[41] lack of zeal and enthusiasm in performing daily tasks, and anger at the difficulties his daily business often threw up at him, as well as manifesting an ability to offend the often sensitive Boucher.[42] We encounter in Stevens's personal correspondence with Boucher all of the normal and rather messy human emotions that even saints experience, and that hagiographers often find tarnish their subjects' reputations.

Of course, other than pointing out the starkly hagiographic nature of Park's biography, none of this detracts, nor is it intended to detract, from the general picture of sanctity presented within it; indeed, there is much to strengthen the claim that Stevens was, to all intents and purposes, a figure imbued with a very high degree of personal sanctity. Boucher, for example, in reflecting upon the impact of Stevens's friendship on him, referred to him as 'one of the prime blessings' of his life and claimed he was 'pious and charitable to an uncommon degree ... a man of very considerable learning, and one of the ablest divines I am acquainted with'.[43]

---

40 Park, *Memoirs*, 46–7.

41 Though Park does not in any way elaborate on it, Stevens does in fact confess in a section quoted in the *Memoirs* that he often possesses a 'melancholy cast' that 'sometimes ... leads him to the habitations of the afflicted': ibid. 81.

42 Williamsburg, VA, College of William and Mary, Swem Library, MS Jonathan Boucher Papers, Bf/2/5–20, letters of William Stevens to Jonathan Boucher, 1789–94.

43 Jonathan Boucher, *Reminiscences of an American Loyalist 1738–1798* (Port Washington, NY, 1967), 146.

Others evidently shared Boucher's opinion. It is reported by Park that Bishop John Douglas of Salisbury (1721–1807) said of Stevens that 'Here is a man, who, though not a Bishop, yet would have been thought worthy of that character in the first and purest ages of the Christian Church.'[44]

Space does not permit a full and complete enumeration of all the aspects of Stevens's life which Park highlighted as conveying his sanctity. However, from this brief survey, it can be seen that, accompanied with a cheerful disposition and a fervent zeal, Stevens's sanctity was above all a sanctity evidenced by practical and pious works. In this Stevens was, as Park phrased it, a 'master in the art of holy living'. It was a sanctity that found its expression and vindication in Stevens's tireless commitment to charitable concerns, his service to the Church and, most importantly, his deep, active and cheerful piety, a piety which refused to separate faith from works and which was evidenced by a strict outward conformity to the Church of England's services and sacraments as well as a rejection of 'enthusiasm'. Put differently, it was a vision of sanctity which was practical and outward-looking and which did not, on the whole, pay much attention to inner feelings, regarding them as untrustworthy.

Seen in a broader context, however, Park's portrait of Stevens's sanctity closely conforms to Peter Nockles's widely cited description of pre-Tractarian High Churchmen as those who 'tended to cultivate a practical spirituality based on good works nourished by sacramental grace and exemplified in acts of self-denial and charity rather than on any subjective conversion experience or unruly pretended manifestation of the Holy Spirit'.[45] Park's account also confirms Nockles's contention that the pre-Tractarian rejection of enthusiasm cannot be read to signify a spirituality that denoted 'lukewarmness or indifference'.[46] Nockles cites a number of pre-

---

44 As quoted in Park, *Memoirs* (1859 edn), 18.

45 Nockles, *Oxford Movement*, 26. Cf. Arthur Burns, *The Diocesan Revival in the Church of England* (Oxford, 1999), 17; Geoffrey K. Brandwood, ' "Mummeries of a Popish Character" – The Camdenians and Early Victorian Worship', in Christopher Webster and John Elliott, eds, *'A church as it should be': the Cambridge Camden Society and its Influence* (Stamford, 2000), 62–97, at 67; C. Brad Faught, *The Oxford Movement: A Thematic History of the Tractarians and their Times* (Pennsylvania, PA, 2003), 35; Kenneth A. Locke, *The Church in Anglican Theology: A Historical, Theological and Ecumenical Exploration* (Farnham, 2009), 70.

46 Nockles, *Oxford Movement*, 196.

Tractarian High Churchmen who, in his view, displayed spiritual lives contrary to the 'high and dry' label. These included Stevens's friends, William Jones of Nayland and George Horne, as well as Thomas Secker (1693–1768) and Samuel Horsley (1733–1806).[47] Given Park's account, Stevens's name deserves to be included among them.

It is, however, likely that Park's portrait of Stevens's sanctity has a much greater significance than simply as evidence that Stevens's spirituality places him among the ranks of notable pre-Tractarian High Churchmen. As evidence for this, it may be noted how widely accepted Park's *Memoirs* were among pre-Tractarian High Churchmen, a fact confirmed by observing how the *Memoirs* became a work increasingly associated with the 'Club of Nobody's Friends', which was founded by Stevens in 1800, the membership of which included virtually all the significant pre-Tractarian High Churchmen who led, or played important roles within, the Hackney Phalanx.[48] Within the 'Club of Nobody's Friends', Stevens, as its founder, was highly revered and Park's *Memoirs* were accepted as an accurate and venerable recounting of his life's deeds (Park, it should be noted, was one of the club's founding members).[49] It may be concluded, therefore, that the *Memoirs*, despite the author's intention that the work be an inspiration for the young, did in fact present a model of sanctity which many pre-Tractarian High Churchmen, clergy and laity, desired to emulate. As a result, the *Memoirs of William Stevens* are not merely an account of one man's holiness but are much more significant for the wider context of pre-Tractarian High Churchmanship. The work thus provides not only a detailed description of what sanctity meant for Park and

---

[47] Ibid. 193–5.

[48] Rowell, *'Nobody's Friends' 1800–2000*, 2. The Hackney Phalanx dominated church affairs in the early nineteenth century. Led by the layman Joshua Watson (1771–1855), it contributed significantly to the upkeep and maintenance of the many church societies that flourished during the first half of the nineteenth century.

[49] The best evidence for this is the 1859 edition of the *Memoirs*. Aside from containing a list of the club's early members (ibid. 168–216, App. III), the preface lauded Stevens's memory. Its author, Christopher Wordsworth, claimed that the members of the club 'may be regarded, in a certain sense, as his [Stevens's] posterity'; furthermore, the club's role was that of 'cherishing and maintaining those sound religious and political principles, which its Founder advocated unswervingly and unflinchingly, but charitably and wisely, in his writings, and exhibited in his life': ibid. iv. The paragraph from which these quotations are taken from is also quoted in [Cokayne] *Biographical List of the Members of 'The Club of Nobody's Friends'*, viii.

how it was displayed by Stevens, it is also a historically significant substantiation of what we know about the spirituality of pre-Tractarian High Churchmanship and of how widespread such views were.

Murdoch University

'A SAINT IF EVER THERE WAS ONE': HENRY ROBERT REYNOLDS (1825–96)

by CLYDE BINFIELD

'saint if ever there was one, but who might have been a
little more effective had there been in his nature some
slight traces of the old Adam'.[1] Thus William Hardy
Harwood (1856–1924) reflecting on a past member of *Sub Rosa*, a
long-established essay club for Congregational ministers in Greater
London. Harwood could only have known this particular saint for
four years and perhaps his recollection is best seen as a businesslike
minister's snapshot of an other-worldliness outside the normal run
of Nonconformist experience. It betrays a degree of affectionate
irritation. It is almost a dismissal. Free Churchmen don't do saints.

Saints are exemplary witnesses. They are intercessors and
confessors; they combine piety with authority. They are credible
Christians, more easily recognized than defined, save in retrospect.
They are people of position in the Christian economy, who might
indeed be bishops. In popular eyes their influence is less quotidian
than eternal; they lift the gaze to extreme, if divine, horizons. If
sanctity is a mark of the Holy Catholic Church, saints are necessary to its understanding. Of course Free Churchmen do saints.

For tradition-conscious Congregationalists, saints are church
members, the men and women gathered in covenanted fellowship.
Each such fellowship is the Church; that is the Congregational
understanding. Here are serious people, in the world but no longer
of it. Their integrity and credibility are manifest among their own
sort; they are consistent exemplars of what are now called Victorian values. Worldly success is a natural consequence for some, a
quality of goodness is an assumption for all, but in popular eyes
that goodness edges into the sort of unworldliness too easily associated with failure.

Henry Robert Reynolds, Harwood's 'saint if ever there was one',
fits this mould. He exemplifies Congregational sanctity, at once

---

[1] Albert Peel, 'The *Sub Rosa*', *Transactions of the Congregational Historical Society* 12.3
(April 1934), 132–41, at 138.

representative and rare. His credibility ranged from the worldly to the other-worldly. He was socially credible; he had private means; his brother was a medical baronet; there were family connections with the legal, military, clerical, academic and landed establishments; and his voice and bearing – he was tall, graceful, and presidential, a superfine Abraham Lincoln – were those of his class.[2] His denominational credibility was unimpeachable; there were family connections with Congregationalism's lay and ministerial establishments and his career, which was also his vocation, cemented this. Abbey Chapel, Romsey, the church in which he was reared, and Old Meeting, Halstead, the church to which he first ministered, were the sort to have had county voters in their congregations; two of Reynolds's sisters married into such families.[3] East Parade, Leeds, then in its golden age, was the church where Reynolds first made his national mark; it was also Leeds's 'Bainesocracy' at prayer and a third sister married into the Bainesocracy.[4] A successful Congregational minister needed to have personal, pastoral, and preaching skills of a high order; he was a bishop as the early Church first understood that office. The church books of Old Meeting and East Parade testify to Reynolds's ministerial skills.[5] As a pastor he was revered, almost worshipped, especially by the women of his congregation, whose education he fostered to university extension level before such a concept was in general currency.[6] As a person he was no less credible, loved, indeed adored, as friend, son, husband, brother and uncle; he had no children. He comes across as alert, companionable, cultivated, the shrewdest but gentlest of

---

[2] The main source is *Henry Robert Reynolds D.D.: His Life and Letters Edited by his Sisters, with Portraits* (London, 1898); Reynolds and his brother, Sir John Russell Reynolds (1828–96), have entries in *ODNB*.

[3] Sarah Fletcher Reynolds married John Bird Best (d. 1902), gentleman farmer of Dorset and Hertfordshire; Harriet Reynolds married John Savill Vaizey: the Vaizeys of Attwoods and Star Stile, Halstead, were an armigerous landowning family. County voters were those who were entitled to vote in county constituencies, by virtue of their property-holding qualifications (the so-called 'forty-shilling freeholders'). Electoral reform from 1832 onwards, of course, changed the basis of the franchise.

[4] Through the influence conferred by their newspaper, *The Leeds Mercury*, the Baines family shaped and dominated Leeds Liberalism, hence the term, 'Bainesocracy', to denote the peak of their influence, which lasted from the 1830s to the 1870s. Susanna Reynolds married Frederick Baines (1811–93).

[5] The interaction of East Parade and the Bainesocracy is developed in C. Binfield, *So Down to Prayers: Studies in English Nonconformity 1780–1920* (London, 1977), 54–100.

[6] *Life and Letters*, 88–92.

teases, politically liberal, enthused by Wordsworth, enraptured by Ruskin, liberated by travel, enchanted by Switzerland and Italy, stretched by Egypt. His appreciation of art, literature and music was discerning if conventional. He enjoyed an encounter with Coventry Patmore in 1867; he wanted to know more of the young J. M. Barrie in 1889.[7]

There is more. After fourteen years in pastoral charge he was for thirty-four years a college principal. At Cheshunt College he flowered as teacher, scholar and denominational heavyweight, credible as each. This childless man came into his own as a father in God; Cheshunt's students, mostly in their twenties, were 'his boys'.[8] He assisted at their ordinations and their inductions. The Reynolds tone could be heard in Congregational pulpits from the 1860s to the 1930s. No wonder that he was first choice to preside at special communion services or that he was urged at least twice to consider the chairmanship of the national Congregational Union.[9] A Congregational college principal was thus a bishop as many fellow ministers were not. He was certainly a public figure. Reynolds breakfasted with Gladstone and welcomed Russell and Shaftesbury as a matter of course to his college platforms; his family knew Palmerston.[10] His learning (rewarded in 1869 by an Edinburgh DD) contributed to this. He published five collections of sermons and addresses; commentaries on Amos and Hosea (jointly with a colleague) and St John's Gospel; studies of John the Baptist, Athanasius and Buddhism.[11] He edited two volumes, suggestively called *Ecclesia*, to which his own contributions were on 'The Forgiveness and Absolution of Sins' and 'The Catholic Church'.[12] He also edited or co-edited two journals and a popular, if unof-

---

[7] Ibid. 208, 430.

[8] [C. Newman Hall], *Newman Hall: An Autobiography* (London, 1898), 302.

[9] In 1883 and 1891: A. Peel, *Letters to a Victorian Editor: Henry Allon, Editor of the British Quarterly Review* (London, 1929), 339–40; *Life and Letters*, 442.

[10] This perhaps surprising link dates from Reynolds's Romsey days: Broadlands, Palmerston's estate, was nearby: *Life and Letters*, 6–8.

[11] [With O. C. Whitehouse], 'Hosea' and 'Amos', in C. J. Ellicott, ed., *Old Testament Commentary for English Readers*, 5 vols (London, 1882–4), 5: 411–34, 449–67; *The Pulpit Commentary: Introduction to the Gospel of St. John, with Exposition and Commentary* (London, 1888); *John the Baptist* (London, 1874); *Athanasius: His Life and Life-work* (London, 1889); *Buddhism: A Comparison and a Contrast between Buddhism and Christianity* (London, 1883).

[12] 'The Forgiveness and Absolution of Sins', in *Ecclesia: Church Problems considered in a Series of Essays* (London, 1870), 243–312; 'The Catholic Church', in *Ecclesia: A Second*

ficial, denominational hymnbook, and he was the joint author of a novel, *Yes and No, or Glimpses of the Great Conflict*, which few seem to have read.[13] His publishers ranged from Macmillan and Hodder and Stoughton to the Religious Tract Society. He served on the committee of the London Library but election to the Athenaeum came too late for his health to allow him to take advantage of it.[14]

Such building blocks for sanctity are easily extracted from an admirable hagiography, Reynolds's *Life and Letters*, edited (with portraits) by his sisters. And was there the unworldliness so easily associated with failure? That is suggested by the *Oxford Dictionary of National Biography*, in which Reynolds is plausibly yet unfairly depicted as theologically conservative, presiding latterly over declining student numbers, financial crisis and defections to the National Church.[15]

The hagiography and the national biography, the one a compilation, the other a distillation, are not the only evidence. There is the testimony of his writings, cumulatively impressive, difficult to compartmentalize. Most interesting of all, there is the question of his influence, its context, nature and extent. Five personal testimonies might here be offered to bolster Harwood's snapshot. They come from individuals, four men and a woman, who knew Reynolds for longer than Harwood and at different stages of his ministry.

Lydia Rawson's family were entrenched in Leeds's professional, commercial, political and cultural life. She recalled the two girls' classes for which she was responsible at East Parade in 1857–8: 'Well, they just worshipped him, and I expect I helped them, for to me he was a sort of impersonated Christ'.[16]

George Burch (1852–1914) was a Cheshunt boy to whom Reynolds lent science books. In due course Burch became one of Reynolds's 'boys' at Cheshunt, training for the Congregational

---

Series of Essays on Theological and Ecclesiastical Questions by Various Writers (London, 1871), 113–71.

[13] Co-editor, *British Quarterly Review*, 1866–74; editor, *Evangelical Magazine*, 1877–82; *The Leeds Hymn Book* (1853); [with John Russell Reynolds], *Yes and No, or Glimpses of the Great Conflict* (London, 1860).

[14] *Life and Letters*, 226–7, 290.

[15] In Reynolds's time numbers fluctuated without declining overall; the constant deficit of the 1880s did not amount to crisis; the 'defections', though painful to Reynolds, did not run counter to Cheshunt's foundation.

[16] *Life and Letters*, 144.

ministry. After five years, first as an assistant at East Parade and then in Oxford, he left the ministry for higher education, a chair in physics and a fellowship of the Royal Society.[17] He was, therefore, one of Reynolds's failures, though neither of them saw it like that. 'If Congregationalism had its saints', Burch wrote of Reynolds after his death, 'he would be one of them'.[18]

James Hirst Hollowell (1851–1909) was another of Reynolds's 'boys' in the 1870s. He remained in Congregational pastoral charge for twenty years before changing course to become the Northern Counties Education League's organizing secretary. As a strenuous exponent of the Nonconformist Conscience, Hollowell might seem to have outgrown Reynolds; he was certainly at odds with some of Reynolds's Baines relations, but he remained unswerving in his veneration for one whom he recalled as 'at once the ideal and the despair of successive generations of students ... [T]o be permitted to know a saint at close quarters is a rare privilege for a student to enjoy'.[19]

R. F. Horton (1855–1934) was not one of Reynolds's 'boys'. He had no formal ministerial training (beyond an Oxford fellowship), indeed he was never ordained, but for fifty years he sustained a north London pastorate of almost legendary intensity. Fifteen years into that pastorate he was invited to succeed Reynolds at Cheshunt. Horton declined, although for him too Reynolds had 'all the qualities of a saint, humility and humour, boundless sympathies and unfailing love of God'.[20]

Newman Hall (1816–1902) was a metropolitan pulpiteer from an earlier generation. Hall and Reynolds were old friends, their friendship marked by a shared Gladstonianism of purest essence and confirmed by Reynolds's sympathetic stance at the time of Hall's divorce and remarriage in 1880.[21] They spoke the same language. 'My dearest and oldest friend went home,' Hall wrote in September 1896:

---

[17] For Burch's ministerial career, see W. H. Summers, *History of the Congregational Churches in the Berks, South Oxon and South Bucks Association* (Newbury, 1905), 253; for his subsequent career, see *Who Was Who, 1897–1916* (London, 1920), *s.n.* 'Burch, George James'.

[18] *Life and Letters*, 546.

[19] W. Evans and W. Claridge, *James Hirst Hollowell and the Movement for Civic Control in Education* (Manchester, 1911), 11–12.

[20] A. Peel and J. A. R. Marriott, *Robert Forman Horton* (London, 1937), 205.

[21] [Hall], *Autobiography*, 332.

He ... sank gently to sleep in Jesus. That afternoon I went to weep with the two loving sisters at Broxbourne. We gave thanks together for his manly strength and womanly tenderness: his learning, wisdom, usefulness, and humility; above all his entire reliance upon and consecration to Christ. How he sympathised in grief and rejoiced in joy as his own! He was an Apostle John. What a treasure is the memory of his love, the consciousness of its perpetuation, and the assured hope of its endless perfection in the love and glory of the Elder Brother.[22]

Christlike, apostolic, saintly: the testimony is uniform. Hall's tribute is the most artful of the five; it aptly introduces us to Reynolds's influence as pastor, teacher of pastors and father in God. Hall's word-picture of friendship, brotherhood and family transcends gendered qualities. In taking us to the sisters at Broxbourne, he takes us back to the sisters of Bethany. Their brother, however, is less Lazarus than John, eternally young at the foot of the cross, the author, it will be recalled, of a well-regarded commentary on the Apostle John.[23] Here, in short, is the carefully suggestive artistry of a High Victorian sermon, almost sentimental, certainly intense. This is not the language of theological conservatism, although theological conservatives might be comforted by it. This was Reynolds's own style, however playfully acute his letters or relatively unadorned his published sermons in illustration and diction.

Reynolds's health determined how he balanced preaching, teaching and pastoring. It was his health which diverted the young Leeds pulpit prince to the self-consciously academic groves of Cheshunt College in sub-rural, semi-metropolitan Hertfordshire, and it was his health which prevented his preaching from the mid-1860s to the late 1880s. Of the eight English Congregational colleges, however, Cheshunt was the likeliest to release Reynolds's strength and turn his health to best use.[24]

Strictly speaking, Cheshunt was not a Congregational college at all.[25] Founded by Selina, Countess of Huntingdon, and opened

---

[22] Ibid. 305.
[23] See n. 11 above.
[24] S. C. Orchard, *Cheshunt College* (Saffron Walden, 1968), esp. 12–13.
[25] The following paragraph is based on the entry placed annually in the *Congregational Year Book* [hereafter *CYB*], in this instance *CYB*, 1870, 333. In 1858 there were

at Talgarth in Wales by George Whitefield on St Bartholomew's Day 1768, it had moved to Hertfordshire on St Bartholomew's Day 1792. It was thus a product of the strand of the Evangelical Revival which was associated with Whitefield, with a particular duty to that distinctive legal entity, the Countess of Huntingdon's Connexion. Its principles were Calvinistic, 'set forth in fifteen articles, substantially the doctrinal articles of the Church of England'. The college's tutors (there were usually four) and students (in Reynolds's time they ranged through the thirties) were required to assent to those articles. That apart – though for the scrupulous it was a considerable barrier – the Countess's foundation was proud of its evangelical catholicity. Its object was 'not to serve the interests of a party, but to preserve the extension of the kingdom of Immanuel by the publication of His glorious gospel, and the doctrines of His grace'. Its young men were 'left entirely free in their choice of the denomination of Christians among whom they may prefer to exercise their ministry'. They were certainly young, Reynolds's 'boys' indeed, unmarried, under twenty-eight, in residence for between two and five years depending on their attainments.

In practice Cheshunt trained men for the Congregational ministry, but the liturgy of its worship was shaped (some felt constrained) by the Book of Common Prayer, and a president who took its foundation seriously was bound to develop an understanding of the Church catholic as opposed to its sects and connexions. And its annual Commemoration furnished a grand occasion for exploiting the unlikeliest unions. As Reynolds wrote to an old Leeds friend:

> A Cheshunt Anniversary Festival is a unique affair. Nowhere else do old nobles and modern merchants, church dignitaries and raw dissenting parsons, liturgical forms and constitutional nonconformity, surplices and extemporaneous effusions, the incense of roses and the memories of the wilderness, ugliness and prettiness so picturesquely blend for an hour or two. Everybody seemed at home, marchionesses and nursery maids, prizemen and old fogies who believe that competitive

---

twenty-two students; twenty-nine in 1869; thirty-nine in 1878; thirty-three in 1893; the college was third in size of the eight English colleges in 1860.

examinations are the modern abomination of desolation in the temple of truth.[26]

That was written in 1875 in the wake of a major centenary rebuilding and enlargement which encompassed a spired tower, a cloister, a boldly apsed chapel and a library on the lines of the famous kitchens at Glastonbury or Fontevrault.[27]

There was a further dimension, this time universal. Cheshunt had a tradition, which Reynolds fostered, of preparing men for service overseas, particularly with the London Missionary Society. The society, like the college, was effectively Congregational but, like the college, its foundation was nondenominational. The society had stations in Africa, India, China and the South Seas; Cheshunt men were thus to be found worldwide, lower-middle-class Britons encountering indigenous cultures and alien world religions in the age of Darwin, Higher Criticism and imperialism. Those challenges were very new. The missionary imperative was also new but it had a head, indeed a heady, start. Reynolds was the man to shape the inevitable meeting of minds and cultures, as his writings tantalizingly suggest.

There is an almost seamless consistency about Reynolds's writing. This may be a matter of style but this style denotes the man. Its keynote is catholicity, or at least comprehensiveness. There can be no doubt as to who Reynolds is or where he stands. The author is preacher, pastor, scholar, teacher; minister, in short, of word and sacrament, although that phrase only became popular among Congregationalism's High Churchmen well after Reynolds's death. He is an evangelical Dissenter (by 1870 he prefers to speak of 'Free Churches') and a Congregationalist. Yet he is impossible to pigeon-hole.

Reynolds could be assigned to no party. Perhaps that was a matter of breeding mixed with temperament; because his foundations were sure, he could build liberally on them. 'Liberal' is an unavoidable word. Reynolds's greatest admirers were old students whose liberalism was notorious in the churches.[28] He was hardly one of them, but his unassailed standing in the churches helps

---

[26] *Life and Letters*, 281.
[27] *CYB*, 1875, 382, 436.
[28] A representative example is William Garrett Horder (1841–1922), notable hymnologist, whose departure from Wood Green to Bradford in 1893 was graced by

to explain the evolution of a Congregational mindset, Congregationalism's position at Evangelicalism's most liberal edge, and its mediating role as Christian bodies moved from evangelical cooperation to interdenominationalism and on to full (if unfulfilled) ecumenism. This suggests political skills, for which Reynolds had the intellect and temperament but not the physical strength, and it indicates a quality of Christian life, attitude and influence. This man, so easily dismissed as a saint, proves to be a deceptively useful Christian leader, with his leadership a function of his saintliness.

Its foundation was the Evangelicalism to which his father, John Robert Reynolds, had been converted in 1809–10 while serving as attaché to the British minister in Washington.[29] John Reynolds was a Congregational minister from 1812 to 1862. In 1865 Henry Reynolds published *Notes of the Christian Life*, nineteen sermons, some preached to his students but others to working men or Sunday school teachers, or on special occasions, perhaps at East Parade; one was for the ordination of a missionary bound for Shanghai.[30] Clear in their diction, reasonable in their logic, mounting and unassailable in their appeal, they are a younger preacher's version of an older generation's measure. Preaching is life or death. It brings men and women to the cross. They might be working men, assembled on the last night of the year, whom Reynolds briefly transports to Canada:

> A party of boatmen on the Niagara river may have a very strong opinion when they are caught by the rapids that it is very pleasant rowing; but neither their shouts nor their merriment will alter the fact that the world's cataract is close at hand. You have a strong opinion that hell-fire is a delusion; that they are superstitious, and cruel and ignorant who ask you to pause, and awake, and prepare for this coming, this continued retribution; but your opinion will not have the slightest, the remotest, the minutest influence on the tremendous fact.[31]

Reynolds and who was to the fore in arranging a Cheshunt memorial for Reynolds: *Life and Letters*, 277, 335.

[29]   For John Robert Reynolds (1782–1862), see *CYB*, 1863, 256–60; *Life and Letters*, 2–8; Charles E. Surman, 'Leaf Square Academy, Pendleton, 1811–1813', *Transactions of the Congregational Historical Society* 13.2 (September 1938), 107–17, at 111.

[30]   H. R. Reynolds, *Notes of the Christian Life: A Selection of Sermons* (London, 1865).

[31]   'The Judgment of God', in *Notes*, 386–411, at 400.

Or they might be Sunday school teachers, the Church's vital auxiliaries in salvation: 'you are ... extinguishing the fires of hell. There they are, those fires, smouldering in young hearts, but you are pouring upon them that water of life which can quench the fires of lust and wash away the ashes of it, which can refresh and animate the whole nature'.[32]

Such passages, however, represent the style rather than the tone of Reynolds's sermons. It is the presence of God and its consequences which are this preacher's true concern: 'No one fully recognises the presence of God unless he has ... been to the cross of our Lord Jesus Christ and there comprehended the righteousness and the love of God, and he has gone back into the great region of conscience, of reason, and of nature, with the lesson he learned *there*'.[33] Good preachers should sense how they might be misheard, especially if speaking to budding preachers. How was Reynolds heard on this occasion?

> I have to announce to you, by God's ordinance of preaching, that you are the offspring of God, the brethren of Jesus. If you will not believe ... you must suffer the consequence of this wilful ignorance ... My brethren, if you will not believe the Fatherhood of God in Christ you are condemned already to the second death ... You are left to the God of the philosophers, to cold laws, to the miserable creations of priestcraft, superstition, and guilty conscience.[34]

What are the trigger words? 'Philosophers', 'priestcraft', 'superstition'? Or 'Fatherhood' and 'brethren'? What are the trigger phrases? 'The life of the holy is the life of God'; 'The life of the Christian is a manifestation of the mind of God'.[35] Life in God was the note which Reynolds struck most insistently. And the consequent mission?

Long before John Oxenham's bestseller, *The Hidden Years*,[36] Reynolds directed his hearers' attention to the hidden years of one 'working in a carpenter's shop in a small Galilean village, quite as much shut out from the rest of the world as some of the hamlets

32 'The Teacher and the Taught', in *Notes*, 311–33, at 322.
33 'The Two Lives', in *Notes*, 1–23, at 16.
34 'About the Father's Business', in *Notes*, 185–206, at 200–1.
35 'The Two Lives', 1; 'Unity in Diversity', in *Notes*, 44–66, at 47.
36 'John Oxenham' [W. A. Dunkerley], *The Hidden Years* (London, 1925).

of Northumberland are now hidden from London, Birmingham, or Paris'.[37] Brushing away 'cobwebs of human fancy', he seized on the one 'point of light' in those years: the twelve-year-old Jesus in the Temple at Passover. That moment, recently captured by a 'great effort of modern art',[38] 'contained the first words of the Word of God, as they have been registered by the Spirit of all truth': 'I must be about My Father's business' (Luke 2: 49). 'The first great discovery that Jesus made ... was this, that God was His own Father'. Those words established in that twelve-year-old boy 'the bond of union between earth and heaven'. The concept gripped Reynolds. Such Fatherhood illuminated the missionary imitation of Christ, Son and Elder Brother. This was not to 'itinerate the country, preach the same message, venture to work miracles, attempt to introduce into England what was peculiar to Palestine'. It was to drink in Christ's spirit.[39] There could be no more intense a privilege; and such fatherhood and brotherhood drew men into the Church:

> In much of His special work it is impossible to imitate Him. We cannot atone for human sin; we cannot confer upon others a righteousness that we can never earn. Still we may have fellowship with the sufferings of Jesus, and be made conformable to His death. We may sympathize in His agony, drink of His cup, and be baptized with His baptism.[40]

This spirit transformed the missionary imperative. Reynolds himself ventured no further than the nearest East but he was an intrepidly vicarious missionary explorer, immersed in distant cultures and religions, convinced by his studies that the 'history of Christian mission is the heroic history of humanity'.[41] 'Do not suppose that *you* take with you the Divine Being', he told the 'beloved brother' whom he was commissioning to Shanghai:

[37] 'About the Father's Business', 187.
[38] Ibid. 188, 192. Was this sermon preached at East Parade? T. E. Plint (1823–61), stockbroker, art collector and Bainesocrat, was a deacon at East Parade; he owned Millais's 'Christ in the Carpenter's Shop' (1849–50); his purchase of Holman Hunt's 'Finding of Christ in the Temple' (1859–60), the sensation of the season, contributed to his financial collapse: Dianne Sachko Macleod, *Art and the Victorian Middle Class: Money and the Making of Cultural Identity* (Cambridge, 1996), 179–86, 460–1.
[39] 'About the Father's Business', 193, 199, 194, 195.
[40] Ibid. 197.
[41] 'The Summons to Holy Work', in *Notes*, 283–310, at 308.

He is there before you in every heathen's soul, in every throb of conscience, in every laudable emotion, in every glimpse of truth, in every predisposition and susceptibility for the revelation of heaven, in all the structure and facilities of that marvellous language ... in all the stupendous march of His providence, and in the wages of sin that He has imposed upon transgressors. Christ is there, ... is there now, in China ... Your heart will tell you, more than any rules of logic, more than any human instructions, where He is working. Discover and use the leverage of good that there is in the hearts of these men, and be faithful to this talent of judgment that God has given you.[42]

Again, what was heard here? The call? The response? The understanding? There are some suggestive, almost disconcerting previews in these sermons from the late 1850s and early 1860s. Reynolds lived in the world of Mrs Alexander's 'All things bright and beautiful' ('He gives to peacocks and hummingbirds, and serpents beautiful dresses; and He gives to the little insect of a day an idle life. But He often clothes His noblest children with rags')[43] but he anticipates T. H. Green with his sense of God's immanence ('God and man are at one with each other ... Viewed on the side of God, it is the Divine Mind working out His vast designs ... ; as consciously realized in the heart of man, all is free, and the desires of his heart are fulfilled'),[44] and there is a foretaste of that Congregational deviation, Christian Science ('All disease is a ghastly parody on the condition of the human soul').[45] Most striking of all, especially when shared with an assembly of Sunday school teachers, so many drawn from society's mental artmen, is Reynolds's gloss on the authority of Scripture and the Reformed economy of election:

> We are working all of us a pattern that we cannot see in the great loom of God. We are writing our own biography and

---

[42] 'Faithfulness unto Death', in *Notes*, 353–85, at 367–8. The 'beloved brother', whom the published sermon leaves unidentified, was Robert Dawson (1836–1906), whose missionary vocation, curtailed in Shanghai by illness, was reborn in the London City Mission. I am indebted to Revd Nigel Lemon for confirmation of this.

[43] 'About the Father's Business', 201.

[44] 'Delight in the Lord', in *Notes*, 111–29, at 119.

[45] 'The Withered Hand', in *Notes*, 207–24, at 208.

our observations of God's ways on paper where already there has been traced the handwriting of Providence. We are playing with the 'loaded dice of God', and working out His designs with our free-will ... And now, my brethren, God has given you a message to convey for Him to those who know it not ... you are entrusted with God's message; you have to convey to them the very idea of a righteous Ruler and of a loving Father. You are workers for God ...[46]

One can see how Reynolds accommodated himself and his students to his college's fifteen doctrinal articles. Such, too, is the preacher's perilous responsibility in churches which regard preaching as an ordinance.

Reynolds's temperament was eirenic, sometimes wryly so: 'it is not impossible that the Lord who gave His image to the Anglo-Saxon and the Bedouin, to the Circassian and the Negro, may have given the life of His Spirit to the Catholic and the Presbyterian. The beginning of the divine life is very varied'.[47] The Church was an earthly end of that divine life and it was in addressing the Church's true working classes, the Sunday school teachers, that Reynolds spoke most naturally of 'the prayers, the wishes, the yearning tenderness of all the Catholic Church of God'.[48] His sense of that Church was as intense as confessed Catholics would have found it diffuse. It inspired *Ecclesia*, the two volumes of essays which he edited in 1870–1 to demonstrate 'the extent to which it is reasonable for Congregationalists to claim the designation of Christian and Catholic',[49] and it lay behind the surprisingly sharp, well-turned, logic of his own essay on 'The Catholic Church':

.... cultivated classes in China, to the present day, hold the civilization of all the rest of the world in undisguised contempt. Surely the tone of the Anglican, Greek, and Roman Catholic Churches with reference to all other communions is profoundly Chinese in its bitterness and unreasoning self-importance. The spirit of Christianity is opposed to this mere *esprit de corps*.[50]

---

[46] 'The Teacher and the Taught', 315–16.
[47] 'The Two Lives', 3.
[48] 'The Teacher and the Taught', 321.
[49] *Ecclesia: Second Series*, ii.
[50] 'The Catholic Church', ibid. 164.

The ultimate opportunity for Reynolds to celebrate his Catholic vision came in October 1889 at the opening of Mansfield, the theological college which Congregationalists had built close to the heart of Oxford. Reynolds, assisted by R. F. Horton, presided at the communion service held in its astonishing chapel.[51] This was an unusual occasion for Congregationalists for no church had been or was likely to be formed in this chapel and the deacons who sat with Reynolds at Mansfield's table were laymen drawn nationwide to serve a congregation of lay people and ministers similarly drawn nationwide. The boldness of the enterprise was exciting, the symbolism impressive. Reynolds drew on two great Oxford movements, the previous century's Evangelicalism and the present century's Anglo-Catholicism, to anticipate 'a greater movement than either'. He placed particular weight on the 'Anglo-Catholic conception', which he thought 'a wonderful step in the right direction': 'And it seems to us that the church principle of which we are the guardians does but carry out to its full expression a similar law of love'.[52] So Reynolds broke the Word before offering the bread and the wine for the first time in the new college's chapel:

> We are seated at a table where the Apostles, Prophets, Martyrs, Saints, and Confessors of every age are feasting still. We join with the Fathers of the Early Church, and with many who were cast out as evil thinkers and wrongdoers, with Reformers and Puritans, and with those who swore Holy Leagues and Covenants in their blood, and we know we are in Him. We are creating no new society, but realising the fact of a brotherhood created by the Holy Ghost. We are not inaugurating but claiming a fellowship with all who love our Lord Jesus Christ in sincerity.[53]

There spoke – in the classic Congregational sense – one of the saints.

After his death, Reynolds was commemorated in Cheshunt College's chapel by a window with two lights, one depicting St

---

[51] *Mansfield College, Oxford: Its Origin and Opening: October 14–16, 1889* (London, 1890), 81–93.

[52] Ibid. 88, 90.

[53] Ibid. 93.

John the Baptist, the other St John the Divine,[54] but a different image might more aptly preface such oral tradition as often characterizes saints. The image is recollected by the daughter of one of Reynolds's tutorial colleagues:

> The yearly photographic groups of the eighties are thoroughly characteristic – they suggest a sort of patriarchal system under a most dignified and gracious leader, Dr. Reynolds. There he sits in the centre with Mrs. Reynolds and the other College ladies on either side, Mr. Todhunter [a tutor] and my father standing close behind with two or three rows of students; in the foreground are the tutors' small children in the careful keeping of their chosen friends from among the students, while completing the group at one side stands the gardener, rake in hand.[55]

The oral tradition comes from the Seventy-ninth Free Church Congress, Sheffield, March 1975. Two Dissenting primates, the United Reformed Church's John Huxtable and the Baptist Union's Ernest Payne, men of equal weight in the British and World Councils of Churches, were relaxing in conversation.[56] Huxtable was recalling Ben Butcher, a hero of the Papuan mission field, who had died not too long before. Butcher was too young to have been one of Reynolds's boys but, as a raw Cheshunt man, nineteen years old at most, he encountered Reynolds in classic student circumstances. Butcher and a friend had determined to teach a bumptious fellow student a lesson. They positioned themselves, each with a bucket of water, by the window of Butcher's room overlooking the college entrance. A figure approached and they tipped the water over him. Alas, the victim was no student; he was Dr Reynolds, the principal emeritus. Butcher, determined to confess and dressed in his best, presented himself at Sandholme, the Reynolds house in Broxbourne. The maid let him in. The Reynoldses were at tea and pressed their visitor to join them. After an agonizing meal Reynolds asked Butcher if he wished to see him privately; and there, in Reynolds's study with its trademark marble bust of Dante,

---

54 *Life and Letters*, 566.

55 Lilian Whitehouse, *Owen Charles Whitehouse of Cheshunt College* (Cambridge, 1916), 55.

56 For William John Fairchild Huxtable (1912–90) and Ernest Alexander Payne (1902–80), see *ODNB*.

Butcher confessed. Reynolds did not seem at all surprised. He merely said: 'next time, make sure it's the right man'. He had, after all, extracted ample punishment during the forty-five minutes of tea.[57] Such stories turn into legends and foster miracles. Such Congregational saints as Reynolds fostered mission and enlarged their contemporaries' understanding of the Church.

University of Sheffield

---

[57] Note taken of the conversation by C. Binfield, 20 March 1975. Reynolds had been a platform speaker at the first Free Church Congress, in November 1892. The story tends to confirm Butcher's recollections during a visit to Cheshunt College, Cambridge, told to me, but not written down, in the early 1960s. For B. T. Butcher (b. 1877), missionary in Papua 1904–41, see J. Sibree, *London Missionary Society: A Register of Missionaries, Deputations, etc.* (London, 1923), 150; N. Goodall, *A History of the London Missionary Society 1845–1948* (London, 1954), 420, 433, 518.

COMMERCE AND CULTURE: BENJAMIN GREGORY'S SIDELIGHTS ON WESLEYAN SANCTITY IN THE LATER NINETEENTH CENTURY

by MARTIN WELLINGS

In September 1790, some six months before his death, John Wesley was pleased to observe in a letter to Robert Carr Brackenbury that an unnamed Methodist, Brother D., 'has more light with regard to full sanctification'. 'This doctrine,' Wesley continued, 'is the grand depositum which God has lodged with the people called Methodists; and for the sake of propagating this chiefly He appeared to have raised us up.'[1]

Born out of Wesley's own lifelong quest for holiness, itself a blend of puritan devotion and High Church piety, entire sanctification, Christian perfection or perfect love became a distinctive and controversial hallmark of the Wesleyan movement. Like other Evangelicals, the Wesley brothers insisted that holiness was the calling of all Christians, and not the preserve of an ordained or cloistered elite. Unlike other Evangelicals, however, the Wesleys provocatively pressed the potential of holiness to an experience of entire sanctification in this life. Although hedged about with qualifications and sometimes expressed with considerable ambiguity, this teaching distinguished the Wesleys' Methodism from other evangelical groups.[2]

The understanding of sanctification in eighteenth-century Methodism has attracted the attention of many historians and theologians.[3] The trajectory of the doctrine in the nineteenth century, however, has been comparatively neglected, with the exception of a brief study by David Bebbington and some suggestive insights from John Munsey Turner.[4] For the first half of the century it

---

[1] *The Letters of John Wesley*, ed. John Telford, 8 vols (London, 1931), 8: 238.

[2] See, e.g., Henry D. Rack, *Reasonable Enthusiast: John Wesley and the Rise of Methodism* (London, 1989), 47, 70–5, 81–3, 334, 395–401.

[3] e.g. Harold Lindstrom, *Wesley and Sanctification* (Stockholm, 1946); Kenneth J. Collins, *The Theology of John Wesley* (Nashville, TN, 2007).

[4] David Bebbington, *Holiness in Nineteenth-Century England* (Carlisle, 2000), 51–72; John Munsey Turner, *John Wesley, the Evangelical Revival and the Rise of Methodism in England* (Peterborough, 2002), 91–5.

would seem that Methodism held firm to the Wesleys' teaching, expounding entire sanctification in line with John Wesley's *Plain Account of Christian Perfection* and expressing its faith and experience through the medium of Charles Wesley's hymns. By the mid-Victorian period, however, new influences were coming to bear. Greater numbers, increasing wealth and growing respectability encouraged a softening of old shibboleths, the restatement of old doctrines and an adjustment or blurring of the boundaries between the Church and the world. Meanwhile a succession of American revivalists and holiness advocates, particularly James Caughey, W. E. Boardman and Robert and Hannah Pearsall Smith, brought fresh insights and approaches which rejuvenated, recast or challenged English assumptions about sanctity.[5] It is against this backdrop of a tradition in transition that this paper will consider two biographies which offer Wesleyan sidelights on sanctity in the 1870s and 1880s. The biographies describe, respectively, an Anglo-Australian entrepreneur and a Wesleyan minister. They both came from the prolific pen of Benjamin Gregory, best known for his account of the conflicts which tore Wesleyan Methodism apart in the early nineteenth century, and it is with Gregory's own career that the story may begin.[6]

Benjamin Gregory (1820–1900) was an eminent member of a distinguished and prolific Wesleyan Methodist dynasty, which produced fourteen ministers over five generations, including Benjamin himself, his brother and his three sons. A son of the manse, Gregory was educated at Woodhouse Grove School, near Bradford, where he served as a junior master before entering the Wesleyan ministry in 1840. Early in his career as a circuit minister he declined an opportunity of a place at the University of Oxford which was conditional on a commitment to take holy orders in the Church of England.[7] Although his moderation during the bitter conflict over Wesleyan Reform in the 1850s sometimes put him in an unpopular minority in the Conference, Gregory's fluency and

5 Bebbington, *Holiness*, 65–7.

6 Benjamin Gregory, *Autobiographical Recollections, Edited with Memorials of his Later Life by his Eldest Son* (London, 1903); David J. Carter, 'Gregory, Benjamin', in John A. Vickers, ed., *A Dictionary of Methodism in Britain and Ireland* (Peterborough, 2000), 141; *Minutes of the Wesleyan Conference 1901* (London, 1901), 125–7.

7 Gregory, *Autobiographical Recollections*, 283; Benjamin Gregory, *Consecrated Culture: Memorials of Benjamin Alfred Gregory, M.A., Oxon.* (London, 1885), 13 n.

erudition as preacher, platform speaker and writer brought him increasing recognition. In 1867 he was elected a member of the Legal Hundred, the permanent core of the Wesleyans' governing Conference, and a year later he was appointed Connexional Editor, responsible for the extensive range of Wesleyan magazines and periodicals. For the next quarter of a century, until his retirement in 1893, Gregory wielded the editor's pen with flair and ruthlessness, recruiting interdenominational contributors to the *Wesleyan Methodist Magazine*, experimenting with new publications, and, latterly, mounting a dogged resistance to the incursions of biblical criticism. In addition to his editorial work on the periodicals, Gregory published a stream of books. His posthumous reputation rests principally on his account of the Reform controversy and its background, *Side-lights on the Conflicts in Methodism, 1827–52* (1897), and on his exploration of Methodist ecclesiology, *The Holy Catholic Church, The Communion of Saints* (1873), but his works also included poetry, sermons and more than a dozen memoirs and biographies.

As a literary genre, a spiritual guide and a profitable publishing staple, biography was hugely important to Victorian Christians, and nowhere more so than in the subculture of Wesleyan Methodism. John Wesley set the pattern, recording, shaping and publishing his own spiritual experience, and disseminating the spiritual biographies of others through his Christian Library and *Arminian Magazine*. The monthly *Magazine* (*Methodist Magazine* from 1798 and *Wesleyan Methodist Magazine* from 1822) typically began each issue with a substantial memoir and included later in the number several pages of brief biographies and obituaries.[8] Book-length biographies became more common in the nineteenth century and they came to occupy a very significant place in the Wesleyan Book Room catalogue. In the mid-1850s, for example, almost half of the catalogue comprised 'biography', 'female biography' and 'missionary biographies', some seventy titles in all. Thirty years later the Book Room printed a separate catalogue of sixty 'biographical works'. Whereas the short biographical paragraphs in the *Magazine* were

---

[8] Martin Wellings, '"A friendly and familiar book for the busy": William Arthur's *The Successful Merchant: Sketches of the Life of Mr Samuel Budgett*', in R. N. Swanson, ed., *The Use and Abuse of Time in Christian History*, SCH 37 (Woodbridge, 2002), 275–88, at 280.

predominantly the stories of lay Methodists, the book-length treatments were almost exclusively the lives of ministers and missionaries, both women and men.[9]

Biography fulfilled a number of purposes for Victorian Wesleyans. In an evangelical constituency where novel-reading might still be regarded with some suspicion, biographies could offer excitement, adventure and even romance without spiritual risk.[10] Didactic, and sometimes ponderous, historical, theological and devotional material could be delivered in a way that sugared erudition with narrative. Above all, however, biography was presented and used as a means of edification, a written form of that testimony to personal spiritual experience which was fundamental to Methodist identity and to Methodist sanctity. Methodism made saints through the face-to-face encounter of believers in the class meeting and the band meeting; this sharing of experience was mediated to a wider circle for instruction, edification and imitation through the printed word.[11] In the judgement of his youngest son, Benjamin Gregory

> believed that the mission of the *Methodist Magazine* was to defend and expound the truth of God, to illustrate God's providential government, to advocate the extension of the kingdom of God, both at home and abroad, to show the power of the gospel as exhibited in the life and death of the saints, to cultivate the deepest spiritual life, and to criticise … all forms of erroneous teaching.[12]

It is difficult to overestimate the importance of carefully chosen and carefully written biographies in accomplishing this mission.

Gregory's biographical writings ranged widely within the accepted boundaries of the genre. He contributed lives of Samuel Bradburn, a former President of the Conference, and John Preston, a colourful poacher turned local preacher, to a series of popular biographies commissioned by the Book Room in the 1890s, and

---

[9] Compare the catalogues appended to Thomas Jackson, *The Life of the Rev. Robert Newton, D.D.* (London, 1855) and Benjamin Gregory, *The Marrow of Methodism* (London, 1886).

[10] Doreen Rosman, *Evangelicals and Culture* (London, 1984), 184–93.

[11] See, e.g., D. Bruce Hindmarsh, *The Evangelical Conversion Narrative: Spiritual Autobiography in Early Modern England* (Oxford, 2005), 130–61, 226–60; Phyllis Mack, *Heart Religion in the British Enlightenment: Gender and Emotion in Early Methodism* (Cambridge, 2008), 22–6.

[12] Gregory, *Autobiographical Recollections*, 429.

his *The Less Known Methodist Writers* brought together sketches of ten minor Wesleyan worthies. His first book, *A Memoir of Emma Tatham*, published in 1859, took for its subject a young woman of exemplary piety, a conventional theme for a Wesleyan author. In two other works, however, Gregory moved into more controversial territory, and the remainder of this paper will consider those volumes in greater detail, discussing how they illustrated, extended or subverted the familiar genre in exploring sanctity in two very different settings.

In 1871 Gregory published *The Thorough Business Man: Memoirs of Walter Powell, Merchant, Melbourne and London*. Walter Powell (1822–68) was a self-made entrepreneur. His family emigrated from Tottenham to Tasmania shortly after his birth, and experienced mixed fortunes in the new colony. This slow start in the Antipodes gave way to wealth and success when Powell found himself running a hardware business in Melbourne in 1851 as gold fever swept through the colony. Powell had become a Methodist in Tasmania in the 1840s, and the biography charted his spiritual development and church involvement alongside his business career and commercial ethics.

Benjamin Gregory was invited to write *The Thorough Business Man* by Walter Powell's English friends; he was not personally familiar with his subject, and relied on Powell's manuscripts and the recollections of his acquaintances.[13] Very different was the second biography to be considered here, *Consecrated Culture: Memorials of Benjamin Alfred Gregory*, published in 1885. Here Gregory's subject was his second son, Alfred (1850–76), who died of diphtheria in his second year of probation as a Wesleyan minister. Alfred Gregory had won a scholarship from Manchester Grammar School to Brasenose College, Oxford, in 1867, taking a First in Classics five years later. His sudden death while serving in a Cornish circuit devastated the family and removed from the Wesleyan ministry its first Oxford graduate since the era of the Wesleys.

Although there were plenty of successful Methodist businessmen by the middle of the nineteenth century, none had hitherto been considered worthy of a full biographical treatment, with the exception of Samuel Budgett, memorialized by William Arthur in 1852. Reactions to Arthur's work, moreover,

---

[13] Ibid. 434.

suggested continuing reservations about the compatibility of sanctity and commerce.[14] Many Methodists also retained deep-seated anxieties about 'lettered learning' and the relationship between Christianity and culture: even senior leaders in the Connexion questioned Benjamin Gregory's wisdom in allowing his son to go up to Oxford.[15] By bringing together sanctity, commerce and culture, therefore, Gregory undertook to show how an exemplary life could be lived in circumstances which might not be regarded as propitious for the making of Methodist saints.

Benjamin Gregory's approach to the lives of Walter Powell and Alfred Gregory drew out many features which would have been uncontentious in mid-Victorian Wesleyanism. First, in both cases, an exemplary life was portrayed as the natural outworking of an inner Christian experience, and the narrative of the subject's journey of faith made much of a pious upbringing and a definite conversion. Even in the rough surroundings of Van Diemen's Land, Walter Powell's mother ensured that everything was done to inculcate 'high moral principles and sentiments' in her son and to 'inspire him with a reverence for principle and piety'.[16] Alfred Gregory recorded in his journal that 'home-influence' was 'amongst the most effective instrumentalities in bringing him to religious decision'.[17] In each case, moreover, the story of conversion combined process and crisis. Powell 'struggled slowly into the clear light of the gospel' through attendance at Wesleyan preaching services and the pastoral ministration of the local Superintendent during a period of ill-health. Although he experienced 'that great change ... which is called *conversion*', it took several months before he was settled and happy in his faith.[18] Alfred Gregory traced his spiritual awakening by fits and starts, recording the effects of various sermons over several years, before he reached the decisive steps of attending the Wesleyan Covenant service in the New Year of 1865 and asking his father if he might join a class.[19] The path to

[14] Wellings, 'William Arthur's *The Successful Merchant*', 275, 282–3, 287–8.

[15] Gregory, *Consecrated Culture*, 66; cf. Tim Macquiban, 'Practical Piety or Lettered Learning', *Proceedings of the Wesley Historical Society* 50 (1995), 83–107, esp. 101–3.

[16] Benjamin Gregory, *The Thorough Business Man: Memoirs of Walter Powell, Merchant, Melbourne and London* (London, 1871), 14–15.

[17] Gregory, *Consecrated Culture*, 15.

[18] Gregory, *Thorough Business Man*, 24–6, 36.

[19] Gregory, *Consecrated Culture*, 16–18.

sanctity, therefore, began for each subject in a Christian home and progressed via the experience of conversion.

In both cases, secondly, the life of faith was nurtured by Christian devotional practices and supported by the structures and organization of the Church. Thus both young men cultivated the disciplines of personal prayer and Bible reading, and each added the keeping of a journal: Alfred Gregory began his journal at seventeen and Walter Powell at twenty-two.[20] For Benjamin Gregory, however, private devotion was only part of the story. In *The Thorough Business Man* he explained in detail the organization of Methodism, its class and band meetings, love feasts, watchnight and Covenant services, all designed to promote 'that deep fellowship which is realized in reciprocal edification'. Gregory asserted that 'a Christian Church is a living organism, wherein the vital force of association is a common and a *communicated* experience'.[21] Faith was expressed, strengthened and developed through a commitment to the corporate spiritual life of the Church. Both biographies illustrated this conviction. Powell, for example, found the weekly class meeting encouraging and challenging as he put his new-found faith into practice. Alfred Gregory had a passion for the class meeting and prayer meeting, taking the initiative to create the first society class for Methodist undergraduates at Oxford. His father noted approvingly that the fruits of a revival at Padstow in the last months of Alfred's life were carefully steered into the regular structures of Wesleyan organization: the pattern of classes to nurture converts rather than protracted revival meetings to prolong excitement.[22]

A faith born in vivid experience and nurtured by the familiar Wesleyan 'means of grace' was expressed, thirdly, in a distinctive lifestyle. Part of that lifestyle involved attendance at the Wesleyan society's activities and commitment to its programmes. Thus Walter Powell quickly became a prayer leader, and then a Sunday school secretary and superintendent, and a class leader. Business success led to involvement in many Methodist enterprises, in Australia and England.[23] Alfred Gregory became a local preacher in 1870, and in the eighteen months between graduation and entering

[20] Ibid. 5; Gregory, *Thorough Business Man*, 41.
[21] Ibid., ch. 5, esp. 67–8.
[22] Ibid. 69–71; Gregory, *Consecrated Culture*, 77, 245.
[23] Gregory, *Thorough Business Man*, 78, 84, 86, 133–4.

the ministry was fully engaged in preaching while employed as a master at Manchester Grammar School.[24]

Church activity was complemented by a commitment to philanthropy, support for temperance, a frugal lifestyle and attention to personal and professional ethics. The biographies recorded, moreover, an aversion to certain forms of behaviour: undergraduate supper and wine parties for Alfred Gregory; and bawdy jokes, 'profane swearing' and dancing for Walter Powell.[25]

Benjamin Gregory was at pains to point out, fourthly, that his subjects combined genuine sanctity and winsome sociability. He recorded Powell's 'heavenly hilarity' and 'effervescent humour'.[26] Alfred Gregory was a cheerful character, active, vivacious, witty, a gifted debater with a talent for repartee.[27] Neither practised a narrow form of piety. Alfred Gregory deplored religious jargon, wanted Methodist students to engage fully with the life of the university, and enjoyed reading fiction, citing *Bleak House* as a formative spiritual influence.[28] Walter Powell enjoyed travel, taking 'a vivid interest in all human matters', and he set himself a programme of self-improvement through study. A friend of Walter Powell's commented: 'Powell was such a fine fellow! I hope his biographer won't make him out to have been a saint!' Gregory found this antithesis 'suggestive', asserting that a real saint, called by the gospel, baptized and justified, could indeed be 'a fine fellow'.[29]

Powell and Gregory, fifthly, trod the path to sanctity through hard work and a steady determination to overcome temptations and faults. Powell struggled with impatience and irascibility. Alfred Gregory was also prone to irritability, particularly in the cut and thrust of debate. Both men strove to control temper, and to live a consistent Christian life.[30]

These characteristics could be replicated in the lives of other Methodist saints of the nineteenth century. In two respects,

[24] Gregory, *Consecrated Culture*, 94, 137.
[25] Ibid. 286, 293, 84 respectively; Gregory, *Thorough Business Man*, 329–30, 280–1, 103, 64.
[26] Ibid. 373.
[27] Gregory, *Consecrated Culture*, 92–3, 289.
[28] Ibid. 283, 68–71, 17.
[29] Gregory, *Thorough Business Man*, 102, 369.
[30] Ibid. 375; Gregory, *Consecrated Culture*, 285–6.

however, Gregory's portrayal broke comparatively new ground and challenged conventional wisdom.

First, Walter Powell's success as a businessman, founded on hard work, shrewdness, attention to detail, and refusal to be distracted from legitimate commercial profit by such sentimental notions as friendship, received general and specific approbation from his biographer.[31] A generation earlier, William Arthur had demonstrated his willingness to criticize some of Samuel Budgett's business practices as inconsistent with Christian ethics. Gregory, however, had no inhibitions in praising Powell's 'sensitive integrity', combined with 'firmness, energy and push'.[32] A substantial section of *The Thorough Business Man*, amounting to no fewer than eight chapters of the book, discussed the commercial ethics of Christianity, a subject Gregory believed to have been woefully neglected.[33] Although various practices were denounced as contrary to Christian principles, Powell's own behaviour and characteristics were exonerated from any blame. Gregory asserted that Powell's personality and success demonstrated that 'there is … no incongruity between business and devotion'. His qualities as a Christian businessman 'had their roots in *holiness*'. The epigraph on the title page of the book confidently proclaimed: 'His career affords one more proof that it is still possible for Christian principle to achieve commercial success', and in the body of the text Gregory exclaimed: 'What a fine pursuit is commerce – business – money making – in the hands of a sensible, conscientious, and believing man!' To Gregory's mind, Powell's achievement was explained by Matthew 6: 33: he 'sought "first the kingdom of God and His righteousness," and found "all these things added unto" him'.[34]

It is important to note that this understanding of the relationship between sanctity and prosperity ran counter to much within the Wesleyan tradition of Christian holiness. John Wesley enjoined and exemplified a lifestyle of extreme frugality, gave away most of his annually increasing income to the poor with indiscriminate generosity, and warned his people against the deleterious effects of wealth. Early Methodists expected to preach the gospel to the

---

[31] Gregory, *Thorough Business Man*, 217.
[32] Wellings, 'William Arthur's *The Successful Merchant*', 281–2; Gregory, *Thorough Business Man*, 207, 209.
[33] Ibid. v.
[34] Ibid. 194, 196, title page, 307, 1.

poor and to encounter the indifference or hostility of the rich. This assumption was challenged in the early nineteenth century when Wesleyanism was reshaped by an alliance of influential preachers and an affluent lay elite, but the frank endorsement of commercial success as an outworking of Christian holiness took time to be accepted. Benjamin Gregory himself remarked privately in 1852 that Arthur's *The Successful Merchant* 'ought to have been entitled "The art of getting a camel through the eye of a needle" '; two decades later, with a son about to enter business life, his perspective had clearly changed.[35]

The second departure from Wesleyan convention concerned the evaluation of culture. In their different ways and spheres both Walter Powell and Alfred Gregory took education and self-culture very seriously. Powell, painfully conscious of his lack of learning, set himself a demanding programme of study, including English grammar, mathematics, history and music. Gregory's biography included extracts from a paper on 'Self-development' given to the Young Men's Mutual Improvement Society at Denbigh Road Wesleyan Chapel, Bayswater, in which Powell urged the young men to strengthen 'your noble resolve to become more intelligent'.[36] Alfred Gregory's considerable educational achievements were detailed in his father's biography, with notes on his breadth of reading, extracts from his undergraduate essays, laudatory comments on his published articles, and outlines of the books he planned but never completed. The bookish son of a scholarly family, Alfred's predilection for study was not surprising; nor, surely, was Benjamin Gregory's delight in the child who achieved the Oxford place which he himself was denied. The elder Gregory, however, added to paternal pride the belief that

> the combination of high intellectual culture, and the boldest reading and thinking, with the most simple, steadfast faith, and the most ardent, plodding evangelic earnestness – the possibility of which is here proved, and the effect of which is here

---

[35] John Walsh, 'John Wesley and the Community of Goods', in Keith Robbins, ed., *Protestant Evangelicalism: Britain, Ireland, Germany and America, c. 1750 – c. 1950: Essays in Honour of W. R. Ward*, SCH S 7 (Oxford, 1990), 25–50, esp. 35–6, 44–50; David Hempton, *Methodism and Politics in British Society 1750–1850* (London, 1984), 85–115; Gregory, *Autobiographical Recollections*, 400; idem, *Thorough Business Man*, iii (dedication).

[36] Ibid. 63, 109, 174–6, 339–41, 343.

illustrated – is still one of the most urgent desiderata of the Christian Church.[37]

In his combination of scholarship and sanctity, summed up in the phrase 'consecrated culture', Alfred Gregory exemplified Methodism's ability to address the needs of contemporary society.

Again, there was plenty in the Wesleyan tradition to challenge this conclusion. John Wesley shook the dust of Oxford from his feet after his excoriating university sermon 'Scriptural Christianity' of 1744 and Methodist sympathizers were not welcome in the university.[38] Neither Tractarian nor Broad Church tendencies were likely to reassure nineteenth-century Wesleyans that Oxford was anything other than a menace to Methodists. Beyond the specific issue of the universities, there was, moreover, an anti-intellectual tendency in Methodism (as in other branches of Evangelicalism), which discounted scholarship, opposed structured ministerial training, and was suspicious of culture and 'lettered learning'. In addressing this constituency it was important for Benjamin Gregory to show that Alfred was a hard-working pastor, a zealous revivalist and an acceptable preacher, as well as an Oxford graduate. The consistent message of *Consecrated Culture* was summed up in the article which Alfred Gregory was planning for a Wesleyan periodical at the time of his death. It was to tell the story of three John Smiths: the 'Puritan captain', the Cambridge Platonist and the Wesleyan revivalist.[39] The seamless integration of leadership, scholarship and evangelical religion was fundamental to Gregory's model of Wesleyan sanctity.

Benjamin Gregory moved beyond earlier biographies in presenting self-culture and prosperity as aspects of sanctity, rather than as distractions or encumbrances to it. This was reflected in the structure of both *The Thorough Business Man* and *Consecrated Culture*, where considerable space was devoted to Walter Powell's business career and character and to Alfred Gregory's university life. Methodist portrayals and perceptions of sanctity were changing, from

---

[37] Gregory, *Consecrated Culture*, v.

[38] Text of the sermon in *The Works of John Wesley: Sermons*, ed. Albert C. Outler, 4 vols (Nashville, TN, 1984–87), 1: 159–80; Gregory, *Autobiographical Recollections*, 407–8.

[39] Gregory, *Consecrated Culture*, 294. The three subjects were John Smith (c. 1580–1631), John Smith (1618–52), and John Smith (1794–1831). The first two are in *ODNB*, the third in Vickers, *Dictionary of Methodism*, 322.

a concentration on conversion, narrowly defined religious activity and a pious death, to a picture of life with broader horizons lived in fellowship with Christ. Addressing a readership of Wesleyan clerks and aspiring middle-class families with Oxbridge ambitions, Gregory, who knew that same milieu as father and pastor, gave a new turn to the long-held Methodist belief that saints, although not of this world, are definitely called to discipleship within it.

Oxford

THE CANONIZATION OF SERAFIM OF SAROV: PIETY, PROPHECY AND POLITICS IN LATE IMPERIAL RUSSIA*

by RICHARD PRICE

St Serafim of Sarov (1754–1833), though not widely known among western Christians, is one of the most popular saints in Russia and among Russians abroad.[1] A discussion of his canonization in 1903 cannot avoid mention of some less than savoury aspects and conjuncts of his cult, but let it be said at the outset that nothing which follows changes the fact that he is both a hugely venerable and very attractive figure. Though a monk in a large monastery, he lived for years as a hermit in a neighbouring forest, loving to be unknown; but in the last years of his life, back in his monastery, he welcomed visitors, who queued in their hundreds outside his cell, day after day. A favourite greeting of his to address his visitors was *moia radost* (my joy). In the words of the synodal decree approving his canonization, 'Spiritual joy had penetrated the starets so much that he was never seen to be sad or depressed, and this joyful mood of the soul he endeavoured to communicate to others.'[2] Equally impressive are such episodes in his life as the occasion when robbers beat him up, leaving him half-dead and with a permanent spinal injury: he not only forgave them but insisted they were not prosecuted, threatening that, if they were, he would leave the Sarov region for ever. Nothing I shall say can besmirch Serafim himself or the devotion to his memory of those who see him as a model of piety and an intercessor in time of need. But this does not alter the strange circumstances of his canonization, and it is these, not his sanctity, that are the subject of this paper.

* I was much helped in writing this essay by information and materials generously provided by Dr Stella Rock.

[1] I am informed by Dr Michael Hagemeister that recent archival research has established 9 July 1754 as the probable date of his birth; see V. A. Stepashkin, *Prepodobnyi Serafim Sarovskii: predaniia i fakty* (Sarov, 2002), 6–10.

[2] *Tserkovnye vedomosti*, 1903, no. 29, repr. in *Serafimovskii Diveevskii pravoslavnyi kalendar-sbornik* (Diveyevo, 2003), 20.

THE CANONIZATION, JULY 1903

In the generally disastrous reign of Tsar Nicholas II of Russia, one of the rare happy moments, perhaps the most happy of all apart from the birth of his son, was when in 1903 together with his family he attended Serafim's canonization, which took place in the saint's own monastery.[3]

On their arrival at Sarov, some two hundred and thirty miles due east of Moscow, on 17 July (Old Style) 1903, the emperor and his family were greeted by a vast crowd that had spent the night in the open fields surrounding the monastery. Doubtless few, if any, had seen their sovereign before, and now the lucky ones could stand within a few feet of him or even touch his uniform; the tight security that surrounded him in the capital St Petersburg (after the assassination of his grandfather) was not enforced in this distant, idyllic retreat of Holy Russia. The emperor commented in his personal diary, 'The crowd was touching and remarkably orderly.'[4] The main celebration was a vigil on the night of 18 July (counting liturgically as 19 July, the day of the saint's death), when a hundred thousand pilgrims filled the monastery for the great moment when his relics would be exposed for veneration. After prayers and litanies the coffin was lifted onto the shoulders of the tsar himself and the grand dukes of the imperial family, and carried from the church, where the relics had lain in preparation, into the Cathedral of the Dormition, where the shrine of the canonized saint was to be. The emperor wrote in his diary: 'One felt an enormous lift, both from the event itself and the extraordinary mood of the crowd.'[5] The climax of the celebration was the opening of the coffin; veneration of the relics continued throughout the night and the following day. During the celebrations several miracles were reported. Such was the press of the crowd that a woman gave birth, almost at the feet of the emperor, who promptly offered to be the godfather. Official communiqués and press reports stressed

---

[3] For the canonization ceremonies, see R. L. Nichols, 'The Friends of God: Nicholas II and Alexandra at the Canonization of Serafim of Sarov, July 1903', in C. E. Timberlake, ed., *Religious and Secular Forces in Late Tsarist Russia* (Seattle, WA, 1992), 206–29; Helen Kontzevitch, *St Serafim, Wonderworker of Sarov* (Wildwood, CA, 2004), 193–200; *Serafimovskii … sbornik*, 112–25.

[4] Andrei Maylunas and Sergei Mironenko, eds, *A Lifelong Passion: Nicholas and Alexandra: Their own Story* (London, 1996), 229–30.

[5] Ibid. 230.

not only the piety of the vast assembly but its representativeness, including as it did pilgrims from almost every nationality in European Russia and beyond. In the words of a modern writer, 'for a delightful and perilous moment the social and national divisions segregating the classes and peoples of the empire broke down, carrying with them for a time the warm breath of hope for a lost solidarity of tsar and people'.[6]

No less striking than the physical proximity of the emperor to his subjects was the absence of the usual protocol stressing differences of station. Before the saint chosen by God all ranks became equal, for a moment which, however brief and exceptional, could be sensed to express a constant truth: the tsar was one with his subjects in dependence on the intercession of the new saint, and his absolute rule found justification in his promotion of the religion that could be perceived as the nation's strongest bond. Of course, this idealistic picture, trumpeted in the official press, was not the whole story: the unprecedented and unpredicted number of pilgrims – 300,000 when 100,000 had been expected – meant that the majority had to stand outside the monastery precinct throughout the ceremonies, and saw and heard nothing. There was also a police presence to control the crowds. But the degree of access to the emperor's person, and his self-effacement before the saint, remained as impressive as they were novel.[7]

The conspicuous participation of the emperor in the ceremony had a particular appropriateness in that it was he who had twisted the arm of the reluctant church authorities to secure the decree of canonization.[8] In the two preceding centuries there had been only five canonizations, and until Nicholas himself took up the cause there had been little support for it outside the region immediately around Sarov. Even when the reported miracles stood up to the

---

[6]   Nichols, 'Friends of God', 206.

[7]   G. L. Freeze, 'Subversive Piety: Religion and the Political Crisis in Late Imperial Russia', *Journal of Modern History* 68 (1996), 308–50, at 324–8, tries to persuade us that the ceremonies, witnessed by only some of the pilgrims, accentuated rather than minimized divisions, and goes so far as to call them 'misstaged'. But even a hostile observer such as the writer Korolenko noted the crowd's 'fanaticism' and 'special devotion to the tsar': Sergei Firsov, *Tserkov v Imperii: Ocherki iz tserkovnoi istorii epokhi Imperatora Nikolaia II* (St Petersburg, 2007), 111.

[8]   Freeze, 'Subversive Piety', 314–19. Freeze's article brings out the tensions in the relationship between Nicholas II and the Russian Church, which resented his arbitrary initiatives.

rigours of formal investigation, the Holy Synod (the governing body of the Russian Orthodox Church) declined to take action; it must have perceived Serafim's cult as essentially a local cause taken up by religious enthusiasts whose judgement and motives were open to question. It needed direct imperial intervention to overcome the Church's passive resistance. In 1902 the imperial couple summoned the Over-Procurator (or Chairman) of the Holy Synod, the scrupulous and arch-conservative Pobedonostsev, and to his astonishment demanded Serafim's immediate canonization. When he pleaded that the proper procedure could not be rushed, Alexandra replied with one of her favourite expressions, 'The Sovereign can do anything.' The best the Over-Procurator could obtain was a postponement of one year till 1903.[9] When the Synod formally approved the canonization in January 1903, its decree drew attention to the leading role that Nicholas had played in 'reminding' the Synod of Serafim's achievements and reputation and expressing a 'wish' that his process should be brought to a successful and speedy conclusion.[10]

Even though the canonization was genuinely popular, an unfortunate detail provided ammunition for the sceptics: when the saint's coffin was opened in preparation for the translation of his remains, they were found to have decomposed. Even though the Synod promptly publicized the fact that the official procedure did not require bodily integrity as a proof of sanctity, popular belief had come to expect it. It was unfortunate that, when Feodosy of Uglich had been canonized in 1896 and his body found to be incorrupt, this fact had been blazed abroad by the church authorities. Both religious opponents of the Church, such as the Old Believers, and political opponents of the tsarist regime gleefully exploited the poor condition of the relics. But it did little to dampen popular enthusiasm. The number of pilgrims who attended the canonization was still far greater than expected, and far greater than the pilgrims at Feodosy's canonization (some 300,000 compared to 75,000), despite the remoteness of Sarov from all the major centres of population and arteries of traffic.[11]

---

9 S. Yu. Vitte [Count Witte], *Vospominaniia: Tsarstvovanie Nikolaia II*, 2 vols (Berlin, 1922), 1: 242–3.

10 Freeze, 'Subversive Piety', 318–19; *Serafimovskii … sbornik*, 21.

11 Freeze, 'Subversive Piety', 320–4. The nearest railway station (Arzamas) was sixty kilometres away.

The *Conversation with Motovilov*

The canonization was accompanied, naturally enough, by the publication or re-publication of materials relating to the life, teaching and holiness of the new saint. His *Life* had appeared in a number of redactions during the 1840s, and is one of the gems of Russian hagiography.[12] It manages simultaneously to present Serafim as a hermit in the long tradition going back to Antony of Egypt and yet to do justice to the peculiar features of his biography and the particular feel of his spirituality.

The year of canonization witnessed the appearance of a work, hitherto completely unknown, that purported to be the verbatim record of a long conversation between the saint and one of his spiritual children, Nikolai Motovilov (1809–79), on the theme of the goal of the Christian life. This conversation, dating to near the end of the saint's life, in November 1831, had been written down at an unknown date by Motovilov, and was now published posthumously in the very month of the canonization by Sergei Nilus, an indefatigable investigator and publicist of Russian monasticism and a man of genuine piety.[13] The work has subsequently circulated under two titles, *The Conversation with Motovilov* and *On the Aim of the Christian Life*. Published when it was, it immediately attracted considerable attention, some of it hostile: when Nilus reprinted the text in 1905, he felt obliged to defend it against charges of unorthodoxy made by some reviewers, and indeed to delete a few pages particularly open to criticism.[14] After the Revolution Russian exiles in the west disseminated the work widely, with translations appearing in numerous languages, and since the fall

---

[12] See T. R. Rudi, 'Le prime "Vite" di San Serafim di Sarov. Problemi di critica testuale', in Adalberto Mainardi, ed., *San Serafim da Sarov a Diveevo. Atti del IV Convegno ecumenico internazionale di spiritualità russa* (Magnano, 1998), 141–56.

[13] For details of the first publication in instalments in a daily newspaper, see Michael Hagemeister, 'Il problema della genesi del "Colloquio con Motovilov"', in Mainardi, ed., *San Serafim da Sarov a Diveevo*, 157–74, at 160 n. 17. I have used the 1905 reprint (for which see n. 18 below).

[14] Vsevolod Roshko, *Prepodobnyi Serafim: Sarov i Diveevo* (Moscow, 2001), 16, 35. Roshko dates the suppression of these pages to the edition of 1911, but they were already excised from the 1905 reprint. These pages (which I have not seen), on the creation and early history of the world, were unorthodox in their treatment of the animal creation, and have been argued to reflect the philosophy of Schelling and Schubert, as transmitted by Feofan Avsenev in the Kievan Spiritual Academy in the mid-nineteenth century: see Roshko, *Prepodobnyi Serafim*, 36.

of communism it has been repeatedly reprinted in Russia itself. It has become perhaps the most celebrated single piece of Russian spiritual writing.[15]

A feature of the text that excited criticism already on its first publication was its stress on the visible manifestations of the Holy Spirit. When Motovilov asks after the goal of the Christian life, Serafim criticizes those who locate it in prayer, fasting, vigils and the like, all of which are necessary (he admits) but only as preliminaries: the true goal is attaining the Holy Spirit, in an experience of the Spirit that will be immediately recognizable. The climax of the work describes how Serafim's face was transfigured by light, so bright that it dazzled Motovilov to behold it. It is this picture of the shining of the saint's face, as he sits with a rapt disciple in the solitude of a forest clearing, while snowflakes fall around them, that gives the dialogue its rare iconic beauty. The narrative continues with Serafim assuring Motovilov, 'You have now become as radiant as I am myself. You yourself are now in the fullness of the Spirit of God; otherwise you would not be able to see me like this.' And the saint proceeds to insist that, once the Holy Spirit has been attained in this way, it is needless and inappropriate to continue to pray, for there is no longer anything to ask for.

Sticklers for orthodoxy may baulk at this point, and begin to doubt the work's authenticity, but our natural presumption that Serafim can never have been unorthodox is not a scholarly argument. In fact, the most obvious ground for doubting the authenticity of the text is a different one, namely its publication by Sergei Nilus.[16] Nilus claimed that Motovilov's widow (a nun devoted to the memory of her late husband) gave him this and other manuscripts in a quite deplorable condition, the pages all jumbled together, and with gems of spiritual testimony mixed up with not only business letters and invoices but also pigeon-feathers and bird-droppings.[17] This story (plus the claim that Motovilov's

---

[15] The most familiar English translation is that by A. F. Dobbie-Bateman, which was reprinted in G. P. Fedotov, ed., *A Treasury of Russian Spirituality* (London, 1950), 265–79. This is, however, a much abbreviated version.

[16] On Nilus, see Ann Shukman, '"The Conversation between St Seraphim and Motovilov"; The Author, the Texts and the Publishers', *Sobornost* 27.1 (2005), 47–57, at 52. On the problem of the origin and authenticity of the text, see Hagemeister, 'Problema'.

[17] Nilus, *Velikoe v malom* (see following note), 203.

handwriting was only decipherable after hours of prayer) was a palpable invention, presumably to deter people from asking to see the manuscript. Add to this the fact that Nilus was the publisher of the most notorious of all anti-Semitic forgeries, the *Protocols of the Sages of Sion*, which he published together with the *Conversation with Motovilov* in the 1905 reprint,[18] and there appear to be the makings of a strong case against the dialogue's authenticity. But in fact no one has gone so far as to accuse Nilus of writing the text himself. Even Vsevolod Roshko, the first critic to raise these and other difficulties, comments succinctly that 'Nilus was a creator of myths but not a forger'.[19] Moreover, it has recently been argued that forgery by Nilus is ruled out by the publication in 1914 of two variant versions of the text (different in detail rather than content), claiming to be based on other Motovilov manuscripts, and edited by one N. P. Popov, who was a serious scholar and theologian.[20]

But our problems are not solved by tracing the text back to Motovilov, for we have now to ask: how reliable was *he*? The conversation was conducted in the open air, while snow was falling. He cannot have been taking notes; and yet we are asked to believe that this record of a long conversation is substantially authentic.[21] Moreover, at the time Motovilov was a young man of twenty-two who had received no theological education: he cannot possibly have remembered a long exposition on unfamiliar doctrine, and with many citations or echoes of biblical and patristic texts. A further difficulty, which does not appear to have struck

---

[18] S. Nilus, *Velikoe v malom i antikhrist, kak blizkaia politicheskaia vozmozhnost. Zapiski pravoslavnago* ['Great in small, and Antichrist as an imminent political possibility; the notes of an Orthodox'] (Tsarskoe Selo, 1905). This was an expanded edition of the work of the same title that had come out in 1903 and contained the first publication of the *Conversation* in book form; it was published by the Committee of the Red Cross.

[19] Roshko, *Prepodobnyi Serafim*, 37.

[20] Shukman, 'Conversation', and Hagemeister, 'Problema', 169. It is ironic that one of these versions concludes: 'On the subject of the canonization of the great starets I [Motovilov] have made, and make, no request to anyone; for he himself during his life said to me by word of mouth, and his words are impressed on my heart, "The Lord raises up his saints, making his Church canonize them, only when she is suffering grievously in her members from whatever impiety." May the Lord deliver our Russian Church from such a misfortune!': *Sarovskoe chudo: O tseli khristianskoi zhizni* (repr. Moscow, 1999), 63. It is understandable that this version was not published at the time of the canonization!

[21] The length in English translation of the Nilus recension of 1905 is around thirteen thousand words. Since the text presents a single, coherent argument, there is little attraction in suggestions that it may have been based on a series of conversations.

other commentators, is that Motovilov was not only a novice in the spiritual life but also mentally abnormal: at this time of his life he was subject to acute depression and a recurrent paralysis of the legs that he himself recognized as what we would term psychosomatic.[22] I find it incredible that any spiritual director, let alone one of the calibre of St Serafim, would have encouraged such a vulnerable individual to look down on the regular practices of the spiritual life and aim at the rarest and most extraordinary manifestations of the Holy Spirit; all spiritual directors are aware that an unhealthy interest in such phenomena is common among the psychically disturbed and has to be firmly discouraged. That Serafim was critical of conventional piety and lauded the rarer charisms of the Spirit could well be true; the Hesychast tradition was available to him through the Russian edition of the *Philokalia* (the *Dobrotoliubie*), which had been published in 1793 and was in the Sarov monastery library.[23] What is not credible is that he chose Motovilov to be his confidant.

Surely the most probable hypothesis is that Motovilov composed the text many years later, after years of steeping himself in the Orthodox mystical tradition, on the basis of a tradition that the saint was sometimes so illuminated by the Holy Spirit that his face shone like light. It is possible that Motovilov had witnessed this himself, but his credibility is not improved by the claim, made in another of his manuscripts, that he had *often* seen Serafim's face shining so brightly that it hurt his eyes to look at him;[24] we are in the presence of a maker of myths with a flexible notion of veracity. Such scepticism is anathema, of course, to the text's numerous admirers both in the Russian Church and beyond: keen to put the *Conversation* on a par with the works of the Church Fathers, they feel obliged to claim that it preserves the teaching and even the actual words of St Serafim.

Nilus had contacts in the imperial entourage, and it is therefore possible that the *Conversation* had reached the imperial couple prior to its publication; they are at least likely to have read it subsequently. If so, their reaction would certainly have been one

---

[22] Nilus, *Velikoe v malom*, 141.

[23] I am informed of this fact by Ann Shukman. The library survives in a state archive.

[24] Nilus, *Velikoe v malom*, 299.

of the keenest enthusiasm. The empress Alexandra had grown up as a fervent pietist in Germany, and, on marrying Nicholas, had adopted the more sober and more communal piety of Orthodoxy with initial reluctance. She and her husband developed a personal piety that owed as much to Protestant mystics, such as Jacob Boehme, as to the native sources of the Orthodox tradition. According to her lady-in-waiting and intimate confidante Anna Vyrubova, she 'read religious books in every language and took an interest in the religions of the whole world', especially those of Persia and India, while Nicholas 'was always mystically inclined'.[25]

At the time of the canonization of St Serafim the spiritual guide of the imperial couple was a Frenchman known as 'Dr Philippe', referred to by the imperial couple as 'our friend' (a term they later applied to his successor Rasputin), who specialized in mystical sessions behind closed shutters, during which (according to a French newspaper report, filed away in the archives of the Russian Ministry of the Interior) he would whisper with the women, at which they 'would seem to rise towards him, as if he were lifting them, making them leave the ground'. The imperial couple (according to the contemporary diary of Grand Duke Konstantin) attended many of these sessions, and would 'return in an exalted state, as if in ecstasy, with radiant faces and shining eyes'. The Frenchman's admirers referred to him as a modest man, but he claimed to be able to cure various illnesses including syphilis, and that after his death he would reappear in a fresh incarnation.[26]

In 1902 he persuaded Alexandra that she would soon give birth to a male child. The result was a hysterical pregnancy and a quasi-miscarriage. Dr Philippe attributed this debacle to a lack of faith, and urged the empress to turn to the intercession of St Serafim, whose miraculous powers had been officially authenticated by a church commission not long before. He assured the empress that, if she bathed in a spring at Sarov associated with the saint, she would give birth as she desired. The hope that devotion to the saint would win the imperial couple the male heir they so longed

[25] Anna Vyrubova, *Freilina ee Velichestva* (Minsk, 2002), 157.

[26] Maylunas and Mironenko, *Lifelong Passion*, 206–8, 218–19. Nicholas, Alexandra and all their children were canonized by the Moscow Patriarchate in 2000, not undeservedly in view of their dignity in captivity and their final martyrdom, but as a result there has been a reluctance to acknowledge that the piety of the last tsarist court was not a model of Orthodoxy.

for must have been a major stimulus to their promotion of his canonization.[27]

THE PROPHECIES OF ST SERAFIM

If Serafim's reputation as a wonder-worker recommended to the emperor and empress by their current spiritual guru provides the most obvious explanation of their devotion to his cause, and if the *Conversation with Motovilov* will certainly have appealed to their taste for mystical phenomena, they were also attracted by a yet more dubious part of the saint's supposed legacy, namely his prophecies. The publication of those still awaiting fulfilment was prevented by the church censorship before the canonization, at the time of the canonization, and down to the Revolution. Some have only been published during the last twenty years, as material confiscated by the Soviet police has come to light. The problems of authenticity, date and provenance are naturally considerable.

The stories of Serafim's ability to read the secrets of hearts and to learn of events by no natural means are likely to have circulated already in his lifetime; such stories are common enough in hagiography. Prophecies attributed to Serafim began to circulate posthumously, in response to later needs. The group of prophecies with the least doubtful claim to authenticity is that relating to the women's monastery of Diveyevo, not far from Sarov. Serafim in his later years was regarded with dubiety by his own brethren, perhaps because he remained sturdily idiorhythmic in what was otherwise a coenobitic monastery, or because he attracted too many visitors to the monastery, particularly women; certainly they tried to dampen the popular devotion towards him by a conspiracy of silence.[28] But at the same time he was acting as founder and spiritual director (at a distance) of the community of Diveyevo, and it is this community, more than his own monastery, which after his death treasured and preserved his memory. The records and memoirs of the early sisters were collected and edited by Leonid Chichagov (alias Archimandrite, and later Metropolitan, Serafim);[29] his work was published in 1896, with a reprint in the year of the canonization. (It is signifi-

---

[27] Ibid. 228–9.

[28] Roshko, *Prepodobnyi Serafim*, 15, 25–7.

[29] As one of the martyrs of the Soviet period, he was canonized by the Russian Orthodox Church in 1997.

cant, by the way, that Chichagov decided to use none of the material collected by Motovilov, because he doubted its reliability.)[30] It was Chichagov who was the most insistent promoter of the cause of canonization, and it is to his influence that well-informed contemporaries attributed the adoption of the cause by Nicholas II and Alexandra.[31] His massive publication (seven hundred large pages) remains, according to modern scholars, the only critical and substantial study of Serafim and the traditions relating to him.[32] What is important for our present purpose is that he included in his work a number of prophecies attributed to Serafim by the sisters of Diveyevo; the publication of these was, however, prohibited by the ecclesiastical censorship. The original manuscript was discovered, however, after the fall of communism in the archives of the KGB, and the suppressed passages were finally published in 1992, and are included in an appendix in a recent reprint of Chichagov's work.[33] Since this material is wholly independent of both Motovilov and Nilus, its value is obvious.

The prophecies include predictions of Diveyevo's future glory as 'a wonder for the whole world', that Serafim's own body would be translated from Sarov to Diveyevo,[34] and that the tsar would visit the convent (which indeed Nicholas II did, at the time of

---

[30] Hagemeister, 'Problema', 171. Compare the judgement of Metropolitan Filaret of Moscow in a letter to the Over-Procurator of the Russian Church in 1861, 'Some details in the notes from Motovilov do not inspire confidence, because they show signs of a restless spirit': *Letopis Serafimo-Diveevskogo monastyria* (Moscow, 2005), 508.

[31] That the emperor's interest in Serafim was due to Chichagov's influence was claimed by Pobedonostsev, in a letter discovered by Freeze: 'Subversive piety', 318 n. 33.

[32] What is needed today is a critical analysis of Chichagov's material. The only attempt at this to date has been Roshko, *Prepodobnyi Serafim*, first published in French as V. Rochcau, *Saint Séraphim: Sarov et Diveyevo. Études et documents* (Bégrolles-en-Mauges, 1987), a short study that only begins the good work.

[33] *Letopis*, 'Prilozhenie' (ed. A .N. Strizhev), 677–83. For details of the 1992 publication, see M. Hagemeister, 'Apokalipsis nashego vremeni: Prorochestva sv. Serafima Sarovskogo o prikhode Antikhrista i kontse sveta', *Stranitsy* 4 (1999), 396–414, at 409 n. 54. There is a German edition of this important article: 'Eine Apokalypse unserer Zeit: Die Prophezeiungen des heiligen Serafim von Sarov über das Kommen des Antichrist und das Ende der Welt', in J. Hösler and W. Kessler, eds, *Finis Mundi* (Stuttgart, 1998), 41–60.

[34] The saint's relics were rediscovered and translated to Diveyevo in 1991, not directly from Sarov, however, but from the State Museum of the History of Religion and Atheism in Leningrad, where, unbeknownst, they had been housed for over sixty years. The Sarov Monastery is now within the enclosure of a large state establishment engaged in nuclear research and closed to all visitors.

the canonization). Of particular interest is a prophecy that invokes the theme of the coming of the Antichrist and predicts its occurrence in the Russia of Nicholas II. Serafim instructed the Diveyevo sisters to dig a ditch round the convent, explaining:

> When the century comes to an end, at first Antichrist will begin to remove the crosses from the churches and destroy the monasteries, and he will destroy all the monasteries. And he will come to your monastery, yes, he will come, and your ditch will stand from earth to heaven. He won't be able to get to you, the ditch won't let him in. Be off!, and he'll go on his way.[35]

This prophecy is so idiosyncratic, and so linked to the development of the Diveyevo convent, that it could surely be authentic.

Most of the prophecies, however, derive, unfortunately, from Motovilov and Nilus. In 1903, together with the *Conversation with Motovilov*, Nilus published a manuscript of Motovilov (dating to 1844) containing exhortations and prophecies attributed to Serafim and relating to the then emperor, Nicholas I (1825–55), whose reign had overlapped with the saint's life.[36] That, when speaking to Motovilov, a young aristocrat with many connections in the imperial service, the saint spoke of the trials of the emperor and the need for absolute loyalty is likely enough, even if one would hope that the rabidly nationalist tone of the prophecies is inauthentic. Motovilov narrates how Serafim spoke to him for hours about the terrible punishment that God was going to inflict on the emperor's enemies and indeed on the whole land: 'The land of Russia will be stained crimson with rivers of blood … , but the Lord will not be angry for ever and will not allow the Russian land to be completely destroyed, because in it alone is preserved Orthodoxy and the remains of Christian piety.' And Serafim predicted of the emperor, 'God will preserve him; he is great before God.' Nilus

---

35 *Letopis*, 681. Other references to Antichrist were not suppressed by the censorship, e.g. 'You [the nuns of Diveyevo] will not live before the Antichrist, but you will live through the times of the Antichrist' (ibid. 367).

36 Nilus, *Velikoe v malom*, 299–304. That this part of the work was already contained in the 1903 edition (which I have not seen) is stated by Nilus in his introduction to the 1905 edition. The prophecy I summarize here precedes a story of Serafim learning of the Decembrist revolt of 1825 by no natural means (ibid. 301–2), which confirms that Motovilov understood all these prophecies to relate to Nicholas I.

prefixed his publication of this prophecy with the remark that it is 'not without prophetic reference, in my opinion, to events and persons contemporary to ourselves'. In other words, he understood a prophecy about Nicholas I to apply equally to Nicholas II.

A letter from Motovilov to Nicholas I himself, dating to 1854 and published in 1995, seems to me authentic according to stylistic criteria and offers a fuller version of the same prophecy. A revolution will erupt, leading to the murder of the tsar's loyal subjects among the upper classes and the clergy, but the resultant civil war will lead to the victory of Nicholas I and the Church over their opponents, who will not be sent to Siberia but put to death, in a great bloodbath that will cleanse the Russian land.[37]

Still more sensational is the so-called 'Great Secret of Diveyevo', that Nilus claimed to have found in the Motovilov archive in 1902.[38] It runs as follows (Serafim is replying to a question by Motovilov):

> 'It was decreed by the Lord God that I should live for far more than a hundred years. But since by that time the bishops will have become so wicked that in their iniquity they will surpass the Greek bishops at the time of Theodosius the Younger, with the result that they will no longer even believe in the most important doctrine of the Christian faith, it is pleasing to God to take me, the wretched Serafim, for the time being from this transient life and afterwards to raise me up; and my resurrection will be like the resurrection of the seven youths in the cave of Okhlon in the days of Theodosius the Younger.'[39]
>
> Having revealed to me this great and dread mystery, the great starets informed me [Motovilov] that after his resurrection he will move from Sarov to Diveyevo and there begin preaching worldwide repentance. At this preaching, but still more at the miracle of resurrection, a great multitude of people will gather from all the ends of the earth ... And when preaching repentance at Diveyevo, Father Serafim will uncover

---

[37] The letter was printed in *Russkii Vestnik* 37–9 (1995), 4.

[38] Its first publication was in the posthumous edition of a work by Nilus (d. 1929) – *Na beregu Bozh'ei reki*, 2 vols (San Francisco, CA, 1969), 2: 192–3.

[39] This is a reminiscence of the legend of the seven youths who entered a cave near Ephesus during the Decian persecution and emerged almost two hundred years later, in the reign of Theodosius II.

four relics there, and on uncovering them he will himself lie down among them. And then there will shortly come about the end of everything.[40]

Equally apocalyptic, but with a different scenario, is a longer text entitled 'The Antichrist and Russia', also deriving from the Motovilov archive, known to have been in manuscript circulation already before the Revolution, preserved by the well-known theologian Pavel Florensky (1882–1937) and finally published in 1990.[41] Russia was destined to experience a disastrous war and revolution, leading to massive loss of life, unparalleled in any earlier revolutions, and to the desecration of her churches and monasteries. But then 'God will have pity on Russia and lead her by the path of sufferings to great glory.' This, the simplest, part of the prophecy claims to be 'in the exact words of Fr Seraphim'. There follows a more specific prophecy of how Russia, in union with the other Slav countries, would capture Constantinople, Jerusalem and Vienna, overthrowing the Ottoman and Hapsburg empires. At this point Antichrist would be born in Russia, and obtain dominion over most of the world, with a political gospel of prosperity and equality. Resistance would come only from the Slavic empire centred on Russia, which, rewarded by God with victory, would become the greatest power upon earth.[42]

Competent scholars believe that most of the material emanating from Motovilov reflects the mounting atmosphere of panic and apocalyptic expectation that began to develop in the middle of the nineteenth century and continued throughout the reign of Nicholas II. Most of it may be ascribed to the fertile brain of Motovilov himself, and so will have existed well before 1903 (since Motovilov died in 1879).[43] A question one would like to be able to answer is how much of it was known to Nicholas II person-

---

40 S. Nilus, *Polnoe sobranie sochinenii* (Moscow, 2002), 4: 756–7.

41 For this text I am dependent on Hagemeister, 'Apokalipsis', 400–1, and A. Strizhev, 'Chevo ne izrekal prepobodnyi Serafim', <http://www.viskres.ru/taina/strizhev.htm>, accessed 19 August 2009 on a site that has now disappeared.

42 Strizhev, 'Chevo ne izrekal', points out that the Pan-Slavism of this prophecy, with its vision of all the Slavic nations united under Russia, points unmistakably to a date not earlier than the mid-nineteenth century.

43 The hostility towards Austria expressed in 'The Antichrist and Russia' in its final redaction seems, however, to reflect the worsening relations with Austria in the early years of the twentieth century.

ally and spurred his insistence on rapid canonization at exactly this stage in his reign. The evidence of contact between Nilus and court circles[44] suggests that all his material could have been known to the emperor. And there are indeed a number of pieces of evidence that point to his knowledge of the prophecies that related directly to himself. One prophecy that must surely have reached his ears was that the first part of his reign would be marked by wars and revolution but that the rest would be 'radiant' and his life a long one.[45] Motovilov's widow was reported to have presented to the emperor during the canonization celebrations at Sarov a letter addressed to him personally by St Serafim and entrusted to Motovilov. On reading the letter the emperor was said to have burst into tears;[46] this letter is most likely to have been one sent by Motovilov to Nicholas I. Likewise the prediction of tribulation followed by triumph is easiest to explain as an application to the last of the tsars of a prophecy originally addressed to one of his predecessors. Such rediscovery and novel application of old prophecies is, of course, a familiar phenomenon (with ample biblical precedent), and it was assisted in this case by the accident of homonymy – with two emperors named 'Nikolai Aleksandrovich'.

The pious and mystical streak in the character of Nicholas II inclined him to accept such prophecies. This inclination will have been strongly reinforced by his own experience on 30 July 1904, when Alexandra finally gave birth to a son, the tsarevich Alexei, the long desired male heir to the throne. This fulfilled the assurance confidently delivered by Dr Philippe that she would obtain this favour if she bathed in a holy and very cold spring near Sarov, associated with St Serafim, as she proceeded to do on the very day of the canonization, nine months before the happy birth.[47] It was a natural result that the trust the imperial couple reposed in the saint became boundless.

[44] Hagemeister, 'Apokalipsis', 408.

[45] Hagemeister, 'Problema', 166; Strizhev, 'Chevo ne izrekal'. Strizhev has found evidence that this prophecy, reported by Motovilov, was discovered in the government archives and sent to the Empress Alexandra in 1906, but an oral report via Nilus could have reached the imperial family earlier.

[46] Anon., *Diveevskie predaniia* (Moscow, 1996), as excerpted in *Serafimovskii … sbornik*, 125; Hagemeister, 'Apokalipsis', 407.

[47] Maylunas and Mironenko, *Lifelong Passion*, 230. I myself have bathed in this spring, and it is the coldest water I have ever encountered.

PIETY AND POLITICS

The canonization deepened the emperor's sense of his own providential destiny, as the protégé of heaven, guided and protected by the saints of the Russian Church. It would be ungenerous to begrudge him this, in a reign so short of consolations, but it had one particular and disastrous consequence.

The great question in the emperor's mind at the time of the canonization was whether to adopt an expansionist policy in the Far East. The fullest English study of the development of his policy at this period concludes that 'it is clear that the pilgrimage [to Sarov] was a profound experience for Nicholas II, and that it had repercussions which were political as well as religious. The tsar returned to St Petersburg determined, apparently, to move resolutely, and to take up the reins of government himself.'[48] On 30 July, a bare fortnight later, he announced the creation of a 'viceroyalty of the Far East', with authority over areas which were not formally within the Russian dominions. This was bound to be seen by Japan as an aggressive move and the prelude to annexation; it was taken on Nicholas's own initiative and without consulting any of his ministers. In such situations Nicholas was reluctant to consult, since he knew he would never win an argument. During the war against Japan that followed, St Serafim shared with St Michael and St Sergius of Radonezh the doubtful honour of being the special patrons of the Russian army and fleet in this, the most humiliating of all Russia's military fiascos.

It would not be fair to describe this as a crass harnessing of religion to the interests of imperialism: church leaders who enjoyed Nicholas's respect argued that a Japan under Russian domination could become a powerful centre for the conversion of the Far East to Orthodoxy.[49] Piotr Badmaev, a Mongol convert to Orthodoxy and a favourite of the emperor, had published a few years before the canonization of 1903 a starry-eyed exposition of Russia's role in the Far East, which contrasted the grasping spirit of western imperialism to the selfless mission of Russia, which was but a generous response to the desire of the peoples of the East for

---

[48] E. H. Judge, *Plehve: Repression and Reform in Imperial Russia, 1902–4* (Syracuse, NY, 1983), 166.

[49] Nichols, 'Friends of God', 223–5.

the beneficent overlordship of the 'white tsar', in line with the teaching of the Russian saints.[50]

It would be an exaggeration to say that trust in St Serafim led the emperor to make war on Japan, but there is good evidence that it made him reluctant to admit defeat. As disaster followed disaster, and humiliation was piled on humiliation, the emperor's continuing optimism began to look to his subjects like indifference to the sufferings his blunders had inflicted upon them. Only when every possibility of continuing the conflict had been exhausted did he reluctantly agree to a peace conference, held in 1905 at Portsmouth. People asked why he was so stubborn; he was at all times a man reluctant to admit to his mistakes, but the most plausible answer is the one given by Count Witte, Russia's chief negotiator at the Portsmouth Conference, namely, that the emperor put his faith in specific prophecies of victory that were attributed to St Serafim. As Witte commented with withering irony, 'Serafim of Sarov predicted, of course, that peace would be concluded in Tokyo [after a resounding victory]; this means that only Jews and intellectuals could think the opposite!'[51]

Although the imperial family's devotion to St Serafim was perfectly sincere, their promotion of the cult had, obviously, its political aspect. Nicholas saw in Russian Orthodoxy a support to tsarist absolutism and a channel through which he could appeal for popular loyalty, above the heads of an elite, both secular and ecclesiastical, that was increasingly disenchanted with his regime,[52] and above the heads of a de-Christianized urban intelligentsia and proletariat, susceptible to revolutionary ideas.[53] The flood of pilgrims drawn by Serafim's canonization can only have strengthened his delusion that the 'real' Russian nation was solidly behind him; as a well-placed observer commented: 'Precisely after Sarov there was heard on the lips of the sovereign more and more often in frequent conversations the word "tsar" and immediately after it "the people" (*narod*). The emperor was conscious of a wall of

[50] P. A. Badmaev, *Rossiia i Kitai* (St Petersburg, 1900), summarized in Nichols, 'Friends of God', 225–7.

[51] Witte, *Tsarstvovanie Nikolaia II*, 1: 243, 345.

[52] For the weighty voices within the Russian Church in this period deploring its domination by the state, see Firsov, *Tserkov v Imperii*, 10–97.

[53] This accounts for the mounting tempo of canonizations in the last, desperate years of the regime – four between 1911 and 1916.

division, but in his heart he denied it.'[54] But it may be doubted whether at this date religion was open to exploitation as a buttress for the tsarist regime. Even the piety of the 'people' was less solid than it seemed: the last decade of the tsarist regime was to witness a startling increase of religious indifference even among the peasantry.[55] And a more particular point can be made. The empire was huge, while Orthodox devotion remained incorrigibly localized, around particular shrines, wonder-working icons, and holy springs. The debate over Serafim's physical remains brings out the importance attached to immediate contact with the heavenly patron of one's choice; quite apart from the unfortunate state of his relics, his tomb and shrine remained out of reach for all but a tiny fraction of the nation. Throughout the land he had his scattered devotees, who cherished icons of the saint and made the pilgrimage to his remote shrine; but this was not sufficient to make the cult a national movement. Before the development of modern mass communications, before the ease of travel and the ease of disseminating images in photographs and films so familiar to us in our own age, the promotion of a saint's cult as a national unifier in a land as vast as Russia could not be achieved.[56]

Can it be achieved today, in Putin's Russia? A linking of the cult, a revived nationalism, and a re-evaluation of Nicholas II found expression in a declaration by Patriarch Alexy II of Moscow on the occasion of the centenary of the canonization in July 2003:

> Today, as a hundred years ago, the saint's memory gathers together bishops, priests, lay people, and state leaders. There is a renewal of the tradition of the joint service by Church and State for the good of the fatherland and its people. Together we are returning to our immemorial path, interrupted by the turmoil of the revolution – to that path taken by the emperor Nicholas Alexandrovich, the church hierarchs, and simple people at the beginning of the last century, when they first paid honour in Sarov to St Serafim.[57]

---

[54] A. A. Mosolov, *Pri dvore poslednego imperatora* (St Petersburg, 1992), 175.

[55] Firsov, *Tserkov v Imperii*, 133–44.

[56] This point is made by Freeze, 'Subversive Piety', 327–9. In a smaller country, with a more developed sense of nationhood and common citizenship, much more could be achieved, as is shown by the successful promotion of the cult of St Joan of Arc in France in this same period.

[57] *Rossiia pravoslavnaia* 2 (October 2003), 1.

But the role of his cult in Russia today would require another paper.

To conclude, the original canonization may be seen as an emblematic event in the twilight years of imperial Russia. My analysis of the misguided politics that accompanied it, and of the wave of apocalyptic expectation that became attached to the name of St Serafim, strangely prescient in some respects and utterly bizarre (or even sinister) in others, is not intended to cast a slur on the vast majority of the saint's devotees either at the time or nowadays, especially the hundreds of thousands who flocked to Sarov for the canonization and had no inkling of the lurid shadows in the background. At this same date the behaviour of the church authorities was exemplary in their refusal to allow the publication of the mass of dubious prophecies that linked the saint's name to hopes and fears about the destiny of Russia. It was in the small circle of the imperial family, and of its ideological agents and abettors, that the cult was burdened with a heavy political baggage. This did not exclude sincerity: what we find in Chichagov and Nilus, and in the imperial family itself, is not a manipulation of piety, worldly in its motivation, but a genuine religious fervour with disastrous consequences. Nicholas II himself, his intelligence unequal to his piety, was not the exploiter of religious enthusiasm, but its victim.

Heythrop College, London

SANCTITY AND MISSION IN THE LIFE OF CHARLES DE FOUCAULD

by ARIANA PATEY

One purpose of canonization, particularly for founders of religious orders, is to present a paradigm for emulation. The legacy of Charles de Foucauld (1858–1916), a Catholic hermit who lived and died in French Algeria as a witness for Christianity to Islam, has been in some dispute. There are nineteen different congregations and associations in the Foucauldian spiritual family, only one of which came to fruition during his lifetime. His beatification in 2005 has sparked a debate about the nature of his vocation, and consequently about which of his characteristics should be emulated. This raises the question of whether he was a monk or a missionary.[1] Careful consideration of his life is an essential prerequisite for answering these questions.

An 'either-or' mentality does not capture de Foucauld's life. He had a vocation to eremiticism, through which he was able to be both a missionary and a contemplative. Based on an understanding of conversion and Islam grounded in his personal experiences, he went to North Africa with the desire to 'sanctify the infidel populations'.[2] Yet this did not conflict with his vocation of silence. He had no desire to preach,[3] nor did he think that conversions were likely.[4] He felt that Muslims, difficult to evangelize and unlikely to convert, were being ignored by the Catholic faithful who were anxious for conversions.[5] He was dedicated to dilating the boundaries of the Church *silently* by making Christ present in North Africa through the eucharist and by imitation. His missionary work was based on the principle of silence; he did not believe in preaching but used himself as a vessel to bring Christ to the Muslims. De

---

[1] See Maurice Serpette, Jean-François Six and Pierre Sourisseau, *Le Testament de Charles de Foucauld* (Paris, 2005); Jean-François Six, 'Les Postérités Foucauld', *Revue des sciences religieuses* 82 (2008) 465–82.

[2] René Bazin, *Charles de Foucauld*, trans. P. Keelan, 2nd edn (London, 1943), 145.

[3] Charles de Foucauld, *Correspondances sahariennes*, ed. P. Thiriez and A. Chatelard (Paris, 1998), 605.

[4] Six, 'Postérités', 477.

[5] Bazin, *Charles de Foucauld*, 307.

Foucauld understood that 'the sanctification of the peoples of this region is in my hands. They will be saved if I become a saint.'[6]

BIOGRAPHY

Charles de Foucauld was born in Strasbourg in 1858. Orphaned at six years of age, he and his younger sister were raised by their grandfather. He went on to become an officer in the French army, and it was in this capacity that he was sent to Algeria in 1881. He had a difficult adolescence: having lost his faith in his teens, he was in continuous trouble, both at school and in the army. On a military expedition in southern Algeria he finally proved himself to his peers and, although he left the army, he went on to achieve distinction through his exploration of Morocco in 1883–4. Moved by his experiences, he began to question his lack of faith and at the age of twenty-eight he returned to the Catholic Church.

After a pilgrimage to the Holy Land, de Foucauld joined the Trappist Order, where he remained for seven years. He then lived as a hermit in Nazareth until his ordination. In 1901 he returned to North Africa, where he offered hospitality and friendship to the Muslims among whom he lived, first at Beni-Abbès and then at Tamanrasset in southern Algeria. He was killed by a bandit in 1916 at the age of fifty-eight.

DE FOUCAULD'S CONVERSION

At the centre of de Foucauld's religious life was the idea of conversion. He worked continually for the conversion of others and prayed ceaselessly for his own.[7] His conversion experience can be understood as having two stages. Before he could accept the teachings of the Catholic Church, or even the reality of Christ, he underwent a period of preparation. This preparation was then followed by exposure to the living Christ and the mystical revelation that this brought about. In the first stage, God 'had broken down the barriers, softened my soul, prepared the ground by burning off the thorns and bushes'.[8] This process of 'softening the soul' undoubt-

---

6　Charles de Foucauld, *Meditations of a Hermit*, trans. Charlotte Balfour (London, 1981), 159.

7　'Dearest Mother … Continue your Visitation; visit the Touaregs, Morocco, the Sahara, the infidels, and all souls, … unworthy me … convert me, I ask you on my knees': Bazin, *Charles de Foucauld*, 224.

8　Jean-François Six, *The Spiritual Autobiography of Charles de Foucauld*, trans. J.

edly began when he was a young man exploring Morocco. It was in Morocco that he came into intimate contact with Islam, a relationship that would influence his vocation for ever.

In preparation for the Moroccan expedition de Foucauld had learned Arabic and studied the Qur'an,[9] but he was an individual who learned through experience; it was the reality of Islam that moved him rather than the study of it. Muslims were the people who taught him to be confident in piety. As a man who had not prayed in almost ten years, he was thrust into a culture that put a high value on prayer and faithfulness. He described his response to Islam to a friend years later: 'Islam created in me a profound upheaval ... the sight of this faith, of these souls living in the continual presence of God, made me catch a glimpse of something greater and more true than earthly occupations.'[10] It was Islam that oriented de Foucauld on the path of spiritual awakening. It prepared him for Christ by turning his mind to God.

The second element of de Foucauld's conversion was his exposure to the living Christ. He experienced Christ through the silent work of his family, in particular his pious cousin Marie: 'A noble soul supported you – by its silence, its gentleness, its goodness and perfection. It let itself be seen; it was good and it spread its seductive perfume around itself, but it never intruded itself.'[11] At the same time he was attending mass and exploring the churches of Paris, opening himself up to the power of Christ's presence in the eucharist. Receiving the sacraments of confession and communion brought about the final transformation of his spiritual life, in October 1886. Through the sacraments he received Christ, which completed his conversion.[12]

EREMITICISM AND MISSION

One argument put forward against de Foucauld's having an eremitic vocation is the amount of time he spent in the world, particularly

---

Holland Smith (New York, 2003), 13.

   [9] Jean-Jacques Antier, *Charles de Foucauld*, trans. J. Shirek Smith (San Francisco, CA, 1999), 68.

   [10] Charles de Foucauld, *Charles de Foucauld: Lettres à Henry de Castries* (Paris, 1938), 86 (translation mine).

   [11] Six, *Autobiography*, 15.

   [12] Ibid. 16.

in his later life.[13] This, however, is a misunderstanding of the vocation of the hermit. One of the most influential books he read when he was in the process of converting to Christianity was *The Lives of the Desert Fathers*.[14] This collection of fourth-century writings described the monastic life of the early Church, when eremiticism had an important civic role. In the early Church it was a rare hermit who lived completely removed from human contact for his entire life. Indeed, while most of the famous hermits lived in seclusion for years, eventually many of them were called by God to live their solitary life in a more public way.[15] As humans who straddled the realms of the physical and the divine, they became a connection between God and the community. As sources of wisdom they spent time dealing with the everyday problems of the people.[16] Their greatest work for humanity, however, was done through their prayer and meditation. It was through their silent contemplation and works of self-transformation that the hermits were able to participate in God, to allow themselves to become 'human vessels' for 'the treasure of God'.[17] Close to God, they became living intercessors: 'the people are supported by their prayers as though by God himself'.[18] As vessels for God they sanctified the community. The hermits 'were like trees, purifying the atmosphere by their presence'.[19]

The Rule of St Benedict describes hermits as 'self-reliant' monks who, having trained in a monastery, are now ready to 'go from the battle line in the ranks … to the single combat of the desert'.[20] Unlike the monk, whose vows of stability to his community tie him to a specific life and function within the everyday running of the Church, the hermit, bound to no one but God and the greater community of humanity, is able to be sent to those areas of crisis

---

[13] Six, 'Postérités', 472.
[14] Maurice Bouvier, *Le Christ de Charles de Foucauld* (Paris, 2004), 37.
[15] Benedicta Ward, ed., *The Lives of the Desert Fathers*, trans. Norman Russell (London, 1980), 104.
[16] The cells in some of the Egyptian hermit colonies were built with rooms for them to receive audiences: Peter Brown, 'The Rise and Function of the Holy Man in Late Antiquity', *JRS* 61 (1971), 80–101, at 93.
[17] Ward, ed., *Lives*, 3.
[18] Ibid. 50.
[19] Ibid. 12.
[20] Joan Chittister, *The Rule of Benedict* (New York, 1992), 32–3.

in which his intercession is most needed – where he is called – making him an ideal missionary. The hermit acts as a missionary in two ways. First, hermits raise humanity up through their own ascetic union with God. Second, through this unification hermits become, not only a piece of humanity offered up to the Lord, but also an imperfect embodiment of the divine. Through their interaction with humanity, however limited, they pass on the message of Christ. De Foucauld wrote that to let Jesus live in man was to make simple human acts 'the acts of Jesus, of infinite and divine effectiveness'.[21]

SANCTIFICATION AS MISSION

De Foucauld's understanding of sanctity as mission was influenced by his devotion to the hidden life of Jesus at Nazareth; he was struck by the idea that God could exist silently among men and bring about their sanctification. He was also influenced by the story of the Visitation, when a pregnant Mary visited Elizabeth, the mother of John the Baptist. In a meditation written in 1898 de Foucauld understood the story as a personal instruction from Jesus:

> I made my Mother take me to the home where John was to be born ... Not only her did I urge along to sanctify others as soon as she possessed me, but I do so to all other souls to whom I give myself ... to all those who possess me but have not yet been given a mission to preach, I say to these, let them sanctify souls by carrying me in silence amongst them.[22]

When de Foucauld entered North Africa in 1901 he answered this call first as a priest. He wrote to a friend: 'Does my presence do any good here? If it does not, the presence of the Blessed Sacrament most certainly does. Jesus cannot be in any place without radiating.'[23] Aside from the eucharist, he was dedicated to living silently within his enclosed hermitage, always offering hospitality and help, but dedicating his life to a strict ascetic regime in an imitation of Jesus at Nazareth.[24] He believed that all men were

---

[21] De Foucauld, *Correspondances sahariennes*, 560 (translation mine).
[22] De Foucauld, *Meditations*, 98–9.
[23] Charles de Foucauld, *Letters from the Desert*, trans. Barbara Lucas (London, 1977), 178.
[24] Bazin, *Charles de Foucauld*, 93.

members of Christ,[25] and he used his work of personal sanctification to bring Algerian Muslims closer to God: 'I must work with
all my strength to sanctify myself. Mortification, mortification,
penance and death. It is when one is suffering most that one is
most sanctified oneself and most sanctifies others.'[26]

After several years in his hermitage a former army friend asked
him to join an expedition into southern Algeria. Recognizing
that he would be able to bring Christ into an area in which he
had been unknown, de Foucauld accepted the offer and eventually decided to build a hermitage in the community of Tamanrasset. He was originally unsure how to respond as a hermit to
the opportunity presented to him. He confessed to his spiritual
director that his desire was to remain enclosed at Tamanrasset and
let the White Fathers[27] take over his hermitage in the north. His
director told him that he needed to maintain both hermitages to
make himself present throughout the country.[28] As difficult as this
was, both physically and spiritually, de Foucauld recognized that
'[h]umans do not choose their vocation: a vocation is a call, the
words "choose your vocation" are nonsense'.[29]

The hermit is often placed in the position of being appealed to
by others. Peter Brown has argued that the hermit is, by his nature,
in a position of power. It is those outside of accepted society that
are expected to take on roles of responsibility.[30] The process of
becoming a hermit is essentially 'a long drawn out, solemn ritual
of dissociation – of becoming a total stranger'.[31] By cutting his
ties with society the hermit puts himself in a position to be an
impartial mediator for the community. De Foucauld fulfilled this
role in French Algeria.

It was at the request of, and with the support of, both the
French army and the White Fathers that he began his journey
into southern Algeria. Evangelization of Muslims had always been
a dangerous and difficult task. From Islam's earliest incursions into

[25] De Foucauld, *Meditations*, 162.
[26] Ibid. 164.
[27] On the White Fathers, see Aylward Shorter, *Cross and Flag in Africa* (Maryknoll, NY, 2006); Jean-Claude Ceillier, *Histoire des missionnaires d'Afrique (Pères Blancs) de 1868 à 1892* (Paris, 2008).
[28] Philip Hillyer, *Charles de Foucauld* (Collegeville, MN, 1990), 127.
[29] Charles de Foucauld, *Directoire* (Paris, 1933), 50 (translation mine).
[30] Brown, 'Rise and Function of the Holy Man', 91.
[31] Ibid.

Europe, the Catholic Church had been reluctant to send missionaries into Spain, aware of the Muslim attitude towards preaching and apostasy.[32] In the nineteenth century, the Ottomans refused to allow missionary activity directed towards Muslims to take place in their territories,[33] and even within French Algeria the White Fathers had to contend with both the anti-clerical French government and the fear of a backlash from the Muslim community.[34] Although de Foucauld had close ties to the White Fathers, he was not bound by their rules. Unlike the large missionary orders that built hospitals, schools and travelled in groups, his methods, and his friendship with the military, allowed him to go where the others could not,[35] like the hermit as described in the Rule of St Benedict.

While de Foucauld ministered to French soldiers when he was needed,[36] and he owed his ability to enter southern Algeria to his friendship with Commandant Laperrine,[37] he was a member neither of the colonial government nor of the army. In fact, General Nieger described how de Foucauld attempted to distance himself from the army in his later years:

> when Laperrine had decided to create a military post in the Ahaggar ... the Father systematically refused to establish himself in the immediate proximity. More than that, finding the contacts were becoming too frequent, he tried to avoid them. He constructed a new hermitage ... far from every route of communication ... He only sought contacts with us again when they were useful to the cause.[38]

While de Foucauld approved of France's colonial ambitions, he was more than willing to voice his disagreement with colonial policies.[39] Affiliated with, but yet not a part of, either the colonial

---

[32] Benjamin Kedar, *Crusade and Mission* (Princeton, NJ, 1984).

[33] Thomas Stransky, 'Origins of Western Christian Mission in Jerusalem and the Holy Land', in Y. Ben-Arieh and M. Davis, eds, *Jerusalem in the Mind of the Western World 1800–1948* (London, 1997), 137–54.

[34] Shorter, *Cross and Flag*, 2.

[35] Six, 'Postérité', 475.

[36] For information on his pastoral role during the battles of Taghit and El-Mungar, see Bazin, *Charles de Foucauld*, 202–10.

[37] Fergus Fleming, *The Sword and the Cross* (London, 2003), esp. 172–3.

[38] Quoted in Hillyer, *Charles de Foucauld*, 136.

[39] Hugues Didier, 'Charles de Foucauld et l'Algérie', *Courrier de la Fraternité seculière*

government or the missionaries, he was the obvious choice to take on the important role of ambassador for Catholicism and France. De Foucauld's policy for the Tamanrasset years was one of evangelization through public action. His work remained an act of sanctification, 'in Him, through Him, like Him, for Him',[40] but instead of sanctifying Muslims through his private relationship with God he used his person to bring Christ to the local population. He decided that he would live amongst them without enclosure and work at becoming their friend. One of the reasons for this shift, which Jean-François Six calls 'l'explosion missionaire de 1908',[41] was that in the years previous he had been deprived of the Blessed Sacrament as a instrument of sanctification. He had been without a permanent server since 1906 and left unable to say mass or to reserve the host in the tabernacle. For years he had seen himself as someone who 'procures [the presence] of the Blessed Sacrament'.[42] With the loss of the eucharist he was forced to re-evaluate his role in the process of evangelization. This new way of thinking coincided with a period of illness. Seriously ill in 1908, it was the local Touareg who nursed him. His friend Laperrine reported that 'he is more popular than ever among them'.[43] Ian Latham has argued that it was this friendship of reciprocity based on a mutual need for each other that allowed de Foucauld to shift from being viewed as an outsider to becoming a member of the community.[44] It was through the intimacy of convalescence that he first began to discuss religion with the Touaregs.[45]

The transition from a more cloistered, stable life to one of intentional interaction with the people of Tamanrasset was not without its complications. De Foucauld would struggle continually with the conflict between his internal vocation and the calling that circumstances had created for him. In 1907 he wrote to the apostolic prefect in the Sahara: 'I am a monk, not a missionary, made for silence not for speech … [although] I make and receive visits,

---

Charles de Foucauld 131 (2007–8), 35–47.
[40] Hillyer, *Charles de Foucauld*, 163.
[41] Six, *Testament*, 224.
[42] Bazin, *Charles de Foucauld*, 262.
[43] Ian Latham, 'Charles de Foucauld (1858–1916): Silent Witness for Jesus in the Face of Islam', in A. O'Mahony and P. Bowe, eds, *Catholics in Interreligious Dialogue: Studies in Monasticism, Theology and Spirituality* (Leominster, 2006), 47–70, at 57.
[44] Ibid. 56–8.
[45] Bazin, *Charles de Foucauld*, 267.

it is not my vocation'.[46] Visiting his hermitage in Askrem in 1911, he declared that '[t]he soul is not made for noise, but for meditation, and life ought to be a preparation for heaven – not only by meritorious works, but by peace and recollection in God'.[47] Even in his final year of life de Foucauld lamented the need to break his solitude, writing to his cousin Marie: 'Deafness is a handicap that hermits long for'.[48]

Even as he struggled with the public aspect of his work, de Foucauld continued to cultivate personal sanctification as a method of missionary work. When Antony, the archetypal hermit, was called down from his mountain to teach and help the people he allowed this intrusion only after he discovered his 'inner mountain'.[49] One of the ways that Foucauld was able to accept the loss of his enclosure was to create one that was 'imaginary and without walls but real'.[50] By 1908 he had decided to 'recapture in the periods in which nothing prevents me from leading a perfectly regular life the time stolen, in other periods, from purely spiritual things'.[51] The three months that he spent travelling between hermitages became the perfect opportunity both for his spiritual regrouping and for his work of sanctification.

Walking can be understood as an act of possession. In southern Algeria, the ability to travel unchallenged was a sign of political dominance.[52] In Genesis God told Abraham to 'Arise, walk through the land in the length of it and in the breadth of it; for I will give it to you.'[53] As de Foucauld travelled the country he sanctified the land for Christianity. He used the opportunity to 'think of the flight into Egypt and the annual journeys of the holy family to Jerusalem'.[54] His migrations ceased to be merely travels but acts of union with God by imitation. Through imitation he made Christ a presence in Algeria because '[b]y union with Christ in life and

---

46 De Foucauld, *Correspondances sahariennes*, 528 (translation mine).

47 Bazin, *Charles de Foucauld*, 297.

48 Hillyer, *Charles de Foucauld*, 146.

49 Athanasius, *The Life of Antony and the Letter to Marcellinus*, trans. and intro. Robert C. Gregg, CWS (London, 1980), 68.

50 Hillyer, *Charles de Foucauld*, 131.

51 Ibid. 124.

52 See Fleming, *The Sword and the Cross*, 32–6, for French expeditions to the region ending in violence.

53 Gen. 13: 17.

54 Hillyer, *Charles de Foucauld*, 131.

act … we do not merely perfect ourselves, we reproduce Him'.[55] As he continued to erect hermitages throughout the country and to travel between them, his understanding of his monastic enclosure, that is to say his sacred space, began to encompass the entire Sahara.[56] The sanctification of Algeria was not only about conversion, but about the sanctification of space and the dilation of the boundaries of the Church through Christ's presence.

Although de Foucauld wrote that he was 'doing everything possible' for the conversion of souls,[57] this statement says more about his understanding of missionary work than about any seismic shift in his ideology. His missionary work was still based on his principle of silence. He never preached to the people; instead his discussions on religion were based on meditating on commonalities between the two faiths and on moral issues. He discussed 'natural religion' with them, offered them advice from the 'holy books' and invented a rosary that could be said by Muslims and Christians.[58] In this way he was fostering their existing piety, a quality he had always admired in Muslims. He saw his work that of 'clearing out' and preparation,[59] similar to the way his own thorns had been removed to prepare him for the living Christ. At the same time he continued to make Christ present for the Touareg through the eucharist and his own example, using the tools of the hermit: 'meditation, discernment, self-control, and godly obedience'.[60]

CONCLUSION

Hugues Didier has described Charles de Foucauld as 'the initiator of a whole missionary and spiritual movement'.[61] De Foucauld greatly influenced people like the French scholar of Islam, Louis Massignon, who considered himself to be de Foucauld's spiritual protégé,[62] and Jules Monchanin, the founder of a Catholic ashram

---

[55] Alban Goodier, *An Introduction to the Study of Ascetical and Mystical Theology* (London, 1938), 94.

[56] Ibid. 133.

[57] Ibid. 160.

[58] Bazin, *Charles de Foucauld*, 243, 282.

[59] Six, 'Postérités', 475.

[60] Cyril of Scythopolis, *Lives of the Monks of Palestine*, intro. J. Binns, trans. R. M. Price, Cistercian Studies 114 (Kalamazoo, MI, 1991), 13.

[61] Antier, *Charles de Foucauld*, 326.

[62] Hughes Didier, 'Louis Massignon and Charles de Foucauld', *Aram* 20 (2008), 337–53.

who desired to use his body to sanctify India.[63] Aside from these famous Catholic figures, de Foucauld's life has also inspired the foundation of congregations throughout the world, comprised of laymen, religious and priests, and including a nondenominational association.

While he had a desire for Muslims to convert to Christianity, his real concern was with presenting what the twentieth-century theologian Karl Rahner has called the 'physical tangibility of salvation'[64] to every nation. Through his eremitic mission of sanctification, de Foucauld strove to make Christ a tangible reality for the Muslims of Algeria and at the same time worked to create friendship between the people of two different faiths. It is, perhaps, this vocation to eremitic sanctification that has allowed de Foucauld's work to encompass so many different modes of religious life. At the centre of his formula for spiritual living is a personal relationship with God, a relationship that is open to all people and can be shared with all people in friendship. He believed that it is this individual sanctification that illuminates the world for the glory of God and the benefit of humanity.

Heythrop College, London

[63] Jules Monchanin, *In Quest of the Absolute: The Life and Work of Jules Monchanin*, ed. and trans. J. G. Weber, Cistercian Studies 51 (Kalamazoo, MI, 1977), 2.

[64] Karl Rahner, Foreword to Eugene Hillman, *The Church as Mission* (London, 1966), 1–13, at 13.

CÉLINE MARTIN'S IMAGES OF THÉRÈSE OF LISIEUX AND THE CREATION OF A MODERN SAINT*

by SOPHIA L. DEBOICK

At the time of the death of Sœur Thérèse de l'Enfant-Jésus (Marie-Françoise-Thérèse Martin, 2 January 1873 – 30 September 1897) the Carmelite convent of Lisieux was a hidden and poor community, destined to remain as obscure and forgotten as Thérèse herself had been during her nine-year career as a nun. Just twenty-eight years later, Thérèse had been made a saint and the Carmel of Lisieux had become the focus of the attention of the whole Catholic world. There was little remarkable about Thérèse's short and sheltered life, but she has enjoyed an incredible 'posthumous life' through her second career as a saint. The autobiographical writings she produced during her time at the Carmel were published in 1898 as *L'Histoire d'une âme* (*The Story of a Soul*) and were an instant success, later becoming a classic of Catholic spirituality. Her canonization in 1925 was the quickest since 1588 at the time,[1] and Pope Pius XI referred to her rapid rise to fame as a 'storm of glory',[2] later calling her 'the star of his pontificate'.[3] Named Patroness of the Missions in 1927, she became Patroness of France, alongside Joan of Arc, immediately after the liberation of France in 1944, and in 1997 Pope John Paul II named her a Doctor of the Church. Only the third woman to earn this title, she became ranked alongside the legendary names of Teresa of Àvila and Catherine of Siena. Since 1994 her relics have been

---

* I am grateful to the Carmel de Lisieux for generously granting access to their archives and for permission to reproduce figures 1, 2 and 4. Thanks are also due to the Office Central de Lisieux for allowing figure 3 to appear here.

[1] See Kenneth L. Woodward, *Making Saints. Inside the Vatican: Who become Saints, Who do not, and Why* (London, 1991), 107. Josemaría Escrivá, founder of Opus Dei, beat her record by over four months when he was canonized in 2002.

[2] Pope Pius XI, address to French pilgrims, 18 May 1925 [the day after the canonization of St Thérèse], in *Les Annales de Sainte Thérèse de Lisieux*, 15 June 1925, 20.

[3] Pope John Paul II, 'Apostolic Letter of His Holiness Pope John Paul II, *Divini Amoris Scientia*' (19 October 1997), <http://www.vatican.va/holy_father/john_paul_ii/apost_letters/documents/hf_jp-ii_apl_19101997_divini-amoris_en.html>, accessed 15 March 2010.

on an almost constant world tour and when they visited Ireland in 2001 the organizers estimated that seventy-five per cent of the total population turned out to venerate them – some 2.9 million people.[4] In September and October 2009 they visited England and Wales, a unique event in the religious history of Britain, which stimulated considerable interest in Thérèse as a historical personality.[5] But while the biographies of Thérèse proliferate, the importance of her posthumous existence for European religious culture continues to be overlooked.[6] This paper looks at the construction of the cult of Thérèse of Lisieux after her death, paying particular attention to the role which the Carmel of Lisieux and its key personalities played in this process, and highlighting the central role played by images and commercial products in the development of the cult.

THE CREATION OF A MODERN SAINT

Thérèse has become famous not as a historical character, but as a carefully constructed religious commodity. From 1897 the Carmel of Lisieux became the hub of the development and promotion of her cult, and an examination of this process in its early years is revealing of the relationship between the commercial and the religious in early twentieth-century Europe, as well as ideas of religious debasement, authentic visual representation and popular notions of the fake in this period.[7] Recent studies of the 'selling' of religion in modern Europe have focused on the late nineteenth century and commercial activity at centres of pilgrimage, most

---

4   Audrey Healy and Eugene McCaffrey, *St Thérèse in Ireland: Official Diary of the Irish Visit, April–July 2001* (Dublin, 2001), 12.

5   On the British visit, see a Catholic Truth Society pamphlet: Keith Barltrop, *Thérèse of Lisieux: On the Visit of her Relics to Great Britain* (London, 2009).

6   The only substantial assessment of Thérèse's cult is Bernard Gouley, Rémi Mauger and Emmanuelle Chevalier, *Thérèse de Lisieux ou la grande saga d'une petite sœur (1897–1997)* (Paris, 1997). See also Thérèse Taylor, 'Images of Sanctity: Photography of Saint Bernadette of Lourdes and Saint Thérèse of Lisieux', *Nineteenth-Century Contexts* 27 (2005), 269–92. Jean-François Six has provided the best historical biographies of Thérèse: *La Véritable Enfance de Thérèse de Lisieux: Névrose et sainteté* (Paris, 1972); idem, *Thérèse de Lisieux au Carmel* (Paris, 1973). Thomas R. Nevin, *Thérèse of Lisieux: God's Gentle Warrior* (New York, 2006) is the most recent major biography in English. The annual Carmelite bibliography published in *Carmelus* (1953–) includes works on Thérèse.

7   My current research focuses on the period from the death of Thérèse in 1897 to that of her sister Céline Martin in 1959, on the eve of the social changes seen in the 1960s and the reforms of Vatican II.

notably the Lourdes shrine,[8] but the emergence of Thérèse's cult on the eve of the twentieth century, at a time when technologies of mass communication were developing rapidly, requires a new assessment of the commercialization of the sacred. The cult of St Thérèse also needs to be situated amongst recent work, most notably that of Robert Orsi and Raymond Jonas, on late nineteenth and early twentieth-century popular Catholicism and the emergence of new devotions to which religious material culture and commercial products were central.[9]

The creation of St Thérèse of Lisieux as a product and the marketing of her to the faithful through a plethora of publications and commercial items were only made possible by the presence in the Carmel of three of her siblings: Marie, Pauline and Céline.[10] Sisters in both blood and religion, they believed Thérèse had displayed exceptional virtue and, building on the autobiography's incorporation of many of the standard tropes for the female saint's life, they used their physical and political presence at the heart of the convent to remould her as a saint. Crucial to the reshaping of Thérèse's image and her subsequent promotion was a highly developed visual iconography, authored and disseminated by Céline (Marie-Céline Martin, Sœur Geneviève de la Sainte Face, 28 April 1869 – 25 February 1959), the sister closest in age to Thérèse and the last surviving member of the Martin family when she died.[11] Céline was an artist of meagre training and limited talent, but in her role as director of the Carmel's iconographical project she sought absolute control over Thérèse's popular representation,

---

[8] See, e.g., Suzanne K. Kaufman, *Consuming Visions: Mass Culture and the Lourdes Shrine* (Ithaca, NY, 2005).

[9] See, e,g., Robert A. Orsi, *Thank You, St. Jude: Women's Devotion to the Patron Saint of Hopeless Causes* (New Haven, CT, 1996); Raymond Jonas, *France and the Cult of the Sacred Heart: An Epic Tale for Modern Times* (Berkeley, CA, 2000); idem, *The Tragic Tale of Claire Ferchaud and the Great War* (Berkeley, CA, 2005). See also Colleen McDannell, *Material Christianity: Religion and Popular Culture in America* (New Haven, CT, 1995).

[10] Pauline (Mère Agnès de Jésus, 1861–1951) entered the Carmel in 1882. Marie (Sœur Marie du Sacré Cœur, 1860–1940) entered in 1886. The middle child, Léonie (Sœur Françoise-Thérèse, 1863–1941), later became a Visitandine at Caen. The sisters' cousin, Marie Guérin (Sœur Marie de l'Eucharistie, 1870–1905), was also a member of the community of the Carmel of Lisieux from 1895.

[11] On Céline, see her unpublished memoirs: Lisieux, Archives du Carmel de Lisieux [hereafter ACL], 'Histoire d'une «Petite âme» qui a traversée une fournaise' (1909); Stéphane-Joseph Piat, *Céline: Sœur Geneviève de la Sainte Face. Sœur et témoin de Sainte Thérèse de l'Enfant-Jésus* (Lisieux, 1963), offers a hagiographical account of her life.

faking photographs of her, suing the producers of unauthorized images of the saint and sidestepping the authority of the men of the Church. The accepted view is that it was Pauline, the second Martin daughter, who 'orchestrated the theresian success'.[12] As 'second mother' to the four-year-old Thérèse after their mother's death in 1877 and Prioress of the Carmel for several terms (then known as Mère Agnès), Pauline has been privileged in accounts of both Thérèse's life and posthumous history, but this has resulted in an overemphasis on her role in the building of the cult.[13] Indeed, Céline played an essential part in the development of the cult of St Thérèse, a project to which she dedicated her life.

THE IMAGES AND COMMERCIAL EXPANSION

In six decades of work on her sister's image Céline produced twenty-six portraits of Thérèse, as well as working in collaboration with other artists to produce scores of other images. Strongly influenced by the Saint-Sulpician devotional art of the time,[14] the most famous of her images were the 'buste ovale', produced in 1899 to provide a frontispiece for the second edition of Thérèse's autobiography (figure 1), and the 'Thérèse aux roses' of 1912, which established the crucifix and roses as St Thérèse's attributes. Céline's images were disseminated through the succession of popular publications released by the Carmel of Lisieux, a principal method of promotion of the cult. Heavily abridged editions of the autobiography, cheaper and textually more accessible than the full-length version, were key marketing tools and the first appeared as early as 1902, only five years after Thérèse's death.[15] *Appel aux petites âmes*, appearing in 1904, was the first truly mass market

---

[12]   Claude Langlois, 'Photographier des saintes: de Bernadette Soubirous à Thérèse de Lisieux', in Michèle Ménard and Annie Duprat, eds, *Histoire, images, imaginaires: Actes du colloque international des 21–22–23 mars 1996, l'Université du Maine (Le Mans)* (Maine, 1998), 261–72, at 267–8.

[13]   On Pauline, see Jean Vinatier, *Mère Agnès de Jésus: Pauline Martin, sœur aînée et «Petite Mère» de Saint Thérèse de l'Enfant-Jésus* (Paris, 1993).

[14]   'Saint-Sulpician' is a term for a genre of Catholic religious art of the late nineteenth and early twentieth centuries which was characterized by a sentimental and 'feminized' representation of Jesus and the saints; see Claude Savart, 'À la recherche de l'"art" dit de Saint-Sulpice', *Revue d'histoire de la spiritualité* 52 (1976), 265–82. Savart asserts that the cult of Thérèse in its 1930s heyday marked the end of the Saint-Sulpician period.

[15]   Anon., *Une Rose effeuillée* (Bar-le-Duc, 1902).

Fig. 1. The 'buste ovale', 1899. © Carmel de Lisieux.

publication produced by the Carmel.[16] Telling Thérèse's story in a concise thirty-three pages and priced at only twenty-five centimes, its small format and affordability meant that it sold over 780,000 copies even before the canonization.[17]

Céline's images were to have their most sustained outing in *La Vie en images*, a visual hagiography, which transcribed the events from the autobiography into sixty-eight tableaux with accompanying eight-line verses.[18] First published in 1923, it cost only four francs to the autobiography's fourteen,[19] and was extremely commercially successful. Like so many of the Carmel's publications, it continued to be published in substantially its original form well into the 1950s. The sale of Céline's images as holy cards

[16] Anon., *Appel aux petites âmes* (Bar-le-Duc, 1904).
[17] Figures from ACL.
[18] Anon., *La Vie en images de la Bienheureuse Thérèse de l'Enfant Jésus* (Bar-le-Duc, 1923).
[19] ACL, May 1923 flyer, archive box S24B, Office Central Catalogues, envelope 2a.

made them commodities in their own right, and the range of these rapidly increased: in 1908 only three different pictures of Thérèse were listed for sale in the commercial catalogues produced by the Carmel's publisher, but by 1911 ten versions of the 'buste ovale' were available, of varying size and quality to suit a range of budgets, as well as nine of Céline's other pictures at three francs apiece.[20] By the eve of the First World War the items available featuring Céline's images included calendars, writing paper and exercise books.[21] After the canonization, the commerciality of the cult flourished and thirty-eight different pictures of Thérèse were advertised in the May 1927 catalogue, along with medals, statues, paper weights, napkin rings, holy water stoups and jewellery, all featuring images of the saint.[22] Céline's images were highly profitable products, the principal commodity of the cult and key to its spread, but despite the huge success of her artwork, Céline was less than content.

CRITICISM AND RESENTMENT

When looking back on her career in her eighties, Céline showed considerable bitterness about her work as an artist:

> I had no permanent studio for painting and drawing. I worked in my cell, in the Chapter house, in the library, [anywhere] here or there that allowed me a momentary refuge. Many of my drawings and paintings were done in my free time: the midday silences in summer, Sundays and free days, but in the Community most of the sisters considered this type of work a waste of time ...[23]

This criticism from other nuns of the Carmel was supplemented by more public disapproval on the part of various commentators who objected to Céline's use of an outdated and, in their opinion, tasteless artistic style in her work. A number of books appeared during the 1920s and 1930s asserting that the sisters' sentimentalization of Thérèse was debasing the cult.[24] The bohemian novelist

[20] ACL, 1908 and August 1911 flyers, Catalogues, 1.
[21] ACL, August 1913 flyer, Catalogues, 1.
[22] ACL, May 1927 catalogue, Catalogues, 2b.
[23] ACL, 'Recueil des travaux artistiques de Sr Geneviève', 39. All translations from the French are my own.
[24] See Abbé Paulin Giloteaux, *La Bienheureuse Thérèse de l'Enfant-Jésus: Physionomie*

Fig. 2. The 'Thérèse-angel' image from the back cover of
Appel aux petites âmes. © Carmel de Lisieux.

and poet Lucie Delarue-Mardrus stated, for example that 'The
loving sisters of the little Thérèse… idealized her face [in the]
smiling images produced by the Office Central de Lisieux' (the
business arm of the Carmel)[25] and stated that 'By an unhappy
miracle recalling one in Holy Writ, it was not into a statue of salt
but into one of sugar that they changed her.'[26] Senior churchmen
also objected to Céline's style and the Vice-Postulator of the cause
for Thérèse's beatification, Mgr de Teil, wrote to the Carmel in
1909 to complain about the 'baby … with angel's wings and bare
legs and arms' featured on the back cover of *Appel aux petites âmes*

---

surnaturelle (Paris, 1923); Maurice Privat, *Sainte Thérèse de Lisieux* (Paris, 1932); Henri
Ghéon, *Sainte Thérèse de Lisieux* (Paris, 1934); Pierre Mabille, *Thérèse de Lisieux* (Paris,
1937).
[25] Lucie Delarue-Mardrus, *La Petite Thérèse de Lisieux* (Paris, 1937), 59.
[26] Lucie Delarue-Mardrus, *Sainte Thérèse of Lisieux*, trans. Helen Younger Chase
(London, 1929), 31.

(figure 2).[27] He added of this angel, clearly representing Thérèse, that: 'Our judges in Rome ... will say that you have placed the Servant of God in a nimbus of light in Heaven, among the stars ... you are pre-empting the process of the Church.'[28]

This image had a complex history, typical of Céline's reuse and refashioning of images. In 1898 she completed a large oil painting representing the Holy Family in which, as she later explained, she wanted 'to represent Thérèse who, in the guise of an infant, was *calling* the "little souls" to surround the sleeping child Jesus. But I did not succeed in giving her the resemblance I desired'.[29] To rectify this lack of resemblance in the angel figure she included in the foreground of the painting, she came up with an effective, although primitive, solution – she cut out Thérèse's face from a photograph of her aged eight and pasted it on to the angel's face, and this bizarre composite image appeared on prayer cards and in popular publications.[30] Later, the figure was cut out and reworked for use on the back cover of *Appel aux petites âmes*. Mère Agnès's response to de Teil was uncooperative, pointing out that 'this little angel has been going for a long time, indeed thousands of copies have been sold!!!',[31] and after he was forced to write to her about the matter again some eight months later,[32] she stated 'Can we leave this little angel? It doesn't represent Sœur Thérèse de l'Enfant-Jésus at all. *We have never had this thought*, it is a simple little angel who expresses one of her sayings'.[33] This small episode demonstrates how the Carmel responded even to authoritative criticism and their determination to represent Thérèse according to Céline's vision.

THE FORTY-SEVEN PHOTOGRAPHS AND RETOUCHING

The sort of creative use of photography seen in the 'Thérèse-angel' case was not unique in Céline's career. The Carmel possessed forty-seven photographs of Thérèse and although most had been

[27] ACL, de Teil to Mère Agnès, 5 May 1909.
[28] Ibid.
[29] ACL, 'Recueil', 16.
[30] Photograph 2 in the sequence established in François de Sainte-Marie, *Visage de Thérèse de Lisieux*, 2 vols (Lisieux, 1961).
[31] ACL, Mère Agnès to de Teil, 5 May 1909.
[32] ACL, de Teil to Mère Agnès, 21 January 1910.
[33] ACL, Mère Agnès to de Teil, 21 January 1910.

Fig. 3. The original photograph in the 'Thérèse aux images'
series, taken in June 1897. © Office Central de Lisieux.

taken by Céline herself (she was a keen amateur photographer and
took her camera with her when she entered the Carmel in 1894)
she did not approve of the final results and heavily retouched the
photographs to achieve the desired 'look'. For example, one of
the set of three photographs known as 'Thérèse aux images' was
considerably sanitized before it was released to the public (see
figures 3 and 4).[34] While the Martin sisters stated that none of the
photographs were a good likeness of Thérèse and that Céline's
retouchings were necessary to show her as she had really appeared,
the release of the photographs in their original form was clearly
unthinkable – they diverged from Céline's original compositions
so dramatically that they would have undermined their credibility
if made public. The sisters had church support in this enterprise,
and in a letter to Céline of 1911 Canon Dubosq, the Promoter of

---

[34] De Sainte-Marie, *Visage*, photograph 43.

Fig. 4. The retouched 'Thérèse aux images' photograph, circulated by the Carmel from the early 1920s. © Carmel de Lisieux.

the Faith in the cause for Thérèse's beatification, wrote to her to encourage the retouching, stating 'it is not appropriate to multiply and *diversify* the type [of images]. They must hold with the sanctioned type, which remains that of the frontispiece of *l'Histoire d'une âme* [the 'buste ovale'].'[35]

Indeed, the retouching served an important commercial purpose, presenting one, recognizable face to the public. To provide more marketable images that also fitted this approved style, Céline 'faked' photographs using découpage techniques. For example, in a picture of Thérèse with her novices and superiors, the figures of Mère Agnès and the Prioress Mère Marie were removed and an image of Marie Guérin, the Martin sisters' cousin and a postulant

---

35 ACL, Dubosq to Céline, 25 January 1911. The Ecclesiastical Tribunal of the Process of Beatification had sanctioned the portrait as the 'authentic' representation of Thérèse: ACL, 'Recueil', 41.

of the Carmel at the time, was inserted.[36] The end result was a conceptually tidier image of Thérèse, in her role as novice mistress, with the newest members of the community.[37] Similarly a group photograph of 1894, showing all the Martin sisters and Mère Marie, was cannibalized to create a composite image of Thérèse in meditation in the convent garden.[38] Such découpage techniques allowed Thérèse to be represented in roles befitting a fledgling saint – in these two cases, those of teacher and mystic respectively.

The Carmel took a position of outright denial on the issue of the manipulation of the photographs, publishing a booklet in 1926 which reproduced a number of heavily edited images it explicitly asserted were untampered-with originals.[39] The editing of the photographs would later attract much criticism,[40] but Céline maintained that in the matter of the retouchings she could not understand 'why anyone who *never knew* Saint Thérèse would suspect the good faith *of her sisters*'.[41] This sense of ultimate authority being invested solely in the Martin sisters was also apparent in Céline's approach to rival images being produced beyond the walls of the Carmel.

COUNTERFEITS AND CONTROL

During the late twenties the Carmel launched a number of legal cases in Belgium, Hungary and Germany against the makers of unauthorized images of Thérèse, and this was a sign that the convent was determined to control the representation of Thérèse, even in the outside world. In a case brought against a Ghent-based manufacturer in 1927,[42] it was alleged that the company had made illegal copies of a statue known as model number five, a three-dimensional version of 'Thérèse aux roses', produced collabora-

[36] De Sainte-Marie, *Visage*, photograph 20.

[37] This example is discussed in Pierre Descouvemont and Helmuth Nils Loose, *Sainte Thérèse de Lisieux: La Vie en images* (Paris, 1995), 510–11.

[38] De Sainte-Marie, *Visage*, photograph 9. On this composite image, see Marion Lavabre, 'Sainte comme une image: Thérèse de Lisieux à travers ses représentations', *Terrain*, no. 24 (March 1995), 83–90, esp. 88–9.

[39] P. Th. Dubosq, *A propos des portraits de Sainte Thérèse de l'Enfant-Jésus* (Lisieux, 1926).

[40] See, e.g., Maxence Van der Meersch, *La Petite Sainte Thérèse* (Paris, 1947), pt 3, ch. 8; Etienne Robo, *Two Portraits of St Teresa of Lisieux* (London, 1957), ch. 2.

[41] ACL, statement of 29 April 1940.

[42] ACL, 'M. Raymond de Bercegol vs la Société Commerciale Ph. Vitalie et Fontana', S24D Office Central Contrefaçons, 3.

tively by Céline and the Trappist sculptor Père Marie-Bernard in 1922.[43] In the case documents we find a complex dialogue about authentic representation and authorial rights being played out, and in fact the case constituted an attempt by the Carmel to establish the crucifix and roses symbol as a trademark belonging exclusively to Céline. M. de Bercegol, director of the Office Central de Lisieux, made powerful claims about the authenticity of this symbol:

> Only an artist habitually practising meditation and who is particularly mystical could have had the idea of this allegory which recalls not the words of Saint Thérèse, but her love for Christ on the cross; and it is very probable that without Mademoiselle Céline Martin, Carmelite nun and the saint's own sister, no-one would have represented her thus.[44]

The assertion of Céline's unique authority, couched in terms of religious inspiration, was central to the Carmel's case. However, the judges were unwilling to establish a precedent giving sole ownership of the crucifix and roses device, Thérèse's essential identifying mark by this time, to the Carmel, and the case was lost. At the same time as this case, the Carmel was also seeking redress from a Hungarian company making statues without the authorization of their official agents in the country. The company was in fact a religious organization, but the Carmel viewed a violation of their rights as a matter for the law whether the offenders were fellow religious or not. Only the intervention of the Provincial of the Hungarian Carmelites, who suggested that the case would be blown up into a scandal by the anti-clerical press and 'Jewish journalists', prevented them from pursuing the case further.[45]

It was not only Céline's original works that the Carmel tried to safeguard; her authority in the matter of the photographs was also strongly asserted. In January 1929 the director of the Third Order Carmelites in Berlin was threatened with legal action for having reproduced and distributed an illicitly circulated photograph of Thérèse, his legitimation of the image by touching a relic of the

---

43 See Pierre Descouvemont, *Sculpteur de l'âme: Un trappiste au service de Thérèse* (Wailly, 2000), 76–9.

44 ACL, 'Réfutation du jugement du Gand', Contrefaçons, 2, farde 10, 1–2.

45 ACL, Fr Brocardus to Carmel, 3 March 1928, and Korda to the Provincial of the Hungarian Jesuits, 23 March 1928, Contrefaçons, 9.

saint to all the copies making the matter all the more serious.[46] Surprisingly, the recovery of lost revenue and the protection of the cult from inferior representations of Thérèse were never central parts of the Carmel's argument in these cases. Above all, these legal actions allowed the Carmel to assert their authority over Thérèse's representation and promotion. Even when they were lost or abortive they allowed Céline to be marked out in public as the authoritative theresian artist, suggesting that images made by others were always in some sense fakes, lacking the authenticity only she could impart. They were an important exercise in self-fashioning, even when legal redress was not achieved.

CONCLUSION

Céline made an extraordinary assertion during her interviews as a witness for the process of beatification. Displeased by the emphasis which other witnesses were putting on Thérèse's 'supernatural gifts', she said that these were rare in her life and stated that 'For my part, I should prefer that [Thérèse] not be beatified if I could not portray her as I believe right according to my conscience.'[47] Behind this seemingly simple assertion of integrity, there is a sense of Céline's desire to designate herself as the superior witness to Thérèse's life and, accordingly, to secure herself as rightful director of her posthumous representation. Her determined approach led to Père Marie-Bernard, the sculptor who worked with her so closely, referring to her as *Sœur Je Veux* (Sister I Want).[48] Céline's tenacity meant she was successful in securing the supremacy of her images, and a fully homogenous landscape of theresian iconography was created in the early part of the twentieth century, with her representations dominating the cult completely. They did so for almost sixty years and it was only with Céline's death and the attendant relaxation of the Carmel's attitude to Thérèse's representation, symbolized by the release of all the original photographs of the saint in 1961,[49] that popular representations of Thérèse diversi-

---

[46] ACL, Reimeringer to Carmel, 24 January 1929, Contrefaçons, 8.

[47] *Procès de béatification et canonisation de Sainte Thérèse de l'Enfant-Jésus et de la Sainte-Face*, 2 vols (Rome, 1973, 1976), 2: 799. This was repeated in Céline's published memoirs: Sœur Geneviève de la Sainte Face, *Conseils et souvenirs* (Lisieux, 1952), 35.

[48] Descouvemont, *Sculpteur de l'âme*, 37.

[49] In de Sainte-Marie, *Visage*.

fied and her 'celinian' representation was questioned.[50] But Céline had remained defiant until the end and in a final statement on her images she asserted:

> Just as refinement of manners or the perfume of a rose are indescribable, so the soul cannot be described, or rather, is sadly hidden behind the physical structure of the face and ... obscured under brutal mechanical processes of reproduction. It is this *'je ne sais quoi'* ... the true picture of the soul beneath the outward appearance ... that I have always and *only* wanted to capture and show to others.[51]

The story of Céline's struggle to achieve this sheds new light on the retailing of the religious within the Church in the early twentieth century and requires a new interrogation of culturally constructed notions of authentic religious practice and 'truthful' visual representation. In telling this story the cult of St Thérèse will finally be situated in the history of modern European religious culture.

University of Liverpool

---

[50] On the transformation of Thérèse's representation after 1959, see Alana Harris, 'Transformations in English Catholic Spirituality and Popular Religion, 1945–1980' (unpublished D.Phil. thesis, University of Oxford, 2008), ch. 4, and Thérèse Taylor, *Bernadette of Lourdes: Her Life, Death and Visions* (London, 2003), 317–18.

[51] De Sainte-Marie, *Visage*, 24.

ANGLICANISM AND SANCTITY: THE DIOCESE OF PERTH AND THE MAKING OF A 'LOCAL SAINT' IN 1984

by ROWAN STRONG

On 23 February 1984, the bishops of the Anglican Province of Western Australia signed and sealed a document promulgating the Venerable John Ramsden Wollaston a local saint and hero of the Anglican Communion in accordance with Resolutions 77–80 of the Lambeth Conference 1958.[1] These four resolutions had allowed national or provincial Anglican Churches to add to the Calendar of the Saints to permit 'supplementary commemorations for local use' according to the following principles where they were extra-scriptural persons. They had to be individuals 'whose historical character and devotion are beyond doubt'; 'revisions should be few and without controversy'; and such additions 'should normally result from a wide-spread desire expressed in the region concerned over a reasonable period of time'.[2]

John Wollaston was one of the first six clergy of the colony of Western Australia, arriving in 1841 and dying as the inaugural Archdeacon of the new Diocese of Perth in 1863. This essay proposes to examine the choice of Wollaston as a local saint for what it reveals about how this Anglican province understood its early history. In other words, using sanctity as an entry point, the paper addresses ways in which the colonial past was portrayed in the service of the present-day Church. It argues that the choice of Wollaston as a local saint involved the Anglican Church in Western Australia in an ameliorating reconstruction of the truth of its colonial past, by a choice of a clergyman who was less radically supportive of Aborigines than one of his other contemporaries, and less sympathetic to their culture than another. It also questions whether the

---

[1] Perth, Diocese of Perth Archives, 'The Promulgation of John Ramsden Wollaston', 23 February 1984.

[2] Lambeth Conference 1958, Resolutions 77–80, 'The Book of Common Prayer – The Commemoration of Saints and Heroes of the Christian Church in the Anglican Communion', The Lambeth Conference Official Website (2008), <http://www.lambethconference.org/resolutions/1958/1958-77.cfm>, accessed 18 June 2009.

Lambeth Conference conditions for proclaiming a local saint were indeed met by the province. The official sources for the promulgation of John Wollaston as a local Anglican saint in 1984 are surprisingly meagre. The file in the diocesan archives consists of just two documents. They are the promulgation document itself, signed by the diocesan and assistant bishops of the three dioceses comprising the province of Western Australia, and a sermon preached by Archbishop Peter Carnley of Perth at the service of promulgation on 23 February 1984.[3] Carnley was an important figure in the promulgation process as it appears to have been largely driven by him, as the metropolitan of the province. There is no mention of any motion regarding Wollaston's sanctification in the 1983 or 1984 diocesan synods. In fact, the first formal mention of the process occurs very late, in the minutes of the Diocesan Council of the Diocese of Perth on 13 September 1984, when the archbishop advised the date and venues for the commemoration.[4] Evidently, by this time the promulgation was an accomplished fact which bypassed the formal synodical process of the Diocese of Perth.

In the formal promulgation document Wollaston is recommended to the faithful of the province for the following:

> for his signal virtues and heroic labours as a faithful pastor of souls, his resolute commitment to the building of the first place of worship at Picton as a sign of his constant devotion to the building up of the flock of Christ, his leadership in all things of the Spirit, his unflagging endeavours on behalf of new settlers and his earnest concern for the welfare of the Aboriginal people of this land.[5]

In Carnley's sermon, Wollaston is singled out for being the Christian who planted and enculturated Christianity in Western Australia; or, in Carnley's phrase, 'an Australian saint who "earthed" the Christian religion in this wide brown land'.[6] Wollaston is

---

3 The sermon by Archbishop Carnley extant in the file is the published version: Peter Carnley, 'John Ramsden Wollaston: The Saint who "earthed" Christianity in the West', in idem, *The Yellow Wallpaper and other Sermons* (Sydney, 2001), 19–26.

4 Diocese of Perth Archives, Perth Diocesan Council Minutes, 13 September 1984, fol. 2, item 4.5, 'Annual Commemoration of John Ramsden Wollaston'.

5 'Promulgation of John Ramsden Wollaston'.

6 Carnley, 'John Ramsden Wollaston', 20.

proposed as 'exceptional', with a 'simple robust faith', and 'an unwavering commitment to the task'. Wollaston's treatment of Aboriginals is particularly attended to in the sermon. Carnley acknowledges the archdeacon's nineteenth-century paternalism, but argues that Wollaston was unusually humane and readily condemned killings by the settlers of Aboriginal individuals as murder.[7]

Archbishop Carnley's boast that Wollaston planted Christianity in Western Australia is open to objection, however, with Major Frederick Irwin, the commandant of the original detachment of soldiers sent with the first colonizing party, who arrived in June 1829, having a better claim. Irwin held the first service, built the first (albeit temporary) church out of rushes, and led services in it, all before the arrival of any clergyman in 1830.

But behind the pious phrases of the sermon and the promulgation document, the concrete characteristics of Wollaston's sanctity which were identified by this Anglican province emerge as being a faithful priest to the new white settlers, building a church, exercising leadership and demonstrating a serious concern for Aboriginal welfare. On the face of it these features of Wollaston's life appear to be no more than would be expected of any conscientious priest in a colonial situation; that is, pastoring people, building churches and caring for the indigenous population.

However, these are characteristics which were, of course, not always evident in colonial contexts, and which were certainly not prominent among the few clergy of Western Australia, or the Swan River colony as it was first named when officially settled in 1829. Until the arrival of the first Bishop of Perth in 1857, there were just six Anglican clergy in the colony, which in 1850 numbered just 4,622 white settlers in a colonial territory encompassing one-third of the Australian continental land mass. Of this settler population just over 3,000 gave their religion as being Church of England, and they and their few non-Anglican counterparts were spread thinly across the vast, sandy, wooded land. Most were congregated on the coastal plain in the town of Perth, and its port of Fremantle, some fourteen miles downstream at the mouth of the Swan River. Some 70 persons lived a hundred miles south at Bunbury, another 150 or so further south in Albany, three hundred miles from Perth; and fewer still in inland hamlets to the west of Perth such as Guildford

7   Ibid. 24–5.

and York.[8] There were a scattering of even smaller settlements and various isolated farms in an area far greater than that of Britain. With substantially the greatest numbers of adherents, the task facing the initial colonial Anglican clergy in Western Australia was a daunting one. However, many of them were demonstrably not up to the task. The priest at York was fortuitously there as a settler rather than a clergyman, having retired as a chaplain in the Royal Navy because of anxiety about preaching! By 1849 William Mears had been forced by increasing ineptitude to resign.[9] John Wittenoom, the inaugural Colonial Chaplain, receiving £250 on the colonial civil list, was hardly a ball of fire either. Despite being responsible for both Perth and Fremantle until the arrival of a clergyman for the port in 1841, the government resident at the port town complained in that year that no service of Holy Communion had ever been celebrated there, and that he conducted most of what services did take place.[10] William Mitchell, the clergyman appointed to the Swan Valley (upstream from Perth along the Swan River) within months of his arrival was still relying on laymen to take services for him.[11] The Revd R. C. Postlethwaite was inattentive to his pastoral responsibilities, perhaps because of his wife's death in 1849. The local man, Charles Harper, was more energetic but because he had been ordained in the colony he lacked confidence in himself as a priest.[12]

Western Australia was not a desirable colony and it is hardly surprising that the clergy who went there were not outstanding exemplars of their profession. It was remote – four months' journey from Sydney by ship – and it was impoverished compared with the other Australian colonies, which had far better agricultural land and also enjoyed gold discoveries in the 1850s. It took the advent of penal transportation in 1853, which the colony requested, to bring in the

---

8   *Western Australia Government Gazette*, 19 December 1848, 2, 5, 6.
9   Perth, State Records Office of Western Australia, ACC 49/26, fol. 86, Colonial Secretary to Mr Brown, Trustee of the York Church, 7 July 1849; fol. 90, Colonial Secretary to Revd Mears, 13 July 1849; fols 93–4, Colonial Secretary to Mears, 21 July 1849.
10   Oxford, Rhodes House Library, SPG records C/AUS/PER 1, George King to Ernest Hawkins (Secretary of the SPG), 28 October 1841; A. E. Williams, *West Anglican Way* (Perth, WA, 1989), 102.
11   J. M. R. Cameron, *The Millendon Memoirs: George Fletcher Moore's Western Australian Diaries and Letters 1830–1841* (Carlisle, WA, 2006), 459 (20 January 1839); 481 (10 February 1840).
12   Rowan Strong, 'The Reverend John Wollaston and Colonial Christianity in Western Australia 1840–1863', *JRH* 25 (2001), 261–85, at 271.

necessary labour and government capital to develop the economic infrastructure for growth until the gold rushes of the 1890s.

Wollaston was, in such modest circumstances, and among his largely unprepossessing colleagues, an outstandingly energetic priest who constantly maintained a concern for the development of his Church beyond his immediate colonial charge. He came to Western Australia in 1841 to be a settler at the age of fifty, because he believed it offered better economic opportunities for his sons than his living of West Wickham on the Cambridgeshire-Suffolk border. More particularly, he expected to be chaplain to the settlement organized by the West Australian Land Company at Australind, near Bunbury.[13] But he arrived with his family and possessions on the beach at Fremantle to discover that the company had failed, and he could not obtain a government stipend until he had a church and was taking services. Wollaston built his church at Picton, near the southern port of Bunbury, in 1842 with his sons, and for the next years was more colonial farming cadet than clergyman.[14] As the only priest in the south-west of the colony, Wollaston made pastoral visits to the families in that region well beyond Bunbury. Moved to Albany by the colonial governor in 1848, and appointed archdeacon in 1849 by Bishop Short of Adelaide (whose diocese encompassed Western Australia as well as South Australia), Wollaston made three long and arduous trips to visit all the clergy of the colony. These trips took months, mostly travelling on his own through the bush of the colony – no mean feat for a man in his late fifties.[15]

But while Wollaston was demonstrably active in the colonial development of the Church of England in this period, he was not completely exceptional either in his energy or his concern for the health of his colonial Church. The Revd George King was an Irishman, appointed as a missionary by the Society for the Propagation of the Gospel (SPG) to the charge of Fremantle from 1841 until he left for a parish in New South Wales in 1848. King not only built a stone parsonage and church in the town, and established a Sunday School, but he itinerated considerable distances south to

---

[13] G. C. Bolton, *John Ramsden Wollaston: The Making of a Pioneer Priest* (York, WA, 1985), 3–4, 8.

[14] Strong, 'John Wollaston', 254.

[15] *Wollaston's Albany Journals*, ed. A. Burton and P. U. Henn (Perth, WA, 1948), 230.

congregations he established among the settlers at Mandurah, the Canning River and Pinjarrah, which was some forty miles south of Fremantle.[16] While Wollaston eventually had greater ecclesiastical responsibilities as an archdeacon, King emulated his initiatives for the growth of the Anglican Church, both in his local charge and well beyond that.

The area other than ecclesiastical development identified by the promulgation document as marking Wollaston's sanctity was 'his earnest concern for the welfare of the Aboriginal people of this land'. This was certainly an aspect of Wollaston's work in the colony, which again differentiated him from most, but not all, of his clergy colleagues. Convinced, like most contemporary missionaries, that the nomadic way of life of the native peoples was detrimental to evangelism, Wollaston proposed to target the children as the most hopeful candidates for conversion.[17] Accordingly, in 1842, the year after his arrival in the colony, he proposed a native institution for children on Rottnest Island, eleven miles off the coast from Fremantle, which was then used as a prison for Aboriginal offenders. Wollaston's proposal, the first one mooted in the colony for institutional welfare towards Aborigines, was nothing short of a radical re-enculturation programme achieved by permanently isolating children from their parents' control. Wollaston did not envisage that this abandonment of their children to his control would cause the parents much grief; it 'w[oul]d be readily done, for there is no stronger tie among these poor savages than that between an animal and its offspring'.[18] The only autonomy parents would be allowed was in the initial decision to give them to the institution; after that Wollaston would permit no further contact between parents and children. 'The Infants I would have baptized forthwith, the Church finding sureties [*sic*], & not allowing them ever to return, after their adoption, to the heathen relatives.' While the Rottnest Island idea remained only a proposal, Wollaston did actually inaugurate a similar institution, principally for mixed-race

16 Rhodes House Library, USPG/CLR/201, fols 117–18, George King to Ernest Hawkins, 28 October 1841; fols 132–40, King to Hawkins, 28 February 1842; fols 141–4, King to Hawkins, 14 May 1842.

17 John Ramsden Wollaston, *The Wollaston Journals, 1: 1840–1842*, ed. Geoffrey Bolton and Heather Vose (Nedlands, WA, 1991), 134–5.

18 Ibid. 134.

children, when he became parish priest of Albany, with government financial support that continued until after his death in 1863.[19]
However, while Wollaston's concern for Aboriginal evangelization was a rarity among his fellow Anglican clergy, again it was not
unique. There were two of his contemporaries who also engaged
with Aboriginal mission. The first of these was George King, who
developed a school for Aboriginal children in Fremantle from 1843
to 1848, when he had fifteen children attending the school. Like
Wollaston, King sought the permission of the parents to enrol the
children. 'I had collected thirteen children from the Bush with the
consent of their parents, the utmost number I was able to provide
for by descending to the most minute economy.'[20] Unsurprisingly,
King's evangelism project was as much tied into the global Euro-
peanizing project for indigenous people as any mission of this
period. He explained to the secretary of the SPG that the children were receiving 'a civilizing and evangelising education' which
would fit them for a subordinate status within colonial society as
'servants & seamstresses for which they have been well educated'.[21]

But King, unlike Wollaston, did not keep the children permanently isolated from their kin, and also demonstrated he was
mindful that the Aborigines had cultural imperatives of their own,
even if he did not much like them. When one of the children
died unbaptized, King permitted her to be buried with traditional
rites, though he did not question his authority to permit this.
'Our original number was thirteen, but two have died; one in a
probationary state, unbaptised, whose remains I permitted to be
interred by the natives with their usual lamentation, inspecting the
proceedings myself, that it might be done decently.'[22] The other
pupil to die had been baptized, but King still involved her family
in the Anglican rite of burial.

> The other was a girl of great promise: she read well, had a
> quick understanding, and evinced a pleasing and amiable
> disposition. I had her carried to the grave-yard by native
> men, and followed by the children of the School. The natives

---

[19] Ibid. 68.
[20] Rhodes House Library, USPG/CLR/201, fols 224–9, George King to Ernest
Hawkins, 27 April 1843.
[21] Ibid., fols 393–5, George King to Revd G. H. Fagan, 15 September 1845.
[22] Ibid., fols 426–32, George King to Ernest Hawkins, 1 January 1846.

remained in reverential silence while the last solemn rite, the most sublime and awe-inspiring of the Church service was performed. This was the first instance wherein the embassage of Jesus, the voice of the Church was heralded abroad the rightful dignity of mankind in this dark and mysterious portion of God's wide domain.[23]

The other colonial Anglican clergyman who engaged with Aboriginal mission in Wollaston's lifetime was one specifically hired for the task by the fledgling West Australian Missionary Society, a small group of elite settlers which included leading colonial officials. Louis Giustiniani was of Italian descent, married to a German Protestant woman. He was ordained an Anglican priest, and arrived as the first Anglican missionary in the Swan River colony in July 1836. Giustiniani was influenced by the Moravian missionary practice of self-sufficient farming by the missionary and his indigenous converts. Accordingly, he set up his mission in the Swan Valley, a site suitably separated from the concentration of settlers, but where the local indigenous people still existed as it was the frontier of invasion-settlement at the time. However, by 1838 the short-fused priest had managed to alienate most of the colonists, including his sponsors, by his militant advocacy on behalf of the Aborigines.

Within a month of his arrival Giustiniani was going into print in one of the colonial newspapers, blaming his inability to instruct the Aborigines on the opposition of the Europeans, 'who stand in nearly as much need of instruction as the natives'.[24] Evidently a confrontational character, the missionary conducted a slanging match in the press with one of the settlers. Notwithstanding this early acrimony, the foundation stone of a new mission church was laid by the governor the following month, with Giustiniani employing some of the Aborigines in his vegetable plot and also holding services for settlers in the valley.[25] But letters critical of him continued to appear in the press, with the missionary answering them all redoubtably. However, in September 1836 one

[23] Ibid.
[24] Lesley J. Borowitzka, 'The Reverend Dr Louis Giustiniani and Anglican Conflict in the Swan River Colony, 1836–1838' (unpublished B.Theol. (Hons) thesis, Murdoch University, 2006), 24.
[25] Ibid. 26.

of the settlers shot dead an Aborigine attempting to steal flour from his barn; the indigenous people speared a settler in retribution in accordance with their customary law, and the governor sent in soldiers.[26] On 1 October 1836 Giustiniani wrote a letter in the local press deploring the killing of Aborigines, along with the custom of so-called 'mercy killing' of wounded ones. His militancy soon prompted the loss of support of the Colonial Chaplain, John Wittenoom, at the time the only other Anglican clergyman in the colony.[27] Public criticism from pseudonymous letter-writers in the press increased and intensified. By April 1837 Giustiniani had become alienated from settler society, partly because of his militant support for the Aborigines, and partly for his goading attacks on previous supporters in ill-considered defences of himself in print. By mid-1837 the missionary was not only writing letters of condemnation about settler treatment of Aborigines to the local press, but also to local government officials, and to the Colonial Secretary, Lord Glenelg, which he subsequently published. In one instance Giustiniani accused the Government Resident at York of firing into Aboriginal huts, and slated the local government policy of control and coercion by the police and military instead of allocating colonial resources to the Aborigines.[28] In October 1837 Giustiniani defended three Aboriginal men accused of stealing in the civil court, urging that they be treated as minors in law, because they were 'too degraded to be put on a level with civilised people'.[29] It came as no surprise to anyone that in November 1837 the missionary society had dismissed him, and the confrontational, acerbic man left the colony with his wife in February 1838.

The conclusion of the historian of the affair is that Giustiniani was certainly a failure, which he brought on himself by a lack of understanding, or acceptance, of the power of the local colonial elites. As a missionary Giustiniani was too different from the expectations of the settlers, the Colonial Chaplain and his initial supporters, who wanted a clergyman more conforming to their values and more accepting of their need to control the Aboriginal population in the competition for land. But she concludes that,

---

[26] Ibid. 27.
[27] Ibid. 33.
[28] Ibid. 44.
[29] Ibid. 50.

while all allowance should be made for the clash of contemporary cultures in that small, isolated colony, Giustiniani simply would not compromise his basic purpose of evangelization for accommodation with colonial culture.[30]

In the varied and contested colonial context, within the tiny group of Anglican clergy, it must be asked if John Wollaston does indeed stand out from his colonial contemporaries in such a way as to qualify him for local Anglican sainthood, as the documents of 1984 attest. The previous evidence has established that he was neither the outstanding example of evangelization to the Aboriginal peoples of the colony nor the only exemplary pastoral priest, though only he and George King were in a class of their own among the mediocre clergy of the period.

The remaining area of Wollaston's life that does remain unique to him among the characteristics singled out by the official promulgation document, and by Archbishop Carnley's sermon on that occasion, is his leadership within the Anglican Church of the colony. This is no mean virtue, and other individuals are commemorated in Anglican calendars, both from before and after the Reformation, who exemplified a similar quality. Those that come immediately to mind are William Laud, Archbishop of Canterbury; George Augustus Selwyn, Bishop of New Zealand; and St Swithun, Bishop of Winchester in the ninth century. No one would suggest that Laud appears in most modern Anglican calendars for his attractive holiness of life rather than his ecclesiastical leadership at another contested period of Anglican history.

The promulgation of John Wollaston as a local saint, however, does raise a couple of important considerations – one about the process of this local saint-making; and another about the reconstruction of its colonial history by the contemporary Anglican Church in Western Australia.

First, with regard to process. There is no evidence at all of any local devotion surrounding Wollaston prior to his official elevation in 1984. Yet this was a criterion the bureaucratic language of the Lambeth Conference resolutions called for – that such candidates for the calendar of saints would be the result of 'a widespread desire expressed in the region concerned over a reasonable period of time'. In contrast, the process in the Province of Western

30 Ibid. 108.

Australia seems to have been more or less the decision of the ecclesiastical clerical elite. Consequently, it is not surprising that the candidate for local sainthood in this instance should have been the colonial clergyman who did most to establish and order the institutional Church, the structure within which the Anglican ecclesiastical elite were authority figures. Given that there were at least two other candidates to choose from among the few Anglican clergy of the initial colonial period, it was the colonial figure most embedded within church structures, and who did most to promote them, who was chosen over two clergymen who were less paternalistic or more confrontational with prevailing colonial culture with respect to Aborigines than Wollaston was. This option for the less confrontational and more institutional person may have much to do with the lack of any local devotion. In church history it has often been the local cult which has promoted the sanctification of figures less comfortable for the local hierarchy. Throughout the Church's history such unconventional figures have generally been the product of local cults only later canonized by ecclesiastical authority. Such localized support for the holy man and woman was generally the practice for the establishment of a saint's cult in the early Church;[31] and a recent example of a similar groundswell of devotion before a reluctant official sanctification was the canonization of Padre Pio in 2002, though the papacy had been opposed to manifestations of a popular cult in the 1930s.[32] A glance through the calendars of recent Anglican prayerbooks suggests a dearth of such radical or unconventional figures compared with those associated with planting or developing institutional foundations or structures. Many Anglican provinces remember, like Wollaston in Western Australia, their founding figures, usually bishops such as Selwyn in New Zealand, Broughton in Australia or Seabury in the United States. Such saints, for all their committed and often arduous lives, were hardly in the mould of martyrs or those who upset the ecclesiastical applecart with their unconventional sanctity.

The second question concerns how the choice of John Wollaston

---

[31] Richard M. Price, 'Martyrdom and the Cult of the Saints', in Susan Ashbrook Harvey and David G. Hunter, eds, *The Oxford Handbook of Early Christian Studies* (Oxford, 2008), 808–25, at 812–13.

[32] 'Religion: Health Campaign', *Time Magazine*, 14 November 1932, <http://www.time.com/time/magazine/article/0,9171,847080,00.html>, accessed 3 January 2010.

as the local saint represents a deliberate reconstruction of its colonial history by this contemporary Anglican province. The evidence offered in the essay clearly demonstrates that when Wollaston is compared with the other two Anglican contemporaries who occupied themselves with Christian outreach towards Aborigines in colonial Western Australia, he is clearly less radical than Giustiniani and more coercively paternalistic than King. Choosing Wollaston as a local saint rewrites the story of British invasion and colonization, with all its attendant cultural and spiritual ignorance and contempt by the British for the indigenous peoples, into a story more comfortable for modern ears to listen to.

The canonization of John Wollaston flies in the face of trenchant criticisms of colonial Anglicanism in recent scholarship. Postcolonial historians have made it evident how supportive Anglican colonial Churches and institutions generally were for the British imperial project during the nineteenth century. In this respect the recent scholarship of Robert Frykenberg on Christianity in India represents similar criticisms by a number of historians. He has drawn attention to the manner in which Anglicans were often motivated by a desire for ecclesiastical dominance and control over local Christians and the conversion process.[33] Jeffrey Cox sees these pro-establishment tendencies of Anglicanism, arising out of its former partnership with the state, as being maintained in the nineteenth century.[34] It also fails to consider the trenchant criticisms of Henry Reynolds, who has argued for a history which offers a fuller account of violence on the Australian frontiers between whites and Aborigines than do those of other historians,[35]

---

[33] Robert Eric Frykenberg, *Christianity in India: From Beginnings to the Present* (Oxford, 2008), 261–7. Similar criticisms of a pro-imperialistic Anglicanism lacking in self-criticism have been made by Carl Bridenhaugh, *Mitre and Sceptre: Transatlantic Faiths, Ideas, Personalities and Politics 1689–1775* (New York, 1965); James G. Greenlee and Charles M. Johnson, *Good Citizens: British Missionaries and Imperial States 1870–1914* (Montreal, ON, 1999), 149; Catherine Hall, *Civilising Subjects: Metropole and Colony in the English Imagination 1830–1867* (Chicago, IL, 2002), 77.

[34] Jeffrey Cox, *The British Missionary Enterprise since 1700* (London, 2008), 98. This prevailing historiography of a pro-imperialistic Anglicanism has been questioned recently, as requiring to be understood more historically as a product of then-contemporary theological constructions; see Andrew Porter, *Religion versus Empire? British Protestant Missionaries and Overseas Expansion 1700–1914* (Manchester, 2004), 13; Rowan Strong, *Anglicanism and Empire c. 1700 to 1850* (Oxford, 2007), 283–94.

[35] Henry Reynolds, *The Other Side of the Frontier: Aboriginal Resistance to the European Invasion of Australia* (Richmond, Vic., 1981).

a viewpoint which has been at the heart of recent 'history wars' in Australian historiography. This more violent 'pacification' of the local Nyungar peoples has been recently attested in the latest history of Western Australia.[36]

Using the insights of this critical scholarship, the canonization of John Wollaston looks like a similarly self-congratulatory expression of Anglican imperial expansion. Both King and Giustiniani, like Wollaston, attempted to evangelize the Aboriginal people in the area of the Swan River colony. King and Wollaston used the classic missionary method of education, targeting indigenous children as likely to be more impressionable and amenable to ecclesiastical control than their parents. However, unlike Wollaston, King seems to have considered that the children still belonged in a relationship with their parents and to have recognized that relationship as one that involved some ongoing authority. Giustiniani, the heroic failure and tactless confrontationalist, nevertheless challenged colonial authority in the name of the gospel, including those in the highest authority in church and state in the colony. Giustiniani was probably the clergymen whose brief time in the colony brought about the greatest Christian challenge to prevailing colonialist cultural assumptions about the place and being of Blacks and Whites. If being a Christian saint means being one who in a contemporary society models the life of Jesus Christ, then Louis Giustiniani certainly comes the closest of all, even to his final failure. Giustiniani certainly represents, more accurately than Wollaston's engagement with the indigenous peoples of the land that British colonization invaded, the contested and multivalenced nature of Christian mission in a colonial context; something which is obscured, if not removed, in the Anglican choice of Wollaston as saint and local hero. It suggests that, as in the colonial period of its foundation, Australian Anglicanism remains, at least in its institutional ecclesiastical culture, a Church which prefers to ameliorate the minority radical elements in its history, is insufficiently critical of its own contribution to oppressive aspects of British imperial history, and prefers to uphold exemplars who are less at odds with prevailing culture.

Murdoch University

---

[36] Geoffrey Bolton, *Land of Vision and Mirage: Western Australia since 1826* (Crawley, WA, 2008), 11–13.

'A SAINT FOR ALL AUSTRALIANS'?

by JOSEPHINE LAFFIN

O n 17 October 2010 Mary MacKillop became the first Australian citizen to be officially canonized by the Roman Catholic Church. This event generated a similar outpouring of patriotic enthusiasm to that which greeted Mary's beatification in 1995. The title of this paper is borrowed from a newspaper article of 1985 by the poet, publisher and self-described 'implacable agnostic', Max Harris, a fervent supporter of Mary's canonization.[1] Saints are the only relatives that you can choose, commented Bishop Ambrose of Milan in the fourth century,[2] and taking this ancient aphorism rather more literally than St Ambrose intended, Dame Edna Everage has claimed descent from a branch of the MacKillop family tree.[3] As Dame Edna's creator, comedian and satirist Barry Humphries, is a shrewd observer of Australian culture, Mary MacKillop's triumph as a saint for all Australians seems assured – but what does this reveal about the meaning of sainthood in contemporary Australian society? This paper will trace some important stages in devotion to saints in Australian history before returning to Mary Helen MacKillop, her status as a national icon, and the threads of change and continuity which can be discerned in her cult.[4]

---

[1] *Advertiser*, 6 April 1985, 39. Similar articles by Harris can be found in *Weekend Australian*, 6–7 April 1985, 6; *Advertiser*, 11 November 1991, 19; *Advertiser*, 20 January 1995, 11.

[2] Ambrose, *De viduis* 11.54; see also Peter Brown, *Society and the Holy in Late Antiquity* (London, 1982), 228–9.

[3] *Advertiser*, 5 February 1999, 3.

[4] I am very grateful to Dr Marie Foale and Dr David Hilliard for their helpful comments on a draft of this paper. For fuller consideration of the themes of this paper, see Josephine Laffin, ed., *What does it mean to be a Saint? Reflections on Mary MacKillop, Saints and Holiness in the Catholic Tradition* (Adelaide, 2010). There is also a growing body of predominantly hagiographical literature on Mary MacKillop. The Jesuit Paul Gardiner, postulator of Mary's cause at the Vatican from 1985 to 2008, is responsible for *Mary MacKillop: An Extraordinary Australian; The Authorised Biography*, rev. edn (Sydney, 2007). Osmund Thorpe's *Mary MacKillop*, 3rd rev. edn (Sydney, 1994) is also highly sympathetic but scholarly. Journalist Lesley O'Brien's *Mary MacKillop Unveiled: Australia's First Saint* (Melbourne, 1994) was written with the cooperation of the Mary MacKillop Secretariat of the Sisters of St Joseph, the religious order

The notion that there could be 'a saint for all Australians' would have been absurd in the nineteenth century. Even after the six independent British colonies came together to form the Commonwealth of Australia in 1901, Protestantism and secularism were too strong. There was, however, a saint for most Roman Catholics (twenty-three per cent of the population of Australia in 1901). As the majority had some Irish ancestry, and most priests and bishops had been imported from Ireland, St Patrick's Day was one of the highlights of the Catholic year.[5] It was commemorated on 17 March with processions, sporting competitions, Irish dancing, Irish music and speeches by visiting Irish politicians: a nostalgic celebration of Gaelic culture spiced with a dose of politics.[6] The political overtones were contentious, especially in Melbourne after the suppression of the Easter Rising in Ireland in 1916. British Empire loyalists were outraged in 1918 when Sinn Féin banners were carried in the procession and Archbishop Daniel Mannix, a supporter of Irish republicanism, did not doff his biretta during the national anthem.[7] Rather than a manifestation of devotion to St Patrick, Melbourne's celebrations underlined the unity and identity of the relatively small, predominantly working-class, Catholic community and they exacerbated sectarian tensions. Yet the militant Irishry evident in Melbourne between 1917 and 1922

co-founded by Mary. From a sociological rather than a historical perspective, Sheila McCreanor's 2001 doctoral thesis for the University of South Australia, 'Sainthood in Australia: Mary MacKillop and the Print Media' is a rare exploration of the growing cult of Mary MacKillop. It was published by the Sisters of St Joseph under the same title (Sydney, 2001). McCreanor, a Sister of St Joseph herself, has also edited collections of Mary's letters: *Mary MacKillop and Flora: Correspondence between Mary MacKillop and her Mother, Flora McDonald MacKillop* (Sydney, 2004); *Mary MacKillop in Challenging Times 1883–1899* (Sydney, 2006).

5   For St Patrick's Day in Australia, see Patrick Mike Cronin and Daryl Adair, *The Wearing of the Green: A History of St Patrick's Day* (London, 2002), 88–93, 113–32, 141–6, 204–10; Patrick O'Farrell, *The Irish in Australia*, rev. edn (Cork, 2001), 41–6, 181–4, 246. For general histories of Australian Catholicism in this period, see Patrick O'Farrell, *The Catholic Church and Community*, 3rd rev. edn (Sydney, 1992); Edmund Campion, *Australian Catholics* (Melbourne, 1987).

6   An editorial in the South Australian weekly Catholic paper, the *Southern Cross*, on 14 March 1890 pointed out that there were two dimensions to St Patrick's Day, one religious and the other national, but in fact it was the latter which predominated in the reports of the festivities the following week. Much attention was paid to the speeches and fundraising activities of two delegates of the Irish Parliamentary Party: *Southern Cross*, 21 March 1890, 7, 9.

7   Cronin and Adair, *Wearing of the Green*, 116–17.

was uncommon in Australia, and as ties with Ireland loosened St Patrick gradually faded from prominence.[8]

In the 1920s Australian Catholics embraced a new saint from France. There are many possible explanations for the worldwide appeal of Thérèse of Lisieux, the 'Little Flower', not least that she was young, attractive, had lived so recently and had encouraged a model of holiness which was accessible to lay Catholics, one based on small deeds of love rather than great acts of heroism.[9] Above all, perhaps, in Australia the supernaturalism of Catholic piety merged with the national tendency toward pragmatism. Thérèse had promised before her death in 1897 that she would shower blessings like roses from heaven, and by the time of her canonization in 1925 she had gained a reputation as a saint who got results. In 1924 Father Cornelius Crowley set out to build a church and school in Colonel Light Gardens, a new suburb in Adelaide, South Australia. Undeterred by lack of money and parishioners, Crowley appealed for funds (under the guise of 'gifts to St Teresa') in 'the Little Flower's Corner', a weekly column in the diocesan newspaper.[10] The money duly flowed in and an estimated four to five thousand people converged on Colonel Light Gardens in 1925 for the dedication of a shrine to the new saint and the opening of the church-cum-school building named in her honour.[11] An even larger crowd attended the blessing of a separate school building the following year. For the latter event, the enterprising Crowley hired an aeroplane to drop rose petals from the sky. Unfortunately, a strong gust of wind blew most of the petals away, but the resulting disappointment 'was happily relieved by the Archbishop's remark that, though the rose leaves had not come down as expected, the money was going up'.[12]

Clearly the institutional church benefited from Thérèse's cult, but it would be a mistake to accuse Crowley and Archbishop Robert Spence of manipulating it in a cynical manner. They both

---

[8] O'Farrell, *Irish in Australia*, 184.

[9] On the development of the cult of St Thérèse of Lisieux, see, in this volume, Sophia L. Deboick, 'Céline Martin's Images of Thérèse of Lisieux and the Creation of a Modern Saint', 376–89.

[10] The column began on 8 May 1925 and featured snippets from Thérèse's writings, accounts of miracles attributed to her intercession, and lists of the contributions to the Colonel Light Gardens appeal.

[11] *Southern Cross*, 18 September 1925, 18.

[12] *Southern Cross*, 21 May 1926, 13.

seem to have developed a genuine devotion to the young saint. Indeed, it is almost impossible to discern in Australia which came first, popular devotion or official promotion of her cult, as both were so closely intertwined.[13] Thérèse indisputably 'struck a chord' with Australian Roman Catholics, but only with Catholics. David Hillard points out that Thérèse's cult:

> demonstrated the huge gap that separated Catholic devotional piety from the English Protestant piety that formed part of the mental world of the great majority of South Australians, with its stress on reading the Bible, hymn singing and preaching. For Methodists, Baptists, Congregationalists and Anglicans, the idea of praying to a deceased French nun for material aid was incomprehensible and certainly contrary to their understanding of Scripture. It confirmed their belief that Roman Catholicism fostered religious practices that were essentially idolatrous.[14]

As Father Crowley commented in the 'Little Flower's Corner', albeit in a more triumphalist tone, 'What an inscrutable mystery must not Catholicism appear to those outside the fold!'[15]

By the 1950s it was the turn of Catholics of Anglo-Celtic descent to feel discomfort when they beheld some of the devotional practices of their co-religionists from Europe. Many of the migrants who settled in Australia after the Second World War arrived with 'saints in the suitcase'.[16] The scale of the transformation of the Catholic community can be seen in the archdiocese of Adelaide, where the number of Catholics doubled in a decade. By 1960 a third of the total Catholic population were newcomers

---

[13] For the cult of Thérèse in Australia, see Katharine Massam, *Sacred Threads: Catholic Spirituality in Australia, 1922–1962* (Sydney, 1996), 127–51.

[14] David Hilliard, ' "Little Flower Land": Devotion to St Thérèse in Adelaide in the 1920s', paper presented to the seminar 'Encountering Thérèse', Catholic Theological College, Adelaide, 2 February 2002, 12.

[15] *Southern Cross*, 22 May 1925, 8.

[16] Stefano Girola, 'Saints in the Suitcase: Italian Popular Catholicism in Australia', *Australasian Catholic Record* 80 (2003), 164–74. See also Adrian Pittarello, *'Soup Without Salt': The Australian Catholic Church and the Italian Migrant* (Sydney, 1980); Antonio Paganoni and Desmond O'Connor, *Se la processione va bene … : religiosità populare Italiana nel Sud Australia* (Rome, 1999); Anthony Pagononi, *Valiant Struggles and Benign Neglect. Italians, Church and Religious Societies in Diaspora: The Australian Experience from 1950 to 2000* (New York, 2003).

who had arrived in the previous twelve years.[17] The new parish which became home to one of the largest Italian congregations in Adelaide was diplomatically named after St Francis of Assisi – everyone knew St Francis – but the church soon filled with statues of more obscure saints like St Rock and St Hilarion. The importance of patron saints in Italian Catholicism can scarcely be overestimated. Rituals associated with the patron saint of a migrant's town or village of origin provided a reassuring sense of continuity amidst the stress of adjusting to life in a new country, as well as an important way of maintaining social networks.[18] This means, however, that the cults fostered neither a sense of Italian national identity nor the successful integration of Italian Catholics into the mainstream Australian Church. Northern Italians were inclined to shrug their shoulders at the feast days of southern Italians which were usually more exuberant than their own, with long outdoor processions, extravagant forms of penance, gunfire and the pinning of jewellery and money onto statues. Anglo-Celtic Catholics were often just embarrassed and bemused. The growth in the popularity of the concept of multiculturalism helped to ease tensions in the 1970s, but the acceptance of exotic feast days by the wider Catholic community probably owed more to pragmatism than anything else. The *feste* proved to be a great way of raising money for the parish church and school.

The first generation of migrant children who went to St Francis of Assisi parish school in Adelaide were taught, like so many other Australian Catholic children in the mid-twentieth century, by Sisters of St Joseph of the Sacred Heart. These women belonged to the religious congregation founded in 1866 by the Adelaide diocesan priest, Julian Tenison Woods (1832–89), and the devout young daughter of Scottish migrants, Mary MacKillop (1842–1909). From humble origins in the small rural town of Penola in South Australia, where Woods was parish priest and

---

[17] Archbishop Beovich calculated in his report to Rome in 1960 that the number of Catholics in his diocese had risen from 66,500 to 120,000, and that 40,000 were recent migrants, a figure which accords with census data collected the following year; the report is in the Adelaide Catholic Archdiocesan Archives: Josephine Laffin, *Matthew Beovich: A Biography* (Adelaide, 2008), 205–13.

[18] See, e.g., the account of devotion to St Hilarion in Daniela Cosmini-Rose and Desmond O'Connor, *Caulonia in the Heart: The Settlement in Australia of Migrants from a Southern Italian Town* (Adelaide, 2008), 68–102.

Mary taught poor children in a disused stable, the congregation rapidly expanded.[19] It became the most successful manifestation in Australia of the wave of new institutes devoted to education, charitable work and mission which swept through nineteenth-century Roman Catholicism. Teaching poor children remained a primary focus, along with the development of orphanages, refuges for the destitute and other forms of social welfare. In the first five years more than a hundred women joined Mary's enterprise, and by the time she died, the tally was over seven hundred. Her sisters were responsible in 1909 for 117 schools and 12 charitable institutions throughout Australia and New Zealand.[20] Numbers continued to rise until the mid-1960s.

Establishing a successful religious order has been one of the best routes to canonization since the papacy assumed control of the process. One of the reasons for this is that an order or congregation can lobby the Vatican on behalf of its founder over a long period of time.[21] It is not difficult to see why Sisters of St Joseph should strive so eagerly for Mary MacKillop's canonization, and with it the affirmation of their own life's work. What, however, is her appeal for other Australians?

An epic tale of eventual triumph over great difficulties will always attract some interest. In addition to the innumerable challenges associated with ministering in urban slums and remote rural communities, Mary endured ill-health, family tragedy and an estrangement from Woods. In 1871 misunderstandings and jealousies led to her excommunication for disobedience by Bishop Sheil of Adelaide.[22] That the decision was revoked by Sheil shortly before his death in 1872 and subsequently deemed to be invalid did not lessen Mary's pain at the time. Even after 1874, when

[19] For the foundation of the Sisters of St Joseph, see, in addition to the biographies of Mary MacKillop, Marie Therese Foale, *The Josephite Story: The Sisters of St Joseph: Their Foundation and Early History, 1866–1893* (Sydney, 1989); Margaret Press, *Julian Tenison Woods: 'Father Founder'*, 2nd edn (Melbourne, 1994).

[20] The figures for the year of Mary's death come from *Southern Cross*, 10 September 1909, 594. See also Foale, *Josephite Story*, 34, 43.

[21] A point made by Peter Burke, 'How to Become a Counter-Reformation Saint', in David Luebke, ed., *The Counter-Reformation* (Oxford, 1999), 129–42, at 138, 140–1 (first publ. in Kaspar von Greyerz, ed., *Religion and Society in Early Modern Europe, 1500–1800* (London, 1984), 45–55).

[22] For Sheil and MacKillop, see Foale, *Josephite Story*, 78–123; Margaret Press, *From Our Broken Toil: South Australian Catholics 1836–1906* (Adelaide, 1986), 182–7.

she secured Roman approval for her institute, Mary encountered strong opposition from bishops who wanted the Sisters of St Joseph to provide a cheap labour force in their dioceses subject to their control rather than under the central authority of a superior general, as mandated in the rule drawn up in Rome. Bishop Reynolds of Adelaide supported Mary for a time, but forced her to leave his diocese in 1883. Ill-founded rumours that she was an alcoholic contributed to his change of attitude.

Throughout her various trials, Mary demonstrated integrity, courage, compassion, pragmatism and egalitarianism, qualities which Max Harris believed made her a more appropriate symbol of Australian national identity than traditional contenders like Ned Kelly, a nineteenth-century bushranger, and Phar Lap, a race horse during the Great Depression.[23] Although Harris died a week before Mary was beatified in Sydney on 19 January 1995, his conviction that she was an iconic Australian was readily taken up by politicians in speeches in the federal parliament in Canberra on 2 February 1995. In response to Prime Minister Paul Keating's motion acknowledging the beatification and the contribution of Mary MacKillop to Australian society, government backbencher Mary Easson proclaimed: 'As we move towards our next centenary of federation, perhaps we should look to seeing Mary MacKillop as a paradigm of an Australian. Her ingenuity, determination, intelligence and plain stubborn courage are Australian values that are accessible to all Australians, whether Catholic or not.'[24] In his own speech, the Prime Minister interpreted the beatification as the bestowal of 'a great honour on a great Australian'. He was pleased that it involved recognition of the often overlooked role of pioneer women in Australian history: 'In honouring Mary MacKillop His Holiness has honoured all Australian women and, I believe, he is honouring us all.' Perhaps conscious of his own Irish Catholic ancestry, Keating, like Easson, stressed Mary's broad appeal. As two of her greatest benefactors were the Jewish businessman Emanuel Solomon and the Protestant philanthropist and socialite Joanna Barr Smith, he was able to declare that 'in a sectarian age she was avowedly non-sectarian'. Keating was also impressed by Mary's

[23] *Weekend Australian*, 6–7 April 1985, 6.
[24] *House of Representatives Hansard*, 2 February 1995, 365 [online edition] <http://parlinfo.aph.gov.au/parlInfo/>, accessed 12 June 2009.

409

determination to establish an institute with central government rather than one subject to the control of diocesan bishops: 'Years before the federation of the nation, her view was national. She thought as an Australian, in Australian terms.'[25] In a rare display of bipartisanship, the Leader of the Opposition, John Howard, seconded the Prime Minister's motion. After expressing his 'total agreement' with Keating's speech, Howard observed that 'it is to me as a non-Catholic and as a member of the Protestant section of the Australian community very humbling and important that the head of the Catholic Church has seen fit to honour this very distinguished Australian'.[26]

That political leaders should adopt a nationalistic perspective is not surprising. What is a little more curious is that they were following the example of the Pope. After arriving in Sydney on 18 January 1995, Pope John Paul II explicitly declared that 'the honour which the Church will give to Mother Mary MacKillop by declaring her among the Blessed is in a sense an honour given to Australia and its people'.[27] In saying this, the Pope went beyond the trend in the Catholic Church since the Second Vatican Council to promote saints primarily as role models. With an 'unshakeable conviction in the "exemplary" value of the lives of holy men and women',[28] John Paul strongly encouraged that approach, but he was also concerned about evangelism and inculturation and realized that saints could be useful allies. Hence on 18 January 1995 he did not only express the hope that Australians would be inspired by Mary MacKillop's 'genuine openness to others, hospitality to strangers, generosity to the needy, justice to those unfairly treated, perseverance in the face of adversity, kindness and support to the suffering'. He also identified these as national characteristics: 'Mary MacKillop embodied all that is best in your nation and in its people.'[29] The following day, in his homily at the beatification ceremony at Randwick Racecourse, the Pope told the crowd of

[25] Ibid. 357.
[26] Ibid. 358.
[27] 'Address of His Holiness John Paul II, Kingsford-Smith Airport of Sydney (Australia), Wednesday, 18 January 1995', <http://www.vatican.va/holy_father/john_paul_ii/speeches/1995/january/documents/hf_jp-ii_spe_19950118_arrivo-australia_en.html>, accessed 12 June 2009.
[28] Michael Walsh, *John Paul II* (London, 1994), 254, 292; see also the 1983 Apostolic Constitution *Divinus Perfectionis Magister*.
[29] 'Address of His Holiness', 18 January 1995.

170,000 that 'the Beatification of Mother Mary MacKillop is a kind of "consecration" of the people of God in Australia. Through her witness the truth of God's love and the values of his kingdom have been made visible in this continent – values which are at the very basis of Australian society.'[30]

'A Nation Consecrated' proclaimed the headline on the front page of the national daily newspaper, the *Australian*, on 20 January 1995. Mary MacKillop's beatification was clearly a publicity triumph for the Roman Catholic Church, which had recently overtaken the Anglican Church as the largest religious body in Australia, with twenty-seven per cent of the population claiming adherence. Since 1995, however, Mary's status as a national icon has proved to be a mixed blessing. It has fostered a sense of entitlement, that a great nation like Australia deserves to have at least one saint, and this has led to impatience with the Vatican and its slow processes. Australians can also feel a vicarious sense of pride in Mary's achievements in the nineteenth century without necessarily wishing to emulate them in the twenty-first.

Moreover, on closer inspection not all aspects of Mary MacKillop's life and piety resonate well with contemporary Australian culture. She refused to criticize her opponents in the hierarchy, and to ease tension with the bishops she obediently relinquished her role as Superior General to a less capable woman for thirteen long years. While such humility and loyalty to the institutional Church cannot have harmed her chances of canonization, they now have limited appeal. The former chief postulator of her cause at the Vatican and author of her official biography, Paul Gardiner, has been accused of defining Mary 'as an idealized woman and saint'.[31] He may well have exaggerated her passive acceptance of suffering and downplayed the extent to which she challenged patriarchal power structures. Nevertheless, this complaint should not be pushed too far. Mary combined a very active ministry

---

[30] 'Homily of the Holy Father John Paul II, Randwick Racecourse, Sydney, Thursday 19 January 1995', <http://www.vatican.va/holy_father/john_paul_ii/homilies/1995/documents/hf_jp-ii_hom_19950119_beatificaz-sidney_en.html>, accessed 12 June 2009.

[31] See, e.g., Kathleen McPhillips, 'Post-modern Sainthood: "Hearing the Voice of the Saint" and the Uses of Feminist Hagiography', *Seachanges* 3 (2003) [online journal], <http://www.wsrt.net.au/seachanges/volume3/html/mcphillips.html>, accessed 15 June 2009.

with what could be called a passive spirituality, one which placed great emphasis on trust in divine providence. Humility, poverty, obedience and chastity were virtues which meant much to her, even if they are not very fashionable today. She associated them with her beloved St Joseph. Male hagiographers have not simply imposed an outdated stereotype of feminine goodness onto her. The name which she chose for herself, 'Sister Mary of the Cross', implies that from the very beginning of her religious life she accepted suffering and self-sacrifice as part of Christian discipleship. Mary MacKillop is thus an ambiguous role model for feminists.

There is also the issue of miracles. Before Mary was beatified, the Catholic Church required evidence that a miracle had taken place as a result of her intercession, and the verification in 2009 of a second physical cure paved the way for her canonization. Both cases involved unexpected recovery from cancer, and represent healings which cannot be explained by scientific means. The thaumaturgical aspect of sainthood, which featured so prominently in medieval piety, retains a significant appeal. On any day of the week, a steady stream of people enter the Mary MacKillop Memorial Chapel in North Sydney and pray before Mary's tomb. On one occasion when I was there a large family group unsuccessfully tried to coax a severely disabled child to relinquish a bunch of flowers and place it on the tomb. It was obvious that they were not there merely to pay their respects to a national icon.

On the other hand, amidst the favourable accounts of the beatification ceremony in 1995, one newspaper editorial noted the 'considerable uneasiness' felt by non-Catholics when the subject of miracles was raised.[32] That was probably an understatement. On Easter Monday 2009 a young Irishman's surprising emergence from a seven-month coma generated a flurry of newspaper reports in Australia (where he had been injured), Ireland and other parts of the world as his family expressed gratitude to Mary MacKillop for her intercession. Ninety-six comments were added to the Australian Broadcasting Commission's internet page devoted to the story on 13 April. Most denounced the notion that a miracle could have taken place ('I think it somewhat ungracious in the least for the family not to focus their praise and thanks on the medical profession'). Some were sarcastic ('It is a pity St Mary didn't intervene

---

[32] *Advertiser*, 20 January 1995, 10.

to prevent him being bashed into a coma in the first place'), and a few vented their prejudice against the Catholic Church ('[it is] an almost blasphemous offence to raise Mary MacKillop to the level of a deity and pray to her'; 'Mary MacKillop is another part of Catholic nutty folklore').[33]

Such disbelief and misunderstandings have not stopped other traditional aspects of the cult of saints from flourishing in twenty-first century Australia. Pilgrimages are made to places associated with Mary, including the shrines (diplomatically known as 'Mary MacKillop Centres') which the Sisters of St Joseph have established in each state. Holy cards and other pious souvenirs are available for sale. In Penola local Catholic men have made wooden crosses from the floorboards of the schoolroom built for Mary in 1867. Other more highly prized relics include the fragments of her original cedar coffin which fell away from the lead lining when Mary's body was moved to its current tomb in 1993. Liturgical services are held annually on her feast day, 8 August, and the hundredth anniversary of her death on 8 August 2009 was commemorated with a variety of special events.

Many are the statues, paintings and stained glass windows which now carry Mary's image. Artists have responded enthusiastically to the challenge of representing a nineteenth-century nun and twenty-first century saint. Brisbane's diocesan shrine is located in the oldest church building in Queensland. St Stephen's Chapel was built in the late 1840s, probably according to a design by the Gothic Revivalist architect Augustus Welby Pugin. The neo-Gothic apse is now dominated by John Elliot's timber sculpture of Mary. A leaflet available in the chapel explains that the rough bark is intended to evoke the Australian bush and the wooden hut in which Mary opened her first school, as well as her 'tough pioneering spirit' and resolute faith in God. While acknowledging that Mary lived most of her life in towns and cities, painter Robert Juniper also chose a bush theme, setting the founder of the Sisters of St Joseph against the iconic backdrop of the Australian outback, his work 'a modern gothic icon' with gum trees against gold leaf.[34]

33 'Bashing victim's recovery "the work of Mary MacKillop" ', ABC News, 13 April 2009, <http://www.abc.net.au/news/stories/2009/04/13/2541282.htm>, accessed 12 June 2009.

34 Andrew Wilson, ed., *Mary MacKillop: A Tribute* (Sydney, 1995), 52.

St Stephen's Chapel and Juniper's icon bring together important strands in Mary's cult, most notably the somewhat uneasy coexistence of her status as a national icon with traditional aspects of Catholic piety inherited from the Middle Ages. If Mary Helen MacKillop really is a saint for all Australians (or at least for a great many of us), it can only be because sainthood has multiple meanings today. Beatification and canonization can be seen as little more than rather strange honours bestowed posthumously on a person of outstanding virtue and achievement. However, older understandings of the saint as a powerful intercessor and miracle worker still have meaning for some and appear as absurd or idolatrous to others. So while at one level Mary MacKillop's popularity demonstrates how well integrated Catholics have become in Australian society, it also contributes to ongoing tensions.

As Australia's first officially proclaimed Catholic saint, Mary MacKillop occupies a unique place in Australian history, but she was only one of 1,341 men and women beatified by Pope John Paul II. A further 482 were canonized during his pontificate.[35] Given this large pool of saints and blessed, exploring the role of sanctity in the modern world should be an interesting and fruitful exercise for historians in years to come. What can be concluded here is that the case of Mary MacKillop provides a remarkable example, along with earlier forms of devotion to saints in Australia, of both the resilience and the adaptability of the cult of saints through Christian history.

Flinders University

---

[35] See, in this volume, Michael Walsh, 'Pope John Paul II and his Canonizations', 415–37.

POPE JOHN PAUL II AND HIS CANONIZATIONS

by MICHAEL J. WALSH

I n his much quoted article 'How to be a Counter-Reformation
Saint', Professor Peter Burke remarks on the 'crisis of canonisations' which afflicted the papacy in the middle years of the
sixteenth century.[1] That particular crisis, of course, was that there
were no canonizations. As the veneration of saints came under
attack from the reformers, successive pontiffs thought it politic to
refrain from creating yet more. In the long pontificate of the late
Pope John Paul II (1978–2005), the longest in papal history apart
from that of Pope Pius IX (1846–78) – whom John Paul beatified,
along with Pope John XXIII, on 3 September 2000 – there was
another crisis of canonizations. In this instance, however, there
were, in the eyes of some, far too many of them, devaluing the
currency. Even the then Cardinal Josef Ratzinger was heard to
utter words of disquiet.[2] Indeed, John Paul's saint-making policy
was a topic almost as much for the secular press as the religious:
'Catholicism turns to computers as the saints go marching in' was
the headline over a piece in *The Sunday Times*.[3]

Writing about the very recent past is, for a historian, problematic.
It is difficult to achieve the appropriate degree of objectivity about
events in which one was oneself to some extent involved. In 1994 I
produced what was, at the time of its publication, possibly the only
critical, not to say hostile, biography of John Paul II.[4] Writing in the
early 1990s I made little comment on his canonizations, apart from
drawing attention to the large number of them, and remarking that
the Synod of Bishops of 1985 had called for more saints from the
ranks of the laity.[5] Even in that most adulatory – and inordinately
long – of papal biographies, *Witness to Hope*, George Weigel spends

---

[1]   Peter Burke, *The Historical Anthropology of Early Modern Italy* (Cambridge, 1987),
48–62, at 49.
[2]   Kenneth Woodward, *Making Saints. Inside the Vatican: Who become Saints, Who do
Not, and Why* (London, 1991), 374–7.
[3]   Rebecca Fowler, *Sunday Times*, 10 May 1992, 6.
[4]   Michael Walsh, *John Paul II: A Biography* (London, 1994).
[5]   Ibid. 154, 253–4.

little time on the canonizations apart from drawing attention to the pope's revision of the process of making saints, something which is discussed below. The number of canonizations and beatifications, says Weigel, is: 'The most visible expression of John Paul II's determination to remind the Church of the universal call to holiness'. And he added, 'Karol Wojtyła's pastoral experience had taught him that saints were all around us, and he thought that the Church ought to lift more of them up as evidence of life's richly, even fearsomely, dramatic texture',[6] whatever that may mean.

In the course of this paper I hope to provide a rather more precise account of the pope's purpose in canonizing so many saints. But before I do so I will give a brief history of the canonization process, dwelling in particular on the changes introduced during the last pontificate, and provide a modest sociological analysis of the saints themselves. Perhaps surprisingly, given the large number of canonizations performed by Pope John Paul, there is little reference to the procedure for making saints in the Church's *Code of Canon Law*, the revision of which appeared in 1983, during his pontificate. The first edition of the Code, that of 1917, had almost a hundred canons on the subject, but in the current version only Canon 1403 deals with it. The first section of the Canon simply states that 'Cases for the canonisation of the Servants of God are governed by special pontifical law'.[7] The expression 'Servants of God', it should perhaps be explained, is a technical one. It is a title bestowed on a candidate for canonization once his or her cause has been formally introduced. The person thus promoted is not yet, however, given the title 'Venerable': this happens only after the cause has been examined, and approved, by the Congregation for the Causes of Saints. The next step is beatification, followed by canonization, though these two stages can be many years, in some instances even many centuries, apart.

There are problems about the distinction between the two stages. Beatification has been defined in the *Encyclopedia of the Papacy* as

> a solemn act by which the sovereign pontiff of Rome declares that a venerable servant of God may be called 'blessed' and

---

6   George Weigel, *Witness to Hope* (New York, 1999), 446, 449.
7   *The Code of Canon Law in English Translation* (London, 1983), 250. The Apostolic Constitution bringing the new Code into force is dated 25 January 1983.

that his or her feast may be celebrated by specific groups of the faithful, in specific places. This declaration is promulgated by an apostolic letter in the form of a papal brief, *sub annulo piscatoris*,[8] signed by the secretary of state. Canonization is a solemn act wherein the pope, having called a consistory of cardinals and prelates, declares that a blessed person is a saint, inscribes him or her in the catalog of saints, and determines that the saint may be venerated throughout the Church. This declaration is promulgated by a letter of decree in the form of a papal bull, signed by the pontiff …[9]

Put like that the differences seem fairly clear. At the first stage the individual given the title of blessed may be venerated, but only by specific groups and in particular places. It is a much less solemn act – and Pope Benedict XVI decided, within a month of his election, that he was not going to preside personally at beatification ceremonies[10] – and the full weight of papal authority is not involved. In reality, however, the distinction is blurred. Beatification is now widely regarded simply as a step towards sainthood, and even before canonization the *beati* are effectively inscribed 'in the catalog of saints' because they are included in the definitive version of that catalogue, the *Martyrologium Romanum*, with no limit indicated as to the extent of their cult. Apart from the use of the word 'blessed' in the text, all that marks out *beati* from *sancti* in the *Martyrology* is an asterisk attached to the name in the index.[11]

Until the later Middle Ages there was no significant distinction between the *beati* and the *sancti*, the terms being used indiscriminately.[12] But with the development of canonization as a papal prerogative the two categories became distinct, the *sancti* being those whose cult had received formal papal approval and the *beati* those who were still awaiting it[13] while being venerated at the level of a diocese or a religious order. In other words, the later medieval

---

[8] The Fisherman's Ring is one of the symbols of the papal office.

[9] Dominique Le Tourneau, 'Causes of Canonization', in P. Levillain, ed., *The Papacy: An Encyclopedia* (New York, 2002), 1: 268–71, at 268.

[10] David Gibson, *The Rule of Benedict* (San Francisco, CA, 2006), 243.

[11] *Martyrologium Romanum … Editio Altera* (Vatican City, 2004). The extremely useful 'Index Nominum Sanctorum et Beatorum' runs to nearly 150 double-column pages: ibid. 697–844.

[12] A. Vauchez, *Sainthood in the Later Middle Ages* (Cambridge, 1997), 85.

[13] Ibid. 98.

practice roughly conformed to the definition of beatification as given in the *Encyclopedia of the Papacy* in that it was understood to be local rather than universal – with the major proviso that since 1634 beatification itself has become a papally controlled process. What we now have, therefore, is a distinction almost without a difference. I say 'almost' because while no one nowadays suggests that papal infallibility is involved in beatification, canonization as a solemn act of the Supreme Pontiff is regarded as fulfilling the requirements for an infallible act as defined at the First Vatican Council. Even before 1870, as Eric Kemp long ago demonstrated, papal infallibility was generally, if not universally, accepted in the case of canonization.[14] Apologists will hasten to add that infallibility is entailed only in the assertion that such-and-such a person is a saint, that is to say, is in heaven. It does not apply to the process leading up to canonization. In other words, it does not apply to the historical investigation into his or her life, or indeed to the theological investigation into the person's writings where there are any. This caveat, however, fails to cover all situations, as will be seen further on.

Clearly there is an issue about the usefulness of beatification within the modern saint-making process. This has not been lost upon the officials of the Congregation for the Causes of Saints who have discussed the issue,[15] but this somewhat arcane debate need not detain us here beyond noting that if Pope John Paul II canonized a large number of presumably holy people, he beatified even more.[16]

In the introduction to a collection of essays on a number of saints, the late Lord Longford remarked that in 1634, when Urban VIII issued his brief *Coelestis Jerusalem Cives* which broadly laid down the procedures which were followed at least until the pontificate of John Paul II, 'thousands of canonisations that had taken place previously were not called into question'.[17] This is, of course, wildly inaccurate. Though there were indeed thousands of

[14] E. W. Kemp, *Canonization and Authority in the Western Church* (Oxford, 1948), 151–68.

[15] Fabijan Veraja, *La beatificazione. Storia, problemi, prospettive* (Rome, 1983); cf. Paolo Molinari and Peter Gumpel, 'L'Istituto della beatificazione: A proposito d'uno studio recente', *Gregorianum* 69 (1988), 133–8.

[16] Woodward, *Making Saints*, 377–80.

[17] Frank Longford, *Saints* (London, 1987), 3.

saints, there have not been thousands of formal canonizations. It has been suggested that the growing consciousness of papal infallibility limited the number who were raised to the altar in the later Middle Ages.[18] I can, however, find no suggestion of this in André Vauchez's study of *Sainthood in the Later Middle Ages*. He prefers instead the explanation that the growing complexity of the canonization process, coupled to its cost, may have had much to do with restricting the growth of canonized saints.[19] But he also adds, rather significantly in the context of the modern debate, that 'popes sought to check the demand in order not to depreciate the supreme honour of canonization by granting it too frequently'.[20]

But how frequently counts as too frequently? Vauchez gives a list of canonization processes, successful and unsuccessful, from 1198 to 1431. Two of the many who did not make it to sainthood during this period were later canonized, Clare of Montfalco by Leo XIII in 1881 and Margaret of Hungary by Pius XII in 1943, but the numbers formally canonized remain remarkably small, just 34 in nearly two and a half centuries[21] as counted by Vauchez, and overall, only 103 in well over five hundred years. Table 1 gives the numbers. From 993 (the first generally accepted papal canonization, that of Ulric of Augsburg) until 1198, and from 1431 until 1588 (the establishment of the Congregation of Rites), the figures are taken from Pierre Delooz's *Sociologie et Canonisations*.[22]

Delooz was, I think, the first scholar to examine critically what sort of people became saints; what their background was; where, geographically, they came from; what they did in life; and so on. He did not restrict his enquiry to formally canonized saints, but I have included only these in the table.[23] Bridget of Sweden seems to have been canonized by three popes: Boniface IX and Martin V – which I have tried to indicate by the bracketed figures in the table – and also by the antipope John XXIII, who has been left

[18]   Philippe Jansen and Dominique Le Tourneau, 'Canonization', in Levillain, ed., *Encyclopedia of the Papacy*, 1: 234.
[19]   Vauchez, *Sainthood*, 64.
[20]   Ibid. 68.
[21]   Ibid. 252–5.
[22]   Pierre Delooz, *Sociologie et canonisations* (Liège, 1969).
[23]   Others have since undertaken even more sophisticated statistical analyses; see, e.g., Donald Weinstein and Rudolph M. Bell, *Saints and Society: The Two Worlds of Western Christendom, 1000–1700* (Chicago, IL, 1982), 121–37.

Table 1. Papal Canonizations 993–1588

Pope	Dates	No. of saints
John XV	985–96	1
Gregory V	996–99	1
Benedict VIII	1012–24	1
John XIX	1024–32	2
Benedict IX	1032-44, 1045, 1047-48	2
Clement II	1046–47	1
Leo IX	1049–54	8
Alexander II	1061–73	3
Gregory VII	1073–85	4
Urban II	1088–99	5
Paschal II	1099–18	2
Callistus II	1119–24	4
Innocent II	1130–43	3
Eugenius III	1145–53	1
Alexander III	1159–81	6
Lucius III	1181–85	2
Clement III	1187–91	3
Celestine III	1191–98	6
Innocent III	1198–1216	5
Honorius III	1216–27	3
Gregory IX	1227–41	6
Innocent IV	1243–54	5
Alexander IV	1254–61	1
Urban IV	1261–64	1
Clement IV	1265–68	1
Boniface VIII	1294-1303	1
John XXII	1316–34	4
Clement VI	1342–52	1
Urban V	1362–70	1
Boniface IX	1389–1404	1 (2)
Martin V	1417–31	2 (1)
Eugenius IV	1431–47	1

Pope	Dates	No. of saints
Nicholas V	1447–55	1
Callistus III	1455–58	2
Pius II	1458–64	2
Sixtus IV	1471–84	7
Innocent VIII	1484–92	1
Leo X	1513–21	1
Hadrian VI	1522–23	2
Clement VII	1523–34	1
TOTAL		103

out. Some of the earlier claims for papal canonizations, especially those listed by Delooz, are problematic.

The situation did not greatly change after Sixtus V had established the Congregation of Rites in 1588. This had responsibility for overseeing the liturgy of the Roman Catholic Church, as well as a number of related issues including the canonization of saints. This latter became the primary concern of the Congregation for the Causes of Saints, created in 1969 by the division of the Congregation of Rites into that of Divine Worship and the Causes of Saints. The table which follows lists the number of saints since 1588 according to each pontificate. This table is similar to the previous one except in two respects. Early canonizations had been individual ceremonies for individual saints. In 1622, however, Gregory XV canonized five saints at one go: Teresa of Avila; Philip Neri; Francis Xavier; Ignatius Loyola; and, rather oddly, Isidore the Farmer, the patron saint of Madrid, who died in 1130 – the others were, of course, all sixteenth-century saints. Table 2 therefore shows both the number of saints canonized and the number of distinct canonization ceremonies. The same remark is true of beatifications: both the number of new *beati* is included, and the number of ceremonies associated with them.

It is obvious from the list of pontiffs that some are missing. Some did not create any saints or even any *beati*. That is often because their pontificates were rather short, though that would not account for the reticence of Innocent X (1644–55), Innocent XII (1691–1700) or Clement XIV (1769–74). These three, however, all confirmed existing cults. That is to say they granted the right of a diocese or a religious order to have a specific liturgy, a mass and divine office, in honour of someone who had long been locally venerated, either as a saint or as a blessed. Among the *beati* thus confirmed is the largest single group of martyrs, the 800 who were killed by the Ottomans at Otranto in Apulia on 12 August 1480. Their cult was confirmed by Clement XIV.[24] Large groups of martyrs are not uncommon candidates for mass beatification or canonization, such as, for example, the 206 Japanese martyrs beatified by Pope Pius IX.

Since the establishment of formal beatification there have been far more people declared *beati* than canonized as saints, largely because of the groups of martyrs such as those just mentioned. But the number of saints canonized remained remarkably small, at least until the beginning of the twentieth century. From 1588 to the end of Leo XII's pontificate there were only 130 canonized. Then things speeded up a little, 25 in twenty years. From the accession of Pius IX to the death of Paul VI, a period of fifty-six years, there were 158 new saints. Canonizations had become more frequent, though not at the rate performed by John Paul II. If these figures are to be trusted, and it has to be stressed again that evidence for papal canonizations is not always secure, before the late Pope 417 new saints had been papally created, while he added 482, more than all other popes combined (table 2).

But the statistics are not quite so straightforward. Some of John Paul's canonizations were of large groups of martyrs. He was, moreover, pope for rather a long time, as I have already remarked. While Paul VI held 20 canonization ceremonies in fifteen years, in other words just over 1.3 a year, during his twenty-six-year pontificate John Paul II held 52 ceremonies, which average out at 2 a year, a not much larger proportion than his predecessor-but-one. The situation is different as far as beatifications are concerned. Paul VI performed two a year on average, while John Paul took part in well over five a year, beatifying more people than had been beatified hitherto. But here again one has to be slightly cautious. The 1,341 new *beati* include many martyrs of the French Revolution, and especially of the Spanish Civil War.

[24] The popes who performed no canonizations or beatifications were Urban VII (1590), Gregory XIV (1590–1), Innocent XI (1591), Leo XI (1605) and John Paul I (1978), whose pontificate lasted only a month. The following only 'confirmed cults': Innocent X (1644–55), Innocent XII (1691–1700), Innocent XIII (1721–4), Clement XIV (1769–74) and Pius VIII (1829–30).

Table 2. Canonizations and Beatifications 1585–1978[a]

Pope	Dates	Saints	Cere-monies	Blesseds	Cere-monies
Sixtus V	1585–90	1	1	–	–
Clement VIII	1592–1605	2	2	2	2
Paul V	1605–21	2	2	13	13
Gregory XV	1621–23	5	1	1	1
Urban VIII	1623–44	2	2	35	11
Alexander VII	1655–67	2	2	2	2
Clement IX	1667–69	2	1	1	1
Clement X	1670–76	5	1	21	3
Innocent XI	1676–89	–	–	1	1
Alexander VIII	1689–91	5	1	–	–
Clement XI	1700–21	4	1	1	1
Benedict XIII	1724–30	10	5	5	5
Clement XII	1730–40	4	1	2	2
Benedict XIV	1740–58	5	1	6	6
Clement XIII	1758–69	6	1	5	5
Pius VII	1775–99	–	–	18	18
Leo X	1823–29	–	–	5	5
Gregory XVI	1831–46	5	1	4	4
Pius IX	1846–78	52	2	222	17
Leo XIII	1878–1903	18	4	112	29
Pius X	1903–14	4	2	73	13
Benedict XV	1914–22	3	2	42	7
Pius XI	1922–39	34	17	499	45
Pius XII	1939–58	33	21	166	52
John XXIII	1958–63	10	7	5	5
Paul VI	1963–78	81	20	61	30
John Paul II	1978–2005	482	52	1341	147[b]
TOTAL		777	150	2643	425

Notes: [a]The information in this table, apart from the figures for John Paul II, is drawn from Jean Evenou, 'Canonisations, béatifications, et confirmations de culte', *Notitiae* 22, no. 234 (January 1986), 41–7. [b]The figures are taken from the Vatican web site, accessed on 25 June 2009: for saints <http://www.vatican.va/news_services/liturgy/saints/ELENCO_SANTI_GPII.htm> and for beati <http://www.vatican.va/news_services/liturgy/saints/ELENCO_BEATI_GPII.htm>, but see also Matthew and Margaret Bunson, *John Paul II's Book of Saints* (Huntington IN, 2007), which provides brief biographies.

Table 3. Martyrs not included in the Analysis

Martyrs of	Dates of Martyrdom	No. of martyrs	Non-indigenous
China	1648–1935	120	33
Vietnam	1744–1862	115	22
Korea	1838–67	99	9
Mexico	1926–28	25	0
TOTAL		359	64

In the essay mentioned earlier, Peter Burke comments:

> most students of the saints have assumed that they are witnesses to the age in which they lived. As individuals they obviously are. However, anyone interested in the history of perception has to treat them as witnesses above all to the age in which they were canonised: there is no other justification for selecting this formally-defined group ...[25]

Martyrdom has been an unfortunate characteristic of Christian life in the twentieth century,[26] so it is hardly surprising that Pope John Paul canonized so many of them. They included Martyrs of China, Martyrs of Vietnam, Martyrs of Korea and Martyrs of Mexico. Apart from the Mexicans, all groups include some non-indigenous missionaries. In the analysis which follows, I have left these large groups out of account for three reasons. First, they seem to me to be rather random groupings from which little specific is to be learnt about John Paul's policy of canonization beyond the fact that he approved of martyrs. Secondly, and this is the main reason why I have not included them in the analysis, for the most part we know very little about the individuals, apart from the missionaries. This is even true of a good many, though not all, of the Mexican martyrs. Thirdly, each group of martyrs died over a relatively limited period, a factor which will be discussed shortly. Separating these large groups from the remainder of the late Pope's canonizations, however, still leaves 38 martyrs about whom a fair

---

[25] Burke, *Historical Anthropology*, 53.
[26] For the figures for the Roman Catholic Church, see Vicente Cárcel Ortí, 'Persecuzione religiose e martiri del nostro secolo', *Monitor Ecclesiasticus* 123 (1998), 647–732.

amount is known among the 117 individual saints who will be analysed.

Of these groups of martyrs, the Mexican martyrs were not only canonized by Pope John Paul; he had also beatified them. The time between the two ceremonies, 22 November 1992 and 21 May 2000, is comparatively short. Eustochia Calafato was 'beatified' in 1482, but canonized only in 1998. The Polish Queen Cunegunde was beatified in 1690, and canonized in 1999. The pope canonized three saints who had been beatified in the eighteenth century, and fifteen from the nineteenth. He canonized nearly a hundred – including the Mexican martyrs – whom he had himself beatified. The shortest time between the two events was a mere three years: Padre Pio, the Italian Franciscan stigmatic, was beatified on 2 May 1999 and canonized, to much popular acclaim, on 16 June 2002. Clearly, the process had speeded up.

It is not necessary here to describe the older form of canonization beyond saying that it was technically a judicial process: 'The trial for sanctity required witnesses, it required judges, and it required the notorious devil's advocate, the equivalent of counsel for the prosecution'.[27] The devil's advocate (*promotor fidei*, to give him his proper title) put forward written objections to the case being made for a candidate's sanctity. Before the *Code of Canon Law* of 1917 there had to be a delay of half a century before a cause could be introduced, by which time, one would imagine, the assertion of sanctity would have been decided by the test of time. As the process came to be started earlier after a person's death, though the possibility of having witnesses greatly increased, so also did the danger that the original claim for sainthood had not been fully established. The debate between the devil's advocate and the supporters of a particular cause might go on for many years before agreement could be reached.[28]

Pope John Paul II's Apostolic Constitution *Divinus Perfectionis Magister* of 25 January 1983 set out expressly to simplify the canonization process – at the request, he said, of the bishops[29] – and

---

[27] Burke, *Historical Anthropology*, 48.

[28] Woodward, *Making Saints*, 81. Woodward provides a detailed account of the older process: ibid. 77–86, but see also Delooz, *Sociologie*, ch. 2, 'La procedure juridique de la canonisation'.

[29] Congregation for the Causes of Saints, *New Laws for the Causes of Saints* (Rome, 1983), 5.

in so doing did away with the adversarial function of the devil's advocate: a fairly recent English-language manual, *Canonization: Theology, History, Process*, does not even mention the famous English term.[30] It correctly explains the current role of the *promotor fidei* as more of a theologian than a lawyer, deputed to preside at the gathering of theologians, and to draw up a report on the discussion. Discussed at these meetings are the documents produced by the local diocesan tribunal, which has now a greater responsibility in promoting the candidate, and the historical disquisition into the life of the saint, the *Positio*, drawn up by an official of the Congregation for the Causes of Saints. They also sit in judgement on any miracles claimed for the candidate. According to the *Code* of 1917, at least two miracles were required for beatification, and another two for canonization, except in the case of those who had died a martyr's death. Historically, miracles proved the power of the saint with God. More realistically, perhaps even cynically, Pope Innocent IV (1243–54) remarked that people whom the public deemed holy might in private be living less than edifying lives: miracles were proof that they were, after all, holy.[31] Since 1975, however, only a single miracle has been required for each stage.[32]

Apart from the theological orthodoxy and holiness of life of the candidate, the diocesan enquiry has to assure Rome that there has been no public veneration of him or her. This is a somewhat paradoxical requirement of the decree of Urban VIII: a person is being proposed for canonization because, locally, he or she has *fama sanctitatis*, in other words, is venerated. But no public liturgical cult is permitted until after beatification. This can make it difficult to promote an individual: the postulators of the cause, as they are called, have to drum up support. It does not always work. In 1992, for example, to commemorate the five-hundredth anniversary of Columbus's voyage to the New World, a group of conservative clerics in Rome and Spain attempted to have Isabella la Catolica

[30] William H. Woestmann, ed., *Canonization: Theology, History, Process* (Ottawa, ON, 2002).
[31] 'Vitam tamen sine miraculis crederem sufficere quoad virtutem, tamen ecclesia non debet tales canonizare propter hoc: quia in secreto potuerunt laxiorem vitam ducere': quoted by Fabijan Veraja, *Le cause di canonizzazione dei santi* (Vatican City, 1992), 81. Cf. also Woestmann, ed., *Canonization*, 60–2, for an address on miracles by John Paul II.
[32] Veraja, *Le cause*, 83. See also Robert Ombres, 'Merits and Miracles: The Causes of Saints', *Clergy Review* 70 (1985), 68–70.

Table 4. Saints Canonized by John Paul II, by Century of Death

Century	12th	13th	14th	15th	16th	17th	18th	19th	20th
	1	3	1	2	3	28	8	22	49

beatified. As she and Ferdinand had driven both Jews and Muslims from Spain there were some who thought her a rather unsuitable role model for a more ecumenical age. Her advocates, or postulators, clearly thought otherwise, and provided counter-arguments for use by their supporters, not least the fact that the pope had beatified Edith Stein 'despite the protests of the Hebrews, Junipero Serra despite opposition in the United States, and some martyrs of the Spanish revolution of 1936, and there continue to be studies of others of the same sort, despite the opposition of socialists'.[33] But their campaign was unsuccessful.

So who were successful? We are dealing here, it will be recalled, with the 117 saints canonized by the late Pope, excluding the large groups of martyrs. As was remarked above, most of the martyrs among John Paul's saints died within a relatively short span of time, and so their inclusion would rather skew any statistical analysis of when John Paul's new saints lived their lives of virtue. The oldest of his saints is Meinard, who was born in what is now Germany c. 1130 and died in modern-day Latvia in August 1196.[34] The most recently deceased, in 1975, is Mgr Josemaria Escrivá y Balaguer, the founder of Opus Dei. The canonizations of both Meinard and Escrivá are significant in understanding papal policy in these matters, and I shall return to them later. Table 4 shows the distribution down the centuries of the new saints. What is surprising, for a Pope who wanted to provide models for modern Christian living, is that only forty per cent came from the twentieth century. On the other hand, it can hardly be a coincidence that six of the seven pre-1500 new saints canonized by a Slavic pope lived and died in Eastern Europe. Two of them, Cunegunde or Kinga (c. 1224–92) and Hedwig (1374–99) were Queens of Poland.

Writing early during the pontificate of Pope Paul VI, Pierre Delooz commented on the geographical distribution of all the saints canonized up to that time, 365 of them: 'One may conclude

---

33 Unpublished and untitled twelve-page document in Italian, in my possession.
34 In all geographical data I have given the current equivalent.

that a third of all canonized saints are Italian. At the very top, the hierarchy of the Catholic Church has been dominated by the Italian model, or more generally a Latin one, for two-thirds of all saints officially declared holy have been born in Latin countries.'[35] He goes on to comment that the situation is a little different when one includes those who have been beatified and others who have achieved the status of saint or blessed by other means than the intervention of the papacy. Four countries alone, he writes, have produced more than half of those he takes into account: Italy, France, Spain and Portugal. Though there are a considerable number of non-Europeans, they tend to be included in the lists of the officially holy because they were directly linked to Europeans.[36] Or, as I put it in an article entitled 'Chances of Sanctity' in 1976, 'the chances of the ordinary Catholic achieving formally recognised sanctity are, statistically, pretty small unless he associate himself in the Far East with some Spanish, French or Italian missionary who is a sure candidate for martyrdom. It will help if that missionary is a Jesuit or Franciscan'.[37] The question is, did the balance shift under the late pope?

Delooz's figures, it must be recalled, are not limited to the formally canonized, and include large groups of martyrs whom I have left out. The analysis of my sample is laid out in Table 5.

Although in this list Portugal is absent, the dominance of the 'Latin' countries which Delooz mentioned is still very evident. The large number of Spanish saints is accounted for in part, but only in part, by the Spanish Civil War, while Italy, which has suffered nothing similar, has still provided the largest number of saints, both of those born there and those who died there. Eastern Europe comes slightly more into prominence, especially Poland (the additional saint who was not born there, is Queen Cunegunde, born in Hungary). Before the election of Karol Wojtyła, Poland, or that region which we now know as Poland, had very few formally canonized saints though, according to Delooz, there were quite a number of *beati* and *sancti* selected by other means. John Paul II added eight.

[35] Delooz, *Sociologie*, 194.
[36] Ibid. 195.
[37] Michael Walsh, 'Chances of Sanctity', *The Month*, October 1976, 336–42. The citation is from 342.

Table 5. 'Nationality' of Saints Canonized by John Paul II, by Country of Birth and of Death

Country	Born	Died
Argentina	1	0
Austria	1	0
Belgium	1	1
Brazil	0	4
Canada	1	2
Chile	1	1
China	0	2
Croatia	2	0
Czech Republic	3	3
Ecuador	1	0
France	10	6
Germany	4	1
Guatemala	0	1
Holland	0	1
Hungary	3	0
Italy	33	33[a]
Japan	9	16
Korea	1	1
Latvia	0	1
Lebanon	2	2
Mexico	3	3
Paraguay	1	0
Philippines	1	0
Poland	7	8
Slovakia	0	3
Spain	30	24
Sudan	1	1
Ukraine	0	1
United States	1	2
TOTAL	117	117

Note: [a]Although both figures for Italy are the same, they do not represent the same individuals.

Table 6. Roles of those Canonized by John Paul II

Abbess	1
Catechist	2
Doctor	3
Founder	44
Hermit	1
Missionary	7
Scholar	4
Teacher	9
Visionary	4

While in no way wishing to belittle Italy's reputation as a nursery of saints, there is another, structural, reason, apart from the dominance of prelates of Italian nationality in the Vatican, why so many saints seem to have died in that country. Founders of religious orders of one kind or another frequently set up the 'mother house' of their institute (i.e. their congregation or religious order) in Rome, and settle there: Escrivá y Balaguer, the founder of Opus Dei, is a case in point. And if one looks at the kind of people who get canonized, founders are at the top. This is understandable. Members of a religious institute are naturally eager that their founder should achieve recognition in the Church at large. This is partly out of *pietas*, but also because they need the legitimacy which a canonization brings. This extends to the founder's 'charism', as religious call it, that is to say to his or her spiritual vision for the members of the institute, and for the work it does. Because a saint's writings are examined for their orthodoxy, it also endorses his or her teaching. This was perhaps particularly true for Opus Dei, which has for long been surrounded by controversy.[38]

Not all of the 117 saints canonized by John Paul II who are being examined here had a clearly identifiable role above their ecclesiastical status as bishop, priest or nun, but as Table 6 shows, of the 75 who did, founders of religious institutes of one form or another counted for well over half.

[38] See Michael Walsh, *Opus Dei* (San Francisco, CA, 2004), esp. viii–ix for the controversy surrounding the beatification and subsequent canonization of its founder.

Table 7. Ecclesiastical Status of those Canonized by John Paul II

Bishop	5
Brother	19
Cardinal	1
Friar	2
Laity	9 (3)
Nun	36
Priest	45
Teacher	9
Visionary	4

The ecclesiastical status of the sample (Table 7) reveals a similar bias to those of clerical rank among the canonized. (Purists would say that nuns and brothers are not clerics, and therefore ought to be included among the laity, but except to the most legalistic of minds, nuns are not counted as lay people.)

The number in brackets after the figure for the laity indicates that three of them were women. Thus, of the 117 saints in the sample, only 39 were women, or just 33 per cent. This figure is far smaller than under Pope Paul VI who, again leaving aside the large groups of Ugandan and English martyrs (22 and 40 people respectively), created only 19 saints, of whom just over a third (7) were women.[39] Even more striking, however, is the tiny number of lay people who have been included among the canonizations, only 7.5 per cent, though in fairness it should be said that were the large groups of martyrs to have been included, the proportion of laity would have been very much higher.

One could see this emphasis on bishops, priests and nuns as evidence that the clerical elite, which, at least in the second millennium, administers the canonization process, only understands holiness in the clerical mould. There is some truth in this, but even in the first millennium bishops, priests and nuns have been the most prolific source of saints. No doubt in the past there have been a

---

39 On the 'invisibility' of women saints, see Michael D. Whalen, 'In the Company of Women? The Politics of Memory in the Liturgical Commemoration of Saints – Male and Female', *Worship* 73 (1999), 482–504.

number of reasons for this, but in modern times this bias towards the clerical state is surely structural. Even now, the complexity of the process is such that much determination is needed, not to mention stamina, to promote someone for canonization. It is obvious that a religious order is more likely to be successful in its campaign than is an individual acting on his or her own. A religious order probably has the financial means, and it has the necessary longevity. Woodward instances the beatification in 1988 of Philadelphia-born Katherine Drexel, founder of the Blessed Sacrament Sisters for Indians and Coloured People, who died in 1955.[40] The total cost for the beatification was $333,250 'in ascertainable expenses'. Katherine's sister had in 1927 established a fund 'to be used for any "extraordinary work" the sisters might choose to undertake. The beatification of Katherine Drexel, they figured, was something extraordinary. In the end, then, the Drexel family – like many a royal family of old Europe – underwrote the cost of beatifying one of its own'.[41]

But there is, in my view, rather more to it than that. In practice, to become a saint one needs a *vita*; one needs a place for people to visit, a shrine in other words, though in the first instance it must not be technically a shrine; one needs relics; and one needs a place where the corpse is interred and revered. It is not impossible for these conditions to be in place for a lay person, but it is undoubtedly more complicated.[42] Indeed, of the nine saints I have listed as lay, four were martyrs in Japan, two of whom, though lay people, were associated with the Dominican Order. Of the remaining five, one, Juan Diego, the visionary of Guadalupe, almost certainly did not exist,[43] a fact which must raise new questions about the infallibility of the process; one was a queen of Poland (the other queen of Poland, Cunegunde, became a nun, and I have listed her as such); and two were twentieth-century Italian doctors, one male, one female. The remaining lay saint was Zdislava Berka, wife of the Count of Lemberk, who founded a Dominican convent near her castle, and died there in 1252. Why was she suddenly chosen

[40] She was canonized in 2000.
[41] Woodward, *Making Saints*, 114.
[42] Cf. R. Rusconi, 'Fame di santità', *Cristianesimo nella storia* 18 (1997), 516–19, where the instance discussed is of a layman, Giuseppe Moscati, whose case, it might be said, is the exception which proves the rule.
[43] D. A. Brading, *Mexican Phoenix* (Cambridge, 2001), 311–41.

Table 8. Social Status of those Canonized by John Paul II

Aristocrats	28
Artisans	12
Labourers	2
Merchants	7
Middle class	31
Peasants	15

for canonization? Undoubtedly because the pope was not far from Lemberk, visiting Olomuc in the Czech Republic.

The late Pope's practice of canonizing or beatifying outside Rome is something to which we shall return in a moment, but I want to complete the analysis of John Paul's new saints by looking at their social background. This is particularly problematic. We do not know much about the early years of some saints, and about many of those included in the large groups of martyrs almost nothing at all, but leaving aside the martyrs and those of whom nothing is known, and using perhaps rather questionable modern categories, we come up with table 8.

The aristocrats include one princess and two queens; artisans are those who have some trade such as shoemaking; labourers are town-dwellers as distinct from peasants; and middle-class is a catch-all category for anyone who is not an aristocrat or a peasant. The category of merchant includes, for instance, shopkeepers.

One final statistic. From Table 2 we have seen that the late Pope conducted 52 canonization ceremonies and 147 beatification ceremonies. Of the canonizations, 38 were performed at the Vatican, either in St Peter's basilica or in the piazza outside, while 14, or just over a quarter, were held elsewhere. Over forty per cent of beatification ceremonies were held outside Rome, performed while the pope was on his travels. To some considerable extent, where John Paul was going dictated who was to be raised to the altars. The case of Zdislava of Lemberk has just been mentioned, but how else are we to account for the rescue of Eustochia Calafato from the 'cases pending' file of the saint-makers, where she had languished since the end of the fifteenth century, except for the fact that the pontiff was visiting Messina where she was born? The same is true of Bishop Meinard, who had died in Latvia as a missionary at the end of the twelfth century: John Paul canonized him during a visit to Riga. Three Jesuit missionaries to what was then Paraguay but is now Brazil were canonized when the Pontiff went to Asunción. And so on.

The practice of performing the canonization ceremony during a visit to a particular place is a clue to what appears to have been Pope John Paul's purpose in creating saints, recalling for people their Christian heritage. We have, however, some more direct evidence. I referred earlier to the call from the Synod of Bishops in 1985 for more lay saints.[44] As has been seen, this did not happen, but it was the pope's intention that it should. In March 1983, more than two years before the synod, the then Prefect of the Congregation for the Causes of Saints, Cardinal Pietro Palazzini, had said in an interview with L'Osservatore Romano, the Vatican newspaper, that the pope had asked the Congregation to prioritize lay men and women so that, said Palazzini:, 'Every category of the People of God should have its own model of sanctity'.[45] In March 1992 the pope expressed his frustration that he had not been able to beatify a married couple. It was not, he said, the fault of the Congregation for the Causes of Saints but of the Christian community which, unlike religious orders, did not put candidates forward.[46] He gave this address almost a decade after simplifying the procedures, but leaving them just as much as before under the control of the Vatican. The spontaneity which the Christian community might need if it were to promote its own candidates remains excluded from the system.[47]

While the present structure survives, it is difficult to see how anything but a clerical concept of holiness can, except in very rare cases, make any headway on the route to official sainthood. The function of saints will remain to display that understanding of holiness which coincides with the perceived needs of the clerical elite. That appears to be the burden of Peter Burke's essay referred to

[44] See above, p. 415.

[45] Quoted by F. de Palma, 'Le cause di beatificazione in Italia', *Cristianesimo nella storia* 18 (1997), 525–55, at 537.

[46] Speech to the clergy of Rome, 5 March 1992, quoted by Woestman, *Canonization*, 63. Woestman points out that a married couple, Luigi and Maria Beltrame Quattrocchi, who lived in Rome, were beatified on 21 October 2001.

[47] The way in which a clerically acceptable version of holiness departs from a holiness popularly conceived has been studied by Candace Slater, *City Steeple, City Streets: Saints' Tales from Granada and a Changing Spain* (Berkeley, CA, 1990).

earlier, and the point is also argued in the context of the Gregorian reform movement of the central Middle Ages by André Vauchez in an article with the thought-provoking title of 'Saints admirables et saints imitables'.[48] Saints are commonly presented as 'imitable', they are presented as exemplars of Christian living as in the words of Cardinal Palazzini just quoted, 'every category of the People of God should have its own model of sanctity'. There are plenty of instances of the pope, in homilies delivered at canonizations, putting the new saint forward as a model to be followed.

The presentation of saints as, in Vauchez's term, 'admirable', by which he means manifesting through miracles the power of God, is largely missing in the canonizations of John Paul II, except possibly in the person of Padre Pio – who was, interestingly, probably the most widely known and revered of all those selected for sainthood. In this style of holiness saints 'are mediators of the transcendental holy', they are 'revelatory tokens, signs of a benevolent power larger than is usually experienced in life'.[49] It could be argued that, in the popular imagination, this notion of sanctity is far more prevalent than the notion of saints as exemplars of Christian living.

Pope John Paul II's use of saints, however, appears to have been different again. As remarked above, a clue to it may be found in his wish to beatify or canonize new candidates in the place where they lived or where they died. When, in Madrid's Plaza de Colon on 4 May 2003, he canonized five Spaniards, one of whom had been executed during the Spanish Civil War, he said: 'To know and to deepen a people's past means to strengthen and enrich their very identity. *Do not abandon your Christian roots!* Only in this way will you be able to bring the cultural riches of your history to the world and to Europe.'[50]

He made an even more specific association between Catholicism and nation-building in his homily in Mexico City on the occasion of the canonization of Juan Diego on 31 July 2002:

---

48 A.Vauchez, 'Saints admirables et saints imitables: Les Fonctions de l'hagiographie ont-elles changé aux derniers siècles du Moyen Âge?', in *Les Fonctions des saints dans le monde occidental (IIIe–XIIIe): Actes du colloque organisé par l'École française de Rome avec le concours de l'Université de Rome, La Sapienza, Rome, 27–29 octobre 1988*, Collection de l'École française de Rome 149 (Rome, 1991), 161–72.

49 John Coleman, 'After Sainthood?', in John Stratton Hawley, ed., *Saints and Virtues* (Berkeley, CA, 1987), 205–25, at 211, 221.

50 <http://www.vatican.va/holy_father/john_paul_ii/homilies/2003/documents/hf_jp-ii_hom_20030504_canonization-spain_en.html>, accessed 10 July 2009.

'*The Lord looks down from heaven, he sees all the sons of men*' (*Ps* 33: 13), we recited with the Psalmist, once again confessing our faith in God, who makes no distinctions of race or culture. In accepting the Christian message without forgoing his indigenous identity, Juan Diego discovered the profound truth of the new humanity, in which all are called to be children of God. Thus he facilitated the fruitful meeting of two worlds and became the catalyst for the new Mexican identity, closely united to Our Lady of Guadalupe, whose mestizo face expresses her spiritual motherhood which embraces all Mexicans. This is why the witness of his life must continue to be the inspiration for the building up of the Mexican nation, encouraging brotherhood among all its children and ever helping to reconcile Mexico with its origins, values and traditions. The noble task of building a better Mexico, with greater justice and solidarity, demands the cooperation of all. In particular, it is necessary today to support the indigenous peoples in their legitimate aspirations, respecting and defending the authentic values of each ethnic group. Mexico needs its indigenous peoples and these peoples need Mexico![51]

In the light of the persecution which the Church had undergone in Mexico in the not-too-distant past, this was a bold statement. Similarly, speaking this time in St Peter's Square on the occasion of the canonization of martyrs of the Mexican persecution, the pope said:

They are a precious legacy, a fruit of the faith rooted in the lands of Mexico, a faith which, at the dawn of the third millennium of Christianity, must be preserved and revitalized so that you may continue to be faithful to Christ and to his Church as you were in the past. Mexico ever faithful![52]

For the late pope, then, saints were markers in a country's history, reminders that the Catholic faith and a nation's culture

[51] <http://www.vatican.va/holy_father/john_paul_ii/homilies/2002/documents/hf_jp-ii_hom_20020731_canonization-mexico_en.html>, accessed 10 July 2009.

[52] <http://www.vatican.va/holy_father/john_paul_ii/homilies/documents/hf_jp-ii_hom_20000521_canonizations_sp.html>, accessed 10 July 2009. This reference is to the Spanish version of the homily.

were closely intertwined. As the Jesuit sociologist John Coleman
has put it, saints 'anchor a sense of tradition by facilitating communities of memory'.[53] John Paul was using saints to recall Christian communities to their culture and their history. In that sense
canonizations were, as the pope always claimed them to be, an
exercise in evangelization.

Heythrop College, University of London

---

53 Coleman, 'After Sainthood?', 208.